D0112987

Generation

at the

crossroads ~~~~~~~~~~~~~~~~~~~~

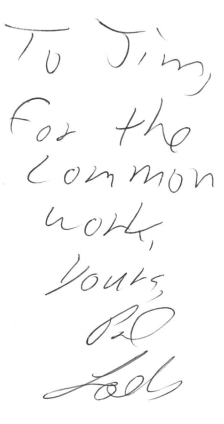

To Jim,

For the

Common

work,

yours,

[signature]

Generation at the crossroads

Apathy and action on the American campus

Paul Rogat Loeb

RUTGERS UNIVERSITY PRESS

New Brunswick, New Jersey

Copyright © 1994 by Paul Rogat Loeb
All rights reserved
Manufactured in the United States of America

Interior design by Ellen C. Dawson

Library of Congress Cataloging-in-Publication Data
Loeb, Paul Rogat, 1952–
    Generation at the crossroads : apathy and action on the American
  campus / by Paul Rogat Loeb.
      p.   cm.
  Includes bibliographical references and index.
  ISBN 0-8135-2144-0
    1. College students—United States—Political activity.
2. Student movements—United States.   I. Title.
LA229.L62   1994
378.1'981—dc20   94-16186
                                                 CIP

British Cataloging-in-Publication information available

Contents ~~~~~~~~~~~~~~~~~~~~~~~~~~~~~

~~~~~~

Generation
at the
crossroads

Introduction **Beyond the myths**

~~~~~~

In a classic *Doonesbury* cartoon, a rumpled professor holds forth from a lectern: "And in my view, Jefferson's defense of these basic rights lacked conviction." His students dutifully take down his words, scribbling away at their notepads. "Any discussion?" he asks.

"Of course not," he says to himself. "You're too busy getting it all down."

"Let me just add," he goes on, "that personally I believe the Bill of Rights to be a silly, inconsequential recapitulation of truths already found in the Constitution. Any comment?"

They continue to scribble away.

"No *scratch* that!" he says, raising his voice and waving his hands, "The Constitution *itself* should never have been ratified! It's a dangerous document! All power should rest with the *executive*! What do you think of *that?*"

The students keep on taking notes, their faces blank.

"JEFFERSON WAS THE *ANTICHRIST!*" the professor screams. "DEMOCRACY IS FASCISM! BLACK IS WHITE! NIGHT IS DAY!"

They take notes as the professor collapses on the podium, announcing, "Teaching is dead."

"Boy, this course is really getting interesting," one student says.

"You said it," another responds. "I didn't know half this stuff."

The cartoon ran in January 1985. At the time I was traveling campus to campus, lecturing on how citizens avoid or confront critical public issues like the arms race, environmental threats, and the growing gap between rich and poor. I began to notice the cartoon posted on faculty doors. For the next five years I saw it at almost every school I visited, until it felt like an icon of the times. It symbolized a split between the teachers who displayed it—often former 1960s activists still involved in or sympathetic to social change—and a new student generation, seemingly docile, unthinking, and wholly uninterested in Jefferson, democracy, or anything else besides making high grades on their tests. The professors tacked up the cartoon to challenge their students, but also to vent their own frustration, their doubts as to whether teaching still mattered.

From the late 1970s through the early 1990s, commentators branded the current student generation as almost pathologically selfish, greedy, apathetic, and unconcerned with higher ideals. In a 1985 *Newsweek on Campus* cover, collegians replaced the old cliché "Don't trust anyone over thirty" with "Never trust anyone under $30,000." A series of *Rolling Stone* ads headlined "Perception/Reality" contrasted the old stereotype of their typical reader—a hippie wearing love beads—with the new model—a well-dressed young entrepreneur, ready for Wall Street; they then offered up contrasting photos of McGovern and Reagan and announced, "If you think *Rolling Stone* readers are taking left turns when the rest of the world is taking rights, consider who they voted for in the last election." A Republican official called the generation perfect fodder for his party: they'd run over their grandmother to make a buck.

Despite the generation's apparent move to the right, cultural conservatives have attacked them as well. Allan Bloom, in his best-selling *Closing of the American Mind*, suggests that students are self-indulgent, isolated, and ignorant, and that we need to salvage the best and brightest with a stiff dose of the classics. E. D. Hirsch, in *Cultural Illiteracy*, declares them lacking in the basic cultural knowledge necessary for coherent communication. Reagan-era secretary of education William Bennett, in speeches and articles, brands their slightest questioning of what colleges should teach as "ignorance, irrationality, and intimidation." *Illiberal Education* author Dinesh D'Souza warns of an unholy alliance of zealous college radicals, self-deluding minorities, and ambitious young faculty, who together degrade the once admirable intellectual life of the American campus.

None of these descriptions match the realities I have found. I began seeking to understand this much-maligned generation in the early eighties, as an outgrowth of my campus lecturing. The more the pundits described the students as callous and corrupt, the more I wondered what those seated before me in classrooms and auditoriums really believed, and why they made their respective choices. I wanted to know why so many seemed to shy away from critical public issues. If they were profoundly cynical, who had taught them? If they were relentlessly pragmatic, why? What did they believe in, beyond personal success? How had some managed to take committed stands, to shift from passivity to involvement?[1]

I questioned students in discussion sessions and workshops that followed my talks, and during visits to various classes. Later, I began doing extensive interviews. From 1987 through 1993, I researched student values at over a hundred campuses in thirty states. I talked with that vast majority who disdained larger public commitments as foolish idealism, and also with the initially isolated students who tried to act on what they believed. I spent time with them at their dorms, apartments, fraternities, and sororities. I went along to their marches, sit-ins, and political meetings, and volunteered with them in soup kitchens. Their observations, insights, and questions appear throughout this book. (I have changed the names of many of the students quoted here to protect their privacy.) I spoke also with their teachers and families, and with others who'd long studied generational change.

I found that these students were not simply greedy or indifferent: their attitudes were far more complex. I found false the images of a generation almost innately deficient, as if missing some key gene for concern. The students hardly led America's retreat from responsibility. Rather, they had come of age under the sway of political, cultural, and economic currents that convinced citizens in general to seek personal well-being over a common social good. How did it shape them to grow up in a dominant national mood of "Don't Worry, Be Happy City," as columnist Molly Ivins described It, "all done on borrowed money, with glitz and mirrors, while the social fabric rotted, the infrastructure crumbled, the environment slowly became nightmarish, and the deficit grew and grew"; to grow up in what Republican analyst Kevin Phillips called "a second Gilded Age," marked by "an ostentatious celebration of wealth, the political ascendancy of the richest third of the population and a glorification of capitalism, free markets and finance"; to grow up with the media fawning over "lifestyles of the rich and famous" while savings and loan institutions collapsed, bankruptcies soared, and average real wages continued to fall, opening up a greater gap between rich and poor than at any point since the eve of the Great Depression? These students were confronted with a future vastly more precarious than the one their predecessors faced twenty years before.[2]

In response, most concluded that the world was inherently unfair, and that they had little possibility of changing it. Buried by outside jobs and by massive debt loads, threatened by a dubious economic future, these students feared they were on their own in terms of personal survival. They suspected they'd have to "work twice as hard" to match their parents' standard of living. Commitments of conscience "would only get in the way." Many also feared that if they failed in their struggle toward the top, they'd end up unemployed and expendable, scraping to get by. They needed to focus, they said, on learning to adapt to whatever circumstances they'd encounter. They could not afford to address the history that had shaped their lives.

This retreat should not be confused with active political conservatism. Although most students backed away from civic involvements, they continued to hold beliefs more liberal than those of the general population. Even in the early to mid-eighties, when the majority voted for Ronald Reagan in the belief that cutting wasteful government would pave the way for economic growth, most also supported national health insurance, a more equitable tax system, greater environmental protection, and abortion choice. A majority wanted to end the global arms race and to cut defense spending. They did not so much endorse the directions of America's leaders as abdicate their own political voice.[3]

Student withdrawal stemmed from more than just economic fear. It was the fruit of a cultural climate in which students learned to mistrust peers who take on causes that go beyond their personal lives. They learned to dismiss politically involved students of whatever style or stripe with an array of often contradictory stereotypes, explaining, "They all wear black," "They all dress like hippies," "They all just say the same thing." They demanded a perfect standard of political proof, as though people should not open their mouths unless they were eloquent enough to debate Henry Kissinger on *Nightline.* And when they *did* admire those who acted, they regarded them as a sort of different breed, explaining, apologetically, "I'm just not that kind of person."

These students learned to view with suspicion those who took controversial stands—not only in the present but also in the past. In particular, they inherited a distorted image of the Vietnam-era movements, whose legacy continues to overshadow American campus politics. That period could be viewed as a model for understanding how ordinary citizens—especially students—worked to end segregation, stop a dubious war, and further democratize this nation. Instead, American culture has focused mainly on its caricatures—ragged crazies spitting on soldiers. Or it has purveyed images of a generation so heroic that the present generation could not possibly match it. Most students remain similarly isolated from knowledge of other historical instances in which citizens have joined together to bring about change, whether antislavery abolitionists, 1930s labor organizers, or fighters for women's suffrage.

With the past thus erased, apolitical students find it hard to imagine how their common efforts might shape a more humane world. Instead, they shrug and explain, "You make your own chances," resolving to work all the harder for their personal dreams. They mistrust all political approaches, from marches and sit-ins to presidential campaigns. Many even balk at the simple act of voting. Although they desire a world more humane, generous, and just, most hope the future will muddle along, whether or not they participate.

Much as student political retreat stems from more than simple callousness or greed, campuses have also been more active than popular mythologies suggest. In the past decade, Columbia students spurred shifts toward South African democracy by helping trigger a nationwide divestment movement. University of Nebraska students fought for family farms they'd grown up on. A University of Michigan group, Greeks for Peace, brought controversial social issues to fraternity row. A University of Washington student body president pushed through a long-delayed campus recycling plan. Financially pressed participants in a tuition strike at New York's Hunter College sought to preserve access to an education: half their parents had not graduated high school.[4] Student community service volunteers worked to heal specific societal wounds, then began to question why there is need in America for food lines and homeless shelters to begin with.

These students act, not because America's dominant cultural thrust encourages them, but because they find models for commitment on the margins. Some have parents long involved in social change. Others encounter teachers, ministers, or friends who consistently stand up for what they believe. Still others find connections to a more general dissident culture: they read about Greenpeace staffers challenging corporate polluters or stumble onto local community groups addressing issues like health care, equitable taxation, and environmental degradation; or they listen to socially committed musicians like U2, REM, Public Enemy, Tracy Chapman, and Pearl Jam. In all cases, strong personal examples galvanize their involvement.

From the mid-1970s through the mid-1980s, politically involved students remained highly marginal on most campuses. Since then they've gradually built a broader base of support, though it remains more modest by far than that underlying the most dramatic moments of the sixties. In contrast with that earlier time, students now juggle more causes, more consciously address difficult fault lines of race, sex, and class, and work to overcome greater resignation and resistance. They cherish fewer hopes that change will come easily.

Though often frustrated, these students feel pulled toward involvement by America's growing crises. They resent being labeled complacent. And their numbers have swelled as students whose parents marched and spoke out at their own colleges in the sixties have begun to join a campus population made up of children of the 1950s' "silent generation." Though only a minority of the sixties generation was ever politically involved, and many soon let their commitments fade, others communicated their values to daughters and sons who are beginning to galvanize renewed campus involvement.

Whatever the roots of the newly committed students, they seek to uphold a vision of a more humane and just world instead of accepting national or global ills as inevitable. They work to build public responsibility as well as private careers. Some act from empathy or solidarity. A Michigan man involved in Greeks for Peace explained, simply, "I thought what we were doing in Central America was wrong." Others act from direct self-preservation. A Puerto Rican woman active in the Hunter tuition strikes got involved because school was her sole shot at a decent future, "and I didn't want to spend my whole life working at Roy Rogers as a biscuit babe." A University of Nebraska woman who had not cared to read the newspaper found herself propelled into involvement on farm issues by the crisis in her rural community. She ended up assistant director of her state Department of Agriculture. These students shared common pressures and uncertainties, yet acted because they could see no other way to build a common future.

Student choices matter because they set a tone for their generation's future directions. Despite "Big Chill" mythologies of generational sellout, studies of those who came of age in the sixties fit an earlier pattern wherein the ways people learn to duck or take on critical moral and political challenges when they're eighteen, twenty, or twenty-two often color their responses from that point on. Contrary to monolithic generational stereotypes, divisions within generations matter as much as divisions between them. This is true of individuals who try to act on pressing social issues, and of those who hold back with disdain. For both, the stage of life when they're first on their own remains a critical period when they sort through identifications, commitments, and dreams; solidify beliefs; and come to grips with what they're willing to fight for. Many establish patterns they'll follow throughout their lives.[5]

The allegiances of this generation are complex. Distant media reporting doesn't always catch the contradictions. In November 1990 the *New York Times* ran a major article, "90's Teen-Agers Echo 60's Spirit," on the resurgence of high school protests. The same week the *Wall Street Journal* announced the "GOP Generation" and heralded the new conservatism of the young. The realities confound neat summations.

In 1965 Yale psychologist Kenneth Keniston, in his excellent book *The Uncommitted*, studied the political and cultural withdrawal of a group of Harvard students. They were responding, Keniston believed, to an adult world that offered little support for involvement. By 1968 America's college mood had so shifted that Keniston did a follow-up study, *Young Radicals*, on students involved in the antiwar effort, Vietnam Summer. He described what almost seemed two different historical eras.[6]

America's recent students are neither wholly radical nor wholly uncommitted. Withdrawal and engagement coexist more closely than in the sixties. Most students still hold back from political concerns, even as growing campus activism echoes more general shifts toward renewed citizen involvement.

The students who attended college from the eighties through the mid-nineties represent the most ambitious and fortunate slice of their generation. Their peers who stopped after high school or dropped out in tenth or eleventh grade share similar rationales for political withdrawal. They have emerged, if anything, more cynical and politically inactive, in part because America's economic decline has landed so hard on their futures. To do justice to their choices would require a separate book.[7]

To understand these students' critical choices, I've looked at both the large majority, who are politically withdrawn, and the minority, who take public stands. I've worked hard to understand their lives and their beliefs, to get beyond quick statistics and instant quotes. In Book One, I explore the world of the students I call the apoliticals, or the adapters, since they represent the dominant current. I use these terms as a shorthand to describe a complex process that has made these individuals unwilling or unable to publicly act on their convictions. In Book Two, I examine students who've tried, despite the obstacles, to work for social change. I call them the activists, the committed, the active citizens, by which I mean something different from media stereotypes of chanting marchers with signs in their hands. Instead, these terms denote a fundamental attitude through which students try to take responsibility for the moral implications of their choices, rather than pass off critical public issues to distant experts. I also explore the intersection of the two groups, their contrasting worldviews, influences, and paths. I continue this discussion in Book Three, in the context of the changing world that active students now inherit. I look at the postcollege paths of both the activists and adapters. I ask what it will take for those who act to continue standing up for their beliefs throughout their lives.

Student choices matter, for now and for the future. What will it mean for this generation that America has become a society in which more than a quarter of the children live in poverty, in which black men growing up in Harlem have a shorter life expectancy than men in the Sudan, in which more than a million men, women, and children live on the streets? What will it mean that, as respected analysts like Worldwatch president Lester Brown suggest, our path of environmental degradation may leave us fewer than forty years to begin reversing its course? Or that they come of age with a heritage of savings and loan bailouts; banking, HUD and insurance scandals; and an unprecedented national debt? Or that young men and women from the wealthiest quarter of American familes will have a nearly twenty times greater chance of graduating college by age twenty-four—after which such achievement grows increasingly less likely—than those from the poorest quarter?[8]

The students are right to fear failure in a society in which those at the bottom pay for the greed and folly of those at the top, right to worry about whether they'll be able to get through school, find decent jobs, pay off their loans, perhaps buy a house and raise a family. But when they—or any of us—abdicate the admittedly daunting task of trying to shape a common future, they leave the fate of this nation, and of the planet, to those whose choices have created these crises in the first place.

Imagine these students twenty-five years down the line. Those now attending college or recently graduated will have reached the age of Bill and Hillary Clinton, Al Gore, Clarence Thomas, William Bennett, Barbara Boxer, Carol Mosely Braun. They will have reached the age of key economic leaders like Bill Gates and Steven Jobs, of prominent media figures like Diane Sawyer and Charlayne Hunter-Gault. How will they treat the power they will hold? Whose voices will they heed? What visions will they forge for the future?

Imagine these individuals as ordinary citizens, facing varied decisions. Imagine them in their PTAs, churches, and temples, in the companies or institutions they work for, in the businesses they run. Imagine them as parents, as voters, involved in their communities. Will they take responsibility for what they perceive to be the common social good? Or will they take the path of greatest convenience, looking out primarily for their personal lives?

This generation faces difficult choices, not of their creation. They will continue to do so. They can resign themselves to steadily worsening social conditions, reasoning that there's nothing they can do. Or they can, with all their uncertainties, work to create a wiser and more humane society. Ultimately, the decisions they continue to make, their contending beliefs and commitments, will shape the future of this nation.

Book one I'm not that kind of person

~~~~~~

One ～～～～～～～～～～～～

You make your Wealth as an
own chances educational goal

～～～～～～～～～～～～～～～～～～

At Fairfield University, a Catholic school on the Connecticut gold coast an hour north of New York City, a group of sophomore men were teasing their friend Rick Vincent, the dorm liberal. "You want to be a teacher?" they asked. "Do you think your parents are paying fourteen thousand dollars a year for you to go into the Peace Corps and become a teacher?"

"What's wrong with wanting to help people?" Rick responded earnestly.

"Nothing," answered Tim Lovejoy, a premed major. "Your goal," he said, "is to teach and maybe go into the Peace Corps. Vigna over there just wants to be a writer. My goal is to make over fifty thousand a year. And George Lipson's is the same."

"Hey, don't sell me short," Lipson broke in with a laugh. "I want six figures at least."

Fairfield's campus is lush and wealthy; the surrounding community is wealthier. But a few miles away, in the city of Bridgeport, crumbling houses and boarded up storefronts line the streets. Unemployment soars. I asked the group whether their six-figure dreams could offer any hope to its residents. Scott, whose dad was a partner in a Wall Street brokerage firm, suggested that improved local education might help: "Starting kids off right is really important." Then he backpedaled: "But that's not my objective. It's not my job to do it."

"God helps those who help themselves," said Tim, whose dad was a doctor and whose mother was a nurse. "I feel sorry for those who get tough breaks, but we'll always have the poor. We gave the blacks a lot. Is it my fault if me or my parents make the bucks and they don't?"

"You make your own chances," Scott added.

These responses seem callous, bluntly so. Yet these students were hardly fervent New Rightists. They consistently mocked a skinny dormmate in Vuarnet sunglasses who idolized William F. Buckley and treated the *National Review* as the revealed word of God. Half were too unconcerned even to vote Republican. But they considered the world inherently harsh and unequal. They intended to do what they considered necessary to get their share.

Consequently, they dismissed the Bridgeport residents as regrettably expendable, perhaps even deserving their fate. And they hammered their own lives and dreams into whatever shape they hoped would spark approving corporate responses. "It would be great if we could come here to learn, and if grades were a real measure," said George Lipson, a salesman's son. "They aren't, and unfortunately the business world just isn't going to care how much I know about Plato. They're going to care whether I show them how hard I can work by getting the best grades I possibly can."

I talked with the group in a dorm lounge that overlooked rolling hills, the trees a fall palette of red, gold, and brown. They wore tailored slacks, expensive sweaters, ragged sweats, worn jeans. They sprawled on couches and chairs, coming and going as the conversation circled from midmorning till night.

Ambition to rise, they believed, was a virtue. Wealth would allow them to "send money to Rick in the Peace Corps. Or maybe give something to cancer." "I feel I owe my parents for sending me here," explained George Lipson . "My dad always says 'I want you kids to do better than I have.' I want to make good and make him proud."

"Rick and I will be living in the Bowery," remarked Paul Vigna, the aspiring writer. "Lipson will drive by in his BMW and flip us some change."

The others razzed him for this, yet for the most part agreed that the world was carnivorous and always would be. "I'm a heavy church goer," said Tim. "The priests say we should help others. But no one's gone out of their way for me."

"College has given me lots of different ideas and thoughts," observed Jim, the one blue-collar student. His dad was a railroad worker and his mom a secretary. "But I'm in school to get a good-paying job. First I want to reward my parents so they don't have to scrimp and save in the future. They both hate their work. They only do it so I can be here. I study to get good grades and to not have to live like they do."

The group's belief that you repay familial affection through economic mobility echoed narratives fundamental to America's history. These students described grandparents who came from Germany, Italy, or Poland with nothing but a willingness to bake bread, pump gas, sew clothes, or do whatever else would allow the family to claw its way up, generation by generation, to middle-class comfort. They believed anyone sufficiently motivated could replicate their passages.

You don't have a life   Nevertheless, they also feared they might lose out in the race for success. For all their talk of six-figure dreams, they worried about the economic ground beneath them eroding, and wondered how long they'd keep the comforts they grew up with. "When I get money . . ." they'd casually state, as if wealth would surely come. "If you work hard, you're going to make a buck." Then they'd repeat, "I don't want to end up poor." "I don't want to end up at the bottom." They dismissed peers who voiced modest social concerns as dangerously impractical.

These Fairfield students were not alone in choosing pragmatic careerism over broader commitment or reflection. In the earlier generation of the late 1960s, more than 80 percent of entering freshmen cited "developing a meaningful philosophy of life" as a prime college goal, compared with 40 percent who selected "being very well off financially." By the late 1980s the figures had reversed. Seventy-five percent picked financial security, while only 40 percent hoped to better understand themselves in the world. Most students viewed college as just a means to material success.[1]

Students with such beliefs don't obsess constantly over their futures. They party, talk, and relax much like their counterparts in other historical times. But most feel their lives have room for only one "serious" concern: preparing to make it in the material world. They believe in a meritocracy—that the wealthy are the most deserving. But they view the success of those who make it to the top as a product, not of intrinsic worth or actual contribution to society, but of how well they manipulate appearances to those who call the shots and make the deals. They worry less about what they'll actually do than about whether they can learn to adapt.

Having grown up during a time when fortunes were built—not by producing railroads, steel mills, or houses, but by the alchemy of junk bonds and corporate takeovers—students in this group remain vague about what they hope to produce, what human needs they wish to serve. They talk mostly of what corporations will require of them, or in vague terms of wanting "an entrepreneur kind of deal." As a student from Texas explained, "I'd really like to get rich. If you have that, everything else pretty much follows."

George Lipson described how his father had spent thirty-five years traveling from store to store selling eighteenth-century furniture reproductions. His dad didn't particularly like the job and felt little excitement about the merchandise he sold. But it enabled him to give their family a comfortable Long Island home, "to buy us things, take us out to dinner, show us how much he cares. He works so hard"—George gestured toward his heart—"to look after us."

"I've got some of that as well," he continued. "When I'm out for dinner with girls or with friends of mine, I want to be able to do that. Not because I'm rich, because sometimes I'm not. Or because I want people to think I'm rich, like this guy from our dorm who drives around in a Lincoln. I just want to be able to do something for the people I care about."

"Helping people is great," Tim added, "and good teachers are great. But you can't help everyone else and throw away Number One. I want to make enough to buy a place of my own, where I can go and if someone's bothering me I can say 'Buddy, buzz off, this is mine. This is what I've paid for.' "

Tim's words portrayed a world without broader claims or attachments, a world full of predators who might seize or disrupt the comfort he intended to work so hard for. He sought a private sanctuary, safe and secure.

"Without money," added Scott, the stockbroker's son, "you have no life."

No one in the group suggested the possibility of redeeming familial love and support with other than material dreams. No one considered using school as a time to learn to think critically, to act on their beliefs, to better understand their world. They considered it wildly unrealistic to even consider trading material success for a larger common good.[2]

They also felt unequivocally hostile to attempts at social change. When I suggested Vietnam-era efforts had made a difference, they called them self-indulgent, misguided, and ineffective. The protestors, they said, made the war longer and spat on innocent soldiers caught in the middle. All but Rick and the ambivalent Paul Vigna, the aspiring writer, condemned the campus political involvements of that time.

In the same vein, the group mistrusted students who currently took political stands. "They're just a bunch of losers," Tim remarked when I mentioned Fairfield students who had protested Reagan's Central America interventions. "They have an unprofessional quality," added a friend named Bob. He called those who'd protested a local nuclear plant "just a bunch of morons." Although Rick's most radical act was to say he might want to become a teacher or to join the Peace Corps, George Lipson wrote off even this as "just trying to get noticed."

The Fairfield students differed from some others in the virulence of their individualism and in the material wealth that fueled it. They allowed no common claims to interfere with their personal chances. But they were wholly representative in denying responsibility for the ills of the world and in disdaining anyone who did speak out.

Campus activists, in the view of one Columbia student, just "protested for the sake of protesting." "They're only in it for a fad and a trend," a University of Washington woman stated, "to jump on a bandwagon, like everyone else." She used to go to Colorado College, "where there was a certain group who put up their little shanties and did their little demonstrations about divestment. They were all just imitative of the sixties. They never drew many people, and no one paid them any attention in any case."

I asked how the same activists could simultaneously be marginal and trendy. Wasn't there a contradiction? "There actually were a lot of the antiapartheid people," she admitted, "but we just called them 'the granolas.' The guys wore grass skirts and beads to go back to nature, and they built their shanties, and to me that's a trend. Because then they got in their new Saabs and drove away."

Did the guys really wear skirts, I asked? Well, just two of them, and that was once at a party. She guessed not all of them had cars, and some who did drove old clunkers. But if they really wanted to be consistent, they'd sell their possessions, give their money to Africa, and know a lot more about what they were fighting for.

Hostile students levied equally condescending charges during the height of the Vietnam era. Had the 1980s been a wholly quiescent decade, there would have been no campus activists to disparage. But when some did take committed stands, they were outnumbered by their far more numerous critics, like students who complained at the height of Columbia's successful antiapartheid blockade about people "who just sit on the steps and try to feel moral." Time and again I saw even the most thoughtful and effective political students cavalierly dismissed along with all the questions they raised.

The same stereotypes were invoked, irrespective of the cause. A Dartmouth student called those who worked on campus racial issues "just marchers with their marcher face on, swept up in their emotions, chants, the attitude they take." Some, he said, were even his friends, but they talked before thinking, constantly demanded attention, weren't nearly as knowledgeable as they ought to be. "Of course, it does seem ironic," he said, after a pause, "that we seem to feel that the people who are marching for one side or another of an issue never understand things as well as those of us who watch from the sidelines."

The mistrustful students included some who shared apparent philosophical bonds with the activists. A Dartmouth student wrote his senior thesis on ways America's military buildup has destroyed the technological and economic base of sectors like the machine tool industry. This seemed precisely the kind of question students should address, not because his judgments mirrored my own, but because Americans so rarely examine the interconnected consequences of our national choices. The student and I discussed his project and conclusions. He mentioned seeing a poster for a lecture on the arms race that I'd given the previous evening. When I excused myself to address a fundraising walkathon for Central America, he was taken aback. "Why would you involve yourself with *that?*" he asked. "Aren't they just a bunch of radicals?"

They aren't my neighbors   Not all the apolitical students are materially greedy. Most just want to get by. But they share a mistrust of those who act. They believe individuals succeed or fail on their own. They view personal futures as having little to do with broad political choices, but rather with individual skill, persistence, the ability to adapt. They share a sense of a world increasingly harsh, in which conscience is a luxury.

A Florida student said he knew the Central Intelligence Agency (CIA) did some dirty business in South America. But so did the Russians. If some people got hurt, they probably deserved it. A young woman at a Seattle-area community college agreed. She described, with a sense of betrayal, how her father's silence regarding his work on MX missile components echoed that of atomic weapons workers I'd interviewed for a previous book. She wanted to confront him, to work to stop the arms race, to found a campus peace group. Then she hesitated. "But isn't it good if we're warlike and frighten other nations?" she asked. "That way no one will mess with us."

In a later conversation, I asked the Fairfield group if they'd ever worried about the nuclear threat. Tim and Scott hadn't. They were Christians and knew they'd be saved to go to "a better place." Switching the conversation to his recent trip to Jamaica, Tim asked, "Why does everyone there hate the U.S. so much?"

"Because we ream people," said Vigna, bluntly. Rick mentioned El Salvador and Iran.

"So stop driving your car," said Tim. "Grow your own cotton and make your own shirt. I like how I live. Are you going to decide what's right or wrong?"

"Then what about all that Christian 'love thy neighbor' stuff?" asked Vigna, who himself was an agnostic. "What about the Jamaicans, or the people in Bridgeport?"

"They aren't my neighbors," said Scott. "Who cares if they hate us? I know my neighbors, and they live in Long Island. No way are those people my neighbors."

The phrase evokes the separations at the heart of the era these students grew up in, separations between individuals across America's widening class divisions, between past and present, and present and future, between notions that citizens have a responsibility to a broader common good, and the judgment that, as Margaret Thatcher pronounced, "There is no such thing as society—there are only individual families." Students with such beliefs hope to do well in their personal lives, even if this means averting their eyes while the world crumbles. They settle for what educator Arthur Levine once called "going first class on the *Titanic*."[3]

Exemption and silence   Students diverge over how much those at the bottom really do make their own chances. In a sociology class at the University of South Alabama, the professor described "driving by a man with a sign that said 'I'll work for food.' It outraged me that to be able to eat, someone in this country should have to sit on a bench holding that sign. The next day, when I drove by again, I didn't feel nearly so upset. It shocked me that I was already getting used to it."

"At first I'd feel sorry for them, too," said a woman in the class. "They're all over Mobile now. But then you feel like, if they wanted a job, they could get one. They could clean houses or something. They don't have to beg."

"But their sign says that," I responded. "It says, 'I'll work for food.'"

She held her ground. "It's not our fault. Why should it be our fault if it's their problem, if they're the ones not trying to do anything for themselves? Why should we make it our problem and do something for them?"

This wasn't the callousness of the elite, but of someone who'd scraped, struggled, and wanted no claims on what she earned. Her dad, she explained, supported five kids on less than $20,000 a year. Her mom, now divorced, lived in a trailer. "I've been working since I was fifteen to put myself through college. Don't y'all tell me you can't get a job."

Other students, from backgrounds equally hard pressed, argued back. One mentioned a businessman friend, "who became homeless along with his family, five years ago. He couldn't find work because he didn't have an address."

We talked of factories leaving town, of the barriers of education and race. "They should be able to see that something's going wrong at their work," a woman commented, "instead of waiting around until things fall apart." "It's easy to say 'He hasn't tried,'" said another student. "Who are we to pass judgment? We don't even know what people are going through."

While the class generally condemned extreme social Darwinism, they blamed the situation of the man who wanted to work for food on poor luck and misfortune. They never mentioned institutional choices that might have left him on the street—a factory shutting down, a landlord raising the rent, a social welfare system that lets people go hungry.

Separation from responsibility builds on a notion of exemption, on a belief that while others might stumble, individuals by their own efforts can keep human tragedy at a distance. Writer Wendell Berry described how this sense played out in commencement exercises of a major California university:

> The graduates of the school of business wore "For Sale" signs around their necks. It was done as a joke, of course, a display of youthful high spirits, and yet it was inescapably a cynical joke, of the sort by which an embarrassing truth is flaunted. For, in fact, these graduates were for sale, they knew that they were, and they intended to be. They had just spent four years at a university to increase their "marketability." . . . But what most astonished and alarmed me was that a number of these graduates for sale were black. Had their forebearers served and suffered and struggled in America for 368 years in order for these now certified and privileged few to sell themselves? Did they not know that only 122 years, two lifetimes, ago, their forebearers had worn in effect that very sign? It seemed to me that I was witnessing the tragedy of history that the forgetfulness of history always is.

The African-American graduates, Berry suggested, could only have worn their signs, "by assuming, in very dangerous innocence, that their graduation into privilege exempted them from history. The danger is that there is no safety, no *dependable* safety, in privilege that is founded on greed, ignorance, and waste."[4]

Strong words, from one of America's strongest critical voices. As I will explore, more whites than blacks believe in this notion of exemption. My Fairfield group lived in a particularly insulating cocoon of privilege, as do Williams students who perform the half-joking football cheer "That's all right! That's OK! You're going to work for us someday!" Or students at Harvard, with a nearly identical version. They could afford to dismiss grave national and global problems as immutable.[5]

Yet even financially pressed students hope that if they can just learn the right moves, they can slide by. They turn college into what Queens College political scientist Michael Krasner calls "survival training . . . preparation so they'll do OK in a lousy world." By the mid-eighties, national surveys of high school seniors found that 90 percent expected things to get better for themselves, but only 47 percent of young men and 34 percent of young women believed the situation of the country as a whole would improve. The split in expectations leads them to prepare themselves for sale to the highest bidder, while keeping larger ideals buried in the remote closets of their souls. Whatever troubles might come, they hope to ride them out through skill, perseverance, and hard work.[6]

Their perspective isn't wholly foolish. America has always let a few individuals rise to the top, even as it becomes more economically polarized than any other advanced industrial nation. With enough money, citizens can avoid immediate crises. They can drink bottled water, live in guarded suburbs with monitored alarm systems, even pay for clean air, as people do who buy inflated real estate on the West Side of Los Angeles. Yet these separations only allow national ills to fester.

More than anything, students' individualism involves a judgment that they can not be the makers of history, but only its recipients. Broad political forces continually frame their opportunities and beliefs, but they see no chance to control them. Real choice, they insist, comes only in private life. As in Tim's dream of saying "Buddy, buzz off," they trade the freedom to shape their communities and their historical times for the right to be left alone.[7]

You don't have Individualism as
a say survival

～～～～～～～～～～～～～～～～～～～～～～～～～

For all their talk of six-figure dreams, most students seek havens more modest than exalted. Their diminished hopes apply not only to America, but to themselves. They give up their chance not only for political voice, but even for work they can believe in. A South Carolina woman decided at age eight to become an accountant, even though she disliked math. Other students wanted to go into teaching but held back because they wouldn't earn enough. Farmers' sons and daughters who loved working the land left it for other careers. Seeing a society of clear winners and losers, fearful of potential false steps, these students want to ensure they are not left out on the street.

At a University of Nebraska agriculture department banquet, the speaker was a successful man, the CEO of a major international seed firm. The students listened as he spoke of the future. The government, he said, was foolish to subsidize land set-asides when we imported commodities like oats from other countries. The market would reward those who worked most efficiently and produced the greatest amount. There were still too many small farmers and small suppliers. More would soon have to fall by the wayside. Students listened quietly as he described the eclipse of the world they had grown up in.

The next day in an agriculture economics class, the professor suggested that students of twenty years ago would have booed the speaker off the stand. He asked for reactions, but the class remained silent. They were used to discussing production curves and market shares, not issues of power and politics. Their other courses ignored such questions altogether. They balked at criticizing a man who'd done so well.

One student, Dale Ottiger, came close to voicing his concerns. He admired the CEO's ability to head boldly into the future. Yet given that the farms predicted to go under would include many his classmates had grown up on, Dale wondered how to reverse this trend. The speaker's judgment, however, seemed hard to fault. Dale thought it would be like trying to fight Wal-Mart or Target in favor of the small-town five-and-dime stores. He didn't even know how to phrase the right questions.

Dale had grown up on a family farm. For the past hundred years his relatives had worked the land in central Nebraska. Until his freshman year of high school, Dale planned to follow his father's path. He loved to tear loose in the combine, surrounded by sun and air, with no one telling him what to do. But by the mid-1980s, American family farmers had hit an economic wall. Because of how federal programs were structured, they'd been getting less and less for their products. They made up the difference by borrowing money against vastly inflated land prices. Then bumper crops and declining exports dropped commodity prices even further. Land values plummeted, leaving farmers drastically overmortgaged as banks called in their loans. Between 1980 and 1987, nearly one-fifth of America's farming population was displaced. Much of the local supporting infrastructure crumbled as well. The entry rate of new farmers also dropped dramatically.[1]

Dale's dad got lucky and narrowly escaped: someone else had topped his bid when he tried to buy a 160-acre quarter section for Dale's brother to farm. The next year, the market collapsed, leaving most of their neighbors with pyramids of debt. Although Dale's dad avoided having his life work put up for auction, he barely scraped by, weighed down by payments on a new silo and feed system. Farming no longer seemed a livelihood for the future.

"Maybe I'd choose differently," Dale said, "if the farm economy had been in a blossom situation when I still lived back at home. But I remember my father saying, 'If you really want financial security, don't farm.' My perception was based on the industry at the time. It's still based on that. I want to see what else is out there."

I have to be realistic   Dale believed the agriculture crisis had little to do with farmers' lack of skill. The giant agribusiness companies, he said, like Cargill, ConAgra, and Dow Chemical, simply controlled too much. They could buy up the local grain elevators. They had greater leverage with transportation, storage, and marketing. They dominated prices for land, fuel, and seed, and called the shots on retail sales, government subsidies, and about every factor you could name. Small family farms barely had a chance.

Yet Dale felt the corporations acted reasonably. Why shouldn't they produce and market their products as well as they could?

The next day, he mentioned plans to open a "door to the future" by taking a summer internship with Dow Chemical.

This took me aback. "Weren't you just saying," I asked, "that companies like Dow helped destroy your community?"

"I can see your point," he said. "But I have to be realistic. At least Dow is in agriculture. They'll give me a chance to test my potential in corporate management and human relations. Perhaps I can make them a better company."

I met Dale at the "Ag Men" fraternity, a red brick house near the university's largely agricultural east campus. We'd been introduced by another member of the fraternity, Lee Wagner, who worked with a new student group called Farm Action Concerns Tomorrow's Society (FACTS). Students involved in FACTS sought to educate and organize around the roots of the rural crisis, holding forums and seminars, speaking at local rallies, and pressuring the university to take the needs of small family farmers more seriously. Lee had been propelled into farm issue activism by his parents' Chapter 11 bankruptcy. He now interspersed his studies and FACTS activities with helping out on the weekends at his considerably scaled down family acreage.

Almost wistfully, Dale asked him what it was like to be back working the land. "It's hard to separate myself," Lee told him, "from my dad telling me what to do. I have to realize he's sixty-four. His son is home, which was his dream. He wants his hands in everything, wants to help and teach me how, but I want to do it on my own. I have to learn to become as bullheaded as he is."

Dale laughed and said, "That does make it hard." He already looked like a manager ready to go golfing in his neat blue sweater, red shorts, and clean white running shoes. Lee wore a faded jean jacket. They'd been friends since Dale first entered Ag Men.

When Lee left, I asked Dale whether he'd return to farm life if it could provide a decent living. "My father never went to college," he responded. "He farmed all his life, always under the gun. He never could take off for vacations. He even missed our high school football games. I remember some seasons when he worked from five in the morning until twelve at night, six days a week. On Sundays, he moved equipment and did his fertilizing. When I left home for school, he told me, 'You have the potential to go beyond this. Don't be afraid to try. *This* will always be here.'" Dale's family viewed him as "the future big wig," the mover—who could talk, cut deals, go as far as he wanted.

Farming wasn't sentimental, Dale made clear. "I talked the other day with a young woman involved in animal rights who grew up in Dayton, Ohio. She thinks all the animals on the farm are like her pet kitty. She doesn't understand that you don't go out there every day to talk to your cattle." He talked more of his prospective internship, and how he'd sell the pesticides Dow manufactured to fight European corn bore. He hoped the job would be his entry into agribusiness.

Dale did worry about where the farm economy was heading, and about land erosion and chemicals in the Platte River Basin. He supported a recent ballot initiative that restricted land purchases by out-of-state corporations. He was glad farm practices had shifted to less disking and fewer tractor passes, leaving less compaction of the soil. Though he credited herbicides, fertilizers, and weed controllers with boosting America's tremendous agricultural production, he mistrusted their excessive use. "Maybe," he said, "I'm just knuckling under to all the hype of becoming a professional, on my way up in a major corporation. But my concern is to find a decent job that will provide for my family. I don't want to have to always think about financial pressure and being forced to sell. I don't want to always be taking it in the shorts."

We drove to Nebraska's new animal science building and its holding stalls for cattle and sheep. Dale put his hand out casually for a Black Angus steer to sniff. Down the hall, a lab technician took a rubber plug out of the stomach of a rather bored-looking sheep. First he twisted off a wing nut, then removed a rubber flange that screwed into an opening surgically cut through the animal's muscle. Digestive rumen spilled out like yellow bile. The lab checked it regularly to see how the sheep digested different feeds. When the technician thrust his glove up inside its stomach, Dale commented, "I'm definitely going to wash my hands."

Another technician repeated a similar check with a black and white Holstein, who sniffed his jeans, licked his leg, and watched the operation with a docile but quizzical gaze. The man pulled out a thick mulch of silage, corn, and hay, inspecting it much as he would a chunk from a compost pile. Nearby, pipes emerged from the throats and bellies of other animals, linking them up with various monitors. It reminded me of a twenty-five-year-old movie, *O Lucky Man*, in which a young Malcolm McDowell stumbles into a lab that grafts human torsos onto the bodies of pigs.

The plugs gave Dale pause as well, but he said the results would help farmers to improve their feed mix. University of Nebraska regularly contracted with corporations to conduct trials for various additives. He suspected large companies would be better able to apply the partially taxpayer-subsidized results. But he still believed the research would benefit both large and small producers.

Perhaps my unease at blood and viscera missed the point. If anything should have disturbed me here, it was the abstraction of the land, the fruits it produced, and the labor of those who worked it—the loss of actual rural life in the mazes of supply-side curves and monitored labs. Professors rarely asked how small-town communities could support themselves, how farmers could pass on a sustainable livelihood to their children. They rarely discussed which state and federal tax policies and which public and private investments nurtured family farms and which helped drive them under. They tended to ignore the consequences of policies that promoted cheap grain, only to bring financial instability, spirals of debt, and a push to produce more and more until both the farmers and their land were exhausted.

Because the school ignored such critical questions, Dale's Ag Men friends treated it largely as a place to learn new technologies and marketing strategies. Even their liberal arts courses rarely gave them a sense of the economic, ecological, and cultural choices that had produced both the culture that they came from and the threats to its existence. They mostly dismissed them as needless distractions.

Dale, too, was skeptical as to how much perspective his classes could offer. In high school he'd learned "just figures and facts," not ways to think through the political choices that directly affected his community, such as tax policies, subsidy programs, the setting of federal interest rates. Here at Nebraska, he'd occasionally had broader discussions, like the one that followed the banquet talk of the seed executive. But even his most useful courses had largely taught "just technical formulas about output and cost. How to manage what you have, and whether to apply more units of fertilizer in which situations. Most classes I just see as BS. Whether I learn anything really isn't the point."

I asked Dale whether Dow didn't have an incentive to sell as many of their products as possible, regardless of economic or environmental impact. I wondered if he worried that the company would use his skills, enthusiasm, and evident goodwill to help damage communities like the one he grew up in.

He told me Dow could only sell so much to each farmer for a given infestation. You had to do something about corn bore. It was either a herbicide, crop rotation, or smaller yields. "I have an open mind to when someone is being taken advantage of. I wouldn't want to represent someone who was corrupt. Maybe I'd never notice it with companies merging and taking over so many sectors. Maybe it wouldn't even be visible. But I can't see myself so hardcore that I'd do anything for a buck." He stopped and smiled. "I don't have the backbone to allow that."

We talked further about agribusiness. Dale saw corporations like Dow and ConAgra as places where he could learn to market new products, "expand my knowledge to have a career as a businessman. I don't look on them as a destructive force against my friends who are back on their family farms. If they did do anything bad I couldn't stop it by being back at home. Maybe if I'm there demonstrating my ethics and values and trying to have a positive impact, I could help. Maybe," he stressed one more time, "I could have an effect from within."

Apolitical students from relatively insulated environments, like Fairfield, dismissed public issues as distant and abstract. In Nebraska, the hammer of economic collapse hit students directly. Even if their own families escaped the worst, students from rural communities across the state witnessed the bankruptcies of neighbors and friends. Most mourned this human toll, then decided either to cast their lot with the winning team—Dow or Cargill—or to leave agriculture altogether, which usually meant leaving the towns they'd grown up in. A smaller number—often their families owned extra land—decided to tough it out on the farm, "working twice as hard" to better apply the high-tech approaches that had already led their communities from boom to bust. Only a few felt able to address the political and economic structures that created the rural hard times in the first place.

These students accept severe limits on the kind of future they can even imagine. It's difficult for any of us to envision ways to create a more humane society or more humane world, not because things seem fine as they are, but because the forces that call the shots seem so immutable. We're not talking about whether individuals can create some utopia, but whether they can maintain any future at all for a family farm culture, whose roots in Dale's case go back a hundred years. He believed that this way of life had unfortunately seen its day.

The sons and daughters of farmers have been leaving the land since America urbanized, often under similar pressures. Yet Dale's choices and assumptions are echoed by students who will never set foot in rural America, but who face comparable economic binds. They, too, worry, with reason, about whether they'll be able to afford middle-class lives. They, too, focus their academic efforts on paths that they hope will produce material well-being. Fundamentally good-hearted, they feel unable to challenge destructive actions by entrenched economic and political institutions. Like Dale, they limit moral judgments to personal concerns.[2]

I'd have to take on the whole world These students respond to major social problems with resignation. "The government won't listen," they say. "Involvement isn't worth it." "Whatever you do, it won't make a real difference." Student resignation both results from and furthers a more general erosion of American political life. Students say they are afraid to act, don't know how, and fear the consequences of even thinking about the urgent issues of their time. "I feel like I'd have to take on the whole world," said a woman from Minnesota's Mankato State University. "I have been taught to believe," wrote a student from southern Missouri's School of the Ozarks, "that world problems do not affect me, and that there is nothing I can do about them. People far away (I don't know where—but far away) must be the ones who make the moves to solve them."

Sometimes these students feel powerless. Or they choose to keep their distance from larger issues because action seems fruitless and involvement risks personal demands. "When you fight the system, you get screwed," said a student at Maine's University of New England. It shook him up to turn on the TV and see grandmothers arrested at the Connecticut Trident submarine yards, but he drew no sense of possibility from their actions. He and others were responding from their history of political withdrawal, not as concerned citizens who'd tried to create change and repeatedly hit a wall. Even when they back away from active involvement, students who stand up and speak out rarely make such blanket generalizations of hopelessness. But for those politically distanced to begin with, it's easy to insist that all efforts will fail.

Like Dale, many have misgivings about their pessimism. They question their political detachment and wish they could reverse it. But as they repeatedly explain, no one has taught them how to act.

"My teachers have always said this is a government run by the people," commented a young woman from Indiana's Saint Joseph's College. "Yet everyone I know says 'You can't do anything. The government will make their decision. You don't have a say.'"

"You don't have a say." I've heard this phrase applied to every imaginable issue—from U.S. interventions in Central America, to toxic waste dumping, to the capricious style of college administrators. It rationalizes politics as the corrupt and distant turf of captains and kings, not as a venue of ordinary citizens. Even on issues that hit as close to home as the farm crisis did for Dale, or even where activist groups have recently won major victories, most students have learned instead to place their faith in individual adaptation and exemption.[3]

Three ~~~~~~~~~~~~~~~~~~~~~~~

I feel a little fearful The reluctance to speak

~~~~~~

In April 1988, I was in Chicago, the second largest Polish city in the world, at the urban commuter campus officially named University of Illinois at Chicago, but which students continue to call Chicago Circle. I spent much of my time there with the Polish American Student Association (PASA), which included students who had grown up in the city's longstanding ethnic neighborhoods as well as others who had come after December 1981, when the Polish imposition of martial law crushed Solidarity's initial hope.

In Poland, meanwhile, citizens were striking. Fifteen thousand workers walked out at the massive Polish steel complex at Nowa Huta. Strikers occupied the Lenin shipyard in Gdansk, the birthplace of Solidarity, while supporters fought with police. In Warsaw, thousands of people marched in the streets, then were beaten and dispersed. Poland had strikes and demonstrations in Krakow and Lublin, Poznan and Lodz. The strikes lasted two weeks, until State security forces stormed the Nowa Huta steelworks and the Gdansk shipyard workers gave in. The challenges seemed to have failed.[1]

Marching in Chicago's annual Polish Day parade with the Chicago Circle group, I met a student named Andrzej. Just two years out of Warsaw, he still burned with memories of marches and strikes. Because America proclaimed democracy as its promise, he assumed that, in contrast with Jaruzelski's Poland, ordinary citizens would routinely participate in shaping their nation's destiny. He found ample career opportunity: part-time jobs with United Parcel Service and with a design firm, training for his intended vocation in economics. But though he saw no one punished for their opinions, political concerns seemed almost wholly absent from his workplace and school.

Responses seemed muted even toward the latest events in Poland. True, Chicago's Polish community sent money and supplies. Parade marshals handed out red and white *Solidarnosc* signs for people to carry alongside floats from restaurants, churches, butcher and sausage shops. But when Andrzej handed out copies of *New York Times* articles on the Lenin shipyard strikes, none but the most recently arrived students were interested.

The parade ended, and we adjourned to a nearby Greek restaurant. "Viva Solidarity. Viva Lech Walesa," the owner said again and again, slapping down free bottles of dark red wine on our table. We talked about Poland and about America. PASA's new members had entered the United States as political refugees, but once here, they pursued just the hope of decent private lives. "People in Poland know what rights they don't have and fight for them," observed a woman studying to be an engineer. "Here, you know your rights. You're satisfied. That keeps people from participating."

At the restaurant, Andrzej talked on as the wine took hold. He spun faster and faster, handsome, charismatic, and drunk. He flirted with the group's president and the other women at the table. "I don't want to be just a mainstream white American," he said. "I want to become a Polish hero." But that meant he had to strike it rich in this land of opportunity, "because ordinary workers don't have power." When he'd earned enough, he'd start a new career, running weapons to Poland, "like another IRA." Or maybe return to be "the next Lech Walesa, the next Martin Luther King." "I'm glad you're not totally selfish," teased his PASA friends, indulging his grand dreams.

Later the group moved to Andrzej's small apartment and put on the music that had gotten them through the darkest times back home. "This brings me back to Warsaw," Andrzej stated sadly as he inserted a Dire Straits cassette into a tape deck. "More than Chopin?" I asked, a bit surprised. Far more, the others agreed. Far more than any music except Leonard Cohen's, whom another student called "the guru of Polish society," relating how his generation was raised on Cohen's mournful dirges.

The night ended with Andrzej crying for everything he'd left behind, repeating again and again, "No one here acts. No one here cares." He was drunk, to be sure, and missed home and family. Yet I believe he missed as well the sense of working to shape a better society. American freedom offered a chance for private gain, and the right to be left alone in personal affairs. But people didn't talk, Andrzej said, about the kind of country they'd like to build. "They just don't talk about it at all."

Isolation set the tone   It's hard to act when dissenting movements are remote or invisible. In times of great upheaval, as at the height of the Vietnam era, students often have to consciously choose whether or not to get involved. In recent years, political withdrawal has been the automatic track at most schools. Students have to consciously work to depart from it.

A student named John from University of Southern Mississippi at Hattiesburg was chosen in his high school senior year as a 1983 Presidential Scholar. Joining 140 other seniors from around the country, he traveled to Washington to meet President Reagan. Although the meeting was purely ceremonial, a New Jersey woman, Ariella Gross, took the audacious step of circulating a letter among the scholars to ask Reagan to support a nuclear freeze.[2]

Gross's actions caused a major controversy, although only a dozen others in the largely conservative student group ended up signing the letter. Like most of the rest, John held back. He felt he didn't know enough to judge, and considered it impolite for Gross to bring her personal concerns into a situation in which she should have just felt honored and grateful. But he left D.C. wanting to learn more about the arms race.

Returning home with his newfound concern, John hit a political void. When he went off to the University of Southern Mississippi the next fall, few students seemed interested in such issues. John knew of no local groups addressing them, and no individuals. He ended up keeping his questions to himself, then barely noticed as they faded away.

In fact, several faculty at the Southern Mississippi campus were interested in issues of global war and peace. And some time later, a group of socially concerned students coalesced around a campus AIDS benefit. But to John, the school seemed wholly isolated and apathetic. He hadn't known where to look.

Some colleges are more politically quiescent than others. Yet until the nascent turn toward concern of the early 1990s, I heard similar explanations of retreat throughout the country. "If I were only at Michigan or Berkeley," students would say, "I'd join in for sure." "I wish I were at Yale or Wesleyan, where people care." "If I was just near Washington, D.C., or had a car . . ." These explanations came from small-town colleges where "problems seem far away and you really can't do anything," from schools in entrenched conservative communities where "if you speak out here, they call you un-American," and from urban commuter campuses where "everyone works and drives straight off to their jobs." They even came from elite residential colleges, including campuses romanticized at other schools as radical meccas. These students, too, talked of "a sort of bubble of insulation," beyond which the outside world receded in the distance.

It's frustrating to want to act, but to find no context. It's frustrating to try to speak out against the current, only to be stereotyped and dismissed. I respect greatly students who worked to forge the first necessary steps toward concern, who persisted even when others of like mind seemed few. Yet most students use talk of isolation not to describe the frustrations of trying to act for change but to justify retreat, to shore up their more general belief that if peers were involved, they were elsewhere, far away.

From the mid-1970s to the late 1980s, isolation set the dominant campus tone. Colleges, by and large, were politically quiet. Surveys found dramatic downturns in the numbers of incoming students who wanted to participate in environmental or community action programs, or who valued goals beyond material success. Most instead focused overwhelmingly on their careers. Even where campus or community activism occurred, the major media rarely covered it, so only those involved enough to tap into alternative information sources got much of a sense that anyone else in their generation cared.[3]

I don't think it's worth it   Politically involved students place large public issues at the center of their lives. Their apolitical counterparts view these same issues as abstract and remote. During a visit to Dartmouth, I crossed paths with visiting speaker Elizabeth Linder, the activist mother of a twenty-seven-year-old University of Washington engineering graduate who was murdered by Nicaraguan contras while working on a dam. I asked two students I was interviewing whether they'd considered going to hear her. They said they probably wouldn't. "It's just something that doesn't directly affect me," explained a junior named Bryan. "Maybe we're drawn into ourselves a little more than people were twenty years ago. But if you take her son's life, he died in El Salvador, no, Nicaragua. As I see my life right now, it just has no bearing."

Bryan lived less for material dreams than many. He made it a point to regularly take classes "just because they look interesting," regardless of how they might contribute to his career. Yet the very autonomy he prized set him in opposition to political involvement. "If you think you can't control things," he said, "you probably won't worry about them. The more interesting question, though, is whether I should radically change the way I live my life to do something about any of these issues. And pragmatically, I don't think it's worth it."

We talked of recent campus demonstrations around South African divestment, and about antiapartheid shanties that right-wing students from the *Dartmouth Review* had burned down. "It's all just a tennis match," Bryan commented. "Watching these people yell at these people, yell at those people. I think the general consensus is not to get involved. Students see it all as more closed-mindedness."

"The apartheid issue was particularly strange," added Bryan's friend Peter, who joined us in an elegantly paneled lounge near a main student eating area. "They wanted to get the college to divest because that would help end apartheid in South Africa, which is questionable. What bothered me, though, was that because I wasn't marching for companies to take their holdings out, everybody who did assumed I was against divestment, for apartheid, and a racist, right here on this campus. I had a little trouble with that. I became almost rebelliously apathetic."

Bryan talked further about the "marchers with their marcher face on," then paused for a moment and reflected. "I don't know why I put in three or four hours a day on the crew team," he continued, "but won't write my congressman or a government that's torturing someone to ask, 'Why the hell are you doing this?' Maybe I just don't want to get involved."

"I know for me," said Peter, "I might still be reacting to high school. I spent it racing from activity to activity, whether with the yearbook, my athletic teams, an Amnesty chapter, or the chorus. I got here . . ." He stopped to take a breath, ". . . and just wanted to sit in the woods, look at the trees, and wander around with no particular destination."

"Is there anything that would involve you?" I asked.

"I don't know," Peter responded. "I joined a pro-fraternity march, because I'm in one, we were under attack, and it felt like the right thing to do at the time. I don't know if it had any impact. But on causes like the South Africa shanties, I've gotten wary. I don't know what people could do to get me involved. Maybe it would have to be personal. I'm getting awfully tired of fliers in my mail box."

Politically engaged students succeed best when they enlist broad support beyond their core numbers. They have to constantly reach out. Yet when they do, skeptical peers accuse them of trying to mandate particular passions as universal concerns. "I've always wanted just to get on with my life," said a student at Western Michigan University. "And I feel you guys get mad at us for not being active. I don't get mad at you if you want to change your carpet from red to blue and I don't approve. That's your choice. I don't tell you what to do or how to act. But when you want me to pay attention to your cause and I don't, you look at me like 'He's a jerk.' "

Educator and theologian Paulo Freire describes a "culture of silence" that emerges when individuals are denied the opportunity to reflect on their situation and to participate in shaping their destinies. Instead, Freire writes, their voice becomes merely an echo of the powerful, of the dominant voices of their time.[4]

Equivalent silences on American campuses leave students who try to act on what they believe in a bind. Nothing has threatened their peers so dramatically as the draft and the Vietnam War threatened a previous generation. More recent shifts to greater concern are related to a growing sense of crisis around issues like environmental degradation, threats to abortion choice, the crumbling of America's cities, and the skyrocketing costs of education. Yet most students still feel uneasy challenging social wrongs. And the less these issues are discussed, the more they recede from view.

Those who try to break this prevailing silence risk being tarred as evangelists. Should they succeed, and mobilize hundreds, hostile students call it "just a fad" or "part of a group mentality." If they draw out only the loyal few, these same critics dismiss them as marginal. "When I see a march on the Dartmouth green," said Peter, "I pretty much know who's going to be there, whether for divestment, or against CIA recruiting, or whatever. There's a certain group who've been involved in every protest since freshman fall. It's OK to feel strongly on many issues, but it undermines them when they constantly go from one to another." Most marched, he believed, "just for the sake of marching."

The adapters call politically engaged students self-serving. They say they plead the causes of peace, the environment, or the poor—yet really want just power or attention. Of course, any group will include individuals who are ego-bound, intolerant, and who seek largely to prove their moral righteousness. But the adapters damn those who make claims on the common conscience, regardless of their actual strengths or weaknesses of character. They do so not because they've known scores of activists who've proven themselves craven and hypocritical, but because they've bought into prevailing myths that levy these judgments against all who question America's dominant political and economic arrangements. They end up blaming the ills of their schools and of America not on institutional choices that promote short-sightedness, callousness, or greed, but on the citizen efforts that challenge them.

The good that they do   Apolitical students, far more than those politically involved, tend to trust America's leaders. Atomic weapons workers I studied for my book *Nuclear Culture* used the phrase "the men who know best" to describe those to whom they delegated the choice of whether or not the bombs they built were necessary. Students of the eighties and nineties grew up in a time that encouraged similar unquestioning faith. They witnessed presidents deriding even token congressional participation in shaping national policy, as when Reagan exclaimed after losing a vote on contra aid, "We have got to get to where we can run a foreign policy without a committee of 535 telling us what we can do." National media constantly celebrated the wealthy and powerful, rarely asking how ordinary citizens might have a say in shaping the common future. If even senators were granted little right to challenge the president, and history was to be made exclusively by those at the top, it's understandable why nineteen-year-old sophomores might feel intimidated.[5]

Some students approved of this antidemocratic current, or accepted its premises as necessary. Fairfield University's George Lipson praised Reagan "because he uplifted our national morale and was a strong figure who made our opinion of ourselves a whole lot better." "We have to leave policy to the specialists," said a University of Minnesota student, "They're the ones who've studied it and made it their careers." "The world would be lots better off," suggested a University of Michigan engineering major, "if people attended to their own work."

In an upper division government class at Saint Joseph's College, I mentioned the 1973 CIA-assisted overthrow of Salvador Allende's democratically elected government in Chile. Only one of the forty students knew the coup had occurred—consistent with responses I'd been getting at other schools—but several nonetheless defended it. It did sound appalling, they agreed. "But there must have been something going on that we don't know. Maybe Chile was shipping drugs or supplying terrorists with arms. I can't see us overthrowing a government or assassinating a leader without a reason." A Dartmouth student defended the Reagan-era CIA in similar terms: "Maybe we just don't know the good that they do."[6]

Surveys throughout the 1980s suggested a substantial number of America's young felt an obligation to believe that those in charge were doing their best. A 1987 Times Mirror study found young adults eighteen to thirty years old the least likely of any generation to criticize business or government for lack of responsibility. In a poll two years later, this group more than any other believed Ronald Reagan would go down in history as "an outstanding or above average president." "We've been taught," explained an Indiana woman, "that God is in control, our leaders are in control, and there's nothing we can do."[7]

Marshmallows and wieners   Stereotypes suggest that student separation from politics stems from active conservatism. If most don't identify with liberal-left causes, why should they get involved? Yet, even in the depoliticized heart of the 1980s, surveys showed students consistently disagreeing with the Republican thrust of expanding the military, attacking sexuality, and allowing an increasingly corporatized global economy to hold sway. The students disagreed on virtually every major policy, even as many embraced Reagan's image of "morning in America."[8]

As a result, conservative student activists found little campus support for their efforts. They hit both specific disagreements around issues and the general antipathy to politics. At the University of Texas, San Antonio, a self-described "staunch young Reaganite" complained that his peers seemed to care about no ideas at all "except how to grub best for the almighty dollar." At a Williams environmental studies seminar, the head of the Young Republicans told a leading campus radical, "No one takes our leaflets either." Williams students, he said, wanted "moderation, the mainstream," were wary of political causes, and mistrusted all sources less respectable than the *Washington Post* and *New York Times*.

National surveys confirmed this mistrust. From the early seventies to the early eighties, the number of students calling themselves "liberal" or "far left" dropped nearly in half before rebounding at the decade's end. Yet the numbers of self-defined conservatives increased only slightly, even at their peak in the early eighties. The real gain was in students who called themselves "middle of the road."[9]

The media has made much of a new crop of campus conservatives, such as *Dartmouth Review* editors who made national headlines by burning an antiapartheid shanty, harassing a black music professor until he quit, and attacking women's studies, affirmative action, minority scholarships, and all other manifestations of what they called a decline in their school's traditional values. Yet the prominence of the *Review* and similar campus publications did not come from widespread student embrace of their viewpoints or journalistic integrity. It came, rather, from massive outside support spearheaded by the money and contacts of a consortium of right-wing foundations that included Scaife, Bradley, John M. Olin, Smith-Richardson, Coors, Earhart, and the corporate foundation of Mobil Oil, as well as conservative alumni.[10]

I'll discuss later the role of these foundations in whipping up media hysteria around "political correctness." For now, it's worth noting that, working through the Institute for Educational Affairs (which later became the Madison Center for Educational Affairs), they helped fund over seventy conservative campus papers, with the John M. Olin Foundation alone giving the *Dartmouth Review* over $300,000 during the 1980s. Their networks supported and nurtured young conservatives, linking them up with legal and journalistic advice, financial support in the form of donations and joint ads, and jobs and internships at conservative publications and think tanks and in government offices. These same foundations also poured millions of dollars into endowed chairs for conservative professors. They joined with the Reagan-Bush administrations and allied networks of right-wing intellectuals and activists to give college conservatives a clout and status vastly disproportionate to either their minimal intellectual contributions or the degree of their campus support.[11]

When I visited Dartmouth in 1987, staffers were regularly leaving copies of the *Review* in the halls of the dorms. One day, while students in the dorm where I was staying were partying and listening to Jimi Hendrix, a man lit a match to one of the stacks. The papers caught fire, triggering the alarms, and the student and his friends threw the burning copies out the window onto the concrete plaza below. As fire marshals cleared the halls, a crowd gathered by the stacks of flaming papers, talking and laughing as if at any fine October bonfire.

Just that afternoon, dorm residents had voiced their mistrust of peers involved in a planned march to challenge U.S. intervention in El Salvador. They were equally skeptical of others who'd built antiapartheid shanties on the quad. But they seemed perfectly delighted about the burning of the *Review*, joking how someone should get marshmallows and wieners, and more copies of the newspaper to feed the fire. Whether politics was left or right, rhetorical or reasoned, they kept their distance.

Even students who admired Reagan and Bush rarely seemed stirred by their specific prescriptions. Particularly as supply-side dreams began to crumble, students less and less praised the vision, wisdom, or courage of America's leaders. Instead they insisted we had no choice but to trust those in charge. "Bush tries," they said, repeatedly. "He's doing the best he can." "If you could meet Ronald Reagan, he'd give you the shirt off his back." "I know Barbara Bush really cares." Until the U.S. economy blatantly collapsed in the early 1990s, and student activism rose, they continued to excuse all manner of dubious actions by America's leaders, insisting that what really mattered was whether they were personally kind.

The perfect standard Apolitical students alternate between feeling they have no right to challenge "the men who know best," and a forgiveness so all-encompassing they find it impossible to hold institutions accountable. They respond to their activist peers, in contrast, with unforgiving judgments, holding up a Perfect Standard that the activists must meet before they will tender their support. They require politically involved peers to know every fact, reference every figure, be eloquent enough to debate Henry Kissinger on *Nightline*, yet remain constantly humble and self-effacing. Maybe then, they suggest, they'll take their arguments seriously.

Mistrust of activism often accompanies faith in those who wield power. "Say you're walking down the street," explained an education major from Minnesota's Mankato State University, "and someone asks you to sign a petition. You'd be reluctant because you don't know enough. Activists at the rallies take a look at what's going on in the country, and immediately find fault with it. But they aren't well informed. The people who are running things, the heads of the corporations, they understand the whole picture. They know what they're doing and are doing it for a reason."

Other students mistrust both groups. It angered a Dartmouth student in an arms control class when, at a campus forum, neither a Defense Department representative nor local peace activists could tell him the accurate range of Soviet SS 20 missiles. "Why is it that a twenty-one-year-old Dartmouth student has been able to discover this, but not the policy makers? The government doesn't know what it's talking about. The peace groups don't either. Nobody knows the facts." This student knew his weapons technologies better than many who acted to challenge them. Yet to insist that citizens understand every policy detail before taking a stand allows them no ethical basis for judgment except technical knowledge.

Some of this is information overload. Too many cable channels. Too many crises. Too many authorities with competing, clashing claims. But to hold to a perfect standard is ultimately a way of reserving judgment not only on any given issue or controversy, but on the entire prospect of taking responsibility for the future.

This standard demands not only perfect intellectual consistency, but flawless moral piousness. At Saint Benedict College in northern Minnesota, a half dozen students slept out in makeshift cardboard shelters to dramatize the plight of America's homeless. "Lots who passed by treated us like a slumber party," one participant recalled. "They acted like we were so cute, then when we kept on for a couple days they began to get annoyed. One girl yelled, 'Homeless people don't have blankets.' I was half asleep and told her, 'Yes they do. They have blankets and friends. They just don't have homes.' She looked like she'd only be satisfied if we stood outside and got soaked in the freezing rain."

If the radicals are truly sincere, this sensibility insists, they'll sleep in their shacks without blankets. They'll "sell their cars and give the money to Africa," as suggested by the University of Washington woman who called them "the granolas." They'll prove their commitment with vows of poverty, and never get foolish or frivolous. But the watchers also accuse them of being too "ultraserious" and holy. Maybe they'd get involved, they explain, if activists had a better sense of humor.

The Perfect Standard creates an abstract hierarchy of issues, in which the causes at hand never quite muster up. "I think South Africa is a reprehensible situation," a Columbia student said, "and maybe I should have made my actions correspond more to my beliefs when they were trying to get the school to divest. But when I watched people protesting, I thought, 'How paradoxical. They're so fervent about how awful it is over there, yet they aren't doing much for immediate situations, like racial issues here at home.' "

Why then, I asked, didn't he get involved when students took on precisely that set of questions two years later? "It all seemed diluted," he responded. "It wasn't so much standing up for fair housing or racial justice. It was almost like standing up for being a liberal or radical. Like the chance to be a protestor supersedes the issue itself."

Students used such arguments not only to challenge peers who acted, but to beat down their own impulses toward concern. "I get a little fearful," said a woman in the Mankato State education class, "when someone approaches me and I don't have enough knowledge about the subject. Instead of diving in and trying to learn about it afterward, I tend to ignore it. We feel we need to know so much just to understand what people are talking about."

A Clarkson student feared political involvement would make him "part of a mob. You'd have no say and lose your individualism." He'd just finished describing his hopes to work for IBM. I asked how much individuality he'd retain as part of that global multinational. "I don't worry about that," he said. "They break things down into different divisions."

Apolitical students also believed they had to agree with each and every aspect of any issue they took on—or else be exposed themselves as inconsistent. At Minnesota's Saint Olaf college, some activists held a "gay jeans day"—one of many nationwide—where students asked peers to support gay and lesbian rights by wearing the clothes they'd most often put on in any case. Some did, either because they were gay or acted in solidarity. Others wore the same clothes as always, then explained sheepishly that they hadn't intended this as a statement. Distressingly large numbers turned preppie.

I was struck by one woman who strongly believed in gay rights, but balked at gays adopting children. Because of that exception, she felt she couldn't wear jeans in support. She saw no way to endorse what she generally believed in, even though she could have readily enough have explained her own particular take on the gay adoption issue if it came up in conversation.

A political science major at Columbia described how she considered getting involved in a series of campus issues, but each time held back. She sat out the school's highly successful antiapartheid campaign, although many of her friends took part. She almost joined a fight over the eviction of a Latina tenant from a Columbia-owned apartment, "but I wasn't sure of my information." She was interested in homelessness, "but you can always doubt conflicting sources." She rejected cause after cause, down to her final conclusion, "I guess I'm just not a political person."

In contrast to more hostile others, she admired political commitment. But she exempted herself from responsibility. She described herself accurately, as did others who explain, "I'm not that kind of person" or "I'm just not the kind who speaks out." These students do hold back from marches, rallies, electoral campaigns, issue-oriented courses, controversial speakers, or any other form of social involvement. They do shy away from trying to change the world. Yet their phrases also reflect deeper assumptions. They draw an absolute line separating the rare few who emerge from the womb with protest signs in their hands and the reasonable majority who leave, and always will leave, these troublesome common issues to others. They judge activists and adapters as fundamentally different human breeds, with the dividing lines never to be crossed.

Character differences and differences in upbringing do play a role in political involvement. Some students, especially men from comfortable professional backgrounds, have been groomed for center stage, and eagerly speak their piece. Others, shy by nature or nurture—including family, class, or gender socialization—may require initial forms of engagement more gentle to their souls. As a Columbia woman said, "I guess I just don't like hearing my voice too loud. I don't speak out in my courses either." But if an entire generation consider themselves so fragile they dare not act as citizens, we cannot write this off to individual upbringings or circumstances.

Fear of speaking unwisely mixes with fear of consequences. "It's almost like, if I make an action," said a man in the Mankato State education class, "then I'm responsible for it. I have to justify it. If I go in and take a side, I'm risking my comfort zone. If I'm wrong, I might be scapegoated."

The students in this class were future teachers, preparing to train a new generation. A woman began to raise her hand, then said she hadn't intended to speak. When I asked if she had any reactions, she mentioned how much she feared creating conflict. "If you have a job in a school and you conform to what the administration wants, they like you. People want to be liked. You might lose job security by doing something different."

"Teachers already struggle for respect," the first speaker continued. He suggested that controversial stands would erode his credibility, and concluded "It's so much easier and safer to keep quiet."

Four ~~~~~~~~~~~~~~~~~~~~~~~~~

The right kind Climbing the
of friends economic ladder

~~~~~~~~~~~~~~~~~~~~~~~~~~~~~~~~~~~~~~~

University of Washington political science major Anna Roselli, the daughter of a barber
and an insurance agent, wanted more out of life "than just the nice house, the nice car,
and the nice boat." She thought the issues of students who marched and spoke out
might well need addressing. But she feared political involvement might "create problems and family tensions. It might separate me from the right kind of friends, the ones
I'm supposed to hang around with."

Anna had been conditioned, she told me, to associate with fellow students
who looked like they were going places, "who could afford the nice cars, nice clothes,
vacations in Europe and trips to Hawaii."

Her friend Patti was going places. Patti was the communications major from
a wealthy Seattle family who'd dismissed antiapartheid activists as "granolas." She
dressed perfectly, lived in an art-filled house with a sweeping view of Puget Sound, had
never known economic uncertainty. "She thinks the same things that I do," said Anna,
"about individualism and how you have to make your money to get ahead. But I don't
understand," she laughed, "how she excuses wealth handed down generation to generation where they pass it all to the family. I almost think I'm right in believing in Ayn
Rand, but she's not. My parents worked to make the American Dream. Patti's didn't.
They were born rich from the start."

No one in Anna's family took success for granted. They had scrimped to send
her to top-notch Catholic schools from first grade on. Her classmates had come largely

from wealthier backgrounds, "and if they didn't, they soon fit the image of preppie girls and boys." Her college sorority offered more of the same, a high status house with lots of pretty women. Anna spent most of her time in a Greek world "so large you never had time or motivation to move out of it. I'm not sure staying there all the time was good." She paused and thought. "But it sure was easy to do."

Twenty-five years before, Anna's parents had migrated from East Los Angeles to Seattle in a battered brown Chevrolet. Her dad had worked in a series of barber shops, finally saving enough to start his own. Her mom raised the kids and then sold insurance. They bought a simple house, then traded up to a low stone rambler with a view of Lake Washington in the distance. Making the best of modest space, her father converted the basement into children's bedrooms and a family lounge.

We talked in that homey, comfortable lounge, with its pool table, piano, TV, bar, and mirrored walls. "My dad's the most right-wing person alive," Anna said affectionately. "'It's not a fair world,' he always tells me. 'No one's going to give you anything. You've got to go out and get it.'"

Anna admired her parents' work and sacrifice, and hoped to redeem it through her own struggle to succeed. This meant, once again, trying to learn from those headed for the top.

"I'm probably a confused person," she said with an apologetic smile. "I grew up when my parents were very frugal and always saving money. Later they had more and we lived more comfortably. The kids I first grew up with are all married now, with children and blue-collar jobs. Those who came later, like Patti, are all pretty wealthy."

Anna lived on a boundary: between a working class world she felt she must leave and a new professional culture, whose rules, loyalties, and obligations were only beginning to come clear. I mentioned the comment of George Lipson, from Fairfield, that "a corporation isn't going to care how much I know about Plato."

"That's defeatist," said Anna. "But lots of people think that way. Someone like me would say 'Over *here*'"—she indicated with her hands—"'you read Plato and think about these things. And over *here*'" she indicated again—"'you get on with your life.'" Yet she accepted the separation even as she decried it.

Anna had recently met some less acquisitive students. "I met some much more interesting people when I started honors classes. I got along with them far better than my much more boring friends who I was used to. But what wins out? These new people are more fun and make me think, but they're not the ones who look like they're going somewhere, look like what society pictures as winners. They're not the ones I'm supposed to hang around with, and maybe I'm not big or brave enough to make a different choice."

The things that seem Anna did feel provoked to think when a
glamorous friend introduced her to Ayn Rand's nov-
els *Atlas Shrugged* and *The Fountainhead*. Like a surprising number of students, she
took Rand's writings not as justification for selfishness and greed, but as a license to
question the gray bureaucracy of mainstream American culture. Recent classes had
made her further question both Rand's approach and her own previous certainties.
"I've started to be a little shakier in what I believe. That's made me more confused, but
in a way that I like. I think a lot of people my age are also confused, but choose not to
deal with it. Maybe they just have less doubts. But I believe they don't really think about
things very much, like my friends who've grown up so cynical. I've only begun to understand why the opinions Patti and I have are so typical.

"Why, then, do I buy into them?" She hesitated. "I'm not sure. I'm trying to
think what else I'd buy into if I didn't. I suppose I could always join the Peace Corps, but
I wouldn't really know why I was doing it. I could become a fundamentalist, like some
of my friends from high school and from my sorority. But I could never spend my life
handing out pamphlets to make people believe in God. I can see problems with the
hypocrisy of trying to get rich. But I like to have wealthy friends, to go out Sunday afternoon and watch the hydroplane races from a speedboat. To be perfectly blunt, going
out on that boat and having friends with money—who are supposedly together, even
though they're really not—these are the things that seem glamorous."

Yet even as Anna described her adaptation, she wished she could learn "ways
to survive that aren't just what our culture thinks of as making it." Her college professors
taught details, not broad ethical questions. An international relations teacher, for instance, had students memorize the entire command structure of the North Atlantic
Treaty Organization. "And if you missed one sentence from his lectures, it would end
up on the test." Her affluent parochial high school had treated larger public issues "as if
they weren't even there." For all of Seattle's large numbers of activist Catholics, her
family church was as silent as her school.

Anna tried to take classes that would make her think, like the one on American political culture where we met. She took them "even if Professor McCann's assignments are hard and it's not so good for my grade point." She remembered another,
taught by a grad student, where she studied Machiavelli, the ways nations demonize
their enemies, and the Milgram experiments in obedience to authority—in which subjects administered what they believed to be dangerously increasing levels of electric
shock to individuals (actually actors) who appeared to fail questions on a test. These
courses challenged Anna's previous certainties, but they were the exception. College
generally gave her little help toward engaging with the world.

Earlier, in McCann's class, Anna had said she didn't understand people who do things "like ranting and raving in front of the White House about the Japanese killing whales. That's doing no good. It just seems irrational." When she was assigned a book on women civil rights workers, she respected them more, because they seemed "courageous individuals, who happened to be involved in a larger cause." She also liked these women more than their contemporaries in the Vietnam antiwar movement, who— glimpsed mostly through the lenses of the media—appeared mostly as stereotypes. "They just seemed like more masses of groups," she said. "I'd see pictures of their sit-ins and demonstrations, with all that violence, then these other people who also opposed things, but in a more structured way. When the activism got too large, it took in people who came for other reasons than just the issues themselves. It was more of a fad, like Patti said."

But the civil rights workers still seemed creatures of a far different time. When I asked Anna if she saw any comparable recent concerns, she suggested possibly homelessness.

"When I was in D.C., once, there were people living in the subway. That's the worst thing I've ever seen. But what do you do about it? Giving money or building shelters helps, but some are mentally ill. So I don't know what you do. I think everything you try is worthwhile, but you have to live your individual life. So you say 'that's a shame,' and help if you can. Maybe there's nothing you can do."

She paused with a look both frustrated and resigned. "I know that's a defeatist attitude, but it's hard to imagine getting involved. When you work on a project to change things, it creates tensions. People can be against you. It takes so much more energy than just working to earn a living and buy your house, buy your boat, and raise your family. It's so much easier just to live your life.

"It's also hard to say I don't care about money. It makes my life comfortable. I work hard, like my parents, so I know I'll do OK. Students I know say, 'make your money first, then you can go make social change if you want to.' But I don't want to become like the wealthy moms on the department store committees for the homeless."

How much, I asked, did she really want the safe and comfortable life? How much was she settling for it by default? Anna thought a moment, and said probably the latter. "It does seem like there's no other path. "I don't think I've ever had to stand up for something I believe in. Maybe I'm just coming into that part of my life where I feel that I can."

Anna remained in a state of flux. She mistrusted activist efforts and believed they made little difference. She was unsure what choices she had except to go after a career that would let her live like her affluent friends. Yet she didn't want to bury her new concerns. While her sorority sisters headed off on vacation to Europe and Hong Kong, Anna finished her final courses, and reflected on what to do next. She felt she was "just starting again and just beginning to learn."

Anna's narrative suggests a complex interplay between the drive for economic security and students' everyday choices. Given an uncertain economy, students worry about making it. Even those born into relative prosperity believe they must jump through endless hoops to maintain their place. Few permit themselves to ask what they most believe in and what they want to fight for. Few ask themselves what important work they want to do in the world, in whatever field they pursue. They feel they have no right to set the terms of their lives.

This process of adaptation leaves them believing that they must make the right friends, that is, useful friends. That they must take the right courses, which track them most efficiently toward successful careers. If, consequently, they ignore their actual interests and passions, they consider it regrettable necessity. They draw the line especially at political involvement. Again and again, students echo Anna Roselli's fears that such commitments would harm their careers and separate them from the right path. "You do see issues that are fairly relevant," explained a Colby woman, "but you say to yourself, 'Well, I could take the time to go down to Portland, or Washington, D.C. But if I do that I'll be stereotyped as that kind of person, that certain kind of radical person.' And that stereotype is definitely not going to help me be successful."

Five ～～～～～～～～～～～～～

America on Coping with
the slide decline

～～～～～～～～～～～～～～～～～～～～

America's economic crunch makes it hard for students to take responsibility for more than just personal survival. Compared to twenty years ago, they work more hours at outside jobs, graduate more in debt, and face a more uncertain economic future. They have fewer choices of what to take and fewer resources to finance their learning. Economic pressures push them to seek careers with whatever institutions will hire them, whether or not these institutions play a constructive role in society.

In 1969, 43 percent of all college students worked outside jobs while enrolled in school. By 1979, the figure had risen to 51 percent, and by 1990, it was 63 percent. Some embraced this increased workload because it bought the good life: the right clothes, car, electronic toys, and money to party on the weekends. Yet even the most frugal felt greater economic pressure than did their predecessors. American myths that glorify the process of working your way through college gloss over what it means to constantly be stretched thin, to come to class bleary eyed, to lack the time to do justice either to your courses or to broader social responsibilities.[1]

"How can I study when I'm at work and have a test the next day?" asked a Chicago Circle student who worked thirty hours a week at a financial management company. "I can't. It's too much. A little job is fine, but this isn't. When I have kids, I want to make enough so they can be a bit spoiled and won't have to do this."

Financial pressures have drastically reduced options for paths other than the most pragmatic. Young women and men conduct alternative cultural explorations best, Barbara Ehrenreich has suggested, "in a sixth-floor walk-up apartment and on a diet of peanut butter and day-old bread."[2] But in much of the country, low-rent walk-ups are gone and student earnings have not kept up with rising costs. In 1973 I was living in New York City, attending the New School for Social Research. Working twenty-five hours a week as a bartender, I averaged $5.00 an hour, which paid the New School's costly private tuition, covered my living expenses, and left enough for a bit of savings. My rent, for a room in a shared house in a marginal Brooklyn neighborhood, cost $75.00 a month. Twenty years later I met a student at City College of New York who split an apartment three blocks from my old house and commuted an hour each way on the subway. He paid $450 a month for his share, yet his part-time job paid just $6.00 an hour, which left him falling steadily deeper into debt. A student at Mercer University in Georgia followed my own path of bartending. He had to work 40 hours a week to match his costs.

Direct educational expenses have risen as well. From the late 1970s to the late 1980s, tuition at public colleges and universities rose one and a half times as fast as disposable income. Tuition at private schools rose almost twice as fast as disposable income. Even relatively comfortable students now feel the pressure.[3]

Students carry greater liens on their futures now than in the past. By the mid-1980s, despite their outside work, more than three times as many students had to take out government loans compared with ten years before. By the early 1990s, the gap had increased to more than four times as many. The students also graduated with higher debt loads and had to spend a greater share of their initial earnings to pay them back.[4]

Such economic pressure rests particularly hard on students from poor backgrounds, who can least afford college to begin with. These individuals have the fewest family resources and support networks to fall back on, will earn less in their ultimate jobs, and will see whatever they make tapped more for other needs, like supporting younger siblings or aging parents.[5]

These pressures have increasingly skewed the composition of the academy along class lines. In 1992, 94 percent of unmarried eighteen to twenty-four-year-olds from families with incomes of $63,000 or more, the richest quarter of the population, graduated high school. Eighty-six percent of these high school graduates enrolled in college. For those from families making $21,000 or less, the poorest quarter, just 64 percent graduated from high school. And just 52 percent of these graduates went on to any kind of higher education, mostly at two-year and other low-status schools. The disparities hit minorities particularly hard, since young African-Americans and Latinos represented 60 percent of the low income group but less than 7 percent of those in the top bracket.

The gaps in graduation rates were even greater. Among college students in the top quarter, 94 percent secured their B.A. by age 24, an age beyond which such achievement grows increasingly difficult; in the bottom quarter, just 12 percent got their degree by this point. Combining the rates of high school graduation, college enrollment, and attainment of degrees, 76 percent of young men and women in the wealthiest quarter secured their B.A. by age 24, compared to 4 percent at the bottom. The gap was bad enough in 1980, when students in the richest quarter of the population had twice the chance to complete college in a feasible time frame as those in the poorest. The gap had now climbed to nearly twenty to one.[6]

Students who take a full academic load, piece together twenty hours a week of geographically dispersed part-time jobs, and expect to graduate $6,000 or $7,000 in debt face tremendous pressures. For some, outside political involvements are virtually impossible. Single mothers, for instance, juggle children, baby-sitters, day care, and study time, and still have to work and take out major loans. The best most can do is get through and still spend some time with their kids.

Yet politically involved students carry no exemption from financial concerns. A University of Nebraska woman who organized fellow students on farm issues logged sixteen to twenty hours a week as night manager of the student union. A friend in the same group made dates with her boyfriend for 1:00 A.M., when she got off her fast food job, because it was the only time she had free. A Columbia activist helped work his way through college by tutoring Hebrew. A single mother at University of Wisconsin at Oshkosh ran the student lecture board. Others worked at law offices and diaper factories, restaurants and bookstores, at jobs no different from those held by their apolitical peers.

Why are so many students in a financial bind that both daunts political involvement and steadily increases class divisions? Why do those with the fewest resources continue to drop out at a time when Americans without a college degree fall further behind economically? To begin with, government aid has been cut. In 1975, 80 percent of federal student support came as grants. By 1988 this had dropped to less than 50 percent. Low- and middle-income students have had no choice but to pick up the slack by mortgaging their futures with debt.[7]

Cuts in federal support for education also fueled college tuition hikes. As government aid programs were slashed, colleges tried to fill the gap by providing more scholarships from internal funds. This in turn left a hole they had to fill either by greater fundraising or by hiking the tuition paid by other students. College expenses also jumped as a result of increasingly top-heavy university bureaucracies. During the eighties, as economist and American Association of University Professors president Barbara Bergmann writes, "administrative budgets—the expenditure for presidents, deans, and their assistants—grew 26 percent faster than instructional budgets—the expenditure for professors." Top administrators joined other elite nonprofit sector representatives in scrambling to match skyrocketing corporate compensations and in establishing new hierarchies that would report to them. By the 1987-88 academic year, the average American institution of higher education spent $1,742 on administrative costs for each full time equivalent student, and the average private university spent $3,417—figures that did not include expenditures for libraries, research, physical plant, or student services like counseling, admissions, or placement. Salaries for administrators and other non-teaching professionals now equal almost half of all money spent on instruction.[8]

University-corporate relationships have also imposed new costs, as universities have developed expensive research infrastructures to conduct joint ventures, which often cannibalize the more flexible funds devoted to general education. The result has been to make college more expensive, to starve traditional liberal arts departments that lack major government or commercial ties, and to foster a general tone that suggests learning only matters when dollar signs follow. The University of Michigan recently chopped a third of the budgets from the schools of education, art, and music. Johns Hopkins sharply cut expenditures for the College of Arts and Sciences. Columbia eliminated its geography and linguistics programs, Washington University its long-respected sociology department.[9]

Growing limits on access to college feed America's more general inequalities. The erosion of decent blue collar jobs makes a college degree almost the base requirement for a decent livelihood, even as vocations like nursing and education now require education beyond a BA. degree. In 1971, for every dollar earned by a male high school graduate aged twenty-five to thirty-four, a college graduate earned 27 percent more, a relatively modest difference. By 1981, the college graduate earned 34 percent more. By 1992 college men earned 60 percent more when they initially entered the work force, and almost twice as much as they moved up in their careers. Men with professional degrees earn still higher incomes from the beginning, while the incomes of young high school educated men have dropped in half in real dollars from the seventies to the eighties.[10]

Young women get a still worse deal. The average college educated woman earns less than high school educated men (the gap is somewhat narrower with younger women), and women high school graduates earn less than male high school dropouts. People of color of both sexes lag behind at every step of age and education, all the more since most start in those economic groups most excluded. As rising costs make the passage through college increasingly difficult for all but the most affluent, they lock out precisely those students who need the opportunities the most.[11]

There are situations in which tightening financial binds have sparked strong student engagement. I'll talk about them later. Yet the economic crunch has pushed most toward solutions more individual and more adaptive. "I'm in enough of a hole as it is," said a student from Michigan State. "The politics are out of my control. I don't have time or energy to waste."

Educational analyst Theodore Marchese suggests that loans prompt "instrumental values . . . because [they] force a responsible student to think ahead to the necessity for repayment . . . to position yourself through your course work, major and degree for a higher-paying job. . . . In effect, college becomes less and less something done for its own sake and more and more something done for what comes afterwards." Such pressures, Marchese says, give students less time to dally with intellectual reflection or social involvement. They feel, instead, that they must sacrifice everything to their practical goals.[12]

Because students first began focusing strongly on jobs and careers in the late 1970s, when more financial resources were available, we cannot wholly attribute their material values to Reagan-Bush policies. Renewed activism at the end of the eighties came amidst visible economic decline. But the crunch of rising scholastic costs and reduced financial aid levies a powerful force to keep students focused on individual survival.

America on the slide   Those coming of age in the eighties and nineties have inherited a worsening economic context in general. A recent Tom Toles cartoon, "The Reading of the Will," shows four befuddled figures who listen, seated in chairs, as a lawyer describes their legacy from the previous time. "Dear Kids," it begins.

> We, the generation in power since World War II, seem to have used up pretty much everything ourselves. We kind of drained all the resources out of our manufacturing industries, so there's not much left there. The beautiful old buildings that were built to last for centuries, we tore down and replaced with characterless but inexpensive structures, and you can have them. Except everything we built had a lifespan about the same as ours, so, like the interstate highway system we built, they're all falling apart now and you'll have to deal with that. We used up as much of our natural resources as we could, without providing for renewable ones, so you're probably only good until about a week from Thursday. We did build a generous Social Security and pension system, but that was just for us. In fact, the only really durable thing we built was toxic dumps. You can have those. So think of your inheritance as a challenge. The challenge of starting from scratch. You can begin as soon as—oh, one last thing—as soon as you pay off the two-trillion-dollar debt we left you.

Not all in the World War II generation shaped these decisions, only those who held the reins of power. But the men who run America have squandered vast national resources on useless or destructive ends. When the cartoon ran late in Ronald Reagan's first term, the economy was supposedly still in a boom phase. Since then, a savings and loan scandal has erupted that will cost at least $500 billion, more in wasted or stolen money than America spent in all of World War II, including veterans benefits, and enough to have bought homes, free and clear, for twenty million citizens. The two-trillion-dollar national debt has doubled to over four trillion. The splits between rich and poor have grown wider.[13]

In the Vietnam era, students came of age during the longest sustained period of economic growth in America's history. Most took for granted that once they had made it through college, they'd find a choice of decent jobs. Students now face both a tougher passage through school and tougher times when they get out.

Given the prevailing economic uncertainty, they are right to fear for their prospects. But their opportunities have been ravaged, not by freak caprices of nature, but by a lack of political and economic accountability, and by a triumph of shortsightedness. They have been ravaged by more than a decade of national choices that have strip-mined a common future.

The students may not know exact statistics, but they know America is in trouble. The landscape they inherit is disturbing to contemplate. Between 1973 and 1991, U.S. average hourly wages dropped 7 percent in real dollars. The country went from being the world's largest international creditor to being the world's largest debtor. With over one million people behind bars, the U.S. has now surpassed South Africa and the Soviet Union to lead the world in the percentage of our population in prison or jail. Between 1970 and 1990, the U.S. suicide rate for young women aged fifteen to nineteen nearly doubled.[14]

Aided by relocation of factories to Mexico and Puerto Rico, by union busting, and policy shifts that dropped tax rates for those in the top income bracket from 70 percent to 30 percent, the richest 1 percent of U.S. citizens have come to control a greater share of national wealth than everyone else combined. Whereas the typical German chief executive makes twenty-one times as much as their average worker, and the typical Japanese executive makes less than twenty times as much, the ratio for CEOs of major American corporations climbed to 40 to 1 in 1980, and 160 to 1 in 1991. The overall disparity of wealth more than doubled in a fifteen-year period, to become greater than at any point since the eve of the Great Depression.[15]

This polarization of resources has combined with what Clinton administration Secretary of Labor Robert Reich describes as a more general withdrawal of the wealthiest Americans from the common life of the society. As federal domestic cutbacks have been passed on to the states, a growing crisis has developed in public schools, parks, police forces, and transportation systems. Those who can afford it retreat increasingly into their own enclaves, whether by sending their children to private schools, living in guarded neighborhoods, spending time at upscale malls instead of in city parks, using cars or taxis instead of buses or the subway, and drinking bottled water instead of working to ensure pure municipal supplies. Students who grow up thus insulated within what John Kenneth Galbraith has called the "the culture of contentment" comprehend less and less the lives of peers who do not.[16]

The high consumption values that dominated this era shaped the dreams of Americans increasingly less able to fulfill them. Between the late 1970s and the mid-1980s, almost 30 percent more high school seniors said they considered it a major priority to acquire expensive consumer goods like new cars, stylish clothes, high-powered stereos, power boats, or vacation houses. Their desire to be very well off financially rose dramatically. So did their eagerness to work in the corporate sector. Three quarters of these students saw no problem with advertisers inducing people "to buy things they don't really need." Definitions of "the good life" shifted, in all age groups, toward materialism and away from either public concern or personal introspection.[17]

These goals didn't dominate students' every waking moment. Some became politically involved nonetheless, or dove passionately into literature, chemistry, or classics. They still flirted, danced, and drank at weekend parties, fell in love or followed out their lust, spent lazy afternoons playing softball or frisbee, watched *Cheers*, *Late Night with David Letterman*, *Days of Our Lives*, and *The Simpsons*, and talked in endless bull sessions with their friends. Those at residential campuses savored the newfound liberty of living away from home. Those without overly demanding outside jobs savored their leisure. For all that the adapters intended to rise, they liked a good time.[18]

Increased material expectations were a core part of Reagan-era mythologies, yet students who embraced them often felt uncertain about their chances to achieve them. Recent U.S. college graduates can expect to log in more paid hours than their counterparts in other advanced industrial nations, and more than other Americans during just about any time in the post–World War II era. Most will be paid less for their work than their parents were at comparable stages of life. In 1979 the median family income of households headed by individuals under twenty-five was $24,000 in 1991 dollars. By a dozen years later, it had fallen to $17,000, a drop of nearly 30 percent, with households headed by women or minorities getting by on much less. Those who didn't go to college carried the brunt of this decline, largely due to a drop in high-paid unionized employment. But even those who made it through and got their B.A.'s faced stagnating prospects. Real incomes of college graduates under thirty increased just one percent a year during the 1980s, a fraction of the growth during their parents' generation.[19]

Certain opportunities did briefly flourish during the time this generation came of age. Fueled by corporate shifts from manufacturing to financial services, students chased six-figure dreams of becoming stock brokers, investment bankers, financial analysts, corporate lawyers, upper-level managers, or other well-paid facilators of speculation and exchange. Yet even on the glamor track, security was precarious. As many as a million and a half midlevel management jobs are estimated to have disappeared during the 1980s. When Wall Street firms crashed at the decade's end, recently hired graduates were often the first to be cut, while top executives retained their million-dollar salaries. Even students who resolutely chased wealth could hardly feel certain of their prospects.[20]

America's social and economic crises have produced some important shifts toward involvement. But economic uncertainty has also pressed more students toward greater adaptation and withdrawal—in ways that have helped allow those at the top to continue taking a greater and greater share. Most students have responded to the general economic tightening by striving that much harder for the promised gold—or just to survive—and averting their eyes from the costs.

The strains of individualism and materialism I describe aren't wholly new. They echo themes apparent to the observer Tocqueville as early as the 1830s. But the period in which today's students have come of age took shortsighted greed to rare heights.

Students who adopted the prevailing ethics mostly disdain others unwilling to fit themselves, Procrustean fashion, into whatever slots become available. They call them "just a bunch of losers," in the words of Tim from Fairfield, a label that hits harder in harsher and meaner times. It accuses those who try to hold America's leaders accountable for their actions of doing so largely from their own internal failings—because they are too weak to succeed. This very notion of "losers" holds a cautionary warning, that to participate politically may be to risk your personal future.

Private solutions   Dale Ottiger, the University of Nebraska student who wanted to work for Dow Chemical, felt no choice but to try and cast his lot with the winners. I met with him again, a few months after his internship with Dow had ended. He'd spent the summer selling pesticides and herbicides, and inspecting fields for corn bore infestations, sometimes going out on his own, sometimes with retailers he served. Because sales demanded friendly relationships, Dale often took customers out on Dow's tab and spent much of his time playing golf and hosting people for dinner.

At first he wondered whether he was earning his pay. On the farm he had worked six days a week, from six in the morning to ten at night, with stress, physical risks, and few ways to take a break. In a good month he'd make a thousand dollars. In other months, he'd work just as hard for nothing. On the sales job, Dale worked regular hours, got paid for socializing, and earned $1,500 a month plus a car and an expense account.

It was funny, Dale said, to see salespeople so biased toward their own brands, whether or not they were really different. He told me he wanted to act responsibly, and asked whom I'd blame if a farmer sprayed his fields with a chemical that didn't work because of drought, and then cutworms ate his crop.

Within the framework of chemical farming, I said, the salesperson acted reasonably—so long as the farmer knew that the product would fail in dry conditions. But what about chemicals that succeeded in their specified tasks yet polluted the land and groundwater?

That, Dale said, was a tough call. He worried about chemical saturation and was glad farmers were beginning to think environmentally. But he saw few productive alternatives, and the market made it as hard to consider these issues as it did to consider the fate of the family farm. "If salespeople aren't productive, if they don't meet their goals and objectives, it won't be good for the company and they'll lose their jobs. Perhaps Dow and ConAgra do try to constantly expand. The bigger they are, the more cash flow they control. But that's just the American Dream. Some people have the touch to manage it. Others work and work and it never comes right."

Dale hoped any institution he joined would respect his individual conscience. Sometimes, he said, corrupt pest management scouts would tell farmers to spray for corn bore when their fields were only 10 or 15 percent infested. "You need 35 percent for it to make economic sense. But they'll say the infestation's just beginning, and the farmers will spray and lose money. The scouts do that because they get benefits based on the amount of product they sell. There aren't a lot of salespeople like that, but there are some, and I'd never be one."

Though I believed him, most farmers who went under had succumbed to no such manipulative tactics. They were too experienced, he acknowledged, to do so. Instead, they hit structural problems—the press of falling prices and rising debt that he felt they just couldn't buck.

Perhaps Dale might have taken a different path had he been exposed to different role models. Nebraska had strong populists in its history, such as William Jennings Bryan, Willa Cather, and Senator George Norris, but he had never read about them. The

University of Nebraska campus was politically quiet. Small-town politeness frowned on visible dissent. If he worried at all about his intended career, he feared that a career in sales might make it hard on his prospective family. "I'm concerned," he said, "that I might end up divorced, like all those other salesmen whose wives and children can't take the strain. But then I'm different from those folks. I know my priorities. If I had a reasonably restricted geographic area, I could make it work."

"Maybe," he suggested, "I'm just too preoccupied with my own life and my goals. Maybe I don't want anything to get in the way. But I'd like to be a positive influence in the company and the agricultural community. Perhaps I've avoided some of these questions"—he thought for a minute, then went on—"because I'm caught in the hype of being a 'professional,' a leader on my way up in these corporations. I like the people who speak out on farm issues. I took their seminar the first year. Maybe what they've done will do some good later, or get them personally in a good career position. But I don't see it as a career position for me, maybe because I have a different dream and haven't studied politics or law. I don't see it as something with wage earning potential."

Like Dale, most students frame their lives in private terms, relegating desires for commitment and meaning to personal life. Their misgivings about their relationships with powerful institutions arise mostly in terms of situational costs—Dale's fear that too much time on the road might hurt his family. They alternate between proclaiming themselves captains of their fates and insisting they have little choice but to fit in.

Building your portfolio   Kenneth C. Green, educational analyst at the University of Southern California, describes the retreat to private life as part of what he calls "portfolio building" behavior. "Like an artist assembling work for exhibit to a potential patron, students attempt to build a portfolio of skills, contacts, experiences, and credentials to present to potential employers. They are making choices—about college, majors, summer jobs, and graduate school—that they hope will serve them well in the job market and protect them from the economic upheaval they have witnessed firsthand in recent years."[21]

From the early 1970s to the mid-1980s, students built their portfolios to the exclusion of nearly all other priorities. As a result, the number of bachelor's degrees earned in the social sciences and humanities dropped by almost half. Those in math and the natural sciences fell sharply as well. So did the numbers of students going on for doctoral degrees. The number of those intending to teach plummeted from nearly a quarter of all students to less than 5 percent, a change fueled particularly by shifts of young women away from this and other traditionally ill-paid and gender-bound fields. Human service careers in general were devastated by federal cuts, and precipitous drops occurred in populations of students pursuing any of those paths.[22]

In contrast, students planning business careers rose from one-tenth of entering freshmen to 25 percent, and most of these majored in business fields. These numbers peaked in 1987, leveling off slightly by the end of the decade, then dropping to 15 percent by 1993 in the wake of economic decline and major Wall Street scandals. During the same period, interest in teaching began to return, to 10 percent. But the academic tracks most popular throughout the eighties promised quick entry and high earnings. They gave students scant context to reflect on broader issues of consequence.[23]

Academic paths track students either toward or away from involvement with controversial public issues. Because of the greater latitude for critical discussion afforded by the social sciences and humanities, students majoring in those areas have long spearheaded America's campus movements. Those in fields like business have remained more remote. As their numbers have grown, this has walled off an increasingly large sector of the campus from social concern.

Students who followed such paths remained curiously detached from the actual content of their prospective labors. A few found genuine delight in the gamesmanship of finance or sales. Yet most flocked to these careers not from intrinsic interest, but from their sense that comfort and security superseded all other goals.

I saw this with the highly individualistic Fairfield students, introduced in Chapter One. For all their talk of magic money—of making a killing in real estate, investment banking, or sales—they had little idea of any specific social needs they wanted to address, products they wanted to produce, or vocations that would provide intrinsic satisfaction.

"If you work hard," said Tim, "you're going to make a buck. That's just the way it is."

"But work hard for what?" I questioned. "Do junk bond dealers and corporate raiders really contribute to society?"

"They make money," said Tim.

"Yeah," Scott agreed, "they make money."

Some highly apolitical students—many engineers and computer jocks who consider financial rewards wholly secondary to the chance to invent and tinker—do love their work. But they also shrug off potential ethical problems. "Lots of us," said a Clarkson electrical engineering major named John, "don't like all the military spending. I'd rather do civilian research, like the space program, than build weapons. But that's where the money is, and where you find the resources."

I suggested America's excess military investments rob the economy of precisely the financial and human resources necessary to thrive. "But the government can't just say 'We'll make a better TV or satellite,' " John replied. "That isn't their role. Most of us," he concluded, "just try to build what we're building to the best of our ability. We like to make little electrical things work better. We don't worry about what we can't change. We don't worry about how what we make will be used."

The adapters believe they have few choices except to just get by, even if this behavior effectively hands America's future over to institutions they mistrust. Their acceptance of runaway corporate power has been encouraged by shifts in campus policies that have increasingly allowed food services to be centrally run by Marriott corporation, bookstores to be managed by Barnes & Noble, and student unions to become surrogate minimalls, featuring brand name franchises like Burger King, Wendy's, and McDonald's. As filmmaker Jim Klein points out, students once questioned such corporations "as off-campus forces that had to be watched and checked," lest they dominate every aspect of American life. Now, their pervasiveness on campus helps them appear as the sole model for America's future. It helps convey a message, as noted by a journalist interviewed in Klein's film *Letter to the Next Generation*: "If you don't do it in the corporate way, it is not going to be successful."[24]

Economic fears, materialist dreams, ethical timidity, and a relentless push to adapt—all flourish in America's current uncertain landscape. Students mostly respond to the constriction of independent paths with a mix of regret and pragmatic resolve. A Chicago Circle student named Gina described how she'd "really enjoy" teaching high school algebra, but considered the money "just so terrible" that she headed instead to market research.

"I can't see living lower than I do now," Gina continued, as I sat with her and a group of her friends on the one of the concrete campus's few patches of grass. Gina's dad owned a pizza parlor, her mother a beauty shop. She put herself through school working twenty hours a week in a grocery. "If I have kids, I want to give them more," she said. "I don't want to have to always work evenings and weekends like I do right now. How can I give them what I want and be a teacher?"

Six ∿∿∿∿∿∿∿∿∿∿∿∿

Divided loyalties Making it from the bottom

∿∿∿∿∿∿∿∿∿∿∿∿∿∿∿∿∿∿∿∿∿∿∿∿

If middle-class students tend to live in a bubble of insulation, students from poor or working-class backgrounds often know America needs changing, but lack the time to act or the faith that their voices will be heard. Their communities are in desperate straits. They see the need to respond. Yet their precarious situations make it hard for them to get involved. Even when issues hit close to their homes and hearts, pressures against involvement ride with them constantly.

Chicago Circle student Raul Ortiz strained at the limits of these dilemmas. He wanted to work and to rise. At the same time, he wanted to stay true to the community that raised him. He wasn't sure both were possible.

Raul's parents divorced when he was five months old; he last saw his father when he was six. He grew up in a Chicago Housing Authority (CHA) apartment in the poor and racially diverse Uptown neighborhood. His mother, with her bad legs and periodic memory loss, supported Raul and his brother through government disability, intermittent work marking prices in a department store, and an eventual job as a beautician. The first in his extended family to go to college, Raul headed Circle Campus's Confederation of Latin American Students (CLAS), through which he administered tutoring and recruitment programs and put together educational, cultural, and social events. Meanwhile, he studied to become an engineer and looked forward to marrying and raising a family, "not necessarily in the suburbs, but in a nice house in a safe neighborhood . . . maybe just across the Chicago city line."

Raul had worked from the time he was twelve, shoveling snow, shining shoes, busing tables, parking cars, and later working at McDonald's. Finally, his priest, Father Michael Rochford, lined him up with a janitor's job funded by a city Comprehensive Employment and Training Act (CETA) program. Raul worked cleaning up the church and the local neighborhood. Unlike some of his college friends who continued to see people they knew engaged in shootings and killings, Raul managed to stay clear of the gangs, although he occasionally played softball with gang members. But for all his hard work, he'd thought little about a professional future.

Father Rochford got Raul the janitorial job to help pay for parochial school. A college prep seminary, Quigley North, required him to improve his English, which would have meant summer school. Instead he went to Saint Benedict's, near Wrigley Field, a frequent source of bat boys for the Chicago Cubs. "That turned out to be a good thing, because Saint Benedict had a better math program than Quigley." Raul felt he learned almost as much in his first year at this school as he had in his first eight years in Chicago public schools.

Father Rochford nurtured Raul socially and became his mentor. "He kept me straight," Raul said. "He had parties where people got together and watched the Cubs and Bears games. There were people from all walks of life—working class, upper middle class, lawyers, doctors, judges, salesmen. I liked how they lived, instead of in CHA houses with roaches and rats. I saw a relationship between working hard and education."

To make it from CHA housing to college, Raul almost had to have a mentor like Father Rochford. Educator Mike Rose, in describing his own journey from South Los Angeles poverty to teaching writing at UCLA, challenges America's Horatio Alger myths by explaining:

> We live, in America, with so many platitudes about motivation and self-reliance and individualism . . . that we find it hard to accept the fact that they are serious nonsense. To live your early life on the streets of South L.A.—or Homewood or Spanish Harlem or Chicago's South Side or any one of hundreds of other depressed communities—and to journey up through the top levels of the American educational system will call for support and guidance at many, many points along the way. You'll need people to guide you into conversations that seem foreign and threatening. You'll need models, lots of them, to show you how to get at what you don't know. You'll need people to help you center yourself in your own developing ideas. You'll need people to watch out for you.[1]

Father Rochford offered this support for Raul. He could not have gone to Catholic high school without the janitorial job that paid for his tuition, bus fare, lunch, and books. He took lots of math and science, edging around the English courses in which he still felt uncomfortable. In his spare time he played baseball, played in the school orchestra, rode his bike, and collected discarded pop bottles so he could afford $1.50 grandstand seats to see the Cubs. His church ran a soup kitchen, "but I stayed away from that, because I never wanted to be like those people."

He didn't consider himself poor. "Everyone else was the same. We'd have soft-ball games against the kids from Arlington Heights, which is a rich suburb. We'd notice they always had nice clothes and brought pop to drink and all kinds of food and stuff. They were better educated. We couldn't invite them to our houses. But we were better in sports. We didn't give a shit about who the governor was. They couldn't walk in the streets like we could."

For a while Raul wanted to be a priest, then changed his mind. He thought of following a friend to the main University of Illinois campus at Champaign-Urbana, but balked at the cost of living away from home with only minimum-wage work available as a busboy or a waiter. Staying in Chicago was cheaper and offered more opportunity. He was eligible for federal and state grants, like the Pell program, without which he probably would have become a carpenter instead of continuing on. Because he had always been good at math, Raul decided to become an engineer.

"People get confused," he said, "whether this should be a place for learning or a place for the professions. I've taken Latin American studies and political science. I'd love to take more liberal arts and philosophy, but the curriculum makes it hard. My time and money are limited. I know I'm good at math and science. I want to graduate at twenty-two and start work."

Raul came to school a Republican. "I didn't vote that way because of pressure from my friends. But I had the American Dream of two cars and the house in the sub-urbs. Maybe I still do. I know I want to get an M.B.A. as soon as I can start working so my employer can pay for it. But this place, talking with these people, has changed me."

He gestured to the muraled walls of the Rafael Cintron Ortiz Center, an on-campus gathering place associated with CLAS that offered a second home to the school's 1,650 Latino students.[2] They studied, napped, played chess, listened to music, and talked and joked with friends. The Cintron Center began in 1976, following years of proposals, negotiations, and demonstrations. Finally, thirty-nine students were arrested for occupying the administration building. The university granted the group an unused locker room, a modest Latin American Studies department, and funds for tutoring and recruitment. Two weeks before the center opened, a young anthropology professor who'd been a strong supporter was killed by someone trying to rob him. The students named the space Rafael Cintron Ortiz Cultural Center in his honor.

The Chicago Circle campus has an almost lunar feeling, with its mazes of concrete walkways. Most students pass quickly through the arid landscape, then head back to work by car, bus, or subway. Inside the center, the murals display a festival of faces and colors—saxophones and city skylines, bare-chested *campesinos*, a jaguar god, a brown Christ on the cross. In one corner, soldiers march with gas masks and guns, facing mothers and priests holding signs for the *desaparecidos*, the disappeared. An armored knight spears a naked Indian in the shadow of a Mayan pyramid. Couples dance beneath a hot urban moon. The walls depict Latino culture's celebration and pain.

Raul looked upscale. He took pride in dressing well, in dark slacks, a black-and-white pullover, and new black loafers. At first, he disliked the Cintron Center. "Hanging out with all you Mexicans," he said, laughing, to his friends Francisco and Victor. "I thought college students were supposed to be mature. I came here and saw people break dancing. It seemed like high school. It wasn't until I was a sophomore that I started to enjoy the programs. Now I like to hang out with these lowlifes."

"Latinos who don't come from the *barrio*," said Victor, "who come from a much better income, think we waste a lot of time here. They consider us just like . . ."

"Like lucky to be in college, lucky to be alive," said Francisco. "They call themselves "high-spanics," like SHIP, the Society of Hispanic Engineers, who just despise the Cultural Center."

"Kind of like me," said Raul, laughing again. "Except I do it differently. I'm part of them but don't like them too much. I get better grades than they do, but I'm too radical."[3]

I asked how Raul's career might change his newfound commitments.

"My mom was on welfare till I was sixteen," Raul said. "I've lived in CHA housing all my life. Working at the church helped me see what life would be like without always worrying about money. I want to be able to enjoy a few luxuries, like a house with a front yard, a backyard and a side yard. I can't have that in the city." Engineers made nearly $30,000 a year fresh out of college. He'd earned $400 a week as a student engineer with People's Gas, Light & Coke company. "I just messed with the computer, did a bit of paperwork, and kept thinking, 'This is the good life.'"

Raul found his new status strange. On a recent job near O'Hare Airport, a union worker his own age took turns with another guy, cutting a large steel pipe. "I got paid simply for watching them. All my life I've been the one doing the dirty work. I felt out of place. I wanted to help the guys work. It was a weird experience, but one I'll get used to. I guess that's why I've gone to school—to avoid jobs like that."

Raul also took on new challenges as president of CLAS. He had volunteered for the position after helping with fundraising for Mexican earthquake relief. He wanted members to "become more like a family, to get everyone on campus involved," then use this base to recruit more Latino students to the school. He put on benefit dance parties, established a regular awards banquet, and set up outreach programs linking Circle's Latino students with those in Chicago high schools. He also took on some of the Cintron Center's other causes, like helping enlist volunteers for Jesse Jackson's 1988 presidential campaign, and organizing a cultural and political awareness week around America's relationship with El Salvador, Guatemala, and Puerto Rico. But he focused mostly on ways to help others from his background replicate his journey.

Raul hoped, in this context, that his new career would buy greater personal security. He could get by on Uptown's streets, but his family's CHA apartment was constantly broken into. After they got hit twice in one week, they moved to the far safer Rogers Park, where his mom found a job in a local beauty salon, and Father Rochford found Raul a job at a new church. "I didn't like living in the inner city," he said after a pause. "Too many people, too many gangs. My mom was mugged. I was mugged. Rogers Park is pretty peaceful."

Harvard on Halsted Street   A few days later, Raul showed me the new red Dodge Colt that he drove to work and to school. He'd made the down payment with part of his summer earnings and paid $170 a month to the bank, which was his main expense since he lived at home. Otherwise, he financed his education with state and federal grants, the summer job with People's Gas, and a twenty-hour-a-week tutoring job, in which, for $5.00 an hour, he helped dropout mothers complete their GEDs.

He drove the Colt with evident pride. We headed first to his old neighborhood where his church continued to hold mass in English and Spanish, but now also in Laotian and Vietnamese. On the vacant grass lot of a burned-out apartment building, Asian kids played soccer where Raul had once played baseball and football. Other kids sat on the stoops drinking beer and talking. We drove past a boys club with a gym where Raul used to swim, a former Holiday Inn that had become a homeless shelter for battered and abused women, and a once-elegant brick apartment that Raul said now housed "the lowest of the lowlifes." Then more boarded-up buildings, a Salvation Army kitchen, and the block where his cousin was murdered ten years before. "Everyone I knew was poor," said Raul. But "it usually wasn't as dangerous back then." When we turned east, the faces got whiter, block by block, as we approached the wealthy lakefront highrises.

We stopped at a brick CHA apartment, and a friend came out in his undershirt to admire Raul's new car. Then we looped back to the Chicago Circle neighborhood. Home of the renowned Hull House founded by Jane Addams in 1889, the near west side melded Greeks, Italians, and Mexicans in one of the culturally richest neighborhoods in the city. Then, as Studs Terkel wrote, urban redevelopment hit, and it became "a complex of institutions, expressways, public-housing projects, and a few islands of old-timers, hanging on."[4] Recently, affluent young whites had begun to reclaim it, returning for its accessibility. New townhouses, with names like Garibaldi Square, sold for $200,000, complete with brick courtyards and bay windows.

Raul and I drove past the university's new technology park—dark buildings with sleek mirrored glass. "For me as an engineer," he said, "this is fine, but I hate to see the poor people have to leave the neighborhoods." New parking lots had replaced modest homes. We passed the vast Saint Luke's and Rush Presbyterian medical complexes, where Circle Campus medical students were trained, and then the university's own separate hospital. A few blocks farther the projects began, and bare lots littered with glass.

Like the neighborhood, Circle Campus was changing. It began as a commuter school with the "urban mission" of serving precisely the diverse communities that its initial 1963 construction displaced. More recently, it had become home for numerous suburban students forced by constricting economics to attend a college cheaper or closer than Northwestern, Loyola, or the University of Illinois at Champaign-Urbana. Circle Campus had recently tightened admissions requirements for its 16,000 full- and part-time undergraduates, and the campus store displayed sweatshirts with the motto "Harvard on Halsted Street."

These shifts made things more difficult for students like Raul. When he began, undergraduate admission required three years of high school English, plus three of math and two of science if he wanted to enter the engineering department. Now incoming students needed to meet a much more comprehensive set of prerequisites that included more courses and straddled more disciplines. They also needed to meet a new threshold level that combined American College Test (ACT) scores with class rank. The shifts gave students a broader academic base, and the school a more prestigious reputation. Fueled by demographic shifts, undergraduate minority enrollment continued to increase from 33 percent in 1985 to 45 percent in 1993. But students from Chicago public schools also found the new requirements considerably harder to meet. In the same period, the percentage of undergraduates who lived in Chicago dropped from 62 percent to 46 percent, replaced largely by students from the inner ring of suburbs.[5]

"When this university was built," Raul said, "it kicked the people out who lived here—Mexican, black, Italian. But they said it would educate their children. Now it's changed its purpose and that's reflected in the requirements. My brother had the same grades and scores that I did, except he didn't take four years of science. For that reason, he was rejected and had to go to community college. It's great for my getting a job as an engineer that the school is changing its image, building new dorms, and finding students who come in better prepared. It's not so great for my peers."

A conservative friend of Raul's predicted he'd soon forget his fine talk of social concern. "Raul claims allegiance with the poor," he said. "But he's just waiting for the day when he finishes engineering school, marries his girlfriend, and moves to the suburbs to make eighty thousand a year."

I wasn't sure, but Raul seemed to be getting what he called "a bad case of the disenchantments" regarding social involvement. At the recent CLAS awareness week on Guatemala, El Salvador, and Puerto Rico, the main events drew just a handful of students. "We put a lot of work into organizing things," Raul told me. "It felt good to be interested in peoples' countries. When it came time for students to support it, they didn't. There was no excuse: it wasn't exam time. This organization's supposed to be two hundred strong, and we're lucky to get ten people at our meetings. I had to call and call to get people out for our organizational elections. They don't take advantage of what's here."

Yet his efforts often yielded fruits. The next week, *Cinco de Mayo*, students packed a benefit dance. Later the center presented a raucous political comedy, written by one of its alumni and performed by a touring San Francisco company, about a bumbling Chicano who flees the *barrio* for the army and accidentally foils a Nicaragua-CIA operation. Three hundred students turned out and gave it a standing ovation.

For all his frustration, Raul liked "hanging out with these lowlifes at the center," bringing in new students through issues like the shifts in admissions requirements. "I feel I've personally grown and enhanced my skills. It's also changed me. If some employer asks me to build a bridge over a neighborhood, I'm not going to just see the dollar signs so much as what the neighborhood would want. I'm not going to forget where I came from."

I feel like a ragamuffin   It takes courage to think beyond material dreams, all the more if you start at the bottom. Students like Raul are right to value the education and credentialing that gives them a shot at decent personal lives. Yet this education can also cut them off from their roots.

America's prevailing culture teaches citizens to identify with those at the top.

As Robert Bellah and his associates explore in *Habits of the Heart*, the notion of a career as an upwardly mobile journey gained currency in the mid- to late nineteenth century. It contrasted with a previous notion of a professional calling, which involved individuals taking up "a definite function in a community" and operating "within the civic and civil order of that community." The new concept of career "was no longer oriented to any face-to-face community but to impersonal standards of excellence, operating in the context of a national occupational system. . . . following a profession came to mean, quite literally, 'to move *up* and away.' "[6]

Students like Raul, Anna, and Dale experience conflicts between personal mobility and community loyalties. The more they groom themselves to adopt the values of distant employers, like Dow, General Electric, or Shearson Lehman, the more they must dismiss the lives of people they've grown up with. Dale faced this in leaving his family farm culture and Anna in wanting to choose the right friends. Raul felt torn between prizing the greater clout of a university that now styled itself "Harvard on Halsted" and the knowledge that the barriers had again increased for people he grew up with who were still trapped in Uptown. As a working-class Colby woman put it, "You don't want to go against what you're going to be standing for in the future."

Students from such backgrounds do become politically active, from solidarity or self-defense, but they also hit barriers to political involvement that are invisible to more comfortable students. They work more hours, go deeper into debt, have fewer familial resources, and feel more uncertain in their educational journeys. They have grown up amidst declining blue-collar wages, a gutting of accessible public services, and a general assault on the unions that once offered their communities some strength and voice. They've watched power in American society increasingly concentrate at the top. Their situation leaves scant time and energy to challenge this.

Tightening circumstances make college itself a chancy venture. Had Raul not been offered his scholarship, he would not have continued on past high school. Chicago Circle's student body vice president described "an unconscious pessimism" that hung in the air for those, like himself, whose families had constantly struggled. "I grew up with a sense," he said, "that I didn't have the money, education, and position to control my own destiny. That someone else was in control."

Sociologists Richard Sennett and Jonathan Cobb explore these tensions in *The Hidden Injuries of Class*. To gain full social respect, they suggest, individuals must climb, and leave working-class roots behind. But when they succeed, they enter an occupational world whose distance from direct productive labor they mistrust, much as Raul felt ambivalent about getting paid to watch men his age cut pipe at O'Hare airport. The journey also stigmatizes onetime friends with failure, highlighting their lack of status and power. Students from these backgrounds often want to speak up for their communities, but to do so jeopardizes their already difficult chances to rise.[7]

Such tugs of loyalty mix with more general uncertainties. Students from poor backgrounds who attend predominantly middle-class or elite schools can easily doubt their right to be there. Peers with similar experiences are rare. Intellectual and social codes are foreign. Fellow students talk differently, wear different clothes, cite different cultural references, take distant vacations. Day-to-day discussions remind these students, by their simple unfamiliarity, that their right to belong is tenuous.

"I fell behind at the beginning," explained a Columbia student named Angelica Garza. Her mother, a waitress in the East Los Angeles *barrio* of Alhambra, never learned English. Her father had run a large Mexican restaurant, but it was robbed too many times; he went bankrupt and ended up with a thirteen-seat café in central L.A. At times Angelica felt isolated and overwhelmed. "I guess I had a pretty crappy education, although people from similar situations are doing OK. There's a different pattern of speech here, more academic, more wordy. We spend a lot of time discussing ideologies and philosophies, taking ideas apart, without dealing with anything day to day. If we're on the subway having a discussion about Plato, people can pick us out as students, maybe even as Columbia students, as opposed to ones from City College, who sound more down to earth. There's no history of education in my family, so I can't tell my pop about my midterms. I don't have much money. I don't have nice clothes. I feel like a ragamuffin."

Even at schools with a mission to serve first-generation students, such as Chicago Circle, or City College of New York, political involvement hits emotional and psychological barriers as well as material ones. People are often moved to political involvement when they begin discussing common experiences of injustice, and therefore validating the need to act. This was true of African-American churchgoers involved in the 1960s civil rights efforts, of the Latin American peasants who gathered in "Christian base communities" to read the Bible together and talk about their common situation, and of feminist consciousness-raising groups that led the 1970s women's movement. Individuals who come from circumstances consistently demeaned or disparaged need to feel that their voices and those of their peers have value. They need to learn why their communities lack power, and how to join with others to change this. They need to learn who they are.

Colleges can help poor and working-class students do this. They can help them better understand the historical circumstances that have shaped their narratives and those of their families, the roots of their assumptions and beliefs. They can introduce them to critical voices capable of shedding light on their dilemmas and dreams.

Sometimes colleges succeed in this. A University of Wisconsin at Oshkosh student named Judy Stahl drank her way through high school classes she considered "wholly meaningless," married her boyfriend at age sixteen, and by two years later was a divorced single mother working as a legal secretary. She was soon frustrated with earning so little and having so few life choices, so returned to school, but nearly failed her first year. Only when she discovered social work did she find teachers who inspired her to learn. "I didn't know I was going to get nearly straight A's. It just snuck up on me. But I liked the courses, liked learning about poverty and family dynamics. I started studying hard and did even better. I got accepted now at Madison, where I'll get my M.S.W. and explore why people like me grow up so alienated to begin with."

More often, the academic hierarchy undermines the chance for learning that gives students like these a context for acting effectively as citizens. Teachers at low-status-schools often treat the wounds of class as immutable givens, insisting that their students can escape only through individual success. Or they resent their own distance from Ivy League heights and decide their classes deserve no more than cursory attention. Many also confirm a judgment, bred in the bone for most of their students, that public issues are the turf of the educated elite.

The frequent result is a still greater silence at these campuses than at colleges with more affluent populations. A man in the Mankato State education class mentioned a sixth-grade teacher "who asked us to write about a controversial issue and then humiliated us if he didn't agree." Almost half a lifetime later, the wound still festered. "No one takes what I say very seriously," said a woman who sat behind him. "I guess I'm just one of those kinds of people who listen a lot to others." A woman at a nearby community college echoed these sentiments. "I've been made to look foolish too often, and now I just don't speak out." I was always taught to be polite and obedient and respect authority," explained yet another Mankato woman. "You get in trouble if you don't."

Cultural starvation   Women in particular are taught to mute their views or undercut them with tentative phrasings. In *Women's Ways of Knowing*, Mary Field Belenky and her co-authors describe subjects bound by silence to the point of seeing themselves almost as invisible objects to be tossed and battered by others. The most quiet were working-class women who believed they had no right to publicly air their troubles.

College women from varying backgrounds share with men certain mechanisms of retreat, including economic fear, a widespread stereotyping of others who speak out, and a reluctance to publicly act on their beliefs. In a 1989 poll, 80 to 90 percent of female undergraduates wanted greater economic equality between women and men. They shared a general frustration with persistent sexual discrimination. Yet only 16 percent of those participating in the survey were willing to call themselves feminists.[8]

One way the sexes differ is that many apolitical men state their opinions more quickly and bluntly than women do, though not necessarily with more knowledge. They feel a greater right to speak, and worry less about the reactions of others. They like to consider themselves captains of their fates.

Young apolitical women, in contrast, remain more tentative, more reticent. They speak out less in general, even in class, and focus their mistrust of campus activists less on specific political differences than on such personal attributes as dress, style, and character, or on the way bringing up controversial issues breaches politeness. These attributes create a measure of judgment many feel compelled to hold up constantly to themselves. They feel the weight of the perfect standard as they explain that they simply don't know enough about controversial questions, repeating again and again, "I don't really have anything to say." They recede into the background, muting their voices and dreams. In attitudes that mirror general male/female divisions described by scholars like Carol Gilligan, Deborah Tannen, and Mary Field Belenky and her colleagues, they are less likely to raise sharp disagreements with particular causes than to insist that they are simply not "that kind of person" who speaks out.[9]

Returning to roots   For women or men, silence of the sort I've described doesn't have to be total. It can coexist with talk of David Letterman or who you're going out with, of music or football, of family and friends and coursework. But this talk skirts taboo areas of politics and power, including the politics of sex, race, and class. If students not born at the top are to take public stands, they must first reclaim the value of their experiences.

Those whose parents are janitors, mechanics, or drugstore clerks, those who go to Mankato State, North Arkansas Community College, or Cal State L.A., often doubt that their judgments and those of their peers can matter at all—and they feel they can do little more than just get by. A painfully shy young man from Texas Lutheran College kept saying he had no opinions on the issues of citizen involvement we were discussing. When I repeatedly asked why this was so, he shook his head, said he still didn't know, then hesitantly suggested that his small rural high school "just didn't teach us to talk about anything."

The solution is not for these students to turn their backs on education and its chances, but to find ways, as Raul said, to be true to their roots. I think of the longshoremen's union leader Harry Bridges. He never took a salary higher than regular workers, and so inspired his union that when he died, nearly ten thousand members contributed to help raise a million dollars for a University of Washington labor studies chair in his honor. These current and retired workers weren't wealthy. No one coerced their contributions. They chipped in because Bridges had spent his life fighting for their cause.

I think of people I know from poor and working-class backgrounds who returned to their old neighborhoods, or neighborhoods like them, to work as doctors or nurses in public clinics, as carpenters and contractors rehabbing local housing, as businesspeople investing in their communities, as teachers or one-time gang members turned social workers. I think of writers who articulate their culture, like Toni Morrison, Latino novelist Arturo Islas, or Tillie Olsen, with her stories of immigrant women ironing in their kitchens. I think of social, political, and legal activists, from Cesar Chavez to Malcolm X to Thurgood Marshall. And of recent students, like Angelica Garza, the Columbia woman who felt "like a ragamuffin," yet ended up with a project to organize homeless street vendors in Los Angeles. These varied individuals saw their experience not as something to run away from, but as knowledge to heed. They identified with where they came from, and used their skills to give back what they could.

Seven ~~~~~~~~~~~~~~~~~~~~~~~

The broken History and
connection memory

~~~~~~~~~~~~~~~~~~~~~~~~~~~~~~~~~~~~~~~

Students act based on what they know. But what if their society shields them from its history, denies them the knowledge necessary to make informed judgments and choices? What if the understanding they need to accurately judge America's crises and their roots gets lost in misinformation and distraction?

I've mentioned a discussion at Indiana's Saint Joseph's College—where only one of forty students in an upper-division government class knew about the 1973 CIA-assisted overthrow of Chile's democratically elected Salvador Allende government. It prompted me to ask about Chile at numerous other schools, and I consistently got the same responses. I did no better when I mentioned the CIA's 1953 overthrow of Iran's democratically elected Mohammad Mossadeq government, in a coup that installed the dictatorial Shah and set the stage for Khomeini, the war between Iran and Iraq, and ultimately America's 1991 Gulf War. I got the same responses when I asked about Guatemala, Greece, and Angola. They had heard about the Soviet use of "Yellow Rain" poison chemicals in Afghanistan—but not that "Yellow Rain" only existed in a Reagan administration disinformation campaign that was finally exposed in sources from the *New York Times* to the journal of the American Chemical Society. Except where large public demonstrations had challenged the CIA's actions, I got blank stares, startled innocence, and only one or two students out of thirty, fifty, or seventy that had even heard of the events I described.[1]

If they had understood something of this history—and our government's propensity to lie—students might have questioned America's right to continue supporting dictators and overthrowing democrats. Since World War II, the United States has intervened in nations as widespread and diverse as Turkey, Indonesia, Guatemala, Greece, Laos, Cambodia, the Philippines, Australia, Brazil, Argentina, Ecuador, Bolivia, Paraguay, Korea, Iran, Iraq, Vietnam, Panama, Pakistan, Zaire, Liberia, Angola, Somalia, Haiti, Santo Domingo, Nicaragua, Chile, and numerous others. If students knew nothing of this past, how could they respond to similar abuses in the present?[2]

Some students openly defended the government's right to censor their knowledge. "If we knew too much," said a Saint Joseph's student, "maybe we'd prevent the president from doing what he needed to do." "I don't have anything to do with the past or history," a Chicago Circle woman stated after a friend described how her father returned from serving in Vietnam and opposed the war. "I mean, it happened. Maybe we can correct past mistakes from looking at it, or correct future mistakes. But what does it have to do with us now? It doesn't have anything to do with me individually."

Most students, however, agreed that they should know more about global events present and past. They explained, apologetically, that they simply lacked time to learn. It was hard to get excited about developments they couldn't change. "By the time I was ten," explained a man from Oregon State, "I knew that politics is corrupt, war is natural, and technology embodies the finest aspirations of man. Life was a game, and if you played by the rules you could win."

Knowledge and power   Pundits have made much of the ignorance of today's young. In July 1988, Gallup and the National Geographic Society announced that Americans eighteen to twenty-four years old ranked last among their peers of nine nations in their ability to locate on a map places like France, Britain, Japan, Central America, and the Persian Gulf. Three quarters of the class of a Gustavus Adolphus International Studies professor placed Nicaragua in Africa. A June 1990 Times Mirror study, *The Age of Indifference*, concluded that young Americans knew far less than their counterparts coming of age from the 1940s through the early 1970s, and less than older Americans. They paid less attention to national and global events, following them only when they related directly to their lives or when they stirred controversies highly visible on campus, such as Supreme Court abortion decisions or developments in South Africa. Regular newspaper readership, the study found, had dropped precipitously among eighteen- to twenty-nine-year-olds from nearly 70 percent in 1965 to 30 percent in 1990. Viewership of television news dropped as well, from 52 to 41 percent. Notwithstanding the desire of many students to get rich, even their awareness of financial news declined.

In earlier periods, the Times Mirror study explained, young Americans were as knowledgeable as their elders about such major news events as the hearings of Senator Joseph McCarthy, Watergate, and Vietnam. During the peak of the sixties they were more knowledgeable. Now, the under-thirty generation joined their elders in following such highly visible events as the Challenger explosion, the Chernobyl meltdown, the San Francisco earthquake, the Panama invasion, and the rescue of a little Texas girl who got stuck in a well. But only 42 percent said they paid significant attention to the November 1989 tearing down of the Berlin Wall. Just 10 percent followed the massive changes in the Soviet Union, the Bush-Gorbachev summits, and domestic events like the savings and loan bailouts or the scandals in the Department of Housing and Urban Development. They were far less aware of political candidates, except through television ads.[3]

Even those who regularly watched TV news suffered from misunderstandings. In a survey taken two weeks into the Gulf War by a group of communications professors at the University of Massachusetts at Amherst, only 29 percent of those aged eighteen to thirty-two knew who Colin Powell was, 26 percent falsely believed Kuwait and Saudi Arabia were democracies, less than 3 percent knew that Syria was also occupying foreign Middle East land, and less than 9 percent knew that when Saddam Hussein first hinted he might use force against Kuwait, the United States had implied it would take no action. While heavy watchers of TV news were more able to identify Colin Powell, they did no better on the other questions, and sometimes worse.[4]

College students were slightly more knowledgeable in these surveys than those who never made it past high school. By the 1992 election, samples of representative students would slightly surpass the political familiarity of a dismayingly unaware American general public. But only 14 percent of student respondents knew that America's poorest economic sector paid the highest percentage of their income in state and local taxes. Only a quarter knew that the Bush administration had responded to the killing of the Salvadoran Jesuits in the fall of 1989 by pushing to continue military aid of more than a million dollars a day to the Salvadoran government. Most believed Bush responded to Tiananmen Square by imposing sanctions on China, even as he vetoed a bill that tried to do so. That students knew more on some issues only highlights the prevailing lack of knowledge among their fellow citizens, although 86 percent in all groups knew the name of Millie, the Bushes' dog. Among both students and the general population, those who watched television the most ended up knowing the least about critical public events and choices.[5]

Day-to-day pressures make it easy for students to disappear into what many called "a bubble of insulation." Political decisions that shape their lives—such as congressional votes to cut financial aid—seem so inaccessible to their influence that most don't feel it worth even following these issues. They respond to political information, as a Dartmouth student put it, as if "it just has no bearing."

They also face the distraction of a more sophisticated and more pervasive media culture than that which existed even in the late sixties. Significant discussions of America's critical issues are carried on, for the most part, in the medium of print. You don't get them in what Bill Moyers calls "the tabloid journalism" of a TV news industry dominated by one-minute sound bites. You don't get them from playing Nintendo. You don't get them from a general cultural context that, as critic Neil Postman warns, all too often leaves us "Amusing Ourselves to Death." If you're going to get beyond the ever-escalating skepticism of the Perfect Standard, you need to ferret out facts and arguments on issues you care about, which usually means finding books and articles that do them justice.[6]

Among students for whom the soaps, MTV, and *Cheers* are a staple diet—the 30 percent of students who spend six or more hours a week in front of the TV—I've seen none involved in political causes. I almost don't expect it, although MTV has undertaken some useful recent forays into public affairs coverage. While CNN devotees seem more thoughtful and ready for serious talk than the norm, they tend to be no more directly involved. Partly, this is a question of time. Politically involved students give broadcast media a low priority. They may take iconoclastic humor from *The Simpsons*, or may occasionally check out CNN or C-SPAN, but to get the political context they need, they read. They find information on issues they care about from mostly alternative sources of books, magazines, newsletters, and the occasional radio show—or the back pages of the *New York Times* or *Time* magazine. They don't rely on major national media to sustain their engagement and vision.

These more active students do not just happen on those alternative sources of information; they actively seek them out. What they learn feeds further critical inquiries. But involvement requires more than having information, as important as that is. It has to do with how these students learn to view their lives and their society. And whether they believe their actions can matter.

Execution class   In an article in *Z Magazine*, Moravian College political science professor Gary Olson describes his attempt to critique U.S. Third-World policies in an introductory class on international politics. Through books, films, and discussions, Olson documented U.S. support for ruthless dictators and for economic arrangements that promoted malnutrition, poor life expectancy, and high infant mortality. He explored case after case where America helped overthrow democratically elected governments and crush popular movements. In assigned classroom papers, most students lambasted these interventions.[7]

One of the few who did not, however, wrote "an 'Ode to Greed' worthy of William Safire or Gordon Gekko's speech in the film *Wall Street*," and Olson read aloud from it. When he asked the class to submit anonymous reactions, three quarters agreed with its sentiments. They'd written their earlier papers just to please him, they said, although course evaluations suggested that students felt free to challenge Olson's opinions. The class had no problem with the core of his critique—both his facts and his judgment that America's actions helped devastate countries and communities. But as one top student explained, "I know what is going on is really bad. But I want a Mercedes 450SL someday and all the designer clothes I can afford. I have the uneasy feeling that if there is too much justice and equality in the world, the good life won't be there for me in the future." "I came to college so I could be rich in the future," said another excellent student. "If our government didn't do these horrible things it might not work out for me. I know it sounds awful, but that's the way it is." "This discussion is irrelevant," added a third. "We can't afford to think about morality and things like that. And if the students in this room were honest they'd admit it."

Olson was dismayed. He'd offered every example he could of who won and who lost by America's national choices. The students themselves had recited damning facts and figures in their papers and classroom discussions. But their disengagement remained unshaken.

Feeling desperate, Olson decided the next week to simulate the execution of a visiting African student, for the crime of opposing apartheid. He insisted his students explain, in terms consistent with their previous judgments, why this man must die. Initially hesitant, they soon enthusiastically took on the role, telling him, "You should have known the consequences of opposing the system. Now you pay the price." But when Olson produced a mock pistol for them to carry out the sentence, they balked, fell silent, and looked away. Olson finally fired the shots himself, then dismissed the class, which slowly departed.

In the following week the students began to talk with each another, with Olson, and with the African student whose "death" they had abetted. They discussed why Olson had selected the material he did, what their backgrounds taught them about power and privilege, and why they'd come to college to begin with. Olson didn't plan to repeat the specific "execution class" experiment: it was so rooted in his own shock at the responses to the callous "Ode to Greed" that replication would have seemed manipulative. But students said this lesson had touched them more than anything in their college experience. Olson concluded that moral empathy requires more than alternative information.

Before the class, Olson's students had a vague sense of national and global events, but they had abstracted the human costs. The consequences didn't seem real. They didn't believe their actions could change things. It felt easier to stay detached. A woman in a Mankato State course on nuclear issues described a similar combination of knowledge and resignation that left her feeling "not at all more powerful, just more overwhelmed." Others explained repeatedly, "it's all just a joke," and returned their attention to private concerns. Only when students saw themselves personally connected to historical events, as occurred in Olson's experiment, did they begin to feel a need to act.

Models for change   If knowledge of institutional abuses can lead as much toward cynicism as engagement, students also need to learn how ordinary citizens have been able to change their societies. Most students remain even more insulated from knowledge of social movements present and past than from the ills of their time. "I want to be active," said a student from Michigan State. "But I don't see stuff in the media that gives me any idea what to do. Because I don't, this adds to my feeling of powerlessness, like when they raised the registration fee four times what it was before, and we didn't even get together to fight it. I feel concerned and I know people can do things, but nobody's ever taught me how to get involved." "The TV news," a friend added, "only shows us the crazies."

Students did of course know the name of Martin Luther King, Jr., and they had heard of the civil rights movement. But for the most part they saw King on a pedestal, as a Nobel Prize winner whom a nation commemorates, certainly not as a twenty-six-year-old preacher heading into Montgomery, Alabama, uncertain of what he could do. Nor as a man who launched campaign after campaign, of which over half failed. Nor as just one powerful voice in a broad and complex movement that succeeded only through the courage of thousands of unheralded citizens. The students understand the civil rights movement through a screen of respectability that lets everyone retroactively approve. By so doing, they blur the brutal realities of segregation, the ways major American institutions helped maintain it, and how hard, dangerous, and seemingly hopeless it was for those who struggled to bring it to an end.

Ignorance of what it took to change past inequities feeds the individualist creed that people make their own chances and have no right to common claims. It feeds the persistent myth that collective efforts are inevitably futile. As I'll explore, this divorce from history has combined with other modes of retreat to fuel a resurgence of campus racial bigotry, often dismissed by the adapters either as trivial and meaningless or as a justified response to unwarranted minority claims. It takes profound insulation to sum up American race relations in the words of Tim from Fairfield University: "We gave them a lot."

Many young women similarly forget that even in this century their great-grandmothers could not vote. Just thirty years ago, they would not have been allowed to apply to many of America's most prestigious colleges. The Supreme Court's 1989 *Webster vs. Missouri* decision limiting abortion rights did spur increasing numbers to act to preserve abortion choice. Yet most young women outside political circles had little sense of how this right, which they sought to maintain, had been won not only by Supreme Court decisions but by a vast surge of early 1970s feminist activity that forced the debate.

Students similarly have little sense of the historical role of the American union movement. They know nothing of how unions fought to bring what was once a more than seventy-hour work week down to the present forty hours, won a livable wage for the core of the American workforce, helped push through programs like Social Security that citizens now take for granted, and formed political coalitions that helped enact the very systems of grants and loans that opened up American colleges to large numbers of those not born affluent.[8]

Apolitical students take for granted personal freedoms (such as the lack of male/female visiting regulations) that were won for them by previous campus activists. They also shrug off more recent successes. Columbia students arriving in 1987 were wholly blasé about the massive spring sit-ins just two years earlier that had forced the university to sell off its South African investments. Students at Mercer University, in Macon, Georgia, had no idea their school had been one of the very first all-white private colleges in the South to racially integrate. In one Colby class, students talked for forty minutes as to why their actions made no difference. Finally, one woman mentioned, almost as an afterthought, that she'd circulated a petition after the school had failed to rehire her favorite philosophy professor. Students signed it in droves, arguing that his teaching quality overrode any supposed lack of high-status publications. They enlisted their parents, and sympathetic alumni. The deans finally reversed their decision. Although the incident had occurred just the previous year and everyone remembered it, no one else thought it worth a mention.

Ignorance of previous social movements limits students' horizons. It denies them past models of sound political strategies, ways to engage communities, and effective styles of leadership. When students do act, they find it hard to locate their efforts in a continuing activist narrative. They find it easy to be demoralized by short-term frustrations.

In contrast, students find themselves empowered when they get a sense of how others have acted in times past. It helps when their courses or outside readings grapple with these efforts seriously enough to convey a real sense of how they emerged, what they meant for those involved, and what they contributed to history. A woman from Maine's University of New England felt so inspired by a class on the civil rights movement that she began a campus nuclear peace group. A woman from Mercer University saw the television series on the civil rights movement, *Eyes on the Prize*, and became involved in a local fight to rectify fiscal irresponsibility in the school's administration. Just about every activist I interviewed spoke of how historical models had helped to sustain them.

Student skepticism isn't instantly eradicated. "You see how many movements and concepts have failed," said a Dartmouth woman, "that might have begun with all the best intentions. Or the idealistic people all over the world who have fought for so many things. It seems like, without exception, these movements have all been perverted, or have failed."

Her friend agreed. "In high school you see what's going on around you and you're eager," he said. "You see the world out there, you're going to college. You think you can make an impact. In college you learn the ins and outs of the system, you read the *New York Times*, you see posters around campus. You learn what's wrong with the system, why it's not working and why you really don't have the ability to make an impact. It's not so easy as voting for free speech or human rights. You learn about so many complicated things that you feel they must know what they're doing. You say 'Now that I know more about the system—well let them run the system.' "

Perhaps these students had studied citizen movements only at a glance, only those that had failed, or only at such a distance that they got little sense of the spirit that drove them. Perhaps they read much of conflicts and tactics, victories and defeats, but not of the visions that sustained participants through their times of despair. Perhaps their professors passed on their own frustration and fatalistic sense that the powers that be will always prevail. Perhaps they learned resignation early on.

If ordinary individuals, of whatever age, are to learn ways to act, I believe they have no choice but to grapple with the legacy of individuals who've gone before them.

Students who get involved draw on earlier efforts for nuts-and-bolts details of how to make change, for lessons on how to act (and sometimes succeed) in the face of enormous odds and sometimes brutal conditions. Most of all, they draw on them to try to understand their spirit—what stirs the souls of others to risk, act, and join together for a broader common good. It's this last understanding that America's dominant culture has denied most of the students now coming of age.

Eight

Spitting on Vietnam revisited **soldiers?**

"You might be right about the need to get involved," remarked a student in a Louisiana State government class. He hesitated, then went on. "But I just can't approve of people going out and spitting on soldiers."

He meant the Vietnam protesters of the sixties, whom I'd mentioned in discussing how ordinary citizens have shaped American history. I agreed that any such incidents were wrong. The question was, how often had they occurred, if at all? In all the activism I experienced, I'd never heard of such a case.

I was surprised, therefore, when students at school after school volunteered stories of protestors spitting on soldiers as their central image of the Vietnam-era peace movement. At every kind of college, in every corner of the country, the slightest mention of antiwar activism of that time would impel them, without the slightest mention on my part, to describe how the peace marchers spat on soldiers, called them names, and drove to bases and airports with the sole purpose of heaping contempt on the already scarred young men as they returned.

"It wasn't the soldiers' fault," a Dartmouth woman commented. "They shouldn't have been maligned and ridiculed." During the 1991 Gulf War, even young peace marchers cited the image to make clear they would not repeat their predecessors' mistakes.

This wasn't my memory of the movement. Peace activists I knew viewed the soldiers as caught in the middle by government lies. Many reached out to them through a variety of projects including a vast network of GI coffee houses, counseling centers, and alternative newspapers. Signs and slogans told the president to "bring the boys home now." Petitions and letters supported GI resisters. Activists I knew damned leaders like Nixon and Johnson, who'd ordered America's escalations in the first place, but I never heard of anyone spitting on a soldier.

How did this myth become omnipresent? Sociologists Richard Flacks of the University of California at Santa Barbara and Jerry Starr of West Virginia University heard testimonies that it "happened to a friend," or heard vets using the phrase as a metaphor for general feelings of rejection, and responded by trying to track down actual incidents of soldiers being spat on. They knew that antiwar veteran Ron Kovic was spat on by a Republican delegate at the 1972 convention, but that wasn't the stuff of media legend. After working through a variety of Vietnam veteran networks, Flacks found no examples whatsoever, and Starr only a single case, and concluded that the stories were mostly urban folklore. Later, Bob Greene of the *Chicago Sun-Times* put out a specific query in his column, syndicated in two hundred papers, as to whether anyone had experienced such an event. He got a mixed bag of responses, which he pulled together in his book *Homecoming.* He writes that he had no way of checking the truth of the more than one thousand letters he received, but that most vets who responded knew of no such incidents and many believed they were pure invention. Some did say it happened to them or their buddies, through stories Greene believed to be true. Others explained, "some things are worse than being spat on," and described a general sense of being rejected by American society, not even necessarily by the peace activists.[1]

I believe that spitting on soliders was, at most, a highly marginal phenomenon, drummed into the American psyche by political leaders and media pundits who continue to regard the Vietnam War as a noble cause. Some at the peace movement's fringe wrongly transfered their anger and frustration at the seemingly endless carnage onto the soldiers who neither initiated America's involvement nor created the fabric of lies that maintained it. It was difficult for some who saw the war's moral horror to respond with appropriate compassion to the men sent off to pull the triggers and drop the bombs. But most in the movement viewed the soldiers as critical potential allies and reached out to them accordingly; for current students to consider spitting on soldiers as even remotely representative of the activist response is to validate a lie.

Images of antiwar protesters spitting on soldiers also conceal the extent to which many soldiers themselves eventually began to rebel. In various combinations of political statement and personal withdrawal, they wore peace signs on their helmets, refused dangerous missions, numbed themselves with drugs. The Pentagon's own studies found that for every hundred soldiers in 1971 there were seven desertions and seventeen AWOL incidents. With the help of civilian peace activists, two hundred and fifty alternative GI newspapers sprung up. One hundred and thirty African-American sailors mutinied on the aircraft carrier *Constellation*, refusing to head off to fight. In the conservative military town of San Diego, more than four thousand GIs turned out to see Jane Fonda's FTA ("Fuck the Army") show. Many vets returned to the United States to work with organizations like Vietnam Veterans Against the War, speaking out at rallies, holding war crimes investigations and, in April 1971, gathering in Washington, D.C., to recite the names of dead comrades and throw their medals onto the Capitol steps. Myths like that of activists spitting on soldiers have erased this history.[2]

Finally, images of peace activists as the soldiers' nemesis ignore the solidly hawkish political leaders who casually sent other people's sons off to war (out of 234 eligible sons of senators and congressmen only 28 served in Vietnam, only 19 saw combat, only one was wounded, and none were killed). When the vets returned, those same leaders closed veterans' hospitals, cut GI benefits, and—with the backing of groups like the American Legion and Veterans of Foreign Wars—refused to recognize claims for Agent Orange exposure or post–traumatic stress disorder. These images ignore the extent to which chapters of the Legion and VFW branded the returning Vietnam vets as whiners, losers, and complainers, dismissing their grievances as illegitimate. The revisions of history also gloss over the extent to which students and others who peacefully challenged the war were themselves repeatedly spat upon, beaten by police, vigilantes, and right-wing students; harassed and jailed in random sweeps; and infiltrated by government agents and provocateurs.[3]

Such distortions matter. Notions like "spitting on soldiers" do more than prevent students of today from taking seriously the legacies of citizen movements that reached their height before many of them were born. They give them further rationales for shying away from all manner of current issues and debates. They serve to convince them that even seemingly worthy causes will be revealed as fundamentally heartless and corrupt.

Apolitical students portray the antiwar protestors as rude, self-indulgent, mindless, and violent, or at best as noble failures. They question their actions, tactics, and commitment. They often suggest that America would have been better off had those protesters remained silent. It was the political pressure of the protestors, they say, that eroded American military resolve, prevented our soldiers from being able "to really go all out," forced them to "fight with one hand tied behind their back," and denied what would have been a worthy victory. "They went in half-assed," in the words of Tim from Fairfield. "The politicians wouldn't let the generals fight."

Almost as often as "spitting on soldiers," students repeated this notion that America lost the war because our military held back. Both notions are equally false.

Attacks on the presumed callousness of the protestors mask the reality that, according to the consensus estimates, American weapons killed between one and two million Vietnamese and wounded four million. Over three and a half million became refugees for an extended period of time, and several million others temporarily, in a country whose combined population, North and South, was thirty-five million people. That doesn't count people killed by American bombs and bullets in Laos and Cambodia, nor those killed by the Khmer Rouge after the United States overthrew a long-neutral Cambodian government and paved the way for Pol Pot.[4]

In the history learned by apolitical students, this carnage is invisible. Instead, popular stereotypes of those who worked to stop this killing make them appear almost to be its cause. The idea that "we fought with one hand tied behind our back" denies the reality that the United States deployed nearly four million troops in eleven years of war that escalated steadily to full-scale dimensions; it denies as well thirty years of involvement stretching back to when we funded up to 80 percent of the military efforts of the French. American planes flew up to two thousand bombing sorties a week, dropped more than eight million tons of bombs—four times as many as during all of World War II. Using napalm, defoliants, and cluster bombs to make the entire country a free-fire zone, the American military held back only in not directly invading North Vietnam and in not dropping nuclear bombs, this due to a combination of antiwar pressure and fear of Chinese and Soviet responses. Even then, the Pentagon tested computerized amphibious invasion scenarios at Stanford, and on at least three occasions American presidents threatened or seriously considered nuclear strikes.[5]

Students are not alone in their misconceptions. Eighty percent of respondents to the U. Mass. Amherst Gulf War survey agreed with President Bush that U.S. forces fought in Vietnam with "one hand tied behind their back." When asked to estimate Vietnamese deaths from that war, they offered a median guess of a hundred thousand, compared to the reality of between one and two million. Such beliefs made it easy for students to dismiss all non-American casualties as faceless, invisible, and lacking in consequences, to enshrine the American vets as the sole victims, and to decide that the true betrayers of humane values were not the leaders who began and pursued that war, but those who tried to stop it.[6]

They talked a good line   Apolitical students also dismiss the motives of Vietnam-era activists. "It wasn't the great cause it was made out to be," a student from the University of Missouri stated. "The majority didn't really believe in what they were protesting. The organizers and the infrastructure, they were devoted, but the rest, they were just followers."

The marchers did it mostly "for a fad," argued Anna Roselli's friend Patti, who'd talked about "the granolas." "Maybe like what we do now in terms of a status thing, like driving a certain car." "They wasted lots of time," concluded a man in the class. "They really made no difference."

Even when students conceded that the Vietnam generation tried to change the world for the better, many blamed them for later betraying their dreams. They cited this presumed failure as proof that those who hold high ideals when they're young inevitably sell them out down the line.

"They all sold out," said a student from Texas A&M. "Now they're all just a bunch of yuppies." "How can they ask us to act," demanded a University of Washington woman, "when they left us the mess we're facing now." "Yeah, I want peace," a Western Michigan student asserted, "but I see the students who were protesting back then, who are old enough now to be involved in government and change it. They're not. They're just sitting at home not being involved. In the sixties those people were pushing peace. Now they're not doing anything." Again and again students echoed the idea that "they talked a good line when they were young."

Other current students, in contrast, looked back to the sixties with nostalgia, yet agreed that those once most radical and dedicated had switched to a gospel of wealth, becoming stockbrokers, lawyers, and born-again Republicans. History proves, they insisted, that dissident politics can never be continued throughout people's lives. They believed students who spearheaded contemporary political efforts at their schools would similarly betray their values down the line.

As with the other myths about the sixties, student images of radicals-turned-Wall-Street-careerists rarely come from firsthand knowledge. Yes, Jerry Rubin went from war-painted yippie to networker of greed. Eldridge Cleaver became a right-wing fundamentalist. Many at the fringes of the Vietnam-era movements soon resumed their previous paths, and even those highly involved often quietly allowed their political activity to recede. Yet it distorts the truth to accept as reality images of the great generational sellout purveyed in movies like *The Big Chill*. Reagan-era *Newsweek* stories told of onetime protest marchers inverting their peace symbols into the Y-shaped emblems on the hoods of their Mercedes'. In a recent *Atlantic* article, later a book, authors Neil Howe and William Strauss have the gall (or sheer incompetence) to quote Berkeley sociologist Todd Gitlin's criticism of the media for perpetuating such stereotypes—Gitlin challenged the myth that "an entire generation had moved en masse from '*j'accuse*' to jacuzzi"—then to pull Gitlin's words out of context to make it sound as if he was criticizing the fate of sixties activists, rather than inaccurate stereotypes.[7]

Students of the Vietnam generation who headed straight to Wall Street were for the most part those most distant from the antiwar movement to begin with—and enamored of the material path from early on. Others, a much larger group, passed through the campuses when the activist presence was still small and marginal, or served in Vietnam when the war went largely unquestioned. Many spent the time simply working and getting by. Among students most involved, significant numbers remained so, in some form or another, even if the intensity of their commitments leveled off.

I saw these patterns in my own high school class, at our twenty-year reunion. There were many from my middle-class West Los Angeles school who would be viewed by current students as quintessential sellouts, living high as lawyers, corporate managers, and stockbrokers. Yet they had always been distant and hostile toward the movements of the sixties. They had no high ideals to abandon.

Students at my reunion who'd been most active during the Vietnam era still, for the most part, worked in jobs consistent with their earlier values—as teachers, social workers, urban planners, labor lawyers, environmental consultants, and as carpenters and mechanics who did political work on the side. Most remained engaged around issues they cared about. Certainly they were not involved as dramatically or as completely as before, but they were by no stretch of the imagination sellouts. I find a similar pattern among most of my long-term friends. They act differently than they did when they were twenty-two, and with less visible heat and intensity. But they retain clear ties to their previous beliefs. I think of prominent public figures who have followed convictions first voiced during that time: writers like Alice Walker, Jonathan Kozol, Molly Ivins, and Students for a Democratic Society leader Todd Gitlin; activists like Gloria Steinem, Marian Wright Edelman, or Earth Day founder Denis Hayes; political figures like Senator Paul Wellstone, Senator Carol Mosely Braun, and former Student Nonviolent Coordinating Committee (SNCC) chairman turned Georgia congressman John Lewis, not to mention the ambiguous path of Bill and Hillary Clinton. I think of the legendary Mississippi civil rights leader Bob Moses returning to the South to instruct teachers in innovative ways to help impoverished students learn algebra skills. Or organizations that evolved out of that period, like Greenpeace, the National Organization for Women, National Abortion Rights Action League, Nine to Five, and the 2.5-million-member community organizing federation Citizen Action, to mention a few. Or successful reform efforts in unions like the Teamsters and the United Mine Workers. Politically involved students repeatedly mention the training sessions put together by the Midwest Academy, a school for organizers developed by a group of core figures in the early New Left. That doesn't count thousands of ordinary individuals who have been the backbone of recent movements around peace, the environment and social justice.

Enough time has now elapsed for long-term tracking studies on students once active at colleges like Michigan, Berkeley, Florida, and UC Santa Barbara. Again, the generation's visible radicalism has lessened. Yet with a few overhyped exceptions, those to whom the politics of that time were central have remained disproportionately involved in issues consistent with their previous beliefs. Studies of former students heavily involved during the Vietnam era find them far more likely now to define themselves as politically radical than apolitical peers of similar backgrounds, to vote for left-of-center candidates, and to involve themselves in political organizations. In his book *Freedom Summer*, sociologist Doug McAdam found that half of those who went down to join the Mississippi civil rights efforts in the summer of 1964 remain involved in at least one social movement (compared to just 6 percent in an analogous sample of the same age and education), and 70 percent belong to at least one political organization. These individuals have not spent their lives chasing wealth, but have concentrated in modestly paid occupations like teaching, social work, and community medicine, in local businesses, or in other fields that make some claim to serving a broader common good. They've tried to stay true to their values, while tempering hopes for fundamental change.[8]

Later I'll address ways to sustain alternative visions and the complex legacy of the Vietnam-era activists. But for now, let's recognize that a vast rightward shift simply did not occur. People compromised, muted their voices, let some of their dreams slip. They did not betray their faith in a manner that would justify any spurning of those who now try to act.

The y'all generation   Some do think of the sixties as a time when students made the world take heed. "When I was growing up," a recent Princeton graduate reflected, "I felt the sixties were the dream." "We grew up with Wall Street. We've sort of been the me generation," said an Emory fraternity man, "versus the sixties, which was more the y'all generation. Maybe it's swinging back with the environmental movement."

"Sometimes I really wish I could have been there," said a woman from Michigan, "that I could have participated. It was really something that they did, and that they accomplished." She'd felt particularly moved when guest lecturers described how they'd begun their still-continuing involvement during that time. Their testaments, she said, had helped inspire her to act. A woman active in Fairfield's nuclear peace group agreed. "I don't want to romanticize all the drugs and negative things," she said. "But I have a sense of people caring, in a way that they don't as much right now. It helped not to take the government's word on everything. It was a time when people really believed in things."

These encouraging images could also make students feel that they were born in the wrong time and place. The more they looked longingly backward, the less they saw any chance to make history themselves. "If students here just cared like they did back then," they'd say, feeling even more displaced in location and time. Somewhere, "I don't know where—but far away," as the Missouri student said, there were students who acted and cared. Somewhere, anywhere but here. I saw this in musical tastes: the Doors and Jimi Hendrix retained vast followings not only because they made powerful music but also because they symbolized rebellion, defiance, and a sense that maybe you could break through to an authentic life. Renewed interest in beads, tie-dye, and peace-sign earrings evoked similarly diffuse yearnings for a presumably kinder and gentler time. Yet too tight a focus on such icons could keep students from learning to act in the present.

I think of a Columbia student named Josh, who played frisbee at the edge of a major campus rally. In his purple tie-dye shirt and his bouncing blond curls, he stayed close enough to hear the speeches and greet friends, but sufficiently distanced to make his separation clear. Later on I visited the "Deadhead Frat" where he lived, amidst hanging parachutes, draped Indian fabrics, and posters of Mick Jagger, Paul McCartney, and Carlos Santana. His t-shirt displayed a marijuana leaf peace sign. An elaborate bong was set on the bureau. Together with his frat brother Alan, who got free tickets through family connections, Josh had gone seventy-three times to see the Grateful Dead in concert. The two prized the Dead's floating protean community and mocked Columbia's straight jocks and grinds. They loved the Halloween smoke-ins at Washington Square Park. But they held themselves back from campus political issues, instead spending their spare time promoting a rock band made up of their friends, called Dreamspeak. They considered direct politics "just a matter of taste, just like music or how you decorate your room."

"This doesn't have anything to do with a social movement," said Alan. "We have lots of sarcasm toward those people who protest for the sake of protesting."

These students weren't entirely hostile toward social causes. Dreamspeak played a Valentine's Day benefit for Amnesty International. Both Josh and a friend named Bob had hovered at the edges of scattered rallies, the divestment sit-ins of two years before, and more recent rallies over racial issues and harsh new restrictions on campus political activity. "I listened to the speakers and heard conversations," said Bob, "but it wasn't the kind of involvement that made me want to do something." The group kept their counterculture identity separate from political engagement.[9]

Burden of dreams   Even for highly concerned students, Vietnam-era history can raise standards of rebellion so dramatic and romanticized that they have a difficult time imagining how they might measure up to them. New Left activists of the early sixties had a similarly mixed response to the epochal movements of the thirties, feeling that their modest rallies of fifty or a hundred could never compare to marches and strikes that involved tens of thousands. The frustration of current activists is reinforced by the condescension of some sixties veterans who feel they invented radical politics and own all the rights. Students today, explained the director of the National Student Campaign Against Hunger and Homelessness, "have to combat the notion that we aren't tough enough, that we haven't yet been through the real fight." "If I get compared one more time to people from the sixties . . ." exclaimed a woman active at U. Mass. Amherst. "What happened then was fine, but I'd like to be my own generation, thank you."

This burden hampers both those wanting to become involved and those who have taken demanding public stands. As 1987 Princeton graduate L. A. Kauffman writes in *Socialist Review*, "Young radicals of the early and mid-eighties tended to see the sixties as period of total, exhilarating politicization, in painful contrast to the greed and quiescence of the Reagan era." Young white activists, she explained, "donned tie-dye, memorized old lyrics, devoured old manifestos, and immersed themselves in the iconography of the decade, in part out of genuine admiration for the past and in part to compensate for the inability to mobilize large-scale political movements."[10]

Current students, Kauffman stresses, felt inferior. "Compared to the apparently heroic and undeniably historic political battles of the sixties, the day-to-day educational and organizing work of the eighties—setting up talks by prominent radicals, collecting signatures for petitions, creating discussion groups, raising funds—could easily feel unglamorous."

With a few exceptions, like the antiapartheid campaigns, recent student involvements have been less dramatic. No one thinks of chanting "the whole world's watching," when the media rarely attends. No one calls contemporary students spearheads of a new and brighter American future. Yet when students frame the sixties in terms of the most dramatic, confrontational events of a few peak years, they forget the long trail of efforts that combined with a seemingly endless war to create the massive movements at the decade's end. In 1964 only two senators voted against the Tonkin Gulf resolution that gave Lyndon Johnson unlimited discretion in conducting the war. In 1965, only 6 percent of students in one national poll favored immediate withdrawal. As late as 1966, no national antiwar demonstration was attended by more than twenty-five thousand people, and more than 70 percent of students at what would become a radical hotbed, the University of Wisconsin at Madison, still approved of America's Vietnam involvement. A spring 1968 *Boston Globe* survey of thirty-nine major newspapers showed not a single voice for pulling out. In March of that year, Robert Kennedy was still opposing military withdrawal as he began to seek the presidential nomination. This was the context that preceded the antiwar movement's peak.[11]

Myths surrounding that period have hampered student dissent in other ways. As Kauffman points out, attempts to embrace hippie styles, build countercultural enclaves, adopt militant rhetoric, or force constant confrontations have helped isolate recent campus activists from fellow students already quick to mistrust them.[12] The period's perceived legacy also tempts current activists to romanticize the very divisive forms of protest that helped tear the anti–Vietnam War movement apart—the trashing of buildings, the riots in the streets, the glorification of "armed struggle" and the "street-fighting man." Although recent student efforts have been overwhelmingly nonviolent, they've at times adopted a similar rhetoric of revolutionary bravado. Casting themselves as the radical vanguard, trying to win their goals through pure willingness to risk, they've made their difficult task even more difficult.

Such approaches emerge from dangerous myths about what tactics did and didn't succeed in the sixties. The focus on dramatic confrontation neglects the humble base building that laid the ground for success. It neglects all the teach-ins, vigils, and marches, all the discussions, large and small, all the meetings, coalitions, and patient organizing, all the nonviolent action, all the efforts that brought civil rights into public consciousness, ended the war, and raised necessary questions about what kind of nation America should be. Romanticizing a few peak moments of confrontation also ignores how much those moments still tar social movements to this day.

Prompted by renewed debates around eliminating the Reserve Officers' Training Corps (ROTC) from campus, a Holy Cross student asked me what I thought about the people who burned ROTC buildings in the late sixties and early seventies. I said the violence of those actions was miniscule compared to that of carpet bombings and napalm raids: one cannot compare the destruction of brick, wood, or concrete with the annihilation of over a million human lives—but they were self-defeating acts nonetheless.

Thinking further, I suggested that the burned buildings and far more common shattered windows and rock-throwing battles with police may well have hastened the war's end. Those actions conjured up specters of American campuses spiraling out of control, more so each day as the Vietnam bombs continued to fall. They pushed national leaders to respond to more mainstream opposition, and finally to begin pulling back the troops.

Yet these actions also marked the movement with an image of blind rage and shifted popular anger away from the war itself and onto those who challenged it. They obscured the massive government violence that lay behind the challenges to the war. They helped gut the best hopes of the time.

Over two decades later, hostile critics still resurrect the images of mindless crazies as a way to bury urgent questions about America's role in the world and the need for citizens to challenge it. Conservative writers like Allan Bloom, Dinesh D'Souza, Neil Howe, and William Strauss use images of barbarians in the streets in general attacks on campus dissent, present and past. Twisting these images out of context, they gloss over the war and the history of official lies that at first motivated activists' most generous and courageous impulses, but led by the decade's end to a self-destructive factionalism. They blur over the thousands of activists who continued to work and to reach out to their fellow citizens until Congress finally refused to continue financing the war. The conservatives use images from that time not to explore how American citizens can more wisely steer this nation down more humane paths, but to damn the act of questioning altogether.[13]

Throughout the eighties, Vietnam-era images held students back from involvement. This began to change as increasing concern led them to learn more about the period's actual legacy. Once they recognized the long, hard effort involved in desegregating the South and ending the Vietnam War, they worried less that their actions would be worthless unless they achieved instant success or made the network news. They felt increasingly part of a continuing effort by citizens toward change. Their understanding of the period impelled them to further question America's long-standing tendencies toward what Senator J. William Fulbright called "the arrogance of power" and its fruit in global interventions and domestic callousness.

"I don't know that much about the movement," explained the Michigan woman who'd been so inspired by the visiting lecturers, "but it makes me believe that something can be done, makes me go 'Hey, if they could do that then, why am I just sitting here now?'"

A more realistic perspective on the time has been spurred by the gradual entry into college of the sons and daughters of those who came of age in it. Although the Vietnam generation remains highly divided politically, compared to the 1950s' "silent generation," it includes more who did take strong stands and who are likely to pass on to their children a sense of why people acted, what they won, and the costs of staying passive and silent.

I think of one Saint Joseph's College sophomore, the son of a Vietnam veteran, who grew up watching his father silently stare at the wall. He visited the memorial with his dad and cried with him when he found the names of his friends. The student began involving his peers in peace activities through his Indianapolis Catholic Youth Organization chapter. At Saint Joseph's he continued his efforts, helping to found a chapter of the national Catholic peace group, Pax Christi, because "I don't want other people to have to go through what my dad went through."

Students have also begun to better understand the sixties through an array of new and highly popular courses. One held each year by UC Santa Barbara religion professor Walter Capps was the first of its kind when he began it in 1979. It has since become the most popular class on campus, with enrollments exceeding nine hundred students. The course includes readings, films, and direct testaments by pro- and antiwar veterans, antiwar protesters, Vietnamese refugees, and others whose lives were changed by that time. Each term there are massive waiting lists for West Virginia sociologist Jerry Starr's seminar on the Vietnam era, in which students research and role-play key debates. Between three hundred and four hundred college courses are now being offered throughout the country that deal significantly with the war; they are matched by belated attempts to address the period in high school curriculums.[14]

Yet for most students during the Reagan-Bush era, the myths and stereotypes predominated. Images like "they all sold out," "they spat on soldiers," and "they didn't let them fight," continue to separate current students from previous campus activism that should serve as political inspiration. Many still use images from the Vietnam era to tar fellow students who take controversial stands. "You should have grown up in the sixties," Holy Cross students teased peers who set up a letter-writing table to protest the Reagan administration's bombing of Libya. "The sixties are over. You don't want to be like that," a friend told a Fairfield student involved with environmental questions. "It's just nostalgia," proclaimed a student from Michigan, accusing others involved in a campus peace group of wanting "to live in an ideal world."

Nine ～～～～～～～～～～～

An unsentimental Ethical detachment **education** in the classroom

～～～～～～～～～～～～～～～～～～～～～～

On the first day of the 1991 Persian Gulf War, University of Washington Student Body President Heidi Wills called for a strike. Normal activities should at least cease for a day, she and other campus peace activists argued, so students could discuss the momentous human consequences of this national choice. Several hundred students gathered in the school's main plaza, then dispersed to enlist support. I headed to a nearby lecture hall where four hundred students sat prepared to learn medieval history.

"Would you vote to walk out?" I asked several students before the period began. They felt disturbed about the war and, without exception, said they would. But no one broached that possibility to the class. When the bearded professor—a man in his mid-fifties—arrived, he said, "I guess people have some other things on their mind today besides medieval history. But this class is medieval history, so we should proceed with it."

Without further comment, he went into his standard lecture on Charles Martel, Charlemagne, and the collapse of the Holy Roman Empire. When the class had begun, most students had been visibly upset, leafing through the special issue of the campus newspaper and talking in muted voices as they filed into their seats. Ten minutes later they were busily taking notes on a lecture the professor might have given every term for the past twenty years. Halfway through the period, the war was invisible.

It's wrong to simply blame colleges for student political withdrawal. Even the much-discussed surveys of generational materialism focus on entering freshmen whose values derive from their families, the media, religion, their churches and temples, and elementary and secondary schools, not from the colleges they've just begun to attend. But for all that some teachers do encourage involvement, the experience of most students in the classroom reinforces detachment from the world.

As a Dartmouth senior and I were talking about his values, choices, and sense of moral responsibility, he said that in all his classes he'd never had an analogous conversation. "What major are you?" I asked in surprise. When he told me he was a philosophy major, I asked what sort of philosophy he was reading.

"A lot of Bertrand Russell," he told me. He had no idea that Russell had spent the bulk of his life raising issues of war, peace, and global injustice. He knew nothing about Russell's incarceration as a pacifist, nothing about his work on Vietnam and the nuclear arms race. His professor presented Russell's analytic philosophy and never mentioned his political legacy.

Professors have strong career incentives to distance themselves from public controversies, given the traditionally conservative culture of the academy. At the turn of the century, University of Chicago president William Rainey Harper justified the firing of mildly socialist economist Edward Bemis for advocating the public ownership of utilities and for speaking out in support of striking railroad workers. A professor was bound, Harper announced, to teach his subject, "not his opinions. . . . He must stand above party lines and be independent of party affiliations." Above all he must not confuse "popular pleading [with] scientific thought."

Historian Page Smith writes, "Harper's doctrine became the rationale for discouraging professors everywhere from speaking out on controversial topics and for punishing those who did. Advocacy of reform in virtually any form was branded as 'unscientific.' On the other hand, those who opposed reform were commonly applauded for their 'objectivity.' The safest stance was a strict neutrality, or simply lying low."[1]

We believe times have changed and that tenure guarantees free speech. Yet tenured faculty were repeatedly fired during the McCarthy period, with fifty-eight professors dismissed in New York City alone. Major universities across the country purged suspect faculty, either on their own initiative or following investigation by government committees. Teachers thus fired were rarely rehired at other schools. The dismissals furthered a broader climate of fear and silence.[2]

This climate persisted until it was broken by the moral crisis of Vietnam. Even then, the number of professors who spoke out was modest, often minuscule. International studies scholars absented themselves almost entirely from dissenting statements on the war. Between 1959 and 1969, the three leading political science journals published exactly one Vietnam-related article, and only a handful on other crises such as urban poverty. Sociologist Patricia Wilner studied the *American Sociological Review* from 1936 to 1982 to see how her discipline addressed developments like the Vietnam War, the cold war, McCarthyism, the civil rights and antiwar movements, and feminist and environmental concerns. During this period of massive social, political, and economic change, less than 5 percent of the journal's articles addressed such questions.[3]

Certainly, the upheavals of the 1960s opened up the academy a bit. Students in the nineties encounter more engaged faculty than they would have in 1960 or in 1965. But the economic crunch of the seventies and eighties had a powerful braking effect on professors who might take controversial stands. Overburdened and underpaid part-timers now constitute more than 35 percent of all instructors at four-year colleges. They have no security, no stake in their institutions, and little time to help students think about their role in the world. Professors with full-time positions feel beleaguered by cutbacks and competition for funds. Conservative assaults on academic dissidence have increased the pressure not to make waves. These have taken the form of denunciations of suspect intellectual currents by officials like Reagan-era secretary of education William Bennett, monitoring of professors by groups like "Accuracy in Academia," and (as I'll discuss) the grossly distorted and often fabricated attacks on "political correctness."[4]

Classroom teaching distances students from civic involvement not only through the subjects it covers or ignores but through its day-to-day approaches. As Russell Jacoby explores in The Last Intellectuals, current academics speak less on broad public questions to an audience of general citizens than to other specialists in a hermetically sealed discourse. Through opaque disciplinary jargon, ethical detachment in research and publications, and avoidance of public controversies, these professors offer no models for students who wish to question the directions and policies of their country.[5]

Technical curriculums particularly encourage political retreat. Most engineering majors never discuss what it means that a third of them have ended up working in the weapons sector, which has also been the destination of three-quarters of federal research and development (R&D) money. Young physicists and computer scientists are similarly shielded. Business students encounter scant discussion around ethical issues except those involving blatant illegality. Even education majors say they've learned a fair amount about how to teach, but little about what purposes their efforts should serve.[6]

I was interviewing students at a University of Michigan fraternity when my computer disk drive jammed. My host, a campus peace activist, called a tall gangly engineer, appropriately nicknamed Stork, who, he claimed, could fix anything. Indeed, it took Stork five minutes to open up the disk drive, strip it down, and begin assembling and reassembling components, bending ever-so-gently misaligned rocker arms, sliding dislocated casters back into place. In ten minutes, the drive was back in order.

Stork admired his friend's peace work. Rather than work in the high-paying weapons sectors, he himself wanted to go into telecommunications, a field that would give him, in the phrase of his twelfth-grade English teacher, "that warm fuzzy feeling of directly helping people."

Yet when I asked if he could see himself working to shift government R&D toward more civilian uses, Stork thought it unlikely. The friend who'd asked him to fix my computer had become politically involved through a class on Central America. Stork's disciplinary path made such electives nearly impossible. He had "too many Omega Three frequencies to learn" to detour from his prescribed course. Engineering had little to do with agonizing over broader import, he said, but dealt instead "with the technical problems at hand."

Marketing success   America needs good engineers, scientists, and software designers. It is worrisome that their numbers have been dropping. Yet those who study the theoretical and practical sciences need contexts in which they can think through how to link their core beliefs with their vocational choices and examine their role as citizens.

Most engineering students draw profound satisfaction from their labors. They like, as the Clarkson student put it, "to make little electrical things work better." Students following the business track sometimes find comparable intrinsic fascination with finance and commerce. More often, however, they see their path only in terms of the wealth they hope it will bring them. Yet their choices, like those of the engineers, will significantly shape America's national future.

Business courses aren't all as craven as a 1988 Columbia offering called "Corporate Raiding—The Art of War," in which takeover specialist Asher Edelman was finally barred from offering a $100,000 bonus to any student who could locate a company for him to seize. Not all follow the lead of the Wharton School dean, Russell Palmer, who hailed speculators Donald Trump, Michael Milken, and Saul Steinberg for possessing a "golden touch" of business intuition, and installed a picture of Milken (the junk bond king later convicted of securities fraud) on Wharton's Wall of Fame. But most business, management, and marketing courses give students scant context to reflect on much beyond how they might best secure the bottom line profits of the companies they work for and personally navigate treacherous corporate shoals.[7]

On every issue, business majors follow most closely the patterns of detachment I've described. They're the most unblinkingly hostile to social movements of all kinds, most narrow in their definitions of self-interest, least willing to challenge the dubious exercise of power. While they may be no more resistant to social responsibility than business students of twenty years ago, their numbers have sharply increased: they constituted 27 percent of entering undergraduates in the peak year of 1987. Their professors, by what they teach and by what they omit, encourage these students' sense of entitlement to earn vastly more than ordinary workers, to sell products of dubious utility, to oppose unions as impediments to success, to shatter communities and the environment if they deem it advantageous. They prepare them to live lives that feed America's growing economic decline and social divisions.[8]

A new crop of courses in business ethics has begun to raise some useful questions. They were catalyzed into existence first by exposés of overseas bribery and illegal political contributions, then by Wall Street scandals, and finally by fears about breeding a generation of sharks. Exploring ways business operations succeed or fail at serving a broader common good, the best of them focus on more than just individual moral conduct. They also analyze institutional relationships: the levels of safety companies owe those who purchase their products; the rights of employees to fair wages, privacy, and information about workplace dangers; how America should best allocate the fruits of its economy. Yet most of these courses remain limited in scope and marginal to the curriculum. Business students rarely get the chance to examine the effect of their intended work on the world.[9]

Concerned science faculty have found similar ways to help students reflect on the social implications of new technological developments and encourage debate on science-related issues. In the spring of 1985, a department secretary prompted physicists and physics students at the University of Illinois at Champaign-Urbana to take the lead in circulating a national pledge in which scientists and engineers promised not to accept funds to work on Star Wars because it was dangerously destabilizing, a fiscal boondoggle, and a major distortion of research priorities. With the help of a parallel effort out of Cornell, they enlisted three thousand graduate students and nearly four thousand faculty members, including fifteen Nobel laureates in physics and chemistry and solid majorities from the leading physical science and engineering departments in the country. Other science professors used organic chemistry classes to discuss biological diversity, ozone depletion, and the greenhouse effect. They developed science and society courses, akin to the business ethics classes, that examined the social implications of the work students were likely to do. Still, these faculty were in the minority. Most of their colleagues remained silent, even on political and social issues that directly touched their disciplines.[10]

Cerebral retreat   In humanities courses as well, scattered professors raise ethical and social issues as matters worthy of attention. But, as the story of the medieval history professor's treatment of the Gulf War suggests, depoliticizing education is the rule across the curriculum. At every school I've visited, activist students cite a handful of key professors, often just four or five on any given campus, who have helped to inspire their stands. Upon reflection they add a few more who have not directly promoted involvement, but who conveyed a general passion for learning, imparted rigorous critical skills, or gave them emotional support. On any given campus, students will list mostly the same faculty mentors, usually scattered through various departments. If campuses are crawling with "tenured radicals," as conservative critics have suggested, why don't politically involved students cite a wider array of faculty as having helped inspire their commitment? The very scarcity of their examples speaks to the failure of other decent and concerned professors, of whatever political stripe, to teach their students to act as involved citizens.[11]

Universities mostly provide models of political detachment. "Armchair liberal professors," stated a Williams student, "create armchair liberal students." "It seems like we're supposed to be aware," observed a Michigan student, "but we're not really supposed to act." Students' sense of fragmentation also furthers retreat. "You memorize who's in the NATO pact," Anna Roselli said of her international relations class, "and the dates of Stalin and Brehznev. If you miss one bit from the lecture, you'll be sure every name, date, and fact will be on the test." Learning these details, Anna said, took up so much time, little was left to think about issues beyond immediate assignments.

Even strongly intellectual students find their studies reinforcing political cynicism. Columbia junior Carolyn Lowenthal loved the academic environment, "reading and writing about wonderful books that I would have wanted to read anyway. When I read Plato's story of the cave, I wondered about thought processes, and what's real and what's just a shadow. When I read descriptions of ideal political states, I look at the U.S. and see how we measure up. I read Dante, Hobbes, and Locke and understand where our politics came from. I've had seminars with professors like Edward Said, who send me out walking on air, wanting to do nothing but think deep thoughts."

"I want to be in a position where I can think clearly," Carolyn stressed, as we talked in a hardwood-paneled dorm lounge. "It's one of the most critical roles I can play, whether I end up teaching in the classroom, as a lawyer in Montgomery, Alabama, or writing a column for the *New York Times*. Whether it's huge or small scale, I want to help people think."

Yet the courses Carolyn admired walled her off from the inevitably muddy and fractious terrain of campus political debates. "I don't believe mass movements work," she said when I asked about the link between knowledge and social commitment. "Sure, they did sometimes in the sixties, and here in 1985 with apartheid divestment. But I don't like the way they work. They're everything Plato hated about the mob, everything Shakespeare makes you see in *Julius Caesar*—people who are convinced their cause is right."

Learning, to Carolyn, meant more than high grades and a lucrative future career. She grew up in an intellectual home, though not a politically involved one. Her mother was a lawyer. Her father taught history at Wellesley. They sent Carolyn to an elite private day school, where she edited the student paper, learned to articulate her thoughts with a casual grace and sense of command, and developed her intellectual passions. Yet this same intellectual style—reinforced at Columbia—encouraged her to regard all forms of direct political involvement as too simplistic, too divisive, and "simply too messy." She applied her ample critical skills only as a detatched and peripheral spectator.

"If you're waiting for me to say I apply these books to the issues of the time, I don't. Maybe it's asking a lot of literature and humanities classes to say that you should both come out with brilliant thoughts and learn to act on them. Not that politics shouldn't take place in the classroom. But I think students need to come to things like that on their own."

What kind of involvement would she view as appropriate? "I'm incredibly cynical," Carolyn said, "on any prospects for reform. My boyfriend's thinking about going into electoral politics, which disgusts me. Activists here spend most of their time marching back and forth with signs across Low Library steps, which accomplishes nothing, instead of sitting down and working with the deans."

If one issue did move her, it was the attitudes of fraternity men toward women. "I'm not antifraternity. This isn't an easy place to have a social life. I don't mind the men having their bonding. I do have a problem when they don't think about what they're doing. They talk about how great it is that they volunteer to paint people's houses, clean stairs, and raise money, but they treat women with the smallest respect. It really boils me when I run into men who say girls who go to fraternity parties are asking to be raped, like a friend of mine who was date-raped freshman year. Or women who say 'that doesn't affect me, because I don't go to the parties.' Or seniors who say 'it doesn't matter to me, because I'm graduating anyway.'"

At what point, I asked, would she really involve herself?

"You mean, at what point would I get off my butt and do something? I don't know. I can't stand the way stuff works here, but I have a huge respect for Columbia. I have huge faith in myself as an individual, but maybe it comes down to my inherent cynicism. I'm ultimately pessimistic about human nature. I don't believe you can change people's attitudes."

Carolyn's critical skills would have helped any effort she joined. She volunteered regularly in a campus-based tutoring program, teaching algebra and geometry to high school kids who were failing math. But she remained remote even from directly political causes she strongly endorsed, like the debates around the fraternities. I could see her carrying a similar disdain throughout her career and—whether she entered journalism, law, or academia—passing it on to her students, clients, or readers.

"Maybe I'm just apathetic," she said, pausing again. "I wonder what I'd have done around the apartheid movement. I probably wouldn't have joined because I would have valued my classes too much. Maybe it's my temperament. In high school, when I was editor of the newspaper, all I had to do was pick up my pen and write an editorial. I didn't have to modify my views or align with any group. Maybe that's why I'm so uncompromising, but I don't like how people here operate. I don't like their tactics. I just don't have the energy to do politics—on a college or any other level. Unfortunately, the people who do aren't necessarily the best at it."

It's possible that students like Carolyn may be just waiting for the right situation and cause. A recent Princeton graduate described classmates who weren't directly involved in campus issues, but who nonetheless wrote highly reflective papers on themes like race, sex, and social class. "I'd often be judgmental," she said, "like 'Why didn't I see you at this rally? What are *you* doing taking women's studies or Afro-American history?' But they'd do very thoughtful projects." In her job at a Washington, D.C., institute that trains young organizers, she had often evaluated applications from students with no apparent political background, but whose essays and interest in the program suggested they had spent much of their undergraduate years quietly thinking about important civic questions. Carolyn herself had had many chances to get involved, but none had quite measured up to her Perfect Standard.

Students' political engagement depends as much on what they bring to their courses as on what their professors teach. I've seen students take classes with excellent, politically concerned teachers, and emerge almost as cynical and resistant as before. I've seen others draw inspiration from professors who would recoil in horror at association with political controversies. "One of my frustrations," said Boston College sociologist Charles Derber, "is the degree to which students are so deeply skeptical about issues of democratization. I talk about worker participation, people taking responsibility for aspects of their jobs. Maybe because they see themselves as future managers, they don't believe workers have the skills and motivation to be efficient on their own. They dismiss it all as 'unrealistic.' " [12]

Making the grade   Political detachment feeds on students' inclination to treat college as a mere means to lucrative future careers. Though cynical about the relationship between their grade point averages and any actual learning, they care about grades deeply, and fear the power of the GPA to affect their personal future. In contrast, they often consider intellectual understanding to be an expendable frill. There have always been students for whom "Will this be on the test?" is the central question of their lives. But for those of the Reagan-Bush era, this became a dominant campus tone. They wanted to be graded, as Fairfield's George Lipson said, not because they considered grades a legitimate measure of achievement, but because they viewed them as pragmatically necessary—a way to prove they could fit into the requisite slots. [13]

Professors can play a key role in encouraging involvement. Those who have the greatest impact insist that student voices can matter. They invite students to wrestle with the issues of the day, to take public stands, to hold political and economic leaders accountable for their actions. They encourage students to trust their tentative judgments, then confirm or change them as they learn more, and to explicitly link their planned futures with their core beliefs. By acknowledging from the start that others may hold different views from theirs, they encourage students to overcome "perfect standard" fears of saying the wrong thing. And they often set strong examples of ways to act as engaged citizens.

In the words of Brown University president Vartan Gregorian, "Whether confronting hard ethical choices in public policy, or issues of personal identity as psychology, or questions about beauty as art or literature, or problems of environmental consequences, we need to admit questions of values to the arena of discussion and debate. The moral argument of a poem, the social implications of a political system, the ethical consequences of a scientific technique, and the human significance of our responsibilities should have a place in classrooms and dormitory rooms. To deny that place is to relinquish any claims or any attempts to link thought and action, knowing and doing." Gregorian suggests that students, faculty, and ordinary citizens need "to be able to engage in new ideas," but also to make public declarations of their convictions and commitments, and translate them "into actions and deeds." [14]

Political involvement requires individuals and communities to take seriously the effects of institutional choices on particular lives. Those who act do so, almost invariably, in response to highly specific stories. A student envisions a Salvadoran peasant being tortured, a child in Brooklyn going hungry, the Colorado River being desecrated. Most academic learning, in contrast, is couched in broad abstractions. While these can be essential for understanding the patterns into which individual acts of callousness or short-sightedness may fit, they often render human consequences bloodless and invisible.

Teachers retreat to scholastic detachment because their disciplines reward it. Detachment offends no disciplinary traditions, no powerful interests. It raises no troubling questions of moral responsibility. It releases professors from having to confront their own doubts about how their efforts rebound on the world.

To take an example from debates over peace studies, political scientist and former nuclear targeting strategist Henry T. Nash suggests that many professors have worried "that if universities were to assume a larger role in educating students about nuclear war issues, teaching would become value-laden, given to emotionalism, over-simplification, and even indoctrination. And indoctrination would erode the process of objective learning." Arguments concerning the kinds of ultimate issues raised by nuclear activists attacked the routines fundamental to "an ordered campus existence." [15]

Nash captures the arguments that keep academics politically detached. But American campuses have rarely been value-free in promoting the interests of powerful institutions. In the time of Chicago president William Rainey Harper, most faculty justified the giant trusts; during the 1960s, Ivy League mandarins shaped and justified America's Vietnam policy. Today Nebraska agriculture professors portray the eclipse of family farms by corporate agriculture as inevitable. The Reagan-Bush era saw a parade of academic experts who filed across the TV screens to justify every military intervention and regressive economic policy.[16]

Added to this, the value given to research over teaching makes it harder for students to find engaged faculty role models. Professors at major research universities often orient themselves toward potential critics in their disciplines, not toward the less prestigious audience in their classrooms. If students find teachers willing to encourage them to take committed stands, this inspiration is as likely to come from overworked and underpaid teaching assistants as from faculty at the top of the academic hierarchy.[17]

During the 1980s, three assistant professors received Stanford's annual Dinkelspiel Award for distinguished service to undergraduate education. Two of the three were subsequently denied tenure, with one being jokingly asked after she got the award, "Don't you know that's the kiss of death?" The 1986 and 1987 winners of Harvard's equivalent Levenson Award also failed to get tenure, as did Harvard sociologist Paul Starr, after a faculty committee branded his Pulitzer Prize–winning social history of medicine mere journalism. A talented young UCLA professor responded to superlative student evaluations by pleading with her department *not* to nominate her for their university award. She feared that if she won, her tenure committee might conclude that too much of her research time had gone into teaching."[18]

Good scholarly research is important. Urgent social, scientific, and philosophical questions need to be explored. But the research of many professors is driven not by the need to explore key issues of our time, but by the pressure to publish regardless of content. This pressure makes it harder for even the most conscientious faculty to take the time to encourage students as citizens.

Expectations to publish damage faculty less at lower-status schools. Yet the lack of prestige at such places leaves many professors resignedly logging their time, having decided that if they aren't at Harvard, Berkeley, or Carleton, what they do hardly matters. Others invest their major efforts in working to move up and out. Either way, they feel strong pressures to treat teaching as drone work, to not jeopardize their situation with controversial involvements.

The avoidance of contentious issues in the classroom adds yet another barrier to social and political involvement. "I went to Notre Dame high school," said a woman involved in Fairfield's nuclear peace group. "President Reagan singled it out as one of the best Catholic institutions in the country. But our teachers never dealt with the arms race or Central America, or any of the other issues I now care about. I'm a politics major here, and these teachers haven't either, except for one class in U.S. foreign policy, where we debated Star Wars. It wasn't until one of my religion courses that I had a chance to sort out what I felt."

I want them to make my job difficult   I'm not suggesting that teachers need to espouse particular political agendas. One Emory peace activist selected as his advisor an ultraconservative political scientist. Their views rarely corresponded, but the professor made him think and hone his arguments, acknowledging even in disagreement that the issues he cared about mattered. Universities in any society need to do more than teach conformity. They need to encourage students to reflect on their choices and plans, to help them develop critical skills, to help them judge for themselves what choices are best for society.

Even when faculty engage urgent issues in their classrooms, scholasticism can drag down their approach. At one college I visited, a student I trusted considered a team-taught war and peace issues class among the most boring of his college career.

We talked afterward with one of the professors, who passionately recalled his own activism twenty years before at San Jose State. The student had not known the teacher had any such experience, or that he could talk with feeling about anything. The professor's background was relevant to the course, and might have added some badly needed grounding. The school's strongly interdisciplinary thrust overtly encouraged such leaps. Nevertheless, the professor resisted making pedagogical use of his experience.

Too often, professors who claim social concern confine their politics to abstruse theories that might be interesting intellectually, but have little relation to the world outside the classroom. Some theories are inherently complex, and therefore difficult to explain, but political visions couched in opaque and self-referential language become comprehensible only to the elect who know the code. They do nothing to challenge academic insulation.

When faculty encourage students to take active stands, both they and the students may incur some costs—at times more difficult intellectual and personal challenges, at times direct threats to their careers. Yet if faculty duck this task, they make it more likely that students will remain silent and passive. Maybe professors need to take the approach of the dean of arts and sciences at Pennsylvania's West Chester University: "I want students to ask the hard questions so I'll have to think and act," he explained, "to push me and the other faculty and administrators to do what is right and not just what is expedient. I want them to make my job difficult."

Ten

I'll work Involvement from within deferred

Midway through my research for this book, a University of Washington professor asked if I'd speak to her mass media class. I began by describing my tentative findings, then asked her students about their choices.

The class spoke of familial pressures, of how sixties activists had sold out, of how hard it was to have to constantly work to build their résumés. An African-American ROTC cadet feared increased activism might bring "too much chaos," then wondered what would happen "if they really did teach us more about social movements." "Maybe I agree with what's already going on," commented a young man in a high school letter jacket who said he liked where George Bush was taking the country.

The sole unexpected response came from a woman whose Spokane church had given sanctuary to Central American refugees. "It was a mess," she said. "We were one of the poorest churches in the community, but we took in these refugees and kind of indoctrinated them into the material aspects of America. We had masses in Spanish. They got into wearing nice clothes. They almost forgot what it was like back home."

Political involvement, I agreed, doesn't always meet expectations. I said I believed it essential nonetheless, and that people had to persevere. A few students talked of causes they'd taken on. One described gradually coming to grips with stories of Chileans tortured under the Pinochet regime. Most gave reasons—economic circumstances, parental pressures, or general isolation—why they simply could not stand up for what they believed. They also implied that America would be better off if more people did. Only the man in the letter jacket justified withdrawal.

I left feeling it had been a fruitful session. But when it came time for the students to sum up the interchange in brief essays, I got some angry responses. Students said I was judgmental, a missionary, a preacher. The sole activist they claimed I recognized was "The Protester," and only for my approved causes. What right did I have to tell them they were bad? Or to consider my generation so terrific and theirs so hopeless? Their private choices were none of my business.

"His agenda is not my agenda," wrote a woman who was one of the most offended. "When he assumed that our time should somehow be linked to his priorities, he was wrong. He is equating worth as a human being with being socially active."

I had mentioned a conversation with a Champaign-Urbana physics major who had wanted to get involved but was overwhelmed with his studies and feared that if he diverted much time, he'd lose his chance at top graduate programs. I'd said that his choice sounded hard and that no one could make it for him. Yet I wondered if there were good programs that would still admit him if he got a 3.8 GPA instead of a 4.0, or if he could spare a couple hours a week and keep his grade point average intact. This might let him act for causes he believed in.

This suggestion outraged the offended communications major. "Loeb was asking me to reprioritize my time, desires, and goals for his goals and hopes in life," she wrote. "He should assume less, expect less, and most of all not set the agenda for someone else's time, social, and political priorities."

This woman had been equally hostile when her professor showed a film criticizing manipulation in advertising, a field she and half the students in the class planned to enter. Maybe my questions hit a nerve. Like most who responded critically, she was enrolled in the section of a teaching assistant who believed strongly in value-neutral social science and who'd complained that I'd tainted my results by prefacing the discussion with my developing themes. Others felt I wrongly mixed the role of lecturer and researcher, or were offended by my taking occasional notes on a laptop computer, something I usually avoid during classroom discussions. Maybe this group was atypically defensive, given that others in the class liked the questions I raised, and said so directly in their papers.

In response to my questioning their fellow students' lack of involvement, several in the class refocused the spotlight on my own Vietnam generation. This seemed fair enough, given how often my peers had lambasted them for apathy, but the arguments on which they built their case were questionable. For example, the woman whose church had taken part in the sanctuary effort agreed that most current students shied away from political involvement, then blamed this on the "hippies of the sixties, who've now become the yuppies of the eighties."

This response fits all the rationales for distancing I've described. It replicates all the standard myths. Yet I don't want to dismiss the impetus behind it: the feeling of being unfairly attacked by critics whose own lives are highly compromised and who do not care to understand the pressures that you face.

Trying to change the world is difficult, uncertain, and fraught with traps. The social, political, and environmental ills I ask individuals to address often seem overwhelming. Who is to say that one ordinary citizen or another is responsible for homelessness, toxic waste, the collapse of family farms, or the Central American wars that drove refugees to seek sanctuary in Spokane? These quandaries have no easy solutions. Yet I believe that if individuals do nothing, the state of our communities and of the world will only grow worse. In seeking to describe why this generation of students has detached from or engaged with the world, I want to place responsibility at least as much on the shoulders of older citizens, who have set the tone for the American culture the students grew up in, as on women and men who are eighteen, twenty, or twenty-five.

Swallowed up   Apolitical students fear that involvement will destroy their identity. "These movements leave you swallowed up," said a student from Western Michigan. A Clarkson engineer mistrusted political groups and feared he'd lose his independence by joining them, but saw no problem working at IBM because "they break things down into different divisions." Even mild forms of involvement conjure up fears that too much virtue can be contagious. A Fairfield student hesitated to join a friend at a local food bank. "I'm afraid I'd see too much," he said. "I'm afraid I'd have to become too moral—like a priest, or even like Christ."

Students feared becoming trapped, caged, buried in demands. "Part of why I don't think of these issues too often," explained another Clarkson engineer, "is that they make everything else seem so trivial. I was going to go bowling with my girlfriend. Then I thought, 'How can I be doing this when people are in trouble and I could be helping them?' But to do that would set back my life and my career. It's hard to draw the line between how much of your life to devote to you, and how much to everyone else."

"Maybe it's the control factor," reflected an African-American education major from Chicago Circle. She taught Christian education at her church and, from a distance, rooted for politicians like Jesse Jackson and Chicago mayor Harold Washington. "Christian education directly benefits people. The church needs volunteers. It's an hour and a half a week, not a lot of time, and you think you're doing something. Political issues take more risk and commitment."

Students may feel the need for greater surety, given the current period. In 1968

Yale psychologist Kenneth Keniston talked of young antiwar activists' "ability to tolerate indeterminacy" because the social, political, and historical process of which they were part was itself indeterminate and uncertain.[1]

Social and political uncertainty now frighten students, perhaps because their future in this society seems vastly more chancy. They fear that engagement will leave them "with nothing left" in their lives. "Politics would be OK," commented a Western Michigan student, "if people could fit it in without pouring everything into it as the one great cause."

Most activists do balance their involvements with personal lives and goals. They have to, if they are to stay committed for the long haul. But from the outside, engagement appears to be all or nothing. Students worry that it will take away from studying time and private concerns. "If you can't control something," said the Dartmouth student who'd read Bertrand Russell, "why worry about it? Maybe I should do something about Central America or the arms race, but that would involve radically changing the way I live my life. And I don't think it's worth it."

The challenge of balancing personal and political commitments continually faces students who act. Most strike a tenuous balance. "It's not as if we activists don't have to work, too," a Seattle University woman commented. "I do what I can," explained a shy, thoughtful Fairfield computer science major, who worked with a national hunger lobby called Results. "If I overstep and do too much, it will affect my studying and I won't be able to continue. I want to be able to keep on." Student activists often alternate flurries of all-encompassing involvement with periods when they recover, catch up on reading and overdue papers, and take time to live an ordinary life.

Apolitical students are right to assume that involvement may radically change them. The activists cite a new sense of responsibility that comes with knowing about issues of homelessness or Central America or the environment: the fears that you might "see too much" and have to become "too moral" aren't baseless. Yet as we'll see, students who become politically involved get much in return. They get a sense of shared purpose and larger social impact rare among those who simply adapt. As the head of the Campus Opportunity Outreach League (COOL), a national student community-service group put it, "You realize that your thoughts have changed, the music that you listen to has changed, you're reading different books, getting to know different people, dreaming different dreams at night." This doesn't erase the difficulty of commitment. Yet individuals who take this path do so through their own choices, at their own pace, and supported by communities that nurture their heart and soul. Those who stay in for the long haul learn to balance political and personal lives.

As I've suggested, students often grow up learning that it is impossible for them to affect history. Even when looking at individuals who clearly changed America, they see only canonized heroism. They think of Washington, Jefferson, and Lincoln, not in their moments of uncertainty and doubt, but as presidents, respectable and proud. They encounter Martin Luther King, Jr., not as a young preacher wrestling with hesitancy and confusion, but as a saint. They envision Lech Walesa, not as a shipyard electrician, but as a Nobel Prize winner. The higher the pedestal on which America places its role models, the more those watching see no choice between leaping in totally and holding back, hesitant and wary. They decide that involvement demands strength of character impossible to muster. Believing they must either throw themselves blindly into a cause or take the practical path toward Rockwell and Dow, most select the latter course, then seek larger meaning in private lives, with family and friends.

Working from within   Students skeptical of politics often resolve dilemmas of conscience by vowing, "I'll work from within." They acknowledge that America is full of corruption, folly, and greed. But when they get some power, they say, they'll set things right. They'll do this, they say, not as part of any political movement, but individually, through their innate moral virtue.

Jill Catalano, a Holy Cross ROTC cadet, had a picture of Oliver North on her door—a fundraising ad from the North Defense Trust. Jill had annotated the photo with the inscription, "The 'Sad Look' (acting class 101)." "Do I hear a violin somewhere?" she'd written next to the part of the ad that described how North worked "so hard to rescue hostages, combat terrorism and fight communism." "The horror!" she wrote where the ad denounced the independent counsel that investigated North. The ad closed by asking for money and listing a toll-free 800 number where donations could be made via VISA or MasterCharge. "While you're at it," Jill had added, "send some to Jim and Tammy too"—referring to the corrupt televangelists, the Bakkers.

I assumed the ad had been annotated by her roommate, a strong campus peace activist. But the comments were Jill's, prompted by her frustration at how North had ducked responsibility. "Maybe he had good intentions," she explained, "but political life was too good to him. He got over his head, started telling more lies. After a while he believed in what he was doing. He couldn't see the harm that his actions created."

It angered Jill that the United States supported brutal military regimes around the world. Our involvement in El Salvador and Nicaragua particularly upset her. A sociology class had also led her to question America's domestic inequalities. At the same time, she believed she could play a constructive role in the military.

Jill joined ROTC at first for the scholarship, seeing the program as a way to achieve her goal of becoming a doctor. Initially, her knowledge of women and the military hardly went beyond the Goldie Hawn movie *Private Benjamin*. But she came to like the sense of self-reliance that came with learning to shoot a rifle, navigate with a compass, and push herself physically. She liked taking charge of her peers "as a teacher and a leader." She valued the ethic of service.

"People come from all over for the military," she said. "They have to work together, enhance each other's jobs. I found a lot of officers in tune with me as a student, supportive of my goals. Most people think the military would breed an emotionally hostile view. But they wanted my development as a whole human being, not a cog in a machine."

Jill seemed slight for a solider, in worn jeans and a West Point sweatshirt. Her father had worked in her grandfather's construction business. Her mother had returned to school for her master's degree, then became a nutritionist for Rhode Island's Women and Infant Children program. Jill had wanted more family support for her ambitions to be a doctor, and her parents believed in what she did, but her grandparents couldn't imagine a girl getting an education and moving away.

Perhaps, Jill hoped, she'd work as a military physician "in a depressed area, like Appalachia, or on an American Indian reservation. Or at a VA hospital. I've heard of some military professionals who've done a lot of work in poor areas near their bases." I mentioned that the National Health Service had financed the medical educations of some of my friends in return for work in underserved communities—but that the Reagan administration had drastically cut the NHS budget. "It makes me furious," Jill said, "that we spend money on Star Wars and more nuclear weapons, when we won't even fund things people need."

Given the Reagan administration's tacit war against Nicaragua, I asked whether she worried about being sent there to fight. "The problem that people have," she said, "especially the Coalition for Peace, is that they see us only as a warfare organization, not a peacekeeping organization. I've talked to so many officers who've said, 'I don't want to go to war, don't want to be the judge of who lives or dies.' The country or the military might not be right all the time. It won't change the stands I believe in. The military won't change if everyone abandons ship."

I agreed that people needed to take responsibility for their institutions. But I questioned whether she would be able to keep an Oliver North ad on her door or speak her mind when she felt the need. "The ad is very caustic," Jill said. "It might make people uncomfortable. I want them to think, but don't want their normal communication with me to be blocked. The military can't function if everyone freely speaks their minds. I don't agree with America trying to throw our weight around. But you can't just have people doing their own thing."

She continued, "Ultimately, it's a judgment call. I have to put my faith in our leaders, the people in charge. If I don't always agree, maybe I don't have the whole story. But I also want to educate myself, find out the reason for doing things. I try to think about the consequences. If something I disagree with strongly comes up, and I have an ethical dilemma, I'll speak to someone. But I won't abandon my faith in my country. I'm taking my stand by going into the military."

Jill's prime concern was "how to live as both a Christian and an officer, to reconcile both." She felt that the only way to have influence was "to be in with the people who make it. Because I think about implications and see things ethically, maybe I could influence people and work to eradicate some of what I don't like, like interventions and more nuclear bombs. Maybe I won't make all the changes I want in my lifetime. Maybe I'll only move things an inch. I know when I'm an officer I can't go rallying in the streets and join antiwar campaigns—not that I would anyway. But I don't think that by entering the military I'm giving up my freedom to speak and believe how I want."

Jill was thoughtfully iconoclastic. Unlike most who talked of "working from within," she was resolved to serve a specific social good through medicine. I hoped she would stay true to her values, keep working to inform herself, keep trying to do good work in the world. I also feared that she would see her best instincts ground down by a military resolved to simply carry out its missions, and find the dialogue she hoped for closed off.

Most who talk of "working from within" have no strong vision of an occupation that might be of use to society or of a way to do necessary work outside their jobs. Their rhetoric simply defers social commitment and critical reflection to some indefinite future time. It can justify any level of greed, as when the Fairfield group talked of earning six-figure salaries, then maybe sending some of the money "to Rick in the Peace Corps." It can also reflect a belief that only the elite can change society, and that the best others can do is aim for the top.

Students at schools like Dartmouth or Columbia suggest that they will be able to serve a greater social good once they become vice presidents of Shearson Lehman or DuPont; those at Nebraska or Central Washington University say they will do so as plant managers or heads of their regional sales offices. They share the assumption that social change comes only from the efforts of prominent individuals, not ordinary citizens. They need first, they say, to "get someplace where I can make a difference."

Such talk of doing good from above misconstrues the cumulative impact of compromises people make to get into positions of power in the first place. It dismisses the degree to which wealth and status constrain so many successful individuals from questioning the privileges they enjoy or examining the consequences of their actions. It ignores how pervasively American institutions reward people for placing expedience over principle. When apolitical students talk of working from within, they don't ask why Exxon scientists universally dismiss the impact of the 1989 Prince William Sound oil spill, why Westinghouse engineers speak on radio talk shows in support of nuclear power, why corporate executives rarely explain that they are closing U.S. plants and opening others in Mexico because they value their earnings more than the lives of affected workers.

Notions like "working from within" fit the Reagan-Bush era in which the students grew up. That time gave ordinary people slim license to shape America's future. Instead, its culture consistently celebrated the rich and famous, concentrated power at the top, and made clear that only those with wealth, position, and standing had voices worth listening to. Real change, these students believe, is made by insiders, like Henry Kissinger, Lee Iaccoca, or at best, Mikhail Gorbachev. Students who buy such rhetoric argue that because they are well-meaning individuals, their mere presence will change whatever institutions they join. The higher they climb, they think, the more good they'll be able to do. They believe that General Electric, the CIA, or Rockwell will automatically play a more constructive social role if these institutions just recruit more decent human beings. They don't envision employees coming together to fight for shared goals, just lone individuals whose innate moral worth will shine through.

"You have to start from the inside," insisted a Columbia student who hoped to work for the securities firm Smith Barney. "Contact the board of trustees if you want to change your campus. Find someone who knows them. For myself, I want to be one of the people in a position to give a lot of money away. Look at how much good Donald Trump could do if he wanted to."

"I'm one of those people who will probably talk with the CIA next year," explained a Colby student. "I'll have to step over fourteen people lying on the stairs with X's on their chests and calling me names. 'You want to kill people,' and all this other stupid stuff. They don't see that I wouldn't join an organization that killed innocent people. I don't like everything they do, but if you have a little power you can control something. Maybe I could do more good than marching around Washington, D.C., with a sign for fifteen years."

Some students genuinely hope to develop specific concerns once they hit the right context. "If you want to change the system you have to get in there, be the inside person, and listen and learn," said a Fairfield woman. She had extensively studied the politics of international trade and the legacy of the Vietnam war, but had involved herself in no social causes. "Maybe ten years from now I'll have learned enough and be in a solid enough position that what I do can genuinely matter," she said.

This student was highly capable and knowledgeable. Perhaps she might find her niche and make a constructive impact. But the prevailing pattern is that adapters remain adapters, so it's more likely that the right time and circumstances will never arise. This doesn't mean students have to cast themselves as outsiders to make a difference. One Williams student specifically called himself "an entrepreneur, not an activist," then used his slot on a university committee to bring in thought-provoking speakers like Wendell Berry. He initiated an independent senior project for which he traveled the country analyzing which alternative energy projects worked and why. "I define being an entrepreneur," he said, "as doing things that really interest you. I'm obviously lucky to be in the position I'm in, at an elite college, and being one of those tall healthy white males who tend to be privileged in our society. I ought to take advantage of it to do some projects that matter."

His approach differed from would-be entrepreneurs who merely held out vague notions that somewhere, after they'd made their pile, they'd find some way to give back. He had a clear sense of his social goals, and acted on them creatively and effectively. He focused on specific institutions, like the convocations committee and the alternative energy projects, and worked to help them take responsibility for a global future. He acted in his present context, instead of indefinitely postponing commitment.

None of this is to say that students should spurn the pragmatic path. Particularly if they come from less than privileged backgrounds, they need skills that will help them be more effective in the world. Social change proceeds best, I believe, when individuals work as stakeholders in their communities, continually raising larger questions in existing organizations like churches and temples, PTAs, unions, neighborhood groups, and Rotary and Kiwanis clubs. Many of the most effective campus activists I know work through existing institutions, whether initiating new classes on urban poverty or developing environmental programs. In her forthcoming book *Conscious Careers*, Melissa Everett writes of such corporate programs as the Day's Inn chain's effort to train homeless people as hotel workers, Stonyfield Farm Yogurt's purchase of milk from family farmers, and Merck pharmaceutical corporation's agreement to hold a massive area of Costa Rican rainforest in trust in exchange for the right to develop medical products from it. She discusses groups like Forest Service Employees for Environmental Ethics, government employees who risk their jobs to protect the forests from unwise and often illegal logging. But these efforts all come from people who have a sense of what they believe in, and who join with others to try to achieve it. They do not simply adapt to the prevailing cultural drift.[2]

Whatever America's future economy, a more humane society will require businesspeople who can distinguish between enterprises that nurture human existence and those that debase it, between ones that help renew ecological capital and ones that squander it, between ones that treat workers with dignity and ones that regard them as mere expendable parts. A humane society needs businesspeople who respect efforts by workers or communities to organize and gain a greater say in their circumstances. The report of the 1989 MIT Commission on Industrial Productivity, a blue-ribbon panel that studied five hundred American corporations, speaks of the need for a "new economic citizenship," in which companies view their decisions in the broadest possible context. Mere talk of "working from within" prepares students inadequately for such distinctions.[3]

Judgments regarding ethical work are tricky, and inevitably personal. I think of Seattle friends who've spent twenty years as commercial fishermen because they like the autonomy, like providing food, and like working on the water, and because white-collar paths they'd prepared for never fulfilled their hopes. Others work as doctors, not as high-priced specialists, but in family practice with needy populations. Still others are teachers who strive to make education more than routinized drone work. I know Microsoft programmers and municipal bus drivers involved in social issues on the side. There are individuals who work for Boeing's commercial airline divisions, or develop satellite monitoring for arms control, but who won't work on cruise missiles or components for Star Wars. One of my closest friends quit a technical writing job with a geological consulting firm when they asked him to justify the construction of a nuclear waste repository. He had a son to support, but felt the project would jeopardize human health, so he refused to do it. As a consequence he was forced to take temporary jobs—building concrete curbs, assembling windows, packing boxes of Harlequin romances—and several years passed before he was able to secure another professional writing position.

Ethical career choices are about more than just mere abstractions in students' intended futures. They're about how students have prepared themselves to respond to difficult situations, and whether they've learned to speak their beliefs. The alternative is to work to fit into a slot and to earn enough to be able to say "Buddy, buzz off."

Most apolitical students take the latter course. The more they strive to mold themselves for sale to future employers, the less likely they are to learn critical perspectives necessary to make "I'll work from within" more than empty words. Without such perspectives, they have no way of challenging dubious projects they might encounter, of joining with others to steer their institutions down socially constructive paths, or of knowing the difference between work that serves a greater common good and work that does not. Their course of adaptation heads them directly away from the intellectual, political, and cultural resources that could help them think through their definitions of a right and just society.

The notion of working from within opens a small window of hope in the adapters' more general social pessimism. But it is a hope of involvement consistently deferred and void of current impact. Those who voice it most frequently root their choices not in what they want, but in what they believe they have no choice but to accept.

They call their poison politics   We might expect students who talk of working from within to embrace the electoral process. They don't. The adapters shun not only campus political efforts of protest, education, and organizing, but also the fourth-grade civics mechanisms of working for candidates, lobbying their legislatures, or often, even voting. Apolitical students stigmatize peers involved in electoral politics less than they do students they call "marchers with their marcher face on." But they grant such efforts little more validity. They consider this sphere inherently corrupt, as when Carolyn, the Columbia student, felt disgusted that her boyfriend even considered running for office. Explaining simply, "They're all just out to manipulate us," even many students who strongly backed Reagan and Bush had little faith that their leaders would respond to the priorities of ordinary citizens.

At the University of Washington, five weeks before the 1988 election, three well-dressed students staffed a table for George Bush. A few stopped to talk or take literature. Most passed by with barely a glance. Later that day, other students held a rally to support Michael Dukakis. In honor of his Greek heritage, they brought huge piles of baklava, intending to hand them out free to the audience. The rally began at noon, with music and passionate speeches about abortion choice and cuts in federal financial aid. Fewer than seventy-five students paid any attention, and half of those were watching distractedly from the steps where they usually sat to eat their lunch. Most continued with their business as if the speakers were invisible. The baklava remained piled high, untouched.

A few years before, a University of Washington political science major had described how friends mocked her when she lobbied for the Equal Rights Amendment at the state capitol. Although they hadn't thought much about the issue, they had no problems with it. But they acted as if she'd gone half crazy by taking a stand. "Why do this?" they asked. "Isn't it a throwback?" "It won't do any good. You're wasting your time."

Students consistently regarded electoral efforts as futile. "We saw a movie on the arms race," explained a student from Michigan, "and I was really into it. But I walked out of the room feeling powerless. Sure I can write my Congressman. Congress controls things. But the politics that go into it, the time I'd be devoting, it just doesn't feel worthwhile."

These students grew up learning that America's official political system was largely a feeding ground for the greediest. Not only did the Reagan-Bush scandals help accumulate a deficit so vast as to drown alternative visions in a sea of red ink, they also permeated the eighties and early nineties with the sense that anything the government touched was corrupt. If this was true, students asked, why hassle with trying to change things? Although campuses sometimes would turn out to see politicians as celebrities, and students occasionally volunteered in campaigns, few made electoral politics a major arena for involvement.[4]

Again, this retreat stemmed from a combination of specific electoral disillusionment and broader cultural impetuses toward withdrawal. Books like E. J. Dionne's *Why Americans Hate Politics,* Thomas and Mary Edsall's *Chain Reaction,* and William Greider's *Who Will Tell the People?* illustrate well how the debasement of America's public sphere, as well as political mistakes by those who've sought to change it, have driven ordinary citizens away from civic participation. But this is only part of the picture. Students' reactions suggest that their involvement has been reduced even more by their experiences in a day-to-day culture that discourages social concern in general.[5]

Young voters were once considered the most left-leaning of Democrats, the only ones to give George McGovern a majority. As late as 1980, voters under thirty identified themselves as Democrats by more than two to one, and gave Carter a one-point lead when they actually went to the polls. By 1984 they'd begun to shift, as Reagan pounded home the notion that he represented the party of the future, in contrast to "the bad old days" of Carter. Young men, and to a lesser extent young women, increasingly cast their lot with the Republicans. Pre-election polls in 1984 showed voters under thirty identifying themselves as Republican in percentages greater than any other age sector of the population, and giving Reagan their overwhelming allegiance, even as they often disagreed with him on particular issues. When election day arrived, the gap closed, however, as some of this volatile population shifted and many more who most embraced the Reagan-era myths stayed home. A similar process occurred in 1988, where Bush went from a 62 to 28 pre-election lead among young voters to capturing those who turned out by just a 52 to 48 percent margin.[6]

Full-time students, including older students, were considerably less enthusiastic about Republican rule. Reagan barely got their vote in 1984; in 1988, 54 percent voted for Dukakis, a higher support level than any occupational group except the unemployed. This was particularly true of students in the social sciences and humanities, who were both more politically liberal and politically involved than their more vocationally oriented peers. After the first blush of the Reagan era, most viewed the available electoral choices as dismal.[7]

Voting represents only one modest political citizenship, particularly when conducted in disgruntled frustration and hampered by complex residency requirements that make student registration particularly difficult. More important, I believe, are the day-to-day individual and collective choices that determine which issues enter the public agenda, how they are framed, and who is granted the right to address them. When enough critical discussion occurs and citizen movements create enough momentum behind a constructive political agenda, this can translate into the electoral arena. The specific votes of the students matter less, therefore, than the ways they do or don't learn to engage with the world.[8]

I'll talk later about the 1992 election—when students and young voters returned to the Democratic fold, spurred by economic collapse and by fear of the religious right's threat to their private liberties. But throughout the 1980s, few national candidates stirred student commitment and passion in the manner of Jack or Robert Kennedy, Eugene McCarthy, or George McGovern. Reagan gained support in his initial years, not as a candidate students actively volunteered for, but as one many cheered from the sidelines for his image as a crusader against government bureaucrats. Some local figures stirred student passions—I think of Chicago Mayor Harold Washington or populist Minnesota Senator Paul Wellstone. But the only other national candidate who spurred major enthusiasm and commitment was Jesse Jackson. Perhaps because students viewed him as both more and less than a conventional politician, Jackson drew large responses, beginning in 1984 with his first campaign. By 1988 he was drawing thousands to campus rallies considerably bigger than those mustered by Bush or Dukakis. Jackson's campaign particularly involved African-American students, who felt that his presence as a candidate was itself a victory, and white student activists who felt vindicated by his stands. But even apolitical students—like sorority women I met in a huge University of Washington crowd—responded to his appeal. They were moved by his parables of how Jesus didn't ask for an insurance card before deciding whether or not to heal someone. They liked his call to involvement. He made them want to feel part of a political movement. But Jackson's message was more in the vein of a moral crusade than of a man preparing for mundane political horsetrading. And when his presence faded, the campuses once again faced an electoral void.[9]

Visions and values   When contemporary students talk of "working from within," this may just reflect their recognition that they have less economic latitude than their predecessors, that it's become harder to live on the margins. But the concept extends beyond vocational choices to an assumption that America needs only more good and caring individuals to cure its ills. It is right and necessary for us to be kind to our families, to be civil to our neighbors and co-workers, to live decent private lives. But none of this by itself will stop corporations from moving factories to Mexico, speculators from looting savings and loans, insurance and drug companies from gouging on health care, banks from redlining urban ghettos, chemical plants from dumping toxic wastes, or military strategists from making decisions that shatter the lives of women, men, and children halfway across the globe. To address such larger ills requires the very common political action that students have been taught to mistrust.

In assuming that acting later on will be easier, students also underestimate the stifling of political dialogue in American workplaces and communities. It is difficult to take committed stands at Mankato State or the University of Michigan. It gets no easier at Dow or at GE. A woman at Florida's Rollins College once tried to put up a poster on her Westinghouse employee bulletin board for a lecture of mine on the arms race. Her manager prevented her: they provided space only, he said, for company approved material. It made me think about the extent to which democracy vanishes at the gates of most American workplaces. Employees at every level can and must find ways to make constructive changes; but to be effective, they need to find allies. These can be co-workers, fellow union members—if unions exist where they work—or outside community groups whose pressure they cite to justify ethical goals. Yet the notion of reaching out to anyone but your superiors flies against everything these students have learned. If they have no experience at extending moral criteria beyond private life, the period when they're trying to climb the economic ladder seems an unlikely time to change this.

As a practical course, "I'll work from within" is a reasonable path of social change, whether for the Williams student interested in environmental issues, or for citizens working to make the institutions of what political theorists call "civil society" take greater responsibility for a global future.[10] But most students who use the words do so to pass off social responsibility to someone else, or to defer it to some continually receding future, when they'll finally be powerful enough to act. The phrase reinforces a mandate to view their lives in terms of individual success, detached from the health of the community. It implies that power is exercised solely from the top, and that ordinary citizens can do nothing to change this. It teaches these students, once again, to quietly adapt.

Eleven ~~~~~~~~~~~~~~~~~~~~~

Diminished Shaping a culture
dreams of retreat

~~~~~~~~~~~~~~~~~~~~~~~~~~~~~~~~~~~~~~

We've been talking a lot about role models. What about the most intimate model—students' families? I'll talk later about the shift in the early 1990s, when students beginning to trickle into the campuses had parents who themselves had been active in the sixties, and who encouraged them to speak out. But through the bulk of the Reagan-Bush era, the parents of most college students came from the 1950s' "silent generation," a group whose activist constituent was small and who passed on considerable mistrust of political dissent.

Some of those parents directly opposed their children's activist involvements. A Mercer woman shied away from the controversy around the college president's fiscal recklessness because her grandfather threatened to stop paying her tuition. Students at Minnesota's Gustavus Adolphus College believed their families would cut off financial support if they discovered their involvement in Honeywell protests. "'Peace studies? I've never heard of that," the mother of a Colgate activist told him. "Stick with poli sci, econ, or English. Go to law school. I'm not paying sixteen thousand dollars a year for you to major in peace studies."

In most cases, these students had been raised in political silence. Their parents might have discussed the nightly news or joked about corrupt politicians. But they avoided difficult public issues, either because they felt uncomfortable dealing with them or because they hoped this would enable their children to grow up protected and innocent, shielded from the ills of the world. They ignored or dismissed citizen attempts at social change.

"My father taught me," said a Minnesota student, "to respect my elders and not talk back." "Just stick to your education," the mother of a woman involved in the controversy at Mercer told her. "If things get really bad, you can always transfer." When another Mercer student argued with her boss over how he treated a fellow worker, her mother warned her that speaking out might cost her job. While such calls for economic caution weren't baseless, they consistently encouraged these students to relinquish their voice.

These parents urge their children to treat college as an investment—and demand concrete returns for the often staggering sums they lay out. Rising tuition leaves even modestly comfortable parents making major sacrifices to help their kids get through. Students work to redeem this support in the tangible coin of material success. They value this goal, in any case, but parental urgings lend it legitimacy. The more the students prepare themselves to do well, the more they can feel a sense of reciprocity, and make proud families who've labored long and hard to give them the chance. "If they're going to pay," explained a Fairfield marketing major, "they're going to want something back. I didn't want to major in business, but all I get is pressure."

General economic constraints furthered this sense. "Even if your parents don't say it straight out," commented a woman in the Nebraska Farm Action Concerns Tomorrow's Society (FACTS) group, "they want you to find a good job." Such pressures bear down particularly hard on students from poor or working-class backgrounds. They face a challenge to understand the social roots of their difficulties—such as lack of sufficient financial support for going to school and unfamiliarity with the conventions of academic life. They face a challenge to treat these difficulties not just as their own peculiar burden, but to join with others to change the institutional structures that maintain them.

Children of privilege, in contrast, grow up isolated from people whose lives they can dismiss in phrases like "they aren't my neighbors." These students may be groomed with confidence to speak what they think and take the helm of history, but many are also taught to pay no mind to those left struggling in their wake. Coming of age insulated and protected, most never notice the moral costs of American social priorities.

Students who grow up on the economic edge face particular pressures to view their education largely in terms of survival. They already lack the resources to casually surmount the kinds of mishaps better-off students barely notice, like spells of illness or the loss of part-time jobs. In the academic environment, they are coping with a culture that is almost foreign. They feel a greater weight of family responsibilities. "My mother works as a salesperson and my dad drives a forklift at the airport for United," explained the Chicago Circle student body vice president. "She already takes care of the two-and-a-half-year-old child of her sister. I feel almost a necessity for me to make enough money to give them a better life when they have to retire."

A Fairfield antinuclear activist named Sue Ballinger had an internship at the Council for a Livable World, based in Washington, D.C. Sue had planned "to stay in Washington, and work with the council, my local congressman, or one of the other peace groups. Then my mom got sick. She was hospitalized and close to death for a week. I got home and she was walking back and forth in the house saying 'Sue, I don't know what to do.' I realized I didn't have to do anything but love her. She took care of me every day when I was growing up. I'm moving back to New Jersey to help take care of her. I'll find some kind of job. I can't plan too far in advance. I just have to have faith that things will work out and this is worth doing for better or worse. Maybe," she stopped and laughed, "I'll even radicalize Lodi, New Jersey."

There's civic work to be done in every community. Sue's values led her to seek a way to continue, even in difficult circumstances. Yet the survival struggles of many students and their families can't be separated from their roots in larger political and economic policies. Students like Sue face the challenge of finding ways to effectively change them.

Neil Howe and William Strauss, in their book *13th-GEN*, attribute much of this generation's focus on material security to their having grown up in a time of high divorce rates and general familial instability. However, with the exception of some young fundamentalists, who seemed disproportionately to come from troubled homes, few students have described this as a factor in shaping their sensibilities. Indeed, some of the most vindictively individualist students, like those in the Fairfield group, had unimpeachable Ozzie and Harriet backgrounds. Student activists spanned the gamut of family settings, including a large number strongly influenced by mothers who became, following divorces, both more independent and more politically questioning.

Divorce rates indeed doubled from 1965 to 1975, but the numbers of single-parent households have stayed relatively constant from 1975 on—the very period when student materialism increased dramatically. Neither Howe and Strauss nor other kindred pundits offer any real evidence that parental divorce influences students to be more pragmatic or shortsighted than parents sticking out troubled marriages, for good or ill. Neither do they offer evidence for the assertion that increases in the abortion rate contribute to a generational feeling of being disposable. If anything, the fact that these students were born in a time when their mothers were not forced to carry them to term might make them feel consciously wanted. Shifts in family situation have rebounded on student values and choices. But I believe they've done so mostly through a passing on of economic fears, a mistrust of citizen movements, and a general distance from public life.[1]

I'll explore later how students nurtured by parents to publicly follow their conscience inherit a different mandate—to learn what they need to take active responsibility as citizens. These students still seek marketplace skills, but tend to trust that they'll find a niche for their abilities, believing they can best redeem the support of their parents by learning ways to stand up for their beliefs. While some still shy away from campus movements (owing to lack of time or a general pessimism), none share the rabid mistrust I've found among so many students from strongly conservative or apolitical households.

The latter learned suspicion of dissenters when they were young. For them to break from it requires a conscious strain on family loyalty. Even when they clearly separate familial love from political differences, involvement remains a difficult choice. "My father is one of the best men I know," said a Fairfield student, "yet he works for Grumman weapons systems. He got me a summer job there, and I liked the people, but I was appalled by their casualness toward the weapons they built. When Grumman F-14s shot down two Libyan jets, people talked about it all day. They were very proud, like 'We did this.' They didn't question the right or wrong of the incident so long as Grumman came out in a good light. I respect my father, but I'm not sure of his work."

Sometimes, as with this woman and the Colgate student who wanted to major in peace studies, students learned to speak out for what they believe, even if it challenged the perspectives they'd learned from their parents. Some directly argued their causes over the dinner table. Others resolved, as did a University of Southern Mississippi woman involved in a campus AIDS benefit, to simply smile and change the subject of conversation when controversial subjects came up on the news. "I love my parents and care about them," she said, "but the things I'm involved in should not reflect on their lives. We should still be able to relate without everything becoming a struggle."

More often, fears of emotional rupture held students back. Even students with generally supportive families worried about their judgments. "It's kind of rejecting them," thought a Fairfield woman, "when you decide, 'I'm gonna do this despite what you say.' There's an emotional balance between doing what you have to and being sensitive to your parents. Next week, I'm driving up to New Haven for a Central America rally, which is something my parents would allow. Then there's a trip to Nicaragua, which I know they're against. I have to decide whether to go despite what they've said."

Such intimate conflicts are always difficult, and especially so when individuals are first out on their own. Some students understood this, even as they resolved to pursue their own course. "It's a harsh world," reflected an African-American Williams activist. "My parents are just trying to be protective, warning that I'll run into a lot of walls because of my commitments. I have to tell them, 'Mom and Dad, I appreciate that. But I'll feel happier making my own mistakes.' " He was the exception in acting and risking family tensions. Most students accepted their parents' boundaries of proper and improper concerns as walls they dared not breach.

All God's will   Apolitical students tend to believe that society cannot change. Global events seem out of their control. They see no gain in taking strong stands. They feel they lack a right to ask what kind of nation or world they'd like to inhabit.

We see this in their religious beliefs, in the absence of that prophetic tradition that speaks to the duty of individuals to challenge public wrongs. Institutional religion usually matters less to college-age individuals than to those younger or older. But to the extent that these students voice their faith at all, it is overwhelmingly private in thrust, reinforcing quiescence.

Consider the case of Dale Ottiger. The father of his girlfriend, Linda, had also been a farmer, until the crisis hit. He'd been doing fine in hogs, Linda said, doubling the size of the farrow operation, buying new trucks and tractors. Then hog prices dropped and the bank took it all. He tried renting two quarter sections of land, fifteen miles from home, and that failed as well. He was now scraping by, trying to sell insurance, filling in occasionally at the local post office.

How did members of Linda's church respond?

"They didn't talk about it much," Dale said. "It was a small congregation and people are proud. It's tough to share hard times when someone else is farming and doing well. It's tough when it might be several years before you make it. But they gave people lots of support by praying."

"God had a plan for her family," he stressed. "That's how her parents believe. Her father's a strong spiritual man even though he lacks business confidence. But God gives him strength every day."

I said it didn't seem fair to blame the agricultural crisis on God. What about government policies and corporate choices?

"But her dad's a strong enough Christian," said Dale, "that he accepts it."

"Things aren't really all that bad," added Linda, shrugging her shoulders, "because we moved to a new town and a larger school. I got voted Homecoming Queen.

Our church prayed a lot for us when it got really bad with the courts and lawyers and when they bolted our machine shop with a padlock. I think it will all work out in the end."

True, religious institutions provide students some ways to get involved. Campus ministry sponsors speakers and concern groups, posts notices of marches and rallies, offers a place to discuss morality and purpose. The churches or temples students grow up in offer a diffuse language of responsibility, and some take on every conceivable cause. Students like Raul, from Chicago Circle, are strongly influenced by individual priests, ministers, or rabbis. But for most, in the congregations where they grow up, concern stops at praying for peace at Christmas or at collecting charity for the poor. As with the Fairfield group who explained "God helps those who help themselves," in the contest between biblical mandates to heed the voices of the poor and dispossessed, and America's civil religion of consumption and mobility, the latter triumphs hands down.

Socially concerned students sometimes draw on a religious notion of stewardship: an ethic that insists humans have no right to destroy what we have not created. As one of Fairfield's more active women explained, "I think everything was put here for a purpose, and if we keep abusing it there will be nothing left. In my eyes that's not God's will. We're supposed to be preserving it. We're not the final owners."

When I asked how she might act on this belief, she remained uncertain. "I look around, and feel I can't do anything about it. I feel so minuscule compared to all the issues."

Her faith led her to question what she considered violations of a sacred trust. But it gave her no assurance that it would matter if she challenged the path of greed and shortsightedness. Older religious peace and justice activists I know often express such a trust—not in a God who directly intervenes in history, but in a force that supports them, in ways they can never fully understand, in their courage, vision, and hope. Today's students, even those religiously and politically committed, seemed bereft of such faith. What they drew from their beliefs was private comfort, "something to lean on," in the words of a woman from the Chicago Circle Polish group, "to rely on if everything fails."

The only students who seem to feel a specifically religious mandate to remake the world are the young fundamentalists. But aside from the abortion issue, where they buck the strong feelings of most of their peers, they are usually so obsessed with private morality as to surrender any chance to hold governmental or corporate institutions accountable for having damaged the modest familial lives they so desperately want to preserve. Crises like hunger, homelessness, and environmental destruction trouble them.

They are angered almost as much as young radical activists by America's worship of consumerism. But they write these ills off to callous personal choices, and explain, "It's not my place to solve them."

Mercer University theology professor Joe Hendricks has suggested that, despite increasing involvement of mainline Protestant and Catholic congregations in social issues, students' spiritual lives have narrowed in the past thirty years. "Students used to pray for the community," he said. "Now they pray for themselves—for their own choices and success." Notions of sacrifice for the common good, Hendricks made clear, can justify dubious actions. Yet they also gave courage to people like Martin Luther King, Jr., and radical Baptist preacher and civil rights activist Clarence Jordan. He cited the Parisian posters from May 1968 that read "All Power to the Imagination." "That's lacking now, along with the prophets who brought the word of God against those who would trample the needy." Moral imagination, Hendricks said, highlighted the tension between what is and what should be. He feared students could no longer even think in such terms.

Winners and losers   I returned for a second visit with the Fairfield group a year after our initial meeting. They still intended to look out for themselves, but they wavered now between defending their material aspirations and acknowledging that it might take more than individual upward mobility to solve America's problems.

George Lipson, the salesman's son, described a party at his Long Island home, where a woman "started talking about the Peace Corps or something. I was purposely being as right-wing as possible, just to get her reaction. I said unemployment should be abolished and I didn't like welfare sucking up my taxes. I felt awful when she almost cried and told me that if it wasn't for unemployment she wouldn't be here, because her father spent eight months out of work."

"I don't think it's idealistic and naive to do something about larger issues," George said, "though that's not the role for me." He liked a comfortable house, he explained, nice cars and winter ski trips. "My grandmother was a cleaning lady. My grandfather owned a gas station. Now one of the jobs I'd never do is work at a gas station or McDonald's."

What choices would the fast track preclude? What economic level would George find sufficient? He mentioned a family friend with a huge mansion, two Rolls Royces, a 160-foot yacht, and several airplanes and helicopters. The man started by singing in piano bars, saving what he earned and investing it "in some really left-field long shots that came through. He just had that Midas touch, where he could start or take over anything and convert it into money."

George paused, pulling back from the allure of the dream. "I guess Ivan Boesky did that, too. I don't need gross wealth. I don't need to be like that, though I'd love to have a Porsche because it's a great car and I'd love to be driving it. I also don't want to have to live like my mother's cousins, whose street is like the drug capital of Long Island. I want to be my own boss and be comfortable."

"Maybe I don't put my first priority on larger issues because I'm concerned with me first. It's going to sound really cold, but that's the way I am. I still feel God helps those who help themselves, and maybe we'd be better off if everyone else admitted that too, instead of using excuses for not making it. Or maybe I'm just selfish. I want to have a family, people I love. I want to do what I can for them."

After leaving George's room, adorned with posters of Porsches, I visited the rest of the group in their rented house, a ten-minute drive from campus and a block from Long Island Sound. When I asked whether their perspectives had changed, Tim Lovejoy, the doctor's son, said he still wanted to get rich. "It's not wrong to be a millionaire, just because there's one millionaire for every 10,000 poor people. If I want the things I have now—a house, a boat, to raise a family—they won't be possible without money."

"I want a place I can call my own," Tim repeated. "I want to be able to say 'Buddy, buzz off. This is mine. This is what I've paid for.'"

Yet events of the past summer had threatened Tim's private dreams. Medical wastes washed ashore on Long Island Sound, littering once pristine sand with used syringes, blood vials, and rags. Health authorities had closed the beaches. Tim joked about "swimming with the syringes," but couldn't go near the water.

Tim "felt violated" by the pollution of his beaches, although the offending corporations had followed his own maxims of placing personal gain above some abstract common good. He'd already been thinking about environmental issues after taking an ecology class as a premed elective. Maybe, he suggested, he could apply his biology training to a career "cleaning up environmental pollution. I can see a big market opening up. If you stop nuclear weapons, you need to keep the stuff for fifty thousand years. There's always going to be dirt. I'd start with picking up trash and recycling, but I see a great entrepreneur deal coming up."

When I asked Rick what had happened with the Peace Corps, he said he'd just received an application. Tim and Scott shot glances back and forth that said, "He's finally gone crazy and done it."

"Rick's too much of a bleeding heart," said Scott. "He doesn't even have a football team."

"You can't be a real man without a football team," said Tim with a laugh. Rick said his mother liked the New England Patriots, and Tim nodded sagely, "That definitely explains things."

Rick still looked an awkward adolescent. He lost his cool in political arguments. Scott, Tim, and the others teasingly called him Nadia, after Romanian Olympic star Nadia Comaneci, because Rick was a gymnast and once tried to impress some young women by doing a series of handsprings. His Peace Corps interest stemmed as much from resignation as idealism. "I don't like this country," he said. "It's hard to fight the bureaucracy. Like with nuclear disarmament. Eighty percent of the people feel we have enough missiles, but we build more each day."

"More! More missiles! We want more!" said Tim and Scott, looking at each other and grinning.

"If they're going to fight the weapons, they'll have to fight the bureaucracy," Rick went on, oblivious to the ragging. "In the Peace Corps I could do something useful. Maybe teach people how to build houses. Put my talents toward work I believe in. Here in America, I feel frustrated."

"I'd love to see nuclear disarmament," said Tim, out of the blue. "But it's crazy to make such a stink about 'The Bombs. The Bombs. The Bombs.' You have such little faith. You don't believe in religion. I believe in God. It's the only guarantee you get."

"I believe in life on this planet," shouted Rick, to which Scott responded, "Yeah, you should be God, Rick, then you'd solve everything."

"It could all have been stopped at one point," commented Paul Vigna, as if sadly watching from a distance. "But now there's too many weapons and too much money. We know it's dangerous, but can't afford to wholly get rid of them."

Paul seemed the most reflective in the group. He took public stands in periodic journalistic forays in the Fairfield student newspaper and in a campus literary magazine he'd helped revive and edit. Yet his cynicism about American culture was equalled only by his quick dismissal of alternatives. "It would be nice to think about a utopian society where no one starved or was poor. But some people will always live off others. Maybe I've grown more realistic. Maybe it's the people I hang out with. But things go on that I just can't change."

"There'll always be winners and losers," said Tim, with a husky laugh. "It's all just like a football game."

Tim shifted roles so fast I could hardly follow. One moment he talked of writing an article on acid rain. The next he insisted "I like how I live" or reiterated the "Buddy, buzz off" theme. When Scott argued for Star Wars, Tim grinned widely and proclaimed, "The Final Frontier."

Yet Tim's budding environmentalism also led him to join a new campus group called Concerned Young Scientists. "It's concerned with environmental issues, nuclear stuff, starvation. We read articles just to get some information, be more aware, put a little pressure on the politicians about their choices. It began with this real intelligent senior who wanted to have it on his résumé, but I've learned a lot from the meetings. I think more information can only help.

"Of course I'm still out for myself," Tim said, half apologizing. "I know this all sounds way too liberal for me. But if there are problems, someone's got to do the work. I'm not sure I want to pick up trash all my life, clean up other people's mess. I learned enough from a summer job pounding in fence posts to know I don't want to end up on the bottom. Maybe doing something environmental could become a career. I still want to be rich, but if I got in on the ground floor, maybe it would give me the same financial reward. Why not kill two birds with one stone and help people out?"

These Fairfield students were torn. Tim's newfound environmental concern was heartening, fruit of the rude disruption of his long-sheltered world. Yet he and the others remained trapped by assumptions that anything less than ending up at the top would mean failure. They wanted economic success and felt sure they deserved it. Porsches and BMWs seemed to them middle-class necessities, along with vacations in Europe and Aspen, and $400,000 homes in Westchester, Long Island, or Greenwich. They worried, with reason, that they'd have a more difficult time achieving these prizes than their parents had. They resolved to work all the harder to make good.

Constricted hopes   Compared to their counterparts in the sixties, recent students grew up part of a generation with lower economic and political expectations. For better or worse, students who acted in the sixties found models of hope in the civil rights movement, in the best of Kennedy-Johnson-era liberalism, in the visions of student organizations like SDS, and in the mushrooming counterculture at the decade's end. At the height of the sixties, hope, imagination, anger, frustration, and a sense of common purpose melded together to give a sense—suggested by the famed phrase "the whole world is watching"—that just about any better possible future might be achievable.

Recent students, in contrast, have grown up in a profoundly cynical time, with foreshortened political visions. They witnessed the retreat of a once-dominant liberal center that offered few alternatives to the Reagan-Bush ethos. Even grassroots community movements have been forced to spend most of their energy fighting gross abuses of power, assaults on rights long assumed to be guaranteed, and attempts to gut over half a century of social progress. They have had little chance to offer broad visions of a more democratic society.

The adapters have responded to this context by pronouncing social change impossible, by projecting the harshest aspects of the present into a perpetual human future. "I read their essays," said the teacher of the University of Washington mass media class that reacted so strongly against my conclusions, "and it all sounds very bleak. I know I didn't feel that way at age twenty. I saw a whole world to discover, all these things I could do, possibilities I could explore. That's not how they see things at all. They talk like people who expect life to be difficult and unpleasant."

Probably, she said, this was because opportunities had closed. "But it's also like they're sitting with this enormous rock or chain on their heads, and don't ever dare to hope."

Complacent times make heroic action difficult, and these students have grown up in a time of profound complacency. Individuals in some periods, critic John Berger writes, experience "national or social crises of such an order that they test all those who live through them. They are moments of truth in which, not everything, but a great deal is revealed about individuals, classes, institutions, leaders. . . . Even those who as a result of the crisis find themselves in total and lasting opposition to one another will nevertheless agree that what was revealed in the moment of truth was undeniable."[2]

"It was like this," Berger writes, "in France in 1940 after the capitulation, in Budapest in 1956, in Algeria during the war of liberation." For many Americans, Vietnam and the civil rights campaigns created such a moral crucible. Individuals were repeatedly called upon to justify their courses of action, to support or oppose the dictates of their government. Ordinary citizens challenged entrenched power. For a brief moment, it seemed this society had the courage to ask the most difficult questions about its past, present, and future. And the political battles of that time continue to be fought.

Recent American students have watched comparable world-defining choices made by young women and men their age in the streets of Prague, Berlin, Moscow, Tiananmen Square, and Soweto. But they've watched this at a distance, on TV. In their own lives, most have faced no similar testing moments or transforming experiences. Students who've taken on issues like homelessness, the environment, or U.S. Central American policy have done so despite a climate that denied the significance of their actions. Apolitical students will recall their college years largely in private terms: who went out with whom, who made it through organic chemistry, who starred in intramural sports, who did or did not get drunk or stoned or make themselves whatever kind of fool with their friends. A few may remember scattered books that stirred their souls. Except during the brief and sanitized military war with Iraq, most students were simply not called upon to respond to major public events.

To demand a wiser and more democratic nation is hard, particularly in a time when citizens expect less and less from their society. Perhaps, as Christopher Lasch suggests, Americans in general have stopped believing in the future. "If young people feel no connection to anything," Lasch writes, "their dislocation is a measure of our failure, not theirs. We have failed to provide them with a culture that claims to explain the world or [that] links the experience of one generation to those that came before and to those that will follow."[3]

Those of us in older generations could encourage students to think about the kind of world they'd like to inhabit—could do so both directly and through the examples that we set. Those in the student generation could act to inspire their peers. Instead, the prevailing American culture, during the time when this generation has been forming its core values, did the opposite. It taught them that societies change only through actions of people at the top, that notions of a greater common good are a mask for hypocrisy, that they should mistrust those who try to shape a better world. It taught them that the best hope, for themselves and America, is to hunker down and do their best to adapt to whatever the powers that be happen to offer. It's not surprising that these students mostly place their faith in private dreams.

Book two **I had to take a stand**

~~~~~~

Introduction   **A stake in the future**

In February 1990, I picked up my copy of *National Student News Service,* a biweekly digest of campus events. Ten thousand students had just marched on forty state capitols to challenge continued deforestation of U.S. public lands. At the University of Southern California, student protests had convinced the faculty senate to call for public hearings on South African divestment. At Rutgers, a coalition of students and union employees had launched a campaign to strip thirteen top university officials of university-provided cars on the grounds that it was irresponsible for the school to provide such lavish perks at a time of rising tuition, declining educational services, and freezes in rank-and-file wages. At the University of New Mexico, the campus chapter of the Nader-inspired public interest research groups, the PIRGS, convinced the student union to ban the use of Styrofoam products in its food service. Students at Allegheny College, in upstate Pennsylvania, boycotted a fundraising telethon, demanding a greater say in college decision making.[1]

Political withdrawal still dominated most of these schools. But something was changing. The spirit characterized by the phrase "they aren't my neighbors" seemed less widespread than just a few years before. The campus mood had shifted since I'd begun my college lecturing nearly a decade before, and had continued to shift as I intensively researched student values and commitments through the mid to late eighties. These shifts emerged in the shadow of the prevailing retreat. Student engagement would continue to grow around a variety of issues including the environment, university governance, rising tuition rates, racial and sexual politics, hunger and homelessness, war and apartheid.

How did students manage to get involved? How did they overcome the barriers I've described? How did their experience and assumptions differ from those of the adapters? How did they successfully enlist others to act, and how did they fail—whether because of the prevailing resistance or their own mistakes? What visions sustained their commitment?

Student concern existed even at the most quiescent trough of the Reagan era. But those who acted were marginal and few. Involvement took major leaps with efforts like the mid-eighties antiapartheid and anti-CIA campaigns. Massive protests in South Africa inspired American students to rally, march, sign petitions, erect protest shanties, sit in at buildings, and attain full or partial divestment at over 150 schools. Their efforts played a key role in long-delayed U.S. government sanctions that helped bring about apartheid's end. Opposition to Reagan-era Central American policies also sparked widespread campus protests. Demonstrations at almost a third of the schools they visited led the CIA to cancel recruiting trips to schools like Princeton, Rutgers, Brown, Columbia, and the Universities of Minnesota, New Mexico, Colorado, and Vermont. Beginning when most participants felt isolated and marginal, such efforts helped seed the ground for later student engagement.[2]

Campus political involvement continued to grow during the final Reagan years and during the Bush administration, when presidential talk of a kinder and gentler America accompanied increasingly visible social and economic desperation. Renewed community service programs took on hunger, illiteracy, and homelessness. Ecological concern sparked a new national organization, Student Environmental Action Coalition (SEAC), whose contacts reached two thousand campuses. Racial incidents spurred students to demand that colleges address America's deep-seated ethnic divides. Rising tuition sparked lobbying, protests, and strikes.

Resurgent concern has emerged from America's growing crises. A worsening national economy has produced collapsing banks, foreclosed farms, and people living homeless in the streets. Ozone depletion, old-growth clearcutting, and toxic dumping signal growing environmental threats. Personal options once taken for granted, like the right to an affordable college education, seem increasingly insecure.

Students have acted because they feel frustrated at being constantly branded apathetic and greedy. Resenting commentators who so describe them, they've worked to prove them wrong. Those who've acted have drawn inspiration from engaged parents, concerned faculty, or older community organizers; then, as their movements slowly grew, they began to inspire each other. Their initial efforts have built, brick by brick, until politically concerned students have begun to find a climate far more hospitable than that of just a few years before. Around the same time, colleges have seen the beginning of a significant shift in generations. Students whose parents grew up in the "silent" fifties were joined by those whose mothers and fathers had come of age in the sixties, and had themselves more often marched, spoken out, and where they did hold true to their values, passed them on. They helped create the return of a socially committed presence on the American campus.

Students who explain their noninvolvement by saying "I'm not that kind of person" feel they have no right to try to shape a common future. It would be nice, they say, to follow out their most generous ideals, but this choice would be naive. They view the world as a hostile place, where they can at best hope to grab some modest personal comforts. In contrast, those who act want their educations and lives to serve more than just personal security or the pursuit of private havens. Where the adapters seek individual exemption, the activists believe that if their fellow humans or the earth itself are brutalized and demeaned, such despoliation wounds us all. Where the adapters link past, present, and future only in personal terms, committed students assume their choices will create the landscape that others will inherit. Seeking to create a country and world they'd be proud to inhabit, they fight, in the words of a Hunter College student, "for those yet to come."

For all the apolitical students' differences in circumstances, style, and vocational choices, their reasons for withdrawal converge. Whether the cause is Central America or apartheid, the environment or homelessness, they step back in similar ways. Politically involved students, in contrast, must consciously break from the dominant paths of their culture. To make this break they have to confront a pervasive mistrust of social involvement, to enlist the participation of their peers, and to effectively challenge institutional policies or arrangements of power. The path they take is inherently uncertain.

Because the goals of these students differ so from their apolitical peers, I've taken a different approach in describing them. In Book One I examined the responses of the adapters through various individual journeys, and through mapping common barriers to engagement. But when students begin to take political stands, they act not just as isolated individuals, but as a part of a community, whose efforts will succeed or fail together. I've therefore chosen to examine politically committed students not just through portraits of representative individuals, but through portraits of representative situations where students have come together to take on various causes. I use these stories of particular people in particular situations to explore the role models and assumptions that help students take their initial stands, and the frustrations and satisfactions that emerge. I look at particular backgrounds or circumstances that separate them from their peers, at the issues that call them to act, and at how they have come to understand those issues. I look at which forms of involvement overcome the political barriers, and which feed into them and fail.

Finally, I've alternated these stories of particular political efforts with more general, reflective chapters. I use them to examine the shared fabric of activist experience: common patterns of student involvement, consistent strengths and limitations of activist community, larger forces that continue to feed renewed social concern. I then move on to Book Three and the challenges this generation faces in the future.

Twelve ～～～～～～～～～～

Fighting for Farm activism
the land returns

～～～～～～～～～～～～～～～～～～～

In earlier chapters, the University of Nebraska served as a model of retreat, where decent and well-meaning students—like Dale Ottiger—saw no way to save their families' way of life from companies like Dow and Cargill, so decided to cast their lot with the winners. Yet the school had another current: a group called Farm Action Concerns Tomorrow's Society, or FACTS for short, who worked to preserve the way they'd grown up as a choice for the future.

In high school, FACTS cofounder Barb Meister had never read the newspapers. Political events had seemed too remote and abstract. She didn't vote in 1984, her first chance, didn't even register. Instead, she worked with the 4-H club and Future Farmers of America, much as she had throughout her life. She lived on her parents' farm in West Point, Nebraska, an hour and a half north of Lincoln, and showed her prize-winning cattle in state and county fairs. As head of the statewide 4-H Awareness Team, she traveled throughout Nebraska to speak. Her high school called her "most likely to succeed." Then the agriculture crisis drove her parents to bankruptcy and thrust her into politics.

Within five years, Barb was a key assistant to populist Texas agriculture commissioner Jim Hightower, and later she became assistant director of her own state Department of Agriculture. *Time* magazine would name her one of a hundred top college achievers in the nation. Politics became her obsession. Yet her vision stayed rooted in the land where she'd grown up.

We met in the spring of 1988, Barb's senior year. I asked her if students had to see their world almost collapse before they'd take a public stand. "That describes me," she said. "I was brought up to be critically minded, but not political. My dad was a member of the National Farmers Organization since he graduated eighth grade and left school to go to work. Ever since I can remember, he'd come in from outside, listen to the commodity markets on the radio, and cuss up and down about what was going on. We'd sit at the dinner table, read the newspaper, and he'd editorialize between the lines. He taught all of us to question, and think beyond what was said on the surface. He encouraged us in high school 4-H, and let us go off to their conferences. I got a lot of confidence doing public speaking for them and Future Farmers of America.

"But I also didn't vote. I didn't read the papers. It wasn't until I went to a huge Iowa farm rally that I felt I'd better wake up and start learning about these issues. I'm very critical that we didn't discuss them in my classrooms or on campus."

Barb's journey began with her family's crisis. They'd farmed for four generations in the West Point area, growing corn, alfalfa, and soy beans, and raising cattle and hogs. Her parents farmed six hundred acres that belonged to Barb's grandparents. Their cattle won prizes throughout the Midwest. They farmed well, with an eye toward conservation, and earned enough to put nine kids through Catholic schools. Then, in 1979, a drought severely cut into their hay and corn production. At the same time, the prices for what they produced fell sharply, below the cost of production. Barb's father took an off-the-farm job as a meat inspector for the National Farmers Organization.

The following year, to eliminate the risk of future droughts, they used a mix of savings and borrowed money and invested $100,000 to put in new wells and irrigation systems. Initially, the gamble worked, producing two strong years of high yields. But in July of 1982, they were heading for a record crop of irrigated corn, when a twenty-minute hail storm destroyed it all. Insurance covered only a fraction of the loss, and they ended up further in the hole. Meanwhile, interest rates on their operating loans jumped to 18 percent, driven by federal monetary policies, while prices plummeted for their cattle and hogs. The interest began compounding faster than they could pay it. Like others all across America in a decade where nearly a fifth of the family farms disappeared, the Meisters could no longer cover their costs.[1]

By summer of 1984, land prices had crashed from $2,500 to $700 an acre, erasing the base that secured the Meisters' loans. What was once a $300,000 loan had ballooned to $700,000. The bank called in the loan and threatened to foreclose. Barb's father was forty-eight years old and had farmed full time for thirty-five years. Their family now risked losing everything.

They hired a lawyer and bought time on a technicality. In their bank's eagerness to lend money during the land price boom, they'd neglected to have Barb's mother sign the papers necessary for a joint husband and wife business. After the process dragged on for nearly a year, they finally reached an agreement to pay the loans and interest by turning over major chunks of their operation. They gave the bank ownership of a tractor, all their hogs, and all but forty head of cattle. Their cattle were top registered breeding cows, and they'd planned to sell them in the fall when people had money from their crops and prices were highest. Instead, the bank sold them in the summer, the worst economic time, with the animals skinny, hungry and pathetic, and fetching just a third of their value. After Chapter 12 reorganization, the Meisters ended up owing $60,000, which they hoped to pay off over time.

Barb's parents tried to shield her and the other kids from this process. Not until they actually received their first foreclosure letter did her father sadly tell them, "We have a little problem." Barb was confused. She knew the family had economic problems, but had no sense of why or of what it would mean. Helping out as best she could with the daily work, she saw no way to do more.

By this time, she was a University of Nebraska freshman. She entered that fall, in 1984, with the family's financial crisis steadily worsening, but with little sense of its gravity. "I went off thinking I was so glad to be away from home. Ready for the big world. Wanting to follow my brother, who was a 'big-man-on-campus' and helped run the Interfraternity Council and Student Union board. Then I got rejected in sorority rush because I didn't try enough houses. I got rejected to be a 'little sister' of my brother's fraternity. I wasn't on top of the world like I expected to be."

Barb felt a spiritual reprieve when she won a statewide 4-H contest and the organization sent her to conferences in Chicago and Toronto. "I felt, this is where I belong. This is what I have to build on."

The following February, a coalition of farm groups held a rally at Ames, Iowa. Barb's parents, still struggling through the courts, decided to attend. Barb had heard some vague information about it, then got a last-minute call from a high school 4-H friend named Jerry. He convinced her to go along on the four-hour trip, and they found a stadium filled with fifteen thousand farmers from fourteen states. High school bands played opening anthems. Farmers described how they'd lost their land. The bishop of Des Moines spoke in support. So did a national Grange leader and a small town banker. Until this experience, Barb had thought little about the reasons nearly everyone she knew was close to economic collapse. For all that she felt angry and powerless about her family situation, she hadn't realized how many others were equally desperate. On the drive back, she and Jerry brainstormed the entire time about what they could do.

Together with a few other University of Nebraska friends, they formed the FACTS group. They sought to educate themselves and their peers on the agricultural crisis, spark a groundswell of concern, try at least to make their fellow students pay heed. Barb wasn't sure she knew enough to speak out. "I was still just a freshman, fragile and self-conscious, but I wanted to do something I felt strongly about, not just put on another spaghetti feed or rodeo. I worried a lot that this would fail like everything else."

Despite her misgivings, they launched the organization later that spring with a series of public forums. They turned out a modest core of interested students. Newly enlisted participants spoke at regional farm and youth rallies. They challenged the university to pay more attention to both the immediate crisis and to the long-term crunch of small farmers. They explored the larger context of farming, like the key shift in the fifties when lobbying by banks and agribusiness corporations and red-baiting by Senator Joe McCarthy led to the repeal of highly successful New Deal stabilization and loan programs that had regulated production, given farmers stable prices for their goods, and boosted soil and water conservation. When Willie Nelson held a Farm Aid concert in Lincoln, FACTS organized an accompanying student conference.

Catholic healing   At a meeting of core FACTS members, current president Julia Kleinschmit opened with "a story about Catholic healing. There's a flood. The waters are rising. A policeman comes by to warn this man, and he answers, 'I have faith in God.' Then a boat comes by, and the man says the same thing. Next a helicopter, and again he answers, 'No thanks. I have faith in God.' Finally the man drowns, and asks God 'Why didn't you save me? I had faith.' God says, 'I sent you a policeman. I sent you a boat. I sent you a helicopter. What more do you want?'"

"A priest told me that," Julia explained, with a laugh, gesturing to her small silver cross. It summed up her approach of working with the situation you are handed, not waiting to be bailed out by someone else. Julia grew up on a dairy and hog farm not far from Barb; where her mom headed the state League of Rural Voters. The year before, she'd been the only freshman in the country to place in the top dozen in national college debate. Then she met Barb at a Jesse Jackson breakfast and switched her passion to working on farm issues.

The core FACTS group met in Barb's spare but functional apartment near the largely agricultural East Campus. It had worn couches, potted plants, a stereo boom box, and a small black-and-white TV. Two pigs on a pink wooden candle holder looked at each other through carved pink hearts. On the mantelpiece, the hands of a clock circled a picture of a cow. A sampler in the bathroom read "Life is fragile. Handle with prayer."

The active members, besides Barb and Julia, included Barb's roommate Lori, an old 4-H friend who'd been in on the organization's founding and who intended to become a veterinarian. There was Lee Wagner, Dale's Ag Men fraternity mate, who'd just graduated as an ag major and who student-taught vocational agriculture at a nearby high school. A new rural organizing project had just secured a grant for him to reach out to small-town high school and college students. He thought he'd keep the job for a year, then perhaps return to his family's farm, where he already grew his own 260 acres of irrigated corn.

Lee had recruited a student named Brad, who was vice president of Nebraska 4-H. Brad, too, had grown up in a small town of fewer than seven hundred people. When his English class read *Hamlet*, he spent a week writing a parody entitled "To Farm or Not to Farm," with lines like "whether to suffer the slings and arrows of outrageous creditors." Already heavily in debt for student loans, he'd recently written a term paper on rural bankruptcy, which he completed just after his own parents filed. Nevertheless, Brad wanted to farm. He had a modest herd of seven Angus cows he'd been breeding since the third grade. Because he'd need an economic grubstake, he planned to apprentice to the Iowa-based financial consultant who was helping their family navigate bankruptcy, then establish his own office to steer other farmers around the traps.

All but one in the group came from farm families, and all had been hit hard by the crisis. Lee and Brad's parents were still in bankruptcy court. Barb's had just emerged. With milk prices low, Julia's family had cash-flow problems as well, but they had their land already paid for, so were In better shape than many others. "I call home three or four times a week," said Brad. "My folks are going through Chapter 12 and I want to be with them. When I go home, my mom's half-crying and my dad is just silent, with nothing to talk about. They're getting more schizy because the land payment's coming up."

The discussion switched to the 1985 congressional farm bill, a direct-subsidy measure whose passage had encouraged overproduction, disregarded soil erosion and dropping water tables, lowered commodity prices below farmers' costs, and allocated over $25 billion taxpayer dollars per year to effectively subsidize cheap grain for giant feedlots, commodity traders, and exporters. The program did little to help family farmers, who continued to go bankrupt, or to improve access for their children.

The students talked of the alternative bill sponsored by Iowa Senator Tom Harkin and Missouri Representative Richard Gephardt, which would scrap this program for a return to a New Deal style parity system, based on giving farmers the chance to vote on limiting production, keeping prices stable with government loans, and spending fewer taxpayer dollars. It got strong backing from liberal sectors like unions and the Congressional Black Caucus, but still hadn't mustered the necessary votes for passage.[2]

The FACTS group had the easy friendship of longtime comrades. They looked like any of the other blonde, farm-bred students at the school, talking crop yields and interest rates while a Peter Tosh tape played in the background. They spoke of professors they admired, critics they'd read, and speakers they dreamed of bringing in. Prizing the best of their heritage, they challenged its passivity and the stolid belief that suffering was God's will. Bankruptcy wasn't, they said. Subsidies that favored Cargill and ConAgra weren't either. Neither were land or grain speculations or takeover wars that left a few giant corporations dominating everything from agricultural research to food production, processing, transportation, storage, and sales. These students wanted to do what they could to challenge this.[3]

Yet their involvement carried a cost. Lee, who'd once won 4-H's National Agriculture Achievement Award, had now dropped out of that organization and "the great chance it offers to reach people" in favor of two dozen other commitments he juggled. Leah Fintel, who coordinated the one-credit seminar on the agricultural crisis that FACTS had organized, had five papers overdue. Julia squeezed in 1:00 A.M. dates with her boyfriend at the end of her fast-food shift at Arby's. In between, she worked on a paper on ways peace and farm activists could work together.

"Sometimes I wish," said Lee, "that I could just say, 'Hey, I'm busy.' Or miss a seminar from time to time. It's like we're always operating, and never take time to ask what we're operating for."

Julia agreed, then praised Leah's job coordinating the ag crisis seminar, which now drew between fifty and eighty students each semester, having progressed from a special class to part of the standard curriculum. "Getting it institutionalized *is* a really big thing," said Julia. "I can't wait until it comes out in the official course guides. Maybe I'll paper my room with it."

University of Nebraska students are divided between the largely urban liberal arts and science majors on the main campus, called City Campus, and those who studied agriculture at East Campus, three miles away. The former encountered more critical perspectives, yet were more economically insulated and privileged. "They don't want to be farmers anyway," said Julia, "so they don't really care. They write off those on East Campus as a bunch of tractor-driving hayseeds and Becky-home-eccies."

East Campus students, in contrast, knew the rural crisis: they came from the communities hardest hit. Yet their courses largely ignored this. The school's program in ecologically sustainable agriculture consisted of just one poorly supported full-time professor. Ag economics taught mainly the perspective of Cargill and Dow Chemical. Even students in the FACTS group took most of their courses in the social sciences and liberal arts.

So the seminar was a real victory, if a modest one. Leah mentioned a researcher from the university's business school who had done a recent study on ways ConAgra could make more money by moving out of state. ConAgra then used this research to secure greater state tax breaks. "Their stock goes up 14 percent a year and they get another government handout. Stuff like that makes it lots tougher to make a living in my hometown. Why does the college always support the kind of research and teach the kind of skills most useful in Kansas City or Chicago?"

Julia agreed. "I'm tired of all these English courses that bash small towns like the one I came from, and just teach me to write my novel and become an elitist in New York. I'm getting really sick of that."

The phone rang, and Barb reported to a friend on the local Jesse Jackson campaign. A thousand people had heard Jesse speak at a Lincoln high school a few weeks before, in anticipation of the spring 1988 presidential primary. Barb had sold a pile of buttons and bumper stickers. The next night a local country band would do a benefit at a nearby Lincoln bar. "This amazes me," commented Leah. "A country band? Students for Jackson? At Chesterfields?"

It's dumb to have to play Later, at the Jesse Jackson benefit, Julia
stupid games and I talked again. The bands were energetic. The eighty students in the audience responded in kind. But they were almost all from City Campus. "I expected more people," Julia said, "but it's a better turnout than last time."

"My mom was always outspoken," she explained when I asked about her family. "The other week we were at the general store and farmers were talking about Jesse Jackson. Someone said, 'We can't have a nigger in the White House because he'd be appointing niggers all over the place and then it would be a Black House.' It was a man I'd always respected, and I wanted to respond. Then my mom said, 'Please don't use terms like that. I find them offensive.' I was really proud of her."

The two were always close. Julia's mom and dad raised cows and hogs on a farm that had been in the family for thirty five years. Her mom and dad started their community involvement with their local Catholic church, then took on their first political issue when Nebraska farmers circulated petitions for the ultimately successful Initiative 300, to limit farmland purchases by out-of-state corporations. Quickly throwing herself into the cause, her mom started a League of Rural Voters chapter in a nearby town, reaching out particularly to other farm wives. Their rallies and forums sparked national attention. She attended farm conferences from Kansas City to Washington,

D.C., and ended up heading the statewide organization, drawing a modest part-time salary that helped family finances. By the time Julia left for college in fall of 1986, the League took most of her mom's spare time.

The resulting ferment left Julia wary of farm activism; her mom really was "swallowed up" by the cause. Instead of politics, Julia threw herself into the debate team, in which she'd been involved since age fourteen. Every other weekend she'd put on a sleek suit and three-inch heels, and garner success after success at nationwide tournaments. She made it, as a freshman, to the national quarter-finals. But she balked at continuing. "It lacked real substance. You don't sleep, eat, see your family or friends. You give up everything just to log rhetorical points and win these little trophies that end up in your closet."

In the midst of this disillusionment, Julia's mom called to say, "I hear there's this FACTS group that Barb Meister started." Barb had invited Julia's mom to a Jesse Jackson luncheon. She couldn't attend, but Julia went instead, and became instantly involved.

"I'm a lot happier now," she said, "than when I was in debate. It has more meaning—trying to challenge the ag college perpetuating the idea that all you have to do is put in the right seeds and chemicals and you'll be fine. They don't tell you that it's dumb to have to play stupid games with the government to make a buck. They teach almost no sustainable or organic agriculture, even though they're starting to get consumer pressure. Most of their funding comes from companies like Ortho and Dow. I'd love us to inspire a few students to feel empowered enough so when their teacher says, 'This will happen when you put this chemical on,' they respond, 'Isn't there another way? Couldn't we try crop rotation?' "

"It's kind of strange," she said, looking around. "Most of us in FACTS aren't in the ag college, though we all have farm backgrounds. We're people who don't necessarily want to be farmers, but we don't want to have the chance taken away by economic constraints. We think there should be family farmers—and more of them—whether or not we want to be them."

"For right now," Julia was majoring in philosophy and broadcast journalism, wavering between wanting a career in radio, in rural organizing, or in farming. She had a job lined up for the coming summer, organizing small farmers in eastern Washington State. "I may get a better sense of what I want to do from that," she said. "I know I don't want to stay in academia. I've been feeling a strong tug to go back and farm."

Community organizing, I said, was a hard career.

Julia agreed. "I've seen organizers lose their farms, their families, their wives or husbands. The ones who stick with it are often involved with other activists. There's a woman from the Youth Project who lives with someone from the League of Rural Voters. They're always on the road, and decided not to have children, which is a choice I'm not sure I could make. I've thought of spending ten or fifteen years doing organizing or maybe broadcasting, then settling down to farm. Have three kids and three dogs. Raise cattle and hogs. Be an activist part time. If I don't find a guy I want to marry who's a farmer, then I'll be one myself. I feel I'm paying dues to make sure it will still be around for me."

What can you do?   In the three years since it began, FACTS had accomplished a lot. They had instituted the class, written newspaper articles and editorials, spoken at rallies and public hearings, sponsored forums and debates, and worked with the agriculture honors society. Together with other schools in the region, they'd assembled materials on what students valued most in their rural backgrounds, what political and economic forces made it hard for family farms to survive, and what alternatives might be possible, both in the choices of individual farmers and in state and national policies.

Yet the organization had only eight to ten core members. East Campus students often knew and respected core FACTS members from mutual involvements with 4-H, FFA, the Ag Men fraternity, or from general university activities. "I know their head girl, Barb, from 4-H," said one woman. "I mean, I don't know her personally. I haven't gone to their meetings. But I hear she's really super." Most, however, had already resigned themselves to agriculture's coming corporate future. "Larger farmers are more scientific," they explained. "Sure, ConAgra is greedy, but what can you do?" "Maybe," one said with a laugh, "I'll change things when I get to be president of Cargill."

Even students directly touched by the organization's efforts hesitated to get involved. Leah's roommate helped make posters, but feared further commitment would overwhelm her life. Dale was convinced by his friend and frat-brother Lee to take the seminar, but remained on what seemed the more practical path. Lots of others, while they didn't revile or despise the group—indeed, wished them well and called their aspirations noble—just couldn't see themselves joining in. As Barb said, "It's safer to get involved in the animal science clubs."

FACTS also ran up against its own organizational limits. The group had the feel, Barb said, "of a good committee of friends. We all know each other and where we're coming from. For new members it can be pretty foreign, and this makes it hard to get involved."

Leah agreed. "We need to not talk over people's heads and not name drop. If we mention a person or bill, we need to say what it's about. We need to prepare information packets for new members instead of just dropping them into things they don't understand. We have to start the seminar real basic, to get people thinking. We've been trying all this, I don't know how successfully."

Still, FACTS touched a variety of students outside the committed core. "For some," Barb said, when we met again later, "just taking time to listen and talk has changed them. Not in a broad way, a life-shifting way, but maybe it's created curiosity or increased their understanding just a bit. We don't always realize our impact. During the Farm Aid benefit, the older people said just seeing college students there rejuvenated them."

Involvement had changed Barb's scholastic focus. She had originally planned to major in microbiology, hoping to develop new breed strains. She'd switched to political science with a minor in agricultural economics. For one class, she did a study of the 1985 farm bill. The school did offer a few decent mentors, including one maverick economics professor who, beginning in the early sixties, was part of a team that used the university's adult education extension service to hold a statewide series of workshops discussing prospective tax code changes. Their efforts sparked so much popular involvement and debate that the state passed a graduated income tax, making a tax burden that had rested disproportionately on family farmers far more progressive.

This professor suggested a similar role for students. After their first couple years at school, they could return to their communities and listen to the perspectives of family farmers and small-business people. They could observe as local citizens argued out their needs on critical issues like taxes, schools, government, transportation, and economic policy—"the gut questions over which people fight." Only then, he said, did it make sense for the students to tap the university's intellectual resources and learn to better help their communities make critical choices.

Barb felt inspired by such visions, which gave her a sense of possibility. It frustrated her, though, how often she gave her schoolwork short shrift. The night before, she'd studied till 3:00 A.M., following her minimum-wage shift as night and weekend manager at the Student Union. She studied when she could at the Union job, and used it to organize as well, "popping in for a few minutes to meetings of the nuclear group or Young Democrats, having them fill me in on what's going on." But she still felt pressed and overextended.

"My past three months," she explained, "have been constant public involvement." She served on the vice chancellor's multicultural committee. She worked on agricultural policy with Robert Kerry's successful senatorial campaign. She served on the University Program Council and on the board of the national campus activities consor tium. Her life seemed an endless round of writing statements, giving speeches, doing research, and logging in her weekly hours at her job.

On one level, the FACTS students were highly traditional. They fought for a way of life that had existed since before their great-grandparents first worked the land. Their involvement also produced a more general questioning. "I'm more politically aware now," said Barb. "I read the papers, watch the news, and look for opportunities to learn. I've connected with whole groups of people I wouldn't have expected to know. Social activists. People from different races and creeds. Gays and lesbians. People concerned with injustice in general, not just injustice in the farming community and in agriculture."

Would these students farm? Or would they make politics their careers? Leah had wanted to work the land since she was a child. "I was always out there, helping my dad in the fields." She spent her freshman year mostly going to parties and hanging out with other people from her small Western Nebraska home town. Then one of her high school friends got involved in FACTS, through knowing Lee Wagner in Ag Men, and invited Leah along to the meetings.

At first, the group's style felt alien. "It was hard to get into, because they knew so much and it was all over my head. I couldn't keep up at all." Even at the ag seminar, Leah felt bored. "Mark Ritchie was speaking—a policy analyst for the Minnesota ag commissioner, and I remember thinking, 'I don't understand this. It's a nice day. I want to be outside.' Now I'm fascinated, Ritchie is one of my heroes, and I could listen forever."

"I want to farm," she repeated. "When I went home last summer to work with my dad, I kept thinking about how important this was to me. It was the kind of life I wanted. But I also get lots of pressure not to. People don't want their small towns to die, but they have this attitude that the only ones who should stay around are the ones who can't do anything else. I have relatives who if I return will say, 'I thought she was smart. She's just throwing herself away.'"

Her father, she said, was supportive, "but won't rock the boat with his friends. He also says I couldn't work a farm as a woman alone. But I could if I had a good hired hand, or a husband, or even with him."

"I never really thought about these issues before," she said. "I worried about weather and bugs, but not these other questions. That's part of the problem with getting farmers organized. They're concerned with getting their crops in the ground and taking care of livestock. They don't have time to sit in meetings."

Yet farming also brought Leah back to what she was fighting for. Her friend who'd gotten her involved had returned to work his family's land, while continuing to work on agriculture issues with the League of Rural Voters on the side. "He's always saying, 'Wait till we get everybody home and then watch out,' but I don't know. I can see myself starting a League chapter in my town. Or trying to make people more aware, encouraging my neighbors and their kids to see things a little differently. I'd like to work my family's land, because of its history. I've wanted that all my life."

A whole generation   Several years into these issues, Barb appeared to be the ultimate political advocate: poised, confident, committed, ready to take on any challenge. A beacon for those who worked for family farms.

In contrast, she viewed herself as still shy and uncertain. She acted, she believed, only because someone had to, and maybe because she liked the challenge. She tried to stand up for her parents, her community, and the hope that she could someday go back and farm—even as this hope grew more distant the more she moved into the political world. "When I was just getting involved," she said, "it hurt a lot when people would label us radicals. I'm still very self-conscious. I still lack confidence in myself. Then I hear people say I should run for office, someday run for the Senate, and it scares me. I wonder why they're saying this. I wonder what I'm cut out for and where the limits of my abilities are. I know that the limits are there."

What impelled Barb's activism, beyond her parents' crisis? "The value of hard work," she believed. "Having responsibility on the farm from an early age. Valuing stewardship and care of livestock. Just being in a large family. Learning to care for each other and respect everyone's rights and needs and wants. Learning how to sacrifice for other people, to do someone's chores when they go to a meeting. A lot of mutual support."

Barb's Catholic beliefs also played a strong part, even through she grew up in a highly conservative archdiocese, where her parish priest studiously avoided the farmers' plight, and the campus Newman Center refused to allow any women on the altar, to help serve or do the readings. "My parents grew up in strong religious traditions, with nuns and priests on both sides of the family. They've become more and more critical because the church has been incredibly slow to respond to the crisis, and minister to those who've gone through it. A very good friend is a Disciples of Christ minister, and he's made this situation his calling. Our parish priest has not. Two summers ago, the farmers had a petition to keep Initiative 300, which protects family farms. They asked if they could circulate it after Sunday morning mass, and he said no. It was too controversial. He said it was too political."

For Barb, faith had less to do with going to mass, "where my mind might be somewhere else, than with my beliefs and my actions. My work is more like a vocation than strictly a career, and I believe in social and economic justice as a Christian value, although it's one of many other religions as well. It's a faith issue in wanting to serve other people." Much as Barb disliked some of the hierarchy and rituals, Catholicism remained "a foundation of my life. I'm trying to separate my own values," she said, "from what I've just learned, accepted, and adopted. A lot of what I feel hasn't really been tested. Mostly, I'm just trying to live out what I believe in."

These were strong ethics. Yet many apolitical students grew up in the same ethical traditions and faced the same crises. How did she overcome a culture that took niceness so far "that people become afraid to be blatant or controversial"? Did she see possibilities other students missed? Feel a hope that they lacked? Stumble into a community that left her less isolated and alone?

"I don't know," she said. "Maybe seeing my neighbors affected—that what happened to my family wasn't an isolated incident. That we as rural people had to give each other support."

She learned a lot as well from her mother's earthy practicality, from her ability to hold together the affectionate floating circus of their household, make it a haven in the most difficult times. Barb learned from her father as well—from his blunt humor and directness and willingness to speak out. From his refusal to paint a blissful landscape in a community of ruin.

Barb followed her parents' lead and that of her faculty mentors. She learned from community workers like those in the Family Farm Coalition, where she'd interned the previous summer. She coordinated with national student groups like United States Student Association (USSA), and met other committed peers through the boards of the Youth Action foundation, based in Washington, D.C., and a new network of young activist women. A program called Leadership America paid for her to study renewable agriculture for three weeks in Holland, where she felt inspired by a student farm organization that had been going since 1968. "They work with a science shop, where students do research for their classes while helping farmers with their needs. The women formed their own national network. Farmers from different areas talk to each other."

Perhaps Barb created her own inspiration, with ample help from others. I met many students with comparable personal crises who never found the necessary context to discover their voices. Or they briefly flirted with social involvement, then returned to private affairs. Barb was launched into commitment by her situation, by her intrinsic character, and by the actions of others, from her friend Jerry who invited her to come to the Iowa rally in the first place, to her enthusiastic co-workers in FACTS. Initially distant from politics, she found key allies at the point when she was ready to act.

"We need to show young people," she said, "that they can make a living in an ethical way—that there's more than just ConAgra. We have the hardest time convincing farm groups that they need to offer challenging internships. Don't just pat us on the back and say what good kids we are. Don't just have us make posters for rallies. Invite us to speak or do workshops. Give us responsibility. Maybe it's the stereotype that young people don't care, are uninterested. But they need us involved or they'll lose a whole generation."

Thirteen

Greeks for peace   Social concern on fraternity row

At the University of Michigan, global issues reached the white colonnaded halls of a chapter of the oldest sorority in America, Kappa Alpha Theta. The Theta house living room was furnished with a grand piano, marble and hardwood tables, and polished brass lamps. Blue floral drapes matched blue floral couches, blue floral chairs, beige floral wallpaper, and the wool skirt of a housemother so primly respectable that she could have been a Daughter of the American Revolution.

On this particular night, a medical student named René was speaking from the National University of El Salvador. In translated Spanish, he described how the U.S.-trained military invaded his university in 1980, killed the rector and fifty students, and held him and hundreds of others face down on the ground, with guns at their backs. For four years the military occupied the campus, while students continued their classes in exile, using store fronts and people's homes, and held periodic vigils outside the campus gates. The medical student mentioned numerous friends now murdered or missing. An accompanying video showed the bloody events and provided historical background. The med student elaborated further, then asked those gathered to challenge their government's policies: a million dollars a day in aid to support a government that had perpetuated these horrors.

These were brutal matters, difficult to confront. The forty-five fraternity and sorority members listened attentively. One man asked why the United States would support such a situation and whose interests we might be protecting. They left saying they'd never known the situation existed.

The talk took place in November of 1987, two years before the Salvadoran military murdered six Jesuits at the country's other major school, the University of Central America. Speakers like René, the med student, came often to the University of Michigan. Even during the low point of concern, this campus maintained a flame of involvement. The Michigan *Daily* routinely debated political questions. A modest but energetic core of students challenged apartheid investment, weapons research, CIA recruiting, and the administration's inadequate response to campus racial incidents. Groups petitioned almost daily on the steps of the Student Union. Posters abounded for presentations on South Africa, Amnesty International, and economic cooperatives. The Student Assembly had recently declared the National University of El Salvador—the med student's campus—a sister university.

But Michigan also had the usual majority who focused on purely personal concerns, and Greek Row was particularly conservative. The group that sponsored the talk, Greeks for Peace (GFP), was founded nine months earlier by Matt Greene, a senior, and a junior named Jean Besanceney. The two met at a statewide Democratic convention, then again through the congressional campaign of an economics grad student who won over 40 percent of the vote against an entrenched Republican incumbent. Noticing numerous fraternity and sorority addresses on campaign volunteer lists, Jean and Matt suspected other Greeks shared their concerns. They formed the organization to find out.

Growing up in Royal Oak, Michigan, a suburb of Detroit, Matt had little interest in global affairs. His father worked his way up from union machinist to foreman at a machine tool plant, logging in fifty-hour weeks of skilled work. His mother worked as a dental hygienist. In high school Matt thought little about politics, and his classes rarely discussed current issues. When he occasionally saw people on TV marching for causes, he paid them little heed. Instead, he played in the school band, acted in student plays, and worked a succession of jobs from paper routes to Taco Bell. He also tutored in a YMCA volunteer literacy program, but viewed the hardships of the kids he worked with "only in personal terms."

At Michigan Matt majored first in psychology, wanting to help people with emotional difficulties. His psychology classes focused on purely individual situations, his science courses on basic theory. Wondering, after a while, what the links were between the problems of his prospective clients and their social and economic surroundings, he switched to the social sciences, thinking he'd teach high school history and economics. It wasn't until sophomore year that he even learned the meaning of the word *apartheid*. For all the school's marches, rallies, and speakers, Matt gazed at students sleeping in protest shanties on the quad "with just about total incomprehension."

Matt joined the Greek system after getting to know several people who were reviving a long-dormant chapter of Phi Kappa Tau. Four friends from his dorm signed up. He decided to go along as well. The house offered a sense of community amidst a 35,000-student megaversity, and the decision seemed almost automatic.

Then he took a sociology class that featured a unit on Central America. It appalled him that the United States had supported governments of wealthy torturers. A woman in the course mentioned a student group called the Latin American Solidarity Committee. Matt went to their next meeting. He felt uncertain, uncomfortable, and overwhelmed by the veteran participants' knowledge.

But he kept on attending. "I felt this was wrong and we needed to do something about it." An architecture class on urban problems and ethical values also shook him up. He began to listen to the news more often and more critically, and to speak out in his courses and with friends. "Even in the science classes, I started thinking about preventive medicine, and all the stupid things that help produce cancer."

He felt awkward politically. To stay involved, he needed a base of support. He could move to the Residential College, to the East Quad area where occupants were called "the Quadies," wore Grateful Dead t-shirts, and lived surrounded by peace signs. He could join activist friends in an off-campus apartment. He could move just about anywhere and find an environment more politically sympathetic than Greek Row.

But Matt didn't like counterculture styles. He liked his Phi Tau friends. He decided to stay and work in the frat system where he lived.

"So much politics," he explained, "is geared for those already in. It was hard being Greek in the activist community—being hurt by the stereotypes. Just because of the pressures, a lot of us involved thought about quitting our Greek houses. We talked about whether they were inherently sexist, classist, and elitist, or whether that was just a few obnoxious members and a few obnoxious frats. We wanted something more basic, for people who were interested but didn't feel they fit the activist stereotype, or didn't know how to act. We wanted a vehicle for people interested in issues to be with their friends and get involved together."

Matt and Jean began their organization by canvassing people they knew. They held a few small meetings, then set things up more formally, with officers, a charter, and classified ads in the *Daily*'s "Greek Gab" section. When the Regents voted on a long-proposed clause restricting military research, their group joined a student vigil. "The Greek system advocates life-improving research," Jean wrote in a letter to the *Daily*, "through the donation of thousands of dollars each year to institutions such as the American Cancer Society. As members, we believe that researching better ways to kill with our tuition dollars is not in accordance with Greek values of community service."

All right, Sandinista I met Matt, Jean, and the others nine months after the organization's founding, just after the visit of the Salvadoran med student, René. Step by step, they'd reached out, until their mailing list included a hundred students in sixteen fraternities and seventeen sororities, including two house presidents. Inside Matt's large rambling frat house, the guys were eating fish-stick sandwiches and ice cream. An old white refrigerator sported a beer tap and a sticker for Amnesty International. Battered armchairs and couches were clustered around a large TV in the living room. The house felt worn but comfortable.

"All right, Sandinista," said a blond guy, teasing Matt in passing, "You missed happy hour. That's it." Matt was now a sixth-year senior, having taken time off to work. Lean of build, wearing a neat wool sweater, a small stud earring, and his dark hair well trimmed, he moved easily among the school's diverse cultural niches. Fellow house members treated his politics as an eccentric pursuit, but some responded with discussion and thought.

I asked the blond student about the organization, and he said peace of course would be great. He didn't go to marches or rallies, however, and didn't think they helped. It angered him when people pointed fingers at the Greeks, like the previous spring, when a sorority woman charged a fraternity man with criminal rape. He wasn't going to take sides on that case, but he didn't like it when people threw around words like "rape culture" or suggested that frat members needed a course on sexual harassment. "I already have enough mandatory classes as it is. People who want to abuse women won't get anything out of it anyway."

"At least," he said, "Greeks for Peace breaks the stereotype" of Greeks in slick suits spending Daddy's millions. I'm definitely not spending mine." He laughed. "Because he works as a horticulturalist and doesn't have any." Another student mentioned being involved a bit last spring, and said he would again when he could.

"I don't push hard in my own house," Matt said. "Sometimes we discuss things. Sometimes we don't. People know it's there if they want it."

"We hear people discussing the issues more," said the current chapter vice president. "They didn't before. If I didn't have all the house meetings, I'd do more with the group myself."

He admired Matt's efforts, though he couldn't always join them. But a few members were harsher in their judgments. "Yes, we're back for another year to educate and activate the Greek community," GFP had announced in a posted flier for the El Salvador talk. Someone had crossed out *educate* and replaced it with *politicize.*

"I definitely disagree," said an engineer named Dick, who'd written the hostile comments on the flier. "What happens if I like things the way they are. This says, 'Either have our view or you're apathetic.' "

I asked Dick if he'd ever attended any rallies, and he admitted he had not. "Maybe, in a personal sense," he said, "I am apathetic. But I wouldn't trust that Salvadoran student. I have enough problems of my own. I think the world would be lots better off if people attended to their own work."

Each time they reached out, the group brought in a few more students who might never otherwise have been involved. Each time they also hit resistance. For most they approached, they brought global issues just a bit closer, as with Stork, the engineering student whom Matt enlisted to fix my computer disk drive. Greeks for Peace, said Stork, had made him more aware. "When I read about some march in the *Daily* I can identify because Matt Greene is part." But his science and engineering classes focused only "on which equations make sense, whereas a Central American course, no way can you put it in an equation." He liked the "look on people's faces when they come to me at the computer lab and I help them figure something out." He wanted to design systems "that help people," even if this earned less than other choices. He felt America put far too many resources into weapons, and not enough into education and our basic economy. But if engineers tried to voice social concern, he said, it would just get quenched by management. "Or we'd say 'I need this job, so I'll do it and forget the consequences.' It's very easy to numb yourself. We engineers deal mostly just with the technical problems at hand."

It just made me mad   Jean Besanceney, the group's cofounder, grew up in a large Catholic family just outside of Pittsburgh. Her father worked as an executive with the Pittsburgh Convention and Visitors Bureau and her mother was a homemaker. Though it took fifteen years for her parents to get divorced, they'd slept in separate bedrooms since she was three; Jean was torn by the tensions between them and responded by worrying, trying to fix the situation, and becoming anorexic. Externally, she grew up sheltered, attending a wealthy suburban public school. Her family never discussed public controversies. Like Nebraska's Barb Meister, she avoided reading the newspaper, which overwhelmed her, and regarded politics mostly as boring civics lessons.

She entered the University of Michigan in 1984. She'd always been good at math and science, and since engineering seemed practical, Jean made it her major and studied diligently. And she voted for Ronald Reagan her first time out. This last was no weighty decision. America seemed in decent shape. Jean believed Reagan made other nations respect us. She heard little talk of the downside. It felt easy to follow the political lead of her brother, a highly conservative Secret Service agent and ex-football player in Miami.

Yet she was also growing restless. Bored in her chemistry class, she found it difficult to keep doing the reading. She briefly tried majoring in business and joined a fundamentalist Bible study group that met in her freshman dorm. But Jean wanted answers "about my own problems and those of the world." When the group suggested only that she embrace Christ as her personal savior, she quietly drifted away.

Jean rushed her sorority in fall 1985, the beginning of her sophomore year. "It just seemed the thing to do." Matt's fraternity was low-key, low status, and inhabited the margins of Michigan Greek life. Theta, in contrast, was known for accepting only the prettiest women, and rested at the top of Greek Row's tacit pecking order. Jean easily fit in, with her blue eyes, small neat features, and blonde pony-tail held back with a mock-pearl barrette. She felt honored to be offered a bid. "Maybe part of me just wanted to be in an elite group." Yet like Matt, Jean also joined for community—to make the school smaller, with the notion that we'd all be sisters, all supporting each other."

At first, the sorority fed Jean's fixation on weight and appearance. As part of a near epidemic of anorexia and bulimia among young middle-class women, 90 percent of Theta's members either binged, purged, and vomited or consistently starved themselves, picking away at their salads, counting every calorie, continually apologizing, "I shouldn't be eating this." By now severely anorexic, Jean started each day with two pieces of dry toast, went for a run or did aerobics to burn that off, ate only vegetables for lunch, then nothing else except diet pills."[1]

Jean finally broke the eating disorder cycle after her brother, the Secret Service agent, asked what was wrong with her that she'd gotten so skinny—and after she took some initial political classes. Angry at first "about Reagan's lies on contra aid," she started asking why almost all the women she knew were needlessly racking their bodies, trying to emulate emaciated models. Until then obsession with food "filled up all the available space in my attention."

Emerging from her personal and political shell, Jean switched from engineering and business classes that bored her to philosophy and theater courses she'd earlier enjoyed. Debates over contra aid in the *Daily* made her want to understand that issue. After she read Marx for the first time in a political philosophy class, she questioned "the impression I'd grown up with that all his ideas were simply evil, so we didn't even have to read or understand them." She found herself asking more questions after a history class on the nuclear arms race, a women's studies course that placed her own anorexia and that of the Theta house women in a larger social context, and a sociology class that dealt with toxic waste dumping, predatory agribusiness, and just about every political issue she could imagine. "They all seemed to deal with the basic problem that people were unempowered—that a very few people routinely make decisions that affect everyone, and most of us have little say. I began making connections between them."

The next half year seemed like a whirlwind. Besides her classes, Jean involved herself in the campus group concerned with Central America, marched in demonstrations, and worked with an Ann Arbor nuclear disarmament organization. "I was learning constantly about our attacks on Nicaragua and wanted to do something with that knowledge."

Her newfound concern led her to attend a spring 1986 campus demonstration against contra aid. A couple hundred students attended. Speakers recently back from Nicaragua described the human toll of the attacks. The group then marched off campus to the office of the strongly pro-contra Congressman whose opponent Jean and Matt would volunteer for the next fall. When they arrived, he was out, and a group of students decided to remain in his office until they were either arrested or he met with them and talked. Jean hadn't intended to get arrested, had in fact worried about that possibility, but she decided to stay and join in. "It just made me mad," she said. "Here our government was doing all this to innocent people and he didn't care. Even after his office was flooded with letters and calls, he never even set up a public forum to discuss the issue."

A law student outlined potential legal consequences. The group sang "We Shall Overcome" as the police came to take them away. The officer who arrested Jean noticed her sorority sweatshirt and remarked sarcastically, "Kappa Alpha Theta, huh?" He seemed annoyed that she didn't fit the ragged hippie stereotype.

Jean felt moved by the sense of shared commitment and angered at her government's actions. The arrest gave her courage to take further steps. But she also felt estranged. "I could tell these people all knew each other, but I didn't know any of them, except Matt just slightly. It was definitely a hippie atmosphere. Birkenstocks and granola. Maybe I'd been with more mainstream types."

The core activists were unsure, in turn, of quite how to regard Jean's presence. "It's really amazing," said one, "to see someone from a sorority here." Jean felt like a novelty—the talking dog. She felt that more needed to be done than just further marches and protests. When the teaching assistant from one of her classes said she didn't have to quit the Greek system to stay involved, she began thinking about peace activists she knew who worked through institutions like churches. She wondered whether she could do the same in her milieu. Forming the organization let her show activists "that they don't have to stereotype Greeks or people who look like Greeks, and show Greeks there are other things to be concerned about than going to the bars."

Women came to sororities, Jean said, in part to be sheltered. Particularly at a campus with Michigan's activist tradition, parents liked their daughters safely protected. They passed on an image of young ladies, watched over by housemothers and courted by soon-to-be-successful young men who waited downstairs for formal dates. Sorority women worried about their place in a status hierarchy where just about everyone in the Greek system could rank the various houses, complete with derogatory names for those currently on the bottom at their particular school—like the Emory women who called Chi Omega "Cow Omega." But their system also offered community, places to retreat from their universities' vast anonymity and to share confidences with their peers.

If sorority life nurtured polite reticence, Jean believed fraternity culture bred the reverse. A good number of men, like Matt, also joined for a haven of friendship, particularly in large state schools. But the aura of drunken debauchery fed a macho bluster. At nearly every campus, fraternity men were far more resistant to dissenting political and cultural viewpoints than their sorority counterparts. Jean commented that fraternity men particularly sought pathways to power through the network of future connections. "'If you meet a head of a corporation,' they say, 'and he's in your fraternity, he'll get you a job.' I wanted those kinds of contacts myself when I first joined Kappa Alpha Theta, because we do it too, though more subtly. At some point, you need to be practical. For me, I hope I'll find work through people I know in the movement."

The more students like Jean and Matt involved themselves, the more they began to see their lives as somehow intertwined with those of people in El Salvador, South Africa, and the poor and desperate neighborhoods of nearby Detroit. Their apolitical peers viewed these worlds as vastly distant—remote from their lives and beyond their power to affect. Like the FACTS members who worked, as Barb said, to keep reaching out to those still politically insulated, those in Greeks for Peace continually balanced newfound political urgencies with the constant need to enlist students who did not yet share them.

The two groups faced different contexts and hurdles. FACTS began their efforts on a campus almost wholly quiescent and built a modest alternative presence through issues immediate to the community they addressed. They butted up against denial of the agricultural crisis's structural roots, the stoicism of those who hoped the problems would pass with time, and resignation about the prospects of changing things. But they took on issues familiar to the students they worked with.

Greeks for Peace, in contrast, worked on a campus with strong activist traditions, but in cultural niches those currents rarely touched. Building on shared experiences and shared identity with their fellow Greeks, they also took up issues that most in the Greek system found unfamiliar, such as the United States' relation to Central America and South Africa. They worked to get these issues taken seriously by individuals used to keeping their distance.

By spring 1988 the year-old organization's regular meetings were attended by fifteen to twenty students. A local bar held a happy hour benefit, advertised with a drawing of champagne glasses clinking and the words "Here's to Peace." Greeks for Peace added their specific voice and outreach network to general campus issues: the push for restrictions on military research, marches against campus racism, and a rally against nuclear testing. A gay member helped pressure the Greek Week steering committee to give part of the $30,000 they raised to AIDS educational efforts. Their representatives worked with campuswide political coalitions, including a student rights party that won control of the Student Assembly. Members spoke at campus rallies, including an Earth Festival.

They also carried out their own projects. GFP responded to the previous spring's rape controversy by bringing in speakers on sexual assault and by holding a forum entitled "Everything You Always Wanted to Know About Sex(ism)." They worked with UCAR, a campus coalition against racism, to set up workshops on Greek Row. Jean wrote an article for Michigan's internal Greek paper, explaining, "critics say that Greeks are selfish and narrow-minded. Greeks for Peace gives us the opportunity to prove them wrong." She talked of trying to convince Theta's national organization to consider a group like SANE or Amnesty International for their next philanthropy. "I want to raise the whole issue of our donating money to charity while we spend so much on arms. Or if we could get the organization going in different houses, we could compete to see which would have the guts to choose something risky. People say you can't be politically active in the Greeks, but no one's really tried."

Like other activists, those in Greeks for Peace discovered both new community and the risk of isolation from more apolitical students. They addressed this by trying to build on their already existing friendships—and on institutions with which they had strong ties. Sometimes they felt they had to make compromises. "I have to still do certain things," said Jean. "Attend fraternity parties even when I don't particularly want to. Take care of how I look, so people will listen to my politics and won't think I've turned into a hippie. I have to remember how I was at first."

Some "ultra-activists" still considered the group "too middle of the road." But most of the initially skeptical now acknowledged their work, and encouraged them to continue. Greeks who casually dismissed other campus activists—as Matt once dismissed the protest shanties—could less easily write them off.

We're watching As with other formerly apolitical students
the Cosby show turned activists, the Greeks for Peace now
served as designated idealists for their friends. "They say they wish they had time to do what I'm doing," said Jean in frustration. "They say I'm so knowledgeable and they don't know enough to act. But at a certain point I think you have to trust your sense of when one side has an interest in lying. You don't need a lot of information to know that killing people is wrong and should be stopped."

Yet the organization touched numerous students on the sidelines. One woman said she'd begun to read more about issues in the *Daily*, had signed a petition on abortion, and thought people should do more than "just sit back and watch MTV." Women in Jean's Theta house rebelled when two of their members spent $200 to send a stripper as a goodwill gesture to a nearby fraternity, and then sought reimbursement. There were several sympathetic Greeks for Peace members in Matt's house.

Others resisted their message and accused them of demanding that everyone else adopt *their* passions. The week before the Salvadoran medical student's talk, Jean, as Theta house "service chair," had booked a speaker to follow the weekly house meeting—a student named Thea from Michigan's Latin America Solidarity Committee. During the week before the meeting, the Theta house president took great pains to stress that attendance at Thea's talk was optional. On the night Thea came, she ran the chapter meeting overtime, effectively preventing house members from attending.

Jean was furious and responded with a letter. "I cannot think of a good reason," she wrote, "that our chapter meeting went on leisurely for *twenty-five* minutes past the time that Thea arrived and *was scheduled* to speak. It seemed like blatant disrespect. . . . The issue of Central America is important. It is timely; and it ought to fall under 'the widest influence' in which we say that we seek 'to promote good.' As college-educated sorority women, we should know what our taxes pay for in Central America and elsewhere."

It was an angry letter, and the president barely acknowledged it. When René came for his talk the following week things got worse. He needed the television to show a video of troops occupying his university and shooting fleeing students. Although the house president had received ample prior notice, she refused to relinquish her spot in front of the TV, where she'd been sitting with a friend. When Jean approached her, she explained coldly, "We're watching the Cosby show," then turned without blinking back to the TV.

"How can you do this?" asked Jean. "He's up here. He's a political refugee. All these people are waiting." The two argued heatedly while guests milled awkwardly in the living room. "OK," the president finally conceded. "But you have to be out by nine, because that's when *Cheers* comes on, and we want to watch it."

Jean felt outraged, politically and personally. Although the program went well, they lost a third of their audience when they had to switch to the front room when the video ended. "Here was this really important event," she said later, "and all their talk of sisterhood meant nothing. I'd mentioned it repeatedly beforehand, but they couldn't care less what I was doing. They weren't even interested in checking it out. Like they were above it or something."

Such resistance left Jean feeling frustrated. But she sustained her spirits through the community she found. After René finished his speech, Jean asked René if he'd like some coffee. He'd love some, he said. Jean served it, thinking earnest thoughts about how coffee symbolized both the hospitality she wanted to offer and the tortured bonds between René's country and hers. But René seemed to be worrying little about such grand political concerns and instead began talking in loud animated Spanish with Alejandro, a Salvadoran refugee given sanctuary at a local Ann Arbor church. During his talk, René had been intent, serious, and restrained. Now his face lit up. His arms gestured wildly. His laugh boomed out across the room. Jean asked his translator what he and Alejandro were discussing, and she said old war stories. René was now miming himself running and ducking, and laughing about how he'd hidden from the soldiers and survived. Alejandro countered with his own baroque tales from his precarious journey of flight. Jean thought of her sorority sisters dutifully reading their textbooks, or worrying about their appearance, a few doors away, infinitely distant.

"This was so different," she told me, "from how René spoke to our group. Everything was wilder, more emotional. It was still tragic, but funny as well. I felt privileged just to be there."

Most students approached by Greeks for Peace still hung on the fence. They were interested but skeptical, concerned but afraid. They edged toward involvement, then continued to hang back. Given the right invitation and context they might at some point find the strength for involvement. If unasked, or approached only by the stereotyped activists they mistrusted, they'd be less likely to wonder whether these issues might be worth taking a stand on.

Greeks for Peace offered a way for fraternity men and sorority women to deal with the difficult questions of their time. A few students responded immediately and found an instant community. Others watched from a distance, wary and reluctant. But the speakers and protest marches no longer sounded wholly alien. Greeks for Peace had closed, just slightly, the divisions between students who took strong public stands and those who did not.

Fourteen ～～～～～～～～～～～

Crossing the line
The genesis of student activists

～～～～～～～～～～～～～～～～～～～～～～～～

How, given the omnipresent barriers, do students like those in FACTS and Greeks for Peace get involved? New information—statistics of gross economic inequality, numbers of dead in covert wars, specifics of environmental degradation—often prompts them to act. But what really awakens what psychologist Robert Jay Lifton calls their "moral Imagination" are stories of specific people with whom they have come to feel linked.

The call of stories   These stories come from varied sources. Greeks for Peace responded to the Salvadoran students and peasants whose lives were described by René, the medical student. FACTS members were moved to action by stories of friends, relatives, and neighbors who saw the work of generations destroyed by the collapse of the family farm economy. Campus divestment activists watched television news coverage of South African police beating and shooting residents of Soweto. Such experiences and stories particularly challenge the Perfect Standard, with its impossible demands for absolute knowledge, certainty, and command. They bring to bear a different basis for judgment—a refusal to accept the shattering of human lives.

Students often get involved when they're directly affected. Student strikers at the City University of New York marched and sat in because devastating tuition hikes threatened their education. African-American students at many colleges have recounted how campus police repeatedly stop and questioned them, how monitors double-check their IDs at the gym, how dormmates treat them like barbarians for playing their music, and how they have found the narratives of their communities wholly absent from the curriculum. A white Emory woman who had grown up in a highly integrated high school said that "when racial issues come up here, I feel connected personally. They aren't just about invisible people who say they're being discriminated against. They're about the situation of my friends."

"You need something on a personal level," reflected an AIDS activist at the University of South Alabama in Mobile. "For me it wasn't just that my friend died of AIDS, but how he died, and the reaction—the apathy and ignorance and lack of concern from his family and friends and his employer. I suddenly realize that how he died is not an isolated issue, that it's happening over and over around the country, and it won't stop unless people take a stand."

For students who grow up insulated and protected, the stories that stir their souls often come through involvement with foreign worlds. Students who volunteer in programs addressing homelessness and illiteracy come to know the children they work with. A woman who participated in an intercollegiate group that spent several months living with Central American families said sharing their lives enabled her "to back up what I believe and get past all the vague abstractions about international dependence and colonial legacies."

Students also learn about these new worlds from those who have been there. The Greeks for Peace weren't themselves threatened by Salvadoran death squads. Until they met René, the medical student, they were unacquainted with anyone who was targeted. But they felt the situation's urgency through stories told by others, who placed a human face on otherwise remote, unrecognizable pain.

Whatever its source, this sense of connection breaks through student beliefs that they are exempt from the pain of the world. They act, as a result, not only because issues affect them personally, but from a larger sense of human solidarity. They feel it is wrong to do nothing while people are hurt or hungry. Students like Julia and Leah of FACTS spoke out on farm issues even though their own households had survived because they knew of too many others that had not. The student at South Alabama felt angered by the treatment of his friend who'd died of AIDS. Even on an issue like abortion, whose restriction directly threatens all sexually active college women, students divided largely between those who remained passive on the issue, stressing that they could always find a way to terminate their own pregnancies if necessary, and those who got involved based on their empathy for others. "What if she can't afford it?" asked students who spoke out, and recounted the situations of friends who'd gotten pregnant when birth control failed. "What if the child isn't wanted?" "What if she'd have to drop out of school?"[1]

These expressions of a sense of connection echoed responses of students who had taken on other larger issues, from apartheid to global hunger. They articulated a common process by which students began to restore what psychologist Lifton once called a "broken connection" between individual actions and a greater common good. They did so through narratives that linked present, past, and future, and geographically disparate lives, and by doing so, they challenged the enclave individualism character-ized by the belief that "you make your own chances." These narratives also described people learning how to act, which helped students overcome fatalism and disdain.

The most successful student groups know this. They consciously work to use stories of specific situations to illuminate broader principles. The FACTS members didn't just toss out a laundry list of rhetorical ills. They focused first on the process that bankrupted their communities, then larger questions of economic justice, environmen-tal sustainability, and the strengths of the small-town culture they struggled to save. When the United States Student Association and the Midwest Academy conduct cam-pus grass roots organizing workshops, they use role-playing and discussion to teach concerned students how to analyze local power relationships, design successful activist campaigns, and understand the potential power of their actions. They have participants make their own history a central focus, for if they understand why they themselves have come to act, they might more effectively enlist others. From the time of myths and bibli-cal parables, lessons drawn from stories have guided individual attempts to live ethi-cally in the world.[2]

Yet stories can be misleading—or outright lies. "You make your own chances" evokes to America's hallowed narratives of Horatio Alger success, yet we rarely exam-ine the flaws in these narratives. President Reagan stirred strong emotions by telling the American public about his valiant role in World War II and by recalling a bomber pilot who, when his plane was shot down, refused to parachute to safety and instead rode along to his death so he could comfort a young wounded tail gunner. The problem with this story is that it only happened in a movie, and Reagan himself never got closer to the front than the Hollywood lots. More dangerously, the Reagan-Bush administrations habitually justified their Central American interventions with stories of Sandinista or Sal-vadoran guerrilla atrocities that were largely the creation of U.S. government psycho-logical warfare specialists. These same official U.S. spokespersons consistently denied true stories—of how, for example, the U.S.-trained Atlacatl battalion massacred more than two hundred villagers in the Salvadoran town of El Mozote in December 1981.

Official denials had such an impact that after reporter Raymond Bonner helped break the El Mozote story and insisted it was true, the *New York Times* transferred him from his Central American beat and Bonner ended up leaving the newspaper. When the *Times* finally confirmed the massacre eleven years later, they never mentioned their own role in helping to hide it.[3]

How do concerned students separate true stories from false ones? To some extent, this depends on whom they come to trust and what other perspectives they encounter. Barb and Julia of FACTS increasingly questioned the promises and prescriptions of Dow, Cargill, and ConAgra. They did this in part by learning to place greater faith in the judgments of their families and others who suggested that farmers' individual misfortunes had larger social roots. Similarly, Matt and Jean of Greeks for Peace saw their belief in a generous and peaceful America ripped apart by revelations of our government's support for dictators and torturers. They no longer trusted Reagan and Bush. They doubted the word of the CIA. They began to place more trust in those who had long questioned national choices. Students who acted on a variety of issues experienced similar profound shifts in faith and allegiance.

These students still question their own actions, assumptions, and sources of information. They work to sort through propaganda, of whatever political stripe, to divide half truths and false conclusions from complex realities. As they become more involved, they view themselves as linked historically with individuals from previous times who worked for civil rights, fought for women's suffrage, organized unions or the poor. They also feel connected with contemporary peasants threatened with massacre and torture, impoverished children denied decent lives, and their own college peers increasingly excluded by rising costs and falling economic support. These links, they believe, give them no choice but to act.

As those wary of being "swallowed up" suggest, heeding such stories can dramatically change people's lives. The assumptions, priorities, friendships, and cultural resources of new activists tend to shift dramatically with their involvement. At the same time, they try to anchor themselves by weaving compelling new stories into an existing framework of ethics they've long embraced—fairness, justice, standing up for your beliefs. They shift, not so much in their assumptions about right and wrong, as in who they hold accountable, which wounds they heed, and what responsibilities they feel.

Models of commitment   Students need to believe that their actions can matter. For them to learn this confidence requires strong role models, examples to carry them through commitment's inevitably difficult passages. For the apolitical students I've described, parents, teachers, and other cultural mentors consistently discourage their concern. Those who act, in contrast, are either encouraged by specific individuals or find role models in the general culture.

The FACTS students drew support from parental examples, a handful of teachers who quickly became their mentors, and older community organizers. They built on friendships, as when Barb went to the Iowa rally after being invited by her friend Jerry. Greeks for Peace had fewer family models of engagement: activists rarely steer their children toward fraternity row. But they learned from engaged professors like the sociology and urban planning teachers who sparked Matt's political interest, or the political philosophy teacher whose class influenced Jean. And they learned from the general climate of a campus where demonstrations, petitions, and newspaper debates were familiar experiences.

Students' primary models remain their families. A slowly increasing number, like Julia in the FACTS group, inherit activist traditions that parents hand down much as others hand down political cynicism or the understanding that their children can repay the debts they owe solely in the coin of material success. "I've gone on peace marches ever since I was little," said a woman from the Mankato State nuclear concern group. "My father was in SDS, and it was just something we did." A woman who coordinated volunteers in shelters and soup kitchens at Connecticut's Trinity College recalled a parade of Soviet visitors, "our supposed enemies," who came through their San Francisco house from grassroots citizen exchanges. Recently graduated volunteers working for the United Farm Workers and the renewed grape boycott of the late Cesar Chavez came almost entirely from blue-collar union homes. The father of one Brown graduate had himself worked in the fields when he first immigrated from Mexico. "I knew about Cesar ever since I was a kid," the student told me. "I knew about the conditions and what he'd accomplished."

Some grow up exposed not so much to advocacy as to less controversial community involvement efforts. A student who worked with the University of Washington PIRG chapter described his parents as politically conservative and possessing a strong sense of civic responsibility: his father spent years helping to create a local park in their sprawling suburb. The mother of a South Carolina peace activist often brought her along to deliver groceries from their church to nearby public housing projects. Although Tajel Shah, USSA's national president in 1991–92, grew up in suburban New Jersey, her immigrant parents had once been active in the Indian independence movement.

Not all families of activists are even tacitly supportive. The more politically engaged the school, the more likely those involved will include large numbers of students from backgrounds overtly hostile toward change, who must therefore look elsewhere for models. But particularly in the germinal stages of campus movements, active students have often been influenced by parents who encouraged them to stand up for what they believed.

What students recall as encouragement of their voices may have been intended as early training for professional careers. But family emphasis on civic responsibility and independent thought parallels the backgrounds of core student activists from earlier periods. When I talk with apolitical students, in contrast, I hear few equivalent narratives of being encouraged to sort through things for themselves and stand up for what they believed. Rather, they describe families who largely avoid political controversy, cynically dismiss it, or insist that American leaders know best and we ought to obey them. Most of all, these students say, they've been taught to keep their heads down and to try to survive.[4]

Students also find involvement encouraged by their experiences in churches that, as they were growing up, took strong stands on issues like the nuclear arms race, Central American intervention, and the crisis of the homeless. Student members of such congregations frequently accompany socially concerned parents, and find their religious message part of a general context that nurtures commitment. Other students find individual church mentors, like the Chicago priest who so influenced Raul Ortiz.

The religious call toward involvement encompasses varied and sometimes clashing perspectives. I've interviewed numerous students from Catholic and Fundamentalist Protestant backgrounds who first marched in right-to-life events, then changed their views on the abortion issue when confronted with the dilemmas of sexually active peers, and with a context in which three-quarters of all students (including solid majorities even at Catholic colleges) support the right to choice. Most of these students then dropped out of politics, but some stayed on in various peace and justice movements.

A Holy Cross peace activist named Mary Raphael grew up in a Catholic parish that was strongly involved in right-to-life activities. Although her mother, who had worked in civil rights efforts, shied away from blockading clinics, she did political lobbying and raised money and supplies for the Catholic adoption support organization Birthright. Mary spent much of her childhood playing among the cribs and toys at the Birthright center. Later she read its antiabortion literature. Then her sister got pregnant following a date rape and decided to keep the child. "It's what the church said you were supposed to do, but they scorned her like she'd committed a crime. It was as if they'd almost rather she'd had an abortion but not told them." Mary's Catholic faith still meant a great deal, yet her sister's experience meshed with her growing anger at church insensitivity on issues like birth control, child care, and the role of women in worship. She felt its leaders often lacked the very compassion they preached. It frustrated her that her Catholic campus offered little institutional support to even question an anti-abortion position.

Yet Mary valued the church community, its emphasis on service, the role of prayer and reflection in her life. She believed still in its message of being true to her convictions. Her political focus shifted to the Catholic peace group, Pax Christi, which used a familiar religious language to address global issues that felt increasingly urgent. It helped her combine her faith and her political vision, "like the other week when I gave the opening Pax Christi prayer, or last night, when I went from a workshop on campus activism to one on the elections and then to Mass. It felt empowering, the right kind of joining."

"My changes aren't like waking up and finding Love Canal in your backyard," Mary said, cautioning. "They're slower and more gradual. I still want to be the person explaining why someone else is holding a sign instead of being the person with the sign. But I want to keep my mind open, keep learning and going to meetings, stay involved in medical ethics, social policy, and in the church. So when my personal Love Canal comes I'll be willing to take a stand."

Teaching for concern   Some role models appear early in students' lives but don't produce involvement until later. As in the case of Jean and Matt from Greeks for Peace, socially committed teachers are often key. In a time when affirmation for citizen involvement is scarce, these teachers encourage critical thought, connect concerned students with valuable intellectual resources, and confirm their right and responsibility to follow their convictions. They also help concerned students find each other, and they serve as models through their own community involvement.

I've described how, at any given school, activist students will cite the same handful of teachers as having inspired them. These professors present their material passionately. They refuse to mute their own voice and vision, even as they incorporate conflicting views and encourage opinions different from their own. They take effective public stands outside the classroom. Though their numbers are modest, their influence testifies to the impact faculty can have when they take seriously the need for citizen involvement. Their influence also challenges that large majority of teachers who consider it academically inappropriate to link their teaching and research to their deepest beliefs, or to current public debates.

Inspirational teachers often come from disciplines expected to deal with topical issues: sociology, political science, environmental science, or women's or ethnic studies. This was true of the teachers who influenced the FACTS group and the Greeks for Peace. But I've met students politically galvanized by professors of music, speech, biology, organic chemistry, physics, and even by a community college accounting teacher who had her students analyze the federal budget.

Students respond when teachers take the risk of engaging them. "I grew up in a small South Dakota town, very sheltered, with no poor people and no dissenting politics," explained a Creighton woman. "Our professor took our class to North Omaha, to the homeless shelters. I didn't know places like North Omaha existed. It totally changed the way I saw things." A Fairfield woman took a class on the arms race to fulfill her international relations minor. The religion professor who taught it inspired her, as he did the newly elected student body president. Later the two students formed a nuclear concerns group.

At Indiana University of Pennsylvania, activist sociology professor Harvey Holtz was turning forty. He'd encouraged students in their challenge to apartheid and in sleeping out in a shanty they had built to call attention to homelessness. He'd helped them negotiate a space behind the Student Union snackbar for a coffee house with tables, dim lighting, and a stage, that they called the Free Zone. It was a place where students met and talked, and where their political community slowly grew. When I arrived, a woman on stage was describing how she had broken from a background of drugs, alcohol, and physical abuse. The student audience was listening thoughtfully. After her talk, a disk jockey played music. Someone in the group dimmed the lights and announced Harvey's fortieth birthday.

With great ceremony, he was called to the stage and handed elaborately wrapped gifts: Rolaids, Milk of Magnesia, and a denture cleaner. Harvey, shaggy haired and hiding a smile, accepted them with sheepish grace. But when he tried to blow out the candles on the cake, he couldn't muster the breath to do so. They were fake. The students laughed with visible affection, making it clear that he was still their inspiration, even if over the hill.

Committed faculty don't seek to produce simplistic political clones. "He lets you learn things on your own," University of Washington's Anna Roselli said of her political science teacher, "like a paper I did on Alexis de Tocqueville. Sometimes the more you learn the more confused you get, with a more complex picture. Not everything simply fits the problems we have to deal with. But it's good to founder a bit if it helps you think."

At its best, committed teaching redeems education as a moral force. One Fairfield student described reading André Brink's *A Dry White Season* for a class on South Africa—a novel, later an excellent film, about the political conversion of a prominent Afrikaner. "I identified so much with him holding back," said the student, "never challenging the system until a certain course of events. He was always waiting for that sometime in his life when he'd get the call and get involved. Some people never hear it. The book made me think about my sense of mortality. That I can't keep separating life into the ideal and the real. I can't keep waiting to get involved in things. It's about time for me to move toward what I believe."

We can dismiss this as sophomore enthusiasm. But I believed this student's sense that Brink's narrative had touched his life, and spurred his first steps toward involvement. The teacher who introduced him to this literature treated it as if it were a mandate for moral choices and actions, not a dead specimen to be dissected. Other concerned faculty similarly helped their students explore the relationships between political means and ends, between individual action and larger social change, between citizen movements of today and those of fifty or a hundred years ago. During a time when America's leaders were fleeing from historical lessons, or ripping them out of context to serve questionable ends, committed teachers helped anchor students in complex and demanding realities. They linked critical events, present and past, with the human choices that created them.

Stoned Malcolm   Models needn't be alive and close at hand to have an impact. USSA's second African-American president, Julius Davis, was inspired by hearing a recorded speech by Malcolm X. Involved in drugs and petty crime as a teenager, he disdained school, except for his involvement in sports. When Julius graduated high school after repeating tenth grade, he washed dishes, worked as an unskilled laborer on construction sites, tried telemarketing, and performed other dead-end jobs consistent with his lack of skills. Mainly, he spent his time smoking pot, hanging out, and partying.

One day he was stoned at his sister's apartment in the Bronx, dejected because he'd just broken up with a woman he'd hoped to marry. Idly, he leafed through a stack of records. He came upon Malcolm's talk, "The Ballot or the Bullet," put it on the turntable, and began listening. He found himself transfixed. He'd never read anything like it, never heard that kind of speech. Ten minutes into listening, he was no longer high.

Julius started thinking about how he'd gotten where he was and what he wanted to do. He began reading intensely—everything on Malcolm, Carter Woodson's *Miseducation of the Negro*, Saul Alinsky's *Rules for Radicals*, and a self-help book that was a gift from his uncle, David Schwartz's *The Magic of Thinking Big*. Feeling for the first time that learning had meaning, he enrolled at Buffalo's Erie Community College, and became involved in black nationalist politics and the Third World Caucus of the Student Association of the State of New York (SASU). At first Julius worked to gain more resources for his particular community. "We had a seven-hundred-dollar budget for the African-American student group. Student government spent seven thousand dollars on 'beach parties.' They paid a Boston organization to put up sunlamps so people could get a tan. I don't need a tan, and neither did any of the other African-Americans on campus." Julius pushed through a people of color conference in SASU, saying if the organization didn't think it had the money to cover the logistics, it had to shift priorities. When the community college student senate told his group they couldn't have an office and phone, Julius brought a hundred students to their next meeting and threatened to occupy their office.

Julius didn't regret these race-specific demands, but he soon realized the need for coalitions. "You win by numbers, where you bring in as many folks as possible without weakening your cause. Also white people would come out of the woodwork who I'd end up trusting, who would learn and appreciate the African-American experience, be sensitive to it, and go a lot farther than I thought they would." He took on a variety of mentors, older recent graduates of all races and backgrounds, then helped others build coalitions first within SASU and the Rainbow Coalition, and later as vice president and president of USSA. At the USSA office, he greeted everyone with "Hey, Homie," automatically making them neighborhood comrades, regardless of background, so long as they were willing to work toward a just society.

Other students found models for nascent political identities in stories they heard on alternative media, such as cultural dissent broadcast by some college and community radio stations. Or copies of *Greenpeace* that they read at the homes of friends or were introduced to by door-to-door canvasses. Young feminists stumbled onto *Ms* at the newsstands, then wrote thanking the magazine for providing a lifeline of validation.

Such confirmation gave newly involved students a sense that their efforts could be worthwhile. It linked them to long-standing traditions of engagement, showed them they had allies, helped them think through ways to best take their stands.

What other influences helped students get beyond rote adaptation? Some found ethical standards in their vocational path. A number of student government leaders began by addressing issues like tuition and financial aid. As campuses grew increasingly restive, they took stands on other questions, brought in provocative speakers, and encouraged the formation of student political groups. While they sometimes took flack for doing this, even the most apathetic students often accepted their outspokenness as part of a general mandate to get things done. This was true, for instance, of a Fairfield student body president who publicly debated William F. Buckley on the value of Star Wars, sparked the school's first nuclear concern group, and was respected as a mover and shaker even by conservative students like Tim Lovejoy and George Lipson.

Peers as well can serve as models. I've often been astounded at the political eloquence of newly involved students—at their ability to meld complex factual information, broader moral contexts, and political approaches that might make an impact. This doesn't mean their fellow students will automatically respond. If the activists seem to betray their ideals even in the slightest, those wary will draw back and the trap of the Perfect Standard will snap shut. Even when they do their best to stay consistent, many will still resist their call. Remember the Saint Benedict's College woman who joined a sleep-out to demonstrate the plight of the homeless, only to be condescendingly told by another student, "Homeless people don't have blankets"? But her example did have an impact. Other students stopped to talk with her, and asked what they could do about an issue most had never considered.

Study groups and Stanford   What caused my own political shifts? Who were my models? What stories influenced me? I started out, like most Americans, trusting our leaders on Vietnam. In 1964, I passed out literature for Lyndon Johnson, who said he was not about to send American boys to fight in a war that Asian boys should fight themselves. The next spring, debating a fellow classmate, I argued that we had to trust our president now that he'd decided the Communist threat in Vietnam had to be stopped. She said we had "a tiger by the tail" and ought to stay out. I answered with a cliché of the times: if we didn't take a stand now, "they'll be landing next on the beaches of California." This was Los Angeles, and the beaches were where we spent our weekends. The class didn't want Red tanks disrupting their sunbathing and body surfing. Almost every student backed my position.

Slowly the myths justifying the war began to crumble. I still vested most of my energy in writing college applications, preparing for the Scholastic Aptitude Tests, and doing whatever else I could to try to get a shot at Harvard. But where I'd previously joined my mother in dismissing what we called "those kooky students" on TV, I soon attended my first candlelight vigil, at UCLA. I bought two albums by singer Phil Ochs, after a student played his song "I Ain't Marchin' Anymore" in our history class, and he sang at the UCLA rallies. By fall of 1969, the beginning of my senior year, America's high schools were erupting. Student rights parties sprang up nationwide, including one at my school. The following spring, Los Angeles teachers walked out, and I joined other class-mates to organize a sympathy strike.

My family backed me up in this. They trusted the teachers and had taught me to stand up for my beliefs, even though they were not involved themselves. My father even helped me get discount rates for fliers at his company printer. We asked students to boycott those classes still being held, leafletted in the face of physical threats from crew-cut shop teachers who broke their colleagues' picket line, and held a brief sit-in inside the main building. Later a group of us also boycotted graduation after the ad-ministration rebuffed a request that students have the option of not wearing caps and gowns at the ceremony and giving money we'd save to a fund for antiwar candidates.

When I went off to Stanford in fall of 1970, I didn't consider myself any kind of radical, but my initially tentative political concerns continued to bloom. Although the antiwar movement had already begun to tear itself apart, a substantial community still helped me explore how America was betraying its most democratic ideals. At first I kept distant, celebrating my newfound autonomy by squeezing in as much hedonism as I could, going to hear music, getting high, and generally having a good time, while still maintaining my studies. President Nixon revived my concern, with his spring 1971 inva-sion of Laos. But what most galvanized my renewed involvement was a study group on the politics of Vietnam and America's global interventions that met once a week in the lounge of my freshman dorm.

Stanford had a rule that faculty could sponsor graduate students to teach pass/fail courses, and this course was led by a graduate student from the German de-partment. I signed up, thinking, "It's an easy three units. I won't have to worry about grades. I'll get to see my friends, and maybe even find out what those crazy radicals are thinking."

The course's content was mixed. The grad student was a moderately rabid Maoist whose political views contained both astute judgments on America's inequities and some fairly ghastly prescriptions about how to address them. I didn't entirely agree with him then and would agree even less in retrospect. But I liked him as a person, and our readings and weekly meetings offered a forum to discuss, in a sustained and serious way, how America betrayed its talk of democracy with endless global interventions. I learned of governments overthrown, dictators installed, and democratic movements shattered. A sense of community grew in the class that gave fresh purpose to our already developing friendships. It encouraged us to voice concerns about the war and its broader context, and to reflect on our own role in social change.

I compare this experience with the sharing of common history that I've mentioned in the context of African-American churchgoers who spearheaded the 1960s civil rights efforts, of Latin American peasants involved in the study and prayer circles called Christian base communities, and of women who participated in the feminist consciousness-raising groups of the early 1970s. Historians Sarah Evans and Harry Boyte describe ways the "free social spaces" provided by churches, unions, and voluntary groups have long offered havens for citizens to discuss common problems and raise critical concerns away from the gaze of those in power. My Stanford dorm group was more elite than most groups that nurture citizen movements. Yet we also sought the chance to understand the roots of a crisis that deeply disturbed us, and to learn ways to effectively act on it. The war's urgency gave this seminar a meaning largely absent in most of our courses. Nearly every participant soon became politically involved. I replicated the process the following year by linking up socially concerned professors and grad students, canvassing the dorms, and setting up a network of similar courses that eventually reached five hundred students.[5]

The study group brought global issues into our immediate context. So did another effort spearheaded by a resident assistant (RA). We had a fund for parties, beer, and other entertainment that totalled roughly $1,000 for the ninety-person dorm. The RA suggested we collectively donate $100 to a Quaker-sponsored organization called Medical Aid for Indochina, which was working to rebuild a North Vietnamese hospital that American planes had bombed. A humanitarian effort to heal the wounds of war, it was also a political statement, to the effect that we did not wish to cooperate with this killing.

Not everyone in the dorm agreed. Several members called the proposed donation partisan and disloyal. Had they remained silent, the gift would have helped the Vietnamese but made few ripples in the lives of these Stanford students. Instead, because these were common funds in which everyone had a stake, we debated it hotly. Discussions lasted the better part of a week. The measure finally passed, with a compromise to also contribute to a group that helped war-scarred children in South Vietnam. I saw students who'd never before taken a political stand begin to speak out.

When dreams and heroes died   The Vietnam-era movements eventually crashed as Nixon's Vietnamization policy substituted Asian corpses for American ones, and the war receded from the headlines. The lottery divided young men who had a stake in the draft from those who did not. The movement eroded from frustration with the seeming endlessness of its task, and fractured as apocalyptic rhetoric meshed with student deaths at the hands of police and the National Guard to feed a sense that involvement could be terminal. The examples offered by the most visible campus activists seemed increasingly arrogant and destructive.

By fall of 1972, when future *New York Times* writer Michiko Kakutani entered Yale, a visiting reporter characterized the mood on her campus as "disappointed, disillusioned, drained and exhausted." Yale president Kingman Brewster questioned a new spirit of "grim professionalism." A short while later, educator Arthur Levine caught the new spirit in the title of his book *When Dreams and Heroes Died*.[6]

Campus political activism continued to decline steadily until the mid-1970s, when it dropped to a fraction of its former strength. By then, the war was over and students most active in opposing it were gone from the campuses. A shaky economy and parental fears helped shift incoming students from the traditionally activist humanities and social sciences to business, prelaw, premed, and various technical fields—a shift that would increase through the 1980s. The election of Jimmy Carter left many who were still concerned feeling they could safely delegate public issues to his more sympathetic hands. Students quietly turned away from political issues and conflicts, while maintaining the more private countercultural legacies of sex, drugs, and rock and roll. Older commentators soon damned the new generation as hopelessly apathetic, a label that has continued to stick.

Overshadowed by the attitudes and conditions I've described, student involvement remained in a trough for roughly a decade—from the mid-seventies through the mid to late eighties. Though students continued to support relatively liberal stands on issues like the environment, abortion rights, the need for a more equitable tax system, and the need to trim military spending, those who tried to act on these causes felt isolated. During these years, students also grew less liberal and more apolitical in their general identifications. In 1971, 38 percent of entering freshmen considered themselves liberal or leftist. By 1981 these numbers had dropped to 20 percent, a shade fewer than those calling themselves conservative, whom the liberals used to outnumber two to one. Until the mid to late eighties, American campuses remained overwhelmingly quiet, leaving those who continued to act feeling frustrated, marginal, and almost incapable of reaching their peers.[7]

Yet even amidst this quiescence, American campuses of the seventies and early eighties weren't entirely politically dead. A number maintained barely visible streams of social concern, which would later grow to feed the broader student movements to come. Feminist visions surfaced in fights for abortion choice and women's rights to greater occupational equality. Environmental concern received general endorsement, if slight direct involvement. Although broad-based questioning of social institutions dropped off, more pragmatic forms of politics continued through organizations like USSA and its predecessor, the National Student Lobby, statewide student associations, and the Nader-inspired PIRGs. These groups worked primarily on campus-related issues like the politics of tuition, government financial aid, and student rights. Later the PIRGs took on other questions, challenging nuclear energy and promoting abortion rights and fairer tax policies. By 1978 their chapters were present at 11 percent of American colleges, then lost ground to an organized Republican counterattack that challenged their support base in designated student fees. But even at their strongest, these organizations involved relatively modest numbers of students directly, instead drawing on common resources to allow their small but committed staffs of researchers, lobbyists, and organizers to take on issues that students largely supported.[8]

Students of this period also maintained a sporadic cultural dissent through campus radio stations and newspapers. Some joined dissident electoral campaigns like the presidential efforts of Fred Harris and Jerry Brown, or worked with off-campus community organizations. A few took on global questions: the late seventies saw the beginnings of apartheid divestment campaigns, opposition to U.S. intervention in Central America, and challenges to Jimmy Carter's reimposition of draft registration. But for over a decade, student politics involved modest numbers and muted approaches. Participants framed themselves less as social visionaries than as consumer advocates, helping their communities get fair value on the educational products they purchased.[9]

Demonstrations and divestment When widespread student activism resumed, it built on these continuing political efforts, then quickly expanded their reach. We see this with the mid-1980s divestment movement, a major signpost of resurgent concern, which sought, in the words of African-American Yale organizer Matt Countryman, to bring "moral and economic pressure on U.S. corporations, forcing them to end their support of apartheid."[10]

At Columbia, where antiapartheid students helped spearhead the nationwide divestment movement, Coalition for a Free South Africa (CFSA), began in 1981, as an offshoot of the university's Black Students Organization. The group initiated a series of forums, discussions, rap groups in the dorms, informational leafletting on the quad, and other efforts that sought to get the university to divest from corporations with South African ties. In 1982, a CFSA spokeswoman convinced the student senate to support full divestment, and the next year got a unanimous endorsement from the far more conservative faculty, student, and administration representatives of the university senate. The trustees stonewalled, calling the recommendation "inappropriate." Columbia President Michael Sovern likewise resisted, kicking the issue back to a committee that, in the judgment of a university senate student member, used "all methods possible to avoid debate and open-minded decision making." CFSA spent two more years in committees, negotiations, forums, marches, vigils, debates, petitions, and even a two-week hunger strike, during which they unsuccessfully sought to meet with the trustees. When President Sovern continued to criticize their rallies and marches, and to spurn their proposals, the group decided to blockade the major administration and classroom building, Hamilton Hall.[11]

They began on April 4, 1985, the anniversary of the assassination of Martin Luther King, Jr., and a nationally scheduled date for coordinated student actions. A dozen CFSA members chained the Hamilton Hall doors and occupied the building steps in an effort they assumed would produce a quick symbolic arrest. Other members led an accompanying rally of roughly two hundred students. After speeches by a representative of the African National Congress and black South African students, they brought participants to the Hamilton steps and announced that their group would not leave until Columbia divested.

To the CFSA leaders' surprise, the bulk of those watching immediately joined in, sat down in front of the building, and themselves risked arrest as well. More students quickly joined. Within two hours, the crowd on the steps grew to 250, expanding further in the next few days, with several hundred others drifting in and out at the margins, bringing food, listening at the rallies, playing frisbee at the edge, and generally lending support.

For three weeks, students camped beneath a makeshift shelter of tarps donated by sympathetic New York City unions and slept huddled in blankets. Administrators, faculty, students, and building workers went in and out through a utility tunnel that CFSA had carefully marked with signs, but the blockade closed normal access in a manner dramatically visible. Participating students studied, made food, held rallies, met with the media, and maintained a twenty-four-hour presence. Friends enlisted others to participate. Students approached sympathetic parents and alumni to help levy pressure. The student-run grocery donated food. A group of African-American alumni helped with photocopying and publicity. Professors discussed the issues in classes as diverse as Italian, art, urban planning, contemporary civilization, and constitutional law. Calls and letters of support came in from the National Conference of Black Mayors, sympathetic congressional representatives, and South African Nobel laureate Desmond Tutu. More than a third of Columbia's undergraduates either joined the blockade or attended related educational events.[12]

Why did so many students participate? Although the core CFSA leaders and blockade initiators were African-American, most of those who joined were white, and new to political activity. Involvement built here, as at colleges nationwide, on long-standing outreach and discussion, including efforts that seemed fruitless at the time. The university senate mandate and years of educational efforts made students feel that those who acted had exhausted more respectable alternatives. In addition, national media helped bear witness to South African brutality, where massive protests challenged worsening economic conditions, substandard education, and a new constitution that would permanently disenfranchise African citizens. Global television gave widespread coverage to the Pretoria government beating, gassing, and shooting peaceful demonstrators. Students felt stirred as well by the risks taken by black South Africans who spoke out and by the wave of arrests, including arrests of numerous celebrities, that began at the South African embassy and at local consulates nationwide, after the U.S. Senate killed a November 1984 bill mandating economic sanctions. Students felt inspired, too, by the willingness of their peers to incur academic jeopardy and personal discomfort in the pursuit of divestment, a commitment that helped overcome the strictures of the Perfect Standard. This was particularly the case with the Columbia students' two-week hunger strike, launched in vain hope of gaining a meeting with the university trustees. It was true at Dartmouth and Cornell, where students slept out in shanties in the bitter cold. By the time the campaigns grew more confrontational, as when Columbia launched its blockade, committed students had effectively explained the narrative of human suffering that called them to act.

Antiapartheid students like those at Columbia, Berkeley, and Cornell inspired other campus divestment activists nationwide, creating a wave of rallies, petition drives, marches, sit-ins, construction of protest shanties, and blockades that pushed through some form of divestment at some 150 schools, totalling over $4 billion. Between two thousand and three thousand students and faculty were arrested. Although only a minority of campuses saw protests, more than 60 percent of these ended up at least partially divesting, compared with fewer than 3 percent of schools where no student movement existed to levy equivalent pressure.[13]

This, combined with divestment by state and local governments of $18.5 billion in pension and investment funds, helped pressure Congress to finally pass a limited sanctions bill over Ronald Reagan's veto in 1986. It also helped galvanize South African reform. Following that country's pivotal spring 1992 referendum, white voters explicitly stated that they would support change in part as an alternative to permanent international isolation. The campus divestment movement not only achieved its political goals beyond anyone's dreams, it began to revive student politics from its ten years of quiescence.

Discussing Rosa Parks This movement succeeded in part because it made distant wounds immediate and salient. Making them visible to ordinary students, it argued that they could steer history in a direction more humane and just by putting pressure on their administration, their campus, their board of trustees. This echoed some of the most powerful student activism in the sixties, that connected issues like the war and civil rights to America's campuses. UC Berkeley's Free Speech Movement began in fall 1964, when the administration imposed restrictions on student efforts to raise money for civil rights efforts and to boycott local branches of stores that helped maintain southern segregation. The 1968 student sit-in at Columbia University was a response to the school's continuing involvement in military research and its decision to erect a new student gym on land the activists considered the property of the adjacent Harlem community. My own Stanford efforts focused on the university's pervasive ties with the Defense Department and leading military contractors.[14]

To act in these contexts, students held up a standard of what their colleges should represent, in terms of furthering human dignity instead of debasing it. Such approaches don't have to involve confrontation, just student efforts to take responsibility for what their colleges should be, and how they fall short of the mark. At numerous schools students raised questions of accountability over issues like faculty hiring and firing, access to education, CIA recruiting, and the authoritarian manner in which administrators ran their campuses.

In 1990 at Mercer University in Macon, Georgia, university president Kirby Godsey refused to resign after his financial high-handedness brought repeated faculty votes of no confidence. In a parallel to Reagan-Bush national policies, Godsey boosted executive salaries and expense accounts, began an ambitious new engineering school with grand new buildings, and even acquired two nearby colleges—all without securing appropriate revenue.[15]

When the economic pyramid collapsed, Godsey unilaterally froze liberal arts salaries and budgets, even though these departments were more than paying their way. He hiked student tuition and fees and closed the school's Atlanta campus—which *U.S. News and World Report* had called one of the top ten undergraduate programs in its category and which was also solidly carrying its own economic weight. Godsey continued to boost budgetary support, however, for business, engineering, and the other professional schools, and to have the trustees award him an additional $900,000 annuity to supplement his personal pension. In response, the faculty and the student government voted no confidence and requested his resignation.

Godsey refused. The trustees backed him up, informing faculty that if they didn't like it, they could leave. Professors began picketing each noon, circling the administration building in their academic robes. Godsey refused to meet with the group of concerned students—until eight of them began a vigil. They brought lawn chairs and signs, and sat down in front of his offices where everyone could see them. Prepared for a siege, some even brought iced tea. But they had to wait just forty-five minutes before Godsey emerged, paternal and solicitous, flanked by dark-suited vice presidents whom students called his "mafia goons."

Because of the intensity of their school's crisis, Mercer students found more faculty models than most. A majority of professors signed a letter asking Godsey to resign. A dozen or so maintained the daily noontime vigil. Someone even added a line to posted fliers that invited students to apply for Fulbright programs in Romania: "Special sessions for disposing of corrupt leaders."

Most students still hesitated to get involved. They feared it might hurt their careers. They thought nothing they could do would really matter. Their parents said they should just keep their heads down and if Mercer went belly-up, cut the best possible deal to finish elsewhere.

Yet a modest group joined their teachers at the noontime vigils, spearheaded the student council no confidence votes, passed out black armbands for others to wear as a daily protest, and kept the issue alive among their peers. Those who acted included the editor of the campus paper, student senators, and members of the student judicial council. They framed their efforts in terms of responsibility, "to ensure that a healthy Mercer University exists for our children." "The current administration," explained their list of grievances, "treats the individual student as an object, as a product to be bought and made, and not as an adult with the right of self-determination."

The phrases could have been taken from the Berkeley Free Speech Movement. Several participants had in fact watched the civil rights film *Eyes on the Prize* for one of their classes, and had read Todd Gitlin's book, *The Sixties*. "We were discussing how Rosa Parks was able to take a stand," explained a woman named Melissa, "and here we have standards and beliefs and what are *we* doing? Just watching the film, we had to do something."

Drawing on this lineage was neither nostalgic nor redundant. The arrogance

of power the Mercer students challenged echoed a similar arrogance students had challenged twenty-five years before. It took their teachers' actions and a sense of historical
precedent to finally stir them to act.

"We were really hesitant," said a friend of Melissa's named Heather. "People
were saying we had responsibilities to keep the newspaper and the student government
neutral. But I felt that was really bogus. I can't do anything for my responsibilities unless
I'm responsible to myself."

Mercer remained a conservative school, with little student dissent, but student
efforts slowly grew. "It felt strange to sit in front of the administration building with our
lawn chairs and signs," said another friend, "and think that twenty years ago people
were doing the exact same things for the exact same reasons. I guess they got through
and survived OK." [16]

Fifteen

A house still divided
The campus politics of race

For his class on black images in the media, Emory University junior Marvin Coleman made a thirteen-minute video entitled *BMOC* (black man on campus). It opens with a black Emory student turning on the TV to a news report that shows the police arresting black suspects for crime after crime. He switches to a Donahue segment in which "Professor Whiteman" explains the various ways that blacks are inferior. Turning off the TV in disgust, the student grabs a boom box, heads out to class, and notices a white woman just ahead who crosses the street, hails down a male friend, and explains urgently, "I think that black man is following me." When the black man approaches to ask the time, the white man offers his wallet in appeasement.

The video then cuts to an Afro-American history class in which the professor quotes Malcolm X and warns against black self-hatred, cuts again to a cafeteria flirtation in which the black student calls a black woman "my African queen," and she teases back, "I've heard that line before." At the gym a student monitor passes several white students who've misplaced their student IDs, but hassles the black man who needs to leave a message for his coach. "Oh you must play basketball," she finally concedes, allowing him to duck in briefly, so long as he doesn't cause trouble.

By this time it's night. The black student heads back toward his dorm. Suddenly plainclothes cops stop him, search him, and demand his ID, belatedly explaining that he resembles another black seen breaking into a car. At last he returns to his room, entering past a poster of Africa. He puts a cassette into the stereo and leans back to relax. Immediately, a woman knocks on his door: "I'd appreciate it if you'd turn that stupid rap music down."

Marvin agreed the video was somewhat exaggerated, and hoped he could do something in the future "where everyone won't be so one-dimensional." The white actors were, in fact, his friends, who'd played their stereotyped roles with ample good humor. But almost all the incidents had happened, if not to Marvin, then to others he knew. He'd seen students get nervous when he walked behind them. He'd watched student monitors casually wave whites through at the library and gym, while they systematically inspected the IDs or book bags of black students. He'd been stopped by campus police, as had several black friends.

We talked outside the gleaming new Student Union, called the Dobbs University Center, or the DUC. Students of all races passed and waved hello. Marvin was lean and muscular, a star hurdler and sprinter who would place in the UAA Conference three years in a row. He had coffee-colored skin, short hair, and a shy, almost hesitant smile. He dressed casually in jeans and a loose shirt, and wore a small Africa pin in the traditional colors of red, green, and gold. Marvin worked hard in school, taking nineteen credits in African-American studies with a minor in communications, hosting a blues and jazz show on the campus radio station, and working fifteen hours a week at the college media center. He wanted to go into broadcasting and maybe teach. He was about to start a summer internship at Philadelphia's major black radio station.

Marvin had grown up in Philadelphia. His father worked in construction and his mother was a clerk and later an auditor for Conrail. Neither had gone to college, but Marvin's grandfather had attended a Baptist seminary and served as minister of a church with a large community outreach program. At thirteen, Marvin got a scholarship to a nearly all-white prep school outside Charlottesville, Virginia. At first it frustrated him when students kept asking if he played basketball and liked watermelon. "But it was also almost a utopia. I didn't have a care in the world except to eat, study, and play sports. They provided us with food and a place to sleep. It was all boys, so I didn't worry about getting in trouble with the girls. I came here, and suddenly, boom. There are all these issues."

Marvin started thinking significantly about racial politics during his freshman year. "When I first got to Emory," Marvin said, "we had special programs for African-American students. They'd assign a junior or senior to be what they called a peer assistant, to look out for us, see that we got our work done, be there if we had problems in the dorm. Especially if you're from out of town, they'd be like your first friend. Mine was a senior from New Jersey, who called and wrote a letter before I came, so I wouldn't feel isolated and alone."

With the encouragement of his peer assistant, Marvin began attending the Black Student Association (BSA) meetings. He felt an immediate bond. When the college English department failed to tenure African-American professor Sondra O'Neale and black students protested, Marvin came along to the first political march he'd ever joined. "I hadn't had her for a class," he explained. "But I knew she had touched students to the point where they were emotional and passionate about keeping her there. These were students I looked up to. I felt it my duty to be part of the cause."

The O'Neale case was complicated, based mostly on her department's judgment that she had inadequate publications. She'd written mostly for non-academic venues like local community newspapers, had published in only a few academic journals, and had not completed a book. Emory's English department competed for top national status with universities like Yale and Duke. When faculty didn't feel O'Neale mustered up, and the administration upheld their decision, a thousand people marched to challenge it, including most of Emory's black students, students from Atlanta's historically black colleges, including Morehouse and Spelman, some local civil rights leaders (though others praised the university's recent minority hiring track record), and a smaller number of white students. "It was a silent march," Marvin remembered. "Everyone wore black. Just a sea of people marching around the quad, then ending in front of the student center for a rally. That was my first march and protest. My only image of southern civil rights marches came from the movies, so I almost expected police to pour out with dogs and hoses at any moment. It was a very powerful thing."

Though the protests around O'Neale's case ultimately failed and Marvin was just another face in the crowd, he felt drawn in by the sense of engaged community and by personal loyalty to the older student leaders. He switched his major from business administration to African-American studies "so I could learn more about my history, and black people's situation in America." Since Emory didn't have a journalism program, he studied these fields on his own, with the help of his highly supportive boss at the college media center. Beginning sophomore year, he began to voice his concerns through efforts like the video project and letters and articles in the student newspaper, *The Emory Wheel.* For example, he wrote a letter questioning the paper's poor coverage of campus Black History Month events.

Death threats and desecration   What propelled Marvin and many of Emory's other African-American students into greater public involvement was a racial incident. On March 5, 1990, an African-American freshman who I'll call Mona Daniels reported to campus police that someone had broken into her room, written "Die nigger die" and "Nigger Hang" on the walls, torn apart her stuffed animals, and stolen her personal letters. Three weeks later she reported that her room was broken into again. Someone had taken her white roommate's wallet, containing a hundred dollars. A notebook Mona had misplaced was returned with racial comments scrawled across its pages. The stolen letters were returned as well, torn to pieces and stuffed in a manila envelope in her roommate's post office box.[1]

Campus police found no suspects, but patrolled the dorm and installed a portable alarm system with a panic button and an infrared motion sensor. On April 3, Mona reported receiving a death threat through campus mail. The dean in charge of minority affairs offered her the chance to change rooms or to complete the semester's studies at home. Mona decided to stay. The next week she went out briefly without turning on the alarm, returned to the dorm, and found another racial threat written in nail polish beneath a rug. She broke down, went mute, and entered the hospital.

Reports of these attacks appalled the Emory community, all the more because they echoed incidents of racial harassment that had been proliferating nationwide. Among the most notorious was a fight at U. Mass. Amherst the evening after the Boston Red Sox lost the 1986 World Series to the New York Mets. White student supporters of the Red Sox began by shoving African-American Mets fans. Then three thousand white students chased and beat black students throughout the campus, leaving one unconscious and nine others injured. At Arizona State, five hundred white students shouted anti-black slurs following an attack by three young black men on a white student. A group of seven Brown University men passed two Asian students on the street and yelled "Chink! Ching, Chong! Chink! Ching, Chong." When the Asian students objected, the jeerers threatened to attack them.[2]

Campus radio stations and computer networks also broadcast slurs, and campus newspapers printed them. In February 1987, a University of Michigan disk jockey joked that the two most famous blacks in American history were "Aunt Jemima and Mother Fucker." Two months later a student logged in to the campus computer system with racist, homophobic, and anti-Semitic jokes, including: "What do you call a nigger with half a brain? Gifted." "What are the three best years of a nigger's life? Second grade." On April 1, 1989, the campus newspaper at the University of Missouri, Columbia, ran an annual parody issue, *The Shiteater*, full of jokes about "homos," JAPs (Jewish American princesses), and two African-American basketball players—one with a "Zulu-looking relative in the stands" and the other with "the biggest cock on the team."

Many of the attacks were anonymous. At Yale a swastika and the words "White Power" were painted on the campus Afro-American cultural center. Vandals carved "Japs and Chinks only" into the door of the ethnic studies department at UC

Berkeley. Swastikas and other anti-Semitic graffiti appeared at numerous schools, including Stanford, Wellesley, Rutgers, Vanderbilt, University of Pennsylvania, USC, and the Universities of Maryland, Minnesota, and New Hampshire. A cross was burned in front of the Black Cultural Center at Purdue. At Brown "Niggers Go Home" appeared in an elevator and "Whites" and "Niggers" was written over "Men" and "Women" on lavatory doors.

Between September 1986 and December 1989, the National Institute Against Prejudice and Violence, monitoring local and national publications, found incidents of racial harassment or violence reported at more than three hundred universities and colleges across the country. They believed this was just a fraction of those that occurred. According to an institute report that drew on surveys conducted at a variety of schools, including Rutgers, Stanford, MIT, Michigan State, the University of Cincinnati, and the University of Maryland–Baltimore County, one out of four minority students—or over one million individuals—are subjected to some form of physical or psychological harassment every year. A quarter of the latter face incidents of victimization repeatedly. Even minority students who are not directly harassed often share the distress of friends who are.[3]

A hostile environment   At Emory, no one knew who had committed the attack on Mona. She had no visible enemies, had participated in nothing more controversial than the soccer team and her premed studies. Concerned students took the events as a call to raise long-standing questions around campus racial relations. Although students of all races wanted to respond, the dominant African-American group, Students Against Racial Inequality (SARI), mistrusted white students. They felt that this was their outrage to deal with. They believed they alone ought to determine the responses. Arguments flared within and outside their group over whether or not the planning meetings should be integrated, and over whether they should act on their own or within a broad coalition. Although Marvin took a back seat in these debates and had not been particularly involved, he ended up being named to SARI's new steering committee. The group's first action was a silent protest on the steps of Emory's old Student Union. An initially all-black effort, it grew to include 250 students of varied races.

A few days later, Emory president James Laney held a public forum before 700 students, faculty, and staff. He'd met in Augusta, Georgia, with Mona's family and affirmed that Emory would do all it could both to support her personally and to catch those who'd perpetrated the harassment. "Yes, racism is a problem on this campus," Laney acknowledged. "Minority students are often subjected to insults or to demeaning behavior." He said that he took the students' broader concerns seriously and that a university task force had already been working on related issues.

The SARI group wanted specific commitments on questions that went beyond Mona's situation. They met again in an all-black gathering at the Black Students Association house where five of them lived. They planned to open the meeting to students of all races at four o'clock, after the initial two hours. But by then little had been resolved, so they continued, debating on and on, while forty frustrated white students waited outside. Some in the white group wondered if the black students were testing them, making them feel for a change like unwanted outsiders. Some got angry. Gradually they drifted away. When the doors opened two and a half hours later, only fifteen remained.

The African-American students defended their actions. They needed to get the sense of their community. They were tired of constantly explaining themselves to mistrustful whites. They briefly apologized, saying the press of events had caught them up in the heat of discussion. Some also questioned the white students' commitment, and expressed fears that they would reveal forthcoming actions to the administration.

Certainly their exclusion of white students had precedents. The women who sparked the 1970s feminist resurgence generally chose to meet without men present so they could work through their common experiences. Black students in the late sixties formed their own distinct groups, yet also joined white activists in broader coalitions. The SARI core had not intended to keep the white group waiting, just to focus on their own responses and needs.

But the image of well-meaning white students spurned produced an immediate backlash. Numerous sympathetic students who'd wanted to join in and do something resented it, as did the more apolitical group who learned about the incident through a *Wheel* editorial that called it "blatantly racist exclusion." Despite SARI's public apology, anger at Mona's anonymous assailants was soon displaced onto the black student activists, a tension compounded by SARI's next march. They billed it as a show of support for Mona. Several hundred students joined, along with Emory professors and several university deans. Linking arms, people marched to the administration building, singing the African-American anthem "Lift Every Voice." At the end, with no previous notice, SARI's leaders presented a list of twelve demands as if they were the consensus of all who'd participated.

"As it stands," read the SARI leaders, "Emory University is a hostile environment for people of African descent." They demanded that Emory pay for Mona Daniels's medical and psychological care; aggressively recruit additional black students and counselors; add enough tenured black professors to equal the percentage of African-American students currently enrolled; create a requirement that two courses in African or African-American studies must be taken to graduate; and establish an African and African-American cultural center that would house archives, a library, and a wholly independent related department in charge of its own faculty appointments. Finally, they demanded Emory Public Safety Director Ed Medlin resign for, in their judgment, doing a slipshod job of protecting Mona and fostering a generally inhospitable atmosphere for African-American students. They demanded that representatives from the Black Student Alliance constitute "at least one-third" of a search committee for Medlin's successor.

President Laney distributed the demands to all students through campus mail. He announced that the school was already paying for Mona Daniels's medical care and had already planned to bring in more African-American faculty through a visiting scholars program and through tapping the resources of metropolitan Atlanta. He also announced a new center to help all faculty address important social issues in their classes, including multiracial and women's perspectives, and a separate multicultural resource and learning center that would provide mentoring and support programs for minority students and more general campus outreach on racial awareness.

Laney rejected the other demands, saying neither African-American studies nor any other department could function wholly autonomously within the university. He believed Emory already had enough undergraduate requirements and would not impose an African-American studies distribution rule, although the next year's freshman seminars would focus on ethnic, racial, and gender differences. He refused to fire Public Safety Director Ed Medlin.

SARI members defended their stands. "If we don't fight for ourselves," they asked, "who will?" "We needed to get together and talk freely," explained a core committee member named Lisa, a senior who'd been trying to address racial issues as part of Emory's Human Relations Committee, and who as a volunteer worked with young African-American single mothers. "People had the impression," she continued, "that we just pulled the demands out of the sky without thinking about them. But other campuses have implemented ones just like them. Lots of things we asked for were mentioned by the President's Commission on Minorities. I can understand that people would want to know exactly what the march was about, but it wasn't like we'd said we'd do one thing and then changed the agenda. The fact that they came along without our specifying our demands seemed a sign of support."

Marvin felt torn by these choices. "We didn't want white students to create their own agenda and impose it on us. We wanted to do something on our own, like this was our problem and something we should deal with from within. Yet we introduced demands to people who weren't familiar with them and they felt used. Like they were supporting something they didn't know about. Then you had all these editorials in *The Wheel* against SARI. The support we did have from white students dwindled. It turned people off and hurt the movement."

Most Emory students were unequivocally critical. In classroom discussions and letters to *The Wheel* they condemned SARI repeatedly for excluding whites from the meeting, for imposing their own demands on behalf of marchers who believed they were simply supporting Mona, for trying to increase their own group's power and numbers at the expense of the school. What seemed reasonable to the black students—for instance, demanding that the multicultural center be named after the long-time head of a modest African-American studies program that borrowed faculty from other departments—seemed pure gall to many white students. For all the validity of many of the issues that SARI raised, they'd neglected to undertake the hard and necessary work of articulating them.

The radically different experiences of most white students made it difficult for them to understand black perspectives. "Maybe we should have explained more what we were trying to do," Marvin acknowledged when I mentioned the common perception of SARI as separatist and elitist. "Maybe before the march we should have told the white students what we were doing instead of just walking them over and then reading our demands."

Marvin communicated some of his perceptions regarding racial mistrust in a guest column that ran in *The Wheel* a week after Mona Daniels entered the hospital. Students were unfriendly to him, he insisted, because he was black; they "look past me when I try to say hello . . . tell the RA that they are scared of me." A white woman in the dorm, he recounted, wouldn't let her black roommate use an answering machine that served their common phone and demanded "that my friend take her visitors to the lounge—four floors downstairs—because she felt that 'black people express themselves rudely.' " "The RA," Marvin wrote, "has made it a habit to say, 'Turn your music down please, or be written up.' " She made Marvin turn down the volume on a taped speech by Malcolm X. He compared her to slave owners who punished slaves for speaking African languages or dancing to African drums.

Another student responded with a letter saying he'd attended lots of multicultural programs and was tired of being "continually called a racist." He believed the RA was only doing her job and would have written up anyone who played their music loudly when people were sleeping or studying.

For all the controversies in his dorm, Marvin was soft-spoken when we talked outside the student union, and when he showed me his video at the library. He was soft-spoken in every encounter I witnessed, casually greeting a wide variety of friends of every race and style. The arguments over the volume of his music, he said, were directed mostly at his roommate, Kendall. "Music is an escape for him. Maybe sometimes he was just not conscious of how loud it was, but if you hear two different tapes playing at the same level, Soul II Soul or Public Enemy coming from one room and the Doors from another, you'll notice the one that irritates you. It might not seem at all loud to Kendall, but very loud to them. It put me over the top, though, when the RA said she'd write Kendall up, because if you get written up several times you get expelled from housing, which is a serious threat for a black student going through on loans."

Marvin described a floorwide dorm meeting that helped clear the air. "The meeting pleased me," he said, "even though some people got rough on what I'd written. I don't have any problem with the RA. I just wished the students who wanted the music turned down had come to me directly instead of putting her in the middle."

Two separate campuses   One Emory student who succeeded in bridging racial divisions while also recognizing their gravity was Sonya Tinsley. Tall and slim, with dark brown skin and a shoulder-length circle of braids, she was the sole African-American student in the campus peace group, one of the few in the campus women's organization, one of two in the Emory Coalition on Hunger and Homelessness. She was also active in the Black Student Association and in the university-sponsored Human Relations Council, and she sang in a largely black gospel choir. Sonya was the only nonsenior to win one of Emory's five undergraduate humanitarian awards.

She felt torn by racial loyalties. "Emory has a general school community," she explained, "but it's perceived as predominantly white. Then there's the black community, the Latino community, and the Asian community. We have our own events, parties, school functions. Not that all ethnic groups aren't welcome in the general Emory stuff, like the activities and concerts. But we perceive it as aimed at white students. What they regard as appealing to the general interest is really culturally specific."

The same held true with campus political groups. At a party the previous week with environmentalist friends, Sonya, as usual, was the only African-American present. She believed students joined such groups as much for the people they met as for belief in the causes, "then you walk in and see people who don't look like you, who listen to different music, who hang out at different places." She believed black and white students attended virtually two separate campuses.

But Sonya was used to bridging. She'd grown up in the 10,000-person town of Covington, Georgia, forty-five minutes east of Atlanta. Her father, co-principal of the local high school, had died when she was six. Her mother taught reading and math but received only a paraprofessional salary, which left the family little money but middle-class educational expectations. Sonya always knew she'd go to college. Her high school was 40 percent African-American, but she and one other student were the only blacks in the gifted track. She was the sole African-American in Girl Scouts and in her ballet class, and one of the few in the 4-H club. "But we were also part of the black church and black community. Growing up I just didn't expect to see black people in certain places and whites in certain others. As I got older I began to challenge that."

She learned an early sense of political responsibility, building on her parents' example. "Girl Scouts, the church, and the PTA were different in our African-American community than in suburbia. Not just that you were doing things for fun, but more about shaping the next generation, trying to prepare kids to swim upstream. It was important to my family, my town, and my extended community, that I be individually successful so that by overcoming the odds I could send a message. But I also felt a sense that what I did had to be more than for just myself."

At Emory, Sonya had to look to find courses that nurtured this feeling, that acknowledged her community and its needs. She considered the English department— English being her prime major—"very strong, but very Western. They do have lots of courses and books thrown in on the margins for spice, and I've tried to make that seasoning my core education." The courses she was just completing included one called Three American Literatures, which focused on writings by Native Americans, Asian-Americans, and Latinos; another on writings by black women from Africa and the Caribbean; a relatively traditional course on literature and philosophy; and one on lesbian writers, "where I was both the only black and the only nonlesbian—and I found it interesting to be part of the dominant culture for a change. It's not your typical Emory education," she told me with a smile. "but it is an Emory education, and it does exist here."

Unfortunately, virtually all the students who took such classes, with the exception of a few whites particularly interested in cultural diversity, were members of the groups on which the literature focused. Courses dealing with non-European cultures were largely by-passed by the white student community.

"I understand," Sonya said, "why SARI is pushing for an African-American requirement, how they see that relationship as so important for this society that students should be required to study it. Some black students argue that other cultures also need to be represented, but they say that isn't our fight and the others can wage their battles on their own. I myself wouldn't make the requirement that specific, but rather some course in non-Western culture. You can't talk about American history without talking about the relations between blacks and whites, but the same goes for Native Americans and the West, or Asian-Americans and the railroads, or the World War II internment camps. You get in a dangerous situation picking one history as more important than the other. But at least if they learn some, they won't think they know it all just because they took Western Civ and studied ancient Greece, ancient Rome, and how the U.S. was colonized. Students need to leave here knowing that they don't know everything they need to."

If SARI made mistakes, Sonya said, "it was in not being open about the direction they were going. They knew all along but were so scared about being sabotaged, about spies, that they tried to do everything in secret. A lot of their problems came from that process."

One answer, she believed, was for different racial communities to work together day to day, "not just in times of crisis, but through organizations doing things together, planning together, sitting and talking informally." She hoped to help this happen the coming year by arranging for the Black Students Association to work with the Coalition on Hunger and Homelessness on links between race and homelessness, and with a feminist group called Choices on the situation of African-American women. "There's so much mistrust now that people almost expect others to be racist or sexist. If they work together, day to day, communication lines will exist. When a crisis happens, people wouldn't have to always jump up and point accusational fingers."

We gave the blacks a lot   How did white students respond to these issues? Particularly where racial attacks were blatant, students generally backed responses like new multicultural distribution requirements, even though this meant more courses for them to take. "It could be like the sciences," thought a white Emory man, "where you have to study something but they don't say you have to take physics." Many, though not a majority, thought increased minority recruitment was fine, so long as it didn't jeopardize "deserving whites." Most recognized that they were going to live in a world "that includes a lot of very different people," and thought learning better ways to get along made moral and economic sense.

Across the country, minority students took the lead, but large numbers of white students joined in pressuring administrators to deal with the racial harassment, stereotyping, and exclusion. A thousand students protested following fraternity incidents at the University of Texas, and similar numbers marched following the racial incidents at Michigan. At Tufts, eight hundred students formed a human chain around the academic quad after an African-American student who'd written on racial issues in the campus paper was beaten and called "nigger" by a group of whites.

Others resented having to grapple with such questions. "Why should we care about black issues?" asked a football player at Maine's Colby College. We were speaking shortly after a star Colby athlete had been disciplined for joining other students in yelling racial slurs at visiting African-American basketball players. In response to the racial heckling, administrators planned an all-day convocation and discussed a possible ethnic diversity requirement. To the football player, these actions represented attacks on his private liberty. He didn't think he or other whites "owed" blacks anything at all. "I don't bother them with my issues. Why should they bother me with theirs?"

"They're going to make black history a requirement," said a friend of the football player who wore an Elvis Costello t-shirt. "Why shouldn't they require Italian history, Irish history, or every other goddamned thing we have in this country? What's to separate them from everybody else? We study American history. We're all Americans. So study that. Why should I be called a racist just because I don't want to go to be lectured at?"

The class split both on the convocation and on political involvement in general. Those who supported "at least trying to increase awareness" believed the Colby community could change, and that efforts like the convocation could help this process. At least, they said, "we have to try." Their opponents dismissed such efforts, locating the problem in a few students "who really need help, and who are going to be about the last people to listen or come."

As with other political questions, students who most dismissed racial problems mixed a broad social pessimism with the narrowest possible definition of personal responsibility. I think again of Tim at Fairfield stating, "We gave the blacks a lot," explaining that economic differences between black and white were "maybe something biological." "We helped them out a lot," a Saint Joseph's student said, repeating Tim's phrase. He blamed America's current crises on "the failed government programs of the sixties."

Is there a link between students who commit overtly racist acts and students who merely resist what they view as unwarranted minority claims on their attention and behavior? Few students consider themselves willfully racist. Even the Colby football player cited friendships with African-American players on his team. Yet students who are absolute individualists—suspicious of institutional attempts to address racial issues and bluntly desiring to be left alone—often echo the phrases of those directly involved in racial incidents.

Both types of white students treat demands for inclusion as competitive threats. Both accept the stereotyping of African-Americans and other minorities that was standard fare in the culture they grew up in: from Willie Horton ads and political scapegoating of welfare mothers, to a resurgence of racial and misogynist jokes, to a rise in conservative campus newspapers that, in the words of sociologist Howard Ehrlich of the National Institute Against Prejudice, "provide the intellectual and moral justifications for social inequalities."[4]

Given the promotion by college administrators of at least token integration and civility, racist actions and words can be nothing more, in the words of African-American rock guitarist Ivan Julian, than "a real immature way of being dangerous."[5] They don't always require overt malice. It is with a kind of innocence that the University of Washington student body president put on blackface to perform a lip synch impersonation of Michael Jackson. When challenged, he said a black fraternity brother told him it was OK. "I was thoughtless," explained a Saint Joseph's College student, suspended after a black RA took his beer away and he said without thinking, "Hey, nigger, where I come from we hang people for that." "It was blown out of proportion," he told me later on. "People are people, words are words. Black people call me nigger back home in Hammond. Still"—he paused and thought—"I don't have the heritage. I can't reach inside myself to see how it is to be hurt."

Student perceptions of racial problems differ widely depending on their backgrounds. At the University of Washington, a student-initiated task force on racism sampled seven hundred students through structured questionnaires. The findings echoed those at numerous other schools: there were major differences in the responses of whites (and to a lesser degree, of Asians), who were generally satisfied with the school's racial politics, and those of African-Americans, Native Americans, and Latinos, who felt consistently alienated. Sixty-two percent of blacks said they'd witnessed or experienced racial discrimination on campus, compared to 28 percent of whites. Three-quarters of white students felt comfortable at the school, compared to a little more than half the blacks. Washington employed just 26 black faculty out of more than 2,100 professors, and only 150 faculty members from all minority groups. Students of color wanted more, but fewer than half of the white students agreed. Only a third thought the university should enroll more minority students. A majority of all students agreed that courses should represent diverse cultural perspectives, but many more whites believed this already occurred.[6]

African-American students face a classic double bind. If they quietly assimilate, white students and professors are more likely to accept them, but their experience and history will remain invisible and unrecognized. If they focus on their particular identity and the claims of their communities, others accuse them of clannish exclusivity or, in the baiting of the conservatives, of "political correctness." As anthropologist Michael Moffatt wrote in *Coming of Age in New Jersey*, a study of Rutgers students in the late seventies and mid-eighties, most whites believed that "if blacks were good Americans . . . they should not want to live only among themselves any longer, because of an interest in black culture or for any other reason. Now that American society, and colleges like Rutgers, had decided to allow blacks to 'integrate,' *they* should want to do so too, or there was something wrong with them."[7]

I can't shave off my color   The sense of estrangement described by Sonya and Marvin is echoed by minority students at predominantly white institutions throughout the country. Buoyed by general demographic increases, students of color presently number one out of six students at America's four-year colleges and just under one out of five if you include two-year community colleges. They are disproportionately concentrated at crowded and underfunded public schools. Eight percent are African-Americans (one-quarter of whom attend historically black colleges), 4 percent are Latinos, 4 percent are Asians, and 0.5 percent are Native Americans.[8]

But their enrollments have fallen behind their presence in the population. The percentage of African-Americans and Latinos who entered college came closest to matching that of whites in the mid-1970s, in the wake of a booming American economy and the pressure of Vietnam-era campus movements. At that point, 27 percent of all white eighteen- to twenty-four-year-olds were enrolled in college, as were 22 percent of African-Americans and 20 percent of Latinos. By 1990, the rate of white enrollment had increased to 32 percent, but that of African-Americans to just 25 percent. The gap between the two had increased. Latino enrollment actually dropped to 16 percent, or half the rate of whites. Instead of narrowing, the divisions continued to widen, accentuated by financial pressures that left students of color taking longer to get through school and graduating at significantly lower rates.[9]

Much of this decline is due to a crisis in poor and segregated urban high schools, but even among high school graduates, the gaps have increased. In the mid-seventies, African-American and Latino students who made it through high school had roughly the same chance as whites of going on to college. Now, even if they surmount this critical hurdle, their chances are less, by as much as 25 percent. Even as college degrees become more essential for success, America's minority students have fallen steadily behind in opportunities to achieve them.[10]

Active student responses to campus racial tensions have produced some new recruitment and support programs, and percentages of minority high school graduates who've gone on to college have increased slightly since the mid-eighties trough. But major gaps in enrollment remain, as do even greater gaps in graduation rates. Add in the increasing devastation of the communities from which many students of color come, and it's not surprising many feel frustrated and estranged.[11]

When the wave of campus racial incidents broke, college administrators responded initially, in the words of sociologist Ehrlich, "by simultaneously denying the existence of a problem on *their* campus and redefining the incidents that occurred as 'pranks,' isolated incidents, or as nonprejudiced in motivation. As the publicity and student pressures have increased . . . the usual bureaucratic devices have been employed: institutional denials, appointments of slow-moving study commissions, attempts at suppressing committee reports, partial acceptance of recommendations, endorsing proposals without implementation, not funding or underfunding new policies, and grandstand gestures of limited symbolic value."[12]

Some administrators did quickly respond, following the lead of their students. At Brown, 1,500 students turned out to hear Vartan Gregorian announce "there are many outlets for racism and bigotry in this country. Brown will not be one of them." Wisconsin fraternities had a series of incidents, including a blackface party featuring a "Harlem Room," with watermelon punch and garbage on the floor, and another in which a party at the predominantly Jewish Zeta Beta Tau (ZBT) house, was crashed by members of another house, who beat up three people and taunted members with "Let's be a ZBT. Let's be a Jew!" Later pledges of the same ZBT house painted their faces black, wore afro wigs, held a mock slave auction, lip-synched Michael Jackson songs, and imitated Oprah Winfrey. Seven hundred students protested the slave auction incident, and Wisconsin chancellor and future Health, Education and Welfare secretary Donna Shalala responded with major programs to increase minority faculty and students, make available minority graduate and professional fellowships, and require ethnic studies courses for all undergraduates. But at most colleges, students of color carried a sense that administrators cared little about their interests.[13]

Blacks were first admitted at Emory in 1963, and in 1990 constituted 7 percent of the undergraduate population. Because this is an elite and selective school, the majority had already succeeded in predominantly white institutions. Like Marvin, they had received scholarships and worked their way through private or parochial high schools. Or they'd taken the high-powered public track, often among only a handful of African-American students in their class. A few faced major transitions, like Marvin's roommate Kendall, who came directly from the South Bronx; but for nearly all of them, racial identity seemed a constant issue. Black students here still walked down fraternity row past antebellum mansions with overwhelmingly white rosters of members. They still ate in student cafeterias where most other blacks were food servers and janitors. When racial issues surfaced in class, everyone promptly turned to them for explanations, as if they could or should reveal what writer Jill Nelson has called "my authentic Negro experience."[14]

"I don't want to speak for all factions of black society," explained the upcoming Black Students Association (BSA) chair, Brian Woods. "I know what this black person thinks." He gestured to himself. "I know something about the kids I tutor. I don't know what everyone else thinks. But if I make a statement, they'll take my word as that of all black people."

In the campus snack bar, a long-haired white student asked Brian why blacks always clustered together to eat. "I feel most comfortable," Brian answered. "I talk with lots of others, but I like being around people who look like me."

"But aren't we all the same underneath?" asked the white student. "Don't we have the same hopes and thoughts?" He got jeered all the time, he told us, when he'd had a Mohawk. "Isn't that similar to racism?"

"You grew your hair back out from the Mohawk," said Brian. "I can't shave off my color."

If their frustrations echoed those of African-American students at other campuses, black Emory students had particular touchstones for discontent. Consider the tenure case that first stirred Marvin's concern, of African-American English professor Sondra O'Neale. To white students, it seemed of marginal relevance. Terrific classroom teachers were denied tenure all the time, at this university and others. Most whites hadn't taken O'Neale's classes in any event, and not all who did gave favorable reports. But large numbers of African-American students knew her personally. Emory had only 13 tenured black faculty out of 618. Though O'Neale was, they admitted, at times disorganized, they found her teaching strong and provocative. She was one of the few mentors they had, and denying her tenure seemed a deliberate affront.[15]

Emory's minority students were troubled by other recent events. Five weeks before Mona announced the initial ransacking of her room, two alleged rapes occurred on the weekend of fraternity rush parties. The first involved a black fraternity member I'll call Lonnie, and his nonstudent black ex-girlfriend. The police had ample physical evidence to convict Lonnie, including scratches on his face and a piece of the woman's jewelry and part of her clothing in his room. They also had a witness, a fraternity mate of Lonnie's, who saw him drag the woman back into his room after she tried to run away—but this would not come out publicly until later. They quickly scheduled his case for trial, and the *Emory Wheel* judged Lonnie immediately guilty, in a front-page article that enumerated his previous violations of university rules.

A second rape charge was levied that weekend against a white fraternity member I'll call Bill. His alleged victim dropped her claim after the police told her they had insufficient evidence to stand up in court. Bill was the president of his fraternity, the son of a stockbroker, a star intramural athlete headed for medical school. He had a mean streak, as he showed by repeatedly teasing a woman from an interracial family by calling her a "zebra." But his alleged rape victim was highly intoxicated at the time of the incident and had gone home and showered afterward, which destroyed physical evidence. In the process of trying to extricate herself, she briefly told Bill "OK," which he read as a sign to continue. After interviewing students present at the party and the woman herself, police concluded that "a brief act of intercourse" probably did occur against her will, but that it was unclear whether Bill knew she wished him to stop. They said they therefore had no case.

Most white students thought the disposition of the cases was fair. But for many blacks on campus, the story seemed only too familiar. The wealthy young white man headed off to medical school, while the black man would probably end up in jail. They resented even more that whites seemed to prejudge the cases from the start. *The Wheel* displayed Lonnie's photo on its cover, while the newspaper referred to Bill only as "the accused attacker." At an open forum, Public Safety Director Ed Medlin kept referring to "the rapes," until Lonnie's friends corrected him, "Could you use the term the *alleged rapes?*" "Whatever," answered Medlin, which the students felt made the distinction seem moot. As SARI leader Erika Jefferson said, "It's like he's just this scum, that 'we've got him now and he won't get out of this.' I don't like someone who beats someone up or rapes someone, but why crucify the man? Let the jury decide."

Others disagreed, yet felt torn by the situation. Choices, the campus women's organization, responded to the events with a vigil on fraternity row, fliers headlined "This Will Not Be Tolerated," and the reprinted *Wheel* article beneath a picture of Lonnie. Sonya Tinsley was one of the few blacks active in the group, and felt troubled by this action. Rape, she stressed, was an outrage. Choices had "an ethical obligation" to take a public stand. "But it never occurred to them that the African-American community would see them as playing into the hands of the college media and the Atlanta press. They promoted the vigil as being in support of this woman and her courage to come forward. But like everyone else, they'd already convicted Lonnie and treated him as the big bad lurking raping monster, while Bill's name hadn't even been released. Whether or not he did it, there's still a certain way his case should have been dealt with, and it wasn't. Maybe if the groups had been working together day to day, the woman who organized it would have had an intuition that it might be interpreted as racist. Or even if everything happened as it did, the African-Americans would have known the women's group well enough to talk about their reactions. I just wish people had been more sensitive."

From Ed Medlin's perspective, he felt hamstrung from the start, unable to release key information due to federal privacy laws, knowing from the start why many students would have questions, wanting them to take Lonnie's violation of a black woman as seriously as they did the image of police arresting a black man. But African-American students weren't frustrated only by Medlin's perceived response to the rapes. In a way that they never fully explained to the broader Emory public, they were also frustrated at how campus police seemed to routinely stop and scrutinize black males, in a manner different than that used with nonblack students. While most acknowledged that Lonnie might well be guilty, they viewed Emory's handling of his case, together with the O'Neale tenure situation, as part of a continuing narrative of insensitivity.

Justice and pride   As Sonya said, these issues weren't "about personal ill will or goodwill," but about how people responded to the challenges they faced. "I don't doubt the integrity or good intentions of James Laney or Ed Medlin, but that isn't the point. Medlin is a nice person who maybe was just trying to do justice to that woman. I don't think he consciously directs Emory security officers to harass black students. It's more like saying 'search for suspicious-looking characters,' but what do you mean by 'suspicious looking?' What kind of look have you been taught makes someone suspicious?

"It's the same thing with Laney," she explained. "He's a good man. He takes ethics and social issues seriously. Emory is lucky to have a president who makes speeches on racial questions, writes essays and sets up task forces, gives you things you can quote and hold him to. That doesn't happen at every institution. But it isn't enough just to say you're trying, or that you've earned your stripes by standing up for civil rights before. It doesn't exempt the Emory community from needing to challenge certain issues of ingrained institutional racism. It doesn't exempt Emory from responsibility."

Just as Sonya distinguished between Laney and Medlin's personal intent and the consequences of their actions, so campus racial tensions are caused by much more than individual callousness or prejudice. They are fed, to be sure, by a handful of individuals who, for whatever reason, consciously act to degrade their fellow human beings. But mostly they are structural; they have to do with different understandings, histories, and perceptions; with the historic absence of students and faculty of color from American campuses; with the growing desperation of minority communities. These structures drag down not only students, faculty, and administrators who steadfastly ignore racial divisions, but also those who work to heal them.

All this only increases the urgency for colleges to deal with precisely the kinds of complex and wounding questions raised in the wake of the Mona Daniels incident. And for students who try to act to address these issues, to reflect as consciously as possible on how their efforts will be understood by communities that do not share their experiences and assumptions. Viewing racism as more a structural than a personal problem should help lend understanding when the actions and responses on both sides are clumsy, and when campuses get tangled in cycles of mistrust.

In contrast with apolitical white students who believe "you make your own chances," most African-American students link their personal narratives with those of their communities. As politically active African-American students often mention, half of America's black preschool children now live beneath the poverty line, more black men their own age are now in jail or under judicial supervision than attending college, and black men in Harlem have a smaller chance of living to age forty than men growing up in Bangladesh. Although plenty of black Emory students differed with SARI's approaches, they cited their own encounters with student monitors at the library or gym, voiced their own frustration at the lack of minority faculty, and agreed that protests were necessary.[16]

Finding the strength and solidarity to speak out was difficult for these students as well. "What makes someone act?" asked an African-American medical student. "For one person, it might take something happening to another black student. To another, it might have to happen to a close friend or a family member. I know some of the white students are sensitized. But for others, no matter how many blacks something happened to, they wouldn't feel it's their business. Whereas lots of blacks wouldn't respond if something happened to a white. You have to view it as happening to another human."

It was this hope of building a human bond that led African-American students to stress the redemptive power of education, and hope that it could live up to its mandate. "It's frustrating," said a SARI leader named Erika. "People don't know that the oldest bones have been found in Africa. That the first civilizations were there. If whites only knew that, maybe it would foster respect."

Marvin Coleman agreed. When I asked why SARI pushed for a specifically African-American studies requirement, rather than one more multicultural, he answered, "I could see taking Asian studies as well. I can show anthropologically or biblically that civilization has African roots. Almost every science has come to terms with it. I wrote a letter for *The Wheel* about how some of the finest Greek scholars went to Africa—to Egypt—to study astronomy and the other mysteries. But I also feel bad because I have absolutely zero knowledge of Asian history—Japanese, Chinese, Korean. I also know there are different Native American nationalities, but I don't know what they are, just as people lump Africa as one big country without any differences."[17]

A search for roots was part of the surging attraction felt by numerous black students for Louis Farrakhan, whom Marvin saw along with sixteen thousand others at the Atlanta Omnidome. Marvin respected Farrakhan for articulating African-American identity and for symbolizing the dream of a proud and uncompromising black community whose members would determine their future, regardless of the response from white America. He dismissed allegations of Farrakhan's anti-Semitism as miscommunication and misunderstanding. He admired Farrakhan particularly as an heir of Malcolm X who, more than any other figure, inspired young African-American activists.[18]

For many African-American students, Malcolm's star burns particularly bright in contrast with that of Martin Luther King, Jr., whose vision they see as having failed. Marvin regarded them both as fighters for justice and dignity, as he did an ecumenical pantheon of black leaders from Farrakhan to Rosa Parks, Ella Baker, Langston Hughes, and W.E.B. DuBois. But many African-American students now denigrate King, lumping him with bland, accommodationist, and outdated civil rights leadership that they believe is taking their people nowhere.

"Malcolm was a man's man," said a student active in a tuition strike at New York's Borough of Manhattan Community College. "I'd always heard him labeled a 'hatemonger,' but he stood for things you learn on the street. Defend yourself. Speak the truth. None of this wimpy nonviolent turn-the-other-cheek nonsense."

Yet as gay African-American film-maker Marlon Riggs writes, the Malcolm young African-Americans most often adopt, frequently via Farrakhan, is "pre-Mecca Malcolm, militant Malcolm, 'by any means necessary' Malcolm, not Malcolm *after* Mecca, when he became more critical of himself and exclusivist Nation of Islam tenets, and embraced a broader, multicultural perspective on nationalist identity."[19]

Riggs links this vision with the romance of "Afrocentrism." "Given the increasingly besieged state of black men in America, and the nation's historic subversion of an affirming black identity, it is no wonder that the community would return to pre-disaporan history for metaphors of empowerment. But the embrace of the African warrior ideal—strong, protective, impassive, patriarchal—has cost us. . . . Black Macho prescribes an inflexible ideal: strong black men—'Afrocentric' black men—don't flinch, don't weaken, don't take blame or shit, take charge, step-to when challenged, and defend themselves without pause for self-doubt."

This style caused tensions at Emory, where some members of SARI spoke in one of their public meetings about the need to "protect our women." To which an

African-American woman in the audience responded, "*Our* women? *Our* women? What do you mean, '*Our*' women? We can protect ourselves."

Some SARI participants wondered whether common ground with whites was even possible. As the SARI core leader and Human Relations Committee member named Lisa expressed it, "Whites are closer to the administration and faculty. They haven't shared our experience. I know it sounds bad, but they are kind of guilty until proven innocent."

Not all of Emory's black leaders felt that way. Brian Woods, the Emory BSA head who explained "I can't shave off my color," worked hard to build broad political coalitions. "I understand," he said in sentiments that echoed those of USSA head Julius Davis, "the fear that as African-Americans we'll lose out by compromising if we work with Latino students or gay and lesbian students, or anyone else. But if you look at the history of struggles, it takes compromise to achieve things."

At the same time, Brian joined most other African-American students in that he lived, ate, studied, and relaxed primarily with other blacks, mistrusting black students who fraternized mainly with white friends. Explaining that he wanted to understand his own identity and background, he suspected the latter of adopting a foreign identity, "forgetting who they are just so they can get ahead." Some black students follow this path no less than highly adaptive white students. One at Emory hung back from campus racial issues precisely because he feared that being identified as a politically involved African-American might hurt his career. National studies have shown that black students who live with black roommates and belong to African-American organizations graduate at a higher rate than those without such support. But even black students like Sonya, who kept strong ties to their community but also spent large amounts of time with white friends, had to continually prove themselves.[20]

If few African-American students mixed in largely white circles, it was even more rare for white students to place themselves in majority black contexts. Brian's historically black fraternity did have one white Jewish member, who'd grown up in an integrated circle in Florida, "where as far back as I could remember I was used to being the only white in a room of twenty or thirty blacks. I also liked Alpha Phi Alpha's strong community service tradition, and decided that I just felt comfortable with these brothers." Although some members hesitated to accept him, others had been his closest friends since he entered the school, and successfully pushed his candidacy.

But mostly, when white students visited with African-American friends, they did so on their own turf. A handful of campus institutions were truly multiracial: campus worship, the gospel choir, the Human Relations Committee, the International Association, and some sports teams. But with these few exceptions, most minorities participated by ones and twos. "When they reach around fifty percent, like some of the cheerleading squads," said Greg Ricks, the African-American director of Stanford's Office of Multicultural Education, "you begin to see the white students rapidly fall away." Sonya Tinsley had the same sense. "The atmosphere is friendly to being the only black person in a group," she said. "But in terms of numbers of blacks it's not. People don't mind one or two stray individuals, but if they come in and want to play their music, that's different." Ricks believed the new community service movement might help surmount these gaps, but stressed that it would take a major conscious effort.

Not all black students at Emory embraced SARI's perspectives. Some denied the existence of major social problems almost as much as their white counterparts. Student body president Aldous McCrory, a black Republican, dismissed SARI's demands as "age-old issues" unrelated to the current situation. He thought the media was paying far too much attention to campus tensions and not enough to developments like the opening of Emory's new $40 million science center.

McCrory accused SARI of seeking "a utopia." Bigoted students, he felt, would "never set foot in a multicultural center except to deface it." He thought a required class would change little. "This campus is conducive to anything you want to do. It's a sheltered environment. If everything's already laid out for you, you won't be prepared when you get out into the real world and there are racists and no one's sitting there with forums and task forces."

However, most of Emory's black students believed the school needed to make significant changes. "We have to look out for our own interest," they said. "We can't rely on anyone else to secure our needs." Others were torn, concerned about the issues, but feeling substantial misgivings about SARI's approaches. The organization's style, they said, had been set by a few angry men who loudly dominated initial discussions though they'd been only peripherally involved in campus black politics. Even Marvin wondered whether SARI's steering committee ended up pushing long-time leaders aside in favor of "students whose voices were the loudest." People disagreed in particular with the demand to fire Ed Medlin and with the exclusive focus on African-American needs.

African-American students, at Emory and elsewhere, hesitated to publicly criticize their peers. They feared that airing political differences would give ammunition to critics eager to resist coming to grips with racial problems. They shared "a sense of pent-up frustration" at the glacial pace of change at their colleges and in American society. They wondered at times whether their efforts could matter at all. "Maybe lots of us did suppress our reactions," said a black woman named Edda, who lived down the hall from Mona and had grown up in a middle-class African-American community in Miami.

"Maybe it was a mistake that we isolated ourselves. Perhaps we let other people run our movement for us. But we did it to reach a common goal. I don't think the core group did it to personally gain power."

Like the SARI committee members, these students felt the attack on Mona as a personal wound. They wanted to discuss it with others who shared their background and experience. Some also affirmed a newfound solidarity. Edda wrote on a message pad by her door, "Black wasn't always beautiful and I wasn't always there. But I'm there now." "When things like this happen," she explained, "it shocks us into recognition. Over the past two semesters of my classes, I've started returning to my history, drawing up a long remedial list of books I should have read all along. I'm beginning to feel I have an obligation to educate, to teach, to help put our story into perspective. This whole incident helped remind me what it means to live as an African-American."

Mistrusted and excluded   Sympathetic white students, again, felt caught in the middle. They wanted to respond, to stand side by side, to make Emory a community where all would participate. Instead, they felt scorned, mistrusted, and excluded as they waited awkwardly outside the BSA house or talked doggedly with other whites to convince them not to dismiss the cause.

"I showed up for the BSA meeting at six P.M. on the button," said a sophomore English major named Katy. "We waited two and a half hours, and every time black students would go in and they'd open the door, we'd get these looks that were just hostile, as if we were a hindrance instead of a help." At the public meetings, black students kept repeating that America would soon be two-thirds people of color, and Katy took that to mean that she would have no place. She'd even lost friends, like Marvin Coleman's roommate, Kendall, "who used to give me a big hug whenever he saw me. But now if I come up when he's with African-American friends, it's like he's embarrassed I'm there."

Others also spoke of their frustration and estrangement. But new bonds were also forged. When Katy wrote a letter in *The Wheel* questioning an article that Edda wrote, Edda responded with a personal note. The two then got together for lunch and quickly became close friends. In an English class, a white friend of Katy defended SARI's position, or at least the need to hang in and support them. "I thought, I will not disband from this," she said, "just because I disagree with some of the extremities. You have to ask for beyond what you want at some point. People said they went too far, but how do you go too far when you just want something in the middle ground?"

To a degree, Katy's frustration was more general. She herself was considering a transfer to Reed, Kenyon, or Rutgers—schools she felt were less preprofessional and more politically concerned. But Katy did support most of the demands. When SARI decided to ask for a moment of silence at an Emory track meet, to reflect on Mona and the issues, she joined the forty students who went along, then ended up reading their request over the mike. "I know there are problems, dilemmas I can't wholly understand because I'm not black. If the students hadn't gotten together and acted, it would have been the end of the story. I just don't support all of how it was done."

Others felt torn as well. "It's not cool to be a racist at Emory, which is a good thing," said a white history major named Scott, who was a deacon in the integrated campus worship group. "In high school I always made it a point on a personal level to talk with a lot of black students, and to say 'I don't like that kind of stuff' if someone made a racist joke. But there has to be a forum where you can say 'I'm not a racist and I support what you stand for at the core, but I don't agree with you.'" He supported a multicultural center and bringing in visiting African-American scholars, but he'd felt manipulated at the march, and disagreed vehemently with the proposed firing of Ed Medlin. Compared to his suburban Atlanta high school, he felt Emory had done a lot to resolve racial tensions. Now it was being attacked, "like we're this incredibly racist place with the KKK running around and rednecks burning crosses." It offended his sense of loyalty.

No time to hate In the midst of these tensions an organizational alternative to SARI emerged called No Time to Hate. The International Students Association initiated it by enlisting other campus clubs to staff tables and to ask fellow students to pledge personal steps toward greater campus racial understanding. The pledge they distributed offered various possibilities for action. It included highly individual ones: "Read a book by an author with a cultural background different from my own"; "Attend minority student programs"; "Say no to friends when they make jokes based on isms." It suggested that students support changes in university policies similar to those advocated by SARI, but that avoided controversial quotas and carried no threat of collective protest. "Write to the administration," the pledge suggested. "Encourage them to hire more minority faculty. Organize hall meetings. Write articles in *The Wheel*. Challenge professors to incorporate diverse cultural viewpoints in their classrooms."

No Time to Hate required neither agreement on specific programs nor clear-cut political commitments. It was easy for campus groups to come up to their table in front of the DUC, and add their names to a large board to show that they cared. The Chess Club, Fencing Club, Spanish Club, Volunteer Emory, Waging Peace, College Republicans, Hillel, Mortar Board, Chinese Students Association, most sororities, and a few of the fraternities—one by one they wrote their names on green paper triangles, then pasted them together into a pyramid of support. Volunteers handed out green cloth armbands as well, and hailed passing students.

"We're *just* asking you to sign this pledge," explained members of the rotating groups who staffed the table. "These are *just* some suggestions we're asking people to try and do." At times the participating students so muted their voices that they virtually stripped their efforts of content. Nevertheless, some students thought wearing an armband was still "too emotional" or explained, "I don't have to prove anything to anyone."

Some participants in No Time to Hate, like African graduate students from Kenya and Nigeria, or members of the environmental group, Students Involved in Resources and the Environment (SIRE), had been involved in the SARI marches. They held lengthy discussions with passing students, but often hit the wall of mistrust that had continued to grow. "We found ourselves stressing, 'This has nothing to do with the demands,'" said a gay activist who cochaired Emory's Human Relations Committee. "I hated myself for saying that."

Other students, less involved, wanted to help and were glad to do something, but remained essentially untouched by this mildest of steps into the world of public issues. They stressed, in the words of a member of the Kiwanis affiliate Circle K, that "learning not to hate is an individual thing."

No Time to Hate emerged shortly before the end of term, leaving students only a week to wear their armbands. The effort's ultimate impact remained unclear. But it offered a way for students rebuffed by SARI's approach to begin to engage campus racial issues. It called people to discussion and concern. By suggesting students had many ways to act, it left fewer excuses for passivity.

What does a college student look like? How did apolitical students treat the racial incident and the varying responses? Initially, most reacted sympathetically towards Mona's personal situation, then resisted SARI's broader demands. "I don't like it when they raise stuff from the past," said Pauline, a student from Maine. "My generation didn't have anything to do with that. All of a sudden I'm a minority because I'm a white person, and they say I have to take an African-American studies course. Why not an Asian course? Why not French or Russian, which is what I am? The demands never took account of my ideas."

"I don't see this as a racist campus," agreed Pauline's boyfriend, John, who sat with her and two other friends, studying in the DUC. "Lots of us went to Forsythe County to march against blacks being excluded. My whole dorm came home after chemistry finals and watched the Cosby show. I have both white friends and black friends. I'm Chinese, but nobody calls me Chink."

Black students griped far too much, repeated Pauline, as in the case of the accused rapist Lonnie, whom she knew from the dorms. She had once seen his girlfriend's face "all beaten up after a fight. But if I say anything I'll be labeled a racist. I'm not a big feminist, but when I see Lonnie beating up his girlfriend . . ."

Yet even her friends were split. "I agree with Pauline and John on a lot of counts," said a student named Sean, "but while a lot of the black students have overreacted, I think there's been an underreaction by the white population. It's hard to only be 7 percent of the campus."

"I get my book bag torn apart every time I come out of the library, said Pauline. "I don't think they get any different treatment. If the cops see someone who doesn't look like a college student, of course they're going to ask them for ID."

"But what does a college student look like?" asked Sean.

"Like you and me," said Pauline.

"But we're white," said Sean.

"I guess that's true," admitted Pauline. "Maybe," she said, "it's how certain black students look. Maybe it's more of a problem than I'd thought."

Pauline agreed that some changes were necessary, said she'd signed her name to the No Time to Hate petitions and might have even worn the armband had the group not run out of them. She wouldn't mind some multicultural course requirements, so long as she could choose from different options: "Going out in the business world, you have to work with people of different races. Maybe if you learn it when you're young it's easier. But I'm poor, too. I work twenty or twenty-five hours a week for books and food. I just don't think they should be catered to."

Students often resisted involvement with campus racial issues for the same reasons they distanced themselves from politics in general. "People come in with certain beliefs," said an Emory marketing major. "Things aren't about to change just because some students march. Rape isn't going to change, and neither will racism." The Colby student who announced he'd "probably go talk to the CIA next year [and] have to step over fourteen people lying on the stairs," also bridled at students or administrators "pushing views all over everybody on race." His choices were his business, he insisted. No one had the right to constrain them.

"I don't want to be swallowed up by the mob psychology of rallies, to lose my individual identity," said an Emory biology major. He criticized career-obsessed students "like all the cutthroat premeds and prelaws who don't care about anything but what they can get on their LSATs or running for fraternity office because it will look good on their résumé." But he also believed black students were, in this case, "crying wolf, trivializing racism by always screaming, so when there is real racism, who's going to listen?" He said he didn't want to align himself with demands he was unsure of. Then he paused for a moment and reconsidered: "SARI is a radical fringe, but I do see the protests as worthwhile. They raise our consciousness. They make people think. That we're talking now suggests they have some educational value."

Wrestling with our soul   The attempts of Emory students to deal with these issues came during the end-of-term crunch. Even the most politically committed kept peeling off to the library and to computer labs, interspersing marches and meetings with all-night sessions to finish overdue papers. Their efforts consequently eased off with no dramatic culmination, fueling some modest specific changes and speeding initiatives already in progress. The university would finally get a multicultural center, initially housed in one of the dorms. A companion center for curricular enrichment would help professors bring diverse cultural perspectives into their classrooms. A new fellowship program would bring in national and local African-American leaders to teach courses and meet with the campus community informally, and efforts would increase to recruit more black faculty and students. Multicultural sensitivity sessions would be held for a variety of employees including the campus police and student workers at the gym and library. Upcoming freshman seminars would focus on the politics of racial and sexual difference, with additional programs on these issues to be held in fraternities, sororities, and dorms.

The import of these changes would be felt over time. On an immediate level, the protests impelled numerous professors to explore racial issues in their courses. Although No Time to Hate quickly ran out of green armbands, their presence spurred talk campuswide. Emory's new, student-run Human Relations Committee sponsored a series of informal discussions in dorm lounges, and others developed spontaneously. Even critical exchanges bore fruit, as students began, however awkwardly, to bridge racial divides, to talk about what separated them and might bring them together. A leader of the Korean students worked to shift her organization from a social club to one that focused on larger issues, such as Emory's dearth of Asian studies. Critics might denigrate all this as mere therapeutic venting, but the issues raised enriched the university.

In a conversation shortly before I left, Emory University President James Laney agreed that the protests raised important issues. We sparred briefly over how much

SARI represented Emory's black community, and why—given widespread student support—Laney didn't initiate a multicultural requirement. Laney told me such issues would be dealt with in the required freshman seminars and through the new faculty resource center. He also believed Emory already had enough requirements and said curriculum was faculty turf, which he wasn't about to invade.

But he acknowledged that changes needed to be made and seemed genuinely hurt by student charges of institutional racism. Just as SARI stressed the twenty-year lineage of their demands, so Laney explained that "the university was already in the middle of a long line of things that had been going on and were being developed, and so our response was not just to start pulling ideas and new moves out of the air as a kind of appeasement or stopgap measure—but rather to reaffirm what we were already doing, to strengthen what we could do better, and in some cases to announce a couple of new initiatives." Black undergraduate enrollment, he said, had increased by 50 percent just during the past five years. Students didn't give enough credit for progress already made.[21]

I could see how campus activists might mistrust Laney's charm. But his stance seemed preferable to the icy condescension of administrators at universities like Columbia, whose trustees refused even to meet with student antiapartheid leaders, where the dean of Columbia College dismissed a one-day sit-in on racial issues as "an act of supreme selfishness," and where President Michael Sovern did not even return the calls of the student paper after bringing police on campus to arrest the protestors.[22]

Laney thought the marches had helped bring serious issues to common attention. For all its tragedy, he believed the Mona Daniels crisis had forced "a sense of reassessment" on the university, had changed both the institution and his own role for the better. The only comparable time he could remember was during Nixon's invasion of Cambodia; he had been a dean at Emory then and had had no choice but to respond. He wished the Emory community had not experienced its recent sadness and trauma. "But it brought me out of a cloistered office into a situation where I had no choice but to talk with the students, the faculty, and the staff as an educator, and not just an administrator. It gave everybody in the community a chance to reassess how we want to relate to each other and what kind of community we want to be." Laney wanted Emory to catch up on these issues, "to be more deliberative, and not always just reactive. It has energized me to see us wrestling with our soul."

Trust and betrayal   Three months after Mona Daniels first reported her room being broken into, reports by the campus and DeKalb County police and by the Georgia Bureau of Investigation suggested the entire series of events was a hoax. A combination of direct and circumstantial evidence, they said, linked Mona with the threatening letters and racial slurs. Mona's lawyer continued to insist that she was an innocent victim. But if the consensus was right, then Mona had fabricated the attack.[23]

We may never know precisely what occurred. When these revelations broke, they seemed to call into question all the complex lessons of how Emory's students had responded to the original incident and the history that surrounded it. I felt the ground I was exploring had crumbled beneath my feet. The entire narrative of how students acted and reacted seemed tainted.

But as I continued to travel from school to school, the same racial tensions continued to surface. Minority students voiced the same frustrations and complaints. White students voiced the same ambivalent concern, bought into the same myths that said you could strip away historical contexts and still understand people's lives. Students of varied cultural and historical identities began working to similarly change their institutions.

Mona's story may be a cautionary one, to remind us that humans of all races and backgrounds can lie to themselves and lie to others. And that even stories illustrating causes we believe in may turn out false. Her fabrication hurt the Emory movement, built resistance to dealing with these issues, and fed interracial mistrust. Yet other racial harassment has unquestionably occurred again and again, at colleges nationwide. Mona's fabrications do not erase the sense of marginalization that students like Marvin and even Sonya felt long before she made her first claims. The more I thought about the situation and talked with those closest at hand, the more the particulars of her case seemed almost tangential to the larger issues raised in its wake. Although the merit of her charges will never be finally resolved, America's most pervasive assaults on human dignity cannot be remedied by merely tracing, as Sonya Tinsley said, "who wrote what in someone's room."

The events left a contradictory legacy. Whatever the particulars of Mona's case, the school still faced, in the judgment of associate chaplain Bobbi Patterson, "the same challenge of how to build a more inclusive community." Most in the movement, as Sonya said, "always felt the issue was much more than the individual case of Mona Daniels. Rather we looked at the divisiveness between different cultural and ethnic communities. The consistent lack of trust. The fact that people never talked to each other. The need to bring different voices into the curriculum, and learn respect for people from different backgrounds. The incident was believable for us because ones like it have occurred. None of us were shocked. It's just that it didn't happen. I feel sad for Mona personally. Most of us feel sorry for her. She obviously needed help and I hope she's getting it. But people who got so obsessed with her individual mental state missed the point."

As a result of student involvement, Emory changed. The multicultural center opened up the following fall, as did a new gay and lesbian center, and later one for women's issues. Training sessions for residence hall advisors began to take seriously issues of race, gender, and cultural awareness. Faculty and students continued to debate the role of African-American studies and larger curricular changes. Most students talked surprisingly little about the incident when they returned to school, but addressed racial issues more than they had. New dialogue continued to take place.

Sixteen

The world of Communities of **the activists** concern

On campus or off, social change is difficult. Even with issues whose moral and political urgency seems obvious, fellow students hang back. Faculty seem too wrapped up in academic specialities to offer much help. College administrations seem hidebound and unyielding. It's easy, in this context, for concerned students to consume themselves with anger at those who do not instantly leap to join them, or to damn themselves for not succeeding more fully.

"I'm a political science major," said an Ohio Wesleyan student who'd been profoundly moved by an intercollegiate trip to Haiti. "But most of my professors tried to talk me out of going. They said I was crazy and was going to get killed. Why didn't I go to Europe, like the rest of the kids. Of course they thought it was noble, and maybe they worried for my safety. But I wanted to see the situation firsthand so I would be credible. They're supposed to be educated professors, interested in seeking the truth. But all they did was discourage me." She got the same reaction, she said, regarding a later trip to Central America. Without her mother's strong support, she'd probably have backed out.

Activists often become frustrated with the political detachment of fellow students. "Maybe it's that I've only been here one semester," reflected a Colby student. "But I keep looking around for people to talk with about certain things. Even on issues like homosexuality or women's rights, they just turn me off, like 'Why do you want to talk about that?' And to me, these are easy issues to understand compared to nuclear weapons or the contras. I mean they're important and I'm interested in them. But it doesn't seem like they should be so difficult to talk about. Some people just don't want to discuss anything that's bothersome."

Frustration often accompanies increased concern. Engaged students want others to match their passion, but instead meet disinterest or hostility. They get branded as the designated idealists, "like we're so great and noble, but no one else wants to help." They get mired in the mundane: sending out endless rounds of mailings; writing meeting announcements a hundred times on classroom blackboards; waiting in line again and again to run off leaflets at the campus print shop. "I can't hold it all up on my own," said a Fairfield student involved with Results, the national hunger action network. "It should be common sense to take care of the world you live in, and make sure everyone has enough to eat. I jumped in figuring I could move very quickly, and maybe I was too impatient. Now I've pulled away. I had to stop. I couldn't do any more."

"It's tiring to work so hard," an Emory environmental activist confessed, "then see the same people over and over again." "Sometimes you want to talk to someone else besides the same ten people every meeting, every quarter, every year," said a Chicago Circle woman. Then she paused. "It's not quite that bad," she said. "We have forty or fifty good people, almost a hundred from the different coalitions. I just wish it were more."

Now I have to do something   In the face of inevitable frustrations, students sustain involvement through community, through sharing beliefs and concerns, hopes and disappointments, with others of kindred spirit. Political community differs from ordinary friendship in its explicit goals of social change. Active students spend time together because they enjoy each other's company, but also to respond to particular crises or challenges. They draw on their newfound community not just to get by, and sustain their everyday lives, but, as sociologist Richard Flacks points out, to "make history," to change the terms under which their lives or the lives of others will proceed.[1]

Yet taking on social causes separates students from their peers. Whether they work for racial justice, or a sustainable environment, or to stop unjust wars or save family farms, new urgencies shape their lives. Most of their fellow students do not share these same priorities, or feel they can do little about them. Politically active students must therefore nurture their bonds with others who share their vision—even as they work to reach out to individuals as yet uninvolved. How they handle the tension between the two will have much to do with both the success or failure of their efforts, and with whether they can continue past their first heat of engagement.

How does political involvement shift community? Fred Azcarate, USSA's first Asian-American president and a mentor to Julius Davis, radically changed his friendship circle when he got involved in SUNY Binghamton's divestment movement. "I was a sophomore still living in the dorm," he told me. "I had my friends from freshman year, who were mostly athletes. Then I got a whole new group of political friends. I tried to get my old group to go to the rallies or meetings, but they'd say no. Then I'd go off with the other people. Involvement consumes all your free time because you're constantly going to meetings and making phone calls. I tried to budget my time, spending a certain amount with each group, then ended up dropping most of my old drinking buddies. It's easier to socialize with people you hang out with."

Fred, who was Filipino, grew up in a mostly white middle-class Long Island neighborhood. His father was an accountant, his mother a nurse. But Fred also spent a great deal of time with his godparents, one of whom worked in a garment sweatshop and the other as a steelworker. "I'd go with my godfather to pick up my godmother where she worked, and think, it's terrible that she has to work under those conditions. It gave me a sense of a need to change things." In 1983, Fred started at Binghamton, intending to get an education, have a good time, and graduate into law school or a corporate job. He'd been a high school debater, which helped him develop persuasive skills, but left him detached from the issues he discussed. He first got politically involved when some people in his dorm invited him to a campus meeting opposing new tuition hikes. Fred ended up running for student government, got elected student body president, and helped pull together a one-day boycott of the campus facilities of the Marriott Corporation, which ran the campus food service and also invested heavily in South Africa. The boycott was part of a successful national pressure campaign: Marriott eventually pulled out of South Africa and disinvested. Fred also worked on reforming the curriculum, helped organize an Asian Student Union, and joined others in the New York state student association, SASU, to beat back a round of tuition raises.

Shifts in communities can strain long-standing relationships. When Fred mentioned his activities to his family, they felt some initial consternation, though his godparents supported him from the start. "They worked hard their whole lives to help me go to school," he said of his mother and father. "They worried that my being an activist meant taking a vow of poverty for life, which is partially true. The first time I got arrested, protesting tuition hikes at SUNY's Albany headquarters, I didn't tell them until Christmas, six months later, when I was visiting. They were confused. They didn't know how to react. It was so out of the realm of their experience that you can do this and still graduate, get a job and be self-sufficient, not screw up the rest of your life."

Fred now worked for Citizen Action, a national network of grassroots community groups, and his parents had become more accepting. "They understand why it's important to organize and work together. I'm also more respectable, working on political campaigns. My father was a mayor of his village. He can understand when I work for local candidates."

Values of involvement bring a sense of responsibility, a judgment, as Sonya Tinsley put it, "that what I did had to be for more than just myself." Jean Besanceney recalled "learning constantly, like about our attacks on Nicaragua," and wanting "to do something with that knowledge." "I felt like I had a duty to the black men and women at Emory," said Marvin Coleman, after organizing a campus NAACP chapter when he was a junior, the year after the Mona Daniels incident.

"Before I got involved," remembered a University of Washington English major, "life seemed more on an even keel, just going along. Now I have different ups and downs, like when someone I know or know about is arrested or tortured in El Salvador. I need to leave time for myself, but can't help having these huge fluctuations. It's more than the time commitment. My head and heart are involved, so I can't pull away from it. But I also feel much more alive now, instead of just watching everything go by."

A sense of linked fates had pulled these students in to begin with. They gradually began to feel their concern less as a life-changing revelation and more as a constant tug of awareness. Causes and issues that, as Matt Greene put it, they once regarded "with just about total incomprehension," now become central to their lives. They wanted to find others who share their new understandings, as when Marvin Coleman explained, "I wish I could surround myself with more people who aren't afraid to speak out in class and say, 'No, slaves didn't enjoy their trip to America.'" Or when Leah Fintel from the FACTS group described her switch from listening to Minnesota agricultural policy analyst Mark Ritchie and thinking "I don't understand this. It's a nice day. I want to be outside," to considering Ritchie one of her heroes and feeling she "could listen forever."

Given the multitude of crises, how do newly concerned students decide which to take on, so that they don't burn out and give up? "You come in as a freshman," explained the student coordinator of Emory's volunteer center, "and say you weren't terribly politically active in high school, like you studied and did band and maybe a sport. Now you come here and people are thrusting a new issue at you every week. You can't suddenly become Joe Cool, veteran recycler, volunteer, racial mediator, and everything else all at once. You have to decide where your commitments will be."

This isn't the Perfect Standard. These students recognize numerous uncertainties, then act nonetheless. They juggle priorities as best they can, and take on issues that most compel them, or ones where peers seem ready to move. They switch from one to another, trying to raise common themes.

As a result of these new concerns, politically active students often anticipate a different professional community. They shift their academic path, seeking to learn more about the issues they take on, and more about how to act and act effectively. Yet they still need to survive financially, and meet the regular demands of school. Most, therefore, are even more pressed for time than students who feel no need to change the world. Barb Meister worked sixteen to twenty hours a week in the Nebraska student union. Marvin worked at Emory's media center. A twenty-three-year-old Denver student juggled tests, papers, outside work, and time with her three-year-old son, while getting through Metro State on an ever-escalating series of loans and helping to run the school's volunteer center. "They think we activists have all the time in the world," said a woman active at Seattle University. "It's not as if we don't have to work too, or have to study or have to worry about where we'll find the money to get through."

This pressure feeds students' broader uncertainties about where their path will leave them. A North Dakota woman told me her parents considered her peace studies major "about as useful as trying to get a doctorate in how to set up literature tables." Most resolve to live modestly and hope that their developing skills of speaking, writing, critical thinking, and organizing will let them both make a social contribution and support an ordinary life. Others follow more pragmatic careers: medicine, law, or computer science. They do so not just to adapt, but from a genuine passion, while squeezing in courses that deal with social and political issues, and pushing their technical classes to explore the moral choices they'll confront in their fields.

The beleaguered white guys Students often define their political voices through specific racial, sexual and cultural identities. I've described ways African-American students worked to make their campuses respond to general visions of equity and inclusion, but also to make them more hospitable for their often marginalized communities. Chicago Circle's Cintron Center offered a haven where Raul Ortiz hoped that Latino students could "become more like a family . . . get everyone on campus involved." Focusing on these identities offers both a necessary sanctuary and the potential trap of isolation from those of different backgrounds or experiences.

We see the mixed impact of identity politics in a growing political gap between college men and women. In the late 1960s and early 1970s male and female students described themselves in relatively similar political terms, with men often slightly more liberal. Recently, college women have become increasingly more involved than the men, and more liberal on just about every issue. This began to shift with the rebirth of feminism. As I've described, both male and female students dropped away from social involvement during the early to mid-seventies. But men became considerably more apolitical and conservative. In 1971, male liberals outnumbered male conservatives in the national freshmen surveys by a twenty-four-point margin. By 1981 self-identified conservatives led by five points. More men have continued to call themselves conservative than liberal in every survey since.

College women also dropped from the 1960s heights of social concern, but their beliefs rebounded more quickly. They too began the seventies far more liberal than conservative, by a twenty-point margin. By 1981, this margin had dropped to just three percentage points, or almost dead even. But it still left the women eight percentage points to the left of the now more conservative college men, and this gender gap would grow even as both men and women became more politically involved. By 1993, 30 percent of freshman women considered themselves liberal and 18 percent conservative, a gap of nearly two to one, with the balance saying they were middle of the road. For men, conservatives led by a 29 to 23 percent majority. The difference between men and women was a staggering 18 points.[2]

Terms like "liberal" and "conservative" carry contested definitions, open to clashing interpretations. Yet these differences in student self-identifications mark real political gender gaps. National studies of college seniors suggest these gaps persist as students make their way through school, even as both sexes become slightly more liberal. College men look even more conservative when we exclude the considerably more liberal male minority students (and as the student gay movement has become more active, male gays). In the 1992 election, young voters had the highest gender gap in the population. Whether in who they vote for, what they believe, or their participation in campus political movements, female students have moved significantly to the left of the men.[3]

In her book *Feminist Fatale: Young Women and Feminism*, 1989 University of Illinois graduate Paula Kamen suggests that apolitical women stigmatize feminism in much the same terms they do other kinds of political engagement. I've mentioned a 1989 poll in which female undergraduates consistently endorsed feminist issues, yet only 16 percent of those asked were willing to apply the label to themselves. Still, feminist perspectives have maintained a diffuse cultural presence, even during the era that writer Susan Faludi aptly calls a time of backlash. Even apolitical female students feel vulnerable to sexual violence and harassment, frustrated by the absence of women's voices in the curriculum, more personally threatened by right-to-life crusaders, and angered that women earn 69 percent of the earnings of male peers. A 1987 survey of six thousand students on thirty-two campuses found that one in six female students reported being the victim of rape or attempted rape in the preceding year.[4]

The feminist movement gives young women a continuing model for involvement. For all that many resist the label, it offers a larger context in which to view injuries and insults they might otherwise regard as purely personal. Feminist classes encourage them to place their specific gender experiences in a larger social framework. A woman from Miami Univeristy of Ohio felt "a breath of fresh air" every time she went into the University Women's Center or attended a meeting of the peace group—most students persistently avoided such issues. Many begin to view their politics, in the words of a Mount Holyoke student, as coming out of "knowing who you are."[5]

Activist male students, whether Matt Greene of Greeks for Peace or Marvin Coleman from Emory, generally welcome the shifts toward equality. They experience, in the words of a Columbia antiapartheid activist, "a sense of partnership, a belief that people should have a voice in decisions that affect them, an egalitarian sense that you carry into other spheres of your life." Feminist perspectives become an explicit part of their vision.

But the same movement that stirs young women's social concern and sense of community can feel like a threat to college men. Apolitical men often view discussion of date rape and sexual harassment as a challenge to codes, assumptions, and ways of acting they've long accepted without thought. They feel far more threatened than equally apolitical women by homosexuality. Forty-eight percent of 1993 freshman men believe homosexual acts should be prohibited (down from 58 percent in 1985), versus 28 percent of the women. Dissidents are readily branded as being unmanly, as when the Fairfield dorm group called would-be Peace Corps volunteer Rick Vincent "Nadia," after the female gymnast Nadia Comaneci, or teased him about not having a football team. Men worry about female challenges to their already uncertain career chances.[6]

Economic pressures hit young white men particularly in their anticipated roles as breadwinners. In the boom years of the Reagan myth, many identified with those at the top, and viewed themselves as inheriting their mantle. Machismo used to be about physical strength, suggested Paul Vigna of the Fairfield group, "beating the shit out of someone in a fight, or driving a muscle car like a Camaro or Oldsmobile 442. For the men I went to school with, fists aren't power, money is power, like making six figures. How much buying power you have, how much control over other people. The kind of clothes you wear and the expensive foreign car you drive. Not being afraid to come off a cold bastard. Students looked up to Milken and Boesky because they were real men."

To not publicly espouse this, Paul said, was to leave yourself vulnerable, like Rick Vincent. "Everyone assumed he was gay, which he wasn't. But he wore a bleeding heart on his sleeve. He'd say he didn't want success and would never kill anyone regardless of the circumstances. At our school, to say that was to come off as a liberal fag. A commie pussy wussy. Women don't have to put up with that."

The downside of six-figure dreams was economic fear, which fed its own conservatism. While young women hoped new opportunities would continue expanding, young men often worried that women and minorities were taking their jobs, scholarships, and slots in law school and medical school. The more women achieved, the more many men felt threatened. "It made some guys angry," said Fairfield's Tim Lovejoy, "losing your power, your hold. You feel you have to compete with guys and women now, not just guys. It's not just a man's world any more."

Economic concerns also hit college women. They had their own six-figure dreamers as well as a far larger group concerned about just getting by. But their efforts to achieve often led them to challenge traditional expectations of what they should and should not be able to do. They mistrusted conservative rhetoric that granted them full acceptance only as mothers and wives. This was true, for instance, in Dale Ottiger's household. His own conservative views matched "the Christian family values that I grew up with." Dale's siblings subscribed to them as well. But his sister was distinctly more liberal than the rest, in part, Dale guessed, because she'd had to overcome constant teasing and derision from his older brothers while she became a star athlete and went on to establish a successful physical therapy business. "They always gave her grief on her ability to achieve."

For all the obstacles placed in their path, young women have many more visible models for social engagement. Emory's Sonya Tinsley remembered growing up admiring women like Gloria Steinem and Alice Walker. "My friends and I were very conscious of a lot of older feminist women we respected. We didn't feel they'd screwed up. We identified with them and wanted to join them." Even when Sonya looked at famous women from the past, they were often feminists because they had to be to buck the odds.

Young men, Sonya thought, had few comparable socially engaged role models. "They had to feel more like rebels and renegades." She knew of lots of famous sports figures, actors like Arnold Schwarzenegger, and speculators like Donald Trump, but few visible current examples of men who spent their lives fighting for high ideals.

This generation of men has, in fact, been specifically targeted by cultural messages that equate empathy with weakness, that support macho posturing by political leaders, and that link the political and individual use of force with the validation of manhood. They grow up playing with toys tied into annihilatory cartoons, and listen to pop songs that often offer much of value and strength, but that at times enshrine rape and killing in endless revenge fantasies. As fifteen- to twenty-five-year-old males have become the major movie-going audience, studios have continually escalated graphic on-screen violence. In films from Stallone and Schwarzenegger street westerns to slasher films in which predators slice up victim after victim—often young women in explicitly sexual roles—the killing in these films dwarfs that in John Wayne or even Sam Peckinpah predecessors. As University of Washington women's studies chair Susan Jeffords points out, action adventure films let young men identify with individuals who ignore the bureaucratic rules and win. Because of affirmative action, civil rights laws, cultural pressures toward civility, and the endless paperwork they have to deal with in school, "they feel constrained in actions they can take and choices they can make. They see Mel Gibson on the screen saying 'I don't have to read you your Miranda rights' They see the hero succeed because he defies these constraints, flaunts the legal and legislative regulations."[7]

Women may go to these films, dragged along by their boyfriends and shutting their eyes when necessary. But it's young men who take ownership of the experience, who withstand barrages of gore to prove they are tough and fazed by nothing. As Tim Lovejoy recalled about his days watching Rambo movies, they "picture the dominant indestructible male, where to have the power is the central focus. You go against the odds, defeat all your enemies. Maybe they give us delusions of grandeur."

Finally, young white men feel beleaguered. They speak in anger about how they're damned for the sins of their fathers, for age-old social inequalities that they did not create. "It's not my fault," they explain. "i didn't do this. How come men get such a bad rap?" Some of this is a reluctance to view themselves as anything other than lone individuals who "make their own chances," a reluctance to acknowledge how America's pervasive inequalities continue to shape their opportunities and aspirations. Women and minorities are more likely to recognize such broader contexts, if only because they've come up against the impact of inequality on their lives. "If you're part of the dominant group," suggested Sonya Tinsley, "you're used to being identified as an individual."

But men also voice a sense that the prevailing campus politics ignores their concerns, which include precarious economic times that leave them wondering if they can still fulfill traditional breadwinner roles, shifting sexual mores that leave them uncertain as to appropriate expectations and responses, and the difficult passages to independent adulthood that are no easier for them than for men growing up when *Catcher in the Rye* became a staple of an earlier generation. "Lots of them are aware of the issues, trying to find their way in the midst of them," said Susan Jeffords. "Then they feel they hit this brick wall that says 'you're a man and you're bad in spite of the struggles you're making to understand these issues. A lot have vocalized a sense of being blamed."

Sonya agreed. "It's so easy to feel ashamed of being a man, that every other man who existed is bad, and you're identified with that. There's a friend of mine, Anthony, who I always give stuff to read, and I wanted to show him a new book by John Stoltenberg called *The End of Manhood.* It had some interesting essays, but I thought about the title and realized there's no way Anthony's ever going to read this. It's not exactly appealing to the average guy."

"If people are given the sense that they're innately wrong," she went on, "that's a problem. I don't feel the majority of the feminist movement does this. But if you're given the impression that you're innately and genetically part of the problem, why bother to change? What incentive do you have?"

Even when campus activists don't stereotype them as generic white males with nothing to say, it's easy for male students to project legitimate uncertainties about their futures on the restless women and minorities whom conservative politicians, intellectuals, and media spokesmen constantly scapegoat for America's ills. Where women or minorities share a sense of being institutionally marginalized, young white men often feel just confused. Even many generally sympathetic to social change remain unclear as to how they personally fit in.

I don't want to overemphasize the differences. Both male and female students hit similar barriers to involvement, although men are more likely to bait those who act and women more likely to explain, "I should be more involved but I'm not." Both sexes sharply dropped their level of political engagement with the collapse of the movements of the sixties, then have begun to turn more recently toward greater involvement. Both have become increasingly liberal on important issues. But the gender gaps remain. While college women continue to move to the left, a significant group of men now view social change with resentment and hostility.

Activist identity   Let's return to how feminism changes women's priorities. Today's young women often first encounter feminist currents scattered through American pop culture. In third or fourth grade, Sonya Tinsley stumbled onto Marlo Thomas's book of feminist children's stories, *Free to Be You and Me,* at her local library. "I'd take out twelve books at once, and I'd always get that one. I checked it out again and again, so many times they should have given it to me. Marlo Thomas also had a TV show *That Girl,* and I watched it and *Mary Tyler Moore* and all these things that were sort of the soft feminism of the time, though I might not see them as all that feminist now. I remember this one commercial for Charlie cologne that really impressed me when I was about six. It was called 'The Charlie Girl,' and showed this independent woman in a pantsuit, a tie, and a little cocked hat who goes into a bar by herself. She sees a man she knows and spins him around in a brief embrace. I think she takes a sip from his drink. Then she strides off with her briefcase, happy and spirited. I was so impressed by that commercial. It made me feel I could do anything I ever wanted."

By the time she went to college, Sonya included feminist issues in the roster she took on. "But feminism is such an intimate movement, it's not just about what happens in the legislature, but about what you do, how you comb your hair, what happens in the bedroom and before the bathroom mirror, how you're going to raise your kids. I have to ask about every choice I make, Am I doing this because I'm socialized, or because I want to? Am I in a particular relationship because I've been taught I should be, or because it's a relationship I value? When I dress in a traditionally feminine manner, maybe it perpetuates some things that aren't good, like a world where people are judged by appearances. Thinking about these things brings up lots of questions, but I'd rather agonize over them than not know they exist."

Barb Meister broke beyond traditional gender roles from an early age. For all the sexual hierarchy of their local Catholic church, Barb's parents raised her and her three sisters with every bit the same high expectations as the five boys. Where political involvement changed Barb's view of gender roles was in recognizing how routinely women's voices were excluded. She remembered "a statewide meeting of about sixty farm activists where people went around the room introducing themselves. One of the farmers got up and said 'My name is so-and-so, I farm 350 acres of corn and 250 acres of beans, and these are the organizations I'm involved with. And this is my wife.' He just pointed to her. He didn't even say her name, which just typifies how farm wives are always there and maybe doing half the work or more, but never get the credit or recognition. It's hard because just about all the farm organizations are headed by men. There'd never been a female state secretary of agriculture anywhere in the country until a woman finally got elected recently in North Dakota. I'm much more attentive to that stuff than I used to be."

Politically involved women from conservative backgrounds faced greater reassessments of their expectations and perceptions. Jean Besanceney began to notice day-to-day life in a different way. "Just small things, like being aware that women tend to be quieter in mixed groups. That they generally don't speak out and don't project their voice. I try to do that even though my tendency is to be more shy and quiet. Because of feminism, I'll take that extra step to break the stereotype."

We shouldn't have Just as feminist visions of involvement are **to be invisible** rooted in women's particular experience, so gay and lesbian students defend their right to declare who they are without being attacked, excluded, or defamed. At most campuses, hostile students routinely tear down or deface posters for their events. Gay men living in the dorms are repeatedly harassed with menacing phone calls, and messages like "Die Fags" and "Queers Get Out" are written on their doors. Western Michigan's Alliance for Gay and Lesbian Rights had its office broken into six times in a single year. Gay groups at some schools even feel compelled to meet off campus, so members cannot be identified unless they choose to be.

Many straight students do accept their gay and lesbian classmates. In 1990, the University of Minnesota elected as student body president a highly articulate and openly gay woman, who even got the fraternity system endorsement on the way to an overwhelming victory. But gay students face constant insults and threats. When they do act, responding to these attacks and to crises like AIDS, they can hardly do otherwise than speak from their particular situations and needs. A University of North Dakota gay activist made presentations on homosexuality to the Interfraternity Council, explaining, "We want to be able to express our affection without physical fear. We want to see the lives of people like us represented in the curriculum. We want the same privileges as every other student." "It's a sense," said a Chicago Circle gay woman, "that you'd better acknowledge my right to exist and you'd better not interfere with me." In the judgment of Shelley Cramer, USSA staff organizer on gay and women's issues, young gays were "moving away from a past trend toward assimilation. Instead we want recognition that we're human beings living on the earth, and we shouldn't have to melt in and be invisible."

Some force that really cares Active students also create communities through shared intellectual and cultural traditions. In the words of Julia Scatliff, the head of the student community service group COOL, "You realize that your thoughts have changed, the music that you listen to has changed, you're reading different books, getting to know different people, dreaming different dreams at night . . . all because of who you're working with."

The adapters read mostly what's assigned for their tests and papers. Except for a few, like Columbia's Carolyn Lowenthal, who are genuinely fascinated with scholarly inquiry, reading seems to have little effect on their lives. Because of their involvements, the activists have even less time to read books unrelated to their coursework. But they also need intellectual scaffolding for their efforts, so strive to take classes and read outside works consistent with their passions. Jean and Matt read Noam Chomsky on American foreign policy. The FACTS group researched the political economy of farming. Marvin Coleman and Julius Davis read Malcolm X and Carter Woodson's 1933 classic, *Miseducation of the Negro*. Students studied activist campus predecessors through works like Todd Gitlin's *The Sixties*. They drew on political fiction to grapple with the emotional context of involvement, like novels by Alice Walker and Toni Morrison. They consistently sought models for commitment.

Contrary to media stereotypes, students most politically involved have been touched little by the widely debated literary/philosophical theories known as deconstructionism, poststructuralism, or postmodernism. Some do read Michel Foucault's analyses of power. A few read Jacques Derrida. But active students tend to justify their actions through notions of a discernable moral order violated when humans are being bombed, tortured, or starved, or when the environment is pillaged, or when families live on the streets. They need faith that they can genuinely understand the patterns they seek to change. Critical works that stress the endless malleability of interpretation rarely provide this.

What of other cultural pulls, like the music that became such a vital countercultural force during the Vietnam era? Current student activists are less likely to take their prime political definitions from rock and roll, though for blue-collar kids with scant prospects, following bands you believe in remains a key source of identity, meaning, and faith. For some active students, music is a minor force entirely. Others drew sustenance from alternative radio or club scenes, through which pass a succession of ACT UP and animal rights activists, anarchists, and Greens. Increasingly through the period I've studied, students drawn into a culture of commitment have found music to sustain them. Bands that have fueled their visions span a range of styles—Tracy Chapman, Pearl Jam, and 10,000 Maniacs, Public Enemy and Metallica, REM, Bob Marley, radical girl bands like L7. This music helps students challenge America's prevailing directions, provides a cultural atmosphere of shared outrage at injustices, and links them with buried alternative traditions. It gives a social vision to dance to, words and images to express anger, longing, and lust; some rude public yowls to remind us that all is not well.[8]

Activist identity rarely breaks completely with the past. Rather, students layer old and new belief systems, taking up ethics of equality and human dignity they've long espoused, but beginning to hold accountable institutions they've habitually accepted. I saw this in students from strong religious traditions. "You grow up thinking of yourself as a Christian, a Catholic, being responsible for your less fortunate brothers and sisters," said Mary Raphael, the Holy Cross senior who'd moved from marches against abortion choice to issues of global peace and justice. "You don't think in terms of making the government or corporations live up to their responsibilities."

Active students who come out of liberal churches often continue to attend, whatever their personal theology, for a sense of engaged community. Others touch back on their faith for basic sustenance. Julia Kleinschmit of FACTS described the comfort of "feeling a personal link to someone or some force that really cares, and will watch out for you no matter what you do." Still others mine dissenting strains within particular religious traditions. A Colgate student explained, "I still can't stand the pretentiousness of mass, but I think the radical Catholics, like the Berrigans and Charlie Curran, are incredible. If anything would draw me back, it would be those kinds of people."

Religious ties don't always erase frustration and despair. But they offer community and a standard of right, a judgment that America's actions violate fundamental covenants when they shatter lives or despoil the earth. Religious belief can also provide a reservoir of hope when times get tough, as with the recent Fairfield graduate and peace activist who returned to New Jersey to take care of her sick mother, and explained "I just have to have a faith that things will pull through and this is worth doing for better or worse."

But such identities can also leave engaged students torn. A Chicago Circle gay activist grew up as a strong Catholic and respected her friends who were involved in peace and justice efforts through the college Newman Center. Inevitably, the church's stand on her sexual orientation distanced her. "It's an absolute difference," she said. "It can't be bargained. How can I agree that my sexuality means less than that of a married heterosexual couple, that I can't raise children or stand proudly with my lover in public. Some choices just can't be bargained."

Only good for canvassers   Given the challenges of their task, engaged students should be able to draw on older activists for a sense of continuity and perspective—and experience that can prevent their repeating the mistakes of the past. As Barb Meister said, "they need us involved or they'll lose a whole generation."

Some citizens organizations have worked closely with student groups. National farm organizations helped inspire the FACTS members, local Ann Arbor activists helped Greeks for Peace, and Atlanta community activists counseled Emory's young African-American students. The Midwest Academy joined USSA to coordinate the Grass Roots Organizing Workshops. The Nader-inspired PIRGs allowed students to walk into an office in the Student Union or just off campus, learn political skills, and immerse themselves in a culture of commitment. The American Committee on Africa played a critical role in helping student antiapartheid activists obtain visiting speakers, research corporate ties, and gain the intellectual underpinnings for their cause.

Yet most active students feel needlessly isolated from broader support. In 1989, the National Abortion Rights Action League (NARAL) set up a joint project with USSA to build a more effective student voice on abortion issues. But they made this commitment only after students and young people marched in unprecedented numbers (two thirds out of 300,000) to challenge the Supreme Court on the eve of its Webster decision limiting access to choice. They moved only after calls from students seeking ways to become involved flooded NARAL's offices in Washington, D.C. In the wake of this massive response, the organization set up a project to work with local campus groups, pulling together the names of students who had signed petitions at the march, and sending them materials to help in their efforts. NARAL also granted stipends to twenty-five student interns for several successive summers and trained them to work effectively with different campus constituencies and to register young voters. But it took the wave of student pressure to make this happen.

When North Carolina students asked the national environmental groups to help them begin what would become the immensely successful Student Environmental Action Coalition (SEAC), most were wary and skeptical. Finally Greenpeace donated a small ad in their magazine that brought in two hundred responses and successfully launched the organization. Even groups that offer youth internships have often been criticized by student participants for slotting them routinely into unchallenging grunt work, for acting, in the words of SEAC chairperson Miya Yoshitani, as if "we're only good for canvassers and signing petitions." In general, politically involved students saw older activists as too often building a dialogue aimed largely at themselves, instead of reaching out to a new generation who could join and eventually succeed them.[9]

Liberal wankers   The same havens that offer hope and respite can also become insular enclaves. They can leave politically active students with no way of recalling what it means to look on apprehensively as others march or speak out for a cause. They wall them off from fellow students who they need to reach and involve if their efforts are to succeed. "By the time you get to be a junior or senior," explained a University of Michigan friend of Jean Besanceney, "you've self-selected whom you hang out with, and don't have lots of time to spend with other people. I seriously don't know students whose politics are different from mine. I listen to their conversations in the Union, and hear them discuss whether someone's a Chi Phi or Theta Phi Rho or whatever. I listen and it doesn't make sense."

At Colgate University a peace and justice house was named after the African-American Nobel prize winner Ralph Bunche. It provided a refuge for students who felt like outsiders at a conservative, fraternity-dominated campus. But it also cut them off from their peers. Drunk fraternity men would cruise by at night singing "Let's be like the Bunchies," and throw beer bottles through the door of a coffee house that the students operated on weekends. Homophobic friends warned prospective residents, "You're going to live there? Don't bend over in the shower." Bunche members of Amnesty International deliberately moved their meeting elsewhere to avoid the stigma. Yet house residents did little to approach those outside, beyond complaining, "We're tired of dealing with all those hockey players."

Isolation can occur even when activists seek to overcome it. As Leah from the FACTS group said, "It becomes hard to relate to someone with a different level of understanding, or who hasn't been personally jolted, like what happened to most of us. Our efforts to educate people often blow them out of the water instead of painstakingly taking them along. It's almost like we have to create another organizational level for those just coming in."

It's when campus activists don't see self-isolation as a problem, don't see the need to reach out to the unconvinced, that insularity can take its worst forms. I experienced this during a 1988 visit to Columbia, three years after the university's highly successful apartheid divestment blockade. The earlier effort worked because it built on several years of patient educational efforts by its organizers. By 1988, their successors were often so tangled in their anger and frustration, so wrapped up in images of themselves as radical heroes, that many of them fulfilled every stereotype the apolitical adapters put forth.

These students faced the challenge of a draconian set of new conduct rules, imposed by Columbia's administration, that had stifling implications for students who wished to challenge university policies. Midway through the fight against the new rules, a campus group that opposed U.S.-backed attacks on Nicaragua decided that fellow activists were responding too passively. Rather than reaching out to build greater support, they took it on themselves to march chanting through campus buildings. Students who encountered them were furious, dismissing them as "fifteen people in front of Low Library yelling about absolutely nothing." Their efforts brought in no one new to help their cause. Rather, they fed their isolation, blurring the core issues at stake behind attempts to muster an image of power and threat that they had neither the numbers nor moral arguments to back up.

A few days later I attended a rally. There were a lot of chanted slogans, but there was little space for persuasive argument, although a few concerned students and faculty had powerful things to say. That evening, the coalition steering committee met in the paneled lounge of one of the dorms. Standing in front of a grand piano, a marble fireplace, and portraits of gentlemen of property, the president of the Nicaragua solidarity group, Kate, argued that Columbia's administration was so arrogant and corrupt that her group had no choice but to respond as they had. "All we can do," she said, "is harass them."

Others disagreed, arguing that such a path would only erode student support. Kate argued for further disruption. "We could go to President Sovern's house at four A.M. and chant 'No justice, no sleep' until the police come and ask us to leave. It's been done before. It's been proven successful."

"We'd better present that to the group," warned another woman. "There'll be opposition. Some people still want things done rationally."

Kate and her supporters justified their isolation through a self-fulfilling logic. Maybe their tactics were alienating. But those who disagreed, they felt, were politically untrustworthy to begin with, and probably unreachable. Given the lack of massive numbers, more moderate approaches wouldn't work. They had no choice but to raise their personal stakes of commitment.

A sociology grad student named Andy lit into Kate's arguments. She knew a lot about Nicaragua, he said, but damn little about how the Sandinistas organized for years. "They were in it for the long haul. It's childish to want a quick fix. We have to organize, not be childish."

Kate argued back, almost in tears. "Columbia isn't a representative democracy. You walk through Harlem and see how they've ruined people's lives. All they care about is money. Having rallies doesn't do anything. We don't have much time. We need action every day and we aren't doing it. People need to know we're serious, not just a bunch of liberal wankers."

One woman suggested that the coalition come up with their own rules of conduct, "so our opponents can't argue that we're just a bunch of hoodlums who don't want to take responsibility." "That's not our job," said Andy, in turn jumping down her throat. "It's one thing to say we should be accountable to the movement, and another to an illegitimate administration."

Frustration comes easily when change is slow. Activist students learn new history, new concepts, new understandings of power. Sometimes they express their ideas clumsily. It angers them when others dismiss the urgency of their cause. At times this anger enmeshes them in messianic arrogance or ineffective rage. It can make it impossible to explain what is at stake in the very issues about which they care so passionately.

At one rally, the assistant director of Columbia's Higher Education Opportunity Programs suggested those in attendance begin by reaching out from their present base. "I can see from the crowd," he said, "that you have a good core group to start with. You just have to find some common ground around which to organize. You have strength in numbers and the rightness of your cause. But you cannot afford to operate in a vacuum." He admonished those listening to avoid self-righteousness and listen closely to classmates who disagreed with them. He hoped they'd become "an intelligent creative force for bringing people together."

But they couldn't get beyond their own perceptions of injustice, couldn't explain them in terms others could understand. At a Columbia forum on fraternities and sexual harassment, the dean running the forum prohibited students from mentioning Greek letter names, Greek organizations, and specific fraternity members. He made it hard for students to cite specific examples of abuses—how friends were date-raped, parties with 150-proof grain alcohol punch and bamboo "smut huts" to which frat members steered available women, and fraternity codes that threatened members who broke solidarity to testify against their brothers. Instead, the students criticizing the fraternities reverted to long and abstract arguments on why frat men were "misogynist and prone to sexual violence," and why sororities reinforced the gender-based hierarchy, in contrast to the attempts of all-female colleges "to counteract inequities between men and women in a traditional white male patriarchal society."

I asked one speaker whether she wasn't losing her audience with her rhetoric. "If I say 'traditional white male patriarchy,' " she replied, "any reasonably progressive person should understand." Within circles of the already committed, such phrases may be a useful shorthand, although their abstraction can easily obscure the complex social patterns they refer to. But for those watching skeptically, the woman at the fraternity forum might as well have been speaking Martian. Other students talked endlessly at rallies and forums about "the bloody hands of American imperialism." America's hands have been repeatedly bloodied while intervening in other nations' destinies. Critics like historian William Appleman Williams have documented extensively our peculiar mix of democracy and empire. But the activists' very use of the term assumed their audience knew this history. The phrases became meaningful only when linked to particular stories and examples. If these links weren't drawn, the words appeared as empty rhetoric.[10]

"We forget that we aren't the whole campus," said another student working to challenge the rules. "We need more than just the declarative statements. Columbia may well be racist and sexist and classist, but simply saying the words doesn't prove anything, except to those who already believe it."

It's hard to be consistent   Even when activists speak out in the mildest manner imaginable, they often find it hard to reach beyond the core committed. They hold their rallies. They post their leaflets. They run their forums. But for all the value of these efforts, they don't easily reach students who aren't already interested.

To do this, they need to consciously approach the habitually apolitical students whom they rarely engage. It helps in this process for them to recall their own often hesitant steps toward initial involvement, and to let these recollections help drive their work, as did Greeks for Peace when they worked in the Michigan fraternity system. They need to engage with existing institutional structures, as did Columbia's initial antiapartheid group in their long-term effort of discussions, referendums, and endorsements—even as they continued to hold rallies and forums and moved toward their hunger strike and blockade. Students need to enter the day-to-day environments of their school, as did Barb and Julia when they took family farm issues into the heart of the University of Nebraska school of agriculture. They need, as one activist said, "to consciously explain things to those students just coming in."

The shift to commitment can feel dislocating. Causes that now burn at the center of your life remain distant or incomprehensible to peers who've not shared your experience. "I find it frustrating when people don't want to hear what you have to say," explained a woman from Ohio Wesleyan, just returned from an extended Central American trip. "I don't want to hide the insights I've gained in the closet."

Some politically involved students treat this resistance as a challenge. "This is a good campus to work on," commented a Chicago Circle lesbian activist from a poor Italian family. "At some schools, like Oberlin, you put up a couple posters and draw four hundred people for a rally. Here we work as hard as we can to get thirty. I'm glad I'm here, though, because there's such a need."

But it's also easy, as Raul Ortiz put it, to get "a bad case of the disenchantments." How do active students avoid becoming so exhausted and brittle that they become ineffective or drop out? It helps to maintain personal havens apart from direct political responsibilities. Sonya sang in the gospel choir. Matt Greene of Greeks for Peace loved the craft of teaching. The FACTS members nurtured themselves each time they returned to work on the farms they fought to save.

Others find cultural sustenance in the daily rounds of play and friendship that accompany even the most serious efforts. The FACTS group interspersed the hard work of their meetings with visits to a local bar. Marvin found himself drawn into involvement by the affection and camaraderie of Black Students Association members who encouraged him as a freshman. I think of Julia from FACTS using speaking skills she'd honed in intercollegiate debate, but using them for more than "just to log rhetorical points and win these little trophies that end up in your closet."

It helps active students to set clear limits. They need to involve themselves as much as they can, but to learn to say no when a friend asks for their participation in yet another worthy project that will tip them over the edge into exhaustion and resentment. It also helps when they ease up a bit on their expectations for immediate results. "You can start out really angry at the world, angry at everything," said a Rutgers woman, "but then you slowly have to sort of channel it together. You see the compromises and you see the realities of the situation, and you say, 'I can't change the world as much as I would like to. I can't rework it completely, but this is what I can do.' "[11]

Forms of involvement vary with students' situations and cultural styles. "I still work for corporate America in the summer," explained a Williams woman. "I still wear my fancy clothes. But I also have positions I believe in. I work to make them happen. It's hard to be consistent." "In the future, I see myself as perhaps not having enough time," said a Dartmouth woman. "But this winter I told myself, 'There comes a point in your life when everybody has a spare amount of time. And when your number comes up, you owe it to the world to do what you can.' So I went to Paris and worked at Amnesty International for three months. I didn't do it to raise my goody pile or anything like that. I felt it was my responsibility. My number was up at that time. And maybe when I don't have time, I'm counting on someone else to do the same thing."

Successful political communities take advantage of differing interests and passions. The art students in Jean Besanceney's sorority hesitated to get involved with Greeks for Peace until they were asked to design fliers and banners. Then they took on the task with energy, enthusiasm, and skill. As a student from Fairfield put it, "If you're by yourself, it's easy to say the problems are just too big. If you're with a bunch of other people, maybe they aren't."

The most productive campus efforts freely acknowledge the existential absurdity of trying to change the world. I think of the Salvadoran medical student at the Greeks for Peace event, mimicking how he ran, ducked, and hid from the soldiers to survive. At a University of North Dakota student conference, a gay activist described his recent presentation for a panel on hate speech. "There was an older woman there, a state supreme court judge. She said that I should become a lawyer." "Lawyers always say that," said one of his friends. "Professors," someone added, "always think you should become a professor." "And florists," said the head of North Dakota State's environmental group, who'd worked as one, "suggest you can become a florist." A nuclear resister, there for the conference, added, deadpan, "We always say that people should go to jail."

A conservative Jew   Participants in even the strongest communities of concern need to maintain ties to some larger social fabric, to connect them with individuals for whom politics is not necessarily the sole central priority of their lives. They need this as a reality check so they don't grow isolated and insular. They need it as well to be full human beings, with dimensions of their lives beyond political activism.

One Columbia student who effectively bridged disparate communities was a religiously conservative Jew named David Gerwin, who headed both the Campus Jewish Organization (CJO) and a group supporting Palestinian rights. His integrity won him respect from every campus faction. David began working with Columbia's antiapartheid coalition during the 1985 blockade. The semester before, a woman in his dorm dragged him to a coalition meeting, where he found himself the only person in the room wearing a *kippah*, the skullcap of a religious Jew. The other students were startled, then greeted him warmly. After the blockade began, David slept outside on the steps and circulated supportive petitions in the kosher section of Columbia's dining hall. When the CJO held a long-scheduled rally for Soviet Jews at the college sundial, he helped lead participants to the Hamilton steps, where they joined in the blockade and spent several hours discussing Israeli–South Africa relationships.

"I didn't come to school a particularly aware person," David said. Growing up in Washington, D.C., he'd attended a Jewish day school that combined secular and religious studies, had attended rallies for Soviet Jewry, and had taken a senior-year seminar on the Vietnam War. He also backpacked with a local wilderness group, volunteered at Audubon, and worked two summers for associations that lobbied in vain to save the solar energy tax credit. But he regarded these involvements as pretty mainstream. David was close to his neurologist father and biochemist mother, both of whom volunteered in a D.C. soup kitchen. He grew up listening to Woody Guthrie and Paul Robeson, and thought it was just the normal thing to play Robeson records and read Carl Sandburg and Robert Frost each Thanksgiving. When David was arrested for committing civil disobedience at a later protest, his parents left a half-teasing congratulatory message on his phone machine.

Students often agonized before becoming involved. Joining an effort like the blockade required crossing major thresholds of fear and hesitation. Yet David regarded his initial participation as a natural outgrowth of his beliefs. "Speaking in a certain rally isn't a lifetime choice," he stressed. "If it turns out to be the wrong move, you go back. I don't have a feeling of one right way to proceed or my actions tainting me forever. I don't need to wait forever until the perfect place and time."

Although he participated in the 1988 movement against the rules changes, David often found it frustrating. "At the rally the other day, people addressed everything but the issue of the conduct rules. The Arab club talked about Palestine. The Nicaraguan group talked about Nicaragua. Others talked about South Africa. I know the issues are linked. But I want people to address the rules directly, so students who don't agree with us on everything else have a chance to respond."

David wasn't asking the coalition to drop related issues. Just to act and organize more strategically. "On the list of demands, the first one is that union employees of a certain rank should have representation in the university senate. It does relate, but if you have six demands about the rules and one about the union, why does the union come first? It's like Sesame Street—'One of these things is not like the others.' Maybe you keep union representation as one of your demands, but you list it as the seventh."

We talked in David's room, and he entered my address in his Macintosh computer. He had a light reddish beard and wore jeans, an old blue sweatshirt, and a white *kippah* with an orange trim. The room itself was crammed with a small refrigerator, a toy elephant, a picture of two birds flying, and posters of Batman and Humphrey Bogart. A family photo was set on a bureau next to a clay leprechaun, a menorah with twin lions curled around its base, and a button proclaiming, "Another Zionist Against Apartheid." The room was neat except for books everywhere: Orwell's *Homage to Catalonia*, Ellison's *Invisible Man*, Kant, Marx, Heidegger, Foucault, and Jurgen Habermas. There were books on moral development theory, histories of Pearl Harbor and of nineteenth-century populism, political biographies of Eugene Debs, Lyndon Johnson, and Ronald Reagan. A bottom shelf held works written in Hebrew.

I asked how religion fit in with his activism. "I can draw from my faith," said David, "but don't feel it's leading my actions. I feel more comfortable with a secular moral reasoning, not based on my particular beliefs. It wasn't Jewish law that prompted me to sit out on the steps of Hamilton Hall, but that everything had been tried, the university senate had voted, and that because this was Columbia, the impact would be heard. I think you can be a good Jew and differ on the blockade."

Then what, I asked, did the *kippah* he wore represent?

"That there's something above us. If I'm not that attracted to the notion of a directly acting God, the idea of something bigger than humankind does inform the way I act. Given that there's something beyond us and above us, it behooves us all to bear in mind that we can't just act freely, and destroy the earth if we feel like it. That a sin against another man is a sin against God. That we have a responsibility to something larger."

How, I asked, could students convey this responsibility to hesitant peers?

"That's really the crux," said David. "Whether you express it in religious or humanist terms. How do you stir people, so they don't just say, 'Yes, it's those protestors again'? Especially if you already have fifty or a hundred people meeting in a room—which is enough to keep you self-referential, but not to win your battles."

A member of a community   David cautioned against romanticizing some "golden mean," an activist Perfect Standard that bridged to all possible constituencies, raised all possible questions, struck precisely the right balance of radicalism and restraint. He didn't wholly dismiss those who acted ahead of the crowd, even when their efforts were clumsy or rude. John Brown, Lloyd Garrison, and the other radical abolitionists led the antislavery debate, and made men like Lincoln seem moderate. ACT-UP angered many with confrontational street tactics, but raised AIDS awareness in a way that benefitted more mainstream groups like Gay Men's Health Crisis. Even my Emory story, he said, sounded if all the mistakes and polarizing language paved the way for some necessary change.

In his own life, David tried to root himself in distinct specific communities: Columbia's activist groups, the temple where he worshiped, the Campus Jewish Organization. He was also rewriting his history honors thesis, composing a commemorative litany to present at graduation, and fighting off a severe cold. He hoped to hear back soon from Columbia's graduate history program, where he already worked closely with several professors. He wanted to follow their paths in mixing political and scholarly commitment, though he worried a bit about being admitted, given that his multiple involvements had lowered his grades. But he liked the idea of making the university a political base.

It was like the traveling SDS organizers, David explained. Their efforts were fine, "but the people who really made a difference then were local, like the Fannie Lou Hamers or the guy who was the head of the Lowndes County freedom organization in Alabama. I'd rather become a member of a community and act from that position than come in from the outside. It's like the difference between the PIRGs canvassing door to door for people to sign up, and being one of the people who signs and then talks with your neighbors. If everyone was involved in their own community, we'd have a different politics."

"The divestment blockade," David said after a pause, "was an impeccable demonstration. Everything was decorous. We didn't use bad language or shout. Sort of 'Clean for Gene,' 1985 style. Since then, the movement's increasingly focused on 'let's run and do something,' rather than on 'how will it work and how will it accomplish what we want?' Students who didn't have the history fell through the cracks."

Seventeen

Tangible The community
fruits service movement

As a response to the standard barriers, and to the real and perceived flaws in existing campus movements, students have begun looking for different ways to voice social concern. They want to act. They want to help. They don't want to deal with complicated issues and factions, or the messy contention of politics. Instead, they've revived approaches to involvement that focus on individual service, and organized volunteering in local communities. Yet these same approaches often then lead them back toward larger social change.

I saw this at the University of Houston, where in the winter of 1989, student Lloyd Jacobson decided to organize a sleep-in outside a local homeless shelter. He invited the head of the campus Young Republicans to join in. "Don't you want to be part of Bush's thousand points of light?" he asked, and quickly got him to agree. Others in the Republican group hesitated, then reluctantly came along. Jacobson then enlisted the Young Democrats: "*They're* participating. Aren't you going to as well?"

The Houston students had perceived homeless people virtually as refuse. But they were unnerved by what they witnessed while trying to sleep on cardboard sheets on the hard cold ground. Huddled together both for comfort and security, they gingerly began talking with shelter residents. The head of the Young Republican contingent returned to write an editorial for the campus paper. He was amazed, he wrote, to find that homeless people actually read books and had comprehensible thoughts. Although he still mistrusted solutions to these problems that relied on "worthless government bureaucrats," something needed to be done. "You cannot possibly know the situation," he concluded, "until you open your eyes."

In the early 1980s, volunteer centers like the one Jacobson established to enable Houston students to work in homeless shelters, soup kitchens, and tutoring projects had a marginal campus presence. Student interest in community involvement had dropped steadily for nearly a decade. Students withdrew from direct service much as they did from all other public commitments.

Like Emory's No Time to Hate group, the campus community service movement began by making an end run around student mistrust of more direct political efforts. Service projects let students perform immediately useful tasks, like feeding hungry men, women, and children without having to challenge entrenched institutional authority. In the process, participants' day-to-day experiences impelled many to begin asking why tragedies like hunger, homelessness, or illiteracy existed to begin with.

The leading national student community service organization, Campus Opportunity Outreach League (COOL), began with a Harvard student named Wayne Meisel. In 1978, this son of a liberal Presbyterian minister was cut from the Harvard soccer team. He responded by convincing 150 fellow students, including other frustrated former high school jocks, to help set up a local youth soccer league. As one of his friends described it, Wayne's encounters with kids who were not middle class, white, or well taken care of, "brought Wayne into the twentieth century." Wayne himself credited his involvement with curing the "anxious paralysis" he felt when he read newspaper headlines or heard political arguments, then hung back, too overwhelmed to act. Having been one of the silent, he felt angry at media stereotypes that branded his generation as apathetic and callous. Although Harvard had long had a community service center, Phillips Brooks House, Wayne wanted to draw in a new group of participants. He soon set to work pairing the school's residential houses with projects in specific Cambridge neighborhoods. He encouraged their students to work in local day-care centers, music and dance programs, boys clubs, and wherever their passions and talents would fit in. After Wayne graduated, he spent the next year extending this approach throughout the Harvard campus. In 1984, he joined with several friends to found COOL as a vehicle to promote comparable efforts nationwide.

Intended to challenge what Wayne called "structural apathy," yet incorporating his wariness of direct political involvements, COOL was launched with what Wayne called a "Walk for Action." To prove that students would respond to a message of personal commitment, he traveled 1,500 miles by foot, visiting sixty-five colleges from Maine to Washington, D.C. Others in the group, including the son of a Kennedy-era VISTA director, soon joined the college-by-college barnstorming. Sleeping on couches, staying with friends, approaching a variety of campus institutions, from fraternities to the activist PIRGs, they helped make the service movement a major campus force.

Such efforts bore fruit because of their participants' passion and commitment, but also because the legacy of Reagan-Bush policies brought previously sheltered students face to face with homeless people on the streets, confronted them with *Time* magazine cover stories on pregnant teenagers, and bred an increasing sense, in even the resolutely apolitical, that "morning in America" was a false dawn. The movement tapped into Bush administration public-involvement rhetoric that downplayed the overt display of greed in favor of patrician benevolence. It played into Clinton administration talk of personal responsibility. It built on student resentment at being labelled materialistic and uncaring.

As a result, attendance at COOL's annual conference jumped from 60 students in 1984 to 120 in 1985, and to 1,700 in 1989. Since then, 1,500 to 2,000 students have attended each year. The organization now includes some 1,000 schools in its network, not counting similar unaffiliated programs. New or revived campus organizations routinely involve several hundred students apiece on a continuing basis. Institutional support for such efforts promises to substantially increase with the Clinton administration's national service initiatives.[1]

Do such renewed involvements merely gloss over deep-rooted social ills? Jerry Falwell runs soup kitchens. The Sun Yung Moon organization sponsors an international student service corps. Service efforts bear an ambiguous relationship to the kinds of direct political advocacy I've been describing. Yet in a time when most students continue to treat politics as poison, the community service movement bypasses many of the obstacles that routinely hamper engagement. You don't need a perfect standard of knowledge to serve soup. You don't need to question the men who know best. You don't have to worry about being stigmatized. By breaking students out of insulated worlds, and by demanding that individuals take seriously those they seek to assist, such efforts introduce thousands of previously apolitical students to social concern.

The influences on service movement participants echo influences on peers who seek more direct institutional change. Role models are important—parents and teachers, clergy and friends—but tend to offer more individual involvement and less political debate. Many students in service organizations grew up volunteering in Scouts, raising money for UNICEF. They grew up in families that took food each week from their churches to the housing projects. Some came from difficult circumstances themselves and could recall how local church and neighborhood groups helped their families and communities survive. Some felt a sense of reciprocity and wanted to "give something back" to society.

Others spoke of new personal bonds. "You do it for yourself," said a student at Berea College in Kentucky, who worked in a tutoring program. "You see a kid get a poem right or understand a concept, and suddenly you feel connected." "I work with a crisis nursing home for abused and abandoned little five-year-olds," explained a Rutgers man. "I've seen more there than I've experienced in twenty-one years. I come in and there's a kid bruised and crying because someone's broken his arm. When I leave, he's smiling. I have to keep going back, because maybe he starts crying again when I leave."

Some students alternate between the politics of advocacy and service. The twenty-three-year-old director of the University of Minnesota community outreach center was arrested protesting nuclear weapons at England's Greenham Common. The student coordinator of Yale's Dwight Hall helped elect a socially concerned mayor for New Haven. A good number of students go back and forth between tutoring or working in soup lines and trying to organize the disenfranchised communities they serve.

University of Houston's Lloyd Jacobson began to think about social concerns while taking the classes of a few key professors, and through stumbling onto Saul Alinsky's classic political organizing text, *Rules for Radicals*, in the back aisles of a Houston bookstore. The year before, the university had slashed funds for handicapped and veterans programs due to athletic budget overruns. Lloyd organized a 300-person march on the president's office to successfully protest the cuts. He saw service programs as a way to get students to begin taking committed stands.

The service movement also includes students who began with the politics of protest, then got "tired of the rhetoric and the rallies," and now want their efforts to yield more tangible fruits. Columbia student Steve Galpern supported the antiapartheid blockade from a distance. "I was in the back of the march," he recalled. "Then everyone occupied the steps, and we ended up right in front of the TV cameras." But Steve grew frustrated at the subsequent posturing and factionalism that began to dominate political activism on the campus. He turned his attention to a new group called Community Impact that ran a soup kitchen and a tutoring program in the basement of a nearby church. "I came from a Pittsburgh suburb," Steve said, "and I'd never seen poverty like this before. It shocked me, people asking for money and sleeping in the streets. I was always a pretty serious kid, with a sense of responsibility. I'd been a Boy Scout and visited elderly people. My dad's a history professor and my mom works for United Way. When I came here I saw some posters and started volunteering. It's been great to see people from the local welfare hotels or the community studying for their GED, but also working side by side with us, getting paid a bit, getting to know the students."

Steve mistrusted peers "interested only in success at their jobs, in law school and on Wall Street." He also mistrusted campus political activists, whom he termed "well-intentioned, but maybe more interested in getting publicity and standing up to authority than practical results. Not like 'Here's an issue and let's solve it,' but 'What issue can we make a fuss about.' Maybe those people would call me afraid of getting involved. They'd say I just do the things that are easy."

"Is that true?" I asked.

"Maybe it's just my temperament," Steve replied. "I'm more into service and less into political statements. Maybe I didn't feel strongly enough to sit on the steps protesting apartheid, even though I supported what they did. There've been lots of other issues, but I never quite felt informed enough to get involved. Maybe I just concentrate on other causes."

At the Community Impact soup kitchen, a friend teased Steve about their respective backgrounds as Eagle Scouts. "I pledge," he recited in a single breath, "to be trustworthy, loyal, helpful, friendly, courteous, kind, obedient, cheerful, thrifty, brave, clean, and reverent." "I'm neither brave, clean, nor reverent," said Steve with a grin, wearing a soiled white apron over his plaid shirt, scrubbing out a huge pot of fat the students had skimmed off the spaghetti sauce. Steve's friend told us Desmond Tutu was lecturing later that evening at the nearby Riverside Church. Puzzled at the lack of response, he asked, "Am I the only one who thinks Desmond Tutu is a big thing?"

Tony, a soft-spoken black volunteer from the community, described coming to New York City from upstate, and working as a security guard at the Metropolitan Museum of Art. Tony loved art, especially African-American art, and wanted to learn to design exhibits in NYU's museum studies program. Then he lost the job and couldn't find another. Descending into alcoholism, he slept in subway stations and all-night porno theaters, "stripped of all my dignity and hope." After two years on the streets, a friend in a drying-out station gave him the name of Community Impact. The organization found him a room in a house and a job washing dishes in a university cafeteria. Regaining his life step by step, Tony still doubted participating students would "really ever understand. They come out of middle-class America, New Jersey or somewhere," he said, "and they're like newborn babies. Some meet black people for the first time. They can dress up like being homeless and go to a shelter, but they can't really understand."

Later, Steve and I talked further. "The divestment campaign changed my mind on a lot of stuff," he said, "especially racial issues. But community service seems more positive. I've learned a lot more about myself, people, the city, and about government. I've learned how people in horrible material circumstances can still have self-respect and strength. I've worked in places I never would have gone to in my life. I've met people who don't get a lot of attention, haven't made the cover of *The Spectator*, but have a respect for human dignity. Next year I'll be part of a city-sponsored program that helps low-income people to fix up their buildings and run them cooperatively. My dad has a letter from when I was a freshman, where I talk about joining the rugby team and the humor magazine, 'and maybe I'll check out the soup kitchen.' The first two lasted about a week. I've been here four years."

Too ideological   When I first talked with twenty-six-year-old Julia Scatliff, COOL's executive director from 1989 to 1991, she stressed that the service movement's task was "to help the person lying bleeding in the street, to put our hands over the aorta and stop the flow." COOL would leave the larger issues, she said, up to America's national leaders, who would respond when they heard sufficiently powerful testaments of need.

Julia grew up in Chapel Hill, North Carolina, where her father was a physician and her mother did volunteer work. In the Girl Scouts, Julia worked with kids and at a hospital, and joined a recycling program. She got further involved at Minnesota's Carleton College, where she took a freshman course from activist professor and future U.S. senator Paul Wellstone. While other students challenged the nuclear arms race or helped Wellstone organize family farmers to fight foreclosures, Julia's passions drew her into setting up the campus service center, where she worked to supply these same farm families "with concrete things like food, clothing, and shelter." Though she respected large political battles, she preferred to meet specific human needs.

Speaking of a ten-year-old boy she tutored, Julia told me that knowing him helped "keep my words simpler, less flighty, more honest." She described student volunteers profoundly changed by what they'd seen and experienced. Author and advocate for the homeless Jonathan Kozol had praised students working with COOL by equating them with the founding generation of Vietnam-era SDS activists, but Julia bridled at the comparison. "We're different," she said. When I asked how, she answered, smiling, "We have Macintoshes and modems." Then she added, "We live our beliefs. If we say something, we back it up. If we talk about housing, we get involved with housing." Julia stressed COOL's authentic commitment, as opposed to the radical posturing that she associated both with her 1960s predecessors and with too many current activists.

Yet commitment and concern do not always promote social change. Volunteer efforts may, in the words of Fordham professor Peter Cucchino, leave primarily "a dissipation of energy into all sorts of charitable activities, without a focus on any kind of reform," averting "people's attention from the real victimization going on." At a recent conference, a Stanford student explained how he'd learned more from volunteering than from all his courses in school. He concluded, "I hope that one day my grandchildren will get to have the same experience working in the same homeless shelter that I did."

He meant no harm by the statement. Other service participants would cite his words as a warning against making day-to-day work too parochial. Yet from its beginning, those involved in the community service movement have vacillated between a fear of taking on explicitly political challenges and a sense that the problems they take on need to be addressed on a deeper level.

The resulting tension expresses itself in a variety of ways. One group of Dartmouth students volunteered eagerly in soup kitchens and brought food to elderly indigents, but wanted nothing to do with an Oxfam fast to combat hunger, which they considered "too ideological." The student coordinator of Emory's volunteer center suggested taking a stand on their campus racial issues and on SARI's demands, but a key woman she worked with "got really quiet and said, 'I don't know,' like 'Let's not talk about this because it's upsetting.' People don't like to disagree. Hardly anyone in the group got involved." In the judgment of student Maura Wolf, who directed the University of Richmond's service center and went on to work for the Points of Light Foundation, a national organization that promotes community service, much of the movement's real impact will come as it influences "students who are going to be bankers, lawyers, wealthy people in high positions." Maura hoped that if these students could only "see what it's like to live in the soup kitchens," they would wield their eventual power more humanely.

Nevertheless, distinctions between political efforts and service efforts have never been absolute, and have blurred even further as students grapple with the lives of those they once knew only as faceless statistics. In March 1988, twelve University of Minnesota students, a campus minister, and the program director for the campus YMCA drove to Brownsville, Texas, to spend a week at the Good Neighbor Settlement House as participants in one of the "alternative spring breaks" that have recently proliferated across the country. They visited Mexico and the Gulf Coast beaches, but also tutored kids, spoke at local schools, rebuilt an old woman's burned house, and stopped at a *colonia*—a shantytown of three hundred dwellings lacking electricity, sewer systems, potable water, and, in many cases, even windows. Later, they met three teenage refugees from Honduras, the last surviving males from their village, who described seeing friends ground down by poverty and others killed by the military.

The group concluded their week at the sanctuary center, Casa Oscar Romero, where they heard more stories of tribulation and pain. When the refugees brought out guitars and invited them to sing, the students led off with the only songs they could think of: the themes from "Gilligan's Island" and "The Brady Bunch." Then the Central Americans offered their own ballads about homes left behind and hopes for peace. Their voices broke with loss and remembrance.

The group drove back to Minneapolis, wrestling with what they had seen through most of the thirty-three-hour van trip. A few days later Minneapolis residents demonstrated to oppose the training of the Minnesota National Guard in Central America. Nearly all the students who visited Brownsville joined in.

Not all service activities result in such dramatically visible shifts. But many carry both complex political lessons and psychological risks as great as those of participating in any march or sit-in. The parents of a University of Southern Mississippi theater major named Patti were appalled to discover their daughter prominently mentioned in the local newspaper under the headline "Gays Unite to Fight AIDS." She had helped put together a campus benefit for Mississippi's first AIDS hospice. The group in fact included a variety of students, both straight and gay, and the paper later printed a correction. Nevertheless, Patti's parents accused her of associating with "the wrong people, as usual." Her father told her this should teach her to keep her mouth shut.

Although the college president gave the event strong support, Patti felt frustrated when students and faculty hung back, as if participation would brand them as pariahs. The dean of the arts college called Patti into his office to tell her she was giving her department a bad name. Most students she and others approached to buy tickets made polite excuses. They succeeded in getting one high-prestige sorority involved, but when the women went to sell tickets in the local mall, shoppers swerved away from their booth, "like something was wrong with us, like we'd turned disgusting to look at or maybe contagious."

Yet Patti and the others felt their efforts were worth it. Patti had never taken on a comparable issue, although she'd frequently gotten into trouble in her rural Mississippi high school for talking back to her teachers and for failing to set a proper role model as a cheerleader. "I don't think I'll ever hesitate again," she told me, "to be involved in any cause I find worthy. It took more commitment than I've ever given a project, but I respect myself for doing something I feel strongly about in Hattiesburg, and not just in a safer environment like New York. It's the first *real* problem I've ever taken on. I know I'll find a way to stay involved."

Just as students involved in the politics of protest wrestle with the tensions between engaged community and insular self-righteousness, so community service participants are beginning to consider ways to broaden the social impact of their efforts. The movement began by consciously distancing itself from political movements. Most of its participants remain wary. Yet the experiences of many impel them to ask whether it is enough simply to care, serve, and help "one individual at a time to beat the odds, or whether we need to be trying to change the odds for all individuals." During COOL's 1989 national conference at Fordham University, students who'd been working in the surrounding Bronx neighborhoods sparked bitter debates when they argued that the 1,200 gathered students had a moral duty to speak out on public issues related to their work. They'd been running soup kitchens on the subway platforms and working to get crack dealers out of buildings. They asked the other students to join a downtown rally the next day for the homeless, and to try to institutionalize peace and justice programs at their schools. COOL staffers and some other participants disagreed, arguing that the movement's strength rested on an ability to transcend partisan politics and reach out to all students, regardless of perspective. People should worry more, answered the Fordham students, about dealing with families torn apart by crack, and less about holding the hand of skittish Young Republicans to make sure their feelings were never offended. The discussion started at 11:00 P.M., lasted for hours, and left no clear resolution.

It could easily have been me Service efforts were different for students who grew up in neighborhoods desperate and poor, and who worked on their own turf when they volunteered. Their choices involved different risks and costs. Francisco Cardenas was a friend of Raul Ortiz, a fellow Cintron Center activist. He came to Chicago from Mexico at age four because he'd caught polio and his parents wanted to get him better medical treatment. His aunt and uncle adopted him, and he learned to walk with braces and crutches, but his aunt, the blood relative, started resenting his presence. "We only have you here because you need treatment," she'd say. His uncle would protect him, but he died when Francisco was thirteen. Things got steadily worse until, at age sixteen, Francisco moved out on his own, got his own apartment, and put himself through high school by combining disability payments with the wages he earned tossing tacos and hamburgers at a restaurant grill.

Francisco was strong and muscular from years of getting around on the crutches. But the restaurant work meant constant motion in hundred-degree heat. "I made minimum wage and finally asked for a raise because I was working really hard and never stole anything, while everyone else always left liquor and meat outside for their friends to pick up. I needed the raise, but didn't get it. I finally quit about the same time I started coming to the university."

Francisco made it through Chicago Circle on grants, a scholarship, Social Security, part-time work as a teacher's aide, and summer jobs at Cook County Hospital and the Westside VA Center. He wanted a career in a lab analyzing medical samples or checking for toxins in food. He studied hard at biology and chemistry, and minored in Latin American studies.

In high school, he'd been involved with gangs. His group began in their local neighborhood, wanting "to have a good time—drink, meet girls, go to the house parties and weddings and high school parties. But the other gangs took us seriously—like we were a real gang with guns, drugs, killing, and all that stuff. We had about three hundred members. We weren't into recruiting or drug dealing. But we turned into a real gang because the others harassed and beat on us. We felt we had to defend ourselves, and that's when people got guns."

"I always saw what we were doing was wrong," Francisco said, "the drugs, drinking, stealing, racing cars, and fighting. I didn't personally get involved, but I'd call the others, and say 'There's these guys coming into the block. Let's take care of them.' I was the only one who had a car with money from my job, so I attracted the others. We'd cruise around, buy beer and drugs, go to parties. I automatically made friends."

People got killed in the neighborhood for the pettiest reasons. Francisco's friend Oscar used to hang around at the edges of the scene. He wasn't a tough guy, didn't even swear. He just liked to carry the name of the neighborhood where they lived. Oscar was twenty, working in a factory like his mother. One Christmas eve another gang came through the alley and shot him six times in the back. The kid who did it was fourteen years old. Oscar's friends killed four other guys in return. Another time, a shotgun blast just missed hitting Francisco; he was driving around with his closest friend Rudy, and two men in a red Thunderbird shot at their car.

Along with most of the party people, Francisco dropped out when his group got guns, but it wasn't easy. If you just went to school, returned home, and kept to yourself, you'd get teased. It helped that Francisco's older brother, Juan, also adopted, returned from the army to study engineering at the Circle campus. Juan co-owned a small apartment building with his father-in-law, and when he wasn't at school or at his job with UPS, he worked to fix it up.

Francisco joined Juan's father-in-law at *Por un Barrio Mejor*, which ran literacy and GED programs, organized block clubs and a bilingual community newspaper, and supported the narrowly successful campaigns of Mayor Harold Washington and a new Latino alderman, Jesus Garcia. "It opened my eyes to the community," said Francisco. "It gave me a model to be part of the Cintron Center, and to come back to help after I graduate with money and time."

Two years after our initial visit in 1988, I stopped in to see Francisco again. I called the phone number he'd given me, but it had been changed. I called the Cintron

Center. The person at the desk asked who I was and why I wanted to get in touch. They said they'd have to get back to me. Later, in the Chicago Circle cafeteria, I ran into Francisco by chance.

Until the week before, things had been going great. He'd had to drop out for a while, but had reenrolled. He and Rudy were sharing an apartment, and Rudy's parents had become almost family. Francisco worked at a hospital to pay rent, food, and tuition, and volunteered at the Cintron Center and in the campus tutoring and counseling program that had helped him get into school. His solid B average would have been higher had he not spread himself thin between classes, political involvements, and outside work.

But the weekend before my visit, the worst had happened. Some gang members came to Francisco and Rudy's neighborhood to shoot a member of a rival group who'd beaten up one of their own. He wasn't home and they got restless waiting. They saw Rudy getting out of his car, returning from a Cintron Center dance that Francisco had organized. They remembered him from his old gang and killed him instead.

"Everything was going great," Francisco told me, still in shock, as if watching his life from a distance. "I'd dropped out of school after having to move four times in one year, then worked in a video store to save enough to come back. I did, and was on the right course. Then this happens. Like my whole life is collapsing. Rudy asked if I wanted to catch a ride, too. It could easily have been me. Two hours before, I was talking, spending time with him, like we had for the past six years. Now that's it. It's over."

Other friends had helped in the week since the shooting. Francisco would still volunteer in the tutoring program and work with the Cintron Center. But he'd lost his closest friend and felt unsafe at their apartment. A family conflict had ended his involvement with the community group, *Por un Barrio Mejor*. He wanted to leave the neighborhood entirely. "It's still all related," he said as I headed out, running late to catch my plane. "All the same goals. Trying to get groups like CLAS and the black groups to push for what we need. Running on a student rights slate for the student assembly. I still want to help my community. It's just going to be at the university instead of in the *barrio*."

How the other half lives   As service efforts have diversified, the movement's predominantly middle-class participants are beginning to examine their relationship to the frequently beleaguered communities they attempt to serve. Greg Ricks, the COOL advisor who headed Stanford's Office of Multicultural Education, explained that the students who began the current service resurgence "wanted to get away from the ugly world of politics. These were preacher's kids and faculty brats. They wanted things fun and honest. They weren't involved in the politics of the world and didn't want to be." But students need to ask, said Ricks, what their involvement actually does for the communities they enter, whether their work helps them gain more power.

At an Atlanta leadership gathering split between Emory and Martin Luther King, Jr.'s alma mater, Morehouse, black Rice junior and future COOL board member Alex Byrd initiated a dialogue on race by stating that he was tired of all the brochures showing middle-class white kids cradling little black children in their arms. A thirty-four-year-old returning student from Southern University of New Orleans described her background of teenaged pregnancy and heroin addiction. She had returned to college along with her twenty-year-old twin daughters and mistrusted patronizing phrases like "celebrating the chance to make a difference." "What you do for fun," she said, "I do for survival." At another meeting, a campus advisor from New Orleans's historically black Xavier University said she didn't think community service should be "just a place where upper-middle-class kids have this wonderful experience and get to see how the other half live or don't live." She believed students were finally beginning to deal with these questions. But her community didn't need any more "white knights to save us from our poverty."

Responding to challenges like these, COOL racially diversified their national staff, rotated their 1991 national conference between the predominantly white New Orleans schools Tulane and Loyola and the predominantly black Xavier and Southern, and made a conscious attempt to address racial issues in their continuing agenda. They also developed a series of workshops in which black students suggested ways white volunteers might have to involve themselves in programs directed by others: "Approach black colleges, the Alpha fraternities, or the Urban League. Relinquish power and work on someone else's project where you're totally outnumbered. Put yourself in the situation a lot of minorities put themselves in every day."

I have to ask more questions   A year after our initial conversation, COOL director Julia Scatliff explained how involvement with a racially and culturally diverse group of movement participants had given her a new circle of friends, altered the daily contours of her life, and consistently enriched her perspective. She still found it belittling to dismiss as mere Band-Aids projects that taught illiterate people how to read or offered job training for unemployed single mothers. But she stressed her discomfort with taking on the messianic image "of being a bunch of Florence Nightingales running out to bandage people's wounds." And she agreed that COOL and the service movement in general were "treading very softly into an advocacy role." Middle-class students could best deal with class and racial paternalism, Julia believed, by being humble and listening carefully. She saw little separation between her efforts to reshape national policy and her volunteer work at a Minneapolis center for Native American children. The service movement allowed students to chip away at major issues bit by bit, in the process changing both its participants and the society. COOL's ultimate politics, she said, came "from educating people on the crises in our communities." She agreed that movement participants had no choice but to eventually confront "the greater systemic questions."

In his book *Making History*, sociologist Richard Flacks suggests that political involvement often begins when a person's private world is suddenly threatened or attacked. People begin by defending what they've had, then move to broader questions concerning power and accountability. Yet this sense of crisis can occur not only when toxic wastes poison the water or the economy crashes, but also when individuals decide that ills that once seemed inevitable should not be allowed to endure, as when black veterans returned from World War II and Korea and helped build the resurgent civil rights movement, or when women who organized Mississippi freedom schools asked why male peers always took center stage. In the case of predominantly middle-class students, a transformation can occur when they witness zones of human devastation beyond the scope of their previous vision.[2]

I saw this with a Fordham student named Chris. He'd wanted to be a Big Brother ever since he was growing up in Texas. An older student got him involved with a campus-based program to give gifts to needy kids, a program Chris ended up running. He also got involved with a ten-year-old boy from the Bronx whom he visited each week to talk, tutor, and play. "I came in as a freshman, the stereotypical conservative," he said. "I loved Reagan, loved all the conservative policies. Up to a few months ago I was against the welfare system because of how it was misused. Now I'm taking a class on the political economy of poverty, and reading from people like Jonathan Kozol how the government will pay $3,000 a month to put people up in a shithole welfare hotel, but won't pay more than $270 a month for an apartment. Before I'd say, 'They're all just lazy. They could work if they want.' Now I see how part is their circumstances and part is this analgesic behavior you get from being beaten down so that after a while, you just stop trying. I used to see a bum and think 'Get rid of him.' Now I question more. I wonder if maybe he was a steelworker whose plant closed, and if he left his family when he couldn't get benefits. I have to ask more questions."

"I was one of the people against COOL going political," Chris continued. "What would make me most happy is to sit back and say this is a great world and people are helping each other and everything's fine. But because of my volunteer experience and because my classes helped me think things through, I recognize that community service has some real limits. I'll always be involved. I'll always be a Big Brother. But its purpose should be so we won't need COOL. We shouldn't have to come here year after year."

To grapple with the root causes of social ills, service participants need contexts where they can gain critical perspectives on their experiences. Sympathetic faculty and administrators have begun to assign community service as fieldwork for existing courses and to introduce it as a general student requirement. The North Carolina–based National Society for Internships and Experiential Education has long explored links between service and learning. New classes like the University of Minnesota's course in social justice and community service examine the legacy of these efforts past and present. Hampshire and Radcliffe programs grant stipends so students can undertake complex research studies of local community needs.[3]

Historically, service projects have fed America's major social movements. In the late nineteenth century, community service was expected from respectable young women, who would bring their "civilizing influence" to bear on a raw and unruly industrial culture. Their experiences influenced their later participation in efforts like women's suffrage. Key New Dealers like Eleanor Roosevelt, Secretary of Labor Frances Perkins, and Works Project Administration director Harry Hopkins encountered political issues in their youth while working at turn-of-the-century settlement houses that sought to assist new immigrants (in both surviving and politically assimilating), and to enact reforms in housing, child labor laws, and workplace safety. In the 1960s, Peace Corps volunteers served their host countries with mixed results, but many returned with concerns that involve them to this day as active citizens. Many early SDS organizers encountered their first social involvement through campus YWCA and YMCAs or by participating in tutoring programs for children.

A goal of inclusion   As the service movement has gained numbers and strength, sponsors and benefactors have at times pushed its participants to avoid difficult questions and controversial choices, to preclude efforts that seek more fundamental change. To what degree did COOL's acceptance of a Bush administration Presidential Voluntary Action Award or the Fordham conference's proud receipt of a solicitous telegram from Barbara Bush encourage those in the service network to temper their critiques of an administration that spoke much of kindness and gentleness but continued redistributing resources from the poor to the wealthy? Did the grant COOL received from the Coors "Volunteers Under 30" program—accepted, true enough, following lengthy internal debate and the end of a national AFL-CIO boycott—place a benign gloss on the Coors family's continuing New Right agenda? Do Exxon donations to the more institutionally based service network of Campus Compact dampen the latter's commitment to environmental accountability? In 1991, COOL secured its largest ever grant: $778,000 from the W. K. Kellogg Foundation for a multiyear outreach project called Into the Streets. But the grant carried limiting terms, which COOL accepted, including the prohibition of voter registration as an outreach option. As Reverend William Sloane Coffin said, in a lecture discussed in the University of Minnesota community service course, "Charity must not be allowed to go to bail for justice."[4]

At COOL's 1991 conference, executive director Bill Hoogterp explained how everyone had "a piece of the puzzle" in working to change America for the better. He argued that people who undertook this task couldn't afford to spurn potential allies just because they might not want to work "with fraternity people, with Republicans or Democrats, or people of a different color, or people whose piece of the puzzle has an edge to it, or people who don't have an edge." No matter how big the mountain seems, he said, we need to reach out across the barriers and solve America's ills. It was a fine message of inclusion but said nothing about accountability. "We're not about figuring out who's right or wrong," Bill continued, "but about getting the job done."

Yet when individual volunteer projects ignore the political context of community problems, they can take the heat off corporate and governmental leaders who continue to slash human resources while America's problems steadily bleed. They can lead service volunteers directly away from asking how America's root social choices continue to betray the very communities they work to serve.

The further students journey into service commitments, however, the more they link face-to-face efforts with the need for deeper institutional change. The new volunteers' highly pragmatic approach at times leaves them unable to see beyond the endless parade of human pain. It also anchors them in the realities they address, and in their complex particulars.

Given a complement of strong advocacy movements, service efforts can provide concrete models for other activists. Like the Constructive Program that complemented Gandhi's civil disobedience efforts, groups like Habitat for Humanity can develop better ways to build low-income housing. Those working in soup kitchens can research the politics of food. Those tutoring kids can shape the future of our schools. The service movement has also discussed ways to funnel students into specific causes, link them up with existing community organizations, encourage collective action among their constituencies.

If the volunteers have a distinct vision of social change, it is one requiring broad-based participation. America will only become a more humane society, they insist, when more than just the committed core work to shape a common future. At one point, I asked University of Richmond's Maura Wolf whether her center would bring people to an upcoming national march for affordable housing. Maura said she'd post fliers so students could see them, and probably attend herself. But she wouldn't make it a center project. "Two years ago, when I was first getting involved, I never would have gone to a political march or been associated with a center that sponsored it. Richmond's a conservative campus. I don't want to scare off someone like me, the way I was two years ago."

Community service participants are justly proud that their centers enlist everyone from conservative Republicans to socialists. Some stake too much on influencing the future elite, and consequently downplay any hint of dissent. But America needs places where people don't always feel judged for their views—where, as Stanford's Greg Ricks said, you don't let people off the hook of responsibility just because they don't agree with your activist politics. The service movement allows individuals to enter social concern step by step, at their own pace, rather than being told, in Maura Wolf's words, "Here's a fact, here's a leaflet, now go out and march this Saturday." Perhaps, as several COOL staffers suggested, their work succeeds best as a "prepolitical" effort through which individuals can pass en route to more direct public stands. At their best, these students work to make their efforts a "free space," a place where individuals can gather for purposes beyond their own private lives, and—for those who make that choice—then grapple with ways to change the world.[5]

Service work can teach students how to care, allow them to hear the voices of people scorned and discarded, and make them more critical of prevailing social choices. As the director of Columbia's Community Impact center suggested, they may allow students "to process their disillusionment" through contact with role models from diverse engaged communities. At their best, those involved have much to teach other activists about ways to reach out across diverse backgrounds and perspectives. They also are beginning to learn ways to pressure entrenched institutions and to articulate visions that go beyond individual caring. They are beginning to link the immediate crises of hunger, illiteracy, and homelessness with tax and budget policies that starve human needs and make expendable the individuals and communities with which they work. They are beginning to to deal with questions of power, conflict, and privilege.

Most current students, for reasons I've described, continue to mistrust political involvement. They enter volunteer projects carrying their badges of wariness, then return to their dorms talking, not about the latest TV show, but about a homeless father's faded childhood dreams, or how much it means to be able "to put a smile on some hungry person's face." Some treat their experiences as exotic tourism, brief sojourns from which to return and continue on as if nothing else had changed. Others, like a student volunteer at Seattle's Family Kitchen, conclude "that an issue such as homelessness can no longer be something that's separate from your life." One Minnesota architecture student wandered into the YMCA to ask about an annual project in which students cleaned streets and parks to raise money for the hungry. Soon he was rehabbing low-income housing in a program called Search for Shelter, "going out to measure this dilapidated building in the middle of winter, in the freezing cold, in disgusting conditions, and with people still too poor to afford it." After trying "to turn around just this one small building that the city bought when the guy didn't want it," he soon began asking why people were homeless in the first place, and began matching up local architects with similar community projects. He decided these concerns were "more important than getting on track to be a principal in a design firm by the time I'm thirty-five."

Eighteen

Shades of green The tree huggers and the politicos

Given strong apprehensions regarding political involvement, students were most willing to act when doing so did not require immediately confronting powerful institutions. In the service movement, a student could serve soup without initially questioning why some people were hungry and living on the streets. In burgeoning campus environmental efforts, students could similarly participate in recycling or in Earth Day activities without, at least at first, asking what national and global choices have steadily degraded the earth. Because entry seemed easy and the crisis self-evident, environmental concern has produced the largest continuing student movement in years.

In April 1990 at Chicago Circle, two weeks before Earth Day's twentieth anniversary, students crowded the table of a new environmental group. They waited to talk, take fliers, purchase buttons, play with an inflatable globe, and ask about ways to get involved. They approached the table freely and lined up five deep, with none of the hesitation I typically see with political causes.

Students had started the environmental group two months before, after a biology major attended a series of lectures at Chicago's Field Museum concerning rainforest devastation. Another student in his program had joined a smaller Earth Day celebration at Lincoln Park the previous year, disliked its air "of a bunch of sixties hippies standing around smoking dope out of a bong," and decided that "maybe I could help do something better." The two roped in a third friend who'd canvassed for Greenpeace, and another who they just thought would be interested. The Earth Support Group now claimed 150 student members.

Thirty feet away sat Chicago Circle's main multi-issue political organization, the Progressive Student Network. They'd done good work and would do more. New posters announced an upcoming speaker on government surveillance. They offered leaflets on their projects and some decent books for sale. But in an hour or more, only a couple of friends stopped to talk. Students treated them either with disdain or as part of the scenery.

Across the country, the 1990 Earth Day gave a clear boost to environmental concern. Twenty years after the original event, IBM ran environmental ads on TV, Phil Donahue talked recycling with actor Raul Julia and with Cosby show "daughter" Lisa Bonnet, as did Arsenio Hall with Kirstie Alley of *Cheers*. President Bush repeated his claim to be "the environmental president." Corporations from hip clothing manufacturer Esprit to megapolluters DuPont, Dow, and Chevron proclaimed new green identities, with Esprit inviting in major environmental leaders to speak to their employees. Who wouldn't want to care for the earth?

As a result of this surge of concern, the leading campus environmental group, Student Environmental Action Coalition (SEAC), now maintains contacts on two thousand campuses. The organization has helped bring together students involved in a range of projects from campus recycling programs to "environmental audits," where schools collect data on resource and energy use by different departments and facilities, with the purpose of suggesting more sustainable alternatives. Between 1986 and 1990 the number of freshman who say it is "essential" or "very important" for them to personally "become involved in programs to clean up the environment" more than doubled, with nearly 90 percent believing the federal government needs to do more to control pollution. The Earth Day anniversary provided a dramatic focus for newfound ecological concern. Since then, campus involvement with these issues has continued to grow.[1]

The president ought   Environmental concern took many forms.
to do something   A University of Nebraska group, the Wildlife Club, consisted mainly of wildlife management majors who educated their peers and local public school students on native plant and animal populations, and on endangered species worldwide. At North Arkansas Community College, a concerned biologist led caving and canoeing expeditions into the lower Ozarks and held discussions on the pollution caused by local chicken ranches. At a small religious college in southern Missouri, fundamentalist students repeatedly warned me about the hidden temptations of Satan and about friends who lost their souls while playing with Ouija boards. "I

don't know if you believe in this," ventured the one who was driving me to the airport. I expected more end-time theology. Instead, he asked whether I thought he was right to worry about aerosol sprays destroying the ozone layer. "I think we're in deep trouble and getting deeper," he said. "The president *ought* to do something. Maybe he won't unless he's pushed."

Just as dramatic increases in hunger, homelessness, and illiteracy spurred student community service efforts, so a widespread sense of global crisis fed renewed environmental concern. Students saw government and corporate leaders strip-mining the future, fostering crises from the ozone hole to the greenhouse effect, from topsoil depletion to acid rain, from toxic dumping to air and water pollution, from the destruction of natural habitats to escalating global population. When Friends of the Earth founder David Brower pointed out at a SEAC conference that during his lifetime humans would consume four times as many resources as in all of previous human history, students viewed this destruction as their immediate inheritance. When Worldwatch president Lester Brown suggested we had forty years to turn the global environment around or face increasingly desperate crises and diminishing resources, concerned students realized the changes had to occur in their lifetime.

Often students first got involved with environmental issues through existing advocacy groups, particularly Greenpeace. When students at SEAC's 1990 national conference were asked about outside environmental organizations they belonged to, almost as many listed Greenpeace as all other national environmental organizations combined. The organization's outreach and canvassing efforts have enabled it to grow from 21,000 U.S. supporters in 1978 to nearly two million in 1993. Student after student spoke of discovering Greenpeace through friends, family, media coverage, or booths set up at concerts of musicians like U2, Neil Young, the Grateful Dead, and Indigo Girls. Membership required no specific actions, and produced no specific involvement beyond receiving a thought-provoking magazine and giving moral support to staffers who climbed polluting smokestacks, sailed boats into nuclear test zones, and researched and challenged global ecological depredations. But the organization's strength let students feel that they were not alone, that thousands of others shared their concerns. Its example gave them a sense that it was right to speak out.[2]

Loving the Lorax   A growing number of students learned environmental concern from the time they were young. At a recent SEAC conference, a speaker asked students to "stand up if you loved the Lorax." Almost without exception the crowd of a thousand rose to their feet, commemorating the Dr. Seuss creature who fought to save the trees. Created in response to early seventies environmentalism, *The Lorax* voiced a steady quiet call from their earliest memories of their parents reading the story aloud to them. Others recalled childhood experiences camping, hiking, canoeing, fishing, and later working as summer camp counselors or in environmentally concerned Scout or Campfire groups. Outdoor activities fueled their involvement— because they brought them to wild and sacred places they could not bear to see destroyed.

Because environmental responsibility included routine choices like recycling or purchasing low-impact consumer goods, it allowed the parents of these students to express day-to-day allegiance to larger ideals. Some of these parents were former activists, for whom more direct political involvements had eroded. Some had never found a political voice, but wanted to do something. Others separated their newspapers and bottles as part of a more general political involvement. They all encouraged their children to make basic gestures of caring for the earth.

"There's been a tremendous increase of people getting out into the country, getting hunting and fishing licenses, finding a reason to walk all those miles," a Nebraska student told me. "They want to get their kids to enjoy the outdoors before the outdoors is gone. Maybe it's more awareness than willingness to act, but I hope that's beginning to change."

Students also got encouragement from key teachers. A Williams senior remembered watching a photovoltaic cell turn a propeller in his seventh grade science class. An Iowa State environmental studies professor had his students research nearby wilderness areas. A Chicago Circle organic chemistry professor handed out materials on ozone depletion, the greenhouse effect, and threats to biological diversity in his class full of career-focused premed students.

The major student environmental organization, SEAC, emerged from a 1986 effort by two University of North Carolina students. They revived a late 1970s campus environmental group and renamed it Student Environmental Action Coalition. Focusing first on campus recycling, then on letter writing in support of the Arctic National Wildlife Refuge, they wanted to coordinate with other schools through an existing national network called Campus Green. But they found it was moribund. They decided to launch their own effort, but when they tried to get support from some of the major national environmental groups, the groups were willing to plug them in as volunteers or canvassers, but wary about helping establish an organization whose direction they'd have no say over. Finally, one of the SEAC members convinced Greenpeace, for which he'd worked as an intern, to run a small notice announcing the new organization in their magazine.

At the time, spring 1989, SEAC's entire annual budget came to $200, raised from bake sales, street fairs, and reselling aluminum cans collected in the dorms. They worked out of a tiny office in a space with other political groups on the UNC campus. Then the responses flooded in, totalling nearly 200 by the end of that summer. "How do I start a group?" the letters asked. "What should we do on our campus?" "How do we join?" The SEAC group responded by phone, by mail, and through a rough and ragged newsletter, helping to coordinate national student efforts on global warming and the Arctic National Wildlife Refuge. The next fall, aided by another small Greenpeace notice, they held their first conference, hoping to draw a couple hundred participants. Instead, 1,700 students showed up from forty-four states. The conference launched SEAC as a major presence.

This allowed the organization's founders to write their first real grant proposals, to hire themselves and a handful of other students and recent graduates at survival wages, and to begin to do some systematic outreach. Consulting with veteran activists from organizations like the National Toxics Campaign, Midwest Academy, and the campus program of the National Wildlife Federation, SEAC organized student marches to thirty-five state capitals, demanding passage of the Native Forest Protection Act, and sponsored Washington, D.C., rallies to support the Clean Air Act. They established an organizational structure with regional representatives. In October 1990 they held another conference, called Catalyst, in the wake of the Earth Day publicity. This time, 7,600 students came to the University of Illinois at Champaign-Urbana from 1,100 campuses, exceeding all imagined expectations. Speakers included Jesse Jackson, Robert Redford, Ralph Nader, Helen Caldicott, Cesar Chavez, and musician Billy Bragg—and some students said there were too many stars and not enough practical networking. But most returned feeling part of a growing movement. They in turn helped build a 2,000-school network of contacts and affiliates.

It doesn't have to be radical   Student environmental concern often begins with limited goals like instituting recycling or replacing Styrofoam cafeteria cups. Students then move to the broader environmental impact of their campuses and communities. In 1986, a small group at Hendrix College in Conway, Arkansas, collaborated with a nearby environmental educational center to conduct a systematic study of their campus meal system. Although Hendrix was surrounded by family farms, 90 percent of the dining hall food came from out of state. Some of the ground beef came from cattle raised in West Texas, then shipped from Amarillo to Chicago, back south to Little Rock, and only then up to Conway. The Hendrix group developed a five-year plan to change purchasing sources, shift cafeteria menus in favor of seasonal produce, and have the school handle more of its own food-processing and storage. Direct expenditures stayed roughly the same. The food was fresher and environmental costs dropped sharply. Though Hendrix enrolled just a thousand students, it managed to pump an additional $300,000 per year into a hardpressed local economy. Hendrix students next embarked on a comparable study of energy resource use. Oberlin and Swarthmore adapted the Hendrix model and extended it further to research and redesign their cafeteria systems. By 1991, students at more than 150 schools had conducted audits of energy use and other environmental costs.[3]

With a similar impetus, Brown University students negotiated utility rebates to help their campus switch to more efficient lighting. Texas A&M students initiated an engineering building retrofit that saved $25,000 a month in cooling costs. University of Minnesota dorms held an Energy Olympics, competing to see which dorm could use the least energy during sub-zero winters and hundred-degree summers.

Student environmentalism affected college intellectual life. At Sangamon State in Illinois, students set up an environmental section in their bookstore. Students at a variety of schools initiated new courses. A group at New Jersey's Stockton State worked with high school students to design a model bill mandating recycling at every private and public educational institution statewide. Students at two hundred New England and mid-Atlantic campuses challenged the purchase of Canadian electricity by local utilities as a way of trying to stop James Bay II, a massive Quebec hydro-project that threatened to dam five major river systems, to displace ten thousand Cree and Inuit people, and to flood an area the size of Connecticut. A new group, Sierra Student Coalition, involves several thousand members within the parent organization, while taking on issues from the preservation of California deserts to urban lead poisoning.[4]

Similar to service efforts (which often included environmental components) and to Emory's No Time to Hate group, these causes offered highly practical approaches. Students could first get involved without having to challenge powerful institutions, vested interests, or entrenched policies. They needed to make no broad political judgments. They could simply suggest individual, voluntary measures to help heal the earth.

"There are lots of things you can be in control of," said a woman newly involved in the University of North Dakota environmental group. "Ride your bike more, or walk to school. Find a shampoo that won't leave a soap scum, instead of the most popular product. Share rides and recycle your cans. Plant trees or grow vegetables. It doesn't have to be radical."[5]

Some students dovetailed newfound ecological concern with career choices.

Nearly a quarter of those surveyed at SEAC's 1990 national conference majored in the natural sciences or in engineering, with another ten percent in environmental studies. The Tufts environmental studies program doubled in a year's time, and the university established a new institute to integrate environmental perspectives into all its courses. At Illinois State, the number of environmental health majors quadrupled in a recent two-year period. Applications to University of Washington's graduate Environmental Engineering program recently increased close to ten-fold. Given the long-term nature of most environmental problems, students felt that training in areas like waste disposal, alternative-energy production, and ecologically sound manufacturing systems might both safeguard their personal futures and prepare them to do good in the world.[6]

I think of Fairfield's Tim Lovejoy, shaken into concern when Long Island Sound was polluted by medical waste. He still talked of the "big market for cleaning up" and creating his own, highly lucrative "entrepreneur deal." But he began to acknowledge responsibilities larger than his personal future.

Practical choices   Environmental careers offer practical rewards, but also alternatives to simply fitting in. They offer more technically oriented students ways to mesh socially responsible visions with particular interests and strengths, and to focus first on scientific questions, then only later on political ones. Some students feel angry at having to address the immense and complex changes humans have wrought on the earth. "We could have prevented all this but we didn't," said one from Emory. But most hope, at least initially, that if people can just voice the necessary concern, appropriate national and international responses will follow.

Campus environmental activism addresses specific technical challenges. How can a university most efficiently heat its buildings during a North Dakota winter, or cool them during a Louisiana summer? How can student groups set up recycling programs that make economic sense for their school and community? An environmental audit found UCLA to be the Los Angeles basin's tenth largest emitter of carbon dioxide. How can such commuter campuses reduce the burden of the cars driven by their students?

These specific dilemmas led students to look for solutions of common potential gain, in which institutions don't have to trade off conflicting interests or make divisive choices. Members of the University of North Dakota's Eco Club at first mistrusted the university's director of plant services: "We felt he was just giving us a bureaucratic runaround." Then the university set up a half-time position in charge of environmentally sound recycling and waste management, and they began working together. The plant services director, who already ran one of the most efficient college facilities in the nation, began soliciting the group's advice and help in researching sustainable alternatives. He even brought several members in to testify at state hearings.

But institutional changes did not all come easily. At the University of Washington, administrators dragged their feet for years on instituting recycling. It was too complex, they said. Students wouldn't participate. It would be too costly. Then 1991 student body president Heidi Wills won her office on a commitment to push through a comprehensive recycling plan, as well as to help develop less car-reliant commuter alternatives and to work for a widely supported ethnic studies requirement.

Heidi grew up in Butte, Montana, where her father worked as a mining engineer and her mother was a volunteer coordinator for battered women's groups. As a girl, Heidi used to cry at her sense of the earth being gouged and torn. She hid the bullets when the family went hunting. When her parents got divorced, Heidi moved with her mother to a Seattle suburb. She felt particularly stirred by a high school history teacher "who gave me a passion for knowing what's going on in the world—for my own sake, not just to regurgitate it for a test."

Heidi acted in high school plays and participated in student government. She was the lone visible Democrat among her class of enthusiastic young Reaganites. She entered the University of Washington in 1986, politically inexperienced but intellectually curious. She joined the high-status Tri Delt sorority, known for cheerleaders, homecoming queens, and academic achievement, because "It just seemed like what you did, what all my friends were doing." Heidi registered her sorority sisters to vote and tried to get them involved in her concerns. Her house even nominated her for Miss Greek, she blushed to admit, and she was elected when the judges liked her arguments for why Greeks should be more involved in the community.

Energetic and athletic with dark curly hair, intent eyes, and a trim muscular frame, Heidi knew how to put people quickly at ease. Though she didn't consider herself politically sophisticated, she liked to get things done. If certain approaches were wrong, she felt there was no excuse to avoid trying to correct them. Heidi got involved in student government by volunteering for an open student assembly slot. She learned in particular from an anti-CIA activist on the student Board of Control, even though the rest of the board often voted down his motions. "He had an impact on me, standing up for what he believed."

Soon, Heidi herself had been elected to the Board of Control. She thought a lot about how to responsibly use her position. Majoring in history, she was nonetheless most influenced by a geology professor who conveyed "a passion for understanding the earth and fighting to preserve it." The city of Seattle had already pioneered a program for curbside recycling of paper, bottles, and cans. Yet the university recycled barely

15 percent of its solid waste, through a program with no student participation. Administration studies to expand it moved at a glacial pace. Heidi jumped the gun and pulled together a coalition that included WASHPIRG, the Institute for Environmental Studies, the Graduate Student Senate, and the Campus Greens. A kickoff rally in the main university plaza, Red Square, drew several hundred students, a huge crowd for this apolitical campus. Heidi told those gathered that it was "OK to be impatient," because the school needed a recycling program "where every person can make a difference." She convinced a Seattle environmental consultant to do a free study of ways to begin a campuswide recycling program, one that the city and the state Department of Ecology judged as first-rate, even while University of Washington Executive Vice President Tallman Trask dismissed it as "a second-year class project."

The university then hired its own consultants for a waste management study that cost $97,000, dragged on for two more years and made recycling only a minor aspect. When Heidi and other students attended public meetings to push the issue to greater prominence, the administrator in charge mostly ignored their raised hands, or when she did call on them, said curtly, "Make it quick."

It frustrated Heidi that so little was happening. "It seemed such a wasted opportunity when all this recyclable waste kept on going into the landfills." By then she was student body vice president. Although the official administration committee refused to help, she secured student government funds so the recycling coalition could begin their own pilot effort following the consultant's suggestions. They built a huge plywood box around a standard dumpster, and painted a picture of the earth on it with a white background. They set it outside the main student center, the HUB, and used it to collect aluminum cans and newsprint. "We decided to do it ourselves to prove that students want to recycle, that they'll participate if we just give them the means to do it. We collected eleven tons from the one collection center. For six months, student volunteers emptied indoor bins into it each day. It worked better than we could have imagined."

The recycling committee circulated petitions as well, and publicized their cause through letters and editorials in the *Daily*. When Heidi was elected student body President in spring 1990, she sponsored a major recycling fair and a five-minute recycling video, done as a slapstick comedy in *film noir* style, and even involving a cameo appearance by the university president. The committee showed the film to thousands of students, borrowing five minutes before classes from sympathetic professors. "The university doesn't have a recycling program," they explained, "but the students do." With the help of the sympathetic director of the university's Institute for Environmental Studies, Heidi secured a $35,000 pilot grant from the national Environmental Protection

Agency, to continue recycling education on campus. She even showed the film at a meeting of the board of regents, trying "to make the administration feel a part of it already, even though at that point we were doing all the work." Using the obvious student enthusiasm and the university's own finally completed studies, Heidi and the others in the committee continued to keep the pressure on, despite Executive Vice President Trask's blunt statement that he had "higher priorities." At last the administration began allocating the necessary funds.

It shouldn't be complicated Students could do some things to make their schools more environmentally friendly. But once they tried to influence institutional policies—of their campuses, communities, or national government—they found themselves in the undeniably political realm of questioning common choices. They also faced questions of accountability. At first, those newly involved often took heart that chemical and oil companies cared enough to protect the deer, dolphins, and seals so lovingly portrayed in their glossy ads. Later, many began to question the split between these fine images and dubious corporate actions. These questions brought to the agenda the difficult challenge of acting not only to make individuals care, but to marshall enough political will to change long-standing policies and to turn powerful institutions away from cannibalizing the future.

Students divide in how broad a net they wish to cast with their environmental vision. It's hard enough to challenge atmospheric pollution and old-growth clearcutting. It may be even more difficult to challenge political and economic choices that disproportionately place the burden of environmental dangers present and future on those with the least wealth, power, and voice. What does it mean for Los Angeles residents to buy clean air (in effect) by purchasing West Side homes where prices begin at nearly a half million dollars? Or for toxic dumps to be sited in the poorest communities? Or for austerity budgets triggered by international debt to force African or Jamaican farmers to switch to export crops that deplete their soil, water, and forests? Student environmental groups that address these questions push against the boundaries of their original focus. They face the same dilemmas of how far and fiercely to carry their vision as newly concerned students entering the service movement.

Some long-active student environmental organizers have tried to draw links from the start. "It's been hard," explained a University of Missouri woman, "to decide whether to work on humanitarian or environmental issues. But whichever you work on, you're challenging the same systems and working for the same vision. It has a similar impact if you're doing it well."

Others slid step by step into more difficult political questions. SEAC ran corporate accountability campaigns to hold multinational companies responsible for environmental degradation caused by their actions. Under the organization's auspices, students boycotted Coors beer, pressured companies like DuPont and British Petroleum (BP) to offer more than lip service on issues like fluorocarbon production and toxic waste dumping, and challenged the James Bay hydro-project. SEAC also helped coordinate an international youth campaign to lobby national leaders attending the 1992 "Earth Summit" in Rio de Janeiro.

Taking on these broader connections produced a commensurate resistance. The job of calling leaders to account for their actions challenged students who wanted to participate but who believed those in charge were doing the best they could and shouldn't be sniped at from the sidelines. Even the most wholesome and nonthreatening ideas could hit the wall of standard dismissal mechanisms, as when the North Dakota group vice president objected to their slogan, "make peace with the planet," for making her organization sound too countercultural and pacifist.

These splits surfaced at SEAC's October 1991 conference in Boulder, Colorado. Responding to criticisms that the student environmental movement, like its older counterpart, was too white and too middle class, organizers tried to establish links to social justice as a central focus. Some students took up these connections with enthusiasm.

But others had misgivings. A half dozen members of the Organization of Students Concerned About Resources (OSCAR), a two-year-old group from Northeastern Missouri State, drove twenty hours to the conference in the hope of renewing their vision and getting nuts and bolts suggestions for ways to organize—"something practical to take back to our school." The group, made up mostly of women, loved Lone Wolf, a deep ecologist who spoke and chanted to a drumbeat, asking students to reach down and feel the grass and earth, "the source of your strength." But they balked at conference discussions on race, class, and economics. "This is bigger than politics," said a group member named Amy. "You shouldn't have to be a Republican or Democrat, Left or Right, to work to save the earth. Everyone can do something. Everyone should work together. It shouldn't be complicated. Students at our school already call us names like 'Ecofags.' I don't want to further divide people."

The group felt particularly bad for one of their members, a Young Republican who'd just started coming to meetings. She was almost in tears after hearing repeated attacks on the Bush administration for opening wetlands to massive development, blocking international action on global warming, and dragging its feet on every other significant concern. "She's feeling really bad, really alienated," said her friend Janelle.

"She shouldn't come to an environmental conference and have her beliefs attacked. She shouldn't have to walk past all the abortion rights tables any more than I should have to have my pro-choice feelings assaulted by being force-fed pictures of aborted fetuses. She just got involved and we don't want to lose her."

"I know all these other issues are important," said Lindsey, another member. "But there are too many names, facts, and legislative issues that aren't necessarily relevant. We came here for the environment, the ozone layer, the rainforests, and the exhaustion of renewable resources. We all want to preserve our habitat so our children don't have to live in concrete tombs underground. I don't know that it has to be so political."

Stumbling across new ground   My sense was that most participants liked the attempt to broaden the movement's focus, although a vocal minority had reservations. Nevertheless, students of color involved in the organization felt frustrated. They'd established their own caucus the previous year at the massive Champaign-Urbana Catalyst conference, in the face of a gathering whose participants were overwhelmingly white and whose speakers were hardly less so. They'd pushed to have SEAC broaden its constituency. SEAC had billed its conference in Boulder as broadly multicultural. They'd even raised money under the flag of linking the environment with racial and social justice. Yet participants here remained as white as ever.[7]

Much of this was due to the gathering's location at the geographically remote and racially homogeneous University of Colorado at Boulder campus. But this itself was a political choice, though one made in a context of few other schools being willing to shoulder the logistical burden. During the Boulder conference, at a meeting of SEAC's national council, a member whose parents had been Indian immigrants joined National Council Coordinator Miya Yoshitani in attacking their white peers for racial hypocrisy. They were tired, they said, of waiting for change. Campus environmental activists, they said, needed to reach out both to students of color and to their communities. They said the movement's efforts would fail if they continued to enlist only the comfortable.

The debate echoed similar questions raised within the student community service movement. Yet SEAC's more overtly radical politics meant it had access to even fewer resources to deal with such issues than COOL. The ten national staffers already put in sixty- to seventy-hour weeks, earning $12,000 a year with no benefits. Most students who attended the conference camped out on a nearby field in twenty-degree weather. Even though it was struggling financially, the organization did tremendously effective work. But the criticisms hit hard, triggering painful discussions on whether in an effort where "the grass roots we started with were white roots" it was hypocritical even to pretend to speak to broader constituencies.

Like COOL, SEAC activists wanted both to expand their initial base and to continue enlisting the kinds of students who'd first responded to their vision. The 1991 Boulder conference did offer a multicultural array of speakers. The organization had hoped that a new cultural diversity coordinator and the people of color caucus would help in further outreach. A few local affiliates had already forged successful multiracial or multiclass coalitions. University of Chicago students helped the South Side community block a proposed garbage incinerator. New York SEAC chapters had joined labor unions to fight the James Bay hydro-project. A number of groups had fought for Native American treaty rights. SEAC also planned a campaign in which interns would work with local community groups in the desperately poor Cancer Alley corridor from New Orleans to Baton Rouge. In recognizing the urgency of racial and class divisions at all, the organization had gone beyond a number of mainstream environmental groups that barely acknowledge their existence, or even celebrate the upscale demographics of their constituents. But as the critics made clear, they had a long way to go in dealing with these issues.

I had mixed feelings watching the overwhelmingly white SEAC representatives beat themselves up over their current homogeneity. Their critics were right in that white middle-class groups represented too narrow a base and too limited a perspective. Yet students can needlessly trash themselves for failing to instantly surmount America's deepest social divisions. SEAC was not three years old as a national organization. The movements it helped coalesce had already given thousands of previously apolitical students new priorities and new commitments. For all that I admired SEAC's lack of complacency, I feared its leaders were so racking themselves with guilt that they risked tearing the organization apart before it could build the strength to face these complex challenges. Like all campus movements attempting to deal with such difficult and divisive issues, student environmental activists were, in the words of a woman from Stockton State, just beginning to "stumble across new ground."

Ultimately I respected them for making the effort. "None of us have the exact same vision for social change," concluded SEAC's national coordinator Miya Yoshitani in her talk leading off the Boulder conference. "We have different priorities, come from different backgrounds. Whether we're working on toxics or old-growth forests, it's political. We shouldn't be afraid of it. Every generation changes the world, consciously or not. We've inherited the changes of others: population increases, Hiroshima, rainforest destruction, the Gulf War. This movement will become what we make it."

Book three **World in motion**

~~~~~~

Introduction **Uncertain times**

American campuses are no longer entirely silent. Social concern has begun to revive.
Students have started to find new role models to help them take committed stands, re-
connect with history, and build engaged communities.

Yet the world in which this activism has returned continues to change. The
cold war has ended. New conflicts have replaced it. With the United States now the sole
military superpower, our leaders continue to discover new potential enemies in the
realms of terrorism, drug trafficking, Islamic fundamentalism, and unauthorized nuclear
states. At the same time, America has hit a persistent economic decline, fueled by a
runaway global economy and domestic policies that have continually strip-mined the
future. This has made day-to-day survival for many, including many students, increasingly difficult. Politically involved students have also faced a strong conservative backlash that has challenged their most significant gains.

I've chosen, in this book's final sections, to look at ways these shifts have rebounded on campus political involvement. I begin by assessing the roots and scope of
resurgent concern, including America's increasingly visible crises, a building activist
presence that makes it easier for new students to plug in, and the influx of a new generation whose parents themselves often marched twenty years before. I take the 1991
Persian Gulf War as a post–cold war test of the student movement's strength, in the face
of a crisis extraordinarily difficult to confront. Massive student strikes at City University

of New York highlight issues of educational access—made all the more acute by an economy in which public dollars grow scarcer by the day—and suggest new coalitions with the potential to demand equitable solutions. The conservative reaction has been to attack even modest student political gains by lumping them together under the instantly dismissive catchphrase "politically correct." In the next chapters, I explore the roots of these attacks and ways students can overcome new obstacles that the attacks have created.

Finally, I return to the world beyond the college gates, and follow the journey of both activists and adapters as they continue their disparate paths. I examine what continues to stop the adapters from taking public stands, and ways the activists have sought to stay true to their developing commitments. I conclude with visions of responsibility that might foster involvement for us all, and how they play out in the recent students' lives.

Nineteen ～～～～～～～～～～～～～

Coming back to concern   The resurgence of student involvement

～～～～～～～～～～～～～～～～～～～～～～～～

How politically active are recent students, compared with the past? How has their involvement changed? In spring 1969, in the words of Berkeley sociologist Todd Gitlin, "three hundred colleges and universities, holding a third of American students, saw sizable demonstrations, a quarter of them marked by strikes or building takeovers, a quarter more by disruption of classes and administration, a fifth accompanied by bombs, arson, or the trashing of property."[1]

In spring 1970, following Nixon's invasion of Cambodia and the killing of student demonstrators at Kent State and Jackson State, protest escalated still further. Strikes broke out at 30 percent of the nation's 2,500 campuses. Two-thirds saw protests of one kind or another. Probably between 50 and 60 percent of the students in the United States, argues Gitlin, at least briefly took part; at least a million students probably demonstrated for the first times in their lives during that month of May.[2]

Such massive outcries were exceptional for the decade: in a 1965 Harris poll, only 6 percent of college students favored immediate withdrawal from Vietnam; as late as spring 1967, half of all students nationwide considered themselves Vietnam "hawks"; even in 1969, half of all undergraduates continued to view their college education primarily in terms of increased potential earnings. But at the height of the war and of the antiwar movement's challenge, unprecedented numbers found ways to take a stand.[3]

During that peak of concern, active students focused primarily on Vietnam, though many also developed a more general critique of America's ills. Now, they take on dozens of different causes from date rape to racial issues, gay rights, South Africa, the CIA, urban poverty, and the rainforests. Most schools now have a half dozen groups taking on different political questions. Ones that used to attract just four or five students to their meetings now draw fifteen or twenty; those larger to begin with, seventy or eighty. Young women and men make up a steadily growing segment of major national marches.

The 1989–90 academic year marked a watershed, with student political efforts breaking out in all directions. Two thousand student leaders gathered in Washington, D.C., to fight for increased student financial aid. Twenty thousand marched to challenge homelessness. Four hundred schools joined a national abortion rights speak-out. Syracuse students boycotted student services to protest tuition hikes. A thousand Rutgers students protested similar hikes at a board of governor's meeting. Berkeley students pushed through an ethnic studies curriculum requirement. Two thousand Cleveland State students marched through the city streets and held an eighty-one-day sit-in to protest the dismissal of a sympathetic vice president for minority affairs. Students attending Earth Day events sent 200,000 postcards to Congress.

Student movements now offer multiple pathways to commitment. If you shy away from blockades, strikes, or marches, you can join low-key educational campaigns, like the FACTS group's. You can work through campus elections, in which radical coalitions succeeded recently at schools from Chicago Circle to the University of Texas. A gay University of Minnesota woman even won the endorsement of the Greek system. You can join organizations like COOL and SEAC and move from seemingly innocuous efforts like helping with recycling or serving food at a soup kitchen to questioning America's fundamental economic inequities. Off campus, a modest musical, theatrical, and artistic counterculture combines with a new crop of struggling alternative newspapers and fanzines. Even among students who don't take active political stands, a growing number have begun grappling with goals beyond fast-track careers.

National surveys confirm the shift in mood. Taking the 1993 figures, a near-record 42 percent of entering freshmen said it was "essential" or "very important" to influence social values. Eighty-four percent wanted to see the government do more on pollution, 64 percent believed that nuclear disarmament was attainable, and 62 percent supported abortion rights. Twenty-nine percent wanted to become "involved in programs to clean up the environment," a slight drop from the 34 percent response shortly after the 1990 Earth Day anniversary, but nearly twice as much as the 16 percent figure from the mid-1980s. Forty one percent considered it an important goal to help "promote racial understanding," up from 34 percent two years before. The numbers of freshmen intending to major in the largely antipolitical field of business dropped for the sixth successive year to 16 percent, down from a peak of 27 percent, and a lower figure than at any point since 1972. The goal of "being very well off financially" also leveled off to 74.5 percent, one percent lower than the peak six years earlier. Twenty-seven percent of freshmen considered themselves liberal or far-left, the highest number since 1976, although the numbers of conservatives also grew to 23 percent. Students also divided in their self-identifications by gender. Freshman women, as mentioned, considered themselves to the left of the men by the unnervingly large margin of 18 percent.[4]

We should not exaggerate these shifts. Two years earlier, the same national freshman surveys reported that a record 39 percent of the current entering class had "participated in demonstrations" as high school seniors, a percentage commentators claimed was even higher than at the height of the sixties. A spate of coverage highlighted this statistic, combined it with real examples of youth activism, and heralded a new political wave about to sweep everything before it.[5]

But the picture is more complicated. The numbers do reflect important growth in concern, and the pattern of their increase has continued. But taking into account all issues and approaches, from fights over faculty hiring and student rights to marches addressing the environment, homelessness, Central American interventions, and both sides of abortion politics, there's no way 40 percent of entering college students have been involved. I've probably talked with five thousand students in classes that I've visited. Because of the kinds of faculty who bring me in, the responses I hear are skewed, if anything, toward greater than average social concern: I've explicitly compensated for this in my other research approaches. But when I ask students to describe any previous social involvement, only a small minority answer yes. No matter how broad a definition I cast, the rest cannot come up with relevant examples from their past.

Perhaps the students responded as they did to the ACE surveys because they wanted to feel concerned. Their answers may well reflect a more general yearning for change. But when students answered that they had "participated in demonstrations," I believe they were referring less to dissident student efforts than to their participation in officially sponsored gatherings opposing drugs, drunk driving, and high-risk sexuality— near-omnipresent rallies that they can easily view as "demonstrations" of a sort. These aren't irrelevant issues, although they are often framed in misleading ways. But most high school "demonstrations" that address them do not require their participants to challenge entrenched authorities or to wrestle with their conscience. Rather, they affirm a prevailing state-sanctioned morality. Involvement is as automatic and costless as marching was in the Soviet Union in a pre-Gorbachev Young Communist rally.[6]

Campus sentiments are changing, and changing significantly. In a 1990 survey of college seniors, 18 percent had participated at some point in campus protests of all political stripes, even if only to listen at the edge of a rally or to attend an institution-wide vigil in the wake of a campus racial incident. A 1990 survey found a quarter of all undergraduates pursuing some level of community service, averaging just over five hours a week on such activities. But this change remains a nascent one. Students are only beginning to believe social engagement is worth the cost.[7]

Standing against the storm   The 1991 Gulf War reflected the building currents of student involvement, even as it tested them. When Bush first deployed troops to the Gulf, students found his actions hard to oppose. Saddam Hussein was a brutal dictator who had gassed the Kurds, invaded Kuwait, murdered his own people, and offered no conceivable framework to view him as benevolent. National peace groups that might have offered leadership, reeling from the cold war's end, were at a financial and organizational low. Key leaders like Jesse Jackson and Daniel Ellsberg backed the initial troop allocations. Few on campus thought a war likely to occur.

Most students remained confused and conflicted, uncertain of how to respond and uncertain of their right to challenge the president. They felt understandable tugs of loyalties to their fathers, brothers, sisters, and friends whose lives were at risk in the Gulf. Yet some quickly spoke out, particularly students who'd long challenged America's overt and covert wars. The first teach-ins began, and scattered marches and rallies, including one at the University of Montana that brought out 600 students in freezing rain. That October, SEAC warned against a pending war at their 7,600-student conference at the University of Illinois. Groups like USSA and Progressive Student Network began to respond.

Then came the November elections, just after which Bush announced that he was sending another 200,000 troops to the Gulf. The threat of war escalated. Students called up from the reserves said good-bye to girlfriends, boyfriends, wives, and husbands. National media, which had presented a steady drumbeat of cheerleading, began including the cautionary voices of Washington insiders, including two former heads of the Joint Chiefs of Staff. Though Bush's timing left just over a month until winter break, campus peace activity increased dramatically. Rallies and teach-ins at Michigan, Minnesota, Stanford, San Francisco State, U. Mass. Amherst, UC Santa Barbara, Berkeley, and again at Montana drew anywhere from five hundred to two thousand students. Antiwar teach-ins sometimes reached over a third of the students on a given campuses. Throughout the country schools debated the crisis.

Students responded best when activists systematically reached out. At the University of Louisville, a large commuter campus, the Progressive Students' League (PSL) began holding Wednesday rallies just after Bush's November deployments. An affiliate of the national Progressive Student Network, PSL already had a strong presence opposing U.S. Central American intervention, promoting international human rights, and supporting a more multicultural curriculum. More than six hundred students showed up at their initial speak-out, milling around concerned and curious. A student spoke whose husband, stationed at nearby Fort Knox, had just filed for conscientious objector status. She wore his army uniform, decorated with bandages, blood, and the word EXXON taped over his name. She was explaining the reasons for his choice when a ROTC man shouted her down, then charged the platform brandishing a stack of PSL fliers he'd ripped up. He tried to get those listening to chant "U.S.A! U.S.A!" to drown her out. Other ROTC men threw firecrackers and cups of ice and shouted down other speakers.

Unable to hear those at the podium, the students began to debate whether it was wrong to silence the peace activists or wrong for the activists to challenge the president. Arguments got heated. People shoved and pushed. But dialogue also began, and the controversy led the local evening news.

PSL's organizers were used to taking heat. Tom Pearce, a key leader, was part Native American, and had long worked with the American Indian Movement. His minister father had worked as a civil rights activist in rural Georgia. His mother was a Baptist minister involved in feminist theology. When PSL held a second rally the following week, the ROTC people and some frat men burned their banner and tore up more of their fliers. The PSL group offered them the mike, and the ROTC men explained that those opposing a possible war were "just a bunch of Communist faggots." When the antiwar students tried to talk, the ROTC men resumed their heckling.

The more the ROTC faction acted like boors, the more PSL gained sympathy. A generally conservative campus newspaper strongly supported their right to speak out, and students started writing letters to challenge Bush's actions. Concerned faculty began their own teach-ins. The PSL held three more rallies, drawing six hundred to eight hundred students each time. Speakers like a PSL cochair with a sister in the reserves described Bush's long and sordid history assisting Saddam Hussein consolidate his power, as well as the long line of United Nations–condemned occupations and invasions by nations Bush still considered staunch allies. They described initiatives for Arab-mediated solutions that Bush had dismissed from the beginning.

Peace groups at other schools conducted similar outreach through dorm meetings, teach-ins, and leafletting at football games. But opposition at most campuses didn't really begin to mobilize until after Bush's November escalation, when the march to war was well underway. Initially, most students denied that a crisis existed. Students deferred to experts they saw on television, like Henry Kissinger, who switched from supporting Iraq as a strategic ally to cheering the march toward war. When they did encounter dissent, they had little context to judge the competing claims of truth. Until the last moment, most assumed Bush and Hussein would cut some kind of a deal.[8]

More than anything, students felt powerless. The month before Bush's November troop escalations, I asked classes at a number of schools whether or not they thought a war was likely. Half believed war would occur, most opposed the prospect, some said it would depend on Bush's standing in the polls. Echoing responses to earlier inquiries I'd made on subjects like nuclear arms, only a handful thought they could do anything about it. Given the razor-close congressional vote, a large enough initial outcry might have tipped the political balance away from the military path. But most dismissed any possible impact of their voices.

These obstacles sometimes defeated all dialogue. When activists themselves considered Bush's initial deployments just bluff, or were so isolated that all they could do was slap up a few fliers, mobilize the hard core of twenty or thirty people, and figure the real protests would start when the body bags came home, they found themselves unable to adequately respond when the bombs started to fall. But numerous students did question the moral implications of Bush's choices, and when they did this early enough and with enough visibility, they laid the groundwork for continuing debate.

A lot more posturing   For University of Washington Student Body President Heidi Wills, the crisis brought a further journey into commitment. When Bush first sent troops to the Gulf, she was unsure what to think. Then she began questioning the growing deployments and holding them to the standards for a just war she'd studied in one of her classes. It angered Heidi that Bush was unwilling even to wait to see if sanctions would work, "that he wouldn't go to every means possible to avoid war. Plus he started out talking about the risk to our energy resources after doing nothing but undermining conservation. Then when people said they wouldn't go to war for oil, his talk changed to freeing the poor Kuwaiti people. But what about South Africa, Tiananmen Square, or El Salvador? Why pick this instance out? Then Saddam Hussein's nuclear threat, which he never mentioned before. I saw Bush doing a lot more posturing than negotiating."

Despite Heidi's successful recycling campaign, UW had been quiet in recent years. Few faculty were politically involved. The state's most socially concerned students tended to enroll in the alternative public colleges at Evergreen State or Western Washington University. Students were slow to react to the Gulf crisis as well, although a UW student reservist died early on when his jeep overturned in the desert sand. The main campus group to respond, U.S. Out, was dominated by a sterile Left sect that squandered most of their energy in endless meetings. A more informal and countercultural group, Dawgs of Peace, spoke out often and early with vigils and rallies, but did little systematic outreach to ensure that people attended. Most who wanted to act saw few effective ways to do so.[9]

In January, when students returned from winter break, war seemed just around the corner. Congress was debating. Students nationwide were holding vigils, marches, and sleep-outs. Heidi found a way to respond with the help of a fellow student government member, a military veteran who showed her an antiwar ad in the *New York Times* signed by major church leaders. They got the idea of trying to get money from campus student finance committees to run their own *Times* and *Wall Street Journal* ads before the congressional vote. The two began calling leaders at other campuses to sound out their level of interest. Most were still out for winter break, but they got tentative support from eight of the first ten schools they reached, including Colorado, Wisconsin, and Stanford universities.

Then the backlash hit. A fellow member of the student Board of Control called the *Daily* and said Heidi was misusing student funds with her efforts. In an executive session, one board member after another attacked her. "We're elected for campus issues, not U.S. issues," they said. "It's one thing to call a few schools and find out their football ticket prices, but another to call pages of schools and ask their position on the Gulf." UW students, argued the hostile board members, had widely differing opinions. Heidi had no right to claim a common position, much less to spend student money promoting it. They demanded she stop making the calls and repay the bills. Some even tried to prohibit her from addressing campus rallies.

Heidi felt she had no choice but to comply on the issue of the phone calls. But the attacks shook her. No one had called her names during the recycling campaign. She hadn't expected these responses. "I didn't realize," she recalled, "that the majority of the Board of Control were strong Bush supporters who believed a war was necessary. I assumed everyone shared my concerns about where our country was heading. Maybe, I started thinking, I shouldn't address this issue at all."

But she felt she had to. It puzzled her that when she'd invited her fellow board members to earlier vigils and speak-outs, they'd never attended, not even to get a sense of what fellow students were saying. They'd hung back as well from the recycling campaign, and had to be dragged into working for the Ethnic Studies requirement that all but one had endorsed in their campaigns. They even refused to join USSA's Washington, D.C., lobbying efforts, even though over 80 percent of UW financial aid came from the federal government. Heidi felt they avoided difficult issues.

"The board and I," she concluded, "didn't just have different political views, but a different sense of our roles. When people say student government officials shouldn't speak out, they could make the same argument about church or union leaders, or anyone else who represents a constituency. You could say that about Bush's right to speak, since lots of us disagree with his choices. My attitude is, you jump in and change things by doing something. Of course you meet resistance. You can't guarantee it will make a difference if we march on the war or send a representative to D.C. to argue for student aid. But I want to do everything I can to get other students to think about these issues, and let our government know how we feel."

Given Vietnam-era echoes, students felt a particular responsibility to act. Many who spurned the activists while the war was building up now besieged them, asking what they could do, who they could call, how they might finally make their voices heard. At a "Last Chance" UW rally the Monday following the congressional approval of force, Heidi expected the usual twenty-five people. Over a thousand turned out, filling a third of the large brick plaza, Red Square, and lining up one after another to voice outrage and concern.

Making it clear that she spoke "for Heidi Wills, not for every student on campus," Heidi blasted the Bush administration for failing to give serious negotiation a chance and for helping Saddam Hussein build his military in the first place. "If Bush says our national security depends on oil," Heidi asked, "then why aren't we looking more into conservation as opposed to exploitation? We make Hussein into some kind of Hitler in that he gassed his own people. But we knew that all along. People say our generation doesn't care," Heidi concluded. "But our lives are on the line. I don't know if they'll listen. But it's time to care now if we ever did."

More students arrived, including several hundred from local high schools. The crowd mixed cultural styles: northwest casual in worn flannel shirts, black-clad punks, tie-dyed neo-hippies, neatly sweatered preppies, and even some ROTC cadets and frat men. After the students held hands and sang "Amazing Grace," some got restive and called for a march. While the leadership hesitated, a group of fifty headed off, and then another. Four hundred more students quickly followed—through the adjacent business district, then—echoing protests of twenty years before—up the exit ramps and onto the freeway.

Cars slowed to a halt. Students filled the southbound lanes. Cops rode up on motorcycles, pushed a few people from behind, then tried to head the group off. Scattered marchers braced for confrontation. "Don't fight the cops. Sit down," said an African-American woman who'd been going to ERA and civil rights marches since she was a kid. "Martin Luther King," chanted others, repeating the name like a litany. The crowd sat, cross-legged, on the tarmac. Then Heidi and other leaders negotiated a police escort to the next exit, where they marched on city streets to the federal building.

Passing motorists overwhelmingly supported them. People honked, waved, and cheered from cars and buses, repair trucks, and semis. The students seemed to be carrying the hopes of their city.

"I felt such a common bond," Heidi remembered. "There we were on the freeway. We looked out from that high bridge over all of Seattle, in shock and amazement at being here with each other for this cause. We were here because we cared, our generation trying to effect change. I didn't know what to expect from people we passed, but so many waved and cheered. People helped each other. We cared about each other, about humanity and peace. I don't think I'll ever forget that day."

On the eve of the congressional vote, the students joined thousands of fellow citizens to try to support a path other than war. An unprecedented number of religious leaders had voiced opposition, including the National Conference of Catholic Bishops and the leaders of nearly every mainline Protestant denomination except the Southern Baptists. So had the leaders of major unions. The Military Families Support Network spoke for friends and relatives of the soldiers. Citizens throughout the country held vigils, marches, and meetings.[10]

The evening following the UW freeway rally, 30,000 people marched in Seattle's streets, sponsored by the metropolitan church council and a local peace coalition. The demonstration was the city's largest in seventy years, larger than any national anti-Vietnam rally until 1967. Portland mobilized 10,000 to 15,000—more than any Vietnam-era rally they'd ever had. Tens of thousands marched in the San Francisco streets. Responses on the East Coast and in the Midwest were hampered by freezing winter weather and by greater factionalism, but 10,000 marched in Minneapolis, 4,000 in Milwaukee, 500 in Corpus Christi, Texas. In Washington, D.C., a 10,000-person religious procession walked from the National Cathedral to the White House—among them George Bush's own Episcopal bishop.[11]

Campuses erupted in a similar last-minute flurry of concern, particularly where students had challenged the build-up from the beginning. More than 4,000 University of California students marched at Santa Barbara and Santa Cruz, 3,000 at the University of Oregon, and 3,000 attended a candlelight vigil at the University of Michigan. Three thousand also marched at Western Washington University, an hour and a half north of Seattle, where students had been conducting teach-ins and staffing information tables since the previous November. Twenty-five hundred turned out at University of Colorado, 1,500 at Ohio State, 3,000 at the University of Cincinnati, some 1,000 at the University of Texas. In New York and Chicago, students swelled the demonstrations in the streets. Indiana students erected a fifty-tent encampment in a snow-covered field outside the Student Union, and slept out for the duration of the war, despite drunken frat men throwing eggs and tomatoes at them, ambushing them with bottle rockets, and calling them SCUDS. Similar tent cities went up and remained at the University of North Carolina and University of Georgia.[12]

Shock and disbelief   In Seattle, the day of the deadline passed in a blur, with more major rallies and marches. Then the storm began. The bombs fell. For the first couple of weeks anti-war students still hoped the bombing could be stopped. Across the country students poured onto the city streets, occupied buildings, marched, and struck—all hoping to stop the process, call a warning, do something to hold back the killing. Four thousand marched at MIT. A thousand marched at the University of Illinois. Santa Cruz and UCLA students initiated strikes. Participants felt they were riding an emotional roller-coaster. "One minute you feel no power at all," said one of the organizers of a sit-in at Western Washington University. "Then you're there with hundreds of people. You feel that, sooner or later, nothing will stop you."

A similar surge of protest erupted off campus. Citizens filled the streets in just about every city north of the Mason-Dixon line. But speaking out soon became harder. Exhaustion set in from days of marching and the weight of dashed hopes. The war's momentum was relentless, as allied bombers pounded Iraq at will, George Bush seemed to call every shot, and the media cheered on the home team. Those who resisted faced news blackouts, accusations of disloyalty, and grave inner doubts about what purpose their actions still served.

With the war now in full swing, the UW *Daily* was filled with attacks on Heidi and others who had opposed it. One student compared campus peace marchers to supporters of the Nazis. "You protestors are so selfish," wrote another. "All you can think about is getting your face on television. . . . You're more violent than anyone else. Half of you don't even know what's going on there."

"I am not a liberal, beret-wearing, peace-rallying, freeway-walking, class-skipping, student government activist," wrote one of Heidi's critics on the Board of Control. "I am sick of opening the *Daily* and our local Seattle papers and being bombarded by pictures of our student body president lobbying people to oppose the war in the Gulf." Students even blamed the peace marchers for not acting earlier, regardless of whether they themselves had spurned their leaflets. "Nuke 'Em Till They Glow," read the banner hung on a UW fraternity house, as members joked about crushing "those sand niggers." "The Iraqis invaded another country," a letter stated bluntly. "They deserve to die."[13]

Given this backlash, many resisters became reduced to mute spectators, watching in silence as TV reporters presented the war literally from the point of view of the bombs. Students who'd once hoped, prayed, and marched to prevent a war from happening, now simply hoped it would end quickly. Even those still speaking out did so with a sense of shock and disbelief. "I felt this can't be happening," remembered Sonya Tinsley, who along with several hundred other Emory students, marched and attended teach-ins. "Like I've been holding onto a mistaken notion that we actually learn from the past. Instead this happens, and everyone gets emotionally bullied into supporting it."

The focus of this bullying was the need to support American troops. As I've discussed, images of Vietnam-era peace activists spitting on soldiers pervade student views of that earlier period. As the Gulf War approached, radio, television, and print media commentators resurrected the image full force, so much so that even students who opposed the war would validate the myth by explaining, "We have to let the troops know that we aren't spitting on them this time." The Bush administration used images of Vietnam-era soldiers harassed and spurned to consciously beat down antiwar voices. Government spokespeople evoked the companion myth of Vietnam being "a war we fought with one hand tied behind our back," a myth accepted by nearly 80 percent of the American public.[14]

As the omnipresent flags and yellow ribbons attested, these strategies worked. People wore them from a sense of concern, a hope that America's brave young men and women would return safely. Even antiwar activists often wore the ribbons, sometimes to honor friends serving in the Gulf. But these symbols, and the flags in particular, also fed a national mood of triumph—one that displaced discussion about why American troops were fighting in the first place, and buried doubts about the war's larger costs in more immediate loyalties to sons and daughters, friends, co-workers, and neighbors who were over there at risk. "If you didn't support Desert Storm," said Emory's Sonya Tinsley, "people took it as a slap in the face to all those giving their lives."

Students who questioned the war faced other barriers. Though most believed sanctions and negotiations could have worked, they found it hard to maintain their belief in this path when faced with the omnipresent quick fix of the bombs. Where they'd largely accepted Bush administration descriptions of Iraq's vast military might, and used them to warn of a potential bloody quagmire, they now had to make the much harder case that the slaughter was tragic and needless even though the dead men, women, and children were Iraqi. Jewish students felt particularly anguished as SCUD missiles landed in Israel. "I have relatives in Tel Aviv," said one of the student coordinators of the University of Pennsylvania's volunteer center. "I marched when the war broke out and I'll keep on doing so. But it's hard and I'm scared. When we see Tel Aviv getting bombed, we have to realize that's what's going on, far more, in Iraq. I work with the homeless every week. We've made more homeless in Panama and Baghdad. People don't realize that to accept war is to accept poverty. We have to find alternatives to violence."

Marches and forums at the University of Washington continued, with much smaller numbers. The Dawgs of Peace built an encampment on Red Square, and for the duration of the war slept out in tents, cooked donated food, studied by plaza flood-lamps, and continued to raise questions with whomever would listen. But whether or not most students agreed with the war, they increasingly felt protest served little purpose.

Students also faced structural hurdles to acting. Teachers hesitated to bring up such a controversial issue in class, so the normal flow of academic routines resumed as if nothing extraordinary was happening. At some schools, hostile administrators prohibited on-campus marching and leafletting and threatened to cut off funds for student organizations that challenged the war. Given pervasive media blackouts of the dissent, students even at relatively active campuses began to feel that few shared their moral reservations, and therefore began to doubt them. Or they began blaming each other for failing to turn back the tide. Because Americans weren't dying by the thousands and the news reports never covered the Iraqi dead, the war's human cost seemed strangely remote. More than anything, students who questioned the war felt isolated, as major national and local media banished voices of dissent. On January 26, ten days after the war began, a broad coalition overcame freezing weather to draw a quarter million people to Washington, D.C. For nearly four hours, they filled Pennsylvania Avenue, marching thirty abreast from the Capitol Mall to the Ellipse behind the White House. The same day, between a hundred thousand and two hundred thousand marched in San Francisco, and thousands more in other American cities.[15]

In D.C., where I attended the march, those who came were astonished at the turnout—ten times larger than the first major national anti-Vietnam demonstration in 1965, and larger than any till the height of that decade's unrest. Students made up a third of the marchers, coming by train, car, and van, pooling money for gas and expenses, financing the trip by loans, student government grants, sympathetic sponsors, and by working overtime and living on peanut butter. The University of Michigan sent 500 students, Columbia 400, Rutgers and Indiana, 250. A fifth of Swarthmore's students came down. A University of Colorado group drove thirty-five hours through blinding snowstorms. "People learned my life-story whether they wanted to or not," said a woman from Louisiana State who had been in a carpool for twenty-two hours.[16]

But few except those on the scene heard their voices. The major media mostly accepted a police claim that the demonstration drew just 75,000, although it packed streets three times as wide as the 30,000-person Seattle march, and took three times as long. The *New York Times* buried a brief story on page seventeen. CBS gave as much time to a group of 150 prowar demonstrators who held signs with slogans like "Smoke Iraq, not Crack." NBC's president vetoed the network's showing video footage of the actual destruction in Iraq and fired the stringer who'd provided it—a man who had worked with NBC for twelve years. National media similarly ignored the large San Francisco marches, the stream of local and regional protests, and almost all the student activity.[17]

I did what I could   As the war wound on, Heidi, along with other activists, struggled to keep from being demoralized into silence. Where she'd drawn praise for her recycling efforts, people now attacked her for her stands, called her a traitor, even insulted her beret. She stayed involved "because it was really all I could do. I couldn't stay home and do nothing." Maybe her actions would have no immediate impact, but after a while that ceased to matter. "I talked with friends and tried to change their opinions. I went to the rallies. I did what I could."

Campus groups that stayed most effective did so by building up a decent base early on, recognizing that whether or not they could stop the daily rain of bombs, their actions would influence the judgment of their peers as to whether the war was a glorious victory or moral betrayal. And recognizing that such judgments could shape America's future choices. Teach-ins in particular continued, as students who felt frustrated at bearing lonely witness still wanted to understand the roots and implications of what was going on. Coordinated events on February 21 reached 250 campuses in thirty-seven states. Continuing to reach out to their student peers, taking on highly specific projects with particular educational goals, active students tried to help their communities critically reflect.

The war galvanized new involvement among campus supporters as well as opponents. Although their rallies generally drew fewer participants, they constituted a genuine grassroots conservative response, in a way that the handfuls of foundation-funded right-wing newspaper staffers did not. They draped signs and flags from the outside windows of their rooms, conducted their own intermittent vigils, and derided their opponents as "malcontent peaceniks."

Even they hit the standard barriers to participation. A University of Pennsylvania fraternity group made a massive effort to pull together a prowar rally by phoning up every Greek in the school, and got scores of promises to turn out for the cause. But only 150 showed, many fewer than for the initial peace protests, though campus polls by now supported the war. When the initiators asked their friends why they hadn't come, they said they didn't feel comfortable taking a public stand—expressing the same sense that led them away from political involvement in general.

Many of the students who had challenged the war felt demoralized and bitter, kicked in the gut—like union members who've lost a strike. "We believed," said a Chicago Circle activist, "that all we had to do was march in the streets and we'd change the course of history. We marched and marched, and none of it seemed to matter." Participants felt betrayed not only by their government, but by an American public that seemed wholly in support of the bombs, and sometimes by peers who'd encouraged them to act.

Yet campus antiwar activism also charted new ground, particularly where concerned students systematically reached out. It's misleading to compare responses to a six-week war with an involvement that lasted more than a decade. Even during the anti–Vietnam War movement's height, political activity surged and receded with the twists and turns of national events, with the academic calendar, and with participants' own sense of energy and exhaustion. The Gulf War was too fleeting to allow for this process to occur. The only sustained chance for students to actively seize the agenda came in September and October, when war seemed a remote possibility. Despite all the obstacles, for a brief moment more students took action than in any other campus movement in years.

Heidi Wills felt the war made her less innocent, yet more resolute in her own commitment. "I'm more aware," she said, "of how our government can lie, and how easily Americans can choose to live a lie that's comfortable than face a truth that isn't. It's also tested my beliefs. Before, I knew what I thought, but it was all pretty easy. I learned from my classes, but except for one or two professors, they didn't make me search my soul about what I really believed in. Now I've put my opinions out for everyone to judge. I know who I am more, and have found others who care as well, who want to work for the improvements we should make or could make or have the ability to make—if we just only pull together the resources. I want to tip the scale toward greater human happiness, instead of misery, death, and destruction. I don't think this war or what brought it on helped do that."

Even movement participants' frustration sometimes firmed their resolve. The information "festers inside you like a sore," one student told me. A University of Colorado woman had been peripherally involved with the local PIRG, then emerged from the war heading a new campus project to challenge the nearby Rocky Flats atomic weapons complex. "The war propelled me," she said, "into doing things I never would have done. Marching in black with a bloody doll, getting arrested, going to court and speaking out. I felt an incredible amount of pain and despair. I was constantly pacing my room, thinking, What am I going to do? How can I respond? How do I know that what I'm doing is right? But I've realized since, that I don't want anyone else to have to feel what we went through—that despair and frustration. I don't want to watch more people being bombed. We have to act for the generations to come."

For most students, the war came so quickly and passed so fast it could almost have been just another TV action adventure series. It widened gaps between the students who acted and those who did not, but common ground soon reemerged around issues like tuition hikes and educational cutbacks. Its long-term impact receded precisely because it was so easy, quick, and costless.

Visible crises   Why did such a broad-based campus antiwar movement emerge despite the odds? Which students spoke out and which did not? How did campus responses reflect new political shifts? To understand these questions we need to briefly return to the roots of renewed concern.

Campus activism has grown in response to America's increasingly visible crises—ones that have continued to jar students out of complacency. Savings and loan institutions went bankrupt. The national debt doubled and tripled. Wall Street glamor tarnished as the empires of men like Ivan Boesky and Michael Milken collapsed. On a personal level, students confronted rising tuition costs, escalating loans, and an uncertain economic future. Those who were racial minorities experienced particular individual or institutional affronts. Supreme Court restrictions on abortion threatened all sexually active men and women. AIDS forced gays to confront their identity.

Other students acted in response to the increasingly visible external crises. Community service participants discovered that a quarter of America's children live in poverty. Divestment activists linked college investment policies with the violence of apartheid. White students joined those of color in pushing for campuses where all students could feel at home. Campus environmentalists were shocked into action by reports of ozone depletion, rainforest destruction, and massive loss of topsoil.

Such crises spur political involvement. They do not by themselves create it. Students still have a choice of how to respond. Some hunch their shoulders and trudge on, resolving to "work twice as hard," or praying, like Dale and his girlfriend Linda, that God will eventually ease the plight of their communities. Some seek private refuge while ignoring others similarly beaten down: an Emory African-American student who feared that involving himself in black issues would jeopardize his chances for a good job after college; a participant in tuition strikes at Hunter College who at first hoped the tuition hikes just wouldn't affect her. Some drown in anger or despair, like the Columbia students who lost their sense of how to get past branding those who disagreed with them "liberal wankers." But America's crises have also served as flash points for students ready to get involved, have given them an impetus to act, reach out, and spark new movements.

Unlike students of a decade earlier, those from the late eighties on have not had to reinvent activism from day one. Rather, they've entered colleges and universities that have already had some years of steadily percolating involvement, where step by step a base has been built. At most campuses, political debates have slowly grown more widespread and issues more familiar. In the absence of internal factionalism or betrayal, the more active groups, organizations, and movements exist at a given school, the easier it is for students to slide into involvement.

Active students have begun to feel part of an international community of concern. Resistance in Soweto inspired divestment activists, and the Salvadoran medical student inspired Greeks for Peace. SEAC chair Miya Yoshitani described how Eastern European students stood up "to take control of their future." At the same time, American student activists have themselves reached out to become less alien to their apolitical peers. As Stork, the engineer friend of Matt's from Greeks for Peace, explained, "When I read about some march in the *Daily* I can identify because Matt Greene is part of it." Renewed activism has also built a base for critical thought and engagement by challenging the university curriculum, feeding overflow classes on the Vietnam era, and creating departments dedicated to the study of women's issues, peace, ethnic and environmental studies. Although the adapters still dominate most colleges, students who want to get involved can readily find existing organizations, programs, and resources.

Alternative currents   Opposition to the war reflected these currents. Students were far more ready to question Bush's pronouncements because they'd seen him lie on Central America, dodge on Iran Contra, dissemble regarding his own son's role in the bankrupt Silverado savings and loan. They were used to challenging American interventions, and believed that if they only spoke out with enough conviction and persistence, their fellow citizens would take heed.[18]

To a degree, this was true. Where schools had created an activist tradition, and mobilized well before the bombs began to fall, enough momentum built that it often allowed effective dissent to continue. This happened, for instance, at Louisville. The

Progressive Students League (PSL) bought six thousand copies of a special Gulf War edition of *Z Magazine* and distributed them, together with their own organizational newsletter, inside the Student Union. They enlisted sympathetic faculty to speak at their rallies and drew a couple hundred students per week to their teach-ins. They organized actions ranging from high-visibility civil disobedience to an all-school week of forums and debates, sponsored jointly with those who had supported Bush's choices. As PSL activist Tom Pearce said, "we worked not just to have rallies of students who agreed with us, but to get the ones on our side to talk to the others who didn't." As a result of PSL's efforts a campuswide poll held during the war's final triumphant week still showed a slim majority of students opposing it. When Louisville held student government elections shortly afterward, every major slate solicited PSL's endorsement, and the multiracial and socially committed group they backed won every seat. Their group emerged with more members and support than ever before.

As with many issues, young men and women split significantly, with women both more dubious and considerably more involved in antiwar marches and speak-outs. In an informal telephone poll a week into the war, reporters from the University of Washington *Daily* surveyed students at UW, University of Oregon, and the highly conservative Washington State University. Men at the three schools supported the war by an overwhelming margin of two and a half to one, while half the women still opposed it. The gender gaps persisted as the war continued.[19]

Gulf War opposition among both high school and college students was far more multiracial than comparable efforts of the Vietnam era. Acutely sensitive to their disproportionate concentration in the military ranks, African-American and Latino students repeatedly described how friends joined the reserves for economic survival, "just two weeks a year and one weekend a month," then suddenly got called up "like just another form of slavery." "Why are black people almost a third of the soldiers in the Gulf?" others asked. "Why does the United States do something about this but not South Africa?" "Why do they get racial with Saddam and the Arabs, just like they do with us?" Many saw the war as one more blatant proof that the U.S. government could always spend billions when it chose to, but never on poor and desperate Americans. Although a sense of greater vulnerability sometimes held students of color back from public action, they remained more skeptical about the war than their white peers, and often more involved in challenging it. As consciously multi-racial organizations like USSA helped coordinate antiwar actions, they brought students together across long-standing divides.[20]

A generational shift toward greater concern also surfaced in tremendous high school student involvement in the initial rallies and marches. Around the beginning of the war, high schools and middle schools throughout the country erupted in a wave of strikes and walkouts larger than at any but the most active colleges. Young students swelled the ranks of Seattle's marches and vigils by coming downtown on the bus to gather at the federal building. Defying threats of detention or suspension, large numbers struck and marched in New York, Minneapolis, San Diego, Louisville, Philadelphia, Eugene, and suburban New Jersey. When a Troy, New York, principal refused a high school student permission to bring in a Marine resister to speak, the student leafletted outside, stirring almost the entire student population to walk out in support and march several blocks to hear him. In Los Angeles, two hundred students left the mainly Latino Montebello High School to help picket a nearby Marine recruiting center. So many high school Latinos joined the citywide antiwar coalitions that the Spanish translators were needed at many of the meetings.[21]

Passing the torch   The antiwar concern of younger students marked a key shift from a generation raised by parents who grew up in the relatively silent fifties, under the shadow of McCarthyism, to one whose families came of age in the sixties. When people assess the Vietnam-era legacy, they think of political, economic, and cultural impact. But many who spoke out during that time have also bequeathed another inheritance—a new generation of activists who they've raised to be socially involved.

Of course only a fraction of parents from the sixties made the movements of the time a central part of their lives. And not all from the fifties generation are hardshell conservatives. Still, among parents of recent student activists, the ones who encouraged students the most, often marched themselves on their own campuses twenty-five years before.

Many of these parents have remained involved, whether challenging Central American intervention, promoting disarmament, working in community politics, or spearheading environmental concern. Their children, students who say they've been "going to demonstrations since I was in my stroller," learn more than blind rebellion. They learn, or the best of them do, how to reflect on the ethics of America's choices, to challenge authorities and institutions when they mislead, and to grapple with how society should be—not just how they might most lucratively fit in. Even when they do not themselves get involved with social causes—for lack of opportunity or from a general pessimism—they generally sympathize with those who do. They have none of the rabid hostility of students from resolutely antipolitical backgrounds.

Alongside expectations of responsibility, these students often learn a repertoire of political skills, including the ability to articulate beliefs, challenge entrenched authorities, engage the differing perspectives of others, and reach out for necessary allies. They learn when to compromise and when to hold firm. They learn ways to view themselves in the world: ones that suggest citizens can live most honorably by working to hold societies up to their highest ideals rather than automatically embracing the dictates of their leaders. They learn political solidarity in their homes, then work to build it on campus.

Growing up with activist parents doesn't always produce intelligent politics. The Columbia woman who told her activist peers that if they didn't join her in marching and chanting in the halls they were "liberal wankers," had been raised by a mother involved in Michigan State SDS. I spoke with a number of active students who felt frustrated at parents who were constantly running out to meetings, demeaning the personal in favor of the political, and voicing mostly cynical critiques devoid of hope. Students tired as well of a broader generational arrogance that treated radical social change as the sole property of those who'd marched in the sixties.

But for most students who grow up on marches, meetings, and grassroots campaigns, public involvement seems simply part of ordinary life. When I visited Minnesota's Gustavus Adolphus College in fall 1989, campus politics were being galvanized by a freshman from a small Wisconsin town whose father had been an early SDS activist. "He stayed in college forever," the student, named Joey, said about his dad, "did lots of general antiwar stuff and a lot of work on Chile. Then he woke up at age thirty-eight and realized the revolution wasn't coming and he couldn't go on forever as he had. Now he teaches at our Community College. They hold lots of debates on nuclear issues and Central America."

Joey spent much of his high school senior year helping coordinate the local Jesse Jackson campaign, galvanizing one of the largest turnouts in Wisconsin. He attended a Rutgers conference that tried to form a national organization of student activists. He'd already begun forging a coalition of concerned Gustavus groups and finding ways to enlist new students. When I asked how he sustained his vision, he mentioned a nineteen-hundred-year-old quote from a rabbi that he'd found in Todd Gitlin's book on the sixties: "It was not granted you to complete the task, and yet you may not give it up." He mentioned Antonio Gramsci's phrase, "pessimism of the intellect, optimism of the will," and spoke of how Virginia Woolf wrote of needing to act regardless of immediate outcomes. He'd grown up learning both organizer's skills and a complex view of his political role. He soared past the standard political barriers almost before he knew they existed.

At Manchester College, an Indiana Quaker school, I saw a passing of the torch between the highly involved coordinator of the college peace studies program and his daughter, who now attended the school. As sometimes occurs, the father was in a slump. He'd worked long and hard for social change, had even helped open up a socially responsible investment option within the largest pension system in higher education. But he felt deeply recent political losses, such as a congressional vote that granted another $100 million in military aid to a death squad government in El Salvador. He seemed tired and worn.

His daughter Kate, in contrast, was energetic, hopeful, willing to try a hundred paths toward the goals they both believed in. Now a junior peace studies major, Kate involved herself in numerous campus groups and lobbied the school to take seriously its Quaker heritage by encouraging students to systematically study nonviolent action. "There've been meetings in my house," she said, "for as long as I remember. I got political buttons and t-shirts for presents. What was hard for me was recognizing that the whole world was not like my family, that we should expect to some extent to be ostracized for speaking out and being political in a small midwestern town."

College brought more demands, Kate said, "than when I was imagining it as a romantic sixth grader. I work at my job, try to get good grades, think about where I might go to grad school." But Manchester also gave Kate a place to apply her ideals. She and her friends, she thought, gave older activists hope.

Parental activism means different things to students of different backgrounds. For students from middle-class families, it often means taking a stand on global issues such as war, peace, and the environment. For those from families harder pressed, it may mean strong community involvement, as in that of Sonya Tinsley's parents in the life of their small Georgia town. For others, it may draw on immigrant memory. A woman involved in a tuition strike at City University of New York recalled relatives involved in the Puerto Rican independence movement.

Young people of color go through different generational passages than young whites. Civil Rights efforts began years before the antiwar movements, and reached out to older citizens through the churches. Their communities rarely have the same false innocence. Even parents who are middle-class professionals have often experienced blatant discrimination. Even when parents were not overtly politically involved, many participated in engaged community work. As Sonya noted, even the Girl Scouts and PTA had a different resonance in the African-American community than in the suburbs. "It's not like you're doing this just for fun. It's more about shaping the next generation, trying to prepare these kids to swim upstream."

Whatever their backgrounds, students brought up in active political traditions learn commitment as a matter of course. Instead of agonizing over whether to get involved, they worry about what approaches will work, and how to balance personal and civic involvements for the long haul. These students sometimes face a shock of recognition, as did the Manchester woman, that not everyone shares their concerns. They face the standard challenges of finding effective strategies for change. But they do so having been brought up with political skills and intellectual and spiritual understandings that promote engagement instead of daunting it. Understandably, they find it easier to get involved.

This propensity for engagement seems strongest in students still in the middle schools and high schools, or even younger. I think of any number of kids of my friends who are growing up learning to act on their convictions. They recycle intensely, scouring family discards for every scrap of aluminum or paper. They nag their parents to buy dolphin-safe tuna. They tease them about their involvements and beliefs, then organize their own social concern groups the moment they get the chance.

The generational shifts have fed renewed concern in young students, from their embrace of socially conscious music, to the Gulf War marches and rallies, to burgeoning environmental clubs and volunteer efforts. Organizations like the Rainforest Action Network are deluged with letters from seven- and eight-year-olds who send in their allowances, hold bake sales and penny drives, and ask how they can help save the trees and animals. Because the most committed young Vietnam-era activists tended to defer having children, and sixties activism did not peak until the end of the decade, most in this new generation have yet to hit America's colleges and help shape their political climate. In the year 2012, the last of them will still be filtering in to make their mark.[22]

Redeeming the vision   The sixties also left a much larger group who marched and spoke out at the time, then sharply reduced their engagement. Retreat often began as a search for respite, for a haven from the constant heat of urgency, and also as a reaction to the movement's factional divisiveness. The war slowly wound down, leaving those who'd worked to stop it exhausted and uncertain of their impact. Participants began shifting from trying to make history with every breath to trying to build more stable lives. Later, individuals who envisioned radical commitment in terms of the barricades found it hard to act in a less dramatic time. U.S. military interventions became less visible, and therefore harder to challenge. Activists built a vision on critiquing the limits of abundance, only to see that abundance begin to slip away, for all but the wealthiest, in a continuing spiral of economic decline. Families, careers, and day-to-day survival added pressures. Without the community or context to sustain them, many individuals saw successively fewer ways to act. For all that many sixties activists did continue on, others became detached and disenchanted political spectators.[23]

What of their kids? What legacies did they find? These parents don't provide the same models as those who've stayed engaged. But it matters that when they look back on their past political efforts, they don't reject them. Even though most from the Vietnam generation do act less often than they did in the sixties, the bulk of those once engaged remain proud of their stands. A handful of hustlers make lucrative careers out of bashing their past—but only a handful. And because there's been no grand disavowal, today's students can more easily hope to pick up the dreams their parents quietly released.

"My family went to the Pentagon," said an activist at Minnesota's Macalester College, "got teargassed, and didn't disown it." They hadn't acted much of late, but at least they backed his efforts. Other students inherited a general attitude of questioning. They grew up encountering hopes postponed, muted, placed on a shelf, sometimes compromised, but never absolutely denied. They learned to regard social engagement as worthy to attempt, if hard to sustain.

In the early sixties, children of the socialists, Communists, labor activists, and Roosevelt New Dealers of the thirties made up much of the initial New Left, whether continuing their parents' engaged traditions or picking up torches they'd let fall. Compared to the late fifties and early sixties, students now have many more cultural models for engagement. Yet, as with environmental activists who grew up loving the Lorax and separating bottles and cans for recycling, students whose parents surrendered their most far-reaching hopes could still feel encouraged by their stands. Their legacy was more mixed than that of students who'd absorbed parental activism with their mother's milk. But many felt a similar mandate to act.[24]

"They were older than most, but they marched against the war," said a Saint Joseph's College woman active in Central America issues. "My mother is a hospital chaplain, so she's involved on a personal level. My father's a lawyer, an ambulance chaser. He did some really cool things in the past, but not anymore. He's out for a buck. I admit it. But they still support what I'm doing."

"My folks were hippies," said a Williams man involved in a student-initiated course on nonviolent action. "They spent years without settling down. We constantly went to protests and rallies, and lived in houses with friends—I guess you'd call them communes. They finally settled down. Not that they rejected what they'd done, but they just weren't living that way any more. I saw a change in them. Mom now works with an adult literacy program. My dad directs a Boston organization that does community gardens. They're sort of resigned to alleviating things."

Most people would consider his parents still highly engaged. To the Williams student, they'd let go of their dreams, settling for token local changes. Still, he grew up much more encouraged to speak out and get involved than friends from families where fear of disagreement routinely banished politics even from conversation. He hoped his own actions could push further. "If I can only keep my idealism in mind," he said, "maybe I can really help change things."

It matters how people judge their one-time ideals. In the early spring of 1971, I was indefinitely suspended from Stanford for a series of civil disobedience protests against recruiting by weapons manufacturers. Shortly afterward I had dinner at the home of my aunt and uncle in Los Angeles. Everyone at the table condemned the war, but none had done much to oppose it. They suggested my political involvement was damaging my future. My aunt, who ran an advertising agency, asked her husband, "Maury, you used to call yourself an anarchist. What do you have to say to Paul?"

I felt as vulnerable as I ever had. I wasn't certain where my political path would lead, but hoped I could continue the journey. Yet for whatever complicated mix of concern and fear, my family could only suggest I turn back. I waited, with everyone else, for Uncle Maury to counsel, in older and wiser tones, that youthful idealism was fine, but I needed to yield to reality.

Maury thought for a moment. He then said quietly, "Just because I couldn't live out my vision, doesn't mean it was wrong."

Twenty

I don't want to be a biscuit babe

The CUNY strikes

Students have acted, as I've suggested, to address broad general crises, like homelessness and hunger, or environmental depredations. They've acted as well to defend their own future. Nowhere has this future been more threatened than through rising college costs and cutbacks in support that make higher education less and less affordable for all but the privileged.

In April 1991, New York's Hunter College was on strike. "For a hundred and twenty-nine years, this system was free," explained a speaker at a rally. "Through two depressions, the Civil War, World War I, World War II, and Vietnam. In 1976 they started tuition, which was supposed to be temporary. Now it's going to be almost two thousand dollars. We didn't want to occupy this building. We'd rather be in class. We didn't have a choice."

"In America, they only teach people to think about themselves, to be concerned with themselves." It was Carol Bullard, president of the Evening Student Government (ESG) speaking now. "I can't eat a sirloin steak if you're eating stale bread. No religion will tell you that's right. The administrators say only two or three percent will be closed out, but that's five hundred students just here at Hunter. It's easy to say that when you have your damn Ph.D., but students here live in the projects."

The strike began after New York governor Mario Cuomo proposed a $500-a-year tuition hike for Hunter and the other schools in the 200,000-student system of City University of New York (CUNY), which comprised seventeen two- and four-year colleges, plus associated graduate schools. The increase would bring full-time tuition to $1,950 a year, following a just-enacted $200 hike that raised it from $1,250 to $1,450. Responding to a general state budget crisis, Cuomo proposed a $92 million cut in the funds available for CUNY. Forty million dollars of this would be recovered through the higher tuition rates. Fifty-two million would be absorbed by the schools, leading them to cut faculty and staff, close class sections, and reduce educational suppport services.

For a stockbroker's son or lawyer's daughter, CUNY remained highly affordable. But this wasn't a system of the affluent. Roughly 30 percent of CUNY's students came from families with combined household incomes of less than $14,000 per year, and nearly half with incomes of less than $21,000. Cuomo supported cuts in financial aid as well, between $100 and $400 for each eligible student. Many now enrolled would effectively pay nearly twice as much as the previous fall, for an education already eroded by previous cuts.[1]

Though Cuomo had already made his mind up, CUNY students hoped to pressure the legislature, which had yet to vote on the cuts. The first school to respond was City College of New York, in Harlem. On Monday, April 8, at 5:30 A.M., students took over their huge North Academic Center, securing the doors with massive locks and chains. Early the next morning, on Manhattan's fashionable upper East Side, Hunter students followed suit, occupying their seventeen-story East Building, which housed administrative offices, the library, and classrooms. Students at sixteen other campuses occupled buildings as well, though some were quickly evicted. By the following week, administrators had cancelled classes at City, Hostos, New York Tech, Borough of Manhattan Community College (BMCC), and at the CUNY graduate center. Classes continued alongside building occupations at Hunter, Lehman, York, Queens, Brooklyn College, John Jay, Medgar Evers, Bronx Community College, and La Guardia. Brief occupations occurred at Baruch and at Kingsborough Community College. Students briefly occupied buildings to express their support at SUNY Purchase and Stonybrook.

At Hunter, cars sped down elite Lexington Avenue beneath a third-floor crosswalk from which banners proclaimed "Hunter on Strike," "No tuition hikes," "No budget cuts," and "Education is a Human Right," this last punctuated by a large black fist. Most Hunter students commuted from poor and working-class neighborhoods. They filed into the narrow entryway of one of the two open buildings, past speaker after speaker warning how tuition hikes would devastate their lives and communities. Four hundred students packed the entryway, a shifting cast of listeners. When some drifted off for classes or work, others replaced them. ESG president Carol Bullard asked students to join a downtown rally of striking home health care workers, to be held the next day. A group of students had circulated a petition to reopen the library, and Carol responded, "I would like to use it myself. But the library occupation is temporary. There are three nearby that people can use. If the tuition increases go through, they're permanent." Circulating the blockaders' petition in support of the strike, which would quickly draw several thousand signatures, she invited students to join those blockading the East Building, or at least "sit in the crosswalk and study."

The stories got personal. An African-American man spoke of his father who'd gone back to school five years ago at age fifty. "He goes to York, my sister goes to La Guardia, and I go to Hunter. He's going to have to drop out for us. I said I'd get another job. He said 'No. You finish. I'll go back later.' " A neatly dressed African-American woman explained, "My younger sister wants to come in two years. She won't be able to. I'm doing this for her. We should all be families for each other."

"My grandmother said 'I'll help you through,' " said another woman, nervous for her first time ever at a public rally, "but I don't want to pull myself up over other people."

"This is my story," each of these people explained. "These are the lives that I know. This is why I've made a choice to fight." They offered a vision worlds apart from "They aren't my neighbors" or "Buddy, buzz off." Most students here grew up barely conceiving of going to college. The risks some took in striking might well foreclose future prospects. They fought both for their own survival and for the opportunities of students to come.

Some students shrugged off the cuts, responding, "I'll work twice as hard," in phrases that echoed the beleaguered young farmers of Nebraska. But a third of CUNY's students already worked thirty-five hours or more a week as janitors or clerks, at McDonald's, or delivering newspapers. Some couldn't find work because previous budget cuts had closed so many class sections that they had to enroll in both day and night classes, and few jobs fit into the intervening space. Others already held full-time jobs as hospital clericals, as postal workers, or as secretaries in New York's massive office towers. In between, they squeezed in classes, studying, sleep, and if they were parents, caring for their children.

The families of most CUNY students had few resources to share. Parents, grandparents, and siblings barely got by themselves, working in stores, as hospital orderlies, driving cabs, or sewing clothes in sweatshops. Even when students' fathers and mothers had clambered up to jobs as transit workers, nurses, or mechanics, they were often threatened with layoffs or saw their resources continually exhausted by aunts, cousins, or brothers who were unemployed, sick, or on the street. Roughly 22,000 CUNY students had immediate family members on welfare. As mentioned, nearly a third came from families trying to cope with New York rents on combined household incomes of less than $14,000, and half were from households earning less than $21,000. Sixty-three percent of these students were racial minorities. Eighty percent were the first generation in college. The parents of half had not graduated high school.[2]

A quarter of CUNY's students supported children of their own, many of them as single parents. Striking City College students even brought their kids along to occupy the college day-care center. Whether they lived independently or with their families, most simply lacked the base of wealth, education, and status that middle-class students take for granted.

I don't want to be   Student after student described the pres-
a biscuit babe   sure of their circumstances. "I came here to Hunter last fall as a freshman," explained an eighteen-year-old woman named Nilda Ruiz. "I didn't know about the previous tuition hikes. I didn't care. I thought it wouldn't affect me.

"Then I started hearing rumors and I freaked. I'm the youngest of seven children trying to get a degree. Right now I work at Roy Rogers flipping chicken and baking biscuits for $4.25 an hour—minimum wage. Is my career being a biscuit babe for the rest of my life? I refuse to be one of those uneducated Spanish chicks who lives in tenement housing and has fifteen kids on welfare. I don't think anyone here has the goal of growing up and being on welfare. But if this thing goes through, I don't know if I can bake enough biscuits to scrounge my way. I don't know if I'm going to be here next year."

Nilda was quick and flip, wearing black jeans, a black top, bright red lipstick, and small silver earrings that set off her short curly hair. We talked in a lounge area near the walkway to Hunter's now-closed East Building, while students checked a schedule of relocated classes. Some also scanned strike literature at an adjacent table and signed petitions of support.

Nilda's father, who'd died six years before, had worked two jobs—as a maintenance worker in a baking company and as superintendent of an apartment building. They'd moved from Puerto Rico in the fifties, before Nilda was born, and he'd tried to put aside money for her future, "so I could do what he never could." Nilda's mother was illiterate, with few skills, and spoke no English. Recently, she'd started extension courses to learn English and basic arithmetic, which made Nilda proud. Since her father's death, the family had survived off a bit of savings and the Social Security Nilda received while attending the highly competitive public high school, Music and Art. Now she was eighteen. The Social Security checks had stopped because the program that continued them if you attended college had been cut. Nilda had only her Roy Rogers wages to help her and her mother survive.

"Like I said, I don't want to be a biscuit babe my whole life. Ever since I was a little girl, I wanted to teach art education, teach kids about culture and beauty. But the arts are always first to go. They say they're not necessary. Like they're going to take away all my dreams. Even if I get through, I may have to change my field, because there won't be jobs for art teachers."

"I had it all planned out," Nilda continued. "I came here with nothing but two tokens and a smile. I saw the job at Roy's and thought I could use that and my grants to pay the $625-a-semester tuition. Then it went to $725. Now it's going to $975. I only work twenty hours a week, and make just $85.00 before taxes, plus a bit from my financial aid checks."

She ran down her costs for a recent week: $23 in subway tokens, $35 on a paperback math book, $10 in photocopied handouts, not to mention food, clothes, and helping with rent. "I have to buy notebook paper, pens, this and that. I'm trying to save for a typewriter or a computer. They have a computer lab at school, but you need to make an appointment three weeks in advance, and then you only get an hour. My future seems to be eroding in little bits and pieces."

At Dartmouth, each entering student purchases a computer, with financial aid covering the costs for those who couldn't otherwise afford it. Other campuses have twenty-four-hour computer labs in every dorm. To finish her last paper, Nilda had stayed up all night, using a typewriter borrowed from a friend in a nearby housing project. "It's like a ghetto within a ghetto," she said, "People doing crack and shooting up outside, children playing with little crack vials. When I was little, I used to play with discarded wood planks. These kids play with vials, syringes, and broken bottles. You literally hear them say 'Cmon, I'll be the drug dealer and you be the cop.'"

Like Raul from Chicago Circle, Nilda wanted a job that would let her leave "the rats, crack dealers, and roaches," but that would also enable her to give back to the community. In high school she'd never involved herself in protests, "because my mom was always afraid the government would send police to beat people." Besides, politics at Music and Art was dominated "by the hippies, and it seemed strange to wear outdated clothes and listen to twenty-year-old music." Instead she became involved in a project called City Kids, which met in schools and community centers to discuss how people were treating teenagers. They produced repertory shows supposed to embody their generation's voice on issues like education, drugs, child abuse, and the environment. Nilda spent untold hours acting, dancing, singing, and serving on the organization's youth board—so many hours that she had to retake two of her art classes.

"But the group turned out to be bogus. Its leader always said we should boycott McDonald's because they used so much Styrofoam and destroyed the rainforest by how they raised their meat in South America. We all boycotted it among ourselves and our friends. I'd plead with people to eat somewhere else. Then all of a sudden we had a fundraiser, and McDonald's was contributing. Instead of trying to get people aware of what was going on and what was important, it turned into just a cute show thing. Dancing and singing for these big companies, getting trips to Scotland, just a way to try and get acting jobs in TV."

The experience left Nilda politically cynical. The month before the blockade, she'd thought of coming along with 3,000 other students who bused to Albany from schools across the state and joined over 25,000 union members and other citizens to protest pending state budget cuts. "But I still felt it would all crumble because of the City Kids thing. I worried about what would happen if I got involved."

The blockade seemed different. "People had so much faith it rubbed off on me. I took it on myself to do this for me and for everybody else who might not be able to. Friday I went to a march at City College. It was so exciting to see a thousand people in the street, even though I almost passed out from the heat with no water, wearing black, and sitting on the pavement. It was my first experience protesting, and I'll be registered soon to vote so I can use that power and get that guy Cuomo out of there. This time, my mom's behind me all the way. She just says 'Vaya con Dios, be careful. If a cop grabs you, go with them peaceful, and we'll get you out.' Everyone's really tired here, but we'll do it again and again until this gets resolved."

Until the color changed   The students defended their vision in terms of responsibility to generations to come. They drew as well from CUNY's own history. A citywide referendum founded its first campus, City College of New York, in 1847, as a free school to serve the working poor. The system has produced Nobel Prize winners, political leaders and corporate heads, and has allowed the children of immigrants to learn and to flourish. Tuition remained free until 1976 when, during a New York City fiscal crisis, the university imposed a fee of $935 a year.

But CUNY's composition has shifted since it was founded. Owing in part to lengthy student efforts in the 1960s that replaced limited enrollment with a tiered system of open admissions, the once overwhelmingly white system is now two-thirds African-American, Latino, Asian, and Native American. City College alone has recently ranked first in the country in enrollment of minority engineering students and third in African-Americans who go on to medical school. Students cite such achievements as proof that the system continues to fulfill its mission, that it gives back to the state and city as its graduates remain to help build their communities.[3]

"Mayor Koch went free to City," they say. "So did Jonas Salk." "So," many state erroneously, "did Cuomo himself." Others correct them: Cuomo attended the private Saint John's—but the belief further damns his role as executioner of their hopes. "It was free all along," they say, "until the color changed."

CUNY students recalled both the school's accessible heritage and the previous movements that had maintained it. They harked back specifically to the spring of 1989, two years before, when, during a comparable fiscal crisis, the legislature tried to raise tuition and fees $200 a year from its $1,250 base.

At that time, a small group of City College students had been meeting, to respond to prospective cuts and to more general threats to their education. Friends had told them about the 1969 building takeovers that had brought about open admissions. They decided to follow suit, occupied the City College administration building, and inspired Hunter and thirteen other schools to hold sit-ins as well.

In the 1989 blockade, students, aided by the refusal of Chancellor Joseph Murphy to call in the police, held their buildings for up to two weeks. Their plight got the support of prominent civic leaders. They held teach-ins, sit-ins, die-ins, and rallies to bring the tuition issue onto center stage. After ten thousand students marched on Wall Street, Governor Mario Cuomo vetoed the projected increases, calling them "an outrage."

The next year, 1990, Cuomo was running for re-election. He said he opposed further tuition hikes because he wanted a public higher education system that was "accessible and excellent." Then, just days before the election, he announced a major budget shortfall and proposed a variety of cuts in the state's core financial aid structure, the Tuition Assistance Program (TAP), and sliced the main budgets of both CUNY and the companion SUNY system. In December, CUNY trustees tried to recover some of the funds by raising tuition $200. With students immersed in finals and political concern focused on the rapidly approaching Gulf War, few publicly challenged these actions—until the additional $500 increase that Cuomo announced just a few months later, which prompted these strikes.[4]

The cuts and tuition hikes damaged lives. Following the 1976 institution of fees, enrollment dropped by more than a quarter, from 250,000 to 180,000 students. In the period since, tuition increased repeatedly, and each hike sliced off another tier of students, or further lengthened their already difficult passage through college. By the time of the 1991 strikes, students' constant juggling of time, money, and outside work-loads left just 27 percent receiving a B.A. within five years, just 38 percent within eight years, and over half not graduating at all.[5]

The 1991 strikers looked back at the successful 1989 actions as a sign that with enough resolve, their actions could matter. They also cited the protests from twenty years before, in the fights for open admissions and black and Puerto Rican stud-ies programs. They now hoped, in circumstances more difficult, to forge another link in CUNY's activist tradition.

At least we'll make some noise   One of those stirred by the earlier strikes was Hunter's ESG president Carol Bullard, now a key blockade leader. A twenty-four-year-old African-American junior majoring in political science and African-American studies, Carol had been on her own for nine years. She wore long beaded dreadlocks, a brightly colored head scarf, red-rimmed glasses, and a dress of West African kente cloth which she draped over one of the black Spandex gym suits that became the all-purpose uniform for tired blockaders with little access to laundry. Silver rings decorated her fin-gers, angular silver African bracelets dangled from her wrists and ankles, making her presence somehow larger and more striking than her five-foot-five frame. Alternating be-tween elation and exhaustion, she described how she'd first held her ESG office as a spring 1989 interim replacement. Working thirty hours a week at an accounting firm, she'd gotten off the Lexington Avenue subway the day of the first protests, "in my little suit, pearls, and diamond earrings—the look you had to have for that kind of job." She saw students blocking the street, and thought "this is what student government should be about, not the miniature bureaucratic BS we're doing in the office. They already had their coordinating leadership. Later that day, we rushed the East Building, just boom, took it over, like that."

To Carol, the 1989 takeover was a revelation, although her involvement had deeper roots. She grew up a precocious child in a middle-class African-American home on Manhattan's upper West Side. Both her parents had started poor, but her mother be-came dean of students at Bronx Community College, and her father directed financial aid at Hostos. As a teenager, Carol wrote poetry, worked as a lifeguard at the YMCA, and edited her school literary magazine. She read about slave rebellions and the civil rights movement, devoured political poets like Nikki Giovanni, knew Martin Luther King speeches by heart. Although her parents didn't necessarily agree with her current stands, they'd raised her to speak her mind.

In 1982, at age fifteen, Carol graduated from Manhattan's all-women Washington Irving High School, and started college at Howard. She dropped out, went to Lehman for a year, then spent a semester at Columbia. All the while, she worked—at a restaurant, at the accounting firm, and at a service agency for tourists. She entered Hunter in 1986, agreed to run the women's poetry center, and found new political mentors like poet Audre Lorde.

A second, unopposed term as ESG president gave Carol a platform, as she made her office a center for political involvement. Elected for the third time for a term that began in the fall of 1991, she sponsored teach-ins and information tables, helped circulate petitions, and coordinated campaigns that generated several thousand letters and phone calls, all to challenge the prospective tuition hikes. That December, she and other students held twenty-four-hour-a-day "study-ins" in the library to ensure it would be kept open all hours during finals time. They also persuaded the administration to fund a couple of buses to drive Hunter students to the Albany march.

It wasn't enough. "If we'd had twenty thousand students in Albany," Carol thought, "we wouldn't have needed to take a building." Instead, the media paid little attention, and most students assumed the prospective cuts wouldn't personally affect them, or would get bargained out in legislative committees. When they finally became real, the takeovers began.

With Hunter's East Building barricaded, the ESG offices became the blockade's most accessible public face. Phones rang constantly as people called in news and rumors. Strike leaders slept by their desks. A parade of students, friends, reporters, and community supporters filed through to hold meetings, to strategize with other campuses, and to respond to events.

Carol and I talked amid the turmoil, in her office where three desks were piled high with newspapers, ashtrays, the debris of hurried meals, and a picture of her niece. News clips recounted previous tuition fights. The door displayed the classic photo of Malcolm X and Martin Luther King, Jr., shaking hands. The walls were layered with posters and fliers.

"People still think we're powerless," Carol explained. "They ask me, 'When you go, Carol, what's going to happen to the movement?' That's diminishing their power." She'd gotten used to standing tough in high school, "acting like I wasn't scared so I never got my ass kicked." Now she wielded that image as a strategic tool: "The administration thinks I'm a little crazy and that some of the people I work with are even more crazy. Some things I can get from them at the drop of a hat. Other stuff we could get if we just had more student backing—like refusing to pay tuition, like a rent strike. I want people to be active. If they're going to screw us, at least we'll make some noise."

A young black man ducked in to say hello. "Congratulations," she told him,

"Mama love says you're getting engaged." A white woman came in to ask for a tape of a recent speaker. Carol said she'd try to find it. "You should keep checking back, though. I'm very disorganized and lose things."

"Oh, my God," she said, "I just remembered that I teach tonight. I need to see if I can skip it." She called the coordinator of a weekly writing class she conducted at a nearby men's prison. "I'm a little concerned about leaving campus," she said on the phone. "I wonder if I can postpone the workshop until this is over. I don't want the men to feel like I'm abandoning them. The minute this is done, I'll arrange for a special program, and I'll bring some friends."

Carol hung up and the phone rang. It was Lehman College in the Bronx, trying to verify rumors that Bronx Community College had surrendered. Carol said she'd just talked to them, and advised them to stay put at least until a court order of eviction. She and the Lehman student talked further about the blockade's internal frustrations, "that fucking macho posturing," on the part of City College leaders, "always concerned with whose occupation is bigger, who's the big man, who has the strongest connections— storming people into meetings as though they're running the show. I'm tired of Puerto Ricans who don't speak to Dominicans. Black people who don't speak to nobody who speaks Spanish even if they're blacker than them. Nobody speaks to whites. I'm just not into it."

"There's always something macho going on when you take over buildings," Carol told me, putting down the phone. She thought CIty's choIce to shut down theIr entire campus was powerful. "They have lots of people. It's always gratifying to go up there." But since CUNY was a commuter system, outreach was hard to do: once classes were cancelled, most students stayed home.

Given the pressures of work and commuting, it's easy to understand why many CUNY students lacked time to get involved. Many had once shrugged off prospective increases, believing they'd slide by somehow. "The first time the issue came up," explained a City College striker, "I was going to La Guardia. A guy approached me from a building they took over, and my attitude was, 'Big deal. If tuition goes up, TAP or PELL will pay for it.' He told me, 'They're cutting back on that as well,' and I thought, 'Even if that happens I can always transfer.' I didn't realize it affected the entire system."

Combined with the actual state budget proposals, the takeovers brought the crisis into high relief. Particularly at places like Hunter, where work on this issue had begun the previous fall, most students generally supported the cause, though frustration sometimes ran high over building closures, cancellation of classes, or in the case of Hunter, the occupation of the library. Some balked at signing supportive petitions "because they might go through the names and suspend us." After enough of this sort of hesitation, the blockaders added an announcement to their petitions: "You will not be suspended for signing this." Other students questioned even the need to respond, dismissing the strikers with the familiar rhetoric, "You make your own chances."

They call you sir   I met such a group of critics one clear spring morning a few days later, on the small plaza that wrapped around the Hunter College subway entrance. They were teasing and flirting, tossing a football back and forth, preening themselves in the sun. They talked of how their parents had come to this country with nothing, then slowly built comfortable lives. Two now lived in the working-class Brooklyn community of Bensonhurst, and one had moved up from there to Great Neck, Long Island. They believed the striking students could do the same, if they were willing to work.

They complained about the closing of the library, then questioned the tuition problem in general. "A five-hundred-dollar increase really isn't that much," thought a student named Alex. "Just a new leather jacket."

His friend Debbie called it "one less trip to the Poconos. The money is there," she insisted. "They just have to go out and get a job."

"Yeah, go get a job," said Alex, laughing. "The state's in crisis. They ran out of money. Why shouldn't we suffer like everyone else?"

What about taxing the rich? I asked, mentioning a long-frustrated legislative bill to place a surtax on incomes of $200,000 or more.

"That's more of the same. They're already paying to send their kids to private schools. Why should they support other people's children? Once the protestors make money, they'll feel the same way."

Alex looked more than comfortable in a sleek new jacket and expensive shirt. But his father had come over from Italy with no skills at all. He'd learned construction, started a business, scraped money together to buy and renovate first one old apartment building and then several more. "Outside his community, they looked at him as a dago. But he had a work ethic. He didn't let it bother him if somebody called him a name. You put money in your pocket and they call you Don Angelo. Then they call you sir."

"My dad worked at his company from when he was seventeen years old," said Debbie. "He didn't go to college, and now he's a vice president. You take what you have and make what you can of it. It doesn't have anything to do with your parents."

For all that I respected their families' journeys, the argument was all too familiar: You worked hard, shaped your own fate, and no one had a claim on you except your immediate kin. Like their peers at schools like Fairfield, these students had no sense that times had changed in America, and it had become perhaps harder than ever to start without skills and work your way up. For all their hardships, the families of these students were also white, and that mattered in a context where most of the blockaders and most of the CUNY students were not. For this group, such political and economic contexts were irrelevant.

Alex and Debbie complained again about the closing of the library. True, they could go five blocks away, where ESG and the Hunter administration had worked out an arrangement with a considerably larger library at the campus of Marymount Manhattan. But why should they? "I don't know the people sitting in. I don't know their financial situations," said Debbie. "But my parents paid for Catholic school from my kindergarten on. These people are lucky to be getting an education."

Debbie bought a pretzel from a nearby vendor, and Alex grabbed for it, then tried to take her hand. "Oh, God, what a thrill," she said, deadpan. "Leave my mustard alone," she added, "you fag with those ugly shorts."

"These are fashionable shorts," he answered, "they're from Bloomies."

"Oh, what a treat, Alex," she repeated. "I wish I had those shorts right now. I told you to leave my pretzel alone."

The urgencies of the blockaders seemed invisible. "You have to take what you have," concluded a third friend. "Say you have three kids. There is nothing you can do but work doubly hard. Get out, into a better situation. Because only you put yourself there. No one else put you in that situation."

To feel you have no chance   For all that critics belittled the obstacles they faced, the CUNY strikers did their best to build decent personal lives. They worked wherever they could, as grocery checkers, hospital clerks, or as biscuit makers at Roy Rogers. They juggled children, ailing parents, and day-to-day survival problems in their neighborhoods and projects, and staggered under more debt than they could carry. They saw their dreams being chipped away, their communities steadily ground down. They fought to preserve choices—both for themselves and for future generations.

Twenty-three-year-old City College architecture student José Rodriguez was born in the Dominican Republic. His father, one of sixteen siblings, left school after the second grade to work on a farm. Now his father worked at the toy department of a downtown Brooklyn hardware store, and the family lived in a Latino neighborhood in Queens. José's mother was literate in Spanish but could speak no English, and she lacked the skills to get a job in a sewing factory. One of José's brothers was in jail. Another was on the street. A third worked a dead-end job, filling 150-pound bags of sand for concrete.

"My brothers are all highly intelligent," José insisted. "None are dumb. But my parents had no hope of social mobility. They couldn't help us with our education. By time any of us were in the third grade, they couldn't help us with our homework. My brothers all dropped out during high school. They felt they didn't even have a chance of going to college."

How, then, did he make it through?

"Maybe by being the oldest. I had a lot of pressure from coming first that generated determination." He played Little League baseball, which kept him out of trouble. He got a paper route to pay for his glove, spikes, and uniform. His parents couldn't help his brothers at all.

"It's so easy to feel you have no chance. My brother in jail is the smartest of us all. He robbed drug dealers with the aid of an Uzi, and now he's in for eight years. The middle one's carrying bags of sand in a construction company in Queens. The youngest dropped out after his freshman year of high school." José's youngest brother would have been a senior by now. But he did nothing but drink and smoke pot, hang out on the street, go to sleep at four in the morning, wake up at three in the afternoon, then hang out some more.

"My brothers don't want to have to go through what I'm living," José continued. "Not having the hundred-dollar pair of sneakers, always working, always being broke, always wondering where I'll get the hundred dollars to spend on an architecture book or to make a model—I spend a thousand dollars a year just on architecture supplies. If college was free they'd be here in a second. They wouldn't have that worry."

I wasn't sure, given that they'd dropped out of high school. But rising tuition stamped education as the domain of the privileged. It made second thoughts and second chances vastly more difficult.

"I was lucky," stressed José. "My parents couldn't help me study, but the student-teacher ratio when I went through in the Newton High School honors program was low, twenty to one. For my brothers it was maybe thirty-five to one. I was lucky, and I pushed myself. I might not have been close to the smartest of those who were striving forward, but I felt I had a shot."

This sounded like the individualist dream, proof that those who insisted "you make your own chances" were right. José said that it was not. "If you don't get the breaks or your timing is off, sometimes you just don't have a chance." He came of age in a situation that gave him scant enough room to dream or hope, but would give those who came later still less.

"My third year of high school," José continued, "I wanted to get out of the English honors program. I thought the people were a bunch of stooges who didn't care about anyone else. I did drop math after the second year, because I felt I was going to be a baseball star and didn't need it. I never saw myself being a professional."

José's skill as a second baseman got him an athletic scholarship to SUNY Buffalo. But he became frustrated that in a city with a huge black and Puerto Rican community, the school, and the architecture department in particular, was overwhelmingly white. Returning home, he worked for a year, then transferred to City, the only other full-scale architecture program in the CUNY or SUNY systems. Living with his parents, he went to school Monday through Saturday, commuting to Harlem two and a half hours round trip on the subway, then worked all day Sunday at a deli. "It's hard," he said, "since in architecture you've got to spend as much time as you can on your drawings and designs. If you can come in on the weekends, certain professors are here to criticize your work, or other students, which is sometimes even better."

We talked in the architecture building, a worn stone structure with gingerbread Gothic spires, a few blocks off the main campus entrance on 138th Street in Harlem. Banners in front proclaimed "Architecture and Landscape Support the Strike" and "Knowledge Comes Only from Action." The lettering was so professional, it might have been produced by a design firm. Students hung the banners by an elaborate system of wires and weights which used water-filled Pepsi bottles for ballast. They occupied the building twenty-four hours a day, working in conjunction with blockaders holding the mammoth North Academic Center (NAC), which occupied three city blocks and contained 80 percent of City's classrooms. Its takeover had spurred college president Bernard Harleston to close down the school until things were settled.

Inside the building, the architecture students seemed bedraggled but cheerful. One read the *New York Times*. Another leafed through *Newsday* while trying to fit a fresh set of batteries into one of the omnipresent beepers. A third worked designing a model house out of a small piece of clay. Down the hall, someone slept on the floor, his head covered with his jacket. The radio gave periodic updates on the success of the BMCC administration in securing a temporary restraining order. Students upstairs worked diligently in their studios. Although the school was shut down, the students ran alternative classes in which faculty, including their deans, led informal seminars and helped on student projects. Everyone was working together, José commented, seniors and freshmen, teachers and students. As with alternative courses held at campuses across the nation during the strikes following Nixon's invasion of Cambodia in the spring of 1970, the seminars gave education fresh meaning. They gave even the most apolitical students reason to come, share common talk and common work, and make modest gestures of support, such as bringing in food.

What we'd always The alternative classes drew people into
wanted to be political discussion simply by their day-to-day context, and pushed participants to think about the social value of the work they would do when they got out. In the judgment of Atim, a young Nigerian woman who headed the student architecture society, the process made the department "what we'd always wanted to be: an active community of students and faculty. It gave the faculty respect for us as students. It gave us respect for them. This isn't just a movement about five hundred dollars. It's a movement about our education."

José began his own architectural path in a high school mechanical drawing class. He designed a house for a Baltimore family of bird-watchers, "which was a wonderful project, even though it never got built." The program at City focused mostly on urban efforts. Students had just finished a group design for housing around Marcus Garvey park in Harlem, which they passed on to the actual architects.

"When the strike began," José related, "we'd just started working on a new housing project in Greenpoint, Brooklyn. It's a mixed-use Polish and Latino neighborhood. We haven't been able to complete it because of the strike, but we're trying to look at whether to make another Battery Park City for the rich or to build something for the poor."

"Designing public housing is hard," added Jose's friend Roland, who grew up in the same Queens neighborhood and whose parents worked in a dry-cleaning shop. "There's very little money, and all these regulations on what kind of door knobs or bricks you're supposed to have. Trying to get the most spaces into the smallest buildings, and ending up creating a sardine can. But it's something people need."

Although City's architectural training was necessarily technical, students talked often about the social needs they wanted to fulfill. José also valued City College's more general intellectual life. He mentioned coming across a copy of Marx's *German Ideology* in a used-book store, and being struck by how it argued for people to continually question those in control—those who make the choices and write the history. "I'd read stuff like that, then discuss it with my friends. I had a good talk about that book with the assistant dean of humanities, one of the teachers who's supporting us. She's Yugoslavian, a feminist, really an inspiration."

As with many students who'd become politically involved, José felt broken out of a previous insulation. Human pain he'd once perceived as caused by acts of God, he now saw rooted in social and political choices. These wounds felt all the more painful, given that they devastated his own community.

The phone rang, and someone answered "CCNY Takeover" as casually as if announcing "Joe's Body Shop." If you called when people were away from the main strike center in the NAC building, a friendly machine explained, "You have reached the Voice Mail system for the City College Takeover," and asked you to push different numbers to reach various occupied offices. A woman knocked on the architecture building door and José looked out through a peephole made of a hinged paper plate surrounded by newspapers and cheerfully decorated with bright orange arrows. The woman at the door was Atim, fresh and clean after a visit home and carrying a load of bread, cheese, peanut butter, and apple juice.

José and Atim teased each other about who'd been involved in the antituition efforts the longest. Then she continued upstairs to work on her drawings.

I asked José whether his parents supported the occupation.

"They don't quite understand it. My mother can't comprehend why this school isn't free, period. 'You're poor,' she says. 'Why is the government asking you for money when you're poor?' My father just wants to rip Cuomo's head off. They don't understand why it was free for a hundred and twenty-nine years and it isn't any more."

Facing the same problems CUNY's students felt their education mattered. For many, it was a sole alternative to a lifetime of checking groceries in a supermarket. "City College was not established," stated the architecture students, "to educate those who could afford to go to Columbia, NYU, or Cornell." They valued their learning both for its promise of mobility, and for its own intrinsic worth. They were unwilling to make it expendable, either for themselves or for others to come. Those who acted initially were, I believe, already inclined to speak out, but other participants were new to the experience of taking a public stand. They felt this situation was so urgent and unfair they could not ignore it.

Students fought for more than lower tuition. Detractors framed them as one more parochial interest group, competing with primary education, libraries, parks, public hospitals, and social services for desperately scarce dollars. They rejected this, insisting that New York State, New York City, and America as a whole had sufficient resources to meet core social needs, but had declined to do so in favor of policies that let wealth concentrate in the hands of the few. They made common cause with others similarly threatened.

As a result, groups who might have viewed the students as competitors supported their efforts. The strike got the backing of the state legislature's black and Puerto Rican caucus. It got strong endorsements from major unions like the Transit Workers, Municipal Workers, Communications Workers, and the Newspaper Guild. Dennis Rivera, president of the 100,000-member Hospital Health Care and Workers Union 1199 helped even further. He spoke at a major City College rally, offered temporary office space and the use of phones, and took the lead in enlisting other unions to contribute food and blankets, oppose the use of police force, and lobby major politicians on the issue. Rivera invited Hunter's Carol Bullard and other strike leaders to speak before a union leadership meeting on the budget cuts, covered the costs of printing a quarter-million publicity fliers for a major student rally on April 24, and even secured the rally permit and sound system.

Rivera gave this support because state budget cuts and resulting layoffs also hit the already hard-pressed community that the union represented. "The students are our daughters, our relatives, our neighbors," he said. "The same problems they're facing, we're facing." The blockaders agreed: "Our parents are being fired. Our cousins are being fired. We have to take a stand." Reciprocally, a thousand students joined a rally of five thousand striking home healthcare workers, who were fighting to increase their $6-an-hour wage.[6]

Many of the schools got strong help from their surrounding communities. This didn't happen at Hunter, located on the wealthy East Side, or at BMCC, located in a no-man's land northeast of the financial district. But at City, York, Lehman, Hostos, Bronx Community, and others based in the poorest of neighborhoods, local stores, restraurants, and organizations like the NAACP jumped in to support the strikers with free food, cleaning supplies, batteries, toiletries, and other materials they hoped would be useful. Ministers and community leaders held local rallies and speak-outs. At Hostos, in the desperately poor Grand Concourse neighborhood of the Bronx, five hundred community members gathered in an auditorium to show their support. When well over a thousand students from City, Hunter, and other schools marched through the streets of Harlem, people left businesses and apartments to join in.

Students also felt supported by their families. While many parents feared for the personal safety of their daughters and sons—"of our baby girl," as the parents of a City premed major called their daughter—they also overwhelmingly supported the strikes. "I think they'd rather I participate in a different way," the premed major explained, "not to the point where my academic status is on the line. But they're definitely behind it."

These fears were understandable, given these students' vulnerability. If they were arrested, the stigma would affect them more seriously than it would more middle-class students. If the worst happened and they were expelled, they'd be barred from all campuses in the system and have no affordable schools to turn to. Not that a college degree guaranteed success. Even if they graduated, most would face a constant scramble to get by. But they'd be better situated by far, and their families worried about their risking that chance.

Students also got substantial faculty support. An intercollegiate group staffed information tables at each school, raised money for legal costs, spoke with the press, lobbied key administrators, and offered to act as observers in case of police attacks. City's faculty senate asked for an end to the occupations so classes could resume, but a majority also opposed police action on campus, and strongly challenged the tuition increases. At Hunter, sympathetic professors held classes in the walkways leading to the blockaded East Building. Over a hundred and fifty faculty and staff from all departments signed a letter of support that praised the students for finally making CUNY's crisis publicly visible.

Other teachers continued business as usual. Concerned students spoke in frustration of those who refused to discuss the situation in their classes, or to cancel sessions for the major rally on April twenty-fourth. On the day of the rally, the majority of the faculty still held their classes as always, refusing to break from their standard routines even in this time of crisis.

Hire a lobbyist   CUNY administrators also varied in their responses. Hostos president Isaura Santiago Santiago met regularly with her occupying students, endorsed their general goals, and slept over in her office to ensure that no one called in the police behind her back. City president Bernard Harleston criticized the takeovers but spoke out against the cuts and refused to call the police onto campus. Other administrators provided buses for the Albany rally and cancelled midday classes for the twenty-fourth.

In contrast, BMCC President Augusta Kappner condemned the disruption of academic life and secured temporary restraining orders to force her students to leave the buildings. Striking La Guardia students won their own restraining order, after they charged that college president Ramon Bowen prevented them from visiting family members or meeting with their lawyer, cut off phone lines and hot water, and turned up the air conditioners to create freezing temperatures.[7]

Hunter president Paul LeClerc wavered. Just after Cuomo's proposal of the tuition hikes on January 31, Carol Bullard and others asked LeClerc to let them use the public address system for thirty seconds during a break period, to announce a citywide rally. He refused, saying it would violate school procedures. Once the students struck, he said he understood their frustration, but issued suspensions for key blockaders and refused to meet with them or to cancel classes for the rally on the twenty-fourth unless they left the East Building. After further student and faculty pressure, he finally agreed that students should attend the rally if at all possible, and suggested teachers could even hold their classes there, but ultimately passed the buck by leaving the choice to cancel or relocate classes to individual faculty. In general, top administrators had done little to encourage students to act through even the most legal and respectable channels, until the seizure of the buildings.

Students involved in the strikes considered W. Ann Reynolds, the CUNY system chancellor, unequivocally hostile. She'd been head of California's state colleges until word broke of a secret trustees meeting at which the board raised her salary 45 percent, to $198,000 a year. Faculty organizations at eleven Cal State campuses had passed votes of no confidence. The chair of the California Assembly's Ways and Means Subcommittee on Higher Education called her actions the "ultimate in arrogance." She resigned and took the $160,000 a year job running CUNY.[8]

Reynolds had argued against the recent cuts before the New York legislature. It was not in her self-interest to support them. But in contrast to her predecessor, Joseph Murphy, she seemed personally offended that students would challenge Albany with their occupations and sit-ins. She'd publicly suggested enrollment at CUNY's four-year colleges should be capped in favor of expanding terminal two-year programs that locked their participants into a lower vocational track. Discarding the notion that the strikers' actions might usefully raise public debate, she condemned them for disrupting their schools, refused to meet with them so long as they occupied their buildings, and from the beginning threatened them with suspensions and legal actions. When city officials resisted using police to eject the students, Reynolds lobbied for a more forceful response. She also sent a memo to all college presidents urging them "to maintain a firm and consistent stance with regard to suspension provisions," and "to reject student demands for total and unconditional amnesty." Even students with mixed feelings about the occupations regarded her attitude as contemptuous and vindictive.[9]

Of course, Hunter strike leader Mark De Palma pointed out, administrators weren't happy with the cuts. "But I'm frustrated when they sit passively watching the destruction of what CUNY has been ever since it started. And the most militant thing they can do is hire a lobbyist for a letter-writing campaign. A lot of them really aren't that upset if we lose students who can't pay."

CUNY was an exception, Mark explained, "created for poor people when slavery was still around and poor people were mostly white. Critics view it as welfare and say horrible things about it, but CUNY works. You get a good education. Maybe it's the racial makeup, when they see our rallies on TV, and they feel like 'Why do we let *these* people go for free?' But it's been free for generations, and none of these schools are easy."

Mark would never have made it to CUNY without open admissions. He grew up in an Italian–Puerto Rican home in Staten Island. His parents started out dirt poor, then worked double shifts to get credentialed as teachers. But Mark disdained academics in high school, spending most of his time hanging out and playing in a rock band. In his junior year, the school administration assigned everyone ID numbers, and students responded with a walkout and t-shirts that said "Tottenville High School Prison." Otherwise school rarely engaged Mark's interest.

"I was immature. I liked my music more than school. I didn't fit in. Who knows why?" Mark could still look like a magazine cover street tough, at six foot two, a muscular two hundred pounds, and wearing a leather jacket, twin earrings, dark moustache and goatee, his head shaved except for a patch of curly hair on top. When he graduated high school, barely, he spent the next few years working as a musician, then got frustrated by the conditions—"people are just animals in that business"—and by constant joking by people who, assuming he was white, casually dropped comments about niggers and spics. He entered BMCC, "which with my pitiful grades was my only choice. School was amazingly hard for someone like me who didn't have good study habits. But it was one of the few places where I could come in not even able to divide or multiply. Later I got A's in physics."

Opening the gates   Behind the battles over aid and tuition lie debates over open admissions itself, the fundamental shift that the university made in 1970, following several years of massive student protests. Using the rhetoric of "excellence," Chancellor Reynolds had already moved toward limiting enrollment. She proposed that incoming students who had not taken a wide range of college preparatory courses in math, science, English, and foreign languages be compelled to complete their equivalents before graduating from either the two-year or four-year campuses of the system—and that these requirements eventually be extended to applicants. "Students simply have to take more solid courses in high school," she said, "if they are going to take advantage of our outstanding faculty and finish college as quickly as possible." [10]

But what if their high schools don't prepare them? Should these colleges freeze out forever students for whom they would make the most profound difference in their lives? Should they force them to take twice as long and further increase their risk of dropping out halfway? Or should they eliminate those, like Mark De Palma, who didn't hit their academic stride at the start?

Open admissions vastly expanded the system. Entry into the four-year schools was based on grades or class rank, but the two-year colleges were accessible to all. CUNY also set up a variety of concurrent tutoring, counseling, and remedial programs. Total freshman enrollment nearly doubled, with minority enrollment increasing fivefold.

The changes weren't a cure-all. Those newly enrolled were encumbered by poor high school preparation, parents unable to offer academic help, and financial hardship that forced them to spread themselves thin with outside work. Forty percent only made it part way. But a long-term study by sociology professor David Lavin, of CUNY's graduate center, found that the changes more than tripled the number of African-American B.A.s, doubled B.A.s earned by Latinos, and sharply increased the participation of economically impoverished students of all races. The changes also doubled the number of students from these groups who went on to complete their masters or other advanced professional degrees, as well as those who earned doctorates.[11]

Tuition hikes threatened this legacy. "We will have open admissions in name only," Kingsborough Community College president Leon Goldstein told the *New York Times*. "It will become more like a revolving door than an open door."[12] Lavin agreed, although he felt the worst damage would come from the accompanying cuts to university programs. Disintegration had been going on for years, as the state and city refused to fund CUNY to keep up with inflation. Hunter had already lost an entire morning class period. Teachers were being laid off or reduced to part-time status. Class sizes were being increased, with forty students commonplace for subjects ostensibly taught as seminars. Tutoring, counseling, and English as a Second Language programs were severely chopped, weakening support systems for students under greatest financial stress. At the community colleges, sympathetic administrators talked of becoming so overcrowded that even basic teaching was threatened, leaving no choice but to cap enrollment and effectively end open admissions.

Lavin agreed that students needed to act. He wasn't certain that massive numbers would immediately drop out, but he expected that degrees that already took forever would take still longer, raising the likelihood that students would sooner or later give up. He also predicted a continuing downsizing of expectations, in which those who would have gone for a master's would settle for a B.A. degree, community college students who would have transferred to four-year schools would stop with the two-year

Associates degree, and numerous others would not continue past high school. Lavin saw the social commitment to New York City's working class steadily unraveling.[13]

The blockades fought for the right of students like José, Nilda, and Mark to continue. "Never let them make you believe," said a speaker named Rob at a Hunter teach-in, "that because the legislatures have mishandled the money, you should be deprived of an education. We're students, too. I've missed two midterms, and I'm late with two papers. If I want my professors to accept them, I'll have to talk a better game than I am right now. This shouldn't have to be the only way we can make a difference. But we have to act. This is about family. This is about community. It comes down to that."

Rob was a Jewish lawyer's son from Queens, one of a minority of middle-class blockade participants. But even those not personally threatened by increased costs would face a school less diverse and culturally rich. They were angered by the exclusion of those who couldn't pay. Students acted out of direct self-defense, but also solidarity, and for a vision of responsibility evoked by an African-American woman who, at a rally, described "the new thing, where people cut up sections of city fences and sell them. That's not what we're about," she said. "Our people stay here and work. We're not about taking from the community, we're about giving to it."

Malcolm D   Many of the blockaders had been involved in civic projects. Carol taught classes at the prison. Nilda joined City Kids. An African-American freshman named Darron learned public speaking in his Seventh Day Adventist church, where his friends used to teasingly call him "Malcolm D" because, although devout and soft-spoken, he'd argue so strongly for what he believed. The sympathetic editor of the Hunter student newspaper had begun speaking out in sixth grade at her Brooklyn Catholic school; she had decided it was unfair that only the eighth graders had dances, so organized one of her own.

Few of these students saw themselves as radicals. But their experiences had given them confidence in their voices, skills in communicating, organizing, and negotiating, and habits of standing up for what they believed. They helped bring along those who were more timid.

The blockade mixed students of all backgrounds—different races, academic majors, political experiences, and cultural styles. "I think everyone in New York should occupy a building for a short while," said Darron. "People would learn to get along better. They'd have to." Darron had held back from the original takeovers, mistrusting all politics. But after attending several rallies and teach-ins he began to speak out.

Darron met people far different from those he'd grown up with. He took his

Seventh Day Adventism seriously; he sang in the church choir and went home each Friday to properly celebrate the Sabbath. He'd been raised to consider homosexuality a sin comparable to adultery. Yet during the blockade he'd become close friends with a gay student named Vinnie. "Before this," Darron explained, "I was never personally aware of anyone who was homosexual. I didn't believe in it religiously. I believed God made man for woman, not man for man. But I've realized since I came here that they're normal like everyone else. The stereotypes and myths, they're not true."

Another freshman named Mike had been a cornerback for the Brooklyn Tech football team. German, Italian, and Slavic in background, "a regular mutt," Mike's mom was a legal secretary, his dad a Transit Authority carpenter. He came to Hunter to study computer science and psychology, lived at home, and paid for everything else with a job as a carpenter's assistant. He'd visited the brief strike of 1990 with several friends from Tech, but hadn't intended to get involved this round. Then he asked whether people needed help making fliers, "and suddenly, I'm in the middle of it."

The takeovers both bridged and accentuated class and racial divides. Because CUNY had charged no tuition before the color of the student population changed, and because most students of color came from the poorest economic circumstances, they felt specifically targeted by the cuts. White students from Westchester and Great Neck felt frustrated, to be sure, by larger classes and curtailed services, but they could better afford to pay more tuition. Indeed, CUNY's open admissions policies made college accessible to large numbers of working-class whites, but these students were resistant to lumping themselves with the have-nots.

Responses also crossed racial lines. A black business major from Baruch insisted that anyone truly in jeopardy "would fall into some category of need and still get helped," while her white friend asked whether Albany expected students to go to school homeless, "sleep in the park, and study with the squirrels." Hunter's strike included a number of highly visible white students like Rob, the lawyer's son from Queens, and like a thirty-eight-year-old single mother who helped coordinate the ESG office, as well as the highly supportive and for the most part white editors of the student newspaper. But the majority of African-American and Latino faces at the rallies made it possible for hostile white students to say "This is just one more case of giving in to *them*," to accuse minority blockaders of once again trying to get special treatment.

The blockaders' vision of the right to educational access challenged this directly. They invited all to participate. At the same time, when African-American and Latino students appropriately linked the cuts to the more generalized impoverishment of their communities, they sometimes neglected to make clear that this impoverishment was destroying the lives of everyone at the bottom of American society, whatever their race. This made it that much harder to communicate with students from different backgrounds. "The leadership has to get beyond the rhetoric about how this is aimed at blacks and Latinos," insisted a sympathetic Hunter student, himself African-American. "We need five hundred people out here, of all different shades. We can't afford to exclude people. We need to realize that this will also affect those like the senior citizens, who are mostly white but won't be able to afford tuition on their pensions and Social Security. It will change the kind of Hunter that everyone goes to, because of all who'll have to leave."

Yet at its core, the blockade created a genuinely multiracial and multicultural community, where students joined for a common goal. "People say it's a black and white thing," said Nilda Ruiz, "but this is the first time I've ever seen blacks, whites, Asians, Hispanics—everyone working together." While some people focused on racial divisions as a way to dismiss the urgency of the situation, the strikes allowed others to overcome long-standing mistrust.

A sense of purpose   The protests gave political newcomers a sense of larger purpose, one lacking in their difficult personal efforts to get through. It gave them a chance to share their hopes and frustrations, and their dreams of helping change the world. They did this, as Nilda said, "working with people of all different backgrounds. Because it doesn't matter what you are, so long as you want the same thing in your heart."

Nilda was, I think, profoundly changed by her involvement. She talked of how hard she'd found high school, "when I never could find anyone who shared my feelings. I've learned so much more here than ever in my neighborhood or my classes. I could be friends with these people for the rest of my life." I mentioned my own closest friend of more than twenty years, whom I met in the midst of a similar political crucible when we were both active in the anti–Vietnam War movement.

No one could tell whether this group would follow through on their newly avowed beliefs and aspirations, or whether commitments now at the center of their lives would fade with time. Yet the crisis they had inherited, and the community they had created, broke their ordinary limits and routines. They began asking all too rare questions about the direction of the institutions they were part of, and about their responsibilities for their future. They began asking what kind of world in general they wanted to work for and hope for. Bonds and priorities forged here might well set a tone for their choices from this point on. Their lives would tell how much this proved to be a defining moment.

Dungeons and Dragons   Students who simply damned the takeovers as indulgent and disruptive echoed the standard categories of retreat: an individualism that insists that you make your own chances; a mistrust of social movements; a separation from history that gives no sense of ways that similar, admittedly controversial, political efforts have sometimes forged a more just and democratic society. As elsewhere, the students who most condemned the activist tactics were also most distant from the issues and the least likely to have marched in Albany, called their legislators, or written letters. They insisted that nothing could be done.

Other students, particularly at schools entirely shut down, agreed the blockaders "did it for a good cause," and helped in low-level ways like signing petitions. But some felt occupying college buildings did little to shake hostile Albany politicians. As the strike wore on, they increasingly worried about losing credit, having to extend the semester into the summer, or falling behind when classes resumed.

By the third week, the blockades began to stagger in a race between sometimes belated efforts at political outreach and the frustration of students for whom the impact of the cuts seemed more remote and abstract than the risk that their present coursework might be wasted. Their sense of being squeezed led them to panic at the thought of possibly having to repeat precious classes and credits. It laid the ground for a backlash.

Among the students who held aloof from the Hunter blockade were those in Day Student Government (DSG), run by an oddly detached DSG president named Lincoln Ng. Lincoln said he opposed the tuition hikes, and that his office had worked on the Albany rally and helped with the letter-writing campaigns. They reprinted the faculty support statement in their newsletter. But they refused to take a stand on the East Building takeover.

Lincoln questioned in particular the closing of the library. He believed students could have followed the lead of some brief protests the previous year, when he and others remained in the building while still allowing normal business. He said this would have left the campus less divided.

But students involved in the previous year's efforts universally judged them a failure. "It didn't work," said Mark De Palma. "It was just humiliating. People were sitting in the corridors. Administrators came in and out of their office to conduct business as usual, and looked over people's shoulders as they planned their strategy. Most students ignored it."

Beyond tactical disagreements, Lincoln simply distanced himself from the crisis. He seemed to live in his own world, like that of Dungeons and Dragons fantasy games whose manuals were the sole books on his shelves. He said he'd spoken privately with one of the deans to oppose punitive suspensions and that he preferred to be involved "behind the scenes . . . working from within." But he made no public statements and his office took no stands. Where Evening Student Government was a hub of political activity, Day Student Government proceeded as if no crisis existed. Students who dropped into the office in the hopes of getting involved were brushed off.

The politics of austerity How did the blockaders respond to their detractors? Political leaders and most of the news media argued that they should acknowledge that times were tough, tighten their belts, and admit they had been getting an undeserved bargain in the first place. But the students considered CUNY's open access tradition intimately bound up with the future of their communities. For poor and working-class students, the closing of access attacked both the chance for a decent individual future and any hope for change in the besieged neighborhoods from which they came.[14]

What if the necessary funds simply didn't exist to meet these needs, to stave off the $40 million a year in tuition increases, the $52 million a year in general cuts, and the additional money sliced from financial aid? "Students Learn Lesson in Economics," stated one *New York Times* headline. The article explained that in such hard fiscal times, few were likely to embrace the blockaders' demands. Yet this argument assumes a zero-sum situation in which citizens have to decide between institutions like CUNY and decent hospitals and libraries, or between having enough firefighters and adequate police protection. In fact, the necessary financial resources exist in New York City, in New York State, and in America as a whole. The question is how we spend them. Given Chancellor Reynolds's $160,000 current salary and her remarkable salary history in California, students found her cavalier attitude toward the tuition hikes insulting. They questioned proposals, like one put forth by the Hunter economics chair, that suggested the school trade lowered enrollments for more faculty research money. In particular, they were outraged by the links between New York's economic crisis and the nationwide era of greed that had recently seen squandered so much wealth. They disagreed that their institutions had become unaffordable luxuries.

The issues raised by the CUNY strikers echo broader debates over whether basic necessities—food, health care, shelter, education, and physical security—should be available to all, and over who should pay for them. The CUNY students came of age in a time of widening social rifts, when the wealthiest 1 percent grew, as I've described, to control more of America's national wealth than everyone else combined. Meanwhile the communities at the bottom—like those of these students—grew poorer and more desperate each year. They faced not an isolated crisis, but one that threatened individuals from comparable backgrounds nationwide.

The money the students needed, they insisted, could be found. American leaders were perfectly willing to spend $300 billion a year on military budgets or to let fester a savings and loan crisis that could well cost $500 billion. The American economy had enough money to pay individual corporate CEOs the $127 million earned, in 1992, by Hospital Corporation of America's Thomas Frist, Jr., when he exercised stock options that accompanied his salary. It had enough to pay United Airlines CEO Stephen Wolf $18 million, in a year when his company profits plunged 71 percent. In 1993 alone, Wall Street investment firm Goldman Sachs would pay out more than $800 million in bonuses of $5 million or more to each of its 161 partners—or enough to cover CUNY's entire $92 million proposed budget cuts for nearly nine years. America's economy had enough fat to continue giving the wealthiest individuals $100 billion a year from the legacy of Reagan-Bush tax cuts, but not enough to educate the country's next generation.[15]

CUNY's fiscal crisis emerged from more than just regressive national politics, however. For all that Governor Cuomo lambasted Reagan and Bush for policies that grossly favored the rich, studies by New York State Senator Franz Leichter suggested that Cuomo's own tax policies did the same. During the 1980s, the share of total state income for the wealthiest 1 percent of New York taxpayers increased one and a half times as fast as the share of income for the wealthy nationwide. And just as America's national leaders provided massive tax cuts to those who needed them least, Cuomo and the state legislature cut the tax rates of the wealthiest New Yorkers nearly in half, further shifting the load to everyone else. Leichter found a similar pattern in corporate taxes. He proposed that New York state raise an additional $1.5 billion per year through a 3 percent surcharge on taxable income over $200,000, and raise more than $200 million more by closing corporate tax loopholes. The Black and Puerto Rican Legislative Caucus offered similar figures in their budget equity proposal. Just 5 percent of this money would have taken care of the entire cut in CUNY's budget that precipitated the tuition hikes and the strike to begin with.[16]

Given this context, could the students be faulted for engaging in admittedly disruptive tactics? They said they'd tried conventional paths and that these had failed. They'd written letters, made phone calls, lobbied the legislature, only to be ignored. In this situation of extreme duress, they believed that only dramatic action could bring the community's crisis to the view of the public and the legislators.

The blockades had worked in 1989. No one called the police. No one got hurt.

Cuomo vetoed the increases. This time, although nothing was guaranteed, precedent suggested that the students' actions might succeed.

An expert on poor people's movements, CUNY graduate center political scientist Frances Fox Piven defended the takeovers as the students' only feasible option. "These students organize in the university much the way they organize in their neighborhoods," she said. "If they try to go to Albany or Washington, it's difficult and expensive, and they don't believe it's effective. To occupy Cuomo's downtown office would be brief, purely symbolic, and wholly detached from their base. So they organize where they live and work, because their main resources are people in the same situation." Piven judged the blockades' success a long shot from the start, but considered the student efforts essential to challenge a "politics of austerity" that was the legacy of the Reagan-Bush pillaging of America's common future. She said they raised essential issues about who gained and who lost by state and national choices.[17]

Mario: Where are you?　　The students created their most imposing presence during the April 24 rally. On a cold rainy Wednesday, eight thousand students gathered in the shadow of the World Trade Center. At first the group was small, but it grew as contingent after contingent arrived. Two hundred students, faculty, and administrators marched over the Brooklyn Bridge from the downtown Brooklyn campus of New York Tech. Hundreds came off the subway from Harlem, wearing purple headbands with the letters CCNY on them. Nearly a thousand came down from the Bronx— from Lehman, Hostos, and Bronx Community. I met students from York, La Guardia, Queens, Baruch, Medgar Evers, Brooklyn College, even a group of a hundred from the so-far-quiet College of Staten Island. Hunter provided by far the largest group, packing ten subway cars; hundreds more came on their own or marched down from a small cluster of dorms. The Hunter turnout alone totalled well over two thousand—a quarter of the full-time student population.

Given the number of CUNY students who worked and could not break away in the middle of the day, attendance was impressive: nearly ten times larger than a tuition protest that had occurred before the takeovers. Significant numbers of faculty marched as well, and even a few deans. Those assembled cheered each new contingent, as if they were the Soviets and Americans meeting at the Elbe. When thunder rolled overhead, people cheered again, as if God were applauding their cause.

The rally ended and the rain fell harder. It poured down in a cold soaking torrent, and many students left with a sense that their duty was done. But five thousand remained and began to march. At times, they consciously forged their anger into an air of threat—a sense that there was only so much they could take before they would tear this city apart. Then the mood would ease, and they'd call out "Mar-eee-oh, where are you?" as if the governor's own mother was calling to chide him.

They repeated their chants in English, Spanish, Creole French, and Chinese. "They Say Cutback. We Say Fight Back." "Whose School? Our School. Whose Streets? Our Streets." "No Justice. No Peace." The students also challenged American culture to match its professed beliefs in equity and uplift. One young African-American man carried a sign reading "Knowledge must come from education"—a quotation from Sophocles taken from the subway ads of a private vocational school. "Yours and Mine with Pride," read the York College banner. "Quality Performance, Quality Results. Inquire at the Admissions Office," read one from Medgar Evers. The marchers gave the innocuous words fresh meaning, embodying the aspirations they fought for.

The parade continued on a snaking three-hour journey through the downtown streets. I heard a Latina woman in a sequined jean jacket speak of dropping out if the cuts continued. A Jewish man in a white and red embroidered yarmulke marched just behind another Latina with Betty Boop silk-screened on the back of her jacket. An African-American woman wore a button that read "Don't be caught dead without Jesus."

"Cuomo lied. Cuomo cheated. Mario Cuomo must be defeated," the marchers chanted. The students felt especially betrayed by Cuomo because most had backed him. As we headed west, a black construction worker raised his fist in support. An old white truckdriver honked his horn. A white woman smiled and waved from the doorway of a shop.

"Mar-eee-ooo. Mar-eee-ooo," the students called out once again. This time, they made it explicit, "You've been bad. You've been grounded. You don't get to go back to Albany." Some Hunter women modified a classic gospel refrain and sang "Amen. Ayayay-men. Mario Cuomo's got to go." Their public message was angry, but the marchers talked, laughed, hugged old friends, then shifted gears once more to call out for the cause. Nilda had decorated her sweatshirt with bright red peace signs interspersed with hearts, and the words "Strike" and "No justice" in black raw graffiti. Running ragged on two hours of sleep, she had a math test and an English report due the next day. Her English professor was marching as well, but she worried nonetheless.

The group spilled briefly onto the West Side Highway, hesitated while police sealed off further access, then doubled back. On Canal Street, they passed billboards advertising cigarettes smoked by smiling people with perfect lives. A group of ten Asian women cheered from a fire escape landing. Their ages ranged from eighteen to seventy. The youngest raised her fist. It seemed the entire city was supporting its children.

Time for the Simpsons   Two days after the rally, a dozen Hunter blockaders sat in an occupied East Building lounge eating a dinner of spaghetti, rice with beans, chicken in tomato sauce, and salad. Several women had pulled together the meal after the men had tried to help but kept getting in the way. The students ate, planned strategies, tried to catch up on their homework. Then Graham, whose parents were Hong Kong immigrants who worked in a garment sweatshop, announced "Time for the Simpsons." Some tried to ignore the show, but one by one they succumbed. It was the story of Lisa Simpson's substitute teacher, Mr. Bergstrom, a Jewish dreamboat who dressed as a cowboy, egging the kids on in making disgusting faces, even encouraging Lisa's genius. In the companion segment, Bart was running for class president against the goody-goody Martin. "This classroom has 1.7 parts per million of asbestos," warned Martin. "More asbestos! We want more asbestos!" answered Bart, and the rest of the class echoed the call. Bart then explained, "Martin says there are no easy answers. I say he's not looking hard enough."

The class cheered Bart on. So did the blockaders. The show broke for a commercial and one woman got up to borrow some correction fluid for her geography lab. Another left to direct a campus play. A janitor was let in through the padlocked doors as part of a complex *modus vivendi* the students had worked out with Buildings and Grounds. The show resumed as Lisa decided she liked Mr. Bergstrom more than her father, Homer, and was heartbroken when he left "for the projects of Capitol City."

As the program was ending, Rob rushed in on overdrive, announcing that BMCC had just been taken back. Earlier that evening, a group of administrators had gathered outside, along with Chancellor Ann Reynolds, several faculty members, a class of nursing students, and others responding to letters the administration had sent out. The nursing students feared they'd lose the course hours necessary for their licensing exams, and the professors encouraged them to confront the students inside. The administration had also called the media, and the nursing students began chanting "Get Out! Get Out! Get Out!" accompanied by a BMCC dean whose resignation the blockaders had demanded. Someone smashed a glass door, and the group poured in.

At first the situation was a standoff, with heated discussions between nursing students and blockaders. Ironically, some of the key blockade leaders were off in Albany, lobbying. Those present had just scheduled a meeting in another hour with BMCC president Kappner to negotiate reopening classes. Some nursing students said they too supported efforts against the cuts. Although none had participated in previous rallies, they wanted to work together after the buildings were reopened, and said that because the blockaders had acted selflessly, no charges should be filed. Others remained angry. The discussion continued for hours.[18]

Hunter students called an emergency meeting. "Those white kids are in there now, probably scared to death," said Rob, and someone suggested Hunter students take the BMCC building back. "That wouldn't work," another disagreed. "All we need is a fight."

"It shouldn't be blacks against whites," argued Jonathan, who was Jewish and gay. "Lots of white people, including me, when we see a whole bunch of black people we get scared. And scared desperate people will do desperate things. Maybe we should get together every white student, like from Queens and Staten Island, then come down and say . . ."—he switched to a clipped British accent—"Excuse us, please. But we think this building belongs to us. And excuse us, but you have to leave now."

But by the end of evening, the BMCC blockaders had given up. Theirs was not the first campus to fall. Queens, Brooklyn, and Kingsborough had ended short-lived sit-ins earlier on. But striking students had made BMCC a symbol of their fight, rallying repeatedly at its gates. Even if those who took it back had been manipulated, their participation left the blockaders feeling isolated and dismayed.

Carol arrived, and stressed that the movement's strength lay not in how many buildings students held, but in how well their outreach succeeded. Some returned to the idea of Hunter students going down to BMCC. "No one likes a mercenary," Carol responded, and argued for political organizing. Hunter had the strongest movement and largest presence at the recent rally "because we've put the most energy into outreach." She left to meet with a sympathetic state assemblyman. The discussion switched to a slate the blockaders were running in the coming student elections.

For all its community, the blockade also taxed its participants and strained their relationships. "My cousin is in the hospital and I was talking to my mother," said a blockader named Terence. "Rob was sleeping nearby and got all upset because I woke him up. I can understand, but I needed to talk to my mother, and family comes first, at least in my book."

"No one anticipated how long this would last, " reflected Mike. "We have to bring in other people, maintain the occupations, run off fliers—and in between it all, go to our jobs, do our school work, and try to catch some sleep." Given the constant meetings and alarms, most slept just three or four hours a night, which seemed fine in the first heat of excitement, then left them more and more frayed each day. Though some would break to go home and sleep, do laundry, and bring back fresh clothes, they never really caught up. The blockade became as much an endurance contest as a political struggle.

The tide turned after the BMCC blockade ended. Students knew from the start that they could be ejected at any time, but the very longevity of their stay had led them to begin treating the building takeovers as an end in themselves. They'd hoped their actions would galvanize a citywide movement, that Cuomo would again change his stance, or that their example would build campus involvement and concern. They achieved some of these goals. Yet they now watched the weaker schools fall in succession, Albany remain visibly impassive, and the remaining semester days tick off one by one.

By the end of Saturday, April 27, only Hunter, City, and Hostos remained under student occupation. Police had rousted blockaders at York, New York Tech, Lehman, and Bronx Community, arresting students who refused to leave. Blockaders at John Jay, La Guardia, and the CUNY graduate center had surrendered their buildings voluntarily.

The remaining blockaders now felt reduced to waiting. They didn't want to capitulate. Yet just as the mushrooming takeovers had boosted their hopes, so the collapse of efforts on other campuses left them feeling more isolated than if they'd acted on their own from the beginning. At City, where striking students had engaged in less outreach activity, the factionalism and rhetorical grandiosity increased each day. At Hunter, the focus shifted to the coming student elections and the continuing teach-ins. Those inside kept their sense of solidarity, forged through common risk and vision. They continued to relax, joke, and play. But their focus shifted from how they might win to the more humble task of seeding the ground for the future.

"Maybe we have to find a better tactic than taking buildings," said a Haitian woman who'd been staffing an outside table and talking with students. "This worked in 1989, so we shouldn't down it. It's raised lots of attention now. But we need to find something that will really hit the legislators who deal with the budget. So they can't just keep raising tuition every year."

"We tried all the normal means," she continued, "rallies and teach-ins. We sent tens of thousands of letters. Before we took over the building, we could hardly mobilize a debate."

A women's studies professor knocked, and announced that sympathetic faculty would keep a twenty-four-hour vigil as observers in case the police came.

"I hate biology," said Terence, trying to make his way through his textbook. "Chemistry is fun, testing for different salts. But God cursed me the day I registered for biology." He looked at his watch and said he had to go tutor a young girl he worked with. Nilda stumbled in wearing sweats and baggy boxer shorts with red checks on them.

"Oh shit," she said, in evident dismay. "I forgot my toothbrush." She ruffled through her gym bag.

"Isn't there a drugstore down the street?" I asked.

"I'm broke," she said, stating it simply as a fact. "I don't get paid till the end of the week."

I was well aware of the students' financial crunch, but this floored me. Nilda couldn't muster up $1.29 to buy a new toothbrush. While she searched furiously, I decided I should just give her the cash. Then she discovered the toothbrush. She held it up for display, announcing with evident relief, "All right. I'm not dumb. I found it."

Nilda and another woman teased each other about whether to keep listening to The Police on the tape player, "It's nice music," said Nilda, "Not what you'd call Eurocentric—well, actually it is—but I like it better than that other stuff, Montego Bay and all that."

"Oh shit," she said again. "I'm late for Chicken Hell," and went off to make biscuits at Roy Rogers.

The boom box played constantly: rap, reggae, pop tunes, house music, and old Rolling Stones cuts. The students studied and strategized to its beat. Later that evening, the group started a jam, pounding away on waste baskets, pots, plastic buckets, and plastic trays. Their music rose and fell with their hopes.

Carol phoned in President LeClerc's latest offer: leave by midnight in exchange for guaranteed amnesty. "That's the same offer we laughed at last week," said Graham. "They think we're demoralized because other campuses went down."

"Why not take it?" I asked. "Doesn't it leave you free to fight again later on?"

"The issue isn't just amnesty," argued another student. "We have other demands about admission policies and remedial resources. We want him to support us against the hikes. We didn't come in just for a publicity stunt. Even if we lose, we can still lift the hopes of future students."

I understood the value of standing on principle. I also feared they were backing themselves into a corner where anything but the most uncompromising stands would leave them feeling like moral sellouts.

Sugar works   Carol and I found time to talk again at midnight, just after LeClerc's latest deadline. "If I've had any influence," she said, "it hasn't been with a microphone. People know where this office is. They sit and we talk. Pretty soon I'm not just the image of someone up there always speaking."

She was tired but spirited. "We can't treat participants like machines," she said. "If you do, they die, burn out. Also personal discipline is very important, what we eat, what we say, how we take care of ourselves. I need more discipline and patience."

The phone rang with a call from City. No, Carol said into the receiver, she wasn't coming up there to a meeting because people just went round and round in the same circles, and she was needed here at Hunter. She hung up, and an African-American professor knocked on the door to suggest she contact another sympathetic state assemblyman. Maybe legislative support could prevent Chancellor Reynolds from pushing through the harshest penalties on those involved. Carol agreed, pulled a sugar donut out of a paper bag, then smiled sheepishly given her recent comments on watching her health. "Sugar works," she said with an apologetic smile. "After two hours of sleep, sugar works."

Mark De Palma walked in next, furious at LeClerc's ultimatum. "He's a sniveling coward," said Mark. "How can you sit as the president of a college with one of the proudest traditions of a people's school and watch it literally being destroyed. He treats us like animals. At least Deans Fishman and Escott came to the rally. It took guts for them to march with all the crazy students in the rain. LeClerc didn't even show. He'll feel proud when he has to arrest his own students."

I asked how Hunter had decided not to occupy their entire school. "It's a political struggle," Carol explained. "The task isn't to shut down a building but to politicize people. It's easy to take a building. It's harder to educate a campus. If people really understood how serious the situation is, every one of these colleges would be shut down, most of the students would be here, and faculty would be walking the picket line."

"In 1989 this was new," she continued. "Now, the media portrays it as an annual rite of spring. That diminishes its meaning. It isn't for fun. It's very hard work. I went home a few days ago for a couple of hours, but I've hardly seen my husband in weeks. I talk to him on the phone every day. He laughs about having bail money ready. I don't want him to view me like this."

Laughter trickled through from the adjacent room, where the political slates for the upcoming student government election were brainstorming last-minute strategies. I asked Carol how she'd changed from when she was working for the accountant and wearing her pearls.

"I didn't really fit that job," she said. "I made good money and had a fur coat. I still have it. I'd like to make money, have a nice house and a nice life. Nothing's wrong with that. It's the maximum profit that keeps making this country so sick."

"But I don't need lots of money," she went on. I don't need diamonds. Poetry readings are cheap. I'd rather go to a house party than a club. I don't feel I'm missing things."

Did she worry about being expelled?

"Who knows when I'll graduate anyway," she said. "I had a 3.8 average when I started student government. Now I have all A's, B's, and withdrawals. I already earn money teaching at the prison. I have a couple of literary agents interested in my poetry. I act. I make a bit doing readings. I can teach creative writing. I can always find some way to make money, which is why I don't understand sellouts."

"Maybe it's because I'm tired," she said with a sigh. "But in terms of myself, I don't care. If they do bring us up on charges, I hope it will just be myself and a few other leaders. I don't want anything to happen to the other people."

You can't help wanting "This isn't a revolutionary movement. **to fight for it** It's a reform movement," said Mark De Palma, when I asked him about the rhetoric of some of the City College leaders. "If you have a revolutionary movement," he went on, "trying to take power from the state, you can't do that with nineteen-year-olds. To approach it as a reform movement, we should have been negotiating since the first week. Instead, people got building fever, caught up in the thrill and the bigness, being on the radio every twenty minutes."

We talked Sunday morning, after Hostos had given up their building. I asked how this compared with 1989. "That was a shorter strike, because Albany suspended the tuition hike and we won our only other demand of amnesty. That also had better food," he said laughing. "A lot of kids, their families would bring in huge amounts of really good cooking—Chinese food, Puerto Rican food, potato pancakes, and bagels."

"In 1989," Mark said, "we had tables outside the library from the start. That's the hardest thing, going student against student. People would curse us out, say 'I want my library books,' knock over our information tables, make racist comments. The first week this time, it was impossible to table. People were just animals. After a while they saw we weren't budging, so it got a little easier and we sat out there to take questions.

"Students didn't argue politically against our taking the library. They didn't say, 'You aren't going to stop it by doing this.' They said 'I need it. It's not fair.' We had a bigger library available two blocks away at Loyola Marymount, but that didn't always solve things."

We talked again about City College, whose organization, Mark felt, was highly undemocratic. "They go upstairs, make a decision behind closed doors, then come back and tell people what to do. I understand it's based on real fears of infiltration, but there could have been a better way of doing it. Here, anything important that happens, we bring it back to decide. People may still question the outcome, but they'll be questioning themselves—choices *they've* made. This whole thing is about dignity. You don't sacrifice people without their consent."

Would he do anything differently, I asked. "Negotiate earlier and get more sleep. If people are going to take leadership, they have to get more sleep. You can't think clearly without it. We also need more outside help, which can't be from the pure radical groups, because they get too manipulative."

Mark wasn't sure about his own future plans. He was one semester away from graduating in black and Puerto Rican studies, and he thought the students on the joint disciplinary committee might acquit the demonstrators. "I don't know what I'll do in any case. I might teach. I might drive a bus. I'm focusing now on this school, and what it means, and how to keep it what it's been. Once you have that sense of history, you can't help wanting to fight for it."

Mark left for Staten Island and his goddaughter's birthday party. "I'll try to just drop off a gift and be back as soon as I can. With my luck, all the good police stuff will happen, and I'll be stuck out there with a stupid hat on."

Why don't you go to Harvard?   Later that afternoon, Carol visited with two friends from her childhood. Her office now served not only as a meeting center and bedroom, but also as a hair salon. Her two friends carefully trimmed each other's long dreads. They wove in brightly colored beads, teased at how stylish they looked, laughed and joked like old times. Carol left to meet with President LeClerc, then returned angry and sad. LeClerc was immovable, she said. He refused to meet with any of the other blockaders until they cleared the building. He acted as if all the others were her puppets.

The phone rang. It was President LeClerc once again. "Why can't you do the right thing and take a stand?" she asked him, her anger rising. "You still can't give a moral foundation for not meeting with the students. Every other college president has met with students while buildings are occupied. Why can't you? Do you think you're too good to sit down and negotiate with people? City is doing it. York was willing. BMCC was an hour away from doing it."

"You only got structural change when people took over buildings," she told him, part a reminder and part a threat. "You only got Puerto Rican studies twenty years ago when the two floors in Hunter North got burned. We could have destroyed your damn office. Maybe we should have. Maybe we ought to. At least you'd remember this."

"No one stays for fun," she continued, answering LeClerc's charge that the students weren't serious. "I haven't seen my husband for two weeks. It's not a slumber party. There are no beds. The heat was up to eighty-five degrees, and now it's freezing. Did you ever stand up for anything in your life? Did you ever risk anything for anyone? You have your Ph.D. and your six-figure salary and your lily-white world. Why don't you go to Harvard or something? This is a public school. Poor people go here. Why don't you be man enough to sit down at a table and if you disagree, say why?"

The two spoke different moral languages. Carol believed in solidarity and risk, insisting that in a crisis this grave, ordinary routines must cease. LeClerc temporized endlessly, believing institutional operations came first, foreseeing no chance that student actions could reverse the cuts. He came off as a man afraid to take a stand.

"Do you think," Carol continued, "that once I'm suspended or expelled or graduated no one will talk about this? The building takeovers weren't my idea. They have a history. I'm not just leading a bunch of mindless people. The sooner you learn that, this school will run better."

She listened, then countered once again. "You're upset because I call you names, but you have no problem throwing people out of school. You can say a lot of things about me, but I've never been questioned morally. People may say I have a big mouth. They may not like me. But they've never questioned me morally."

"We've come to the end of this conversation, " President LeClerc told her. "We've come to the end of a lot of things," Carol answered.

Carol got off the phone, covered her face with her hands, then lit a cigarette. "He just repeats 'I refuse to move on this,'" she explained to the friends who'd sat listening. She seemed exhausted and, for all her blunt realism, betrayed.

On Thursday May 2, at 2:00 A.M., students occupying City College's mammoth North Academic Complex (NAC) building walked out in silence after negotiating amnesty. Maintenance crews used heavy-duty bolt cutters to clip $1500 worth of inch-thick locks and chains from more than a hundred doors. The following morning, the building opened for normal use.

Traps in the path   Hunter had fallen the previous day. The blockaders had decided, after tense debate, to peacefully wait for the police to arrest them. Instead, at seven thirty in the morning, those nearest to the doors heard strange scraping noises. It was Buildings and Grounds, who LeClerc had instructed to clip the chain and then remove the doors by their hinges. Several administrators walked in, accompanied by campus security guards, and rousted out the sleepy blockaders. The group argued briefly on the walkway. Rob and another blockader had a minor scuffle with a university lawyer over a video camera. Then the students dispersed and headed home to get some sleep.

Could the blockaders' vision of responsibility for all in their communities have made a greater impact? Hunter's effort bred a strong solidarity, reaching out effectively to other students. Outreach was more limited at schools where classes were suspended. As Mark and Carol stressed, participants often confused possession of a building with political organizing. And the City group's factionalism and mistrust severely damaged the systemwide coalition.

The latter, I believe, was fueled by the very economic marginalization that the strikes sought to challenge. Students at City College came from all over, not just from the adjacent communities of Harlem. But they were the poorest of the poor, the most distant from America's dominant culture, with the fewest ties to conventional institutions of power. Their actions also made it harder for their message to get out.

While poor people's movements may have ample reason to mistrust the media, the initial articles on the strikes were supportive. Yet a *Village Voice* reporter who'd already published one favorable piece couldn't get into City's NAC building to do further interviews. The most sympathetic reporters from the *New York Times* were similarly denied access to interview anyone except the (entirely male) designated spokesmen. Even when profoundly moved by students' initial testaments, journalists found it increasingly difficult to convey the heart of the blockade—the diverse stories of its participants. After repeatedly quoting the same lines from the same core spokesmen, they soon began to treat them like PR flacks of any stripe. Or they went elsewhere, to campuses less obsessed with their role at the center of the world. The blockade soon lost sympathetic major media coverage, as journalists at the major papers and TV stations began to frame their stories almost exclusively in terms of students wanting to return to class, and the need to make these tough but necessary cuts.

A more open stance at City College might not have changed this. But City had the visible radical history: participants and media alike treated it as the activist hub. Closing off access made it more difficult for the press to grapple with the real economic and social roots of the takeovers, and with why those involved persisted.

City's obsession with security also fractured the activist community. A week into the blockade, I watched two African-American women from BMCC wait endlessly at the NAC building door, after being told City could help feed their strikers. Though they offered their student IDs, the guards at the door wouldn't let them in. They waited longer and longer, whipped by a cold bitter wind. At last, one woman grew angry. "I'm not going to stand outside and freeze any more," she told the man peering out from the padlocked door. "I came here to work out food. Hunter doesn't have any and BMCC doesn't have any. We were inside the other day. Now you won't let us back in. People can't strike if they can't feed themselves."

She was wearing a jean jacket and a Simpsons t-shirt. She shivered in the cold. Finally a woman in long dreadlocks came out, carrying a twenty-pound bag of carrots. "I know sister," she apologized. "I agree with everything you said. We didn't have food for the first couple days either. Sometimes they won't even let me in. Sometimes they won't let anyone in."

"I've spent an hour in the cold," the woman who'd been waiting said, still furious. "My daughter is waiting at home. The strike isn't going to break me down, because I believe in God. I believe in Allah. But I'm not going to be treated like a beast. I understand this is the nerve center and all. But we have needs as well."

Later, I watched another African-American woman, a student from John Jay, wait in similar frustration. At that point, her school had not yet occupied any buildings. Its students felt apprehensive, given police attacks on the students who went on strike the previous year. She'd been told City's Day Student Government president, Rafael Alvarez, might give her some advice.

Instead the guards at the door brushed her off. "Why don't you go to the information table?"

"But there's no one there," she insisted with increasing desperation. She asked again about Rafael. He was gone, someone from an opposing faction told her. They didn't know when he'd be back. No one else had time to talk with her. She waited a half hour more, getting colder and angrier each moment, reiterating plaintively, "I'm just a student from another college. They told me I could come up here for help."

At times City students themselves couldn't get in. Professors and staff were explicitly banned, and one sympathetic English teacher waited an hour, holding her own calico blindfold, and pleading to be led up to her office to water her plants. Granted, large numbers of students went in and out without any problem. But each time I passed, I saw someone with a reasonable claim spurned, turned away, or made to wait while their patience slowly burned.

Enlisting further support seemed a low priority for City's blockaders. They had secured their building with massive locks and chains, scouts with beepers and walkie-talkies, and barricades of piled-up chairs. But the sealed-off building separated them from others and offered scant invitation for new students to join. Holding it soon became a purpose in itself.

The students' mistrust was understandable, if only because of the constant pain they had felt as they watched their communities steadily disintegrate. City students were, again, more overwhelmingly poor and estranged than those at Hunter. They were a step closer to the desperation of the young men and women who would riot in Los Angeles when the Rodney King verdict came in. The feeling of being pushed over the edge hit all those who watched their hopes being ground down.

Yet students who threw around phrases like "by any means necessary" begged both moral and practical questions about the relationship between ends and means. They avoided asking how their efforts would be understood by others whose support they needed to politically succeed.

Images of radical martyrdom seduce white middle-class students as well. This was true of Columbia students who paraded the halls shouting against the new conduct rules, explaining, "All we can do is harass them," all the while isolating themselves from what was once a highly supportive student populace. Both groups saw themselves at the center of history. Both felt a messianic passion, mixed with desperation, that helped them act for what they believed, but also made it harder to think strategically about the impact of their actions on their goals. Casting themselves as the radical shock troops, willing to take any risk or bear any burden for the cause, they were less willing to work at building the broad base necessary to succeed.

As the Hunter leaders argued, whether or not the police broke up any particular blockade, whether or not students could stave off suspensions or expulsions, whether or not their efforts would sow the seeds of further engagement had little to do with the thickness of padlocks. It had little to do with how much time they invested in security, or in endless drills on what to do if the cops came. It had to do, rather, with mobilizing enough people, so that even if draconian punishments occurred, they would catalyze further involvement.

To their credit, the core City group had spearheaded their school's massive letter-writing campaign and had organized a large contingent in the Albany march. They'd triggered the successful strikes of two years before, and were the first to go out this round. They tried hard to assist the more isolated campuses, helping them in their efforts, talking constantly on the phone, and sending continual delegations to reinforce their ranks. But they were better at taking over buildings than at mobilizing support.

They faced a difficult physical situation. The NAC structure spanned three interconnected buildings, with a maze of tunnels and entrances many believed were designed explicitly to make student occupations nearly impossible. Its design turned its back on the adjacent Harlem community, offering, in the judgment of an architecture student, "just a cold grey wall, broken by vents through which it literally excretes its waste products." Its sheer size made occupation complicated. Because the building was such a prize, students feared all the more that by making a careless mistake, they would lose it.

They had ample historical reasons for caution. They wanted to avoid any taint of the vandalism that had tarred some previous strikes. Although college president Harleston had faxed them a signed promise that if occupations remained peaceful he would bring no cops on campus, they worried about police violence, which had occurred at New York Tech and (the previous year) at John Jay. They also feared university sanctions, like the suspensions that Harleston promptly issued to strike leaders who held student government office or who signed their names to initial statements. That these students were wary was understandable.

Yet all the security would make little difference if the cops decided to come in. The administration could easily enough discover participants by monitoring them going in and out. It became too easy for students to feel that merely by occupying forbidden ground they were shifting the course of history.

Unfortunately, the tensions in City's blockade went beyond lack of attention to political outreach. Although their initial takeover had broad support, the core occupation was quickly dominated by a small group of students and recent graduates based in Students for Educational Rights (SER) and the Dominican Club. Setting up a self-selected steering committee from their own ranks and those of their allies, they rammed decisions through in closed meetings, and issued arbitrary decrees and threats of physical force. They pushed DSG president Rafael Alvarez out of leadership because they considered him insufficiently radical. They ejected others they disliked from the occupation itself. Their machismo left many participants feeling manipulated and betrayed.

Because City regarded itself as the movement's nerve center, and students at many of the other campuses agreed, its factionalism damaged more than just its own particular effort. City College activists fought constantly with students at other schools over claims to leadership and their insistence that they—rather than some campus more centrally located—should be the location for all citywide meetings. They resisted representative systems of delegates that would prevent them from packing these meetings. They even tried to cancel one meeting after they discovered Rafael Alvarez on the list of participants. Other college leaders accused them of having "no strategy except for taking over buildings."

They also severely damaged relationships with the unions. Halfway through the occupations, a group of labor, community, and political leaders invited student representatives to a citywide coalition opposing the budget cuts. The idea was to build a joint effort for the major downtown rallies, involving as many people as possible. But as the students entered the room, a member of the core SER leadership, supported by a few of the other campus representatives, began attacking the 1199 leadership as opportunists. "They're using you," he said. "Why are they doing this? What do they have to gain?" He demanded that the students caucus to rethink their participation. They delayed the meeting for an hour and a half, while other participants waited outside, increasingly frustrated.

President Dennis Rivera of 1199 was outraged. So were local community leaders, one of whom asked the City College student whether he was an agent intentionally sent to disrupt things. Though other blockaders worked hard to repair the damage, as did some of the union leaders, the students never regained the labor-community coalition's full trust.

Most schools encountered the factionalism only in the systemwide meetings, although a few—Lehman College in the Bronx was one—replicated similar internal fights. But even schools not plagued by factionalism faced major problems drawing students into the strike as soon as they shut down entirely.

Closed campuses did hold teach-ins and rallies, and worked at reaching out by telephone and word of mouth. City participants met repeatedly with local community leaders, held an initial Friday march of 1,000 students, and each afternoon drew 100 to 150 students, who would hang out in the plaza, play soccer, toss footballs, and listen to speakers and to music. Hostos filled a 500-person assembly hall with families from the surrounding Bronx neighborhood, who consistently turned out to their rallies. York worked closely with its community. Even geographically isolated campuses, like BMCC in lower Manhattan, had daily events with reggae and rap music, to get students to come in support.

But without the pull of regular classes, student participation in events at the closed campuses steadily declined. Attempts to reopen closed buildings for study and teach-ins were made too late to reverse the trend. Many sympathetic students never even found out about the major downtown rallies.

Sympathetic spectators   These dilemmas led the Hunter leaders to deliberately occupy only the one symbolic building. As Carol and Mark stressed, they needed to do something to make the crisis visible, but also wanted to keep reaching out. They understood that most who attended school here were busy, preoccupied, resistant to political involvement, and would not automatically throw themselves into even the most urgent cause.

Hunter's efforts built strong morale, in which new participants like Nilda and Mike left eager to continue the labors of social change. They sparked broad general support, which helped them carry both their day and evening student government electoral slates to solid victories. They turned out by far the largest contingent to the citywide demonstrations. Still, I wondered whether they might have been able to draw in even more active participation.

"We asked people to get involved," said Darron's friend Vinnie at one of the meetings, "But we never offered specific things they could do, besides come to the rallies, sign petitions, contact their legislators, and talk about the issues." In the first days, the Hunter group did invite in all who wanted to participate, and people continued to bring their friends. But a gap opened between the core committed and those outside, who were asked only to stand in support. The locks and chains made it easy to hold a building with as few as a dozen participants. They also made it easier for students to say, "I'm really proud of them, but I'm not the kind of person who can imagine myself sitting-in in the library." They made it harder to significantly involve new people.

I talked to a great many Hunter students who shared the blockaders goals, attended the rallies and teach-ins, and wanted to find a way to help further. But although they considered possibilities like making posters, playing music outside, initiating classroom discussions, or asking if they too could come in through the closed doors and sleep over, no one helped them become more than sympathetic spectators.

Maybe Hunter's occupation had to be closed, given participants' fears of police entering at will, of provocateurs causing vandalism, of hostile administrators casually identifying them. Yet I've seen blockades that did not seal their doors, and therefore allowed supporters to get involved step by step. This happened in Columbia's antiapartheid movement and in CUNY's 1989 occupations, where City students occupied only their administration building, while classes continued systemwide. In the present strikes, City's architecture students checked IDs at the door, but anyone who was part of that community could enter, and students were encouraged to join in and give tacit support by remaining there to study and to link their education with the questions raised by the blockade.

These strategies allowed many students to directly take part. They reached out effectively to the previously apolitical. Although they necessitated giving up some control over the movement's direction, they widened the alternative community that so changed the lives of those who participated.

"The news refers to us as a small group," reflected a Hunter blockader. "We don't like to admit it, but realistically it's true. Our strength now resides in our ability to construct a just case, and in our numbers in a few demonstrations." As political scientist Frances Piven stressed, those who criticized the blockaders for being a minority missed the point: so were the civil rights activists and most who opposed the Vietnam War until the very peak of those movements. At the same time, the strikers needed to reach beyond their initial ranks, to stir enough active support to carry the day.

Certainly, Hunter students reached out through teach-ins, petition drives, and electoral campaigns. They enlisted new participants, as when Mike followed up on his initial involvement making posters, or when Nilda and Darron joined, following the initial public protests. But barricaded movements can too easily isolate themselves from the very ferment and discussion their example creates. They can reduce politics to an endurance test, where success depends on sheer will, on proving they care enough to hold out and take the consequences. It can become easy to forget how much success depends on being able to convey their perspective to the initially uncomprehending, and on coming up with creative ways for new students to participate.

Different possibilities   How successful were the CUNY blockades in meeting their goals? Media critics dismissed them for not putting their full force toward lobbying Albany, and for fighting a fruitless battle to begin with. Yet they mustered the only real force they could, the commitment of their fellow students. They used their community to make visible the consequences of allowing an institution like CUNY to surrender its historical promise. They brought discussion of these consequences into the media, into their schools, and into the awareness of many who were previously unconcerned. They spurred greater administrative involvement on these issues, as when the same BMCC president who'd fought them with a restraining order also established a centrally located Budget Fightback Center, where she encouraged students to write letters, make phone calls, plan rallies, and otherwise organize to pressure their legislators. They won back some of the TAP scholarships, reduced the budget cuts, and deferred part of the tuition hikes.[19]

The students gained only a small part of what they hoped for. But it's misleading to judge social movements solely in terms of pragmatic goals. Sooner or later, they knew they'd have to leave the blockaded buildings. They could not expect to stay forever, nor to instantly change the political direction of America. But their actions helped students previously uninvolved raise new questions and take new stands. They raised key issues regarding the right of all in America to have a shot at a decent economic future. They helped CUNY teachers begin to address, in their classrooms, the university's common plight. They helped involve a new generation of future potential leaders, like Nilda and José, who may well look back, twenty years from now, and consider this a turning point in their lives. They helped give students a sense that their education could matter.

"Events like this are transforming," observed Frances Piven, who'd taught at various CUNY campuses for a dozen years. "In the everyday life of these schools, students are very individualistic and very upwardly mobile. They set their eyes on getting ahead for themselves and their families. They work. They commute. They don't want to hear about politics. Events like this give a sense of joy, different ways of acting, different possibilities." They also make clear, she stressed, the real social priorities of America.

The blockades reminded me of a statement made by dissident Polish intellectual Adam Michnik, just after Solidarity took power. He described his own political genesis as a protesting student in 1968, and the difficult journey that followed. He rooted Solidarity's victory in what he described as "mostly the experience of defeat, of faithfulness to a defeated cause." Speaking of the then-recent events at Tiananmen Square, he thought maybe only those causes were valuable "for which you have to pay dearly. . . . With all my heart," he said, "I support those students. . . . I believe that the blood they shed will not have been wasted. That kind of blood is never wasted."[20]

It would be arrogant for the CUNY students to claim equivalent historical impact to the Eastern European revolutions, or to suggest that they took risks comparable to those taken by the students in China. Yet as the Polish example suggests, we cannot always tell which necessarily uncertain efforts will seed vast changes down the line. Given the steady economic and political shifts that increasingly damp the hopes of their communities, CUNY's students were right to view their cause as part of the same battle for human dignity as that of the young Chinese or Poles or Czechs. They were right to hold America to its promise.

Twenty-one

Whose history, whose voice? The politics of political correctness

I have one more story to tell about the students and their world. It's a story not about how they think or live or have learned to speak out or stay silent on critical social issues. It's a story, rather, of myths that have been spun to miscast their attitudes and actions, and present their reality in a distorted mirror.

Because this book focuses on students' actual lives, I had thought about ignoring these distortions and myths. But they have become too pervasive, and obscured too many real and urgent issues. They have, in fact, become a new major bar to continued involvement, both on campus and off. The myths have come to so dominate American cultural assumptions that it seems essential to challenge them.

Though they had long-standing roots, these myths surfaced most visibly as student social commitment began to revive in the early 1990s. Speakers for the political Right attacked the new currents of involvement as dangerous, misguided, and totalitarian. They did this primarily by wielding the label "politically correct," PC for short, which they used first to bait students who spoke out on issues of racial or sexual politics, and then those who took on other programs for social change.

The phrase "politically correct" surfaced initially in the sixties and seventies. Activists used it, for the most part, as an in-group joke, a way to chide comrades too zealous for the cause. Occasionally individuals used it when asking whether a particular action, choice, or strategy fit specific designated goals. Activists virtually never used the phrase in the puritanical, censorial style that current cultural stereotypes suggest. If anything, they used it to warn their compatriots when they started to lose their sense of balance and proportion.

How did the meaning of these words get so inverted? How did they become an American cultural commonplace, apparently as self-evident in meaning and historical import as the words *table* or *chair*? How did they become a brush capable of tarring any dissenting movement, whatever the cause? Is there any link between the debates they generated and the actual life of the campuses?

The attack on "political correctness" exploded in the public eye in fall 1990, as the United States was gearing up for the Gulf War. Within a matter of months, major articles warning of the PC danger broke in the *New York Times, Newsweek, Time, The New Republic, New York Magazine,* and *Reader's Digest,* and on the major television networks. Coverage subsided while the war dominated public attention, then resumed with greater force that spring, following the publication of former *Dartmouth Review* editor Dinesh D'Souza's book, *Illiberal Education,* its two-part serialization in *The Atlantic,* and the barrage of respectful media attention that it garnered. Quickly reaching the national best-seller list, the book helped solidify media stereotypes of a conspiracy of zealous campus activists, self-deluding minorities, and ambitious "tenured radicals," whose unholy coalition was degrading the once rigorous intellectual life of American colleges.[1]

The media attack was spearheaded by a group of conservative intellectuals, New Right foundations, and political figures like Reagan-era secretary of education William Bennett, and Reagan-Bush National Endowment for the Humanities (NEH) director Lynne Cheney. These individuals seized on the phrase "political correctness" as a way to counter a variety of real and perceived shifts on American campuses. These shifts included debates over the kinds of books students would read, support programs for women and minorities absent or marginal on many campuses twenty-five years before, and efforts to create campuses that would nurture the learning of everyone enrolled, including programs that attempted to respond to abusive language and racial and sexual harassment. Answers to the questions surrounding these shifts were rarely easy ones, but conservative critics turned them into caricatures, using the term "politically correct" to attack political dissenters in general, from citizens concerned with environmental issues to those who challenged dubious military interventions or opposed Republican causes like the nomination of Clarence Thomas to the Supreme Court. They did this in a series of grossly falsified stories, words and phrases taken out of context, and broad-brush allegations that turned out to be baseless. Unfortunately, the major media picked up these distortions and gave them full coverage.

Let's look at examples that those I'll call the PC-baiters have put forth to make their case. They've warned about the degradation of the curriculum, and its replacement by trendy courses of marginal worth. In a September 1990 *Atlantic* story that anticipated the barrage of attacks, Caleb Nelson, a former editor of the conservative *Harvard Salient,* complained that "in the 1989–90 Harvard course catalogue no core Literature and Arts course lists any of the great nineteenth-century British novelists among the authors studied, nor does any list such writers as Virgil, Milton, and Dostoevsky. In the core's history areas even students who . . . took every single course would not focus on any Western history before the Middle Ages, nor would they study the history of the Enlightenment, the Renaissance, the American Civil War, or a host of other topics that one might expect a core to cover."[2]

It sounds terrible. The problem is, it's not true, as recent Harvard graduate Rosa Ehrenreich writes in *Harper's*: "I have the 1989–90 catalogue in front of me as I write, and a quick sampling of some of the entries gives us, from the Literature and Arts and the Historical Study sections of the core curriculum, the following courses: Chaucer, Shakespeare, The Bible and Its Interpreters, Classical Greek Literature and Fifth-Century Athens, The Rome of Augustus, The British Empire, The Crusades, The Protestant Reformation."[3]

Ehrenreich cites Nelson's complaint that students will have "no broad look at . . . philosophy," then lists authors from the Moral Reasoning section of the Harvard core: Aristotle, Thucydides, Machiavelli, Locke, Kant, Rousseau, Hume, Mill, Nietzsche, Marx, and Weber, as well as one course on Confucius, one on the writings of "Aristotle . . . [and] Maimonides," and one on "Jesus as presented in the Gospels."

Nelson's evidence was simply false, as were his conclusions about Harvard's being dominated by trendy curricular radicals. A magazine with the stature of *The Atlantic* should have caught such a distortion before printing it. Instead, they accepted it without question.

Harvard was the scene of a much-discussed incident in the PC-baiters' repertoire in which historian Stephan Thernstrom had a brief run-in with some African-American students. Again, the media grossly distorted and falsified the events in their description. *New York* magazine published the initial story, opening its PC article (which *Reader's Digest* then reprinted), by describing black students verbally harassing Thernstrom as he walked through the campus: "'Racist. Racist!' they exclaimed. 'The man is a racist! A *racist!*' Such denunciations, hissed in tones of self-righteousness and contempt, vicious and vengeful, furious, smoking with hatred—such denunciations haunted Stephan Thernstrom for weeks. Whenever he walked through the campus that spring, down Harvard's brick paths, under the arched gates, past the fluttering elms, he found it hard not to imagine the pointing fingers, the whispers."[4]

Indeed, the pointing fingers and vengeful whispers were imagined. They never happened. Thernstrom himself found the article's "artistic license" appalling, though he said it captured his emotional mood. As Rosa Ehrenreich makes clear in her *Harper's* piece, and as UC Irvine historian Jon Wiener writes in *The Nation*, the picture of the incident painted in John Taylor's *New York* magazine article, in D'Souza's best-selling *Illiberal Education*, and in a proliferation of spin-off columns and reviews, has almost no relationship to reality. According to the account as it proceeds in *Illiberal Education*, three African-American students charged Thernstrom with "racial insensitivity" in his introductory history lectures. They supposedly accused him of saying that Jim Crow laws were beneficial and of reading from white plantation owners' journals that painted a "benevolent" picture of slavery. Rather than approaching him with their complaints, writes D'Souza, they went to Harvard's Committee on Race Relations, and then to the campus newspaper, the *Harvard Crimson*. In response, Thernstrom charged the students with a "McCarthyism of the Left," and said he was open to anyone who wanted to talk. D'Souza then cites an open letter that Harvard dean Fred Jewett issued to the Harvard community, condemning "all kinds of prejudice, harassment, and discrimination." "Far from coming to his defense," he writes, "Jewett appeared to give full administrative sanction to the charges against Thernstrom." Thernstrom was so frustrated, D'Souza says, he decided not to teach the course again.[5]

Wiener contacted Paula Ford, one of the initial complainants, and she explained that D'Souza interviewed neither her nor any of the other students involved in the controversy. D'Souza claims the students never voiced their concerns directly to Thernstrom, but Ford said they tried "a couple of times," including once after a lecture on the black family, where "he said black men beat their wives and then their wives kick them out. We complained to him after class that this was offensive and inaccurate. He said, 'If you don't believe me, read Toni Morrison.' I felt that was completely trivializing what's out there."

Wiener also interviewed Wendi Grantham, the Black Students Association officer whom D'Souza portrayed as ringleader of the complainants. In fact, she had not participated in the initial exchanges, and only responded to a *Crimson* reporter who'd heard about them. D'Souza didn't interview her either, presenting her instead through a letter to the *Crimson*, in which she wrote that although she did not charge Thernstrom with being a racist, she challenged his framing of affirmative action and was "left to question his sensitivity when I hear [Thernstrom claim] that black men get feelings of inadequacy, beat their wives, and take off." In her letter she explicitly states, "I am not judging his character; I am simply asking questions about his presentation of the material," a part of the letter D'Souza chose not to acknowledge.

None of the students involved, and none of their organizations, ever suggested that Thernstrom should stop teaching the course. No one attacked him with personal epithets, in contrast to harassment conducted by staffers of D'Souza's former newspaper, the *Dartmouth Review*, against black Dartmouth music professor William Cole, whom they attacked until he quit, calling him a "used Brillo pad," "a mud pie," and "a cross between a welfare queen and a bathroom attendant." The Harvard students simply questioned specific approaches of Thernstrom they found inaccurate, condescending, or limited in perspective—at first privately, then through the pages of the *Crimson*. The antiharassment statement of Dean Jewett was wholly unrelated: he had distributed it before the Thernstrom controversy broke. In the judgment of African-American Harvard government professor Martin Kilson, whom D'Souza quotes as an authority to prove that race and gender are loaded issues, "There is no Thernstrom case. There were 680 black students at Harvard at the time. A couple of them complained about his interpretations of black experience. That got translated into an attack on freedom of speech by black students. Nothing like that ever happened at Harvard."[6]

Conservative polemicists like D'Souza and Reagan-era secretary of education William Bennett criticize strongly what they consider dangerous changes in American university curriculums. A prime example is Stanford's modest 1988 broadening of its Western civilization core requirement; spiking their descriptions with phrases like "The Visigoths in Tweed," the critics make it sound as if American colleges have been taken over by barbarians. Let's look at the changes at Stanford. In 1988, the faculty senate replaced a three-course program once called Western Culture with a set of eight optional tracks, called Culture, Ideas, and Values (CIV), which was designed to give greater representation to women and minorities. CIV was developed in response to lengthy student efforts, including marches, petitions, debates, meetings with concerned faculty, and seemingly endless rounds of negotiations and compromises. The faculty senate spent two years in their own complementary discussions, then voted to change the requirements by an overwhelming majority of 39 to 4.

The new required courses continued to be dominated by traditional curricular materials. Yet conservative critics like Bennett, Allan Bloom, Charles Krauthammer, John Leo, Roger Kimball, and later D'Souza falsified this fact and made it appear as if pressure applied by militant students had successfully banished works by authors like Aristotle, Plato, and Shakespeare from undergraduate education, replacing them wholesale with such books as Frantz Fanon's *Wretched of the Earth* (grossly caricatured as a brief for the mass murder of whites), and the autobiography of Guatemalan Indian leader Rigoberta Menchú. (Menchú was an easier target then, before she won the Nobel Peace Prize.) In a *New York Times* editorial column Bennett accused Stanford of succumbing to "ignorance, irrationality and intimidation."[7]

A *Wall Street Journal* editorial repeated the phrases about "capitulation" and "political intimidation," then lumped together as leftist political tracts Navajo creation myths, the UN Declaration of Human Rights, Menchú and Fanon, the work of the brilliant and culturally traditional African-American novelist and folklorist Zora Neale Hurston (dismissed as a chic feminist), and the largely apolitical Mexican novelist, Juan Rulfo, one of Latin American literature's half dozen most-hallowed figures. The writers of the editorial took these examples from one optional track—Europe and the Americas, taken by a total of forty-eight students that year—and implied they represented new core requirements to be studied by all. The *Wall Street Journal* mourned the loss of works by Aquinas, Locke, Mill, Virgil, Cicero, and Tacitus, who were never part of Stanford's core curriculum to begin with. They cavalierly dismissed books from the Stanford course list that they'd never even read.[8]

In fact, Stanford's new requirements did not consign traditional classics to the dustbin of history, any more than did the Harvard core. To take the school's 1990 core requirements, all eight of the CIV tracks included the Bible, Freud, Shakespeare, Aristotle, and Saint Augustine. In six, students read Plato, Machiavelli, and Aquinas. Professors repeatedly assigned Rosseau, Descartes, Homer, Euripides, Dante, Locke, Luther, and Montaigne. Frantz Fanon was taught in just two tracks, and Rigoberta Menchú in only one, the much maligned Europe and the Americas. The main shift was in adding a scattering of previously absent voices, like Sappho, Marie de France, Virginia Woolf, Mary Shelley, Ralph Ellison, and Toni Morrison.[9]

I could recite a voluminous list of further incidents in which the PC-baiters falsified, distorted, exaggerated, and pulled events out of context. Many are explored in Patricia Aufderheide's terrific anthology, *Beyond PC: Toward a Politics of Understanding*. But to understand how and why the PC myths were created, and what they mean to the students and to their campuses, we need to explore the history of the attacks.[10]

Distort D'Newsa   The Right began to apply the phrase "politically correct" in earnest in fall of 1990, soon after their old Communist enemy collapsed. Articles attacking the PC menace ran first in the *Chronicle of Higher Education* and the *New York Times*. Then in *Newsweek*, which less than two years before had run a cover story on campus racial incidents entitled "America's Youthful Bigots." Now the magazine warned of the new "thought police," and, with a couple dissenting sidebars, questioned every proposed attempt to address these tensions, from shifts in the curriculum, to restrictions on hate speech, to human relations workshops in the dorms. *Time* ran an only slightly more temperate story. A *New Republic* cover story was titled with a warning: "The Chilling of Intellectual Life"; and a January 1991 *New York Magazine* article (the piece reprinted by *Reader's Digest*) warned of the "new fundamentalists," displaying a cover picture of a beleaguered preppie and the question "Are You Politically Correct?" with pictures inside of Nazi book burnings and of the parade of dunces from the Chinese Cultural Revolution.

The Gulf War accelerated a media climate of hostility toward dissenters. When Dinesh D'Souza's *Illiberal Education* was released that spring, it garnered not only the major two-part *Atlantic* excerpt, but a stream of sympathetic comments and reviews, including ones by such liberal stalwarts as Yale historian C. Vann Woodward, Morton Halperin of the ACLU, and Marxist historian Eugene Genovese, as well as a torrent of national print and broadcast coverage. A few months later, in a University of Michigan commencement speech written by a former staffer at the Sun Yung Moon–owned *Washington Times*, President Bush weighed in as well, attacking "the notion of political correctness" as an "Orwellian" assault on free speech, and proclaiming that American universities were no place for a philosophy that "declares certain topics off-limits, certain expression off-limits, even certain gestures off-limits." [11]

As much as any other individual, former *Dartmouth Review* editor D'Souza spearheaded the attacks on PC, using images that continue to dominate popular discussion of campus racial and sexual politics. Yet D'Souza's examples consistently collapse under critical scrutiny. And considering all the talk about the virtues of classical scholarship, it's disturbing that those who so readily endorsed his work did not seriously examine either his previous track record or *Illiberal Education*'s repeated departures from truth.

I've described how D'Souza miscast the Thernstrom case at Harvard, as well as Stanford's new core requirement. His willingness to twist or to invent facts for questionable political ends has long-standing roots—going back to the days when Dartmouth students and staff jokingly referred to him as "Distort D'Newsa." [12]

When sympathetic reviewers mention D'Souza's days with the *Dartmouth Review*, they characterize the *Review*'s unsavory actions as adolescent pranks. But even apolitical Dartmouth students considered the "antics" of D'Souza and his group not harmless fun, but vicious bullying. D'Souza was editor in chief when the *Review* printed a virulent parody of black English, entitled "Dis sho' ain't no jive, bro."

This column so angered Jack Kemp that he resigned from the *Review*'s board in disgust. Other prominent conservatives kept their association, including William F.

Buckley, William Simon, Pat Buchanan, *American Spectator* publisher R. Emmett Tyrrell, and *National Review* publisher William Rusher. Supply-side economics guru George Gilder and black conservative Walter Williams came in to replace Kemp on the board. Massive donations continued to funnel in to the *Review*, like the $150,000 that the John M. Olin Foundation authorized for it in 1991.[13]

D'Souza was also a key member of the *Review* staff when the group mocked an Oxfam hunger fast by hosting a lobster and champagne dinner on the lawn. He was editor in chief when someone broke into a secured resource room of the college center where a women's journal was kept. The *Review* printed sections from the private student writings in that journal. Also under D'Souza's editorial leadership, the *Review* obtained stolen documents from Dartmouth's Gay Student Association Alliance and printed private membership information and quotes from personal letters. During D'Souza's tenure the paper printed such witticisms as "Genocide means never having to say you're sorry," "The only good Indian is a dead Indian," and "The question is not whether women should be educated at Dartmouth. The question is whether women should be educated at all."[14]

D'Souza was notorious for his recklessness with journalistic accuracy. Dartmouth faculty and administrators recalled that he consistently invented "facts" in the service of his cause, or distorted them beyond recognition. In one case, a highly respected Jesuit priest and Harvard Divinity School professor came to lecture, and D'Souza asked about his stand on abortion. The priest replied that he personally opposed it, but understood that others could differ. D'Souza reported the talk accurately in the *Dartmouth Review*, but in a conservative Los Angeles–based paper, the *National Catholic Register*, he invented a new closing quote in which the priest supposedly said "You can favor abortion and be a good Catholic." A major controversy ensued. The Vatican's Apostolic Delegate investigated. Dartmouth's Catholic chaplains were forced to write and assure both the priest's Jesuit superiors and the papal representative that the priest had said nothing of the sort. Campus observers wondered why the two columns differed so, with the falsehood occurring only in the venue three thousand miles away.[15]

The *Review* specialized in personal attacks. In one case, associate chaplain Richard Hyde gave a talk called "A Christian Understanding of Love and Sexuality," in which he argued that moral rules had to take account of the complexities of our time. One religion professor who attended characterized the talk as "nothing you wouldn't find in 'Dear Abby' or 'Ann Landers.'" Then a student asked about the North American Man/Boy Love Association, which endorsed sexual relationships between older men and teenaged boys. Hyde paused, taken aback. He understood, he said, that Western literature had a long tradition defending adult-child relationships. Still, Hyde said, an adult man seducing a teenager or child seemed a clear matter of exploitation, legitimate to oppose or to ban.[16]

D'Souza attended the talk, dutifully taking notes. The *Review* then published an unsigned squib entitled "Hyde and Don't Seek," opposing Hyde's consideration for a vacant head chaplain's job. Condemning Hyde's opposition to nuclear weapons and U.S. Central America policies, the writer accused him of defending "not only extramarital sex and homosexuality, but even, albeit with some reservations, the Man/Boy Love Association." The statement completely reversed what Hyde had said, then used the lie to challenge his potential promotion. Later, the paper ran a second column, signed by "Deep Throat," attacking various liberal-left faculty members as "The Dartmouth Liberation Front." The column repeated the libel against Hyde without any qualification. Hyde was "barely a Christian," it said, and wanted "to disarm the United States so he can be seduced by the sexy Soviet bear. . . . Hyde sometimes has a good word for the North American Man/Boy Love Association, which may be his idea of perfected Christianity. Last fall he married a girl he had met only six weeks earlier."

Hyde sued for libel, and produced a tape of the actual talk. The *Review* agreed to a cash settlement out of court, and in a printed retraction, apologized to Hyde for presenting "a false and misleading account of his views on certain aspects of Christian morality and life" and for printing "false and misleading information about the Reverend Hyde's personal life."

Couched now in more sophisticated language, D'Souza's thrust remains the same. He promotes the same values and demonizes the same enemies as he did at Dartmouth, and at Princeton while editing the *Princeton Prospect*, a publication sponsored by alumni angry at developments like the opening of the university to women. He follows the same dubious star as he did while writing an admiring biography of Jerry Falwell, while working at the Reagan White House, and in his initial and continuing work with the American Enterprise Institute. He then wrote and promoted *Illiberal Education* under the mask of the naive seeker of tolerance and truth, drawing on grants and sponsored fellowships from the ubiquitous Olin Foundation, which between 1988 and 1993 would total nearly a half million dollars. His pattern of inaccuracy and distortion continues in that very book, in which he purports to defend hallowed scholarly traditions against the new barbarians.[17]

Illiberal Education is rife with misstatements, too many to cover fully here. I've mentioned the case of Stanford's core requirements and Harvard's Thernstrom case. D'Souza offers numerous other inaccuracies and distortions, such as his claim that Michigan's new black professors flocked mostly to departments "such as education, physical education, and sociology, the fields in which the most blacks get Ph.D.'s." Except that Michigan doesn't have a physical education department, and no one in the group D'Souza cites was hired in education either. D'Souza moreover remains silent regarding the role he and his *Dartmouth Review* colleagues played in stirring up the very bigotry and polarization he now purports to heal, even as their actions and ones similar are spurring so many of the hate speech laws, curricular changes, and human relations workshops he and the other PC-baiters so vehemently oppose.[18]

In each of his examples, D'Souza evokes an image of innocent fellow seekers after truth, blindsided by the baseless hostility of discontented women or minorities. He treats questions students raise about racial or sexual issues as inherently groundless, describing African-Americans, women, Third-World activists, and gays as "groups claiming to have been victimized." "It is hard for minority students to admit," D'Souza continues, "that any classroom difficulties they experience are the consequence of inadequate academic skills."[19]

In other words, those students should stop complaining, buckle down, and leave the running of our universities to those who know better. This contradicts the experiences of just about every minority student I've ever talked with. And whatever the merit of particular student complaints, mandated silence is dangerous. Students must have the right to question professors of all ideological stripes, or all pretense of learning as dialogue disappears.

Scorched communists   The attacks of the PC-baiters are not about creating more effective learning situations. They are about shutting down critical discussion altogether, silencing the voices of human pain, and dismissing worldviews they do not care to understand. D'Souza focuses much on attacking what he calls "the victim's revolution," which according to him subverts a once pure and neutral academy with baseless minority claims. Texas English professor Alan Gribben uses the equally derisive term "oppression studies." But though D'Souza and Gribben would deny it, American society does produce victims, and we need their perspectives.

Throughout the Stanford debates, the PC-baiters had no greater icon of scorn than the book *I, Rigoberta Menchú*, the dictated autobiography of the Guatemalan Indian who would later win the 1992 Nobel Peace Prize. Their responses to this book exemplify their politics of contempt.

Menchú's story begins with the day-to-day world of her remote mountain village: rituals of marriage and birth, of planting and harvest, her coming of age as a

Catholic catechist; her work for starvation wages on the huge coffee plantations and later as a maid. She tells of the government evicting her village from the remote mountain land they'd painstakingly cleared and farmed. Of a brother dying of malnutrition and lack of medicine. Of a childhood friend who is hacked to death with machetes when she refuses to sleep with the son of a powerful landlord.[20]

Menchú tells how her family tries to save their lands, pooling the community's every *centavo* to travel to the capital and hire lawyers and interpreters. They begin to organize their village, and others nearby. In response, the army jails and tortures her father, accusing him of being a subversive. They abduct and kill nearby villagers, then kidnap Menchú's sixteen-year-old brother, smash his eyes with stones, drench him and other "subversives" with gasoline, and burn them alive in the village square. Later, they rape, torture, and kill Menchú's mother. When Menchú's father and other Indians try to draw international attention to their plight by occupying the Spanish embassy, Guatemalan security forces ignite a fire in which thirty-nine of those inside burn to death. While Menchú's two sisters join the guerrillas, Rigoberta organizes strikes, unions, and a protest march to the Congress, then finally flees to Mexico, where she continues to speak out.

D'Souza seizes on *I, Rigoberta Menchú* in his attacks on curricular reforms. Although the autobiography was assigned in exactly one Stanford core course, which is taken by 50 to 150 freshmen per year, D'Souza entitles his chapter on canonical debates "Travels with Rigoberta," and claims the book "best reveals the premises underlying the new Stanford curriculum." After some snide remarks about Menchú's autobiography being dictated, he takes on what disturbs him most—"the development of Rigoberta's political consciousness."[21]

"Her parents are killed for unspecified reasons in a bloody massacre, reportedly carried out by the Guatemalan army," writes D'Souza, quickly getting past the history, "and Rigoberta vows to fight back." No mention of her brother burned alive in front of the village. No mention of coups, rape, abductions, torture, or dictator Efrian Rios Montt's classic statement, "We have no scorched earth policy. We have a policy of scorched Communists." No mention of the pain of a country whose U.S.-backed governments killed more than fifty thousand peasants between the early eighties and the mid-nineties, and more than twice that number since the CIA overthrew democratically elected president Jacobo Arbenz in 1954. Instead, he uses the phrase "reportedly carried out by the army," as if Menchú might have made the whole thing up.[22]

After breezing over Guatemala's history, D'Souza does his best to tar Menchú as a hard-line leftist ideologue. He quotes one of her chapter titles, "Rigoberta Renounces Marriage and Motherhood," to make her sound like the Vietnam-era Weathermen denouncing "bourgeois monogamy." But Menchú never makes such an argument. Instead, she speaks eloquently of her bonds with her parents and grandparents, but she also says that the situation of being an Indian standing up for your rights "makes women think very hard before getting married, because who will look after the children, who will feed them?" Finally, D'Souza dismisses Menchú for representing not her people or her continent's pain and experience, but for being "a mouthpiece for a sophisticated left-wing critique of Western society . . . a modern Saint Sebastian, pierced by the arrows of North American white male cruelty. . . . Now it is her turn to be canonized—quite literally for her to enter the Stanford canon."[23]

If you haven't read Menchú's book, and aren't familiar with Guatemalan history, such charges may sound convincing. Shortly after the release of *Illiberal Education*, *New York Times* columnist Flora Lewis wrote a piece called "Old Rebels Are Training the New Thought Police," in which she complained that "the text of an oral history of her daily problems by an illiterate Guatemalan woman is accorded equal deference with historic masters." Respected Yale historian C. Vann Woodward repeated D'Souza's attacks on Menchú in the *New York Review of Books* (he later acknowledged that he'd accepted as truth "some serious and irresponsible factual errors" in D'Souza's presentation). For all the PC-baiting rhetoric about the decline of excellence and of critical scholarship, scores of respectful reviewers of *Illiberal Education* never questioned D'Souza's gross caricatures of Rigoberta Menchú's life and words—even though her autobiography was readily available to read. The scorn with which they so quickly dismissed her voice only echoes the brutalization of her people in the story that she tells.[24]

But Menchú's narrative is about more than wounds needlessly suffered. It portrays a rich and complex culture that has sustained her through appalling brutality. It embodies a complex view of the world, with roots that go back thousands of years. It puts forward a view of life and work and hope from which we all might learn profound lessons. Critics like D'Souza demean her worldview with quick epithets as "leftist," "romantic," or "primitive," much as they dismiss brilliant African writers like Chinua Achebe and Bessie Head, great Latin American writers like Gabriel Garcia Marquez, Eduardo Galeano, and Juan Rulfo—the author of the novels so blithely caricatured in the *Wall Street Journal* editorial on Stanford. When conservative critics like Saul Bellow pontificate, "When the Zulus have a Tolstoy, we will read him," they display mostly their own insularity and ignorance—an ignorance ironically parallel to that of neo-Nazi David Duke who, while condemning the decline of American culture because of racial mongrelization, exclaimed, as a prime example, "Saul Bellow—that's not literature."[25]

The dollars of Olin   How did the PC backlash emerge? It was the creation, not of skeptical students, but of New Right intellectuals, their backers in conservative foundations, and of a small group of senior professors resistant to being challenged and questioned. The roots of the attack date to the late 1970s when a group of ultraconservative foundations coalesced to spearhead what would become the intellectual arguments for the Reagan-Bush agenda. These included the John M. Olin Foundation, the Lynde and Harry Bradley Foundation, the Sara Scaife Foundation, the Smith-Richardson Foundation, the J. M. Foundation, the Adolph Coors Foundation, and the corporate foundation of Mobil Oil. The largest, the Olin Foundation, has allocated as much as $55 million per year (and consistently $15 to $20 million) to pushing a conservative educational agenda. Olin's dollars are the philanthropic legacy of a major weapons producer and general manufacturing corporation that has been found guilty of illegally shipping arms and bullets to South Africa, and that has a history of price fixing, strike breaking, illegal toxic dumping, and questionable payments to foreign government officials.[26]

Throughout the eighties, these institutions backed a variety of right-wing causes, including Star Wars, supply-side economics, general military buildups, support for the Nicaraguan contras and for Jonas Savimbi's Unita guerrillas in Angola (fueling a war that took a half million lives), anti-union "right to work" laws, and attacks on abortion, homosexuality, and dissident voices in the media and the arts. They did this directly and also by providing support for an interconnected network of think tanks like the Heritage Foundation (whose 1990 budget was over $16 million), American Enterprise Institute, and Phyllis Schlafly's Eagle Forum; pressure groups like Accuracy in Media, Committee on Media Integrity, and the Center for Media and Public Affairs; campus organizing efforts like the Institute for Educational Affairs (later called the Madison Center), the Leadership Institute, and the National Association of Scholars; publications like *Commentary, The Public Interest, The American Spectator, National Review, Heterodoxy,* and *The New Criterion;* and Olin's investment of millions in endowed chairs for conservative faculty. These groups represented different and sometimes contending factions of the conservative movement, but would join in attacking the PC menace.[27]

This network supported the efforts of virtually all the major PC-baiting players, including Bloom, D'Souza, Robert Bork, Irving Kristol, Linda Chavez, Herbert London, Diane Ravitch, Roger Kimball, and former leftists turned red-baiters David Horowitz and Peter Collier, as well as Harvard historian Thernstrom's wife Abigail Thernstrom, who would play a key role in miscasting the perspectives of Bill Clinton's nominee to the Civil Rights Division of the Attorney General's office, Lani Guinier. The efforts of these individuals and institutions gained legitimacy and strength from the strong support of Reagan-Bush officials like then secretary of education William Bennett (to whom Olin gave a $175,000 grant after he left the administration) and assistant secretary of education Chester Finn. Their backing ensured that when individuals like D'Souza and Allan Bloom took on what they described as the subversion of the academy, they did so from highly visible pulpits.[28]

The new class   The developments that these right-wing commentators are attacking have emerged from profound shifts on America's campuses. As Queens College English professor Louis Menand writes in a *New Yorker* review of D'Souza's book, "In 1960, a year well within the memories of most senior professors and university administrators, ninety-four percent of college students were white. . . . Of the students making up the remaining six percent, a third attended all-black or predominantly black institutions. Sixty-three percent of college students were men; almost nine of every ten Ph.D.s awarded were awarded to men; and nearly eighty percent of university faculty were men. Some of the most distinguished private colleges in the country did not admit women, and there were several public universities (not to mention private ones such as Duke) that did not admit black students."[29]

Now, in contrast, about 55 percent of college students are women, and almost 20 percent are students of color. The white men who once dominated college life are rapidly becoming one voice among many. Demands for inclusion by students once at the margins, like those at Emory, have consequently become louder and more insistent.[30]

Inevitably, doing justice to these shifts is difficult. Sometimes those trying to make changes or adjust to new situations slip and stumble. Or they proceed well and wisely, but challenge ingrained cultural ways and entrenched power. The PC-baiters deny the roots of the resulting conflicts in the complex realities of specific human lives, in the shifting nature of American campuses, in the difficulties of securing necessary change. Instead, they brand moves toward a more multicultural education or new minority access programs as insidious power grabs fueled by blind resentment. They leave no way to understand them.

PC attacks by conservatives like Irving Kristol, Norman Podhoretz, Michael Novak, and William F. Buckley echo charges that many of the same group have been raising since the early 1970s. At that time they began to blame America's problems on the rise to power of what they called "the new class" of liberal and leftist professionals. Fifteen years before, Yugoslavian dissident Milovan Djilas had used this phrase to condemn a Yugoslavian political bureaucracy that furthered its own power under the pretense of building socialism. Radical theorists of the sixties talked about a "new working class" of individuals who, working in the knowledge industry, could become what Michael Harrington called a potential "constituency of conscience" for social change. Talk of the new class floated around American intellectual circles with fairly neutral connotations until neoconservative Michael Novak used it in a 1972 *Commentary* article to attack student radicals who concealed their own "lust for power" and "class interests" in "an aura of morality so thick it would make the righteous Anglo-Saxons of a century ago envious." Fellow neoconservatives Kristol, Podhoretz, and Seymour Martin Lipset soon amplified Novak's themes, attacking teachers, journalists, psychologists, social workers, government administrators, public clinic doctors, and other professionals who questioned corporate America. This group, in Podhoretz's words, "represented itself as concerned only with . . . the good of others (especially the poor and the blacks), but what it really wanted to was to aggrandize its own power." Conservatives would continue to brandish these pseudopopulist themes as a club against any who challenged their vision.[31]

The Right has replaced warnings about the "new class" with attacks on the "politically correct," but key players remain the same, joined by younger protégés like D'Souza. They take a similar rhetorical approach: creating images of a spoiled and elitist group using taxpayer dollars (or parental tuition) to subvert America's hallowed values. It doesn't matter that the students whose actions they attack tend to be the poorest and most marginal, or that the faculty who support those students are mainly overworked and underpaid lecturers and assistant professors, not academic jet-setters flush with research contracts. Neither does it matter that the well-funded right-wing intellectuals themselves can be considered perfect "new class" representatives, who have done a fine job of advancing their personal interests through currying favor with the powerful. They reserve their condemnation for individuals who question the rule of private wealth.

The conservatives also attacked a more general presumed lapse in American moral values. In 1987 Allan Bloom's *Closing of the American Mind* became an unlikely best-seller by focusing on the new disease of "cultural relativism," a fancy way of saying American intellectual life had no standards. Bloom takes on a range of supposed abominations, from rock music and premarital sex to peace studies, ethnic studies, women's studies, and the influence of Margaret Mead. He accuses American academics of making moral choice impossible for the young, yet when he mentions Vietnam-era students who acted on what they believed, he dismisses their political stands as posturing and cant, the present equivalent of "the counsel of the sophists." America, he says, holds "the responsibility for the fate of freedom in the world," but this is a responsibility to be exercised by leaders, not citizens.[32]

Bloom's views were buttressed by the companion best-seller, E. D. Hirsch's *Cultural Literacy.* In contrast to Bloom's avowed elitism, Hirsch did argue for a knowledge accessible to all. But he downplayed the importance of teaching broader social contexts in favor of being able to recite dictionary definitions of specific cultural references. His view of what knowledge was significant was narrowly traditional. "The culture that determined where we were going," Hirsch claimed, "was pretty well established on these shores in 1776, and it all came from Western Europe."[33] Critics like William Bennett amplified such arguments, taking on developments like Stanford's modest shifts with dire warnings of civilization's pending fall.

Thought police   All too often, the major media embraced these claims with scant question. In the *Newsweek* article entitled "Thought Police," an accompanying photo displays a montage of political buttons, with the caption "For those who wear their politics on their denim: PC Buttons." What did these buttons say? "A Woman's Place Is in The House, And in the Senate," "Against Abortion, Don't Have One," "Outgrow Militarism," "Demilitarize Space." What was the point of showing them, except to lump vague warnings about the new totalitarians with blanket dismissals of any of these causes. It was almost as if the buttons had become so chic as to be required attire for fraternity rush, while the truly independent thinkers were now the stolid antipolitical students who wouldn't be caught near a controversial statement in their dreams.

The same piece describes the "PC Person"—"a student in a tie-dyed t-Shirt, with open-toed sandals and a grubby knapsack dangling a student union-issue, environmentally sound, reusable red plastic cup," instantly recognizable from Wisconsin to Princeton. What, again, was the point? That those who push these issues are sixties wannabes? That drinking from reusable cups is more trendy faddishness? That socially concerned individuals look the same from campus to campus? The description serves its cause, trivializing any student impulses to change American society.

PC-baiting could not have succeeded had America's national media questioned the truth of the distorted, exaggerated, and fraudulent examples that they so blithely passed on—examples repeated in article after article. A variety of thoughtful rebuttals did challenge the rhetorical stampede. (Many of the best articles, as mentioned, are collected in Patricia Aufderheide's *Beyond PC: Toward a Politics of Under-*

standing). But rarely did they appear in major national venues. Their presence was limited, rather, to liberal-left publications of modest circulation, to scattered newspaper editorial pages, and to periodicals aimed at the academy itself. In contrast to the attacks of the PC-baiters, they were barely visible. The phrase "politically correct" has meanwhile become a taken-for-granted phrase in American culture, used to describe everything from citizens taking out their recycling to enforced niceness in everyday speech.[34]

Do the PC attacks raise any legitimate questions? As I've described and will explore further, activist students have their flaws. Because their task is difficult, they sometimes grow judgmental, bluntly shutting down those who disagree with them. They sometimes separate themselves from important historical perspectives, dismissing rich and vital literature as the mere testaments of dead irrelevant white men. Their efforts to address America's profound divisions, of race, sex, and class, leave them at times off balance or awkward. Inevitably, they take some false steps, which the critics then attack.[35]

How else do student activists fall into the traps that conservatives have so effectively caricatured? Some do wrestle to absurdity over how to make their words inoffensive to all possible groups. At times this creates their own perfect standard of language, and it can leave newcomers so afraid they'll have to act and talk a certain precise way, that they balk at getting involved. Other activists voice their arguments for social change in language so opaque and jargon-encrusted as to almost set themselves up for attack. The politics of racial and sexual identity can often factionalize, as occurred with Emory's SARI group. At a time when poor and minority communities have been devastated by America's political and economic choices, a sense of outrage and solidarity can make it tempting to vent frustration on targets close at hand, such as university professors, administrators who may or may not be culpable, or equally beleaguered white working-class students. It can be tempting to justify questionable actions in terms of clear larger wrongs. As I've explored, students often need to draw support from their specific communities and to build on common experiences and understandings. But when they judge whether people are trustworthy solely on the basis of skin color or gender, they veer onto dangerous turf.[36]

Yet such flaws are peripheral to contemporary student movements. They occur largely at their margins and affect mostly those directly involved in the cause. Although they sometimes make the important work of these movements more difficult than necessary, by no stretch of the imagination do they cast the kind of intellectual and emotional chill over their campuses that the PC-baiters describe. Real issues exist behind the caricatures, as I'll later explore, but the hype of the critics has made them harder, not easier, to address.

Miscast claims   The errors and misstatements of the PC-baiters are pervasive. Even when they get specific facts right, they mislead by miscasting context and significance. They warn repeatedly of a "new McCarthyism" while blurring fundamental distinctions between students raising discomforting questions, right or wrong, and universities firing professors whom the government has targeted. They conjure up images of a pure and apolitical time before the upheavals of the sixties, while ignoring the vast numbers of women and racial minorities who during the fifties were excluded from American colleges, not to mention that period's consistent suppression of critical questioning. They blur widely disparate currents, confusing engaged student activists with the efforts of the frequently opaque and politically cynical deconstructionists, who rarely get involved in campus or community issues. They endlessly repeat absurdities, such as the notion that people are seriously campaigning to replace the term "pet" with "animal companion." They get away with their distortions because the media pass on their stories without bothering to check them.[37]

Just as notions of omnipresent PC-police are conservative myths, so are the claims of campuses suddenly overrun by "tenured radicals" and unruly women and minorities. In her excellent *Harper's* article, Rosa Ehrenreich describes the faculty conservatism she encountered while she was recently a student at Harvard. "I got through thirty-two courses at Harvard," she writes, "majoring in the history and literature of England and America, without ever being required to read a work by a black women writer, and of my thirty-two professors only two were women. I never even *saw* a black or Hispanic professor." Her experience was typical, considering that, of 373 tenured professors in Harvard's College of Arts and Sciences, only two were black. Meanwhile, half of Harvard's undergraduates dutifully enrolled in an economics course taught by former Reagan economic advisors Martin Feldstein and Larry Lindsay.[38]

Once we exclude historically black colleges, the percentage of African-American faculty has remained roughly the same nationwide since the late seventies: barely over 2 percent, and disproportionately concentrated, along with Latino and Native American professors, in lower academic ranks and at low-prestige schools. The tenure gap between whites and nonwhites has actually increased slightly since then, so that 72 percent of white tenure-track faculty are now tenured, compared with 61 percent of minority faculty. An even greater gap—16 percentage points—exists between tenured men and women.[39]

The notion of omnipresent cadres of radical faculty is also simply false. This is confirmed by national surveys in which fewer than 5 percent of faculty members describe themselves as politically far left, 37 percent describe themselves as liberals, and the vast majority claim to be either moderate or conservative. For all that conservative professors warn of a new "McCarthyism of the left," none have lost their jobs, their endowed chairs, or their national podiums. The worst that has happened is that students have challenged their ideas.[40]

The only student to be recently expelled for "saying the wrong things" was a Brown undergraduate who after repeated violations of university conduct rules, drunkenly shouted insults outside a dorm at two in the morning, yelling "fucking niggers" and other racial epithets. When a student in the dorm asked him to quiet down, he yelled, "What are you, a faggot?" and called the other student a "fucking Jew." He then yelled at a black woman, "My parents own your people," and had to be restrained from starting a fight.[41]

Despite pervasive rhetoric about forced minority hiring, senior professors at most schools remain overwhelmingly white, male, and moderate or conservative politically. The boards of trustees, who wield the ultimate power, remain overwhelmingly so. PC-baiters remain silent about such conservative bastions as business, engineering, and law schools. They speak only of a few dissident corners of the social sciences and humanities where, even so, the radicalism is often more rhetorical than real, or else highly marginal compared to mainstream disciplinary traditions that tend to ignore the pivotal issues of our time.[42]

When a recent American Council on Education survey tried to discover the extent of debate around racial and sexual issues, for good or ill, on campuses throughout the country, faculty members at only 5 percent of colleges reported any pressure at all from students or fellow professors to question the political and cultural content of their courses. Only 11 percent in the same survey said they used undergraduate readings that even slightly address racial or gender issues.[43]

Suppressing dissent   PC-baiting began with the campus politics of race and sex. Thirty years after warning, in a debate with Martin Luther King, Jr., that integration would erase "every distinction of race" in our society, columnist James J. Kilpatrick argued that actions like "coddling blacks and pandering to militant feminists" risked not only "the decline of great institutions" but "the decline of the West." But the label PC continues to be used to condemn a more general questioning of existing institutions; it is cast at everything from campus environmentalism to advocacy for the disabled.[44]

PC-baiting tars all students who take stands on racial issues, however thoughtful, effective, and ecumenical. It dismisses all sexual politics, from issues of date rape, abortion choice, sexual harassment, and gay rights, to the study of gender roles in history.[45] It dismisses the efforts of groups like COOL to become more than "just a place where upper-middle-class kids have this wonderful experience and get to see how the other half live—or don't live." It attacks any student who challenges institutional choices and priorities, from Carol Bullard of the Hunter CUNY strikes, to Barb Meister challenging the University of Nebraska agriculture curriculum, to the University of Washington's Heidi Wills, working to push through that PC hallmark—recycling.

Politically active students find this highly frustrating. "It's made it easier to write off anything we do, any issues we raise," said a University of North Dakota woman, "by saying we're 'just trying to be PC.' " The head of the University of Washington Black Students Commission felt furious when the faculty reversed itself after the PC media barrage, withdrawing a mandate for an ethnic studies requirement that it had previously passed. Most professors, he believed, had never even glanced at the three years worth of debates in the UW *Daily*, or the voluminous task force and committee reports. They treated bigotry as if it were a harmless fraternity prank. "They don't even consider our history worth learning."

Students of color have felt particularly frustrated by PC-baiting. Many already carried a sense of estrangement from their colleges, feeling a distinct minority in a situation where faculty and fellow students had little sense of their culture. American society as a whole responded to their communities' most urgent questions with apathy or condescension. While they'd finally been invited to the table of college life, they had little role in setting the menu of what was studied. They learned from a professorate that remained overwhelmingly white, and at senior levels, overwhelmingly male.

"By making these issues something you can ridicule," said Emory's Sonya Tinsley, "people no longer have to take them seriously. Now you can just make fun of someone instead of weighing the merit or lack of merit of what they're trying to accomplish."

I asked if she'd read D'Souza's *Illiberal Education*. She had. "Parts literally made my stomach turn. Like his explanation for groups like the Black Student Association, women's groups, or ethnic cultural alliances. He referred to them almost as reject grounds, places where people could make each other feel better about their inferiority. If I see black and Latino women's groups, or gays and lesbians of color, that's a sign of a healthy community. Sometimes they work together and with other students. Sometimes they work apart. To me, that makes people stronger. Whereas D'Souza views these groups as a sign that their members can't deal with mainstream society. Like the barometer of their health is how many white Anglo-Saxon Protestants they surround themselves with."

"I also disliked assertions," she said, "that some of the books that mattered most to me were second-rate, inconsequential, and of only the slightest enduring value. And that areas like African-American studies were some kind of weak pseudodiscipline. No one suggests someone British is teaching British history because it's easy for them. Or that they're only giving a limited perspective. As if one didn't need to be just as skilled to be involved in these things."

"We have to ask," Sonya stressed, "what's important for us to know. *Illiberal Education* says teaching the canon in a new way would be disrespectful to classic works. If I have to choose between students being able to quote Shakespeare and make witty references to certain writers at cocktail parties, and students learning to have respect for the diversity of people they're going to have to interact with every day, I'd definitely go with the latter. But you don't have to choose between the two. We're not talking about throwing away Shakespeare. Change isn't about saying such and such a writer is stupid, racist, and imperialist for not including certain people in their work. It's about reading a book and asking who isn't in that text? Whose experience is ignored? And why didn't it occur to this person to include these people? Those are very valuable questions."

Sonya agreed that certain works continued to speak generation after generation. "People say, 'I recognize myself in this. This has something to do with me.' But there's a problem if writers can only maintain their status because those who read them have never been exposed to anyone else. I sometimes think those people who claim to be looking out for the best interests of the canon care more about the canon than the human beings that the canon was created for."

Old and new McCarthyism I've mentioned the evolution of PC-baiting from the "new class" rhetoric of the 1970s. The current attacks have even more disturbing parallels to the key intellectual justifications of the McCarthy era. Works of that time, like Sidney Hook's 1953 essay "Heresy Yes, Conspiracy No!" and William F. Buckley's 1951 book *God and Man at Yale: The Superstitions of Academic Freedom*, laid the groundwork for academic purges of Communists and supposed Communists by arguing that they were neither independent-thinking citizens nor free intellectuals deserving respect for dissident views. They judged them, in rhetoric repeatedly cited by academic institutions desirous of eliminating suspect faculty, as slaves to a conspiratorial party that demanded absolute allegiance and conformity, and as therefore lacking in any liberties worth respecting. "The enforcement of the proper professional standards," explained former radical turned red-baiter Hook, "is a matter of ethical hygiene, not of political heresy or persecution." Buckley, who continues to be a major player in these issues, took the argument against intellectual freedom a step further, proclaiming that professors should teach values supported by their college governing boards. He offered a list of Yale professors who needed to be cashiered, one that included not only presumed Communists, but also socialists, Keynesian economists, "collectivists," and one professor who had the temerity to endorse premarital sex.[46]

Critics who have spearheaded the current attack on PC warn, in similar terms, of a "neo-Leninist movement" through which one-time 1960s radicals have infiltrated our universities with the goal of subverting American values. The politically correct, these opponents imply, have no independent mind, but are ideological slaves who need to be stopped. For all their rhetoric about a "new McCarthyism" in which faculty and students with conservative views are supposedly being attacked and banished, the PC-baiters remain disconcertingly accepting of the real McCarthyism that purged American institutions of a generation of dissenters. The National Association of Scholars has even established an annual $2,500 Sidney Hook Award—which they present to a professor who publicly combats the new fifth column threats they now perceive.

PC-baiters minimize and distort the actual legacy of McCarthyism much as they distort present realities. "Professors were not fired," Allan Bloom bluntly claims. "In major universities [McCarthyism] had no effect whatsoever on curriculum or appointments."[47] In fact, as discussed, Communist and non-Communist professors alike were repeatedly dismissed. In school after school, Ivy League and obscure, McCarthyism drove faculty with socially critical views either out of the academy or into silence. The structures of the current arguments ring disturbingly familiar. Critics first brand their opponents as PC, eliminating any need to seriously grapple with their ideas. They tar them with allegiance to a new totalitarian faith, a mutant offshoot of the now dead Soviet menace. Neither the dissenters nor their ideas, they argue, have any place on a civilized campus.

D'Souza promotes the idea that corporate elites should exert greater control over American universities. In a recent *Forbes* article, he urges the magazine's wealthy business readership (subscribers have an average annual household income of $220,000, and an average net worth of $1.6 million) to use their financial clout to defend "our Western, free-market culture," and refuse to countenance dangerous changes on campus. "Don't just write a check to your alma mater; that's an abrogation of responsibility. Keep abreast of what is going on and don't be afraid to raise your voice and even to close your wallet in protest."[48]

In a time of widespread academic budget cuts and decisions over which departments and professors to keep and which to slash, PC-baiting has made more precarious the situations of individuals and programs it has targeted. It has made more difficult a common response to situations like the CUNY cuts, or their equivalent in the other state systems. Some schools, like University of Texas and University of Washington, have reversed entire programs that were the fruit of lengthy and careful deliberation. PC caricatures have added numerous stereotypes to the burdens student activists already bear.[49]

Canons in contention   Because these attacks rest so much on myth, I've felt it important to explore some of their representative falsehoods. But there are genuine and complex issues behind the rhetoric. For instance, what, if any, shared canons of knowledge should American colleges teach?

Canonical fights are nothing new. In the 1880s most scholars opposed the teaching of English and other modern literatures instead of Latin and Greek classics. Later others resisted serious consideration of writers like Joyce, Kafka, Garcia Lorca, and Faulkner. Even a current standard like *Moby Dick* was, as late as the 1920s, written off as a "travel" or "adventure" novel. The furor over cultural dissidents "watering down" a hallowed canon echoes earlier battles to place once-belittled American and twentieth-century literatures in the curriculum.

As Henry Louis Gates points out, it's tempting to confuse literary criticism with social change, and to believe that paying "homage to the marginalized and demonized" means as much as challenging actual injustice. Yet if education means anything beyond mere credentialing, books and classes do matter—or can matter to the degree they offer a sufficiently compelling vision of responsibility for a broader common future. But this vision has to be one of inclusion. Student reading needs to reflect America's diversity in order to break from what Gates described as "the teaching of an esthetic and political order, in which no person of color, no woman, was ever able to discover the reflection or representation of his or her cultural image or voice."[50]

As I've suggested, students of different races often have sharply differing views of history and of their relation to it. Most white students describe their narratives in individual terms—how their parents and grandparents worked their way up, sacrificed and struggled, and for those most fortunate, achieved some modest comfort. Depending on their background, they may worry about their place in the academy and in an uncertain economy. But they view the hurdles they face more in personal than in social terms, just as most ignore the historical roots of advantages they gain by their race. Because they are white, they take for granted that they will not be singled out for special scrutiny when applying for a job, moving into a neighborhood, or seeking credit at a bank. They've grown up with curricular materials that affirm the place of people who look like them in America. (Although poor whites may feel equally estranged because others assume they've grown up economically privileged.) Most take for granted, as Wellesley's Peggy McIntosh has pointed out, having "received daily signals that my people counted, and that others either didn't exist or must be trying, not very successfully, to be like people of my race."[51]

Minority students, in contrast, talk more about the overall situation of their race, and about historical legacies that continue to damage their communities. As Berkeley's Troy Duster points out, they therefore judge well-meaning white students less by individual friendliness than by how they respond to issues that touch this collective burden of pain.

Courses examining racial issues can allow a dialogue to occur between students of these vastly differing experiences. Not dialogue as a club of guilt, or as a salve that will heal all ills, but as a way to engage and understand widely differing experiences and assumptions.

This is not to dismiss the role of traditional canonical works in this or in any other task of importance. In their anger at the familiar canon's limitations, concerned students sometimes dismiss its worth altogether, assuming that the only works worth studying are from non-Western traditions. To dismiss the entire Euro-American past as a mere creature of "dead white men" lumps together those who fought for liberty and those who suppressed it, the wealthy and the poor, those who developed still vibrant democratic visions and those who supported authoritarianism and silence. As Irving Howe cautions, works casually dismissed as "Eurocentric" form the core of a tradition that political radicals have long embraced in their fights for democratic rights. "There were the Labor night schools in England bringing to industrial workers elements of the English cultural past; there was the once-famous Rand School of New York City; there were the reading circles that Jewish workers, in both Eastern Europe and American cities, formed to acquaint themselves with Tolstoy, Heine, and Zola. And in Ignazio Silone's novel *Bread and Wine* we have a poignant account of an underground cell in Rome during the Mussolini years that read literary works as a way of holding itself together."[52]

"I grew up," Howe continues, "with the conviction that what George Lukacs calls 'the classical heritage of mankind' is a precious legacy. It came out of historical circumstances often appalling, filled with injustice and outrage. It was often, in consequence, alloyed with prejudice and flawed sympathies. Still, it was a heritage that had been salvaged from the nightmares, occasionally the glories, of history, and now we would make it 'ours,' we who came from poor and working-class families." Such culture, Howe says, can "foster historical imagination . . . moral imagination, a sense of other ways . . . [and] create kinship with those who had come before us, hoping and suffering as we have, seeking through language, sound and color to leave behind something of enduring value."[53]

Howe is right about the need to cherish the best of this heritage. Columbia students cited works of Aristotle, John Stuart Mill, and Thoreau in opposing the draconian rules changes. Yet Americans need to grapple with both the strengths and the limits of these texts and traditions. As African-American theologian Cornel West writes, "Don't just read Voltaire's great essays on the light of reason—read the 'Peoples of America,' in which he compares indigenous peoples and Africans to dogs and cattle. Don't read just Kant's *Critique of Pure Reason*, read the moments in *The Observations of the Sublime*, in which he refers to Negroes as inherently stupid. It's not a trashing of Kant. It's a situating of Kant within eighteenth-century Germany, at a time of rampant xenophobia, along with tremendous breakthroughs in other spheres."[54]

Similarly, West argues, "You can't find too many insightful formulations in Marx about what it is to be black. You don't go to Marx for that. . . . If you want to know what it means to be black, to be African in Western civilization . . . you go to the blues, you go to literature, you go to Du Bois's analysis of race, you go to Anna Julia Cooper's analysis of race. For what it means to be politically marginalized, you go to a particular tradition that deals with that."[55]

Such approaches require engaging in precisely the "oppression studies" that the conservatives mock and despise, because these are the banished voices. Sentiments like "you make your own chances" and "I'm not that kind of person" arise when students grow up with no context in which to question the chasm between the opportunities and privileges they take for granted and the desperation of those at the bottom of the well.

I'm not just talking about empathy for victims. I'm talking about the chance to grapple with worlds that offer fertile ways people can survive, live, and find joy, even amidst terrifically painful circumstances. I'm talking about exposure to literatures as rich as any coming out of the Western tradition, rich because they convey human characters and dilemmas that are rooted in their cultures, but that resonate beyond those particulars and illuminate universal aspects of humanity.

Students need to grapple with these visions, not as an instant solution to social ills, but as a way of hearing different voices, thinking about different choices, and reflecting on different ways to live. They need to use them to ask which aspects of America's present society feed or demean human dignity, and what other models exist. They need to find examples of courage that suggest that lives of commitment are worth the cost. Works from the traditional canon contribute to this task, yet need to be placed side by side with new voices—those traditionally excluded. This may make possible precisely the (at times painful) self-examination from which real learning blooms.

As Sonya Tinsley pointed out, the issue wasn't whether to throw away Shakespeare, but to ask whose experiences are ignored in his works, and then bring these missing voices into the discussion. Were I choosing a direction for curricular changes, I'd look closely at Stanford's Europe and the Americas track on which the conservatives vented so much fury, but which even some initial opponents at Stanford have come to respect. In this track and in a pilot course used in developing it, students read Shakespeare's *The Tempest*, juxtaposed with Caribbean poet Aimé Césaire's takeoff on that play, *Une Tempete*, which casts Prospero's struggle with the monster, Caliban, as a parable of European colonialism. They studied Augustine's *Confessions* side by side with the Navajo creation myth, *Son of Old Man Hat*. They read Alexis de Tocqueville on the French Revolution coupled with the diary of Equiano, the son of a West African prince, who was captured into slavery. You get a different Augustine from the juxtaposition, explains Stanford anthropologist Renato Rosaldo, a different Tocqueville when you place his discussion of French prosperity in the context of Haiti and the slave trade, a different Aristotle and Rousseau when you juxtapose their notions of political liberty and those in Equiano's diary.

Rosaldo believes it a false dilemma to have to choose Ralph Ellison over Aristotle, Simone de Beauvoir over Plato. The trick is to bring these voices into dialogue, to recognize that curricular choices "touch a nerve about who belongs here, has a place here, has a voice here," and about "which groups have a stake in determining the future of American culture." The new curriculums can provide a necessary coherence, he points out, not through single perspectives that claim to speak for everyone's experience, but through difference, argument, and contrast—through "juxtaposing books and writers that are not ordinarily put together."

English professors Gerald Graff of Chicago and William Cain of Wellesley suggest a similar need to understand the roots of current debates. It's a dead end, they argue, to simply add a few minority names to a preformed canon, or to endlessly fight out "which cultural interests are universal and which are merely special." Or even to play "Let's Make a Deal, [in which] the radicals will teach their pet texts and theories in their curricular enclaves while the traditionalists go on humanizing away in theirs."[56]

Instead they propose to "teach the conflicts": to acknowledge contending views and to focus a unified curriculum on their differences. Advocates of each perspective, they suggest, could offer their best arguments throughout the term—exploring how a society chooses the books it values and which voices will speak from the past to the present. They hope this will allow students to challenge myths of scholarly objectivity and also to refute the cynical view that since all positions are equal, none is worth taking a stand on. Such an approach, they suggest, could give students and faculty alike a chance to debate their most fundamental assumptions about whose voices should be heard, what values are important, where America should head as a nation.

The right to question   Faculty resist the opening of academic traditions for varied reasons. Some are simply ignorant of the subjects on which they pontificate. Some resent the complications produced by new faces and new questions in the classroom. Most act for reasons as experiential as political—reasons having to do with training and credentialing, careers and identities, the initiation rituals of their academic guilds. Traditionalists fear the displacement of works they've grown up with, made their mark with, and sometimes taught with care and passion. For those who themselves worked their way up from working-class roots, the canon may represent their passage to intellectual respectability and a hope for others to follow their path. Academic backlash also has its practical side. Professors defend turf they have become accustomed to exploring, defend their status within their departments against challenges from new methodological approaches or new voices not part of their experience.

This brings us back to students' basic right to question. This path will, inevitably, spark disagreements. When students challenge faculty for statements they believe are problematical, or when they question perceived omissions—as happened with Stephan Thernstrom at Harvard—they challenge their professors' status as masters of the classroom. This is neither censorship nor barbarism, but a necessary intellectual dialogue. The difference is that those who've increasingly begun to argue back are not traditional guardians of knowledge, but freshmen, sophomores, and seniors.

These students may err through overzealousness. They may find it easier to pin a quick label of racist, sexist, or Eurocentric on philosophical thrusts they disagree with than to figure out precisely which examples and arguments give them problems and then articulate why. Not all their claims will be justified. But their right to question transcends the merits of their particular cases.

I believe recent conflicts between students and professors have emerged largely from increased student readiness to question their teachers' views. Conflicts have erupted most often when students view their professors as arrogant, inaccessible, and unwilling to seriously discuss contrary opinions. This was very much the student perception in the Thernstrom case, and in almost every case that the PC critics have cited. As Santa Barbara sociologist Richard Flacks has pointed out, "If you believe in critical education, you have to encourage students to challenge your perspectives, your curriculum, your teaching methods and your assumptions. I think cases like Steve Thernstrom's happen when professors react with defensiveness and anger instead of saying 'let's discuss this.' Where instead of explaining their position and justifying it intellectually, they call it intimidation, or shut up and withdraw."[57]

Fighting words   PC-baiting has encouraged college professors, administrators, and trustees to dismiss the challenge to create a more inclusive academic community. How *can* colleges once overwhelmingly white, male, and upper middle class incorporate students from increasingly diverse backgrounds and bring their concerns into the curriculum? How *should* teachers explore America's historical and cultural legacy in a way that does justice to all who shaped it? How *can* schools respond to bigoted actions that attack those already most vulnerable on campus? Though these questions have few easy answers, they emerge not from some arbitrary PC litmus test, but from America's most deeply rooted conflicts.

Let's briefly explore the issues around hate speech and abusive language. As I've described, incidents of bigotry have occurred at numerous schools. These include a group of University of Washington men who dumped flour on a Native American who was taking a shower, telling him it would teach him "what it means to be white"; the race riots at the University of Massachusetts at Amherst after the Boston Red Sox lost the 1986 World Series, and again in 1992, after a white student's friend punched an African-American resident assistant and left racial graffiti on his door; and, at the University of Michigan, fliers under black students' doors announcing "open hunting season on jigaboos and porch monkeys." A quarter of all minority students have directly encountered abuse.[58]

The same period has seen consistent harassment of lesbians and gays. A Rutgers study found that 55 percent of gay students had been verbally assaulted and 18 percent had been physically attacked. Surveys at the University of Massachusetts at Amherst, Penn State, Yale, Oberlin, and the University of Illinois found similar results. Gays received death threats at Northwestern, the University of North Dakota, and the University of Delaware, and were beaten up at the University of Hartford. They experienced verbal harassment and defacement of their posters and fliers at virtually every school in the country.[59]

How, then, should students, faculty, or administrators respond to such cases? Verbal abuse can make campus life a gauntlet for those who already feel most uncertain about their very right to be there, and are often in precarious financial straits. To a gay student whose friends have been repeatedly beaten up, someone yelling "hey fag-got" is a tangible threat. Racial slurs evoke a similar emotional resonance. Colleges cannot afford to let students be harassed or driven out simply because someone happens to think campuses would be better off all white, all male, or entirely heterosexual. For vandalism, physical attacks, or cases of gross personal harassment, campuses have every responsibility to levy whatever penalties will protect the rights of innocent students.

Things get complicated, however, when we talk about legal restrictions on general speech, even the most obnoxious, inflammatory, and wounding. Certainly such speech needs to be challenged. Yet when administrators step in with prohibitions, students can too easily turn bigots into martyrs, or focus on their abstract right to say what they choose, rather than on the impact of their words. Restricting bigoted language to secure campus order and tranquillity can also set a dangerous precedent. Justice Oliver Wendell Holmes made his famous statement that citizens have no right "to shout fire in a crowded theater" to justify the jailing of World War I–era socialists who had merely advocated the repeal of America's draft law. College administrators citing the need to maintain peace in the community have repeatedly restricted the political speech of dissenting students, from the bans on student support for civil rights efforts that triggered the 1964 Free Speech Movement at UC Berkeley to prohibitions on Gulf War demonstrations.

As of 1994, the drunken and repeatedly abusive Brown student mentioned earlier was the only student expelled from any school under any of these laws. It is grossly misleading for PC-baiters to imply that students have been thrown out for saying *black* instead of *African-American*, for disagreeing with affirmative action, or for failing to acknowledge the contributions of gays in their papers.

Yet rules against hate speech contain profound traps, which may explain why they've been instituted more by administrators attempting a quick fix for complex problems than by the efforts of activist students. Campus antiracist coalitions have at times directly opposed them. A well-meaning but seriously flawed policy at Tufts was successfully challenged by a coalition that included everyone from the Young Republicans to Democratic Socialists of America and the Latin American Society. Although student activists disagree on such restrictions, the sense of most is that colleges need to respond to racial bigotry, not by banning the objectionable symbols and words, and not through the conservatives' malign neglect, but by raising an outcry and educating the community.[60]

This means marches, rallies and forums, newspaper letters and editorials, classroom discussions, expressions of solidarity like Emory's "No Time to Hate," and formal institutional initiatives like ethnic studies core requirements. These responses let it be known that bullying and destructive words are publicly recognized as necessarily legal but thoroughly reprehensible, and that they have no place in a community of learning or in American society.

Students have the right to question damaging language. A Columbia woman described an engineering class in which students learned to memorize the names of circuits with the mnemonic sentence "Boys Rape Girls But Women Want It Anyway." The words were repeated day after day as part of the course; she didn't know how to respond. I've heard story after story of students walking blithely along, thinking of nothing related to race, gender, or controversy, only to be rudely brought down by calls of "nigger" or "faggot," or by casual racist jokes. It's easy for those never targeted to dismiss these occurrences.[61]

Yet it's self-defeating for students to jump down the throats of their peers for the slightest failure to measure up to a standard. Students are not necessarily racist or sexist because they call young women "girls" or African-Americans "blacks," from force of habit. Campus activists do, at times, spend so much energy obsessing over which words to use that they end up exhausting core participants, and leave already hesitant newcomers likely to give up on social movements entirely rather than scramble to learn new hidden rules and codes.

Excessive focus on language may also stem from a more general powerlessness. In the time of mean and cramped social visions in which these students came of age, it has been easier to focus on how people speak than to grapple with seemingly intractable political and economic structures that cause war, poverty, and injustice. It has been easier to call to account fellow students who slip up by using the "wrong" phrases than to confront that distant strata of Americans who control most of this country's wealth and whose daily choices shape the lives of the rest of us. The power of semantics pales in comparison. Campus activists who spend too much time particularizing the precise words that are inoffensive may have scant energy left to deal with the root task of reaching out to enough of their peers to help change society.

Picking up the clichés   PC-baiters offer a sophisticated rationale for political withdrawal. They articulate a highly individualist doctrine of responsibility, insisting that citizens arrive at their varied fortunes wholly through work and intrinsic merit, never by the force of social circumstances. They damn anyone who questions the authority of America's leaders to order the world as they see fit, reinforcing the image of "the men who know best." Their attacks resurrect every conceivable social activist stereotype, from the tie-dyed hippie of *Newsweek's* "PC Person" to constant warnings against the "new barbarians." PC-baiting provides ample justification for students to back off and insist "I'm not that kind of person."

Before PC-baiting surfaced, student opposition to such shifts as the broadening of curriculums was cast in the language of individual choice. This was true of the Colby football player who asked, after a star fellow athlete had been disciplined for yelling racial slurs, "Why should we care about black issues? Why should we all of a sudden have to take a course in African history if we're not interested? Why should we even be asked to get involved?" Now this rhetoric has changed. Those opposing attempts to redress long-standing racial or gender ills now pose as valiant defenders of freedom. They are no longer merely seeking their right to do what they want unhindered by broader social claims. They are no longer merely seeking private havens where they can say "Buddy, buzz off." They are now striking a blow for Western Civilization.

Whatever the individual behavior, PC-baiting offers a means of excusing it. At New Jersey's Glassboro State College, Alpha Phi Delta fraternity posted a series of fliers in the student center. They were printed in their house color, purple, and advertised their rush week with the photo of *Playboy* model Morgan Fox lying nude on a bed and exclaiming "Oooh, purple turns me on." Numerous female students called the fliers demeaning and asked that they be removed from the common public area. The fraternity president claimed they'd put them up to warn of the dangers of censorship.[62]

Granting the Alpha Delts' right to post obnoxious materials, PC-baiting let them drape a fundamentally sleazy publicity effort in the mantle of a defence of civil liberties. Since the media furor, students, faculty, and citizens in general who've wished to delineate their turf against assertive gays, blacks, or women have suddenly been able to feel sanctified. *American Scholar* editor Joseph Epstein can take pride in comparing feminists to pit bulls in the respectable literary journal, the *Hudson Review*. Students can justify any sort of heedless, bullying, mean-spirited, or simply apolitical behavior as a way of combatting the "liberal thought police."[63]

Identity politics   What are appropriate roles and visions for students who wish to make their campuses a home for all who attend? Students most involved have continued to pushed their administrations to bring to the curriculum previously excluded voices, to expand minority recruitment and retention, to support campus centers for women, gay students, and ethnic minorities, and to provide a base for a more diverse collegiate future. They've taken up issues of wounding and demeaning language, first challenging overt bigotry, then addressing the more slippery business of unintended offense. They've challenged professors they deemed grossly insensitive or simply wrong, who sometimes in turn have lashed back. All have agreed that racial polarization needs to be addressed.

Organizing around common racial or sexual identity can anchor students in common experience and history. It can help them challenge the myths that all Americans begin with equal chances. It can unearth the pain of wanting to succeed while knowing that it might mean having to leave behind family, friends, and community.

Yet politics based on particular identity also carries traps. Its adherents can too easily play one-upmanship games with oppression, arguing that they are specially worthy of trust because they are African-American, or female, or gay—romanticizing their own identities in a mirror image of the old hierarchies, deciding that individuals have no right to speak on particular issues because they happen to be white or male or heterosexual. In this vein, Asian-American writer David Mura cautions against "using our victimhood as a mask for sainthood . . . letting whatever sins the white race has committed against us become a permanent absolution for us, an excuse to forgo moral and psychological introspection."[64]

For American students to examine their particular identities means examining the narratives of work, love, migration, and struggle that have created this nation of immigrants. It means looking honestly at the darker side of America's history—the repeated violations of human dignity that continue to this day—and then moving on to recognize that humans do share common bonds, and need to find ways to equitably live together.

Identity politics cannot by itself produce this vision of the common good, though it's an improvement on listening only to white men and calling their perspective universal. Taking diverse experiences into account is essential to a democratic vision. It can't however, substitute for the vision itself. It can't do justice to what holds us together as humans on this planet.

Identity politics can displace a politics that seeks what is wise and humane for all individuals with rhetoric that is constrained to respond to the needs of one particular group. As Hunter's Carol Bullard remarked of the City College factionalism, "I'm tired of Puerto Ricans who don't speak to Dominicans. Black people who don't speak to nobody who speaks Spanish even if they're blacker than them. Nobody speaks to whites."

Identity politics can also err in focusing on race and sex to the exclusion of the more slippery categories of class. It's a historical irony that what's called "the new social movements" have emerged at a time of growing class polarization and economic decline. But this irony has fostered profound rifts between groups that ought to be able to work together for a more just and humane society.

In her book *Families on the Fault Line*, sociologist Lillian Rubin suggests that working-class whites often respond to the proliferation of claims based on race, and to a recent wave of immigrants of color, by stressing the pain and struggle of their particular ethnic backgrounds—the difficulties their families faced when they came from Italy, Germany, or Poland, and labored to make a decent life in America. These individuals increasingly feel, Rubin says, that they need to formulate their own identity as victims, so that, in the words of one man she interviewed, they can "take their place at the multicultural table." The more they do this, the more they resist what they view as the unwarranted claims of outspoken minorities, and the harder they find it to build common ground.[65]

I saw such a response with the highly individualistic Fairfield students, who justified all manner of social ills because of their grandparents' struggles. I saw it with the Hunter College Bensonhurst group, who said their parents, in contrast to the CUNY strikers, "had a work ethic" and were willing to "take what you have and make what you can of it." And with the Colby student who said, "They're going to make black history a requirement. Why shouldn't they require Italian history, Irish history, or every other goddamned thing we have in this country? What's to separate them from everybody else?"

Students need to explore America's often brutal racial history. They need to examine the deep divisions between the sexes, including the historical roots of rape, domestic violence, and dismissal of women's voices and perspectives. The stories of gays can no longer be buried. Yet students also need to discuss the equally taboo questions regarding the ways American society divides increasingly between haves and have-nots, and not just between whites and blacks, Asians and Latinos, men and women, gays and straights. The experiences of white students' Italian, Polish, and Irish grandparents are part of this historical legacy, and need to be studied, though not in a way that glosses over America's painful racial divides. Gaining a sense of such interwoven history may help students understand and challenge the growing gap between that increasingly hard-pressed majority—of all backgrounds and races—who struggle just to get by, and the top 1 percent of Americans who control more wealth than all the other inhabitants of this country combined.[66]

Conservatives cynically play upon the omissions of class within current identity politics. D'Souza offers the image of "a black or Hispanic doctor's son, who has enjoyed the advantages of comfort and affluence," yet receives preference "over the daughter of an Appalachian coal miner or a Vietnamese street vendor." Yet critics like D'Souza, Bennett, Cheney, Bloom, Kilpatrick, George Will, and Rush Limbaugh use such images only to deny other claims to equity and justice, not to open opportunities for the children of impoverished miners or street vendors—or students like those at CUNY. They remain as quick as ever to bait individuals who dare to question America's fundamental divisions of wealth and power.[67]

Identity politics can also discourage political involvement. Individuals who can't or don't choose to frame their beliefs in terms of membership in a particular oppressed group can be left out in the cold, feeling guilty, illegitimate, and angry. This may be a major factor influencing the gender gap in student politics whereby young women are increasingly more liberal and more involved than their male peers. I've met many young white men who involve themselves effectively in contemporary student movements and take liberal or radical stands. But many more buy into a dangerous innocence regarding power and privilege, and a resentment focused not on those who have squandered America's wealth and pillaged its economy, but on those at the margins who serve as scapegoats.

The conservatism of young white men comes, as I have suggested, in part from being more insulated, experiencing fewer routine indignities, and encountering no equivalent harassment. Men feel a greater urgency about ending up on top and a greater anxiety about being able to fulfil traditional breadwinner tasks in an uncertain economy. They worry about the demands of changing sexual roles. People tell them again and again, "You and your kind need to change." They lack their own specific identity movements, unless they want to join Robert Bly and the wild-man circles. They often feel dismissed as archaic representatives of a problematic culture.[68]

When political debate focuses solely on collective identity, individual student lives can get lost. Students want to be recognized as African-Americans, Native Americans, or gays, for these aspects of their being matter profoundly. They also want to be recognized as distinct individuals, with distinct hopes and fears, and their own right to speak for themselves. As Emory Black Students Association chair Brian Woods said, "I don't want to speak for all factions of black society." Students want to be treated with respect not just because they fit into a particular group, but because they're somebody's daughter or son, and are eighteen, twenty, or twenty-two years old, doing the best they can to get out and build their own life. This is as true for the much-maligned straight white males as for those in specific identity groups, though they face different constraints and opportunities.

Students involve themselves in political causes not only because of specific experiences resulting from their racial, ethnic, or gender identities, but also because they feel compelled to act on larger visions of human dignity. The 1960s movements flourished in part because students responded to broad moral causes that drew them across America's cultural and economic divides. This has been true of much recent campus involvement as well. In the words of Greg Ricks, the African-American head of Stanford's Office of Multicultural Education, issues like the global environmental crisis, the decline of America's economy, and the emotional costs of a culture of material insatiability give "even the blond-haired rich kids from Greenwich, Connecticut, some legitimate reasons to feel disenfranchised." Highly specific experiences often drive students to enter politics, but the students need to reach beyond them.[69]

How can they bridge these divides? The successful citywide Washington, D.C., group, D.C. Student Coalition Against Racism and Apartheid (DC-SCAR), deliberately established a multiracial organization with majority nonwhite leadership, modeling itself consciously after the early phase of the key civil rights group, the Student Nonviolent Coordinating Committee (SNCC). As executive director Ray Davis said, SNCC at that point neither excluded nor included anyone on the basis of race, but core leadership was black, even as members "married across racial lines or developed strong friendships across racial lines, and these personal relationships kept them from going backwards and declaring, 'Well, you're white, so you can't join in.'" For students of color to have their own organizations, he believed, and learn their own history, culture, and traditions, made possible more durable, principled, and equal coalitions with whites.[70]

Sonya Tinsley suggested that students could work together day to day, across racial and cultural barriers, "not just in times of crisis, but through organizations doing things together, planning together, sitting and talking informally. . . . If they work together on things that have nothing to do with issues and crises, communication lines exist." African-American sociologist Troy Duster, at UC Berkeley, noted the success of professors who assigned collaborative classroom projects to draw students out of their separate enclaves.[71] Dartmouth students mentioned extensive human relations workshops, which gave those from different backgrounds at least a glimpse of each others' hopes, frustrations, and fears. A number of schools started successful community service efforts that brought together diverse campus communities.

Student political movements have themselves created strong multicultural bonds. During the Gulf War, for instance, African-American and Latino students (who consistently opposed the war in greater numbers than whites) ended up working with once predominantly white campus peace groups. In the CUNY strikes, students sought the common goal of keeping their campuses accessible, speaking out in a chorus of voices as diverse as their schools. Students have also built bridges through consciously multicultural organizations. USSA has developed a complex system of group and constituency representation to ensure that all voices are heard. Other groups, like SEAC and COOL, have taken similar steps to broaden their core staff and national executive councils. More and more recognize that they cannot presume to have students of a single particular background speak for all those they wish to involve.[72]

Education for democracy   America is a nation of people with vastly differing beliefs, experiences, and identities. Its citizens accept no single moral or theological framework as a common standard of rightness. But we should be able to agree that this country faces profound crises that will only be resolved with the participation of all of us, and that these issues consequently need to be debated in every possible venue.

Critical education requires acknowledging widely differing experiences. It requires continually asking how to create a society that is more just, more peaceful, more sustainable in its varied directions and choices. It requires asking how ordinary citizens can shape national choices in reality as well as in civics rhetoric.

Neither teachers nor students are likely to agree on every specific prescription toward these ends. But the very process of arguing issues out, whenever possible, leads students to take their education more seriously, to replace a vision of cynicism and withdrawal with one that recognizes the profound consequences of their actions. That students have begun to critically question their professors, push for a broadened curriculum, or even take that dangerously radical step of ensuring that their cafeterias provide reusable cups, seems to me to redeem higher education's democratic promise.

As students have begun to question, they've also challenged deeply rooted institutions of power. It is for this reason, I believe, that they have been so vehemently attacked and baited with labels like "politically correct," that their opponents have denied their right to speak out about the world they will inherit and sought to drive them back to passive silence. Yet I believe these attacks will ultimately fail. The crises in American life are too grave, the shifts in the student population too profound, the growing commitments of a significant minority too strong.

Twenty-two ～～～～～～～～～～～

Sustaining Every generation
the vision changes the world

～～～～～～～～～～～～～～～～～～～～～～～

How can students best sustain their newfound social concern? How can they stay involved after they leave the college gates? What do the shifting currents of student life
portend for America's future? I've examined the shaping of the students who came of
age in the eighties and early nineties and how they've formed their core values and
commitments. They don't represent all of their peers; rather, they are the more or less
privileged half who make it, at least briefly, to college. But just taking those who entered
institutions of higher learning in the twelve-year Reagan-Bush era, they represent nearly
thirty million men and women.[1]

If experiences of previous generations hold true, students' choices of retreat
and engagement matter beyond their immediate political impact. Many use their college years to settle on fundamental ways of understanding their role in the world, and
to embark on paths that will set the directions of their lives. This is as true for those who
frame their choices in purely personal terms as for students who consciously seek social
commitment.

I've mentioned tracking studies of Vietnam-era campus activists. While many
found their involvement substantially chipped away, students who took strong stands
during that period have remained significantly more politically involved and more supportive of social change than have their apolitical peers. Radicals from the 1930s faced
more daunting barriers to continued involvement: both the political betrayals of Stalin-
ism and McCarthy era attacks on dissent. In response, sizable numbers turned conserva-

tive or dropped out of politics entirely, although the Vietnam War brought some of them back. Still, significant numbers of thirties activists continued to work in various ways for a more humane society.[2]

The perspectives of current students aren't static or immutable. Those who are politically active face a challenge to continue their involvement in a time when movements that embody their ideals are often fractured and scattered. It is to their advantage that the political detachment of their peers has given them the feel of swimming against a prevailing current. Conversely, apolitical students who've attended campuses where activism was invisible or peripheral may take on social causes at a later date, under the pressure of emergent social crises or a general resurgence of concern. No student's future is carved in stone.

Nonetheless, college is a time when many students develop a base of cultural assumptions they will use throughout their lives. They set habits of speaking out or remaining silent, of engaging with difficult public issues or avoiding them, of embracing or mistrusting the power of ordinary citizens to have a political say. They embark on self-reinforcing paths in their careers, friendships, and goals. On or off campus, they will face similar dilemmas of engagement or withdrawal, similar issues to respond to, similar arguments for passivity.

It will take ten or twenty years to see whether the men and women of this generation maintain their present course. Yet for the students of the eighties and nineties whom I've studied, the patterns hold true. Those vehemently antipolitical have generally remained hostile or distant toward America's contemporary social movements—even causes, like the environment, whose goals they often support. Those on the fence—disengaged but questioning—often continue a mix of withdrawal and concern, holding back from taking direct stands, yet wondering if they ought to be more engaged. Students with strong political backgrounds continue trying to address issues they care about.

Those I've called the adapters have no less moral goodwill than their activist peers. They share similar concerns about how to get by in tough economic times, similar desires to live decent personal lives. But they have been taught, in a variety of ways, to stay politically silent. Many endorse a carnivorous individualism that buttresses both material greed and the passive stoicism of those just scrambling to survive. They remain ignorant of and distant from citizen movements, present and past. They frame their personal narratives, not in terms of addressing some nebulous common good, but of working toward a separate private peace. While many would like to see a more compassionate world, they do not consider it their role to try to create it. In the often repeated phrase, they continue to consider themselves "simply not that kind of person."

This pivotal period   For recent graduates involved with social causes, continued engagement requires adjustments. Jean Besanceney of Greeks for Peace graduated from the University of Michigan in June 1988. At the main commencement ceremony, Reagan-era U.N. ambassador Jeane Kirkpatrick was awarded an honorary degree. Jean attended an alternative graduation ceremony keynoted by African-American graduate student Barbara Ransby. An eloquent speaker who had pushed through Columbia's initial divestment resolutions while still an undergraduate, Ransby thanked the gathered parents for raising children with the courage to speak out. She asked the new graduates to stay committed to their dreams. Jean felt slightly awkward at the mostly black gathering, since her activism had only peripherally addressed issues of race. But the ceremony validated her beliefs. She felt honored to be there. "It even gave my parents a sense of why I acted."

After college Jean moved with her boyfriend Neal, an industrial designer, to the conservative 27,000-person town of Holland, Michigan. She found a peace group based in a church, and some decent local Democrats. "But mostly people just talked. They did very little about outreach." Uncertain how to act, Jean felt isolated being out of school. "College is really safe," she said. "I'm realizing now how much easier it was to be active there."

Jean wanted to live her life in a way that mattered. "I can't forget what I know. My life wouldn't have meaning if I stopped caring about all I've learned." But the alternative culture she found provided few obvious niches in which to act. Jean applied for a state job working with migrant farmworkers, even mentioning Greeks for Peace as a credential. Then, feeling she was living too much in Neal's shadow, she moved to Cleveland, roomed with an old high school friend, and got an interim job as a hostess at the Red Lobster restaurant.

"Cleveland Heights is way cool," Jean wrote in a letter. "Racially integrated. An art museum. Ballet and famous orchestra, renovation of warehouses, university culture, pseudo hippie culture. It's a nuclear free zone! (No more work to do here!—Ha!) I like city living except for traffic and tacky development strips." But she wanted a different job than working at the Red Lobster, which felt "ultimately meaningless—unless I can psych myself up for how wonderful an institution Red Lobster is and the simple idea of making the customer happy." She liked the racial and cultural mix of the people she worked with, except for two waitresses who requested that she not seat "tables of niggers" in their sections, which prompted Jean to speak up, outraged. But she earned just $4.50 an hour. "I have a college degree!" she wrote. "I have student loans to pay off!"

Jean systematically tried to research long-term choices, paging through *What Color Is Your Parachute, Life After Shakespeare*, and the interviews from Studs Terkel's *Working*. She applied for a job as a neighborhood organizer dealing with fair housing and redlining. "I don't know if I should pursue low-paying social change work," she wrote. "I know it's meaningful and challenging, although I never want to canvass again. But would I be happier making money in some mainstream job and doing political work on the side? What if the job sucked out all my energy? I still want to join an aerobics class, study art, and have a social life. What if I 'accidentally' sell out, steer myself into a meaningless career and become an alcoholic Republican? I hate this pivotal period in my life."

"Maybe," she reconsidered, "I don't want to be an organizer even if it's meaningful. I know I don't want to be a hippie." In the long run, she hoped to be some kind of professional, perhaps doing city planning or environmental work. For now, she wanted "just some semi-interesting job that pays the bills and lets me worry about the meaning of my life later on."

Jean looked for work through every channel she could find, including University of Michigan alumni parties and the get-togethers her sorority held. People at these gatherings seemed mostly into reciting stale football cheers or telling her she should meet some great young doctor and get married. But they did lead her to a near-miss interview for a marketing job with a local playhouse. She thought the Left needed "better networks in addition to political work."

Jean also sought a supportive social milieu. "Just like a newcomer to town joins their church, I want to find the progressive community." She called the local office of the major peace group, SANE/FREEZE. The woman who answered "seemed like an instant friend." Volunteering to help with a mailing, she got a list of further job leads for places like the Rape Crisis Center and an alternative United Way. Finally she found a job as information and research coordinator for the Lutheran minister who served as Cuyahoga county ombudsman. Jean also visited a couple recommended by someone in the Holland, Michigan, peace group. Invited to their house for dinner, she found a milieu of books, records, and conversations that recalled her Ann Arbor community. Their bulletin board displayed familiar buttons and bumperstickers. Recyclables were piled in the corner. Jean worried briefly that because none of women were wearing makeup, they'd think her less of a feminist for doing so. Then she described how she'd become involved with Greeks for Peace. Others recalled their own political journeys. She began to feel at home.

A financial harvest   Just as Jean continued with social involvement, so students more politically detached continued to choose other priorities. Nebraska's Dale Ottiger completed his summer internship with Dow, then another with the chemical company ICI Americas. But when he graduated in 1989, ICI made a belated job offer and Dow failed to come through with one at all. Dale was courted instead by Cargill, Iowa Beef, and the giant Farmland Cooperative. He joined Farmland's Petroleum Products Division, out of Kansas City.

Farmland had been established by a consortium of local rural co-ops to supply them with seed, fuel, herbicides, and fertilizers. When I asked if the company played a role more supportive of family farms than private conglomerates like Dow, Cargill, or ConAgra, Dale said this might be true, but that he took the job because it came along at the right time, required no major relocation, and because the company was a familiar presence while he was growing up. He liked it that Farmland let him stay in the Midwest, crisscrossing Nebraska, Kansas, and Missouri to supply lubricants and diesel fuel to traditional co-op markets and to new ones like trucking companies, construction firms, and convenience stores.[3]

Dale was still with Farmland In 1994 as I was completing this book. Living in Kansas City, married to his college girlfriend, Linda, he had a new plan for his future. He spent his spare hours building up his own business as a broker for a four-billion-dollar-a-year direct distribution network, through which people could buy household goods, insurance programs, faxes, computers, and even automobiles. Like Amway, Shaklee, or Mary Kay Cosmetics, it used multilevel marketing, an approach Dale credited with producing one-fifth of America's millionaires. He hoped his personal sales network would grow to encompass a thousand families.

"In my vision," he said, "the network's not so different from farming. Instead of cultivating the land, I'm cultivating people. I'm involved with people from all walks of life, from all around the world, people who are not willing to accept defeat and will choose to defeat the odds. My brothers are still home farming. They'd rather pay interest to the bank than income tax, but one day that attitude will pop up and kill them. They'll have one devastating season and lose everything. I probably put in as many hours as they do, but that's the sacrifice I make to secure my future."

"In a way," said Dale, "I am still planting, cultivating, nurturing, and helping others experience their own harvest. It's just a harvest of financial freedom."

Making the bucks   When I recontacted the Fairfield group, it didn't surprise me that Scott, the stockbroker's son who believed that "you make your own chances" and who had explained that "love thy neighbor" applied only to his wealthy Long Island community, had followed his father's path and joined a New York securities firm. As a friend in the group commented, "Some people stumble into Wall Street because that's what's available. Scott went after top-dollar work from the beginning. He hates his job. He'd switch to any other that paid better. But he's making the bucks, which I guess is all right." George Lipson, who'd explained that "the business world just isn't going to care how much I know about Plato," worked at first for IBM, where he ran marketing seminars but felt his advancement opportunities would be limited, and then attended law school. George quit a brief job selling insurance because the company "seemed so utterly sleazy that I didn't want my reputation associated with them," and now followed politics somewhat more than he had at Fairfield, "like I try to read the *New York Times* and I even went to a Ross Perot meeting just to see what he stood for." He spoke mostly of wanting a comfortable life with nice vacations.

Others in the group also continued their earlier paths. Rick, the token liberal whom the others had called "Nadia" and teased for wasting $14,000 a year of his parents' money by wanting to be a teacher, did exactly that and now taught social studies in a Massachusetts high school. Paul Vigna, the writer who straddled cynicism and social concern, got a job at a small-town New Jersey paper and volunteered occasionally on a local Habitat for Humanity newsletter. He might never earn as much, he acknowledged, as the others in the group. But he learned something even from reporting on car crashes and high school football teams, and was delighted when he could occasionally cover community issues that mattered.

The most interesting shift in the Fairfield group was that of Tim Lovejoy, the doctor's son who began as a vehement individualist, wanting to get a place where he could tell the world "Buddy, buzz off" and asking about the urban poor, "Is it my fault if me or my parents make the bucks so that they can't?" Tim had been profoundly shaken by medical waste washing up on the shore of his beloved Long Island Sound. Within two years he had made environmentalism his profession. He worked first at Connecticut Audubon, where he helped schoolchildren build aquariums and brought in a live spotted lizard to discuss habitat destruction. Then he did asbestos removal and industrial hygiene inspections for a D.C. consulting group that monitored renovation of government buildings. Earning $25,000 (instead of his six-figure dream salary) Tim felt was OK, though he hoped to ultimately make more through his own environmental firm. Between jobs, he'd even spent a few weeks canvassing for Greenpeace, although he felt culturally estranged from his largely countercultural co-workers, and felt skeptical about supporting civil disobedience when "offering practical solutions would make more sense, like don't just protest or pass another law to stop people cutting down forest for the spotted owl. Figure out how to move the owl to another part of the forest."

Once wholly scornful of social concern, Tim now wondered whether the Reagan-Bush years promoted a culture of too much greed. "I'm still very conservative, but I think about who I serve and whether I do enough for others. Whether I live up to my Christian beliefs. Just getting a paycheck at the end of the week doesn't do much for anything." Social ills, Tim still believed, could best be addressed through private rather than public solutions. He still felt the rich had a right to keep as much as possible of what they made, since they ultimately provided the jobs. But he also said the government should cut military spending, offer incentives for fuel-efficient cars, and maybe even open up the basements and garages of official buildings at night to give homeless people a place to sleep. He admired Jimmy Carter for building low-income housing.

Maybe, Tim acknowledged, the very corruption of the Reagan-Bush era accentuated his mistrust of government solutions. "Plus working in Washington, D.C., you see so much sloth and hypocrisy. I still feel the government can't spend money as well as I can, that they have too many opportunities to spend it and waste it." But he asked many more questions than before.

Even Tim's material needs had gotten simpler. When I asked him about the fancy boat, car, and house he'd wanted, he laughed and said, "Nice stuff is still nice to have. But the bottom line is that if I don't need it I probably won't buy it. If I did get a boat it would have to be a sailboat, which would maybe replace the house. But I'd rather live humbly and happy than wealthy and unhappy. Right now, I have a place to sleep, a place to shower, a car that runs, a decent stereo, and food to eat when I want it. I have all the things I really need in my life. I guess maybe I have changed."

Apolitical students don't necessarily end up conservative. Just largely detached from social involvement. Anna Roselli, the barber's daughter from the University of Washington who worked "to meet the right kind of friends," went on to the University of Michigan law school and a job with Seattle's second largest firm. The affluent crowd she'd deliberately hung out with still centered their lives around the tennis club and jobs they'd gotten with the help of their parents' contacts. They remained as hostile as ever toward efforts at social change. Anna was considerably more sympathetic, but still distant from those taking on controversial public concerns. She considered getting involved in various worthwhile causes as she made her way through law school, but never quite found the time or venue. She considered volunteering for Clinton and

Gore in the 1992 election, but was just getting settled in her new job. She thought she might someday shift to environmental law or work as a labor lawyer, but these remained vague thoughts for the future.

Columbia's Carolyn Lowenthal remained similarly ambivalent about larger social concerns. She graduated from Columbia in 1989, spent a year in the research department of the *New Yorker*, then attended the University of Chicago law school. Gearing up for a year-long clerkship with a federal judge, she said she'd always envisioned herself as a district attorney or public defender, working in the trenches of the criminal justice system. "I wouldn't make much money, but I'd be in the courtroom. The work would matter. I feel I'd be cheating myself if I didn't give it a try." But public-sector jobs were overworked and underpaid. "You start at twenty-six thousand instead of sixty-eight, which is hard when you're forty-five thousand dollars in debt. The Xerox machines don't work. You don't have a secretary. Sometimes you don't even have voice mail. You don't have time to give the attention you'd like."

"It's important," Carolyn stressed, "that my work be as good as it can get, whether it's a court appearance, filing a brief, or negotiating with an opposing attorney in the hallway. All my life, from when I started at the Shady Hill School at age four to when I worked this summer in a Washington law firm, I've been taught to produce a perfect product. One of the things that people like me face in public-sector jobs is whether we'll be able to do that. Not that you have to go to a private firm, but the public sector's always going to have a larger caseload. You're going to have fewer resources. You won't be able to just spend money, because you're working for the taxpayers. Maybe I'll work a few years in the district attorney's office, then join a private firm."

Or perhaps, Carolyn said, she'd switch careers entirely. From Columbia on, she'd been tutoring low-income kids. By her senior year she was doing this ten to fifteen hours a week. Education remained a core concern. "It's interesting that I had such an utter disgust for politics, because I have a strong interest now in state or local government, which is where I think things get done most effectively. Maybe I'll import the analytic and writing skills I've learned from studying law, and use them in some other area, like becoming a principal and trying to save a public school. I figure my law school skills are a lot more useful than skills people get in those ridiculous education programs where all you do is tell teachers who've been teaching thirty years how they're doing it wrong."

Carolyn remained doubtful about organized social movements. She did serve on the board of the law school's long-standing women's organization, and take part in discussions of why women were often marginalized—out of twenty-eight students selected for the Law Review only one was a woman and none was African-American. But she was critical when some fellow law students organized a one-day walkout they called "Awareness Day" over the University of Chicago's lack of minority law faculty. "Of course they did it when prospective students were visiting, just as the groups did at Columbia. There were lots of speeches, some inspiring and some annoying. It got major TV coverage because Chicago's a conservative school. I didn't disagree so much with their ideas but with how they tried to get them across. Not that pressure shouldn't be put on the administration to hire minority faculty, but they make decisions in a certain way, and the best way to make change is to sit down and meet with the appointments committee. I just don't see how cutting classes did any good, except waste our parents' money when they're paying four hundred dollars for every session we take. People did get together a petition asking the school to carefully consider the role of women, minorities, and openly homosexual people on the faculty and consider bringing more in. That I can work with. That's responsible citizenship."

I asked Carolyn if she helped circulate the petition. She hadn't, but she did sign it after a lengthy conversation with one of its initiators. I suggested she was still struggling with the Perfect Standard. She laughed and agreed. "I either throw myself all the way into a cause, like education, or I hold back. If I care about something enough, I'll talk about it, I'll hand out leaflets. I'll get passionately involved." But she hadn't actually leafletted on any issue yet, because "the right cause just hasn't come along, and I wouldn't leaflet just because a position is generically consistent with my views." It infuriated her when the Gulf War broke and her professor in a property class "just went on as if nothing had happened, as if it didn't matter that we were at war. It infuriates me that the school can take these five hundred incredibly smart people and teach them that they're above the fray and that their work is more important than anything else that happens, all the worries of the riff-raff." But she stayed away from local antiwar protests. During the 1992 elections she considered volunteering for future senator Carol Moseley Braun. But she spent the summer in New York, and when she got back to Chicago in October, she wanted to do more than just make phone calls, hold up a sign, or stand on a corner handing out fliers, which was at that point what the campaign needed.

"I'm more aware of the real world," Carolyn said, "but my basic values are the same. I think more about paying the bills and my career. It's my VISA bill now, not my parents'. I'm getting married next year and in the next five years will probably have a kid. I think about more things. But the same issues are still important. The same things still disgust me. It's awful but true, but as I said, maybe politics is just too messy for me. I don't like groups and what they do, don't like being part of the messy way they act. Maybe that's a liability. I don't know how I'm going to balance the side of me that wants to go out and save the schools with the side that wants all the resources and everything done right. But even if I go into the private sector I have every intention of not only doing pro bono work but also tutoring, advising kids, being involved in the community. Maybe you should call me in five years."

For all of Carolyn's mistrust of citizen movements, she nonetheless believed in civic commitment. The same was true with Jill Catalano, who went from her Holy Cross ROTC scholarship to the Uniformed Services University of the Health Sciences (USUHS), the U.S. government medical school for the military and for associated public health programs. Again, economics played a role in Jill's choices. Her home state of Rhode Island had no public medical school. Attending a private university would have meant incurring a debt of $8,000 a year, even with a four-year public health commitment. At USUHS, the military covered all expenses and Jill earned a lieutenant's salary that even let her donate to charities she believed in, like a Washington, D.C., rape crisis center and programs for the homeless. In return she'd give the military four years, which would pay for ROTC, and another seven years, which would pay for medical school, all following her three-year residency. It was a huge chunk of time, but she had access to fantastic teachers and the newest equipment. She could work in local community hospitals and with students from every background. She'd be doing work she cared about.

"I love patients and helping people," she said. "I don't see myself as this all-powerful professional god to whom people should pay big bucks because I'm so wonderful and educated. I feel I have a trade and that people need my craft. I can give them support even when I can't always heal them, like with terminal cancer patients. I also get a lot back. Some days I ask why I am spending all this time at the hospital when people my age are outside enjoying their leisure and families. But it's a passion and a calling. It gives me a way to serve."

In the face of this calling, other issues receded. I asked about the Gulf War and Jill thought it probably necessary, though Bush's previous support for Iraq could not be justified. She still opposed Reagan-era Central America involvements, thought the military budget should be cut, and was delighted "when people got outraged over six-hundred-dollar toilet seats." She hoped she'd never have to be involved in military policies she opposed, "but would just have to hope my commander in chief had weighed all the risks and benefits." Mostly, these kinds of decisions seemed distant from her role as a doctor, although she hoped someday to be able to speak out on health policy. For now, she focused on the immediate human bonds in her work.

Students who graduate distant from politics find it easy to continue this stance. The weight of American culture reinforces it. So do their jobs, as with Anna

Roselli's suspicion that her firm would respond poorly if she involved herself in the radical National Lawyer's Guild or the ACLU. Rather than helping them to resist cultural norms of political silence, their individualism furthers quiescence, separates them from any sense of broader responsibilities or potential historical power. Most have only to follow along, focus on private concerns, and leave large social issues to others. Even when public crises emerge, they lack the habits of political involvement that would allow them to easily respond.

Yet a growing number of students have learned to take strong stands. Their presence remains small among those who came of age in the early to mid-eighties, larger among those who've hit college in the period since. Although they remain a distinct minority, their numbers have continued to grow.

Electoral shifts   The 1992 elections reflected shifts toward renewed student involvement. USSA mailed out detailed scorecards, contrasting candidates' positions on issues from abortion rights to government financial aid programs. NARAL targeted the overwhelmingly pro-choice student majority as voters and volunteers. Together with an MTV campaign, "Choose or Lose," Rock the Vote registered thousands of young men and women through ads on key radio stations and booths at rock concerts.

In contrast to Michael Dukakis's 1988 campaign, which largely ignored youth and the campuses, the Clinton-Gore campaign made a conscious effort to target young voters. They ran interviews on MTV and the *Arsenio Hall Show*, ads on major rock stations, and national satellite hookups. They hired two national student coordinators who were themselves products of recent college activism addressing hunger, homelessness, and abortion choice. The campaign held back resources for local state organizers that might have mobilized student voters still further, but enough students were disgusted with Bush that decent numbers involved themselves nonetheless.

Students did not universally vote Democratic. Some endorsed Bush's individualist creed, some Perot's mystique as the maverick billionaire. In 1988, among the Fairfield dorm group, everyone but Rick, the aspiring teacher, either voted for Bush or didn't vote. Four years later, Tim Lovejoy felt torn. He felt Bush had done a miserable job on the economy and the environment, but supported him in his opposition to abortion, and mistrusted Clinton's political evasiveness. He considered supporting Ross Perot as a protest vote, then ended up voting for Bush. George Lipson felt similarly torn, feeling Bush was out of touch and that Clinton was too slick and would raise taxes. He ended up supporting Perot, who at least, he felt, was honest. Nebraska's Dale Ottiger once more backed Bush, because he respected his Gulf War stand and hoped his talk of God and family would encourage Americans to respect Biblical morality and turn people away from homosexual lifestyles.

The standard political barriers held other students back from active participation and sometimes from voting. They feared being critically judged for taking public stands, even when Clinton strongly led the polls. Many who disliked Bush for his damage to the economy or his pandering to the religious right, nonetheless levied their own Perfect Standard by refusing to vote for anyone unless they had unequivocally positive feelings. Others in the less political stream, such as Anna Roselli, Carolyn Lowenthal, and Jill Catalano, supported Clinton and Gore to ensure their access to education, to maintain abortion choice, and to reverse the economic decline that Bush had begun to symbolize. They approved of Gore's stands on the environment and resented Bush's inaction. They disliked Republican rhetoric, which threatened their private liberty by stigmatizing all but the most whitebread of lifestyles. Even many who'd once leaned toward the Republicans felt betrayed by Bush's performance in office, and worried whether there'd be any jobs at all by time they graduated. Far more than in previous recent campaigns, they tuned into news reports, raised issues with their friends, and actively discussed the choices involved.

For the activists, the election seemed a mixed opportunity. Most initially supported other candidates, like Tom Harkin or Jerry Brown. They'd opposed Clinton on his Gulf War support. They mistrusted him for hedging his bets on an array of critical issues: NAFTA, the death penalty; his refusal to significantly address the crisis of America's inner cities. But they feared Perot as an unaccountable autocrat and saw Bush as embodying the worst of American politics: callous, expansionist, and racially divisive. While some still held back disgruntled, most finally slapped Democratic campaign buttons on their jackets and bumper stickers on their cars, hung Clinton-Gore signs in the windows of their dorms, and turned out to vote in solid numbers. Though they were less committed than they would have been if Clinton had taken stronger stands, many also volunteered to staff noontime tables, hand out literature, canvass the dorms, and work at local campaign offices. They wanted to ensure Bush's defeat.

Clinton's campus support held on November third. On the eve of the last two elections, young voters had registered solidly Republican in the polls. Those who actually voted supported Reagan and Bush by narrower ultimate margins but gave them a solid lead. Full-time college students remained considerably more liberal, giving Reagan just a five-percentage-point lead over Mondale in 1984 and in 1988 actually backing Dukakis by ten percentage points. Now, bearing the brunt of economic insecurity, young people gave George Bush the lowest support of any generational group. Thirty-seven percent turned out to vote, up from 29 percent the previous round.[4]

Clinton got 44 percent of their support, Bush 34 percent, and Ross Perot 22 percent, his highest age-group total. Among full-time students, the gap was greater: 50 percent for Clinton, 35 percent for Bush, and 15 percent for Perot. The generation also split sharply by sex, with young women backing Clinton over Bush by thirteen percentage points more than men—a gender gap greater than the male/female gap in every other age group combined. Together with other Americans, students helped bring the Reagan-Bush years to a close, and usher in the more politically ambigious period that has followed.[5]

You've got credibility   Times change. Issues change. The divisions within the student generation continue. The eighties and early nineties launched two political streams on the campuses and among recent students now out in the workforce. One was marked by relentless individualism, exemplified by the phrase "you make your own chances." The other took up a contrasting vision of common responsibility. The conflict between these two tendencies will continue as those who came of age in this time pass through American life. It will continue to shape the values of students to come.

Campus activists know from the beginning that their path will be challenging, that they'll have to work consciously to make their voices heard. Involvement has shifted their priorities, their sense of who they are, what matters in their lives. They've involved themselves with issues from the environment to homelessness, from challenging questionable military interventions to working to make higher education accessible to all. They have emerged with a sense that ordinary citizens have no choice but to speak out.

If they are to continue their involvement once outside of school, these students need more than just their sense of concern. They need paying work they can link with their commitments, or complete and put behind them to leave time for causes they believe in. They need a supportive community to provide the strength of numbers and sustain them when times get tough, confirming the worth of their efforts. They need specific contexts in which to act, and ways to translate personal moral urgency into tangible social impact. They need a broader vision, or at least basic principles, to help guide them on their path.

When recent graduates find clear ways of acting, many feel more powerful than during their student years. People take their efforts more seriously. They no longer have to spread themselves thin between politics, classes, and outside work. They reach out to others besides just transient students. "You've got credibility, a job," said Barb Meister, "people you're working with, an organization you represent. Whereas students don't carry as much credibility. People say, 'That's idealistic. That's nice. Now be on your way.' "

Nine years before, Barb had started out "just a fragile and self-conscious freshman." Her college involvement had now launched her to make changing American agricultural policy her life's work. "I developed expertise when I was a student. I learned far more from my activism than from my classes, but I wasn't just protesting. My jobs came from what I'd done, what I knew, issues I was grounded in." During her senior year, Barb wrote a major paper analyzing the impact of federal farm policy on rural culture, the natural environment, and local economic institutions. Through one of her professor's contacts, she presented it at the Western Social Science Association, then published it in a respected economics journal. She was organizing young farmers out of Des Moines when the teacher who'd advised her on the paper got a call from the office of populist Texas agriculture commissioner Jim Hightower. They were looking for an agricultural economist and the professor had recommended Barb. Hightower's office hired her to represent Texas farmers in national policy debates. Working with local farm groups, she researched material for speeches, wrote a booklet explaining Hightower's positions, and arranged statewide meetings for farmers to build a common voice. "It wasn't always the most organized shop, because Hightower was such a visionary. But it was an amazing collection of creative folks he pushed to produce, to use their talents and resources, and do things that hadn't been done to better the farmers' situation."

Then Hightower lost the re-election, narrowly defeated by a massively financed conservative opponent whose challenge he hadn't taken sufficiently seriously. "It was like a death in the family. Everyone scattered all over the country. I really miss it, but I keep in contact with all the people I worked with."

Barb was next hired by a newly elected Democratic governor of Nebraska as assistant director of the state Department of Agriculture. The director was a conservative Democrat opposed by progressive farm groups, and the higher echelon staff was entirely male. It was a choice job with major responsibility, but Barb felt pigeonholed as the token woman and liberal, and quickly ran up against an entrenched bureaucracy. When she spearheaded a major performance review, staffers balked for fear it would lead to job cuts. Examining the department's comprehensive budget, she questioned excess spending on areas like travel, but "they told me that no assistant director had ever asked to see the budget before. Like I was supposed to just sit up front and look cute." Barb also vetoed the appointment of a man hired to deal with alternative crops but whose background as a ConAgra broker had not even taught him the definition of organic produce, and who'd been hired through a job search that totally ignored family farm constituencies.

After challenging such practices, Barb got fired. "It was a bit of a blow. I could have just sat there, sucked up a forty-eight-thousand a year salary and been on my way, but I couldn't have lived with myself if hadn't tried to make changes, make an impact, do something for the farmers." She next worked on agricultural issues and as a field organizer for Senator Tom Harkin's presidential campaign, and later as a staffer in Harkin's senate office. Figuring that she'd have more leverage with academic credentials, she then enrolled for a master's degree in public policy at Harvard's Kennedy School of Government. "I wanted to formalize what I'd learned and broaden what I know. Learn to better communicate on the issues, and connect them with each other."

Barb planned to then return to farm issues, and work on ways to link family farm groups with unions and environmentalists, challenge corporate lobbies, and fight for the kind of communities she'd grown up in. Compared with her campus political work, she felt her efforts now carried both more risks and greater potential impact.

Other recent graduates also found jobs in political organizations. Former USSA head Fred Azcarate worked for Citizen Action, an organization that coordinates efforts between local community organizing groups representing two and a half million members. His friend and successor, Julius Davis, married the head of NARAL's campus organizing project and worked first for the Children's Defense Fund and then for Public Allies, a new organization that places socially concerned young men and women in apprenticeship programs with public service projects nationwide. Julia Scatliff of COOL ran a Lyndhurst Foundation program that sponsors young southern activists in innovative community organizing. Barb's FACTS co-worker Julia Kleinschmit now split her time between a group based in Des Moines, Iowa, that worked to organize midwestern farmers, and a Catholic-sponsored effort that sought to convince churches to sustainably farm any land they owned and to rent or sell it to beginning, restarting, and minority farmers. Carol Bullard, under suspension for her role in the CUNY strikes, worked first doing outreach to young women of color for a New York–based reproductive rights project, and then for a campaign that challenged the incursion of Whittle Corporation's commercial-laden video feeds into American public schools.

Like many student activists, Sonya Tinsley ended up in the social service sector. She ran a youth program in Atlanta's desperately poor Summerhill neighborhood, where she recruited volunteers, worked with families, and planned community activities. She'd intended it as a way station before graduate school, but now thought of staying on with the program's sponsor, a nonprofit corporation that developed low-income housing, supported local businesses, and sought to return hope to the neighborhood. "When I first started coming from Emory," she said, "I didn't have a car. I took the bus, and it was like crossing a national boundary. All the issues are intertwined here: child neglect, homelessness, racism, poverty, drugs, environmental problems. You can't just look at one and ignore all the others." I asked Sonya to what degree her work addressed the roots of these ills, and she called it useful, but limited. "It needs to be done. When you're cut you do need a Band-Aid. But lots is just patching up what the system has caused. Hands-on service is important, vital, and necessary. For me personally, it's almost like communion, so you don't just talk about theory, programs and isms. But it's not any ultimate solution."

Sonya wanted a path "where we won't be just caught up in a cycle of reacting. Going to marches, holding up signs, and shouting. Then waiting for the next big crisis and reacting again. I remember telling a friend right after the Rodney King riots how tired I was of constantly marching in response. At Emory. During the Persian Gulf War. During the Anita Hill hearings. In response to the riots. It's important to make those symbolic statements. I still drove however many hours to Washington for pro-choice. But I want the marches to be part of something else, something substantial in terms of building alternatives and solutions."

I don't believe in gimmes   Coming out of the sixties, student activists consciously pursued the bohemian path. They founded alternative newspapers, co-ops, law communes, low-income medical clinics, and collective print shops. Many sought to live on next to nothing, logging the minimum possible paid working hours while spending their remaining time trying to create social change. They consciously positioned themselves on society's fringes.

Some of the current postcollege activists follow similar countercultural approaches, cramming into shared houses, living on spaghetti, tofu, and peanut butter, shopping at Goodwill, riding the bus instead of owning a car. They take demanding and low-paying jobs as door-to-door canvassers or staffers at alternative bookstores or cafes. They wait tables or run copy centers while vesting their prime energies in local political groups or in cultural efforts like socially conscious bands or the new crop of alternative newspapers. Wherever they land, they hope to continue to live close enough to the ground so they can vest their souls in work they believe in. "I wouldn't mind," said a North Dakota woman, "spending my life in a cheap apartment and buying groceries with leftover pennies from the bus, so long as I can continue this work. I think this is the real world and I want to stay with it."

The bohemian path is more difficult now than it was a generation ago. America's declining economy has made basic needs like housing and medical care more expensive, decent jobs less available, the future less secure. Recent student activists aren't immune to this tightening. They worry about how to get by day to day, what will happen down the line, whether they'll be able to afford to have children. But they want to continue to act.

Not all these students can maintain their commitments. While the initial engagement of many brings successively deeper involvement, others back off, shifting their goals under the pressures of school, outside work, and frustration with political efforts they've taken part in. Two years after our initial visit, I met again with Raul Ortiz, the former head of Chicago Circle's Confederation of Latin American Students (CLAS). Raul was still in school, in his sixth year, inching through at eight credits a quarter while working thirty-five hours a week as a Federal Express courier. His blue Federal Express uniform made him look younger, poorer, less upwardly mobile than before. He wasn't certain he'd complete his degree, since he already earned $15.00 an hour plus excellent benefits, and would make little more as a newly minted engineer. (He finally did graduate a year and a half later and moved into a new Federal Express job as an industrial engineer.) Aside from work and school, he was focusing mostly, these days, on ways to use what he made to buy an inexpensive home on the city's south side and enable his family to leave public housing. He was also beginning to talk marriage with his girlfriend Olivia, an elegant marketing major from a middle-class Mexican background whom he'd been dating for the past four years.

All these concerns pressured Raul's time, but he'd also been rethinking his convictions. When we'd first talked, it had angered him that his brother had high school grades and test scores equal to his own, yet had to go to a community college because Circle had tightened its requirements. His brother had since dropped out of school for lack of money, but Raul now defended the situation, saying it was his brother's own fault for being inadequately prepared. "If I were a senior and needed an eighteen on the ACT, should I get mad at the university for having such high standards? The students who are ready come and do well."

What about his earlier argument that the university had begun to unduly favor students from the suburbs?

"I don't get family support," he said. "I don't get financial support. I think it's up to the individual. It's too bad the Chicago public school system is so screwed up that some can't make it, but my brother wouldn't have gotten through high school if I hadn't tutored him in algebra. Maybe he isn't meant to go to college. I'd hate to see the university lower its standards and become a third-rate school. I'd hate to see my degree become worth less than one from Illinois Institute of Technology."

What had shifted his perspective? "All the tax money taken out of my checks, but mostly that I worked really hard to get where I am. I never saw racism for me, never experienced racism against me. I play with the cards I'm dealt, and do the most I can. If Lee Iacocca is looking down from the top, I'd still be a peasant, but compared to where I began . . ."

I asked if his tenure as president of CLAS had been just an experiment, trying on a set of beliefs like the fit of a suit.

He was unsure. "At first I had ideas to recruit more Latino students and graduate more from the school. I read somewhere that only twenty percent of those who come in here get out in four or five years. That concerned me and still does, but I also discovered part of the job was being politically aware. CLAS was always a left-wing organization because of its past presidents. So I became more of a left-winger."

Yet Raul disagreed with some of the causes. When the CIA recruited at a minority career day, CLAS joined a student protest. "But I have no problem with the CIA coming in. I'm not saying I like everything they do. But if students want jobs, why stop them?"

CLAS also opposed, together with other organizations, the university's expansion into the nearby Maxwell Street neighborhood. "They're against that because the communities will be pushed away," Raul said, "like when they built this place before. But to me that community is very ugly, with lots of crime and garbage in the streets. It's fine to move them out."

"They say that this university was for the students of Chicago, the sons and daughters of the Mexicans and Italians that they displaced, and that now it isn't. They have an attitude that the university owes them something. I don't think it does. It's ludicrous to say a university should have a mission. If I wanted a cheeseburger, fries, and pop that was three-fifty at McDonald's and I only had two and a half dollars, I wouldn't ask them to give it to me for less. I'd go to White Castle and order something else, or work harder and earn more."

"I don't believe in gimmes," Raul said. "If my brother wants to borrow my car, he has to do certain stuff. Everything has a price tag. Maybe it would have been different if I'd grown up with money."

"I still come by here sometimes," he said, gesturing at the murals on the Cintron Center walls. "Mostly to argue with all these liberals. But I don't get involved."

Looking back, he wondered whether his work with CLAS was worth it. It took so much time and effort. He didn't like having to put up his own scarce money when the center rented a hall for a benefit, or when he and four or five others ended up doing everything for an organization of two hundred, or when students praised what he did, then failed to show at events. "As far as my personal development, I learned how to speak better in public, to organize events and be a leader. Maybe if I could have been more of a manager . . ." He paused and shook his head. "I wanted to reach more people."

These days, Raul mostly just went his own way. "I'm more of a regular person, reading the sports section, watching ESPN, like the guys at work. I'd encourage education, if a high school student asked me, but I won't get involved with it." He smiled apologetically. "I guess I'm just a lost soldier."

But he also denied the notion of a conservative friend that he'd become a closet Republican. "I still vote Democratic out of guilt for the poor people of the world, the have-nots. I've become more pro choice from lots of women I know who've had to have abortions. I believe in big business" he laughed. "I want to become part of big business. But I also like people who challenge. I like Jesse Jackson. I like the underdog. I'm always going to be a die-hard Cubs fan. Maybe I'll come around and maybe I won't."

Vocations for change　　How students respond to leaving their campus base depends much on the climate of their former schools. For Jean Besanceney, Michigan had offered a ready-made political base, with a long tradition of speaking out. In Cleveland, political community was harder to find, though she found an eventual niche at the ombudsman's office and with SANE/FREEZE. She felt more isolated when she moved to the small California coastal community of Half Moon Bay, married her long-time boyfriend Neil, and worked for a series of software and design firms. While Jean debated going back to school in holistic medicine, the two joined a nearby Green Party group that worked on pesticide education and on a local currency project that attempted to build the economy of small coastal towns. She found a new sense of community when she explored and converted to the Jewish faith of her husband Neil and of many of her closest activist mentors and friends. She valued its highly personal relationship with God and drew spiritual and emotional support from a new community of Jewish feminists. For major political marches, like the ones protesting the Gulf War, she and Neil drove forty-five minutes to San Francisco or an hour to Berkeley. At one point her employer at a small multimedia company began repeatedly sexually harassing her. Jean finally took him to court with the help of a San Francisco legal rights organization and won. Although she hadn't sought the harassment fight, standing up for herself seemed part of the same struggle for justice and respect as her other political efforts.

But the levers for social change seemed now more elusive. Change in general seemed to come harder. "Maybe," she said, "I was simply more angry back then, and now I'm getting more jaded, less shocked at the hypocrisy in the world, and therefore less energetic to act." Uncertain what personal path would best serve her broader visions, Jean missed the ways to take a stand that were so readily accessible during her days with Greeks for Peace. Yet she felt forever changed by her college activism, and couldn't imagine quietly slipping back.

Recent student activists don't dismiss issues of economic survival, even though they're willing to live with more modest earnings and greater financial uncertainty than those aiming for the top. Only a minority will make their long-term livelihoods as organizers. Most therefore seek work that they can combine with some way of voicing their beliefs, work that contributes something useful to society, like teaching, or at least that causes no harm and lets them readily pursue their political efforts on the side. "I worked two years on seven thousand dollars a year as an organizer," said an MIT computer whiz involved in challenging campus military research. "I'll make fourteen thousand in the next couple of months, and plow it back into covering phone bills and doing photocopying and mailing for organizations that I work with. I don't want to always be economically desperate."

Greeks for Peace founder Matt Greene went back to urban planning school after two years of teaching English in Korea. "I don't want to work for the interest of just a single company," he explained, "but for the community as a whole. I wanted skills to fight lifelong for what I believe in." Graduating from planning school in the midst of the 1992 recession, he ended up scrounging intermittent jobs as a waiter, borrowing money from his brother, and "going out to look for work each week while my watch breaks, there's a hole in my sock, and I'm twenty-four thousand dollars in debt for grad school loans." He found it hard to plan for the future "because by now I'll take work in any city, or maybe overseas." His family was also financially shaky, with his father worrying that GTE would close down the machine tool plant where he worked, and this left Matt still more precarious. "I feel empathy for guys on the street with no skills at all," he said, "even as I have friends making fifty thousand a year in corporate jobs." But while he focused for the moment on survival, he felt confident in his path.

Lee Wagner, Dale's friend from the Nebraska FACTS group, followed his graduation with a brief stint with a rural organizing project, then returned to western Nebraska to raise corn and cattle on family land and on additional acreage he rented nearby. He also spent fifteen to twenty hours a week chairing the Nebraska League of Rural Voters, and this choice fed a chronic shortage of time. "If you skip a college class," he said, "you can stay up late cramming and studying, or borrow someone else's notes. But when the corn needs to be cultivated, it's either do it at that point or not at all. There's no one else to sit in and take your place."

As a result, he tried to plan his political work with ample lead time. "Most gets done in the winter. I don't hold meetings when people are planting or harvesting. I have less time, but concentrate more of my energies. Grand Island, where I live, is a conservative town. After five years, a lot of people still treat me as new to the community, where in college, the community's constantly changing and it's easy to become part. I've learned to work slowly, with more patience. To know the limits of each person or each crowd, and sometimes push those limits, like trying to bring together farmers and environmentalists, or making clear that I don't like racial jokes. I take what victories I can. Without being involved in FACTS, I wouldn't even be here on the farm."

A Marvincentric way of figuring Marvin Coleman also tried to find a career consistent with his values. When we first talked, he was new to political involvement, but the next year took the lead role in resurrecting a campus NAACP chapter. Designed to bring more student resources to bear on black issues, the group enlisted students, faculty, and staff of all races to work on its programs of cultural outreach. The chapter sponsored speakers, and a film series with accompanying discussions that showed everything from rap videos to *Eyes on the Prize* and a PBS documentary on campus racism. It also put together a major cultural festival that Marvin called the Block Party. The festival brought in jazz musicians, a dance troupe, poetry readings, art, drama, rhythm and blues, and rap artists. They reached out to Atlanta's black community with stories in local papers and announcements on the radio stations. The first year the Block Party drew five hundred people to its events; the second, six thousand, including families, schoolchildren, teenagers, and older community people. "We did a media blitz that Emory had never seen. We had people coming from Alabama, Florida, Tennessee. The school got nervous, because they'd never seen so many black faces, but there were no incidents. It was sort of my swan song. To bring Atlanta to the school and show that black students cared about the city. It ended up being good PR for Emory."

But Marvin also became frustrated. "When I first got involved, I felt like if I went out on a limb, stood up to a big institution, the black community would cover me, back me up. If something happened to me they would protest. Toward the end I felt like they wouldn't for anyone. NAACP and BSA meetings were sparsely attended. We'd bring in famous black academicians and students would say, 'Oh, I forgot. I had something else to do.' When we did the Block Party I couldn't get people to volunteer until a few days before the event, then everyone wanted to get involved and meet the artists. It pained me because I'd come to the school during that golden era when black students really cared for each other. If something went down, we were together. Now people who never lifted a finger were always criticizing, spreading nasty rumors, like the one that a black women's group that Sonya helped start was just man haters and lesbians. I helped a sophomore I knew put out a new black newspaper, *The Fire This Time*, but they didn't trust him because when he was a freshman he hung out mostly with whites. People attacked my roommate Kendall just because he was BSA president."

In response, Marvin wrote an article in his friend's new paper, questioning black students "who were selfish to the community, rumor mongers, who didn't join organizations that only cost five dollars in dues, and wouldn't come to events unless we provided refreshments. At the end I said, 'Here are some people who are doing things,' and put in the names of people I admired. It was almost a total transformation for me, like Malcolm X. I don't want to compare myself to him, but it's like when he went to Mecca, learned that whites were not all devils and became a harsh critic of the black community. I also learned that all that glitters isn't gold just because people are black and that people could be negative regardless of race. That everything we did that was positive, some rumor detracted from it. It was a painful close to my Emory career, but I devoted most of my senior year to trying to make the black community more like it was when I came in."

Marvin wanted to continue doing public events and media work. He got a master's degree in journalism from Columbia, where he worked closely with the Black Student Association, "because maybe I didn't spend enough time at Emory nurturing the freshmen and juniors, teaching them how to negotiate a contract or deal with student government. Maybe I didn't help newer students like people helped me." He continued his summer internships at Philadelphia's major black radio station, working with a senior journalist long involved in local African-American affairs. He began looking for work as a media producer or doing publicity for organizations that served the community. He wrote for the local black papers and for a magazine that covered rap. Once the *Philadelphia Daily News* ran an article that criticized a highly successful picnic for two hundred thousand African-American Greeks from across the country—and linked it with an unrelated shooting that happened after people left. Marvin sent in an op-ed piece correcting the inaccuracies, and the paper ran it along with his photo.

When I asked Marvin how his journey had changed him, he said he'd become more tolerant of people who don't have time. "I realize that not everyone can have the same priorities. I figured that if I could do it, anyone could—getting involved, working at the media center, running track, and keeping my grades up. But that's a very Marvin-centric way of figuring it. Not everyone has the same energy. I've stepped down from trying to save the world by myself. But I want to be involved through my journalism, what I write about. Or have my own PR business and employ black and minority students. The same kind of lifting-as-you-climb that helped me when I first came to Emory."

Finding a base   Professional tracks, like Marvin's work in journalism, can mix the pragmatic with the political. It was for this reason that striking CUNY students like José and Nilda doggedly continued working toward their degrees, even as they hoped to make their skills serve new social concerns. Student activists in general pursued professional skills and credentials differently from peers who were seeking purely personal advancement. They wanted not only to secure their individual futures, but to use the position and autonomy conferred on them as levers for change. They wanted to build institutional bases that would help support social commitment throughout their lives.

David Gerwin followed this path. He entered Columbia's doctoral program in history, then took two years off to teach at the Jewish high school he'd attended in Maryland. He liked the sense of working in a face-to-face environment where it was harder "for people to abstract you into a symbol, some anonymous radical, but where you're part of a community, where members are responsible to each other for what they say and do." During the Gulf War he wore a black ribbon of mourning and protest, which angered some other teachers. Yet they worked with him day to day. They knew David's fiancé and his brother were in Israel and at risk. They couldn't easily dismiss him. David discussed the war in his classes, making sure "not to pounce on students who are just learning to articulate their thoughts," but using historical examples to examine the difficulties of occupying armies imposing political values, and to question the war's roots and goals. He started a class that linked social justice and community service, and took field trips to a D.C. food pantry and free medical clinic. As he was getting ready to return to Columbia, the high school tried to fire the original mentor who'd first taught him as a student. David joined a walkout of six faculty members that, together with legal proceedings, helped save her job.

Now working on his doctoral dissertation (a history of an SDS organizing project in Newark) David repeated his desire "to be able to speak as a member of a community, having that legitimacy, rather than always coming in from outside." He thought he could do this as an activist professor, teaching students to think critically, involving them in the community, writing and researching on issues he cared about. David found his own nurturing community in a politically supportive synagogue on New York's upper West Side, and taught current affairs at an affiliated seminary. He also worked on Israeli peace politics, did an oral history project at the Jewish Home for the Aged, and volunteered periodically at a homeless shelter. He'd keep raising questions "because I couldn't live with myself if I didn't."

Communities of concern   Recently graduated activists sought not only vocations congruent with involvement, but specific ways to keep on acting, and communities that would nurture their concern. Except at the most isolated and silent campuses, colleges had offered distinct advantages: central quads for tables and leaflet-ting, budgets for mailings, forums and speakers, fellow-students getting through the same transitional and relatively unbound period in their lives. Even harried commuter schools could bring together individuals from disparate backgrounds to critically reflect on the world. On residential campuses, groups like FACTS and Greeks for Peace built on existing college communities, as did the City College architecture department dur-ing the CUNY strike.

On campus or off, activists face comparable challenges of reaching beyond existent core groups, overcoming the hesitation and mistrust of individuals watching skeptically from the sidelines, and balancing political priorities with personal lives. Yet those outside the college gates must even more consciously seek ways to stay involved.

Recently graduated students sustain their commitment through activist organi-zations: the SANE/FREEZE chapter with which Jean worked in Cleveland; local projects tackling environmental issues, tenant's rights, or affordable health care; the theatrical sexual politics of groups like ACT UP. They support hope and commitment through in-formal networks. A group from Chicago Circle's Cintron Center helped Francisco Car-denas continue on after his roommate Rudy was shot by gang members. He graduated eight years after he'd begun and got a job working with Latino youth in his West Chi-cago *barrio*. In Atlanta, Sonya Tinsley helped start a multiracial circle of young feminists that participants called the Amazon Salon. Recently graduated activists support their in-volvement through still-existing bohemian neighborhoods that provide political book-stores, cafés, and coffee houses, through alternative magazines and books, through a new surge of music that speaks to their lives and to America's ills. They join dissenting streams diffused throughout the country in churches, unions, and community groups.

Much of the most visible current citizen politics—Greenpeace is an example—is organized on the basis that most supporters will be represented by their organizations more than directly involved. Greenpeace canvassers, often recent college activists, promote a general climate of concern and support a skilled and committed staff involved in everything from plastering banners on polluting factory smokestacks to helping negotiate international environmental treaties. But they offer few specific ways to get involved beyond writing a check, lobbying legislators, or being urged to join whatever worthy campaigns happen to be occurring in their area. This organizational model is echoed, in various degrees, by other national groups working on issues that range from the environment and reproductive rights to the arms budget and economic justice. They fight well and hard on important issues, local and global. They lobby well and effectively, and turn out volunteers for worthy candidates. At times they launch major demonstrations and conduct important educational efforts. But they offer relatively few opportunities for the direct, day-to-day participation that activists become used to in their college years.

As a result, recently graduated students often remain uncertain of how to fit in. While they wait for the right situation, they risk the slow chipping away of direct involvement that saw many from the sixties generation end up disengaged and reluctantly silent. Avenues for involvement do exist in most communities, but they aren't always visible. Young activists need to assertively seek them out if they want to do more than just attend sporadic marches or become relatively passive organizational supporters. They need to find continuing ways to take effective stands.

Ambiguous promises   Besides concrete ways to act, these students need sustaining visions. What kind of world do they want? What kind should we all want? At first glance, the answer seems obvious: we need a world where people can live modest decent lives, where they can find useful work that meets their basic needs, and where their labors will protect the earth's future and nurture human community instead of despoiling it. We need a world where everyone has access to food, housing, education, and medical care, where no one starves, beats, shoots, evicts, tortures, or otherwise degrades other human beings for any reason, and where individuals can worship as they choose and speak what they believe. We want a world where democracy is more than an vague civics slogan masking cynicism and greed, where it is a genuine invitation to participate.

In the abstract, these goals stir little controversy. Most, including the rights to food, housing, medical care, and education, are formally enshrined in the United

Nations International Bill of Human Rights, signed by almost every nation in the world. But this is mostly lip service, routinely violated. America's political and economic leaders breach them daily—at home, by neglecting millions of our citizens at the bottom of the economic pyramid, and globally through support for repressive regimes. Citizens learn to dismiss these rights as impossible to achieve, and to focus instead on their personal lives.

Involvement requires solidarity: an ethic that encourages people to act not only for themselves and their immediate families, but for others with whom they feel a basic human connection. "In America," as Carol Bullard said, "they only teach people to think about themselves, to be concerned with themselves. I can't eat a sirloin steak if you're eating stale bread." Solidarity insists that human fates are intertwined. The classic labor phrase argues "an injury to one is an injury to all." So does the notion that we are all God's children, sharing a common covenant.

Yet solidarity is the fruit of involvement as much as its cause. It surges and recedes with the tides of popular movements that at their best embody the sense of compassion and common purpose that Martin Luther King, Jr., called "the beloved community." Individuals trying to act in the present moment face particular obstacles when they try to envision a more human future. In the 1930s the Soviets seemed an inspirational model. Unions marched and sat in. Capitalism visibly crashed. Activists, including those on America's campuses, felt part of a global historical promise. In the 1960s, active students largely distanced themselves from the Communist left and its sectarian heirs. American capitalism was never more economically triumphant, but revealed grave moral flaws, from the barbarism of the Indochina war to the desperation of the inner cities and the quiet irrelevance of many middle-class jobs. Student activists drew inspiration from an American past of populists, Wobblies, socialists, suffragists, and the often romanticized promise of Third World revolution, as well as from democratic ideals that insisted it was wrong for citizens to be beaten down because they were black, brown, or poor, wrong for the United States to support dictators and coups, wrong to make war on other nations. When social change movements erupted worldwide, American students saw themselves as kin to their counterparts in Warsaw, Prague, Paris, London, Mexico City, Berlin and, with some of that dangerous romanticizing, to the Vietnamese, who survived the daily American bombs.

These days, grand historical promises seem elusive. Citizen activists can take heart from the epochal revolutions in Eastern Europe and the South African freedom struggle. But in the United States of the 1990s, politics-as-usual seems mired, and fundamental change so distant as to feel nearly impossible. Given the difficulty of pushing national leaders to pay more than token heed to omnipresent crises, it feels even harder to ask what economic, political, and cultural shifts would reflect America's highest ideals.

Such a national self-examination should have a better chance with the death of Soviet Communism. U.S. political leaders have less excuse than ever for a war system that bleeds off immense amounts of capital, many of our best engineers, technicians, and scientists; the very ability to look beyond a world of endless enemies. For the moment, though, those who set America's dominant political and cultural tone continue to evade the most important questions about national directions. Even as the Soviet threat has collapsed, bloated Pentagon budgets are only slightly lessened: military-related expenditures continue to take up nearly half of all federal income tax dollars. Resources that could meet pressing economic and social needs remain mortgaged to expedience. Instead of finding a middle path between the traps of their previous Soviet rulers and those of an unchecked market, Eastern Europe's new leaders have embraced capitalism's most predatory forms. Here in the United States, we've seen an unstinting celebration of a global corporate order, with few questions asked about how it risks making us all expendable bit players in scripts designed without loyalty to people, place, or planet. It's a hard time for envisioning root social change.[6]

Pathways of commitment   Because it will require sustained popular movements to shift this climate, students need to learn ways to continue their involvement throughout their lives. It helps if they can keep talking and listening to those outside the already committed core that Barb Meister once called the "good committee of friends." It helps, as former USSA head Fred Azcarate said, to take heart not only from their specific political achievements but also from "seeing new people come in, and do amazing things, and then go out and bring in more."

Long-distance runners need a sense of balance. A sense, as Fred said, "of when to push. When to stop when you hit your limit, and not work twenty-four hours a day so you end up burned out and ineffective." They need bounds between public and private life, so politics doesn't swallow every aspect of their being, and they can break from the fever pitch of the struggle. "I can talk farm all day," Julia Kleinschmit's mom would always say, "but when night comes, I have to go out and have a beer and forget it." They need to know when to laugh at their own efforts, no matter how high the stakes, as when Hunter's Mark De Palma left the CUNY strike for his goddaughter's birthday party, worried that the police would come and the blockade would end with him "stuck out there with a stupid hat on." They need a sense that true and lasting work takes time.

A culture of cynicism is hard to change. Campus activists these days, compared to those of the Vietnam era, experience less breaching of illusions. They know American society is often callous and corrupt—have known this, in many cases, since they were young. Their fellow students know it, too, for all the talk of six-figure lives. Those who seek change face a challenge more complex than overcoming false innocence. They need to convince others that their actions and choices can matter.

They can't do this with absolute promises of social redemption—whether of technological utopia, the dialectic of history, or now tarnished Reagan-era supply-side dreams. Unlike their 1960s predecessors, those now active carry few hopes of achieving the world they seek in a single generation, or even a single lifetime. But they undertake the task nonetheless, knowing that to stay silent further erodes the ground of democracy and human dignity. Their actions build new ground for others to stand on.

A focus on the immediate tends to make active students pragmatic, to leave them placing less stress on grand ultimate visions than on the consequences of specific actions or choices. Heidi Wills embodied this pragmatism as she pulled together her recycling coalition, then graduated to work in a municipally sponsored theater group that educated school kids about conservation. She also coordinated a phone bank for the King County Democrats, and helped run tours to the Canadian Rockies. After numerous attempts to find a job congruent with her core interests, Heidi landed a position as an aide to a liberal county councilwoman. "I see the improvements we should make or could make or have the ability to make," she said, "if we only pull together the resources. I see politics as something I'm good at, and a way to change the society. I want to work on all the issues I care about."

Pragmatism has its strengths. It provides a check on abstract rhetorical politics with no links to complex social realities. It allows activists to work from what is, and to discover what ought to be through specific concrete successes. Those of us who want to change America would do well to recall the words of the priest who founded Spain's 21,000-member Mondragon worker co-op: "We build the road as we travel."

Pragmatism also cautions against trying to make social movements meet their participants' every personal need, and against an excess of righteousness. As political theorist Harry Boyte points out, it's dangerous to load politics up with needs for love, family, and a chorus of agreement on every issue. "In private life," Boyte writes, "we associate with people who share similar outlooks and values. In public life, we meet people from backgrounds unlike our own. The first principle should not be that 'we're all the same'—an assumption privileging dominant cultural groups—but rather the presumption of dissimilarity. This leads to a recognition of the moral ambiguity of politics, the awareness that we cannot expect simply to impose our values."[7]

Yet those who want to change this society should not accept a limiting of their dreams. They should accept neither the judgment of distant men of power that the routine indignities and needless tragedies of ordinary humans are inevitable, nor the more subtle cultural damping that breeds resignation and complacency even in those with power to speak. The students need to be willing, as Heidi was during the Gulf War, to speak out even when it seems their words and actions do little apparent good. Activists need the practical, step-by-step march, but they also need to explore the deepest roots of particular ills—what the late Michael Harrington calls "visionary gradualism." They need to ask what kind of society would best do justice to human dignity and allow its members to live sustainably on the earth. They need to then ask how best to create it.[8]

An ethic of responsibility   For many recent graduates, the principles they uphold emerge directly out of their work. Environmental activists fight for global sustainability. The FACTS group works to preserve strong and independent rural communities. The Greeks for Peace demand a society that does not constantly assume the right to determine other nations' destinies. Students involved in the service movement seek to heal specific communities, schools, and neighborhoods. Individuals who take on racial and sexual issues support a vision of broad-based inclusion, where the voices of all in our society will be heard. The CUNY students and others fight for accessible education.

As students get further politically involved, they try to link various causes. Sometimes this creates overload or friction. This occurred at the Columbia rallies where, as David Gerwin pointed out, people piled on so many different issues that students who did not already agree with every one of them felt excluded. Tensions erupted at the Colorado SEAC conference over the organization's attempt to link environmental concerns with issues of power, privilege, race, and class. In the words of the woman from Stockton State, students were only beginning "to stumble across new ground."

As I've suggested, the visions that move these students are almost always rooted in highly specific stories. I think of Greeks for Peace members learning from the Salvadoran medical student. Or of the teach-ins of the Hunter blockaders, where individual after individual explained how the cuts threatened both their ability to go to school and the future of their community. Activists need to pay heed to such actual human narratives, then trace the way they link to broader social choices. Citizens debating issues of accessible education need to know, for instance, that for all the talk of government fiscal crisis, resources do exist to adequately educate a new generation—

they're simply in the hands of a narrow slice of the affluent whose taxes are a fraction of what they were in America's boom years of the fifties and sixties, and who have come to control more wealth than all other American citizens combined. Such frameworks root specific violations of human dignity in their broader contexts, as they do the individual and collective choices that challenge them. They suggest that a society cannot not simply make people expendable without poisoning its soul.[9]

To draw these connections requires an ethic of responsibility. Julia Kleinschmit called her work "paying dues—to make sure the farms will still be around for me down the line." As an Iowa State environmental activist said, "If I want these changes to happen, I have to do something."

Hope and sustenance   For all that students take important stands out of feelings of solidarity with others, or the need for self-defense, or a sense of moral outrage, for them to continue through their lifetimes, they need something more. They need to believe in a human capacity to redeem the world. They need an explicit framework for hope.

Some sustain commitment through religious faith, as with Barb's Catholicism, or David Gerwin's sense "that there's something beyond us and above us." Others take less theological paths to nurture their spirit. They draw on the complex web of life of the natural world and their sense of its fundamental order. And on a historical legacy of ways that ordinary women and men overcame the most difficult circumstances to end slavery, child labor, and legal segregation, organize unions, achieve women's suffrage, and challenge militarism and war. They draw as well from day-to-day communion with family and friends: the mundane human exchanges that nourish us all.

Just being young and energetic feeds a certain optimism. "Maybe it's because I'm twenty-two," said Sonya, laughing, "and twenty-two-year-olds always feel this way. Maybe I'll feel differently next month when I turn twenty-three. But I really think we're beginning the next big wave of social change, with so many things going on. Abortion and Anita Hill and the monumental slaps in the face of women. So many people homeless. So much damage to the environment. I remember watching the Rodney King stuff on television, feeling that anyone who doesn't believe we're all connected, this has to show them how much each one of us has the power to destroy or save other people's lives. To make or break everyone around us, whether we know them or not. You see a man being pulled from a truck by people he didn't know beforehand even existed. Then being rescued by others he also didn't know. That human connection is always there, though we might not pay attention until something tragic happens. But you see it and can't bear not to do something."

These individuals continue to act because they have to. They feel they've learned too much to pull back and allow a society of meanness and bitterness to prevail. They see how acts of faith and courage cumulatively build new ground for the future.

For some, ethics of connection have been bred in the bone. "So many of the things I believe," said Sonya, "I was taught as a child. Maybe I believed them on a deeper level than anyone intended. But I believed every word about equality and justice and every person having the right to be who they are. I always took it seriously, and think I was right to do so."

Others embraced social commitment later on, but came to a similar sense of responsibility for the future. "I've thought about quitting," said Lee Wagner, the former FACTS activist, "especially when I don't see results. But I've seen so many people in harder situations who don't give up. A friend of mine who works with League of Rural Voters had a tornado hit their farm. He and his wife were injured in an auto accident. He has two kids. But he's kept on staying active throughout. I feel if I want things changed, I don't have a right to quit. I know too much about social injustices. Plus," he laughed, "people won't let me. Whenever I slack off, someone will give me a call to perk me back up."

For all the hurdles, these newly committed citizens felt compelled to stay involved. Only by consciously taking on America's major political and economic challenges could they hope for a more humane future. Most came to see their responsibility in terms of a larger chain of history, one that began with struggles long past and nearly forgotten, to which they would now contribute their part.

Historical portents can be ambiguous. As Vaclav Havel wrote before the 1989 Eastern European upheavals, "Hope is not prognostication." We never know when the world will shift and a chance will open up for major change, as it did in 1989 in Warsaw, Berlin, and Prague, in 1968 worldwide, or in 1985 when the Columbia blockade helped spark the nationwide student divestment movements. Sociologist Richard Flacks remembers visiting Berkeley in September of 1964 and hearing SDS members complain that students were apathetic, concern was dead, and nothing they did seemed to work. A few weeks later, the Free Speech Movement erupted. In the final stages of writing this book I visited the Rochester home of Susan B. Anthony, who fought through a life of nearly ninety years for women's right to vote. Fourteen years after she died in 1906, the suffrage amendment was ratified.[10]

If we look at America's most significant social movements, from women's suffrage and the abolition of slavery to the union drives of the thirties and the civil rights and antiwar efforts of the sixties, those who acted hit repeated frustrations and failures. At no time could they prove their efforts mattered. The reverse often seemed true, although movement participants took heart from the courage and vision of their comrades. Only looking back can we see how fundamental change grew and bloomed.

Students adopting the Perfect Standard want guaranteed success. Social activists must live with ambiguity. Sometimes, as with the 1985 antiapartheid campaigns, they get lucky and their efforts bring quick visible results. But even there, most of the successes were built on years of painstaking work that bore little apparent fruit. Activists have to accept that the results of their labors will often be intangible, that they will rarely have every answer or relevant fact, that they'll often be uncertain about what they've achieved. They need to recognize as well that even in the darkest times they can find ways to spur discussion and thought, and build, as David Gerwin said, "a taste of that world that we're working for."

As I've suggested, students learn their sense of responsibility through role models that teach either commitment or withdrawal. The adapters remain silent not because of some missing gene for concern, but because choices made and abdicated by those they respect—and by society in general—have taught them that social involvement is not worth its cost.

Students who chose paths of engagement act, conversely, because key individuals convince them of the worth of this choice. They help teach skills and offer resources, connect them with others similarly concerned, give them a sense that history is theirs to create. These role models also inspire through strength of character—carrying off their involvement with enough spirit, humor, and hope to embody their vision in how they live and act.

"If you really have a sense of the history and struggles that came before," said a friend of David Gerwin's who'd headed Columbia's Black Student Association, "you embrace an obligation to move forward." Now getting his doctorate at Emory, this student came into the movement through the social commitment of his parents, and through learning from a generation of black student leaders at Columbia, all of whom had remained politically active. "I gave a talk to Emory's black students," he said, "and pointed out that 'we're here not just because we're good students, or on our intrinsic merits. We're literally here by the blood of our people.' I'm only twenty-seven, but I'm beginning to come to grips with the reality that I probably won't be around to see the fundamental changes I want. It helps to know that there are many folks before us and many more who will follow."

We might view the future of this student generation as a contingent one. Their paths will depend on whether they and their successors can connect with enough historical and personal examples to demand more of their lives than resigned adaptation. At the beginning of the 1980s, students mostly followed paths of withdrawal. By the early to mid-nineties, modest but growing numbers began trying to work for a more humane and just society. Their next step is to find enough models of engagement and enough contexts in which to act so that they can continue to voice their concern.

Though we should be heartened by renewed student involvement, no single generation can bear the sole responsibility for healing the world. No matter how skilled and courageous their stands, the students, and young men and women in general, will remain just one modest sector of America. They will only be able to act and act effectively if others stand beside them, and join in common cause. We therefore honor their resurgent commitment not by handing them the burden of the future, but by viewing the issues they take on as a challenge to us all. This challenge calls us to take committed public stands not only during the brief passages through college, when some of us first learn the habits of engagement. It calls us to take these stands throughout our lives.

Notes

Introduction: Beyond the myths

1. The very phrase most commonly used to label the students' generation is a product of the insularity I've described. Media commentators often call young men and women in their twenties and early thirties "generation X," after Doug Coupland's widely selling novel by that name. The novel is flip, cynical, and in my judgment shallow, though Coupland comes up with plenty of catchy phrases to package the standard clichés, as when he categorizes individuals who cling to 1960s liberal dreams as "bleeding ponytails." Since the book's success, the media has proclaimed Coupland a generational spokesman.

But this spokesman, like all the other pundits, writes mostly from the inside of his own head. Coupland's second novel, *Shampoo Planet*, is set in a town he calls Lancaster, modeled after the Hanford nuclear complex that I wrote about in my own first book, *Nuclear Culture*. A mutual friend passed *Nuclear Culture* on to him, and one day Coupland gave me a call to say that he'd read it right after completing *Shampoo Planet*, and liked it very much. We chatted amiably about his books and mine. I asked what he thought of Hanford when he went there.

He didn't go, he said. He thought it would mess up his process of writing. He might or might not make it over before he finished his revisions.

I was stunned. Hanford was only a six- or seven-hour drive from Vancouver, where Coupland lives. He'd written an entire book without bothering to check out the place he described. When I called our mutual friend, he said Coupland did this all the time, and had sparked controversy with a magazine article on the atmosphere of a local rock club he had never visited.

I'm not saying novelists should work like journalists. Coupland has a right to research as he chooses, from whatever combination of sources. But the media has made him a spokesman, and his pronouncements have been treated as gold. To me, they mostly repeat the same stereotypes that I suspect he's absorbed from the media to begin with. It's disturbing that one of the few individuals granted the standing to speak for his generation is one with a habit of pronouncing on the world without engaging it.

See Doug Coupland, *Generation X* (New York: St. Martin's Press, 1991); *Shampoo Planet* (New York: Pocket Books, 1993). Also Paul Loeb, *Nuclear Culture* (Philadelphia: New Society Publishers, 1986).

2. Kevin Phillips quote from *The Politics of Rich and Poor* (New York: HarperCollins, 1991), pp. xvii–xviii. Molly Ivins quote from *Molly Ivins Can't Say That, Can She?* (New York: Vintage Books, 1992), p. 103. Income disparities from Sylvia Nasar, "Fed Gives New Evidence of 80s Gains by Richest," *New York Times*, Apr. 21, 1992, p. A1. And from Sylvia Nasar, "The Rich Get Richer, But Never the Same Way Twice," *New York Times*, Aug. 16, 1992, p. D3.

3. The general population also supported most of these stands, but the students did even more so. See Alexander W. Astin, Kenneth C. Green, and William S. Korn, *The American Freshman: Twenty Year Trends, 1966–1985* (Los Angeles: Higher Education Research Institute, UCLA). This is a compilation of the Cooperative Institutional Research Program (CIRP) annual nationwide surveys of American freshmen, originated by the American Council on Education (ACE) in 1966 and administered by the Higher Education Research Institute at UCLA since 1973, still under the sponsorship of the ACE. Hereafter, this work will be cited as Astin et al., *Twenty Year Trends*, and referred to generally as the CIRP studies.

See also the subsequent year-by-year CIRP surveys, also published by the Higher Education Research Institute at UCLA: Alexander W. Astin, Kenneth C. Green, William S. Korn, and Marilynn Schalit, *The American Freshman: National Norms for Fall 1987* (hereafter Astin et al., *The American Freshman, 1987*), Alexander W. Astin, William S. Korn, and Ellyne R. Berz, *The American Freshman: National Norms for Fall 1989* (hereafter Astin et al., *The American Freshman, 1989*); Alexander W. Astin, William S. Korn, and Ellyne R. Berz, *The American Freshman: National Norms for Fall 1990* (hereafter Astin et al., *The American Freshman, 1990*); Alexander W. Astin, Eric L. Dey, William S. Korn, and Ellyne R. Riggs, *The American Freshman: National Norms For Fall 1991* (hereafter Astin et al., *The American Freshman, 1991*); Eric L. Dey, Alexander W. Astin, William S. Korn, and Ellyne R. Riggs, prepublication summary for *The American Freshman: National Norms for Fall 1992* (hereafter Dey et al., *The American Freshman, 1992*); Alexander W. Astin, William S. Korn, and Ellyne R. Riggs, *The American Freshman: National Norms for Fall 1993* (hereafter Astin et al., *The American Freshman, 1993*).

On student beliefs on national health insurance, tax equity, environmental protection, abortion choice, etc., see Astin et al., *Twenty Year Trends*, pp. 97–99.

4. Hunter statistics on parents and high school from phone conversation with CUNY Director of Public Information Rita Rodin, June 1991 (based on CUNY's internal studies).

5. Monolithic generational stereotypes are exemplified by books like Neil Howe and Bill Strauss's, *13th-GEN* (New York: Vintage Books, 1993). For the actual patterns of sixties activists, see Jack Whalen and Richard Flacks, *Beyond the Barricades* (Philadelphia: Temple University Press, 1990); Doug McAdam, *Freedom Summer* (New York: Oxford University Press, 1988), p. 215; Lauren Kessler, *After All These Years: Sixties Ideals in a Different World* (New York: Thunder's Mouth Press, 1990); Myra McPherson, *Long Time Passing: Vietnam and the Haunted Generation* (New York: Doubleday, 1984); M. Kent Jennings and Richard G. Niemi, *Generations and Politics* (Princeton, N.J.: Princeton University Press, 1981).

6. Kenneth Keniston, *The Uncommitted* (New York: Harcourt, Brace & World, 1965); Kenneth Keniston, *Young Radicals* (New York: Harcourt, Brace & World, 1968).

7. For a superb look at white suburban kids on the dead-end track, see Donna Gaines, *Teenaged Wasteland* (New York: HarperCollins, 1992).

8. According to the *Washington Post*, "among children under the age of six, one out of every four lives in poverty as the government defines it—last year, no more than $14,228 for a family of two adults and two children." From "Who's Poor," *Washington Post*, Oct. 7, 1993, editorial on p. A22. Black male longevity from *Human Development Report, 1992* (New York: Oxford University Press, 1992, published for the United Nations Development Program). Cited in R. C. Longworth, "U.N. Data Offers Disturbing View of U.S." *Chicago Tribune*, Apr. 24, 1992, p. 1. Environmental statistics from Lester Brown, "Earth Day 2030," *Worldwatch*, Mar.-Apr. 1990. On differential college graduation rates, an estimated 4 percent of those from the bottom quarter in family income will earn a bachelor's degree by age twenty-four, versus 76 percent from the top quarter. See Thomas G. Mortenson, "It Helps to Be Born Rich: Family Income Backgrounds Continue to Determine Chances for Baccalaureate Degree in 1992," from p. 7 of the Sept. 1993 issue of the newsletter *Postsecondary Education Opportunity*, published by Thomas G. Mortenson, P.O. Box 127, Iowa City, Iowa 52244.

One: You make your own chances

1. The figure for "a meaningful philosophy of life" dropped to 50 percent by 1980 and to barely 40 percent by 1989, before rebounding slightly to 44.6 percent by 1993. "Being very well off financially" began at 39 percent in 1970, hit 63 percent in 1980, and continued climbing steadily to 76 percent in 1987; it leveled off to 74.5 percent in 1993. See Astin et al., *Twenty Year Trends*, p. 97; Astin et al., *The American Freshman, 1987*, p. 60; Astin et al., *The American Freshman, 1989*, p. 56; and Astin et al., *The American Freshman, 1993*, p. 24.

2. For excellent discussions on the fears and realities of middle-class downward mobility, see Barbara Ehrenreich, *Fear of Falling* (New York: Pantheon, 1989), and Katherine S. Newman, *Falling from Grace* (New York: Vintage Books, 1989).

3. Thatcher quoted in Greil Marcus, "Obituary: The 60s," *Cake*, issue no. 4 (1991); Levine quote from Arthur Levine, *When Dreams and Heroes Died* (San Francisco: Jossey-Bass, 1980), p. 103.

4. Wendell Berry, *The Hidden Wound* (San Francisco: North Point Press, 1989), p. 128.

5. Williams cheer from Williams student Hal Hermiston, personal interview, April 1989. The Harvard cheer, identical except for the phrase "You'll work for us someday" (instead of "You're going to work for us someday"), noted in John Trumpbour, *How Harvard Rules* (Boston: South End Press, 1989), p. 5.

6. Krasner quote from phone conversation, Sept. 1988.

See *Monitoring the Future: A Continuing Study of the Lifestyles and Values of Youth* (Ann Arbor, Mich.: Survey Research Center, Institute for Social Research, University of Michigan), volumes from 1980 through 1992. The data for these annual national surveys of high school seniors are collected under the direction of Jerald G. Bachman, Lloyd D. Johnston, and Patrick M. O'Malley. Bachman is the lead author in even-numbered years, Johnston second, and O'Malley third, with Bachman and Johnston switching positions as lead and second author in odd-numbered years. Hereafter, this body of work is cited as Bachman et al., *Monitoring the Future* (for even-numbered years), and Johnston et al., *Monitoring the Future* (for odd-numbered years). Gaps in high school seniors' expectations that things will get better for themselves but worse for the country, from *Monitoring the Future*, 1984 survey, form 4, questions A02 and A04.

7. On the notion of private liberty in American life, see Bob Blanchard and Susan Watrous, "An Interview with Frances Moore Lappé," *The Progressive*, Feb. 1990, and Richard Flacks, *Making History: The American Left and the American Mind* (New York: Columbia University Press, 1989).

Two: You don't have a say

1. On the collapse of commodity prices, between 1983 and 1984 the price of wheat dropped from $5.25 a bushel to $3.46, losing a third of its value. By 1984 U.S. farm debt totalled $215 billion, or forty times farmers' total net income of $5.4 billion. See Bruce Brown, *Lone Tree* (New York: Crown, 1989), pp. 46, 110, 198–203. Farm bankruptcy rates for 1980s from Mark Ritchie and Kevin Ristau, *Crisis by Design: A Brief Review of U.S. Farm Policy* (Minneapolis: League of Rural Voters Education Project, 1987), p. 7. Ritchie and Ristau also present an excellent overview of federal farm policies.

Defining the precise number of family farmers to go out of business is a slippery task, as the U.S. Department of Agriculture has changed the definition of a farmer to include more hobby farmers whose prime income is derived elsewhere. But the number of Americans residing on farms has steadily dropped, from 35 percent in 1910, to 25 percent in 1930, 10 percent in 1950, 5 percent in 1970, and 1.9 percent in 1990. From Oct. 1993 phone interview with A. V. Krebs, research director of PrairieFire Rural Action, Des Moines, Iowa.

Decline in entry rate of new farmers is from A. V. Krebs, *The Corporate Reapers* (Washington, D.C.: Essential Books, 1992). See also Jerome M. Stam et al., *Farm Financial Stress, Farm Exits, and Public-Sector Assistance to the Farm Sector in the 1980s*, Agriculture Economic Report no. 645 (Washington, D.C.: U.S. Department of Agriculture, 1991). Stam and colleagues say that between 1980 and 1988, 200,000 to 300,000 farmers became bankrupt, were foreclosed upon, and/or were financially restructured because of financial stress in the farm sector. They stress that voluntary exits from farming may have declined because of the drop in land prices and uncertainties in the general economy, while involuntary ones increased. Moreover, they report that the most dramatic feature of the eighties farm crisis was the dearth of new farmers entering the profession.

2. In 1880, 54 percent of the male juniors and seniors at the University of Illinois came from farm backgrounds, yet only 15 percent would return to work the land. Joseph R. DeMartini, "Student Culture as a Change Agent in American Higher Education: An Illustration from the Nineteenth Century," *Journal of Social History* 9 (1975–76): 529.

3. As part of their annual *Monitoring the Future* surveys, Jerald Bachman and his colleagues asked high school seniors whether or not they agreed with the statement "I can do very little to change the world as it is today." Through most of the eighties, students who agreed, to some degree, with this statement led those who disagreed by 15- to 20-point margins, with the balance unsure whether or not they agreed. Toward the decade's end, the gap began to narrow, and it reversed with the growth of social concern in the early 1990s. By 1992, 44 percent said they disagreed, implying that they felt their actions indeed could matter, while only 33 percent suggested they were powerless. Bachman et al., *Monitoring the Future*, questionnaire form 4 from 1984 through 1992, question D10B.

I suspect the numbers of those who said they felt powerless would have been still higher had this response not clashed so much with official civics verities. It's also possible to read these surveys as indexes not only of resignation but also of disenchantment. In the concurrent CIRP surveys of college freshmen by Astin and his associates, the numbers of those who agreed that "realistically, an individual can do little to bring about changes in our society" increased from 35 percent in 1967 to 52 percent in 1975, even as student movements were dramatically expanding. The researchers stopped asking this question from 1976 until 1985, by which point student activism was just beginning to re-emerge from a ten-year trough, and the numbers who said they were powerless registered 40 percent. See Astin et al., *Twenty Year Trends*, p. 98.

Comparisons between the two eras are tricky, however; most students in the sixties entered college believing in America as a land of near perfection, then saw their faith dashed on official lies about Vietnam. Their disillusionment was greater, as was their anger. Recent students are more cynical and resigned to begin with.

Three: I feel a little fearful

1. Lech Walesa, *The Struggle and the Triumph* (New York: Arcade, 1992), pp. 137–146.

2. See Ariela Gross, "Showdown at the White House," *The Nation*, Aug. 6–13, 1983.

3. During this period, the numbers of incoming freshmen who wanted to participate in community action or environmental programs dropped by a third. Astin et al., *Twenty Year Trends*, p. 97. The *Monitoring the Future* studies of high school seniors found similar declines in those wanting to address social and economic equality in general. See *Monitoring the Future* studies cited in Eileen M. Crimmins, Richard A. Easterlin, and Yasuhiko Saito, "Preference Changes Among American Youth: Family, Work, and Goods Aspirations, 1976–1986," *Population and Development Review* 17, no. 1 (1991): 115–133, Table 8.

4. Paulo Freire, *Cultural Action for Freedom* (Harmondsworth, Middlesex: Penguin Books, 1972), p. 52.

5. Reagan quote from Steven V. Roberts, "Foreign Policy: Lot of Table Thumping Going On," *New York Times*, May 29, 1985, p. A16. On the responses of atomic weapons workers, see Loeb, *Nuclear Culture*. On media silence and political retreat, see Mark Hertsgaard, *On Bended Knee* (New York: Farrar, Straus & Giroux, 1988). On cultural distraction from critical realities, see Neil Postman, *Amusing Ourselves to Death* (New York: Viking Penguin, 1985).

6. On Chile, the coup, and its implications, see Seymour Hersh, *Kissinger: The Price of Power* (New York: Summit Books, 1983), especially pp. 258–296. William Appleman Williams, *Empire as a Way of Life* (New York: Oxford University Press, 1980), pp. 194–213.

7. The 1987 Times Mirror survey is cited in *The Age of Indifference* (Washington, D.C.: Times Mirror Center for the People & the Press, 1990), pp. 26–28. Survey on Reagan, also from *The Age of*

Indifference, pp. 2, 27. Seventy percent of those aged eighteen to twenty-nine believed he would be viewed favorably by history, versus 56 percent of those aged thirty or older.

8. Astin et al., *Twenty Year Trends*, see Introduction, footnote 3.

9. In 1971, according to Astin's annual CIRP surveys, 38 percent of entering freshmen considered themselves "liberal" or "far left." This fell to 20 percent a decade later in 1981, remained at 21 or 22 percent throughout the decade, then rebounded to 27 percent by 1993. Self-defined conservatives began at the beginning of the seventies with 17 percent; pulled slightly ahead in 1981, at 21 percent; fluctuated between 18 and 21 percent for the balance of the decade; and ended up at 23 percent in 1993. Those calling themselves "middle of the road" began in 1971 at 47 percent, rose to 60 percent in 1980, then dropped slightly, spent the remainder of the decade at 54 to 56 percent, and dropped further to 50 percent in 1993. They constituted an even broader psychological norm in terms of students' willingness to actively advocate what they believed. See Astin et al., *Twenty Year Trends*, p. 97; and Astin et al., *The American Freshman, 1993*, p. 25. For representative samplings of the intervening period, see Astin et al., *The American Freshman, 1987*, p. 61; Astin et al., *The American Freshman, 1989*, p. 57; Astin et al., *The American Freshman, 1991*, p. 26.

10. Sara Diamond, "Campus Right Wing Organized and Loaded," *The Guardian*, Oct. 17, 1990; and "The Funding of the NAS," originally published in *Z Magazine*, Feb. 1991, as "Readin', Writin', and Repressin,'" reprinted in *Beyond PC: Toward a Politics of Understanding*, ed. Patricia Aufderheide (Minneapolis: Graywolf Press, 1991).

11. The newspapers are officially sponsored by an institution called the Collegiate Network, part of a larger New Right institute, the Madison Center for Educational Affairs. Intellectuals who helped support the young New Rightists included William Simon, William F. Buckley, Irving Kristol, William Bennett, Pat Buchanan, Jack Kemp, and Michael Novak. Olin alone spent between $15 million and $20 million a year funding ultraconservative faculty and the support networks that surrounded them. Much of the $295,000 Olin donated to the *Review* in its largest grant went to pay the legal expenses of *Review* staffers called up on college charges for harassing a black professor, but the foundation, through the Madison Center, also gave the paper repeated annual grants of $10,000 or more. See Fox Butterfield, "The Right Breeds a College Press Network," *New York Times*, Oct. 24, 1990; Diamond, "Readin', Writin', and Repressin' "; Jon Wiener, "Dollars for Neocon Scholars," *The Nation*, Jan. 1, 1990; and Gregory Jay and Gerald Graff, "The Best Ideas That Money Can Buy," *Democratic Culture*, Fall 1992, the newsletter of Teachers for a Democratic Culture, Evanston, Ill., p. 5.

Five: America on the slide

1. Shift in hours worked at outside jobs, from Eileen M. O'Brien, *Outside the Classroom: Students as Employees, Volunteers, and Interns*, Research Brief Series, Vol. 4, no. 1, (Washington, D.C.: American Council on Education, 1993).

2. Barbara Ehrenreich, "Hope I Die Before I Get Rich," *Mother Jones*, Sept. 1986.

3. Between 1980 and 1987, tuition and fees at public universities and colleges increased 83 percent, and tuition at private schools, 95 percent. Disposable income during this period increased 56 percent, and the inflation rate was 38 percent. Arthur M. Hauptman and Jamie P. Merisotis, *The College Tuition Spiral* (Washington, D.C.: College Board/American Council on Education, 1990). See also the biweekly newsletter of the San Francisco–based *National Student News Service*, Dec. 4, 1989; Nicholaus Mills, "Are Colleges Fixing Prices?", *The Nation*, Mar. 19, 1990.

4. Increases in students taking out loans, from Laura Greene Knapp, assistant director for policy analysis for the College Board, Washington, D.C. The Guaranteed Student Loan programs comprise the vast bulk of government college loans; in the 1973–74 academic year, 938,000 students borrowed from these programs. By 1979–80, the number of students enrolled had more than doubled to 1,940,000; it was 3,147,000 by 1983–84. The population climbed steadily throughout the decade to 4,071,000 by 1992–93.

In terms of student debt loads, 34 percent of 1977 college graduates owed money on college loans when surveyed between eight and twenty months after graduation. They owed an average of

$2,000 (or $4,137 in 1990 dollars). By 1990, 45.5 percent graduated in debt, with an average load of $7,000. Increasing debt levels continued to outpace the rate of inflation and weighed particularly heavily on groups that would not earn high salaries when they graduated, like humanities and social science majors, or students who ended up in low-paid service jobs. The average humanities major had to apply 7 percent of their yearly pretax income as payment toward college debt, the average social science major, 5.2 percent. By 1990, 8.3 percent of new graduates carried debt burdens exceeding 10 percent of their initial income. Calculating all loans at the 1990 interest rates and repayment terms, median debt burden rose from 3.2 percent in 1977 to 4.7 percent in 1990, a 50 percent rate of increase. See Kari Alexander and Alexander Ratnofsky, *Debt Burden: The Next Generation* (Rockville, Md.: Westat Inc., for the U.S. Department of Education, 1993). See also Cathy Henderson, *College Debts of Recent Graduates* (Washington, D.C.: American Council on Education, 1987).

5. See Frank Newman, *Higher Education and the American Resurgence* (Princeton, N.J.: Carnegie Foundation for the Advancement of Teaching, 1985), p. 77. Also Janet S. Hansen, *Student Loans: Are They Overburdening a Generation?* (Washington, D.C.: The College Board, Feb. 1987), p. 28. As of 1984, college-educated women aged twenty-five to thirty-four made only 74 cents for every dollar earned by college-educated men in the same age bracket. Significant splits also occurred by race. See also Thomas G. Mortenson, *The Impact of Increased Loan Utilization Among Low Family Income Students* (Iowa City: American College Testing, 1990), p. ii.

6. As of 1992, top-quarter families earned $63,500 or more, while families in the bottom quarter earned $21,600 or less. Some of the gap was due to far lower high school graduation rates among poorer students. But even among ones with the strength, skill, and perseverance to surmount the innumerable hurdles and get through, just 52 percent continued on to college, compared to 85 percent of wealthier students. For all income groups, the 1992 college participation rates among high school graduates rose markedly, probably because major corporate layoffs and military downsizing eliminated some previous alternatives. Three years earlier, college attendance figures had been 45 percent for the bottom quarter and 78 percent for the top quarter; but this still included only students who graduated high school. Gaps between those with good chances of getting a degree and those with poor chances continued to grow.

Since 1980, the class-based gap for the rate of college enrollment among all unmarried eighteen- to twenty-four-year-olds has widened by eight points. From a gap of 62 to 27 percent, it's grown to 76 to 33. In 1979, top income high school graduates had a 50 percent chance of graduating college by age twenty-four, and those in the bottom category had a 27 percent chance. By 1992, the odds had changed to 76 percent and 4 percent respectively, a gap of nearly 20 to 1. See Mortenson, "It Helps to Be Born Rich," pp. 1–8. See Thomas G. Mortenson and Zhijun Wu, *High School Graduation and College Participation of Young Adults by Family Income Backgrounds, 1970 to 1989* (Iowa City: American College Testing, 1990), pp. iii–xxiii, 43–44, and Table 39. Mortenson figures derived from the Current Population Survey data of Dr. Robert Kominski, Chief of the Education and Social Stratification branch of the U.S. Census Bureau. Figures checked during Paul Loeb phone interview with Kominski, Mar. 15, 1994. In terms of when students attain their degrees, a 1991 study of the National Center for Education Statistics found that 75 percent of all B.A.'s were secured by age 25. From telephone interview with NCES educational analyst Peter Stowe, April 5, 1994, based on 1991 NCES study of 1989–90 recent college graduates.

Educational inequality also affects the type of higher education students pursue. In a study for UCLA's Higher Education Research Institute, Kenneth Green has suggested that economically struggling students often follow a "buying down" pattern, wherein "students who might have enrolled in private institutions opt for public campuses. Students who would have preferred to attend the state university opt in increasing numbers for public colleges closer to home. And increasing number of students are matriculating as commuters, living at home while attending a local four-year or community college." From Kenneth C. Green, testimony for House Committee on Education and Labor, Congress 100, Session 1, presented to the Subcommittee on Postsecondary Education, hearing on "Higher Education Costs," Sept. 15, 1987, p. 7. As part of this trend, the percentage of college freshmen who come from the lowest 10 percent in family income dropped by over 40 percent between the years of 1978 and 1986, as financial aid programs shifted from grants to loans. From Mortenson, *The Impact of Increased Loan Utilization*, pp. 10–12.

7. From a United States Student Association (USSA) brochure, "Issues and Answers" (Washington, D.C.: United States Student Association, 1988).

8. On impact of government aid cuts, see Green, House Committee on Education, p. 1, and Henderson, *Impact of College Debts*. Green and Henderson suggest public and private institutions alike have been forced to increase tuition in part to maintain and modernize college physical plants, to pay decent faculty salaries, and to provide up-to-date labs, computers, and libraries—but more than anything, to cover the shortfall of federal aid.

In 1930, according to Bergmann's study, higher education institutions spent 19 cents on administration for every dollar spent on instruction; by 1950, that figure was 27 cents; by 1988, it had climbed to 45 cents. These figures include salaries for professionals who provide some clearly useful services, such as counseling, staffing the residence halls, and running computer labs, but, as Bergmann explains, they also included payments to scores of new speech writers, special assistants, creators of fancy brochures and newsletters, and writers and monitors of reports. At the University of Maryland, Bergmann once collected a pile of twenty-four different newsletters that ended up in her mailbox, and her department had to get comments and approval from twelve different administrators to hire a new colleague they were courting. Barbara R. Bergmann, "Bloated Administration, Blighted Campuses," *Academe*, Nov.–Dec. 1991, pp. 12–16.

9. On university-corporate ties, Leonard Minsky and David Noble of the National Coalition for Universities in the Public Interest, and Thomas Ferguson, political scientist at the University of Massachusetts at Boston, suggest that universities have been seduced by 1980 patent act changes that allow them to license out the fruits of federally funded research.

"To compete successfully with industrial as well as academic institutions," write Minsky and Noble, "a university must recruit and equip the most commercially promising researchers—most of whom will do very little undergraduate teaching—and it must provide them with the most advanced equipment and laboratories. . . . The University of Washington assembled a $2.3 million package to lure a bio-organic chemist. Brown University paid a quarter of a million dollars for one chemist, a recent Ph.D. The University of Utah put together a half-million-dollar package, including new equipment and three assistants, for one solid-state physicist. Stanford University paid nearly a million dollars for another physicist." Minsky and Noble suggest the massive expenditures to launch these projects end up coming not only from specific government and corporate contributions but also from more flexible general funds that are derived from tuition. Leonard Minsky and David Noble, "Corporate Takeover on Campus," *The Nation*, Oct. 30, 1989.

See also Elliot Negin, "Why College Tuitions Are So High," *The Atlantic*, Mar. 1993. Negin gives examples of major humanities cutbacks at Columbia at a time when the school spent $62 million on a major research center for engineering and physical sciences. Examples from Michigan, Johns Hopkins, and Washington University appear in Jim Blivens, "Socialism and Higher Education," *The Activist*, "Democratic Socialists of America Youth" section, Jan. 1990.

10. Figures on ratio of college to noncollege earnings, from Mortenson, *Postsecondary Education Opportunity* (newsletter), Nov. 1993. See also L. L. Leslie and P. T. Brinkman, *The Economic Value of Higher Education* (New York: American Council on Education, 1988).

While the percentage of the U.S. population enrolled in higher education is larger than in any other country in the world, our percentage of college graduates is no higher than Canada's or Japan's. And we rank fourteenth out of sixteen advanced industrialized countries in the percentage of our gross domestic product (GDP) spent on elementary and secondary education. If we compare our primary and secondary systems to those of Japan and Germany, we find that we spend a greater percentage of our money on buildings and administration, and less on teacher salaries. See Robert Rothman, "U.S. Not Biggest Spender on Education, Study Finds," *Education Week*, Sept. 30, 1992, p. 14; Ralph Nader and Mark Green, "Passing On the Legacy of Shame," *The Nation*, Apr. 2, 1990; and Barbara Kantrowitz and Pat Wingert, "The Best Schools in the World," *Newsweek*, Dec. 2, 1991, p. 52.

Were other tracks to decent livelihoods readily available, college graduation would not be such a critical divide. But as well-paid blue-collar jobs disappear and a bachelor's degree becomes a minimal threshold for an adequate chance at earning a living, limitations on the affordability of higher education play more and more into America's growing class divisions.

11. Male/female comparisons from Susan Faludi, *Backlash* (New York: Crown, 1991), pp. xiii, 65, and from Thomas Mortenson, "What's It Worth?" in *Postsecondary Education Opportunity* (newsletter), Sept. 1993, pp. 9–12.

12. Theodore J. Marchese, "Five Articles, One Tough Issue," *Change* 18, no. 3 (1986): 4–5. As Arthur M. Hauptman points out, the "on your own nickel" designation isn't strictly accurate for student loans, as the government effectively subsidizes them at the rate of 40 to 50 cents for each dollar lent (*National Student Loan Bank: The Road Less Traveled* [Washington, D.C.: National Association of Independent Colleges and Universities, Feb. 1986]).

13. See Robert Sherill, "The Looting Decade," *The Nation*, Nov. 19, 1990.

14. Prison statistics from "Prison Rate in U.S. Highest in World," *Seattle Times*, Jan. 5, 1991. See also Nader and Green, "Passing On the Legacy of Shame." Suicide statistics from Ronald K. Fitten and Carol M. Ostrom, "Suicide: The Plague That Haunts Generation X," *Seattle Times*, Apr. 24, 1994, p. A1. Decline in real incomes and increasing disparities in wealth, from phone interviews with Jared Bernstein of the Economic Policy Institute, Sept. 27 and Oct. 3, 1993. See also Lawrence Mishel and Jared Bernstein, *The State of Working America* (Armonk, N.Y.: M. E. Sharpe, 1993).

15. Figures on the decline in the incomes of individuals under twenty-five and increasing disparities of wealth, from Bernstein phone interviews (see note 14). See also Bernstein and Mishel, *The State of Working America*. The 1980 ratio of executive-to-workers pay from Kevin Phillips, "A Capital Offense: Reagan's America," *New York Times Magazine*, June 17, 1990. Pay ratio in 1991 and German and Japanese ratios from Karen W. Arenson, "The Boss: Underworked and Overpaid?", *New York Times Book Review*, Nov. 17, 1991, review of *In Search of Excess*, by Graef S. Crystal (New York: W.W. Norton, 1991). Additional information on income disparities from Nasar, "Fed Gives New Evidence" and "The Rich Get Richer" (Introduction, note 2). See also Donald L. Barlett and James B. Steele, *America: What Went Wrong?* (Kansas City: Andrews & McMeel, 1992). On the particular situation of women, see Gertrude Schaffner Goldberg and Eleanor Kremen, *The Feminization of Poverty* (New York: Greenwood Press, 1990).

16. See Robert Reich, "Secession of the Successful," *New York Times Magazine*, Jan. 20, 1991, and for a general look at this issue, John Kenneth Galbraith, *The Culture of Contentment* (Boston: Houghton Mifflin, 1992).

17. From Crimmins, Easterlin, and Saito, "Preference Changes Among American Youth" (see note 3, Chapter Three). Drawing on the 1977–1986 *Monitoring the Future* studies, Crimmins and her colleagues noted that responses of high school seniors who wanted to have clothes in the latest style jumped from 41 to 56 percent in this period; that those who wanted a high-powered stereo grew from 45 to 57 percent; and that those who wanted to own a powerboat, snowmobile, or other motorized recreational vehicle climbed from 16 to 25 percent. Eagerness to work in the corporate sector nearly doubled during this same period, increasing from 14 to 27 percent, and disagreement with advertisers inducing manipulated consumption dropped from 44 percent in 1981 to 27 percent in 1986. These last figures come also from *Monitoring the Future*, and are cited by Margaret Mooney Marini in "The Rise of Individualism in Advanced Industrial Societies," a paper presented to the annual meeting of the Population Association of America, May 1990, Toronto, Canada; copies are available from the Department of Sociology, University of Minnesota, Minneapolis.

18. In a 1990 survey of college sophomores, nearly half of those at four-year schools spent more than sixteen hours on classes or labs, and more than ten hours on studying or homework each week. Over 40 percent spent more than ten hours on outside jobs, almost 20 percent spent three or more hours commuting to campus, not counting traveling to their work. But 36 percent also spent more than sixteen hours a week socializing with friends, 34 percent spent six or more hours a week partying, 30 percent spent playing sports, and 29 percent watching TV. From Tamara L. Wingard, Eric L. Dey, and William S. Korn, *The American College Student, 1990: National Norms for 1986 and 1988 College Freshmen* (Los Angeles: Higher Education Research Institute, UCLA, 1991), pp. 26–27 (hereafter Wingard et al., *American College Student, 1990*). This work is a follow-up study of college sophomores and seniors who had been interviewed two and four years earlier for Astin's annual surveys, *The American Freshman*. Three years earlier, Sylvia Hurtado, Alexander W. Astin, William S. Korn, and Eric L. Dey, had done a follow-up survey, with similar results: *The American College Student, 1987: National Norms for 1983 and 1985 College Freshmen* (Los Angeles:

Higher Education Research Institute, UCLA, 1987), hereafter, Hurtado et al., *American College Student*, 1987.

According to a 1992 Roper survey, the favorite TV programs of undergraduates included *Cheers, The Cosby Show, Late Night With David Letterman, Days of Our Lives, The Simpsons, Saturday Night Live, In Living Color, Married . . . With Children*, and *Beverly Hills 90210*. From Sara Rimer, "Television Becomes Basic Furniture in College Students' Ivory Towers," *New York Times*, Oct. 27, 1991, p. A18.

19. Drop in family income from Mishel and Bernstein, *State of Working America*, pp. 36–38. Comparisons with time worked by parents from George Lipsitz, "Hours Not to Reason Why, Hours Just to Work and Die" (review of *Our Own Time*, by David R. Roediger and Philip Foner), *In These Times*, Sept. 27–Oct. 3, 1989, p. 19. Figures on decline in real income from Peter Kilborn, "Youths Lacking Special Skills Find Jobs Leading Nowhere," *New York Times*, Nov. 27, 1990, p. A1., based on data from an Economic Policy Institute study.

20. On middle-management job loss, see Phillips, "A Capital Offense." On corporate compensations, twenty-nine executives of the bankrupt Drexel Burnham Lambert continued to receive over a quarter million dollars a year in compensation, and two made $1.45 million a year each. Kurt Eichenwald, "Drexel Still Pays Millions in Salaries," *New York Times*, Dec. 24, 1990, p. A29.

21. Kenneth C. Green, "Children of the Upheaval," *Educational Record* (Summer/Fall 1989).

22. In 1968, 38 percent of women intended to be elementary or secondary teachers; by 1982 the numbers had dropped to 7 percent. Ehrenreich, *Fear of Falling*, p. 210, drawing on Gene I. Maeroff, "Shifting Away from the Liberal Arts," *New York Times*, Mar. 26, 1985, and from Andrew Hacker, "The Decline of Higher Learning," *New York Review of Books*, Feb. 13, 1986, p. 35.

Reagan-Bush policies directly cut social service programs and dried up the community block grants that had provided significant funding to the states. They also fueled a backlash against state taxes, as local governments tried to garner income to cover curtailed funds and services, only to hit community resistance. Those that profited from the shift in resources were what Kevin Phillips calls the traditionally Republican constituencies of "military producers and installations, agribusiness, bondholders and the elderly," and most of all, the wealthy and those who served them. Phillips, "A Capital Offense."

23. Twenty-four percent of students majored in education in in 1968, 5 percent in 1982, and 10 percent in 1990 and 1993. In 1972, 11 percent planned business careers; that increased to 25 percent at the peak of interest in 1987, then dropped to 22 percent in 1989, and 15.5 percent in 1993. Although both sexes dropped off from teaching, women moved in the largest numbers away from this and other traditionally female fields (see note 22, above). Between 1968 and 1982, men bound for teaching dropped from 14 percent to less than 2 percent, which was a higher amount proportionately, but far smaller in terms of overall numbers. Women's interest in these fields would then climb back to 12.3 percent by 1993, and men's to 5.1 percent. See Astin et al., *Twenty Year Trends*, pp. 91–93; Astin et al., *The American Freshman, 1987*, pp. 53, 55; Astin et al., *The American Freshman, 1989*, pp. 65, 66; Astin et al., *The American Freshman, 1993*, pp. 17–18.

24. *Letter to the Next Generation* is an excellent look at Kent State twenty years after the shootings. It can be ordered from New Day Films, 22D Hollywood Ave., Hohokus, N.J. 07423. Telephone (201) 652-1989.

Six: Divided loyalties

1. Mike Rose, *Lives on the Boundary* (New York: Penguin, 1990), pp. 47–48.

2. University of Illinois at Chicago had 1,650 Latino students as of 1988, and 2,300 by 1992.

3. On the political divisions between self-identified "Latinos" and "Hispanics" see Rodolfo Acuna, *Occupied America* (New York: Harper & Row, 1988), pp. ix–xii.

4. Studs Terkel, *American Dreams: Lost & Found* (New York: Random House, 1980), p. 126.

5. Between 1985 and 1993 the Latino undergraduate population increased from 9 to 15.5 percent, and the Asian population from 12 to 18 percent, while African-Americans held steady at 11 percent and Native Americans at 0.3 percent. In 1985 there were 10,400 (64 percent) undergraduate students enrolled whose residences were in the city of Chicago; in 1992, there were 9,200, or 50 percent (from letters from the assistant vice chancellor for academic affairs at the University of Illinois at Chicago, Roger Nelson, Sept. 9 and 20, 1993).

6. Robert N. Bellah, Richard Madsen, William M. Sullivan, Ann Swidler, and Steven M. Tipton, *Habits of the Heart* (New York: Harper & Row, 1986), p. 119. See also Burton Bledstein, *Culture of Professionalism: The Middle Class and the Development of Higher Education in America* (New York: Norton, 1976), pp. 1–5, 120, 172, 176.

7. For a general look at these aspects of social class, see Richard Sennett and Jonathan Cobb, *The Hidden Injuries of Class* (New York: Vintage Books, 1973); Paul Willis, *Learning to Labor: How Working Class Kids Get Working Class Jobs* (New York: Columbia University Press, 1977); and Lillian Rubin, *Worlds of Pain* (New York: Harper & Row, 1976).

8. Paula Kamen, *Feminist Fatale: Young Women and Feminism* (New York: Donald I. Fine, 1991), pp. 31, 35–36.

9. As Carol Gilligan and her colleagues have explored, many of these women were once brash and loud, but silenced themselves when they reached adolescence, to fit the expected roles. See Carol Gilligan, *In a Different Voice* (Cambridge, Mass.: Harvard University Press, 1982); Lyn Mikel Brown and Carol Gilligan, *Meeting at the Crossroads: Women's Psychology and Girls' Development* (Cambridge, Mass: Harvard University Press, 1992); Deborah Tannen, *You Just Don't Understand* (New York: Ballantine Books, 1990); and Mary Field Belenky, Blythe McVicker, Nancy Rule Goldberger, and Jill Mattuck Tarule, *Women's Ways of Knowing* (New York: Basic Books, 1986).

Seven: The broken connection

1. The United States first attacked Allende by funneling millions of dollars into a series of covert funding programs to defeat him in the 1958, 1964, and 1970 elections—more than $20 million in the 1964 election alone. When he finally won a plurality of the popular vote in the last of these campaigns, the CIA first attempted to bribe the Chilean Congress to install the opposition candidate, then helped plot the assassination of the strongly constitutionalist head of the Chilean armed forces, General René Schneider. Under the direction of President Nixon, and closely supervised by Secretary of State Henry Kissinger, U.S. intelligence organizations worked with corporations like ITT, Kennecott Copper, the Chilean newspaper *El Mercurio*, and multinational institutions like the Inter-American Development Bank to foment strikes, marches, sabotage, and ultimately a coup that replaced the longest democratic tradition in Latin American with Pinochet's brutal regime.

The overthrow of Allende and other democratically elected regimes has left nations that want to find an independent economic and political path in a bind. Those that the United States branded as leftist and that respected too finely the liberties of their opponents risked a similar fate. Those that tried to limit a hostile press or individuals working for their overthrow were branded totalitarian, faced escalating American attacks, and found their internal chances for democracy in jeopardy. Either way, the United States refused to let them find their own destiny. See Hersh, *Kissinger: The Price of Power*, especially pp. 258–296. For a more general discussion of the U.S. inability to let other nations find their own paths, see Williams, *Empire as a Way of Life*, and Noam Chomsky, *Deterring Democracy* (New York: Verso Press, 1991).

On Yellow Rain, see Martin Lee and Norman Solomon, *Unreliable Sources* (New York: Lyle Stuart, 1990), p. 128. See also Julian Robinson, Gene Guillemin, and Matthew Meselson, "Yellow Rain: The Story Collapses," *Foreign Policy*, Fall 1987.

2. See Williams, *Empire as a Way of Life*.

3. Geography study from Barbara Vobejda, "Many Americans Lost When It Comes to Geography: Nation's Young Adults Ranked Last in an International Comparison of Knowledge," *Washington Post*, July 28, 1988, p. A4. Knowledge of global events from Times Mirror's *The Age of Indifference*.

4. To conduct the Gulf War survey, communications professors at the University of Massachusetts at Amherst (hereafter U. Mass. Amherst) hired a national research firm to conduct a statistically valid survey in the representative city of Denver. The survey uncovered widespread ignorance among all age groups, of the kinds of key information I've cited. But individuals aged eighteen to thirty-two knew even less, by an average of ten percentage points apiece. Heavy TV watchers among the generation were particularly misinformed, by an additional seven or eight points, and even those who constantly watched the news did no better than average on questions like whether Kuwait or Saudi Arabia were democracies, what we told Saddam Hussein before he rolled into Kuwait, or their knowledge that other Middle East nations like Israel and Syria were also occupying foreign land. See Justin Lewis, Sut Jhally, and Michael Morgan, *The Gulf War: A Study of the Media, Public Opinion, and Public Knowledge* (Amherst: University of Massachusetts, Department of Communications, 1991), pp. 6–11, 32, 39–45, 50.

5. See the results of a spring 1992 survey of U. Mass. Amherst students, in Justin Lewis, "What Do We Learn From the News?" *Extra*, Sept., 1992, published by the media watch group Fairness and Accuracy in Reporting (FAIR), New York, N.Y., pp. 16–17. See also the Oct. 1992 national survey of likely voters by Justin Lewis and Michael Morgan, *Images/Issues/Impact: The Media and Campaign '92* (Amherst: University of Massachusetts, Department of Communications, 1992), pp. 4, 5, 10 (excerpted in the Dec. 1992 issue of *Extra*). Comparisons of students and the general public, including their noncollege peers, from phone interview with Justin Lewis, Jan. 1993.

6. Moyers quote from Feb. 1993 Seattle lecture, sponsored by KCTS-TV. For a general discussion of recent media politics, see also Postman, *Amusing Ourselves to Death*, and Hertsgaard, *On Bended Knee*.

7. Gary Olson, "Execution Class," *Z Magazine*, July/Aug. 1988.

8. See, for instance, Richard Boyer and Herbert Morais, *Labor's Untold Story* (New York: United Electrical Workers, 1979).

Eight: Spitting on soldiers?

1. Sociologist Flacks was an early mentor to SDS who'd long written about the politics of youth and social change. Starr, together with the Vietnam Veterans of America Foundation, developed a program to promote teaching about the Vietnam War in American high schools. Its centerpiece was his curriculum, *Lessons of the Vietnam War* (Pittsburgh: Center for Social Studies Education, 1991). See also Bob Greene, *Homecoming* (New York: Putnam, 1989).

2. GI movement history from Greg Gaut, "It's Time to Tell Truth About Peace Movement's History," *In These Times*, May 15–21, 1991. Drug use from Todd Gitlin, *The Sixties: Years of Hope, Days of Rage* (New York: Bantam, 1987), p. 418. See also David Cortright, *Soldiers in Revolt* (Garden City, N.Y.: Anchor/Doubleday, 1975).

3. On service of congressional representatives' sons, see McPherson, *Long Time Passing*, p. 165. On government harassment and infiltration, see Frank Donner, *The Age of Surveillance* (New York: Vintage Books, 1981); also Gitlin, *The Sixties*, especially pp. 243, 244, 378, 414.

4. On casualties, see Starr, *Lessons of the Vietnam War*, p. 266; and Lewis et al., *The Gulf War*, p. 12. Refugee figures from James S. Olson, *Dictionary of the Vietnam War* (New York: Greenwood, 1988), p. 387; and McPherson, *Long Time Passing*, p. 577. Combined Vietnam population, as of 1968, was 35,500,000 (*World Almanac* [New York: Doubleday, 1968]).

5. America's Vietnam involvement began when we supported French military efforts to regain control of their previous colony after World War II, eventually funding 80 percent of their military expenses. The United States installed South Vietnam's initial president, Ngo Dinh Diem, who'd been living in Maryknoll seminaries in New Jersey and New York, helped him scuttle the 1954 Geneva accords, and armed and trained his secret police, using advisors from Michigan State University. When Diem bred disaffection and rebellion, the United States gave tacit approval for his generals to overthrow and execute him in 1963, and then backed a series of dictatorships until American troops finally withdrew in 1973 and Congress cut off military aid two years later.

For a general history of Vietnam see Frances Fitzgerald, *Fire in the Lake* (New York: Vintage, 1973), and Committee of Concerned Asian Scholars, *The Indochina Story* (New York: Bantam, 1970). Numbers of troops and bombing sorties from Gitlin, *The Sixties*, p. 242. Total tons of bombs from Gitlin, p. 378. The total number of U.S. troops in the Indochina war zone was 3,780,000; from McPherson, *Long Time Passing*, p. 7. On the level of U.S. involvement, see also James William Gibson, *The Perfect War* (New York: Atlantic Monthly Press, 1986), p. 9.

Indochina-related nuclear threats included two 1954 discussions by Secretary of State Dulles with French Prime Minister Bidault. In the first, Dulles offered tactical nuclear weapons to use against the Chinese Communists, and in the second he offered to relieve troops besieged by the Vietminh at Dien Bien Phu. Public discussions occurred in 1968, in newspapers and in the Senate, regarding Nixon's deliberations on using atomic weapons to defend the Marines surrounded at Khe Sanh, Vietnam. In 1969, Richard Nixon gave what he later termed his "November Ultimatum"—a threat, which Henry Kissinger conveyed to the North Vietnamese, that if they did not capitulate and force the National Liberation Front to do the same, they would face massive escalation, including possible nuclear strikes. Targeting was planned, down to mission folders containing photographs of the sites for potential atomic attacks. Nixon then backed off, owing to massive domestic protests. See Daniel Ellsberg's introduction to E. P. Thompson and Dan Smith's *Protest and Survive* (New York: Monthly Review Press, 1981), pp. v–vi.

    6. Lewis et al., *The Gulf War*, p. 11.

    7. On *Newsweek*, see "The Year of the Yuppie," *Newsweek*, Dec. 31, 1984, p. 14; the misappropriation of Gitlin by Neil Howe and William Strauss from "The New Generation Gap," *The Atlantic*, Dec. 1992, p. 69. Actual Gitlin quote from *The Sixties*, p. 433.

    Best-selling books that have purported to analyze the current generation consistently present gross caricatures of the Vietnam-era movements. This is true of Allan Bloom's *Closing of the American Mind* (New York: Simon and Schuster, 1987), Dinesh D'Souza's *Illiberal Education* (New York: Free Press, 1991), Neil Howe and William Strauss's *13th-GEN* (see note 5, Introduction), and novelist Doug Coupland's *Generation X* (see note 1, Introduction). Bloom wrote an entire chapter damning the sixties through distorted anecdotes and false stereotypes, without ever mentioning the Vietnam War except in one tangential and incomprehensible aside about Vietnamese trade markets, and he gave just a single peripheral mention to student civil rights participation. See Bloom, *Closing*, pp. 313–336, 364. D'Souza ascribed the bulk of American colleges' present ills to the baleful influence of former sixties radicals turned tenured professors. The less overtly political Coupland seems obsessed with talk of "bleeding ponytails" and stereotypes of left-over sixties hippies. Howe and Strauss present an odd pastiche of statistics and recycled quotes, computer conferences and cartoons, that not only subordinates complex realities to historically misleading clichés and a dubious political agenda, but also gives the feel of having been assembled by database search. In addition to inverting the "'*j'accuse*' to jacuzzi" Gitlin quote, they constantly caricature generational peers who've tried to maintain their earlier ideals. See Howe and Strauss, pp. 36–44 and 122–126.

    Unlike some of the other misleading works of recent years, *13th-GEN* got dismal reviews and made little impact as a book (see "The Boomer's Babies" by Andrew Leonard in the *New York Times Book Review*, May 23, 1993, p. 9). But Howe and Strauss have gotten continual press as promoters of Lead or Leave, a youth organization founded by Jon Cowan and Rob Nelson that has attracted national attention by promoting a neo-Reaganite politics of deficit-cutting. The Lead or Leave spokesmen say nothing about a more progressive tax structure or trimming bloated military spending, but focus instead on cutting entitlements like Social Security. The organization's main base comes from money provided by Ross Perot and by Republican financier Pete Peterson. Despite grandiose claims it has few ties to anything occurring on campus, but helped by the eager promotion of Howe and Strauss, it has gotten coverage on outlets like *Nightline* and *Good Morning America* that have pretty much ignored more representative student involvement.

    Howe and Strauss have also helped promote Lead or Leave's much-hyped cousin organization, Third Millennium. For an example of the coverage both have received, see Chrisopher John Farley, "Taking Shots at the Baby Boomers," *Time*, July 19, 1993, p. 30. Lead or Leave is excellently critiqued in Andrew Cohen, "Me and My Zeitgeist," *The Nation*, July 19, 1993. Miles Seligman and Aimee Strasko discuss the hype around both Lead or Leave and Third Millennium in "What's Behind the Twenty-Something 'Movement,' " *Extra*, Mar./Apr. 1994. As Seligman and Strasko point out, Lead or Leave claims 450,000 members, but when it held a major demonstration in front of the Washington, D.C., headquarters of the American Association of Retired Persons, only a hundred people showed up. And I've found no sign of it on any of the campuses I know. The only general portrait of the generation that does not succumb to the stereotypes is recent Harvard Law graduate Michael Lee Cohen's oral history, *The Twenty-Something American Dream* (New York: Dutton, 1993).

    8. Statistics on the subsequent paths of Mississippi activists from McAdam, *Freedom Sum-*

mer, p. 215. For a general look at the subsequent path of the 1960s activists, see Whalen and Flacks, *Beyond the Barricades*; Kessler, *After All These Years*; Stephen I. Abramowitz and Alberta J. Nassi, "Keeping the Faith: Psychological Correlates of Activism Persistence into Middle Adulthood," *Journal of Youth and Adolescence* 10 (1981): 507–523; Richard G. Braungart and Margaret M. Braungart, "Political Career Patterns of Radical Activists in the 1960s and 1970s: Some Historical Comparisons,' *Sociological Focus* 13 (1980): 237–254; Joseph R. DeMartini, "Social Movement Participation: Political Socializations, Generational Consciousness, and Lasting Effects," *Youth and Society* 15 (1983): 195–233; James M. Fendrich, "Keeping the Faith of Pursuing the Good Life: A Study of the Consequences of Participation in the Civil Rights Movement," *American Sociological Review* 42 (1977): 144–157.

9. Although similar splits occurred in the sixties, they're replicated now with fewer students involved in both the political and countercultural alternative strains.

10. L. A. Kauffman, "Emerging from the Shadow of the Sixties," *Socialist Review*, Oct.–Dec. 1990, pp. 14–15.

11. *Boston Globe* survey from Martin Lee and Norman Solomon, *Unreliable Sources* (New York: Carol Publishing Group, 1990), p. 107. Size of antiwar rallies from Gitlin, *The Sixties*, p. 183. Wisconsin survey from Loren Baritz, *The Good Life: The Meaning of Success for the American Middle Class* (New York: Knopf,1989), p. 257.

Kennedy reference from Gitlin, *The Sixties*, p. 309. See also Lewis Chester, Godfrey Hodgson, and Bruce Page, *An American Melodrama: The Presidential Campaign of 1968* (New York: Viking, 1969), pp. 339–349.

12. Kauffman, "Emerging from the Shadow."

13. In addition to the works by Bloom, D'Souza, and Howe and Strauss cited in note 7 above, see also Peter Collier and David Horowitz, *Destructive Generation: Second Thoughts About the '60s* (New York: Summit Books, 1989).

14. See Starr, *Lessons of the Vietnam War*, as an example of the material used in some of these courses. In 1985, the Project for the Study of the Vietnam Generation at George Mason University found 347 college and university classes dealing with the issue.

Nine: An unsentimental education

1. Page Smith, *Killing the Spirit* (New York: Viking Penguin, 1990), p. 78.

2. Ellen W. Schrecker, *No Ivory Tower: McCarthyism and the Universities* (New York: Oxford University Press, 1986). Numbers of New York City professors fired, from Russell Jacoby, *The Last Intellectuals* (New York: Basic Books, 1987), p. 126.

3. Political science and sociology examples from Jacoby, *The Last Intellectuals*, pp. 153, 156, 158. See also Robert A. McCaughey, *International Studies and Academic Enterprise: A Chapter in the Enclosure of American Learning* (New York: Columbia University Press, 1984), p. xiv; David M. Ricci, *The Tragedy of Political Science: Politics, Scholarship and Democracy* (New Haven: Yale University Press, 1984), pp. ix–x; Patricia Wilner, "The Main Drift of Sociology Between 1936 and 1982," *History of Sociology* 2 (Spring 1985): 1–20.

4. Combined figure for regular and temporary part-time faculty at four-year schools is 35.8 percent. From 1988 survey by U.S. Department of Education, cited in *Chronicle of Higher Education*, Aug. 28, 1991, p. 30.

5. For a general look at the undermining of intellectual life by abstruse academism, see Jacoby, *The Last Intellectuals*.

6. The percentage of R&D money has been over 65 percent from the mid-eighties on. See Marcia E. M. Molmen, "Secrecy on Campus: The Price of Security," *Peace Issues* (Grand Forks: University of North Dakota Center for Peace Studies, 1988), p. 2.

7. See David Zinczenko, "Business Schools That Shun Ethics Courses Should Go Straight to Jail," *Los Angeles Times*, Apr. 14, 1991.

8. On prevalence of business majors, see Astin et al., *The American Freshman, 1987*, as described in Chapter 5, footnote 23.

9. As an example of the material studied in the new courses, see Manuel G. Velasquez's top-selling text, *Business Ethics: Concepts and Cases* (Edgewood Cliffs, N.J.: Prentice-Hall, 1991). See also the work of the Business Enterprise Trust, a Stanford-based organization founded by Norman Lear and a dozen corporate leaders to encourage "acts of courage, integrity and social vision" in corporate life. Case studies include the ethics of investment in South Africa, Brown Lung compensation, falsification of safety tests, and factory relocations for the sake of lower wages.

10. Groups like the Boston-based Science for the People and publications like the *Bulletin of the Atomic Scientists* have long worked to foster social responsibility. In Holland and Denmark, university-based science shops explicitly place technical knowledge at the service of nonprofit and community groups; scientists and engineers who volunteered with the somewhat similar U.S.-based Science for Nicaragua helped Nicaragua develop alternatives to expensive imported pharmaceuticals, trained local students in groundwater hydrology, and established an electronic repair shop at the National Engineering University. Engineering ethics courses have explored questions like workplace safety, the role of whistle-blowers, and price-fixing in contracts. See Mike W. Martin and Roland Schinzinger's *Ethics in Engineering* (New York: McGraw-Hill, 1989).

11. On the implications of a comparable disengagement in literature, see Carol Bly, *Bad Government and Silly Literature* (Minneapolis, Minn.: Milkweed Editions, 1986).

12. Charles Derber, in conversation, Apr. 1989.

13. For instance, sociologist Howard Becker entitled a study of University of Kansas students in the late 1950s and early 1960s, *Making the Grade*. Howard S. Becker, Blanche Geer, and Everett C. Hughes, *Making the Grade: The Academic Side of College Life* (New York: Wiley, 1968).

14. Vartan Gregorian, "Three Challenges for Higher Education," *Brown Alumni Monthly*, May 1989.

15. Henry T. Nash, "Thinking About Thinking About the Unthinkable," *Bulletin of the Atomic Scientists*, Oct. 1983.

16. On the role of American intellectuals in promoting and excusing the Vietnam War, see Noam Chomsky, *American Power and the New Mandarins* (New York: Vintage, 1967). On ways the Reagan-Bush era media promoted the intellectual justifications of the political right, see Hertsgaard, *On Bended Knee*, and Lee and Solomon, *Unreliable Sources*.

17. For a terrific look at the moral and political ambiguities of intellectual workers, see Alvin Gouldner, *The Future of Intellectuals and the Rise of the New Class* (New York: Seabury Continuum, 1979).

18. Stanford historians Estelle Friedman and Paul Ferrulo won the 1980–81 and 1983–84 awards respectively. Both initially failed to get tenure, although Friedman filed a grievance after her department voted to give her tenure and the dean overruled them, and got her job back after a two-year fight that included major student protests on her behalf. Paul Starr example from Constance Holden, "Sociology Stir at Harvard," *Science*, May 10, 1985, and from Russell Jacoby, "Radicals in the Academy," *The Nation*, Sept. 19, 1987. Levenson award example from Nicholaus Mills, "The Endless Autumn," *The Nation*, Apr. 16, 1990. UCLA example from Rose, *Lives on the Boundary*, pp. 197–198.

Ten: I'll work from within

1. Keniston, *Young Radicals*, p. 42.

2. See Melissa Everett, *Conscious Careers: Your Guide to Making a Living, a Life, and a Difference* (New York: Bantam, forthcoming).

3. MIT Commission on Industrial Productivity, *Made in America* (Cambridge, Mass.: MIT Press, 1989).

4. In 1969, at the height of nonelectoral protest, 16.4 percent of incoming freshmen also volunteered in campaigns. By the mid-eighties, with far less going on outside, the figure dropped to under 9 percent. Twelve percent of students at four-year schools, and four percent of those at two-year colleges volunteered in campaigns at some point during their college careers, but not with any regularity. See Astin et al., *Twenty Year Trends*, p. 86. Hurtado et al., *American College Student, 1987*, p. 72.

5. E. J. Dionne, *Why Americans Hate Politics* (New York: Simon and Schuster, 1991). Thomas Edsdall and Mary Edsall, *Chain Reaction* (New York: Norton, 1992). William Greider, *Who Will Tell the People?* (New York: Simon and Schuster, 1992).

6. McGovern figures for those under twenty-five from Whalen and Flacks, *Beyond the Barricades*, p. 78. In 1980, voters under thirty gave Carter a 44 to 43 percent lead over Reagan, as well as 11 percent to John Anderson, with the Carter and Anderson figures the highest of any age group. In 1984, 59 percent of young voters voted for Reagan. Young voters in 1988 finally gave Bush 52 percent. "Portrait of the Electorate," *New York Times*, Nov. 5, 1992, p. B9.

On the quote from the Republican consultant and the shifting allegiances of young voters, see E. J. Dionne, *"Lure of the Young to Reagan Turns Into Capital for Party,"* *New York Times*, Oct. 31, 1988; E. J. Dionne, "If Nonvoters Had Voted: Same Winner, but Bigger," *The New York Times*, Nov. 21, 1988; and Adam Clymer, "Some Subtle Problems Undermine G.O.P Victory," *New York Times*, Nov. 14, 1988. According to Dionne, the 40 percent of the 1988 nonvoters who were under thirty supported Bush more than both the general populace and their generational peers who did vote. Young voters who were not registered said they would have chosen Bush over Dukakis by a massive 54 to 31 percent margin, or a gap 19 points wider than among those under thirty who voted and 15 points higher than Bush's 53- to 45-point lead in general.

Between 1972 and 1988, voting rates for eligible voters aged eighteen to twenty-four showed the largest decline of any age group in the population. Their participation rate was 50 percent in 1972, dropped to 41 percent in 1984, and then to 36 percent in 1988. Participation figures from *The Age of Indifference*, p. 25.

7. Reagan got 52 percent of the student vote in 1984, and Dukakis won by 54 percent in 1988. *New York Times*, "Portrait of the Electorate." In terms of divisions within the campuses, an internal University of Michigan survey shortly after the 1984 election found that only 39 percent of undergraduate humanities students and 48 percent of social science students had supported Ronald Reagan, versus 68 percent of those in the natural sciences. Sam Eldensveld, "Student Political Activism at the University of Michigan," Department of Political Science, University of Michigan, 1985.

8. For a general sense of the interaction between grassroots social movements and shifts in national policy, see Flacks, *Making History*; Gitlin, *The Sixties*; Taylor Branch, *Parting the Waters* (New York: Simon and Schuster, 1989).

9. Six thousand students, for instance, came to hear Jackson at Arizona State, and several thousand at the University of Washington. Arizona State numbers from Doreen Carrajal, "In New Speech, Jackson Gives Proposal for Producing Deficit," *Philadelphia Inquirer*, Apr. 8, 1988. University of Washington estimate from Terry McDermott "Jackson Hoists Liberal Banner Here in Support of Dukakis," *Seattle Times*, Oct. 13, 1988, p. A1. McDermott of the *Seattle Times* wrote that despite short notice, the crowd was as large as any Dukakis had drawn in six visits to Seattle.

10. "Civil society" is that sphere of independent culture between the economy and the state. See John Feffer, *Shock Waves: Eastern Europe After the Revolutions* (Boston: South End Press, 1992).

Eleven: Diminished dreams

1. Howe and Strauss, *13th-GEN*, pp. 49–56. On the link between the leveling off of the divorce rate and a continued increase in generational materialism, see Crimmins, Easterlin, and Saito, "Preference Changes Among American Youth," p. 22 and Figure 5.

2. John Berger, *A Fortunate Man* (New York: Pantheon, 1967), pp. 161–162.

3. "The I's Have It for Another Decade," Christopher Lasch, *New York Times*, Dec. 27, 1989, p. A23.

Introduction to Book Two: A stake in the future

1. Lee Neil Maher, "Students March to Save the Nation's Forests," and various news briefs, including "Campus Security Meets USC Demonstrators with Billy Clubs," "Students and Employees Fight Free Cars for Administrators," "Momentum Builds for Campus Styrofoam Bans," and "Student Boycott Fund Drive to Protest Administration Decisions," in *National Student News Service*, Mar. 5, 1990.

2. On student opposition to the CIA, see Ami Chen Mills, *CIA Off Campus* (Boston: South End Press, 1991).

Twelve: Fighting for the land

1. Ritchie and Ristau, *Crisis by Design*, p. 7.

2. For a concise history of federal farm programs, see Ritchie and Ristau, *Crisis by Design*. On the Harkin-Gephardt supply-reduction approach versus the current path supported by both the Reagan administration and Democratic congressional leaders like Tom Foley, see Ritchie and Ristau, pp. 11–17.

3. On the impact of leveraged buyouts for firms like Beatrice and Safeway, see Krebs, *The Corporate Reapers*, pp. 36–41, 101–110.

Thirteen: Greeks for peace

1. Statistics on the prevalence of anorexic and bulimic behavior vary widely, depending on how observers classify eating disorders that by their very nature are intermittent. But Joan Jacobs Brumberg, professor of human development at Cornell, puts the number of anorectics at 5 to 10 percent of all American girls and women, primarily those young, white, and disproportionately middle and upper class. On some campuses, she believes, one woman out of five is anorexic. Eating disorder specialist Dr. Charles A. Murkovsky, of New York's Gracie Square Hospital, says 20 percent of American college women are bulimic, and binge and purge on a regular basis. See Naomi Wolf, *The Beauty Myth* (New York: Anchor, 1992), pp. 182–217. Also Joan Jacobs Brumberg, *Fasting Girls: The Emergence of Anorexia Nervosa as a Modern Disease* (Cambridge, Mass.: Harvard University Press, 1988), especially pp. 12 and 22. Kim Chernin in *The Hungry Self* suggests, according to Wolf, that at least half the women on American campuses suffer at some time from bulimia or anorexia. See Chernin, *The Hungry Self* (London: Virago Press, 1986).

Fourteen: Crossing the line

1. Granted, a good number of students join antiabortion protests through right-to-life church organizations when they are in high school. These efforts also frame their argument in terms of stories—those of the helpless fetuses that they say are capriciously murdered. But antiabortion participation drops sharply when students get to college, where three-quarters of students favor keeping the decision a private one, and sexually active peers make far more concrete the implications of women being forced to unwillingly bear children.

In the 1990 follow-up to the annual CIRP surveys, 72.6 percent of sophomores at four-year schools, 68 percent of sophomores at two-year schools, and 76 percent of seniors supported the right to choice. This had climbed significantly from figures in a 1985 survey, where the respective levels of support were 64 percent, 52 percent, and 61 percent, but in both cases pro-choice students were a solid majority. See Wingard et al., *American College Student, 1990*, pp. 16, 100; Astin et al., *The American College Student, 1985* (Los Angeles: Higher Education Research Program, UCLA, 1985), pp. 51, 83; and Hurtado et al., *American College Student, 1987*, pp. 37, 61. Some, to be sure, continued to follow what Catholics like Chicago's Cardinal Joseph Bernardin calls a "consistent life ethic," opposing abortion, war, capital punishment, and the marginalization of the poor. But most involved in student political movements have decided that, whatever their personal qualms, limiting abortion will not create a more just world; students who believe it desirable for the state to make abortion illegal remain mostly those most accepting of authority in general.

2. The Midwest Academy, a labor and community organizing institute, emerged out of theories of organizer Saul Alinsky; early on, it was staffed by key former SDS members, and between 1986 and 1993, helped USSA train 4,500 students in intensive weekend workshops.

For a general discussion of the moral use of story, see Robert Coles, *The Call of Stories* (Boston: Houghton Mifflin, 1989), and Belenky et al., *Women's Ways of Knowing*, pp. 168–189.

3. In Feb. 1988, for instance, the *New York Times* printed a lengthy story of Salvadoran guerrillas executing two peasants who wanted to vote in upcoming elections. As Martin Lee and Norman Solomon describe in *Unreliable Sources*, p. 298, *Times* correspondent James Le Moyne never indicated that he had simply lifted the story from a right-wing San Salvador newspaper, which in turn had been fed it by Salvadoran psychological warfare specialists. Eleven years later, the *Times* finally acknowledged the El Mozote massacre and Bonner's contribution to unmasking it, but made no mention of the paper's pushing Bonner out of his job. See "Truth, Lies and El Salvador," *New York Times*, Mar. 16, 1993, editorial on p. A18. U.S. government human rights reports have also consistently understated the magnitude of human rights violations taking place inside Guatemala, where security forces have killed on the order of 150,000 civilians since 1970 and 50,000 since 1980. Guatemalan figures from Lee and Solomon, *Unreliable Sources*, p. 305, and from Larry Birns, Council on Hemispheric Affairs, Washington, D.C., phone interview, Oct. 1993.

4. On backgrounds of previous student activists, see Keniston, *Young Radicals*; Richard Flacks, *Youth and Social Change* (Chicago: Markham, 1971); Helen Lefkowitz Horowitz, *Campus Life* (Chicago: University of Chicago Press, 1988), pp. 82–97, 151–173; and Robby Cohen, *When the Old Left Was Young: Student Radicals and America's First Mass Student Movement, 1929–1941* (New York: Oxford University Press, 1993).

5. Whether in official institutions like this study group or church circles, or in informal conversations among activist participants, popular movements always have their places of sanctuary. As Providence College sociologist Eric Hirsch writes regarding the student antiapartheid movement, "Consciousness-raising is facilitated in nonhierarchical, loosely structured, face-to-face settings that are isolated from persons in power; in such *havens*, people can easily express concerns, become aware of common problems, and begin to question the legitimacy of institutions that deny them the means for resolving those problems." See Eric Hirsch, "Sacrifice for the Cause: Group Processes, Recruitment and Commitment in a Student Social Movement," *American Sociological Review* 55 (1990): 243–253, quote from p. 245. See also Hirsch's draft paper, "Consciousness-Raising and Political Protest," available from Eric Hirsch, Department of Sociology, Providence College, Providence, R.I. For a general look at the role of such havens, see Sarah Evans and Harry Boyte, *Free Spaces* (New York: Harper and Row, 1986).

6. See Michiko Kakutani, "New Haven Blues," in *My Harvard My Yale*, ed. Diana Dubois (New York: Random House, 1982), p. 282, and Levine, *When Dreams and Heroes Died*. In fall 1970, a Harris poll reported the first drop since 1965 of students calling themselves "radical or far left," down to 7 percent, from 11 percent the previous spring (Gitlin, *The Sixties*, p. 417).

7. Astin et al., *Twenty Year Trends*, p. 97.

8. Arthur Levine and K. R. Wilson, "Student Politics in America," *Higher Education* 8 (Nov. 1979): 627–640. Also Levine, *When Dreams and Heroes Died*, pp. 48–49.

9. Levine, *When Dreams and Heroes Died*, pp. 40–42.

10. Matt Countryman, "Lessons of the Divestment Drive," *The Nation*, Mar. 26, 1988.

11. My discussion of Columbia's antiapartheid movement comes from interviews with participants and from the extensive interviews, observation, and surveys of sociologist Eric Hirsch, then teaching at Columbia. For a general look at Columbia's movement, see Hirsch's "Sacrifice for the Cause" and "Consciousness-Raising." See also Tony Vellela, *New Voices* (Boston: South End Press, 1988), pp. 19–39. (Some of Vellela's other chapters are sloppy, but the one on divestment is accurate.) Quote about university divestment committee using "all methods possible to avoid debate" is from the report of Columbia disciplinary hearing officer Lewis B. Kaden, Aug. 30, 1985, p. 7, attachment to "Notice of Charges" delivered to Columbia student Carl Parham for his participation in the divestment blockade. From personal files of Carl Parham.

12. According to one of Hirsch's extensive surveys, 37 percent of a random sample of undergraduates participated in blockade rallies and/or slept overnight on the steps of Hamilton Hall. Hirsch, "Sacrifice for the Cause," p. 248.

13. The more accountable public universities divested in the greatest numbers, including the entire University of California system—which withdrew $3.1 billion in July 1986, after House Speaker Willie Brown and other legislators threatened to hold up the university's budget and the Republican governor, George Deukmejian, reversed his opposition under the pressure of a coming re-election campaign. Other public universities to fully divest included Wisconsin, Michigan State, Vermont, Wyoming, Arizona State, Maine, Kentucky, and City University of New York. In the cases of Columbia, Smith, Ohio State, Rutgers, the University of Massachusetts at Amherst, and others, protests pushed the schools from partial to full divestment. Private schools with some of the largest endowments, such as Stanford and Princeton, pulled out only token amounts, while some partial divestments—like Harvard's $204 million, Missouri's $80 million, and $41 million from Michigan—were substantial. Campaigns securing full divestment ranged from major public institutions to such private schools as Columbia, Swarthmore, Georgetown, Middlebury, Fairfield, and the University of Rochester.

For a general portrait of the student antiapartheid movement, see John L. Jackson, "The Student Divestment Movement: Anti-Apartheid Activism on U.S. College and University Campuses" (Ph.D. dissertation, Ohio State University, 1990). Figures on state pension funds and corporate disinvestment from Jackson, p. 61; on prevalence of student divestment activism, from pp. 76–79; and for comparative divestment rates of colleges that did and did not have major protests, from pp. 156–165. Estimates of antiapartheid arrests, revising earlier estimates from Jackson, p. 10, from Nov. 1993 phone discussions with Jackson and with Richard Knight of the American Committee on Africa/Africa Fund. For a general study of the antiapartheid movement's policy impact, see Fredrick Ira Solop, "Public Protest and Public Policy: The Anti-Apartheid Movement and Political Innovation," *Policy Studies Review* (Winter 1990). See also Fredrick Solop, "From the Margins to the Mainstream: The Anti-Apartheid Movement and the Politics of Agenda-Setting in the United States," (Ph.D. dissertation, Rutgers University, 1990), pp. 176–184 for further examples of activism; pp. 227–228 for a look at year-by-year levels of divestment for colleges, universities, and city and state governments; and pp. 215–216 for the political impact of sanctions on South Africa. Figures and examples also from *Divestment Action on South Africa by U.S. and Canadian Colleges and Universities* (two-page fact-sheet), (New York: The Africa Fund, 1988). Other examples of divestment movement activism from Philip Altbach and Robert Cohen, "American Student Activism: The Post-Sixties Transformation," in Philip Altbach, ed., *Student Political Activism* (Westport, Conn.: Greenwood Press, 1989), pp. 464–468; and Vellela, *New Voices*, pp. 19–39.

According to an estimate by the American Investor Responsibility Research Center, international sanctions caused South Africa's gross domestic product to be from 20 to 35 percent lower than would otherwise have been the case. Cited in George M. Frederickson, "No Going Back for Either Side," review of *The Future of South Africa*, by Sebastian Mallaby (New York: Times Books, 1992), in *New York Times Book Review*, Apr. 5, 1992, p. 3.

14. At the time, Stanford ranked among the top fifty military research, development, testing, and evaluation contractors nationwide. Stanford information from phone discussion with Lenny Siegel, Pacific Studies Center, Mountain View, Calif., Jan. 1994.

15. The two other colleges subsequently closed down by Mercer were Tift, in Forsyth, Georgia, and a nursing school in Atlanta. On Jan. 11, 1990, a DeKalb county jury concluded that Mercer University's trustees had "acted in bad faith" in deciding to close the Atlanta campus without consulting the faculty or students, and forced the university to pay restitution. Sources for the Mercer controversy from my interviews with Mercer faculty and students. See also the *Macon Telegraph News*: Don Schanche, Jr., "Lawyer Says Godsey Knew about Deficit," Dec. 5, 1989; Don Schanche, Jr., "Griffin Bell: Mercer's Deficit Gave Me a 'Great Shock,' " Dec. 8, 1989; Audrey Post, "Mercer's Actions Apparently Fueled Faculty Discontent," Dec. 10, 1989; Don Schanche, Jr., "Godsey: I Didn't Realize I Was Hiding Deficits," Dec. 20, 1989; Don Schanche, Jr., "Ex-Mercer Finance Chief Says Figures Rearranged Annually," Dec. 21, 1989; Audrey Post, "Faculty Members Protest Mercer Finances," Jan. 4, 1990; and Audrey Post, "Jury: Mercer Broke Contract," Jan. 12, 1990. See also *Atlanta Journal and Constitution*: David Goldberg, "Mercer University's Financial Crisis Checked, But Morale Low," and unsigned editorial, "Mercer's Bad Day in Court," Jan. 18, 1990, p. A10. Quote from jury findings that Mercer had "acted in bad faith," from professor of English Kenneth Hammond, in documents presented to the American Association of University Professors. Student letters from the *Mercer Cluster*, Feb. 6, 1990.

16. After months of marches, vigils, newspaper editorials, and wrenching campus debates, Godsey retained his post, but the trustees endorsed a major college restructuring, acceding to numerous demands regarding the school's fundamental direction and need for administrative accountability. Though it wasn't a total victory, the professors who were most involved considered it a significant one, and said student pressure played a key role.

Fifteen: A house still divided

1. The actual name of "Mona Daniels" appeared widely in the Emory and Atlanta press, but given the eventual consensus that her allegations were probably spurious, I believe it serves no useful purpose to cause her further public humiliation. For the same reason, I have also changed the names of the two men in the alleged date rape incidents detailed in this chapter.

2. In other incidents, a white Farleigh Dickenson student and his fraternity brothers attacked two black students sitting in a car. White students also attacked blacks at Marquette, Cleveland State, and the University of Michigan. These and racial incidents described in the text are from Jon Wiener, "Racial Hatred on Campus," *The Nation*, Feb. 27, 1989; Joseph Berger, "Deep Racial Divisions Persist in New Generation at College," *New York Times*, May 22, 1989, p. A1; Task Force on Racism of the Associated Students of the University of Washington, *Report to the University: Racism and Discrimination in the College Environment* (Seattle: University of Washington, 1989), pp. 1, 20; and Howard J. Ehrlich, *Campus Ethnoviolence and the Policy Options* (Baltimore: Center for the Applied Study of Prejudice and Ethnoviolence [formerly the National Institute Against Prejudice and Violence], 1990), pp. 41–72 (hereafter: Ehrlich, *Ethnoviolence and the Policy Options*). Brown incident is from p. 58 of this work by Ehrlich.

3. Prevalence of harassment from Ehrlich, *Ethnoviolence and the Policy Options*, p. iii. For a more detailed survey of research on minority victimization, see Ehrlich's follow-up study, *Campus Ethnoviolence: A Research Review* (Baltimore: Center for the Applied Study of Prejudice and Ethnoviolence, 1992), pp. 1–26 (hereafter: Ehrlich, *A Research Review*).

Fraternities are often involved in racial and sexual incidents, fueled by racial exclusivity, machismo, and ample supplies of alcohol and drugs. A house at Dan Quayle's alma mater, DePauw, sponsored a "ghetto party," with racial slurs decorating the wall. A fraternity at the University of Pennsylvania hired two black strippers, whom house members showered with racial and sexual remarks. Fraternities performed blackface skits at UC Irvine and Oklahoma State, as well as at the University of Washington. At the University of Texas, in spring 1990, members of one house spray-painted "Fuck coons" and "Fuck you nigs, die" on a car, and a group from another house distributed a t-shirt on which the head of Sambo had been printed, superimposed on Michael Jordan's body. Fraternity members have also harassed fellow students on sexual grounds; for example, at the University of Oregon fraternity members disrupted a gay-sponsored film, blocked the exits of the room, then shouted comments at women who were leaving. See Ehrlich, *Ethnoviolence and the Policy Options*, pp. 55–68; and Ehrlich, *A Research Review*, p. 16. Texas incidents from Karen Houppert, "New Campus Radicals," *Ms*, Sept./Oct. 1991.

4. Ehrlich, *Ethnoviolence and the Policy Options*, pp. 21–22.

5. Ivan Julian quote from "The White Noise Supremacists," collected in Lester Bangs, *Psychotic Reactions and Carburetor Dung* (New York: Vintage Books, 1988), p. 275.

6. Associated Students of the University of Washington, *Report to the University*, pp. 9–18. Other studies with comparable results were conducted at Stanford, University of Virginia, MIT, Michigan State, the Baltimore County campus of the University of Maryland, St. Cloud State, and the University of Colorado at Colorado Springs (Ehrlich, *Ethnoviolence and the Policy Options*, pp. 12–15; Ehrlich, *A Research Review*, pp. 9–14).

7. Michael Moffatt, *Coming of Age in New Jersey* (New Brunswick, N.J.: Rutgers University Press, 1989), p. 144.

8. Total 1990 enrollment at four-year institutions was 8,529,000. Total minority enrollment was 1,450,000, 17 percent. African-American enrollment was 715,000, or 8 percent, including 208,000 at historically black colleges and universities. Latinos were 344,000, or 4 percent. Asian-Americans were 343,000. Native Americans numbered 48,000 (one-half of one percent). Ten years earlier, the comparable figures were 2 percent for Asians, 3 percent for Latinos, and 6 percent for blacks. These and the following figures come from Deborah J. Carter and Reginald Wilson, *Minorities in Higher Education: Tenth Annual Status Report* (Washington, D.C.: American Council on Education, Office of Minorities in Higher Education, 1991), pp. 43, 46.

9. Carter and Wilson, *Minorities in Higher Education*, pp. 7–8, 36–37.

10. Carter and Wilson, *Minorities in Higher Education*, pp. 36–37.

11. On shifts in minority college enrollment and graduation rates, see Carter and Wilson,

Minorities in Higher Education, pp. 19, 36–37, 48. The economic crunch and cutbacks in financial aid have hit all races, but minorities especially hard. Among low-income high school graduates, participation in higher education for blacks has dropped from 40 percent in 1976 to 30 percent in 1988, and for Latinos, from 50 percent to 35 percent. Low-income white high school graduates, though under major duress, nonetheless managed to hang on and increase their percentage during this same period from 37 percent to 39 percent. See Deborah J. Carter and Reginald Wilson, *Minorities in Higher Education: Eighth Annual Status Report* (Washington, D.C.: American Council on Education, Office of Minorities in Higher Education, 1989), p. 39.

12. Ehrlich, *Ethnoviolence and the Policy Options*, p. 17.

13. Ehrlich, *Ethnoviolence and the Policy Options*, pp. 48, 49, 59–61, 69; Wiener, "Racial Hatred on Campus"; Brown incident and Vartan Gregorian quote from Pete Hamill, "Black and White at Brown," *Esquire*, Apr. 1990.

14. Emory black enrollment figures from *Lovejoy's College Guide* (New York: Simon and Schuster, 1987), p. 281. See Jill Nelson, *Volunteer Slavery: My Authentic Negro Experience* (Chicago: Noble Press, 1993).

15. Figures on Emory's tenured faculty from 1990; tenured black faculty increased to 20 out of 748 by 1993. As of 1993, Emory's tenured and nontenured black faculty amounted to 87 out of 1,518. Figures from Emory public relations director Jan Gleason, letter of Sept. 13, 1993. The school had also recently added a black dean of graduate arts and sciences and a highly articulate black assistant dean for minority affairs. The latter would also direct the Multicultural Center.

16. When the Washington, D.C.–based organization, the Sentencing Project, studied black men between age twenty and twenty-nine, they found that more than 25 percent were under judicial control. This figure was higher for the younger men on the spectrum. "Prison Rate in U.S. Highest in World," *Seattle Times*, Jan. 5, 1991.

17. On the controversies surrounding the role of Egyptian influences on ancient Greece, see Martin Bernal, *Black Athena* (New Brunswick, N.J.: Rutgers University Press, 1987).

18. Student admirers of Farrakhan linked him with Malcolm even though Farrakhan remained part of the main Nation of Islam group that attacked Malcolm when he left, and that may well have ordered his death. See the documentary "Malcolm X—Make It Plain," aired as part of the PBS series, *The American Experience*, Jan. 26, 1994, produced by Blackside, Inc., Washington, D.C.

19. Marlon Riggs, "Black Macho Revisited," *The Independent*, Apr. 1991, published by the New York–based Association of Independent Video and Filmmakers.

20. For a general look at these issues, see Walter R. Allen, Edgar G. Epps, and Nesha Z. Haniff, ed., *Colleges in Black and White: African-American Students in Predominantly White and Predominantly Black Public Universities* (New York: State University of New York Press, 1991).

21. African-American undergraduate enrollment at Emory College went from 192 in 1985, to 301 in 1990, to 357 in 1992. The size of the college also grew during the same period from 3,443 to 4,473 students, but the proportion of African-American students still climbed from 6 to 8 percent. From Emory public relations director Jan Gleason, letter of Sept. 13, 1993.

22. "Supreme selfishness" quote from Columbia College dean Robert Pollak, from "Sovern Calls In Police to End Blockade," *Columbia Spectator*, Apr. 22, 1987. Michael Sovern incident from "The Invisible Man," *Columbia Spectator* editorial, Apr. 27, 1987. This editorial blasted Sovern for "patent unwillingness to deal with the students he's been hired to handle."

23. "Mona's" handwriting was similar to that on the threatening notes and a grammatical error in the notes also appeared in a message she'd left for a friend down the hall. Her fingerprints appeared at the top of the notes, upside down, as they would when one has pulled a letter out of the typewriter after having typed it. And Mona's story contained numerous discrepancies. Letters from her boyfriend that she said were stolen were found over the break in her room. Her prints were on a coffee can belonging to her roommate that was tossed around the room, but Mona didn't drink coffee. At one point she told a woman in her hall that her roommate had just left the door unlocked again. When the woman said she'd seen the roommate lock the door and turn on the alarm, Mona said it must have been someone else breaking in—then never reported the incident to the police. See Peter Applebome, "Woman's Claim of Racial Crime Is Called a Hoax," *New York Times*, June 1, 1990. Anne Hardie and Anne Cowles, "[Daniels] Won't Be Prosecuted," *Atlanta*

Journal Constitution, June 1, 1990, p. E10. Marilyn Milloy, "Cast as Exploited—Exploiter: Georgia Student Under Suspicion in Racial Attacks Against Her." *Newsday,* May 13, 1990, p. 3. Phone interview with Emory Police Chief Ed Medlin, Sept. 1993.

Sixteen: The world of the activists

1. Flacks, *Making History,* pp. 1–4.

2. In 1970, 39 percent of freshman men considered themselves liberal or far left, compared to 19 percent who called themselves conservative. The gap among women was similar, at 35 to 17 percent, though slightly smaller. By 1981, male freshman conservatives outnumbered liberals for the first time, by 25 to 20 percent, a five-point margin. They have continued to do so, with a more or less similar gap, throughout the period since. Freshman women, however, remained far more skeptical of the Reagan-Bush crusades. Their margin of liberals over conservatives dropped from 13 percent in 1976 to a narrow 3 percent in 1981, which was still eight points to the left of the men. Then college women began to move back to the left, with the margin of liberals over conservatives reaching 7 percent in 1985, 11 percent in 1991, and 12 percent in 1993. In that year, 30 percent of freshman women considered themselves liberal and only 18 percent conservative, while among men, conservatives continued to lead by a 29 to 23 percent margin. The men continued to call themselves slightly more conservative than liberal, though their responses were liberal on nearly all social issues except those having to do with crime and homosexuality. But the women had moved sharply to the left, and the eighteen-point gap between the sexes was greater than ever.

In terms of specific issues, abortion, surprisingly, was the sole exception to the differences: nearly two-thirds of both male and female freshmen consistently supported the right to choice, with support rising to nearly 75 percent as they made their way through school. But to take the 1993 figures, 29 percent of female freshmen wanted to participate in community action, compared to 21 percent of the men. Forty-five percent of women wanted to work promoting racial understanding, versus 37 percent of male freshmen. Both sexes believed the government should do more to control handguns, but the women endorsed this by a margin of 90 percent, the men by 72 percent. Both wanted the government to do more to protect the consumer, but women led 76 to 68 percent. Twenty-four percent of women believed the death penalty should be abolished, versus 19 percent of men. Eighteen percent of 1993 freshman men insisted that racial discrimination was no longer a problem, compared to just 11 percent of women. Astin et al., *Twenty Year Trends,* pp. 49–51, 73–75; Astin et al., *The American Freshman, 1991,* pp. 42, 58; Astin et al., *The American Freshman, 1993,* pp. 43, 61.

3. Both men and women would also register more conservative if the statistics were confined to whites. Though the national survey reports do not break down responses by race (the information is part of their internal master data base), they do give separate figures for all black colleges, whose students represent something of a cross section of the African-American community. To take the 1993 figures, the responses from males at those schools are 19 points to the left of freshman men in general, and those from women are 14 points to the left. I believe Latino students would present a similar response. If both were factored out, both men and women would come off more conservative, and the gaps would be slightly greater. Astin et al., *The American Freshman, 1993,* pp. 43, 61.

Tracking studies of college seniors show these splits holding true or increasing. In 1983, 22 percent of male freshmen called themselves conservative, narrowly leading the 21 percent who called themselves liberal. Among women, liberals led by 21 percent, versus 15 percent who called themselves conservative. The overall gender gap was 7 percent. When this same cohort was surveyed in 1987 as seniors, 36 percent of the men called themselves conservative, and 25 percent liberal, while among senior women, liberals continued to lead by 29 percent to 24 percent. The gender gap had grown from 7 to 16 percent.

A similar pattern held true in a 1990 survey of students who'd entered in 1986, the last national tracking study as of this writing. Their freshman gender gap was unusually high for the mid-eighties: 18 percent, with male conservatives leading liberals by a margin 28 to 23 percent, and female liberals leading conservatives by 27 to 14 percent. By the time these same students were seniors, 31 percent of men called themselves conservative, and 29 percent liberal, still leaning slightly to the right. Among senior women, 33 percent called themselves liberal, with only 18 percent conservative—barely half. Although the differences in political involvement were more modest, the gap in self-identification totaled 17 percent. See Hurtado et al., *American College Student, 1987*, pp. 85, 96. Wingard et al., *American College Student, 1990*, pp. 126, 152.

In the 1992 election, Bill Clinton led George Bush by a fifteen-point margin among young women, 48 to 33, compared to a nearly dead even 38 to 36 split for young men. *New York Times*, "Portrait of the Electorate."

4. See Kamen, *Feminist Fatale*, pp. 31, 35–36. Rape surveys from Liz McMillen, "Colleges Urged to Step Up Efforts to Prevent Rape, a Major Menace to Students on Campus," *Chronicle of Higher Education*, Sept. 1, 1988. See Susan Faludi's book, *Backlash*.

5. On male/female wage gap, see Lindley H. Clark, Jr., "The Pay Gap Narrows—Slowly," *Wall Street Journal*, July 2, 1993, p. A6. In 1971, women working full-time in America earned 58 percent of the weekly wage of men; in 1981, 62 percent; and in 1988, 69 percent. The gap in the United States remains considerably larger than in other advanced industrial countries. Mount Holyoke quote from Kamen, *Feminist Fatale*, p. 25. Wingard et al., *The American College Student, 1990*, pp. 122, 148.

Women's studies courses are now offered at half of all four-year colleges and at two-thirds of all universities. There were 621 programs as of 1990, with 425 offering either a minor or area of concentration, and 187 offering majors. As of 1990, nearly a quarter of all graduating women and 5 percent of all men had enrolled in at least one women's studies class. Kamen, *Feminist Fatale*, p. 277.

6. Both men and women have gotten more tolerant regarding homosexuality. In 1985, 58 percent of the men and 38 percent of the women thought it should be prohibited. By 1993, the corresponding figures were 48 percent and 28 percent. Such judgments would shift among both sexes toward greater tolerance as students continued their passage through school, but the gender gaps would remain. Astin et al., *Twenty Year Trends*, pp. 49–51, 73–75; Astin et al., *The American Freshman, 1993*, pp. 43, 61.

Young high school–educated white men in particular have bought into the conservative myths. As their once-decent economic prospects have been devastated, a high percentage have not responded by questioning the wealthy and powerful who have chosen to close down plants at which they would once have worked, bust the unions that once gave them protection, and shift the tax burden onto their paychecks. Instead, they've blamed their situation on those, like blacks and women, whom they have perceived as edging them out. A national survey by the Yankelovich polling organization called this angry and resentful group "The Contenders," and described their consistent sense that other, specially favored, groups had left them behind (Faludi, *Backlash*, pp. 65–66).

7. From phone interviews with Susan Jeffords and Myriam Miedzian, Jan. 1994. Also see Susan Jeffords, *Hard Bodies: Hollywood Masculinity in the Reagan Era* (New Brunswick, N.J.: Rutgers University Press, 1993). And on more general links between masculinity and violence, see Myriam Miedzian, *Boys Will Be Boys: Breaking the Link Between Masculinity and Violence* (New York: Anchor Doubleday, 1992).

8. On blue-collar rock as hope, religion, and rebellion, see Gaines, *Teenaged Wasteland*, especially pp. 175–217.

9. See Judy Karasik, *Young People Working in the Public Interest: What Are They Doing and How Can We Help?* (Chicago: The John D. and Catherine T. MacArthur Foundation, 1990), pp. 136–143.

10. See Williams, *Empire as a Way of Life*.

11. Rutgers quote from Paula Kamen, *Feminist Fatale*, p. 271.

Seventeen: Tangible fruits

1. Other key organizations include Campus Compact, an organization founded in 1985 by the presidents of Brown, Stanford, and Georgetown Universities, and which gives administrative support and resources to campus service activities.

2. Flacks, *Making History*, pp. 68–97.

3. Other model efforts include USC's Joint Educational Project, which integrates an extensive volunteer program in the surrounding low-income communities of Los Angeles with classes on related issues.

4. William Sloane Coffin, Jr., "Justice, Not Charity," keynote address to 1988 Outward Bound Conference.

5. For a general look at this subject, see Evans and Boyte, *Free Spaces*.

Eighteen: Shades of green

1. Desire to become personally involved in environmental issues grew from a low point of 16 percent in 1986 (down from 45 percent in 1972), to 34 percent in 1990, before dropping back slightly to 29 percent in 1993. Astin et al., *Twenty Year Trends*, p. 97; Astin et al., *The American Freshman, 1990*, pp. 5, 56; Astin et al., *The American Freshman, 1993*, p. 24.

2. Comparisons of student members of Greenpeace versus other environmental organizations from sociologist J. Allen Williams's survey of participants in SEAC's 1990 national "Catalyst" conference at Champaign-Urbana, Ill. Printout of *Conference Evaluation and Student Survey* responses available from J. Allen Williams, Department of Sociology, University of Nebraska. Greenpeace information on printout p. 42.

3. *A Proposal to Supply the Hendrix College Food System with Locally Produced Commodities*. Available from Meadowcreek Project, Fox, Ark. 72051. Student Environmental Action Coalition, *The Student Environmental Action Guide: 25 Simple Things We Can Do* (Berkeley, Calif: Earth-Works Press, 1991).

4. Many of the preceding examples come from *The Student Environmental Action Guide*, 1991. On Sierra Student Coalition, see John W. Bartlett, "Young Crusaders," *Sierra* magazine, Sept./Oct. 1993.

5. One personal choice many of these students make is vegetarianism. John Robbins's *Diet for a New America* has become their new bible, with its attack on meat production for polluting soil and water, increasing global energy use, and furthering the gap between rich and poor. Whatever its validity, the vegetarian choice allows large numbers of environmentally concerned students to feel they are making their private lives consistent with their beliefs. If everyone followed suit, they explain, the resulting grain savings "could feed the entire population of the world." See John Robbins, *Diet for a New America* (Walpole, N.H.: Stillpoint, 1987).

6. Illinois State example from my interviews with students at SEAC conference, Boulder, Colo., Oct. 1991. University of Washington example provided by environmental studies department, Nov. 1993. The young did remain less concerned than those older: a 1989 Gallup poll found only 31 percent of those under thirty calling themselves strong environmentalists, compared to 49 percent of those fifty and older. But the gap was closing rapidly. From Times Mirror Center for the People & the Press, *The Age of Indifference*, p. 28.

7. In surveys from SEAC's 1990 conference, 58 percent of students who responded supported a broad definition of environmentalism that included a social justice component, 38 percent supported a more narrow definition, and the remainder weren't sure. See Williams, *Conference Evaluation*, printout p. 39.

Nineteen: Coming back to concern

1. Gitlin, *The Sixties*, pp. 342–343.

2. Gitlin, *The Sixties*, p. 410.

3. Harris polls cited in Jerold Starr, "The American Youth Movement in the 1980s," paper delivered at World Congress of Sociology, New Delhi, India, Aug. 1986. Number of 1967 students who were Vietnam hawks from Baritz, *The Good Life*, p. 257. Percent of students viewing education in terms of increased earnings, from Levine, *When Dreams and Heroes Died*, pp. 4–5.

4. The 1993 surveys did see a small shift back toward the right from the year before, with several indexes of liberal social concern lower by a couple percentage points. This was particularly true among young men, and may reflect a larger political mood of sour resentment. But statistical surveys of this type inevitably fluctuate. They are at best general guides to student beliefs. I believe the shifts in student experience will continue to point toward increased liberal involvement. Freshman responses from Astin et al., *The American Freshman, 1993*, pp. 24, 25, 43, 61.

As indicated in Chapter Two, note 3, *Monitoring the Future*, a series of studies of high school seniors, showed a similar trend toward concern. In 1984, 48 percent of their national sample agreed, to some degree, with the statement "I can do very little to change the way the world is today"; 29 percent disagreed. By 1992, 44 percent said they disagreed, implying that they felt their actions indeed could matter, while only 33 percent agreed that they were powerless. Bachman et al., *Monitoring the Future*, questionnaire form 4, question D10A, 1984 and 1992 survey responses.

5. Among sources that seized on this figure were the *New York Times*, the Associated Press, *Harper's*, the *Chronicle of Higher Education*, and *The Nation*. The exact 1990 figure was 39.4 percent. The figures for 1966 and 1967 were 15.5 percent and 16.3 percent respectively, but the survey stopped asking the question just when political involvement took off, and didn't pick it up again until 1979, when it was 16.8 percent. See Astin et al., *The American Freshman, 1990*, p. 45; Astin et al., *Twenty Year Trends*, p. 86.

6. In January 1990, I mentioned this inadvertent flaw to ACE/UCLA survey director Al Astin. In ACE's fall 1991 survey, in the wake of the Gulf War, 39 percent once again said they had participated in organized demonstrations—a percentage that climbed slightly to 40.5 the next year. But the surveys also asked whether incoming freshmen "demonstrated for change in some military policy," to which just 9 percent responded yes. The vast bulk of politically active students marched at least briefly to protest the war either as it was approaching or right after it started. A much smaller number marched to support Bush's policies, though they might not have counted themselves among the 9 percent. I'd suggest the actual number of politically active incoming freshmen is actually closer to this figure than to the 39 percent figure given the widespread coverage. Astin et al., *The American Freshman, 1991*, p. 15; Dey et al., *The American Freshman, 1992*, p. 1.

Another relevant statistical index is the number of incoming freshmen who expect to participate in student protests (6.2 percent as of 1993), or those who would like to participate in community action (a constituency of 25 percent who are most disposed to involved themselves in the service movement). Astin et al., *The American Freshman, 1993*, p. 24. According to the 1990 National Postsecondary Student Aid Study, 26 percent of undergraduates pursued some level of community service, averaging 5.3 hours a week on such activities. Forty-seven percent of students in education programs volunteered, roughly 40 percent of students in the social and behavioral sciences, but only 20 percent of those in engineering or computer science, and 23 percent of those majoring in business. Volunteer participation correlated inversely with desire for financial success. From O'Brien, *Outside the Classroom*, pp. 1, 6.

7. Number of college seniors who'd participated in campus protests from Wingard et al., *American College Student, 1990*, p. 96. See note 6, above, for undergraduates involved in community service.

8. Kissinger's firm, Kissinger Associates, had in fact recently helped lobby through nearly $400 million of U.S. government loan guarantees that went to Iraq under a Department of Agriculture program called the Commodity Credit Corporation. See Alan Friedman, *Spider's Web* (New York: Bantam, 1993), p. 223.

9. University of Washington had been particularly compromised during the McCarthy era, firing three tenured professors, cooperating extensively with a state equivalent of the House Un-American Activities Committee, and developing rationales for purging suspect faculty that became a nationwide model. The resulting climate set a particularly cautious political tone among faculty who entered the university in the years that followed. See Schrecker, *No Ivory Tower*, pp. 94–112.

10. Unions opposing the pending war included the United Auto Workers; Machinists; Communications Workers; Oil, Chemical, and Atomic Workers; National Education Association; International Longshoremen; and Service Employees International.

11. Estimates of demonstration crowds are always slippery and highly politicized, but the size of the Seattle march was agreed on by both its organizers and local media, with the reporter at one network affiliate judging the total as high as 60,000. Until the April 1967 New York City march, whose attendance Martin Luther King, Jr., estimated as between 300,000 and 400,000 people, the largest national anti–Vietnam War rallies were an Apr. 17, 1965, SDS demonstration in Washington,

D.C., of 20,000, and one in New York City the following March, of 22,000. See Thomas Powers, *Vietnam: The War at Home* (Boston: G. K. Hall, 1984), pp. 76, 168, 233.

12. These and following student examples from interviews I conducted with antiwar students who attended at various conferences, particularly a national meeting of the major student antiwar coalition Jan. 27, 1991, in Washington, D.C., and COOL's annual conference, Mar. 7–10, 1991, in New Orleans, as well as follow-up calls to individual campus activists and to editors and reporters at various campus newspapers. See also Stephen Braun, "New Voices Shout Message from the '60s," *Los Angeles Times*, Jan. 20, 1991, p. A3; and Larry Gordon, "College Freshmen More Likely to Join Protests, Survey Shows: Researchers Say Marches Since Start of the Gulf War Confirm Their Findings," *Los Angeles Times*, Jan. 28, 1991, p. A3.

13. See University of Washington *Daily*: Heather Brooke and Angie Galloway, "Student Opinion Polarizes Over War," Jan. 17, 1991; Stephen Marty, "War Protestors Misguided," Jan. 18, 1991; Heather Brooke, "Wills Asked to Reimburse ASUW," Jan. 18, 1991; Letters pages, Jan. 17, 18, and 23, 1991.

14. In the Gulf War survey described in Chapter Seven, footnote 4, researchers discovered widespread ignorance of key events, such as the April Glaspie conversation and comparable illicit occupations by nations the Bush administration continued to consider staunch allies. The small minority who did know of those occurrences were far more likely to oppose the war.

Responses of belief that the United States fought the Vietnam War "with one hand tied behind our back" come from this poll, with 79 percent in agreement. In the same poll, respondents believed the total number of Vietnamese dead to be, on the average, one hundred thousand, compared to a reality of one to two million. Lewis et al., *The Gulf War*, pp. 7–8, 39–42, 50, 55, 57.

15. Figures for the San Francisco march were, as always, disputed. Organizers estimated 175,000 to 225,000; San Francisco police, who consistently downplay the numbers, claimed it was just 50,000. Participants who compared it with previous rallies on other issues judged it close to the organizers' estimates. San Francisco was full of massive protests throughout the first couple weeks of the war, including an earlier march of almost the same size on Jan. 19. A march in Los Angeles on Jan. 26, was estimated by police at 2,500 and by participants at 15,000 to 20,000. See Eric Brazil, "Biggest Peace Rally Since '71," *San Francisco Examiner*, Jan. 20, 1991, p. A1; and Eric Brazil, "S.F. Anti-War Rally Draws Groups Throughout West," *San Francisco Examiner*, Jan. 27, 1991, p. A5, photo on p. A1. See also the following *San Francisco Chronicle* articles: Jim Doylek, Lori Olszewski, and Don Lattin, "600 Arrested in Day of Anti-War Protests Around SF," Jan. 16, 1991, p. A1; Lori Olszewski, Bill Wallace, and Don Lattin, "Demonstrators Fill the Streets to Protest War," Jan. 17, 1991; Torri Minton and Jerry Carroll, "The New Faces of Protest," Jan. 17, 1991, p. B3; Susan Sward and Ramon G. McLeod, "SF Police Arrest 1,000 Protesters," Jan. 18, 1991, p. A1; Nanette Asimov, "Young Protestors of the Gulf War: Junior High and High School Students Quickly Take to the Streets," Jan. 21, 1991, p. A7. See also Sarah Thalling, "Massive Anti-War Rally Held in SF," *Oakland Tribune*, Jan. 27, 1991; Scott Harris, "Marchers Urge End to Conflict," *Los Angeles Times*, Jan. 27, 1991, p. B1; Craig McLaughlin, "Taking It to the Streets," *San Francisco Bay Guardian*, Jan. 23, 1991.

16. Percentage of students from *Washington Post* survey, in Elsa Walsh and Paul Valentine, "War Protest Draws Tens of Thousands Here," *Washington Post*, Jan. 27, 1991. The *Post* also found that a third of the crowd had friends or relatives in the Gulf. Numbers from various schools from march participants and from checking with their respective student newspapers.

17. The *Washington Post* gave the D.C. march front-page coverage, and printed both the police and the organizers' estimates of its size. But this seemed to have little ripple effect; other major media outlets either ignored or minimized its import. My figures for the D.C. march come from its sponsor, the National Campaign for Peace in the Middle East, but seem consistent with comparisons of its relative size to the 30,000-person march in Seattle two weeks earlier. From my perspective as a participant in both, the one in D.C. certainly seemed eight to ten times larger. See also Walsh and Valentine, "War Protest Draws Tens of Thousands."

The national networks blanked out dissident voices, not only after the war began but before it started. For the first month of *Nightline*'s Gulf crisis coverage, not one guest argued against sending U.S. soldiers to the desert sands. From the initial commitment of U.S. troops to the eve of the war, just 1 percent of all Gulf-related stories dealt with popular opposition to the U.S. buildup, including all coverage of protests, peace organizations, conscientious objectors, religious dissenters, and antiwar veterans, as well as hostile or sympathetic comments on the peace movement and its role. The networks interviewed none of the movement's associated scholars, such as Edward Said, Noam Chomsky, or Eqbal Ahmed. The major media gave no sense that ordinary citizens had either the right or power to affect our nation's policies. See "Gulf War Coverage: A One-Note Chorus," a special issue of *Extra*, May 1991. See also Lee and Solomon, *Unreliable Sources*, pp. xv–xxiii.

Framing the war from the start as a national crusade denied citizens any broader context in which to judge it. In the University of Massachusetts Gulf War survey (see note 14 above), respondents who watched the most TV had overwhelmingly heard of the Patriot missiles. But they knew even less than the national norm about key aspects of the war that cast U.S. policy in a more dubious light. Among all who responded, only 13 percent knew that Ambassador Glaspie had told Saddam Hussein that the United States would take no action if Iraq used force against Kuwait. Less than a third knew about Israel's occupation of the West Bank, and less than 5 percent knew about Syria's occupation of Lebanon. Just 14 percent knew that the United States and Israel were among the 3 nations out of 156 to vote against a U.N. political resolution attempting to settle the Israeli-Palestinian conflict. Lewis et al., *The Gulf War*, pp. 34, 39–42, 49, 50, 61.

18. As a director of the Silverado savings and loan, Neil Bush accepted a $100,000 "loan" from a major customer whom he never repaid. He also voted to approve $106 million in loans to another investor who loaned him $1.75 million. Eventually the savings and loan folded at a cost to the taxpayer of $1 billion. See C. Yang and D. Harbrecht, "Neil Bush: Now the S&L Mess Has a Name and Face," *Business Week*, July 30, 1990, p. 19; C. Yang, "Why Silvarado Bought the Ranch," *Business Week*, Dec. 3, 1990, pp. 146–147; and Jeff Cohen and Norman Solomon, "How Media First Botched Coverage of Whitewater," *Seattle Times*, April 2, 1994, p. A9.

19. Among men, supporters outnumbered opponents by 66.6 percent to 24.5 percent, with the balance undecided. Among women, students split nearly evenly, 45.6 percent in favor of the war, and 43.5 opposed. S. Komarnitksy, "Poll Finds Students Split Over Gulf War," University of Washington *Daily*, Jan. 23, 1991.

20. South Africa, as black students pointed out, not only oppressed its own population but also defied a U.N. order to relinquish control over Namibia and repeatedly sent troops across its borders into neighboring countries Mozambique, Zimbabwe, and Angola.

21. Troy, N.Y., example from July 1991 informal conversation with Fellowship of Reconciliation youth coordinator Jo Becker. Los Angeles examples from May 1991 phone interview with USC student activist Jill Nichols.

22. As John Kerr of the Nature Conservancy's Adopt-an-Acre project points out, elementary school children often learn about the rainforests through classroom projects. They study the region, write reports, create maps and models, raise money for preservation efforts by pooling their allowances or selling baked goods and animal pins. Teachers repeat the projects each year in their classrooms, then they extend to other grades as the kids themselves initiate further interest. The Rainforest Alliance says that half their inquiries come from students of less than college age. Conversations with Nature Conservancy and Rainforest Alliance, Nov. 1993.

23. For perhaps the best general look at the subsequent journeys of 1960s student activists, see Whalen and Flacks, *Beyond the Barricades*.

24. On the generational continuities of the initial crop of 1960s student activists, see Keniston, *Young Radicals*, pp. 307, 309.

Twenty: I don't want to be a biscuit babe

1. Tuition figures from Evelyn Nieves, "Students Protesting New Tuition Rise Shut 2 CUNY Colleges," *New York Times*, Apr. 11, 1991, p. B1, and Joseph Berger, "At Heart of CUNY Protests, Its Role in Educating the Poor," *New York Times*, Apr. 15, 1991, p. A1. Percentage from households making $14,000 a year or less was 28.3, $21,000 or less, 47.7 percent, from June 1991 phone interview with Rita Rodin, CUNY director of public information.

2. Thirty-seven percent of the students at City University of New York are white; 31.5 percent, African-American; 22.5 percent, Latino; 8.6 percent, Asian-American. Figures from "1989 OIRA Student Experience Survey," Table 1, an internal CUNY study available from CUNY's Office of University Relations. Number of students with family members on welfare derived by multiplying 200,000 by 10.7 percent, figure cited in Table 10 of the OIRA survey. See also Eric F. Coppolino, "End of an Era," *Village Voice*, Jan. 22, 1991, and Berger, "At Heart of CUNY Protests." CUNY's director of public information, Rita Rodin, in a June 1991 phone interview, said that 23.1 percent supported children.

3. In 1976, tuition was $935 a year for senior colleges and $775 for community colleges; tuition was $1,250 for both by 1983. Fifty-four percent of Hunter students and over 80 percent of City College students are people of color. Rankings in engineering enrollment and entrance into medical school from Aug. 1993 phone query to Charles DeCicco, City College public relations director. (City and Hunter are individual colleges within the larger CUNY system.)

4. On Cuomo's responses, see Coppolino, "End of an Era," and Nov. 1990 through Sept. 1991 articles in the now defunct *Student Leader News Service* (SLNS), back copies of which can be purchased from Eric Coppolino, Box 255, New Paltz, N.Y. 12561. See, in particular, Coppolino, "Cuomo Calls for $500 SUNY/CUNY Tuition Hikes," Feb. 4, 1991.

5. Rising tuition costs were not the sole factor in student attrition. They fed into a larger context of cutbacks in financial aid, a declining economy, a more impoverished student population, and new CUNY admissions policies that made it harder to get into its four-year schools, and that tracked students instead toward two-year programs from which it became increasingly difficult to transfer. See Berger, "At Heart of CUNY Protests."

6. Sarah Ferguson, "Labor Signs On," *Village Voice*, Apr. 23, 1991.

7. La Guardia temporary restraining order was issued in the students' favor on Apr. 23, 1991, by New York State Supreme Court Justice Bruce Wright, though later overturned by another court. From press release issued by City College student blockade leaders Day Student Government President Rafael Alvarez and Ricardo Pons of Students for Educational Rights; verified in Mar. 10, 1994, phone conversation with attorney Ronald B. McGuire, who represented a number of CUNY's student governments and secured the initial order.

8. Samuel Weiss, "California Educator Chosen in New York to Head University," *New York Times*, June 1, 1990, p. A1; Michael Lev, "A Tough Administrator," *New York Times*, June 2, 1990, p. 29; Larry Gordon, "Meetings Will Probe Cal State Pay Hike Furor," *Los Angeles Times*, Apr. 17, 1990, p. 7; Larry Gordon, "Cal State System Trustees Planning to Sell Chancellor's $2 Million Bel-Air Mansion," *Los Angeles Times*, Apr. 27, 1990, p. A38. Also see Jack Lyons, "CUNY Chancellor Escaped Pay Scandal in California by Coming to New York," *Student Leader News Service*, June 10, 1991.

9. Reynolds memo about rejecting demands for amnesty from Eric Pace, "37 Suspended After Protests in City System," *New York Times*, Apr. 15, 1991, p. B4. On Reynolds's response to CUNY's fiscal crisis and to the strikes, see Ferguson, "Labor Signs On"; Berger, "At Heart of CUNY Protests"; and Joseph Berger, "A CUNY Lesson in Goring the Wrong Ox," *New York Times*, Apr. 29, 1991. Pervasive criticisms of Reynolds from my student and faculty interviews, including harsh judgments levied by students also skeptical of the blockaders.

Later Reynolds tightened CUNY bylaws to restrict the political activity of student groups and successfully demanded that the CUNY trustees fire longtime Staten Island president Edwin Volpe after he resisted her plans to centralize various programs and refused to prosecute or turn over the names of students who turned their backs on her in protest when she attended the opening of a new Staten Island campus (from Nov. 1993 phone discussion with attorney Ronald B. McGuire).

10. Samuel Weiss, "CUNY Plans Tougher Standards That All Must Meet to Graduate," *New York Times*, Jan. 23, 1991, p. A1.

11. See David E. Lavin and David B. Crook, "Open Admissions and Its Outcomes: Ethnic Differences in Long-Term Educational Attainment," *American Journal of Education* (Aug. 1990): 389–425. Also see the forthcoming book by Lavin and David Hyllegard, tentatively entitled *The Value of College: Open Access Higher Education and the Life Chances of the Disadvantaged* (New Haven, Conn.: Yale University Press).

12. Berger, "At Heart of CUNY Protests."

13. David Lavin, phone interview, July 1991.

14. U.S. college attendance now encompasses roughly 50 percent of the relevant age cohort, compared to 20 percent in Germany, France, and Scandinavia. But those countries also have organized apprenticeship programs that have traditionally led to well-paid, generally unionized blue-collar jobs, so college is less essential for a decent life. The United States is also number one in spending on higher education, but low among industrialized nations in per capita investment in elementary and secondary education. Combined with a more stratified workforce, that makes the economic necessity to finish college much greater. (See Chapter Nine, note 10. Also lecture by SUNY Buffalo educational historian Philip Altbach at Indiana University of Pennsylvania, Oct. 19, 1989, and phone conversation with Altbach, Sept. 1993.)

15. Tax savings based on an estimated lost return of $950 billion during the 1990s, from Tom Wicker, "A Time for Action," *New York Times*, May 29, 1991, p. A23. Thomas Frist salary from Judith Nemes, "HCA Execs Pocket Millions with Stock Option Payouts," *Modern Healthcare*, Mar. 29, 1993, p. 3. Salary of United Airlines head Stephen Wolf from "Pressure to Perform," *U.S. News & World Report*, Apr. 6, 1992, p. 49. The $5 million plus bonuses for Goldman Sachs partners from Mark J. McGarry, "Short Cuts," *Newsday*, Dec. 7, 1993, business section, p. 43.

16. Income for the top 1 percent of New York taxpayers increased by 137 percent, compared to an 86 percent increase nationwide. Leichter also found, regarding corporate taxes, that by using state tax credits, the largest companies paid just over a third as much on their earnings as did businesses of more modest size. For proposed tax changes and summaries of the existing tax inequities, see "News from State Senator Franz S. Leichter," Jan. 28, 1991, and May 15, 1991, from the office of Franz S. Leichter, New York, N.Y. See also Leichter's more extensive accompanying reports: *Brother, Can You Spare a Dime? Inequalities in Income and Taxes in New York State*, released in Jan. 1991, especially pp. 4, 9–10; and *New York: The Cadillac of Corporate Welfare States*, released in May 1991, especially pp. 2, 3, 11. Link to budget equity proposal and to CUNY budgets from phone interview with Leichter aide Bill Zwart, Sept. 2, 1993.

17. Frances Fox Piven, phone interview, June 1991. See also two books by Frances Fox Piven and Richard Cloward, *Poor People's Movements: Why They Succeed, How They Fail* (New York: Pantheon, 1977), and *The New Class War: Reagan's Attack on the Welfare State and Its Consequences* (New York: Pantheon, 1985).

18. BMCC description from Evelyn Nieves, "Protest Group Is Confronted at a College," *New York Times*, Apr. 26, 1991, p. B1; from interviews the following day with students either active in the blockade or opposed to it; and from June 1991 phone interview with James Blake, professor of counseling in BMCC's Department of Student Life.

19. After several go-rounds with Governor Cuomo, the legislature finally restored some of the cuts from the Tuition Assistance Program, but ended other programs, like the Regents scholarships. CUNY tuition increased $400 for the next year at the senior colleges (instead of the originally scheduled $500), and $300 for the community colleges. The state's contribution to CUNY's general budget was slashed by $56 million instead of $92 million. Although students won back only a small part of what they'd hoped for, and Albany would levy another $73 million in cuts the following year, I believe the outcome would have been worse without the student efforts. Whatever their immediate success, the questions that they raised remain as urgent as ever.

Figures on cuts and tuition changes from letter from Rita Rodin, CUNY's director of public information, Dec. 3, 1993, and letter from Bill Zwart, office of State Senator Franz Leichter, Mar. 3, 1994. See also the following fact sheets, available from City University of New York, Office of Governmental Relations, Albany, N.Y.: "City University of New York, Historical Funding Analysis: Funding and Funding Changes" and "City University of New York, Historical Funding Analysis: Enrollment and Funding Per FTE." For excellent coverage, from a student perspective, of the heat of the strike and then of its wrap-up, see Eric F. Coppolino, "CCNY Leads CUNY Uprising," *City College of New York Student Leader*, Apr. 1991 (a special *Student Leader* edition), and Eric F. Coppolino, "Tuition Is Up, Financial Aid Is Down, and SUNY/CUNY Budgets Are Cut," *Student Leader News Service*, June 10, 1991.

20. "The Talk of the Town," *The New Yorker*, June 19, 1989.

Twenty-one: Whose history, whose voice?

1. Outlets that praised D'Souza's book ranged from the *New York Review of Books*, *Washington Post*, and *Wall Street Journal*, to *Good Morning America*, *Face the Nation*, *The MacNeil/Lehrer NewsHour*, *Firing Line*, *Crossfire*, and *This Week with David Brinkley*. See C. Vann Woodward,

"Freedom and the Universities," *New York Review of Books*, July 18, 1991; Diane Ravitch, "Illiberal Education," *Wall Street Journal*, Mar. 28, 1991, p. A12; and Elizabeth Fox-Genovese, "Education and Its Discontents," *Washington Post Book World*, Apr. 7, 1991, p. 6.

2. Caleb Nelson, "Harvard's Hollow Core," *The Atlantic*, Sept. 1990.

3. Rosa Ehrenreich, "What Campus Radicals?" *Harper's*, Dec. 1991.

4. John Taylor, "Are You Politically Correct?" *New York* magazine, Jan. 21, 1991.

5. This and following material from D'Souza, *Illiberal Education*, pp. 194–197. For an unmasking of the incident, see Jon Wiener, "What Happened at Harvard," *The Nation*, Sept. 30, 1991, and Ehrenreich, "What Campus Radicals?"

6. Wiener, "What Happened at Harvard." D'Souza also made a point of repeatedly interviewing freshman Afro-American studies majors, asking them esoteric questions designed to reveal their ignorance, then using this to supposedly prove the shallowness of their academic program—although what they did and did not know was at that point wholly the fruit of what they had learned in high school. In a letter in the May 29, 1991, *Chronicle of Higher Education*, headlined "Disputing D'Souza on Political Correctness," educator Scott White explores similar distortions in D'Souza's examples of supposedly harassed professors at Penn and at Michigan. Like Wiener, White called numerous participants in the incidents, collated articles from the respective student papers, and again got sharply different stories and perspectives than those conveyed by D'Souza (also from a phone interview with White, July 1991).

7. William Bennett quoted in Robert Lindsey, "Bennett Says Stanford Was Intimidated Into Changing Course," *New York Times*, Apr. 19, 1988. For a case study of one of columnist John Leo's distortions, see Jon Wiener, "'Rape by Innuendo' at Swarthmore," *The Nation*, Jan. 20, 1992.

8. "The Stanford Mind," *Wall Street Journal* editorial, Dec. 22, 1988, p. A14. See also "Stanford and the Marketplace of Ideas," a letter by Stanford provost James Rosse critiquing the editorial, *Wall Street Journal*, Feb. 24, 1989.

9. Raoul V. Mowatt, "Stanford's Revolution That Wasn't Quite," *Washington Post Educational Review*, Apr. 7, 1991, and reprinted in Aufderheide, *Beyond PC*, p. 129, as "What Revolution at Stanford?" The PC-baiters often cite a Stanford student chant, "Hey, Hey! Ho, Ho! Western Culture's gotta go." D'Souza uses it to lead off his chapter on canonical debates. Roger Kimball uses it in his book *Tenured Radicals*. The chant continues to be recalled by conservative writers more than five years after the events at Stanford. The critics never mention what participants and observers nearly universally understood the words to mean, including many who disagreed with the students' stand. As participating students made clear to me, those who chanted weren't trying to banish everything to do with Western culture from the University's curricula, but questioning and trying to change a particular required course.

Some critics have noted that Jesse Jackson admonished the students against use of the "Western Culture chant." That hasn't stopped PC-baiters from attacking Jackson by association with it, but it raises the question of whether commentators like D'Souza misinterpreted it innocently. As Stanford anthropologist Renato Rosaldo notes, however, Jackson's criticism of the chant was a strategic one. He suggested students change it because it made them vulnerable to precisely the kinds of off-campus media distortions that have occurred. From Renato Rosaldo, phone interview, Aug. 1992, and interview with former Stanford *MECHA* head Alicia Ybarra, Jan. 27, 1991, in Washington, D.C.

10. See Chapter Three, note 10, for full information on Aufderheide's book.

11. Maureen Dowd, "Bush Sees Threat to Flow of Ideas on U.S. Campuses," *New York Times*, May 5, 1991.

12. The epithet "Distort D'Newsa" originated with the campus humor magazine, *The Jack O'Lantern*, then became a standard on campus. From Fasaha M. Traylor, "Controversy on Campus," *Philadelphia Inquirer*, June 30, 1991, p. 2J. Also part of general discussion on D'Souza with Dartmouth religion professor Charles Stinson, based on my June 1992 and Sept. 1993 phone interviews with Stinson, and his follow-up letters of June 12, 1992; Aug. 29, 1992; and Sept. 16, 1993.

13. Resignation of Kemp and continued support of other *Dartmouth Review* board members reported in the Mar. 15, 1982, and June 14, 1982, issues of the *Review*. Buckley, while not a board member, continued as a supporter listed on the masthead, and Simon continued to funnel money to the *Review* through the Olin Foundation. Amount of Olin grant to the *Review* ($150,000), from Teachers for a Democratic Culture. This money went largely to pay the legal expenses of staffers involved in the harassment of black music professor Cole, but nonetheless represented major support of the publication's approach. See Keeney Jones, "Dis Sho' Ain't No Jive, Bro," *Dartmouth Review*, Mar. 15, 1982 (an issue that lists D'Souza as editor-in-chief), and "Our New Advisors," *Dartmouth Review*, June 14, 1982.

14. Information on break-ins at women's writing room and gays being beaten up, see Dinesh D'Souza, "Profiles on Homosexuality at Dartmouth," *Dartmouth Review*, May 18, 1981; "Did We Goof?" *Dartmouth Review*, June 1, 1981; Dave Goldberg, "Review Claims GSA Material Was Provided by Inside Source," *The Dartmouth*, May 26, 1981; and Dudley Clendinen, "Conservative Paper Stirs Dartmouth," *New York Times*, Oct. 13, 1981. Also from June 1992 phone interviews with Stinson (see note 13), Director of Student Activities Stephen Nelson and Reverend Janet Cooper Nelson, associate pastor and campus minister at a local United Church of Christ congregation whose members included numerous faculty. The *Review* claimed they did not steal the Gay Student Alliance letters that they printed, but rather received them from an "undisclosed source." *Nation* columnist David Corn, however, specifically recalls D'Souza bragging about the *Review*'s feat of obtaining them. See David Corn, "Beltway Bandits," *The Nation*, May 13, 1991, and exchange of letters with D'Souza in *The Nation*, July 8, 1991.

15. General information on D'Souza's Dartmouth years from Goldberg, "Review Claims GSA Material"; Clendinen, "Conservative Paper Stirs Dartmouth"; Corn, "Beltway Bandits"; as well as D'Souza's own previously mentioned articles and documentation from Dartmouth College archives.

See also "Liberal Catholicism," *Dartmouth Review*, Feb. 7, 1983; "The Dartmouth Liberation Front," *Dartmouth Review*, Apr. 16, 1984; "Hyde and Don't Seek," *Dartmouth Review*, May 9, 1983; "Apology to Reverend Richard Allen Hyde," *Dartmouth Review*, June 4, 1986; and Dinesh D'Souza, "Biblical Scholarship Defended: McCrae Questions 'Unsophisticated' Interpretations," *National Catholic Register*, Feb. 6, 1983. Information also comes from June 1992 and Sept. 1993 phone interviews with dean James Breedon of the Dartmouth Tucker Foundation as well as Stephen and Janet Cooper Nelson (see note 14) and Charles Stinson (note 12).

16. Description of Hyde's Apr. 1983 talk from Charles Stinson, based both on Stinson's recollection and on notes that Richard Hyde made from Stinson's tape recording (see note 12).

17. Beginning in 1988, the Olin Foundation sponsored American Enterprise Institute fellowships for D'Souza, totalling $30,000 in 1988, $50,000 in 1989, $50,000 in 1990, $98,000 in 1991 (the year *Illiberal Education* was released), $107,000 in 1992, and $109,500 in 1993. They also contributed $20,000 to the Madison Center for Educational Affairs to purchase and distribute copies of D'Souza's book. From phone conversation with Olin Foundation program officer Bill Voegeli, Nov. 29, 1993. To Olin's credit, they were forthcoming and nonevasive in listing their figures.

See also Liz McMillen, "Olin Fund Gives Millions to Conservative Activities in Higher Education," *Chronicle of Higher Education*, Jan. 22, 1992; and Ellen Messer-Davidow, "Manufacturing the Attack on Liberalized Higher Education," *Social Text*, 36 (Summer 1993): 40–80. *Illiberal Education* also benefitted from the support of the more general network of conservative thinktanks and campus-related institutions, not to mention its rave reception by highly credulous major media outlets.

18. D'Souza, *Illiberal Education*, p. 140, and Scott White's conversation with Walter Harrison, University of Michigan executive vice-president. White, "Disputing D'Souza." See also Alice Jardine, "Illiberal Reporting," *Women's Review of Books*, Feb. 1992.

19. Dinesh D'Souza, "In the Name of Academic Freedom, Colleges Should Back Professors Against Students' Demands for 'Correct' Views," *Chronicle of Higher Education*, Apr. 24, 1991, Sec. 2, p. 1.

20. Rigoberta Menchú, *I, Rigoberta Menchú: An Indian Woman in Guatemala* (London: Verso, 1983).

21. This and following quotes from D'Souza, *Illiberal Education*, pp. 71–73.

22. Conservative defenders of the Reagan-Bush policies have argued that the United States did not support the Guatemalan military, since Congress cut off military aid for human rights violations in 1977. But the United States continued to give economic aid throughout the eighties, which the Guatemalan government then funneled back into military efforts to control and coerce peasant communities like Menchú's. They also, according to the Washington-based Council on Hemispheric Affairs, retrofitted for military use a number of U.S. helicopters, sold to them allegedly for civilian use. On Arbenz overthrow, see Eduardo Galeano, *Guatemala: Occupied Country* (New York: Monthly Review Press, 1969). On recent atrocities in Guatemala see John Maslow, *Bird of Life, Bird of Death* (New York: Dell, 1987).

23. Menchú quote on having children from *I, Rigoberta Menchú*, p. 223.

24. Flora Lewis, "Old Rebels Are Training the New Thought Police," *New York Times*, July 12, 1991; Vann Woodward, "Freedom and the Universities." Vann Woodward's acknowledgement that D'Souza had misled him from the reprint of his article in Aufderheide, *Beyond PC*, p. 29.

25. Bellow quote from John Searle, "The Storm Over the University," *New York Review of Books*, Dec. 6, 1990, reprinted in Paul Berman, *Debating PC* (New York: Dell Laurel, 1992), p. 90. David Duke quote from Ros Davidson, "The Politics of Evil," *Image Magazine, San Francisco Examiner*, Mar. 8, 1972.

26. Olin's 1988 report lists grants of $55 million, and $15 million to $20 million in most other years. Wiener, "Dollars for Neocon Scholars." Information on Olin's corporate background from Jacoby, *The Last Intellectuals*, p. 270.

27. These foundations began their focus on the universities with Olin's investment of millions of dollars for endowed chairs and programs in business, law, economics, and social theory, that supported conservative professors, including Allan Bloom. In 1978, key neoconservative Irving Kristol and future Olin head William Simon created the Institute for Educational Affairs (later called the Madison Center). The organization spent a million dollars a year funding and promoting young conservative activists, and helped support sixty conservative campus papers, including Dinesh D'Souza's *Dartmouth Review*. (The million-dollar-a-year figure was as of 1990, and included $330,617 to support the conservative newspapers.) Institutions like the Leadership Institute and the National Journalism Center provided training and placement for young conservative journalists. In 1982, John Jay College government professor Stephen Balch founded the Campus Coalition for Democracy, which would become the National Association of Scholars (NAS)—an organization established to challenge intellectual currents like multiculturalism, feminism, deconstructionism, peace studies, Latin American studies, critical legal studies, and policies like affirmative action. See Sara Diamond, "Endowing the Right-wing Academic Agenda," *CovertAction*, Fall 1991, and Messer-Davidow, "Manufacturing the Attack."

The foundations I've mentioned also supported sympathetic PBS shows like *Firing Line*, *American Interests*, and Milton Friedman's *Free to Choose* series, as well as an array of books, films, conferences, and policy studies. See Josh Daniel, "Uncivil Wars: The Conservative Assault on Public Broadcasting," *The Independent*, Aug./Sept. 1992.

28. Information on Olin, the IEA, and the NAS from Sara Diamond, "The Funding of the NAS," in Aufderheide, *Beyond PC*, p. 89, and Diamond's longer original version, "Readin', Writin' and Repressin'," in *Z Magazine*, Feb. 1991. Sara Diamond, "Notes on Political Correctness," in *Z Magazine*, July/Aug. 1993. See also Jay and Graff, "The Best Ideas," and Pamela Wilson, "Politics on Campus," *Interface*, Spring 1989, available from AFL-CIO Department for Professional Employees, Washington, D.C. Abigail Thernstrom's role in the Guinier nomination from Kathleen Quinn, "Author of Her Own Defeat," *Lingua Franca*, Sept./Oct. 1993.

29. Louis Menand, "Illiberalisms," *The New Yorker*, May 20, 1991, p. 104. Harvard Law School, for instance, did not admit women students until 1950, and Stanford Law School did not graduate its first African-American student until 1968. See also A. Leon Higginbotham, Jr., "An Open Letter to Justice Clarence Thomas from a Federal Judicial Colleague," in Toni Morrison, editor, *Race-ing Justice, En-Gendering Power* (New York: Pantheon Books, 1992).

30. Current racial and sexual figures from Menand, "Illiberalisms," p. 104.

31. Novak cited in Ehrenreich, *Fear of Falling*, p. 149; and Podhoretz cited in the same work, p. 151. See pp. 144–195 of Ehrenreich's book for a more general discussion. Both Ehrenreich and Gouldner, in *The Future of Intellectuals*, stress the liberatory possibilities of intellectual autonomy, as well as the pressures toward moral compromise. They see the "New Class" as a potentially democratic force, as does Michael Harrington, in *Toward a Democratic Left* (New York: Macmillan, 1968).

32. Bloom, *Closing of the American Mind*, pp. 33, 85–86, 332, 382.

33. Hirsch quote from Joseph Berger, "Ibn Batuta and Sitar Challenging Marco Polo and Violin in Schools," *New York Times*, Apr. 12, 1989, p. A1.

34. See Chapter Three, note 10 for bibliographical details.

35. One of the best sympathetic critiques is Barbara Epstein, "'Political Correctness' and Identity Politics," *Socialist Review*, Dec. 1991, reprinted in Aufderheide, *Beyond PC*, p. 148.

36. As I've described, for all the PC-baiters' attacks on new critical methods like deconstructionism, students who make these approaches their central intellectual focus are not usually those most involved in direct political efforts on campus. These efforts are spearheaded primarily by students and faculty who tend to believe more in some intrinsic, at times even traditionalist, principles of an existent moral order, and who challenge institutional choices that violate these principles.

37. At the University of Texas, for instance, a faculty committee decided on "Writing About Difference" as the focus for the introductory writing class. The class examined Federal Court opinions dealing with discrimination in education and employment, and students used them in exercises to develop critical thinking by sorting through the varied perspectives of the plaintiffs, judges, and defendants. Right-wing intellectuals quickly jumped on the proposed course, calling it leftist indoctrination and "a new fascism of the left." Critics in publications ranging from the *New York Times* to *Newsweek* and the *New Republic* accused it of dropping the literary classics, pushing left-wing ideology, and serving as a bashing session on "white male racism." But the course had never taught classic canonical works in any of its previous versions. It dealt with a wide variety of discriminatory claims, not a demonized "white male racism." It had no single political thrust, but rather the varied perspectives of its numerous instructors.

The major book the critics attacked, Paula Rothenberg's *Racism and Sexism: An Integrated Study* (New York: St. Martin's Press, 1988), had been dropped early in the development of the syllabus because it fell outside the prime focus on the court cases, and perhaps because of early attacks on the class. But none of this made the papers, and it continued to be the focal point of the critics in their ultimately successful efforts to cancel the course. When a *New Republic* writer interviewed Rothenberg at length over the phone, he wrote condescendingly that she couldn't name a single book that was so racist and sexist that it should be dropped from the canon. But Rothenberg had specifically refused to suggest that any works should be dropped "on the grounds that transforming the college curriculum was not about banning books." She added that other teachers might effectively use works she personally found objectionable. None of these comments made it to print, however. See Linda Brodkey and Shelli Fowler, "Political Suspects," *Village Voice*, Apr. 23, 1991, reprinted in Aufderheide, *Beyond PC*, p. 113, as "What Happened to English 306." Also Paula Rothenberg, "Critics of Attempts to Democratize the Curriculum Are Waging a Campaign to Misrepresent the Work of Responsible Professors," *Chronicle of Higher Education*, Apr. 10, 1991, B1 and B3, reprinted in Berman, *Debating PC*, cited quote on p. 264.

In another instance, D'Souza writes about University of Washington business major Pete Schaub, who enrolled in an introductory women's studies course and then was asked to leave. In D'Souza's portrait, Schaub was yet another assaulted innocent who rightfully spoke up when a professor called the traditional American family dysfunctional and said lesbians could raise children better. When Schaub asked for the source of these judgments, D'Souza explains, both the teacher and fellow classmates began harassing him.

Like all the other incidents D'Souza cites, it sounds terrible, from the content of the course to the treatment of Schaub. But students who actually took the class told a different story. Schaub was belligerent from the start, they said, baiting fellow students in the course, following undergraduate facilitators to browbeat them, interrupting so constantly that class could not continue, exclaiming "Fuck you, bitch," to a female student he was arguing with, and physically threatening other fellow students. Schaub's description of the course's content, they said, was grossly distorted.

Schaub continued his baiting at a public rally, calling women in the class "whiny little babies," telling one, "You can borrow my shaver if you need to shave," and responding to accusations of sexual harassment by saying, "Why would I harass any of *you*? My God, that's sick." His story seemed to me far more like the *Dartmouth Review*'s successful harassment of African-American music professor William Cole than like a genuine attempt to get an education. From University of Washington *Daily* articles including Paula Reynolds, "Rally Defends Women, Ethnic Studies," Apr. 4, 1988; Paula Reynolds, "Schaub v. Women 200: The Skirmish Persists," Mar. 31, 1988; Pete Schaub, "Pete Schaub Speaks Out on Women Studies 200," Apr. 12, 1988; Paula Reynolds, "Under the Glaring Lights of the Media," Apr. 12, 1988; and Sally J. Clark "Making It Big: Schaub Reaps Benefits of Conflict," Apr. 29, 1988. I also discussed the Schaub case with women's studies graduate student Karen Stoldrier and women's studies professor Nancy Hartsock in June 1991, and with *Seattle Times* education reporter Sally Macdonald in Nov. 1993.

38. Ehrenreich, "What Campus Radicals?"

39. In terms of the percentage of minority faculty with tenure, the overall rate rose negligibly from 1979 to 1989, from 60.3 percent to 60.7 percent. For whites, it increased from 68.9 percent to 71.9 percent. Women also fell behind men 59.2 percent to 74.9 percent, a gap which has stayed consistent over time. See Carter and Wilson, *Minorities in Higher Education*, pp. 31, 63, 64. See also "Few Colleges Have Had 'Political Correctness' Controversies, Study Finds," *Chronicle of Higher Education*, Aug. 7, 1991, p. A23. As of Dec. 1993, the ACE had not released a later major status report, but Deborah Carter, assistant director of the ACE's Office of Minorities in Higher Education said, in response to my phone query, that the proportions had stayed roughly the same.

According to an ACE study, women are also concentrated "overwhelmingly" in the lower academic ranks. As of 1991, women held 15 percent of full professorships, 28 percent of associate professorships, 40 percent of assistant professorships, and 46 percent of instructor and lecturer positions. Women of color held only 2 percent of full-time faculty positions. While 75 percent of full-time men were tenured, just 58 percent of women were. Women also earned less than men of comparable status at every step of the academic ladder. From "Women Post Gains in Higher Education But Still Lag on Many Indicators," *ACE News*, press release dated June 4, 1993, American Council on Education, Washington, D.C. Release describes the study of Cecilia Ottinger and Robin Sikula, *Women in Higher Education: Where Do We Stand?* (Washington, D.C.: American Council on Education, 1993).

40. On the political views of faculty, a 1989–90 national study conducted by UCLA's Higher Education Research Institute found 4.9 percent of faculty called themselves far left, 36.8 percent liberal, 40.2 percent moderate, 17.8 percent conservative, and 0.4 percent far right. From "Attitudes and Activities of Full-Time Faculty Members," *Chronicle of Higher Education*, Aug. 26, 1992, p. 30.

41. Susan Dodge, "Campus Codes That Ban Hate Speech Are Rarely Used to Penalize Students," *Chronicle of Higher Education*, Feb. 12, 1992, p. A35.

42. On academic disciplines and social issues, see references in Chapter Nine to Jacoby, McCaughey, Ricci, and Wilner.

43. *Chronicle of Higher Education*, "Few Colleges Have Had 'Political Correctness' Controversies," Aug. 7, 1991.

44. James J. Kilpatrick's "decline of the West" statement from his syndicated column, James L. Kilpatrick, "Colleges Paying Price for Appeasing Leftists," *St. Louis Post Dispatch*, Nov. 20, 1990, editorial page 3b. His quote from 1960 debate with King, cited by Jeff Cohen and Norman Solomon in "Media 'Balance' Aids GOP Gay Bashing," *Seattle Times*, Aug. 22, 1992.

45. Two years after the initial PC-baiting wave, Princeton graduate student Katie Roiphe weighed in with her own attacks on campus feminism, ridiculing women concerned about issues like date rape as neo-Victorians eager to play the role of victim. She cited conservative Berkeley social welfare professor Neal Gilbert's attack on the National Institutes of Mental Health–funded study by psychologist Mary Koss, who was then at Ohio's Kent State University and now at the University of Arizona medical school. As a woman who herself claimed to be a feminist, yet attacked just about all existing campus feminist activity, Roiphe got an instant media podium, including a *New York Times Magazine* cover story and a largely sympathetic front page *New York Times* review for her book, *The Morning After: Sex, Fear and Feminism on Campus* (Boston: Little, Brown, 1993). See Katie Roiphe, "Date Rape's Other Victim," *New York Times Magazine*, June 13, 1993, p. 26. And Wendy Kaminer, "What Is This Thing Called Rape?" review of *The Morning After* in the *New York Times Book Review*, Sept. 19, 1993, p. 1.

But as Paula Kamen writes, Roiphe picked up Gilbert's miscasting of the Koss study verbatim, without ever bothering either to talk with Koss, or—given that Roiphe's footnotes never cite the

Koss survey directly, but only Gilbert's articles attacking it—very likely without ever even reading the actual study. Gilbert, Roiphe's prime source, had neither done direct research on rape and its prevalence nor published anything on the subject until he began his attacks. Nonetheless, Roiphe used his arguments to jump on Koss's widely cited finding that 28 percent of female college students had at some point been the victims of rape or attempted rape, and to suggest Koss had now stretched the definition of rape "beyond bruises and knives, threats of death or violence, to include emotional pressure and the influence of alcohol." Roiphe then singled out the category of "emotional pressure" to suggest that campus feminists encouraged women to refuse to take responsibility for their actions. But as Kamen pointed out, Koss never included "emotional pressure" in her definitions, all of which were taken not from "campus feminists" but from an Ohio penal code, which included a category for having sex with someone who you've gotten so drunk or so high—as in fraternity parties with grain alcohol–spiked punch—they cannot meaningfully consent. When Koss used this definition to determine that 15 percent of the women had been raped and 28 percent had experienced attempted rape, her numbers rang consistent with subsequent studies nationwide.

Roiphe's other main point, as Kamen pointed out, was that 73 percent of the women identified by Koss as having been raped do not identify themselves as such. "These are not self-proclaimed victims, then," Roiphe writes, "they are victims according to someone else." But the Koss survey was conducted before the more generalized awareness of date rape that it helped trigger. Numerous respondents simply did not know that their experiences with men they had initially considered acquaintances or friends fit the legal categories. Of the 15 percent who described to the surveyors incidents legally defined as rape (whether or not they used the term or had reported the instances to the police), 30 percent considered suicide afterward, 31 percent sought help from a therapist, and 82 percent reported being changed by the experience. Paula Kamen, "Erasing Rape," *Extra*, Nov./Dec. 1993.

46. Even organizations in charge of professors' rights refused to challenge the witch-hunts, explaining, in the words of American Association of University Professors founding secretary Arthur Lovejoy, that members of the Communist party were "engaged in a movement which has already extinguished academic freedom in many countries and would—if it were successful here—result in the abolition of such freedom in American universities. No one, therefore, who desires to maintain academic freedom in America can consistently favor that movement or give indirect assistance to it by accepting as fit members of the faculties of universities, persons who have voluntarily adhered to an organization, one of whose aims is to abolish academic freedom." Buckley cited in Jacoby, *Last Intellectuals*, pp. 203–204, 207. Hook quote from Schrecker, *No Ivory Tower*, pp. 105–110. Lovejoy quote from Schrecker, p. 106.

47. Bloom, *Closing of the American Mind*, p. 324.

48. Dinesh D'Souza, "The Visigoths in Tweed," *Forbes*, Apr. 1, 1991. Figures on annual income and net worth of *Forbes* readers from *Forbes* advertising department, Sept. 10, 1993.

49. In note 37, I've described the withdrawal of a new and innovative University of Texas freshman writing program. At the University of Washington, a series of racial incidents prompted three years of task forces, committees, negotiations, and the eventual proposal that a one-quarter ethnic studies requirement be instituted. The faculty senate passed this requirement in the spring of 1991, then reconsidered after the barrage of "PC" attacks in the media, and finally sent it to the entire faculty, who voted it down by a more than two-to-one margin.

50. Henry Louis Gates, "Whose Canon Is It Anyway?" reprinted in Berman, *Debating PC*, pp. 192–193, 196–197.

51. See Peggy McIntosh, *White Privilege and Male Privilege*, Working paper no. 189, Wellesley College Center for Research on Women, Wellesley, Mass., 1988, p. 11.

52. Irving Howe, "The Value of the Canon," *The New Republic*, Feb. 18, 1991, reprinted in Berman, *Debating PC*, pp. 156–157.

53. Berman, *Debating PC*, p. 157.

54. Cornel West, "Diverse New World," *Democratic Left*, July/Aug. 1991, reprinted in Berman, *Debating PC*, p. 328.

55. Berman, *Debating PC*, p. 328.

56. Gerald Graff and William Cain, "Peace Plan for the Canon Wars," *The Nation*, Mar. 6,

1989. For a more general discussion of this approach, see Gerald Graff, *Beyond the Culture Wars* (New York: Norton, 1992).

57. Issues of faculty arrogance seemed at the heart of similar examples D'Souza cites at the University of Pennsylvania and University of Michigan. See Scott White, "Disputing D'Souza." Comment on Thernstrom from Dick Flacks, phone conversation, June 1992.

58. Ehrlich, *Ethnoviolence and the Policy Options*, and Wiener, "Racial Hatred on Campus."

59. Ehrlich, *Ethnoviolence and the Policy Options*, pp. 55, 63, 68; Ehrlich, *A Research Review*, pp. 8, 13; North Dakota example from conversation with North Dakota peace studies coordinator Kristin Sorensen, Apr. 27, 1992.

60. Tufts example from Christopher C. Blanker, "Tufts Students Oppose Rules Against Racist Speech," *National Student News Service*, Oct. 12, 1989. See also Jon Wiener, "Free Speech for Campus Bigots," *The Nation*, Feb. 26, 1990.

61. Columbia story from former women's center head Nichole Hyland, interviewed at Columbia, Apr. 1988.

62. "Students Attack Fraternity Flyer as Sexist," *National Student News Service*, Oct. 24, 1991.

63. Joseph Epstein example cited in Joel Conarroe, "How I'm PC," *New York Times*, July 12, 1991, p. A20.

64. David Mura, "Strangers in the Village," in *Multicultural Literacy*, edited by Rick Simonson and Scott Walker (Minneapolis: Graywolf Press, 1988), p. 147.

65. See Lillian Rubin, *Families on the Fault Line* (New York: HarperCollins, 1994), p. xiv. On the level of recent immigration, Rubin writes that 2.5 million immigrants from Asian countries were admitted to the United States during the decade of the 1980s, compared to less than half a million during the 1960s. Close to three-quarters of a million documented Mexicans crossed the border in 1990, compared to less than half a million during all of the 1960s. The 1980s brought more than a million immigrants from Central America and the Caribbean. The percentage of immigrants in the U.S. population is less today—6.2 percent—than in 1920, when they were 13.2 percent of all U.S. residents, but because most are people of color, they are far more visible. See Rubin, *Families on the Fault Line*, p. 181.

66. As of 1989, the top 1 percent of the population controlled 50.3 percent of net financial assets. From Jared Bernstein interview, see Chapter Five, note 14.

67. See D'Souza, *Illiberal Education*, p. 252.

68. On male socialization toward violence, see Miedzian, *Boys Will Be Boys*.

69. Greg Ricks, phone conversation, July 1990.

70. Ray Davis, "Anti-Racist Organizing, Then and Now," *Socialist Review*, Oct.-Dec. 1990, p. 32.

71. Troy Duster, "They're Taking Over! And Other Myths about Race on Campus," reprinted in Aufderheide, *Beyond PC*, p. 182.

72. In the case of USSA, the organization began in the mid-seventies to work out a succession of affirmative action guidelines for students who attended their annual conventions. College delegations would still be based on campus size, and small schools could send whomever they wanted, but the larger colleges, with their bigger delegations, had to include both specific numbers of women and students of color. The organization later refined the guidelines to encourage participation of other traditionally marginal groups, like gays, disabled students, and veterans.

USSA leaders themselves made clear their approach could hardly be exported as a universal model, but was highly specific to their situation, working to represent the breadth of American students. Yet from what I could tell, the system worked. In 1984, USSA elected its first African-American president, and in 1990 its second, Julius Davis, the Buffalo student who'd been headed for jail and the streets until he heard the Malcolm X record. Fred Azcarate became its first Asian-American president. Rutgers student Tajel Shah, whose parents emigrated from India, was the first woman of color to serve as a USSA officer, and later served as president as well. These students came from state universities, not Harvard or Yale. Few of them came from families with money, and many of their parents had not even graduated high school. Owing to their life experiences, they felt close to the majority of students—who are constantly struggling to get through—and they were as effective as anyone I've seen at creating a milieu where students of all backgrounds felt accepted.

I've described the new initiatives of COOL. In SEAC's case, continuing discussion of the need to broaden their racial and cultural base led to a new structure where half the national board members and half of those on key committees had to be students of color. If this did not occur by the normal voting process, the People of Color Caucus would fill additional seats to balance things out.

Twenty-two: Sustaining the vision

1. Totals for generational size from "High School Graduates Compared with Population 17 Years of Age," in *Digest of Educational Statistics, 1993* (Washington, D.C.: GPO, 1993), p. 108, Table 98. It's difficult to get precise figures for the percentages of a given age cohort attending college, since students can enter at any point in their lives. But analyst Robert Kominski, of the Education and Social Stratification Branch, Population Division, of the U.S. Bureau of the Census, suggests we can use the figures for students who've been out of high school long enough that most of those who will go back to college have already done so. Those who were eighteen in 1980 have, for instance, been surveyed fourteen years later, at which point, 11.3 million out of 22.3 million had completed one or more years of college, representing a shade over 50 percent. From the figures generated through the eighties, Kominski believes this percentage has stayed relatively consistent, and is a reasonable estimate for the share of the generation who've at least briefly attended college. From phone interview with Robert Kominski, Mar. 15, 1994.

2. Whalen and Flacks, *Beyond the Barricades*; McAdam, *Freedom Summer*, Kessler, *After All These Years*; McPherson, *Long Time Passing*; Jennings and Niemi, *Generations and Politics*.

3. Farm activists said Farmland played a mixed role in agricultural politics, offering some lower prices for small family farmers, but also putting its financial clout behind legislation that worsened their situation in favor of the large grain interests. Phone conversation with Julia Kleinschmit, Oct. 1993.

4. The voting turnout of eighteen- to twenty-four-year-olds was 42 percent in 1972, dropped to 29 percent in 1988, and then returned to 37 percent in 1992. Figures from Sept. 1993 phone interview with Curtis Gans, Committee for the Study of the American Electorate, Washington, D.C.

5. In 1984, voters aged eighteen to twenty-nine went Republican by a 59 to 40 percent margin, and by 52 to 47 in 1988. Full-time students gave Reagan a 52 to 47 percent lead over Mondale and backed Dukakis 54 to 44. In 1992, young men in general gave Perot his highest age-bracket support of 26 percent, compared to 19 percent of young women. Among young women, Clinton led Bush by a 48 to 33 margin, compared to a 38 to 36 split among young men. From *New York Times*, "Portrait of the Electorate."

6. In President Clinton's proposed 1994 fiscal year budget, military spending continues to account for 26 percent of total general federal allocations, excluding monies from specifically designated trust funds, like Social Security. The military component includes allocations for the Department of Defense, the atomic weapons programs of the Department of Energy, foreign military aid, and other military-related independent agencies. Another 19.3 percent goes to the cost of past military efforts, including veterans' benefits and interest on the nearly 60 percent of the federal debt accountable to past military spending—from Lyndon Johnson's Vietnam-era deficits to the debt-financed buildups of the Reagan era. The combined military-related share is 45.3 percent. From Friends Committee on National Legislation, *Analysis of the Federal Budget* (Washington, D.C.: Friends Committee on National Legislation, July 1993), Table 2.1 and chart titled "The Federal Budget Pie"; and *FCNL Washington Newsletter*, Apr. 1993. In terms of discretionary spending, excluding mandatory pensions and entitlements, 51 percent of the 1994 budget goes to current military spending. From *Economic and Budget Outlook: An Update* (Washington, D.C.: Defense Budget Project, Sept. 1993).

7. Harry Boyte, "The Pragmatic Ends of Popular Politics," in Craig Calhoun, ed., *Habermas in the Public Sphere* (Cambridge, Mass.: MIT Press, 1992), p. 352.

8. See Michael Harrington, *Socialism Past and Future* (New York: Arcade, 1989), pp. 248–278.

9. Philosopher Richard Rorty suggests the best way to promote human solidarity is not through trying to articulate the universal bonds that tie us all together, but by telling highly specific stories about human suffering. And by expanding "our sense of 'us' as far as we can," so we can't simply write off those who are different. See Richard Rorty, *Contingency, Irony, and Solidarity* (Princeton: Princeton University Press, 1989), pp. 189–198.

10. Havel quoted in Richard Rorty, "For a More Banal Politics," *Harper's*, May 1992, p. 16. Flacks story in conversation, Dec. 1990.

Acknowledgments

Books that take seven years don't get written without help—lots of it in my case. Students opened up their lives to me, voicing stories, thoughts, and hopes. Faculty hashed out ideas and offered perspectives. An array of individuals and institutions provided intellectual brainstorming, financial support, emotional sustenance, places to stay, and a wealth of other kinds of assistance. Thank you Architects of Travel, Ark Foundation, Harriet Barlow, Ann Bartley, Michael and Corie Benedetto, Laurel Blossom, Dick Boone, Harry Boyte, Beth Brent, Betty and Charles Brink, Leslie Brockelbank, Craig Brown, Lucille Bullert, Blanche Cashman, Laura and Richard Chasin, Craig Comstock, Cook Brothers Educational Fund, Gloria Cooper, Eric Coppolino, David Crowe, Sam Day, Lenny Dee, John Deklewa, Gary Dreiblatt and Nancy Sinkoff, Jim Driscoll, Larry Egbert, Jane Ellis, Wendy Emrich, Marge Fasman, Gordon Fellman, Gary Ferdman, Ellen Ferguson, Carol and Ping Ferry, The Flow Fund, Nancy Friedhoff, Jorge Garcia and Barbara Schinzinger, Lane Gerber, Ian Gilbert, Adrienne Hall, Nora Hallett, Harburg Foundation, Frances Close Hart, Jane Hatfield, The Edward Hazen Foundation, Richard Healey, Wray Herbert, Bill Hess, IACS Foundation, Hylah Jacques, Jennifer Jett, Lisa Kahane, Anis and Julie Karam, Alan Kay, Corrine Dee Kelly, Kristine Knutson, Pete Knutson and Hing Lau Ng, Kongsgaard-Goldman Foundation, Jenny Ladd, Beth Lamont, Norman Lear, Joel Levin, Rodney Loeb and Carol Summer, Kelle Louallier, McKenzie River Gathering, Shirley Magidson, Gertrude Marshall, Dick Mayo Smith, Dorothy Morrell, Ken Mountcastle, Josephine Murray, Jeffrey Newell, Joan Palevsky, Bill Patz, Don Pennell, Jennifer Perry, Dan Petegorsky, Puffin Foundation, Alan and Andrea Rabinowitz,

Bernard Rapoport, Rick Rapport and Valerie Trueblood Rapport, Denise Rose and Larry Spivack, Kathy and Don Rouzie, Samuel Rubin Foundation, Ruth and Jacques Sartisky Foundation, Leonard Schroeter, Florence and John Schumann Foundation, Stanley Sheinbaum, John and Janet McKee Silard, Paul and Ann Sperry, Florence Sponberg, Jerry Starr, Karen Starr, Evan Stover and the late Nancy Stover, Kate Thompson for designing a terrific cover, Tides Foundation Pequod and Small Grants Funds, Peter Titcomb, Bill Vandercook and Betsy Elich Vandercook, Lisa von Mettenheim and the late Jack von Mettenheim, Magda and Fred Waingrow, Jerry Wald and Sondra Kaplan, Joan Warburg, Marion Weber, Bert Weeks, John Weeks and Jeana Kimball, Cora Weiss, David Williams, Ron and Jaki Williams, Heidi Wills, Blaikie and Bob Worth, Robert Zevin, and Katy Zimmerman.

Though my research is primarily qualitative, thanks for continuing statistical surveys of student life to Alexander Astin, William Korn, Ellyne Riggs, and their colleagues at UCLA's Cooperative Institutional Research Program, and to Jerald Bachman and his colleagues at University of Michigan's Institute for Social Research. Thanks to Tom Mortenson and his excellent journal *Postsecondary Education Opportunity* (P.O. Box 127, Iowa City, Iowa 52244), for steering me through American higher education's growing class divides. To the Times Mirror Center for the People and the Press for their continuing studies of contemporary American values, Jared Bernstein of the Economic Policy Institute for studies of recent economic shifts, Larry Birns of the Council on Hemispheric Affairs for Latin America fact-checks, Howard Ehrlich of the National Institute Against Prejudice for campus racial politics, Gerald Graff and John Wilson of Teachers for a Democratic Culture for the debates surrounding "political correctness," and Jeff Cohen and Norman Solomon of FAIR for media politics. Pete Knutson helped me recall our shared history as Stanford anti-war activists with his tape *Hell No We Won't Go! Vietnam at Home* (text by Peter Knutson, music by David Hahn, distributed by Bookpeople, Berkeley California, 1992). National Student News Service has helped me trace student involvement throughout the country. They can be reached at 116 New Montgomery Street, Suite 530, San Francisco, California 94105. The staff of the Seattle Public Library and University of Washington's Suzzalo Library helped tremendously with my fact-checking. Jack Litewka and the Kinesis ergonomic keyboard saved my wrists halfway through the project. My conversations with University of California Santa Barbara sociologist Dick Flacks have been invaluable in sorting out the complex currents of youth and social change.

Thanks to all the organizations that represent the core of contemporary student activism, and go beyond the media hype. They include SEAC, COOL, University

Conversion Project, Progressive Student Network, USSA, DC-SCAR, Student Action Union, and Save Our Students. They didn't all make it into the book, but their efforts have helped shift American campuses toward greater social concern.

Thanks for providing an institutional base to the Institute for Global Security Studies and its director Charles Meconis, and to the Church Council of Greater Seattle and its staffers Joy Estil and Alice Woldt. Thanks to Abby Brown and Public Relations Services for getting me on more radio and TV shows than I could possibly imagine. Thanks to my Seattle local of the National Writer's Union, a source of friendship, business acumen, mutual aid, and a grounding in why we do this work to begin with. And to my Rutgers support group of Marilyn Campbell, Steve Maikowski, Beth Apone Salamon, Bonnie Kaplan, Arlene Bacher, Kate Harrie, Tricia Politi, and Leslie Mitchner, as well as Kate Fuller for her meticulous copy-editing. This book has also benefited from comments made by Lisa Peattie, David Gerwin, Frances Fox Piven, Glenn Pascall, Sonya Tinsley, and Wayne Grytting.

Finally, six individuals helped sustain this project through its most difficult moments, and to its ultimate fruition. My agent Jonathan Dolger kept insisting *Generation at the Crossroads* was worthwhile even when it seemed the book would never see the light of day. Liz Gjelten tamed and helped organize a first draft that approached the size of a major market telephone directory. Priscilla Long worked each phrase and each line to make sure it read with clarity and grace. Ed Dobb brainstormed on everything from basic structural questions to philosophical concepts and magazine serializations. Former Rutgers Press director Ken Arnold bought the book with a commitment solid enough to give it a real chance in the marketplace, edited it down to its final version, and was a delight to work with at every stage. Finally, my wife, Bette Jean Bullert, endured each moment of a process that turned out to take seven years. Thanks, B.J., for helping me stay human.

Index

Brown, Lester, 250

Brown University, 97, 161; CIA recruitment at, 128; and environmental issues, 253; racial incidents at, 180, 181, 191, 349, 359; research expenditures at, 407n9

BSA. *See* Black Student Association

Buchanan, Pat, 338, 405n11

Buckley, William F., 337–338, 344, 351–352, 405n11

Bullard, Carol, 286, 287–288, 350, 392; on City College factionalism, 295, 362; and collapse of the blockade, 316, 318–320; family influences on, 293; and President LeClerc, 303, 321–322; post-graduation activism of, 381

Bulletin of the Atomic Scientists, 414n10

Bush, George, 111, 337; and the Persian Gulf War, 266, 267, 268, 272, 278, 376; young voters for, 377–379, 436n5; youth vote for, 112, 415n6. *See also* Reagan-Bush administrations

Bush, Neil, 426n18

business ethics courses, 93

business majors, 54, 91, 92–93, 264–265, 490n23

Byrd, Alex, 242

Cain, William, 356

California, University of, divestment by, 417n13

California, University of (Berkeley), 173, 264, 266, 354; Free Speech Movement at, 174, 359, 397

California, University of (Irvine), 334, 419n3

California, University of (Los Angeles), 99, 254, 272

California, University of (Santa Barbara), 78, 88, 266, 271, 357

California, University of (Santa Cruz), 271, 272

California State University (Los Angeles), 66

Cambodia, 80

Campus Coalition for Democracy, 431n27

Campus Compact, 245, 422n1

Campus Green, 251

Campus Jewish Organization (CJO), 227

Campus Opportunity Outreach League (COOL), 104, 218, 264, 381; and corporate grants, 244–245; history of, 232–233; and political action, 236, 239, 243–244; and racial diversity, 242, 366

Capps, Walter, 88

Cardenas, Francisco (pseud.), 239–241, 390

career choices, ethical, 109–110

Cargill, 21, 25, 136

Carleton College, 236

Carter, Jimmy, 112, 170, 171, 373

Catalano, Jill, 105–107, 376, 378

Center for Media and Public Affairs, 343

Central America, U.S. intervention in, 14, 158, 159–160, 171, 376, 430–431n22; and Greeks for Peace, 145–146, 147, 151, 154–155

Central Intelligence Agency (CIA), 33, 68, 108, 341, 410n1; recruitment by, 128, 146, 384

Central Washington University, 107

CETA. *See* Comprehensive Employment and Training Act

CFSA. *See* Coalition for a Free South Africa

CHA. *See* Chicago Housing Authority

Chain Reaction (Edsall and Edsall), 112

character differences, 38

"Charlie Girl," 217

Chavez, Cesar, 67, 161

Chavez, Linda, 343

Cheney, Lynne, 332

Chicago, University of, 90, 98, 260, 374–375

Chicago Circle. *See* Illinois, University of (Chicago)

Chicago Housing Authority (CHA), 56, 57

Chicago Sun-Times, 78

Children's Defense Fund, 381

Chile, 33, 68, 101, 410n1

Choices (Emory women's organization), 193

Chomsky, Noam, 219

Chronicle of Higher Education, 336

churches. *See* religion

CIA. *See* Central Intelligence Agency

Cincinnati, University of, 271

Citizen Action, 210, 381

City College of New York, 45, 287, 292, 295. *See also* City University of New York strikes

City Kids, 290–291

City University of New York, 157, 353, 381, 389, 390, 393; activist tradition at, 292–293; budget cuts, 287, 288, 292; and City College architecture department, 299–300; divestment by, 417n13; history of, 291; minority students at, 426n2; and open admissions, 291, 292; restrictions on student political activity at, 427n9; student attrition at, 427n5; students' family income, 287, 288–289; tuition, 428n19. *See also* City University of New York strikes

City University of New York strikes, 157, 365; accomplishments of, 329–330; and administrators, 303–305; April 24 rally, 313–315; and BMCC nursing students, 315–316; as bridge across differences, 307–309; and City College factionalism, 320–321, 323–327; collapse of the blockades, 317–320; and Day Student Government, 310–311; and debate over open admissions, 305–307; and faculty, 303; family and community support for, 302–303; and Hunter College supporters outside the blockade, 327–329; and labor-community

City University of New York strikes (*continued*)
coalition, 301–302, 326–327; post-graduation activities of participants, 381, 389, 390, 393; President LeClerc's refusal to negotiate, 321–322; and sense of larger purpose, 309; and state and national economic issues, 311–313; student critics of, 296–297; student support for, 295–296; and tuition hikes, 286–289. *See also* Bullard, Carol; De Palma, Mark; Rodriguez, José; Ruiz, Nilda

civil disobedience, 373

civil rights movement, 42, 73, 75, 121, 196, 282

CJO. *See* Campus Jewish Organization

Clarkson University, 37, 54, 103

CLAS. *See* Confederation of Latin American Students

class inequality, 38, 65, 116–117, 362–364; and education level, 45–46, 406n6; and income, 47, 49. *See also* poor and working-class students

Cleaver, Eldridge, 81

Cleveland State University, 264

Clinton, Bill, 82; student support for, 377, 378, 379, 436n5; women's support for, 422n3

Clinton, Hillary, 82

Clinton administration, 233, 436n6

Closing of the American Mind, The (Bloom), 345–346, 412n7

CNN, 71

Coalition for a Free South Africa (CFSA), 171, 172, 173

Coalition on Hunger and Homelessness, 187

Cobb, Jonathan, 63

Cohen, Leonard, 28

Colby College, 74, 108, 189, 207, 361

cold war, end of, 261

Cole, William, 335

Coleman, Marvin, 210, 211, 213, 219, 225; dorm conflicts and, 184–185; family background of, 178; on Louis Farrakhan, 196; on multicultural education, 195–196; and Sondra O'Neale protests, 179; post-graduation career, 387–389; and SARI, 181, 183–184, 198; video project of, 177–178

Colgate University, 115, 220, 222

college costs, 73, 405n3, 407nn8, 9. *See also* City University of New York strikes

Collegiate Network, 405n11

Collier, Peter, 343

Colorado, University of, 128, 259, 269, 271, 274, 276, 395

Columbia antiapartheid movement, 15, 74, 171–173, 225, 227, 234; administration reaction to, 172, 204; decorum of, 230; and Per-

fect Standard, 36, 37; as source of hope, 397, 398

Columbia University, 38, 46, 64, 84–85, 246; activists' reactions to sexual harassment and fraternities, 224; business courses at, 92; and CIA recruitment, 128; Steve Galpern, 234–236; David Gerwin, 227–230, 389–390, 395, 396, 398; linkage of issues at, 395; 1968 student sit-in, 174; 1988 movement against the rules changes, 228; and Persian Gulf War, 274; and political correctness, 355, 360; program cutbacks at, 47; students' attitudes toward "working from within," 107, 108; students' detachment at, 94–96; students' post-graduation activities, 374, 388, 389; and U.S.-backed attacks on Nicaragua, 222–224, 225. *See also* Columbia antiapartheid movement

Coming of Age in New Jersey (Moffatt), 189–190

Commentary, 343, 345

Committee on Media Integrity, 343

communism, failure of, 393

communities of concern, 370–371, 390–391; as different from ordinary friendship, 208–211; and feminism, 216–218; and frustration with political detachment, 207–208; and gay and lesbian students, 218; and insularity, 221–225; and intellectual and cultural ties, 218–220; international, 278; and men students, 211–216; and older activists, 220–221; and ties to larger community, 227–230

Community Impact, 234, 235, 246

community organizing, 138–139

community service movement, 128, 266; as alternative approach to social change, 231–236; compared with earlier movements, 236; employment in, 381–382; and goal of inclusion, 244–247, 365; and middle-class paternalism, 241–242; as part of college curriculum, 244; and personal risk, 238; and poor and working-class students, 239–241; and racial diversity, 242; relationship to political advocacy, 233, 234, 237–239, 243–244, 245; role models for, 233, 234, 236; as way to avoid political controversy, 236–237

Comprehensive Employment and Training Act (CETA), 57

computer networks, 180

computer scientists, 91

ConAgra, 21, 24, 137

Concerned Young Scientists, 124

Confederation of Latin American Students (CLAS), 56, 58, 60, 383, 384, 385

United Farm Workers, 161

United Nations International Bill of Human Rights, 391–392

United States Student Association (USSA), 143, 166, 171, 197, 209, 218, 381, 393; group and constituency representation in, 366, 435–436n72; and 1992 election, 377; organizing workshops by, 159; and Persian Gulf War, 266, 269, 279

upward mobility, 63

urban folklore, 78

U.S. Out, 269

USSA. *See* United States Student Association

USUHS. *See* Uniformed Services University of the Health Sciences

Utah, University of, 407n9

value-neutral teaching, 102

vegetarianism, 423n5

Vermont, University of, 128

videos, 256

Vietnam-era activists, 42, 85–87, 263, 276, 412n7, 424–425n11; children of, as activists, 87–88, 280–283, 284–285; and generational continuities, 367, 368; and later retreat from activism, 169–170, 283–284; Paul Loeb's experiences as, 167, 168–169, 174, 285; and the "sellout" myth, 80–83, 102–103; and the "spitting on soldiers" myth, 77–80, 273. *See also* sixties, the

Vietnam Veterans Against the War, 79

Vietnam War, 90–91, 411–412n5; ignorance regarding, 425n14

Vigna, Paul, 11, 12, 16, 213–214, 372

Village Voice, 323

Vincent, Rick (pseud.), 11, 122–123, 372

visionary gradualism, 395

visions, sustaining, 391–393

voter registration, 377

wages, hourly, decline in, 49

Wagner, Lee, 22, 135, 136, 213, 397; post-graduation activities of, 386–387

Walesa, Lech, 105

Walker, Alice, 82, 219

Wall Street, 372

Wall Street Journal, 269, 336, 342

Washington, George, 105

Washington, Harold, 113

Washington, University of, 39, 81, 101, 125, 161, 210, 215, 373; committed faculty at, 164; electoral politics at, 111, 113; environmentalism at, 254, 255–257; labor studies at, 67; during

McCarthy era, 424n9; and the Persian Gulf War, 89, 268–272, 274, 279; and political correctness, 350, 353, 358, 432n37; racial incidents at, 189, 358, 419n3, 434n49; research expenditures at, 407n9

Washington State University, 279

Washington Times, 337

Washington University, 47

Webster vs. Missouri, 74

Weiner, Jon, 334

Wellesley College, 354, 356

Wellstone, Paul, 82, 113, 236

West, Cornel, 355

West Chester University, 100

Western Michigan University, 81, 103, 104, 218

Western Washington University, 268, 271, 272

Westinghouse Electric Corporation, 108, 114

West Virginia University, 78, 88

Wharton School, 92

When Dreams and Heroes Died (Levine), 170

Whittle Corporation, 381

Who Will Tell the People? (Greider), 112

Why Americans Hate Politics (Dionne), 112

Williams, Walter, 338

Williams, William Appleman, 224

Williams College, 34, 94, 109, 119, 226, 251, 284

Wills, Heidi, 255, 394; and the Persian Gulf War, 89, 268–271, 272, 275, 276; and recycling projects, 256–257, 350

Wilner, Patricia, 90

Wisconsin, University of, 46, 65, 269; divestment by, 417n13; racial incidents at, 191

Wolf, Maura, 237, 246

women: on faculty, 348, 433n39; income of, 47, 422n5

women's studies courses, 422n5, 432n37

women's suffrage, 397

women students, 409n23; and abusive language, 360; and early 1970s feminism, 74; in law school, 431n29; and the Persian Gulf War, 279; relative liberalism of, 211–212, 214, 216, 265, 364, 421n2, 421–422n3, 422n6; reluctance to state opinions, 65–66, 410n9; and ROTC, 105–106; in USSA, 435–436n72

Women's Ways of Knowing (Belenky), 65

Woods, Brian, 192, 197, 364

Woodson, Carter, 166, 219

Woodward, C. Vann, 337, 342

work ethic, 296–297

working from within, 114; and ethical career choices, 109–110; and military service, 105–107; as rhetoric of deferred involvement, 107–109, 110–111

Wretched of the Earth (Fanon), 335

Xavier University, 242

Yale University, 104, 170, 171, 234, 342, 358;
   racial incidents at, 180
YMCA, 244, 247
Yoshitani, Miya, 221, 259, 260

Young Republicans, 258–259
Youth Action. *See* United States Student
   Association
YWCA, 244

Z Magazine, 71, 279

About the Author

Paul Rogat Loeb is the author of *Nuclear Culture: Living and Working in the World's Largest Atomic Complex*, and *Hope in Hard Times: America's Peace Movement and the Reagan Era*. He was born in Berkeley, California, in 1952, and attended Stanford University and New York's New School for Social Research. He is a former editor of *Liberation* magazine, and has written for a variety of publications including *The Washington Post, Los Angeles Times, Psychology Today, Village Voice, Utne Reader, Seattle Times, St. Louis Post Dispatch, New Age Journal, Mother Jones, Los Angeles Herald-Examiner, National Catholic Reporter, International Herald-Tribune*, and Knight Ridder News Service.

An Associated Scholar at Seattle's Institute for Global Security Studies, Loeb has conducted over four hundred TV and radio interviews, including nationwide appearances on CNN, National Public Radio, C-Span, *The Michael Jackson Show*, Studs Terkel's *Almanac*, and the *NBC Nightly News* with Tom Brokaw, as well as national German and Canadian radio. He has lectured at nearly two hundred colleges and universities, including Harvard, Stanford, Dartmouth, Chicago, Michigan, MIT, Yale, Cornell, Wisconsin, and Columbia. Comments on Loeb's presentations include:

"In this politically conservative state, I was amazed that the small-group question and answer session following your lecture lasted for three hours. Clearly the students were very stirred by your message."
—*Marjorie Wheeler, history professor and director of the university forum, University of Southern Mississippi*

"The response from both faculty and students has been outstanding. Your analysis of the dynamics which drive persons into public protest or political withdrawal was striking."
—*James Breedon, Dean of the Tucker Foundation, Dartmouth College*

"Excellent and extremely well received. You very nicely combine a journalist's sensibilities with an academic's care in gathering and using information and ideas."
—*Gordon Fellman, sociology professor, Brandeis University*

"You helped people feel they *can* effect change even if they don't live in D.C. and don't feel they could debate Henry Kissinger on *Nightline*. Your combination of vision and practicality has enriched us."
—*Charles Wallace, university chaplain, Willamette University*

"The videotape of your lecture has been requested by groups as diverse as the Music Department, the Honors Committee, and the Women's Center. You served as a powerful model of commitment and motivation. Our students are almost desperate to see how people are balancing their values with action in an environment which does not always value risk-taking and speaking out for what you believe."
—*Sally Sharp, director of student leadership, Miami University of Ohio*

"Your lecture drew 400 students from a population of 1,000. Not even General Westmoreland, following the end of the Vietnam war, drew such a large crowd. Few speakers have the gift for lifting us from the pessimism and cynicism which surround serious global issues. We owe a debt of gratitude."
—*Rick Hinterthuer, biology professor, North Arkansas Community College*

Mr. Loeb is currently lecturing throughout the United States and is available for speaking engagements and workshops. For further information, contact him through the Institute for Global Security Studies, 3232 41st Avenue SW, Seattle, WA 98116. (206) 935-9132.